D1572809

child development and behavior

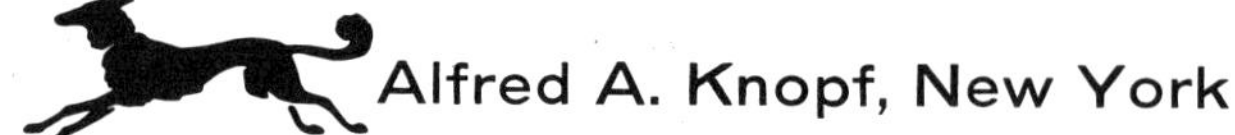

Alfred A. Knopf, New York

child development and behavior Second Edition

Edited by Freda Rebelsky Boston University
and Lynn Dorman Boston University

To Bill and Sam

THIS IS A BORZOI BOOK
PUBLISHED BY ALFRED A. KNOPF, INC.

98765432

Library of Congress Cataloging in Publication Data

Rebelsky, Freda, 1931- comp.
Child development and behavior.

A collection articles.
Includes bibliographies.
1. Child study—Addresses, essays, lectures.
I. Dorman, Lynn, joint comp. II. Title.
[DNLM: 1. Child behavior—Collected works.
2. Child development—Collected works. WS103 R291c 1973]
BF721.R345 1973 155.4'18'08 73-14640
ISBN 0-394-31816-1

Second Edition

Manufactured in the United States of America

Cover photos by James M. Wall and Mike Nelson

acknowledgments

MARY JO BANE and CHRISTOPHER JENCKS, "Five Myths About Your IQ," from *Harper's* (February 1973), pp. 28, 32–34, 38–40. Copyright © 1973 by Minneapolis Star and Tribune Co., Inc. Reprinted from the February 1973 issue of Harper's Magazine by special permission and permission of the authors.

SILVIA M. BELL and MARY D. SALTER AINSWORTH, "Infant Crying and Maternal Responsiveness," from *Child Development* (1972), *43*, pp. 1171–1190. © 1972 by the Society for Research in Child Development, Inc. Reprinted by permission of the authors and the Society for Research in Child Development.

URIE BRONFENBRENNER, "Who Cares for America's Children?," from *Young Children*, Vol. 26, No. 3 (February 1971), pp. 157–163. Reprinted by permission of the author and the National Association for the Education of Young Children.

BETTYE M. CALDWELL and JULIUS B. RICHMOND, "The Impact of Theories of Child Development," from *Children* (March/April 1962), pp. 9, 73–78. Reprinted by permission of the authors and *Children*, U.S. Department of Health, Education, and Welfare, Social Security Administration, Children's Bureau.

JOHN B. CALHOUN, "Plight of the Ik and Kaiadilt Is Seen as a Chilling Possible End for Man," from *Smithsonian* (November 1972), pp. 27–32. Copyright 1972 Smithsonian Institution from SMITHSONIAN Magazine, November 1972. Reprinted by permission of the author and the Smithsonian Institution.

GORDON N. CANTOR, "Effects of Familiarization on Children's Ratings of Pictures of Whites and Blacks," from *Child Development* (1972), *43*, pp. 1219–1229. © 1972 by the Society for Research in Child Development, Inc. Reprinted by permission of the author and the Society for Research in Child Development.

KORNEI CHUKOVSKY, Excerpts from *From Two to Five*, originally published by the University of California Press 1963; reprinted by permission of The Regents of the University of California and the author.

FRANK CURCIO, OWEN ROBBINS, and SUSAN SLOVIN ELA, "The Role of Body Parts and Readiness in Acquisition of Number Conservation," from *Child Development* (1971), *42*, pp. 1641–1646. © 1971 by the Society for Research in Child Development, Inc. Reprinted by permission of the authors and the Society for Research in Child Development.

CAROL O. ECKERMAN, HARRIET L. RHEINGOLD, and RICHARD A. HELWIG, "A Laboratory for Developmental Psychologists," from *Journal of Experimental Child Psychology* (1971), pp. 54–62. Reprinted by permission of the authors and Academic Press, Inc.

LOIS G. FORER, "The Rights of Children," from *Young Children* (1972), pp. 332–335. Reprinted by permission of the author and the National Association for the Education of Young Children.

SUSAN GOLDBERG, "Infant Care and Growth in Urban Zambia," from *Human Development* (1972), pp. 77–89. Reprinted by permission of the author and S. Karger AG Basel.

LOIS GOULD, "X: A Fabulous Child's Story," from *Ms.* (1972), pp. 74–76, 105–106. Copyright © 1972 by Ms. Magazine. Reprinted by permission of the author and International Famous Agency.

CHARLES F. HALVERSON, JR., and MARY F. WALDROP, "Maternal Behavior Toward Own and Other Preschool Children: The Problem of 'Ownness,'" from *Child Development* (1970), *41*, pp. 839–845. © 1970 by the Society for Research in Child Development, Inc. Reprinted by permission of the authors and the Society for Research in Child Development.

LAWRENCE V. HARPER, "The Young as a Source of Stimuli Controlling Caretaker Behavior," from *Developmental Psychology*, *4*, 1971, pp. 73–88. Copyright 1971 by the American Psychological Association and reproduced by permission of publisher and author.

MARTIN L. HOFFMAN, "Father Absence and Conscience Development," from *Developmental Psychology*, *4*, 1971, pp. 400–406. Copyright 1971 by the American Psychological Association and reproduced by permission of publisher.

JOHN HOLT, "Not So Golden Rule Days," from *Center Magazine* (1968), pp. 83–87. Reprinted by permission of the author and Center Magazine.

JEROME KAGAN, "Attention and Psychological Change in the Young Child," from *Science*, Vol. 170, pp. 826–832, issue 20, November 1970. Copyright 1970 by the American Association for the Advancement of Science. Reprinted by permission of the author and the publisher.

BONNIE J. KAPLAN, "Malnutrition and Mental Deficiency," from *Psychological Bulletin*, Vol. 78, 1972, pp. 321–334. Copyright 1972 by the American Psychological Association and reproduced by permission of publisher and author.

WILLIAM KESSEN, "Research in the Psychological Development of Infants: An Overview," from *The Merrill-Palmer Quarterly* (1963), pp. 83–94. Reprinted by permission of the author and The Merrill-Palmer Institute.

JONATHAN KOZOL, Chapter Two from *Death at an Early Age*. Copyright © Jonathan Kozol, 1967. Reprinted by permission of the author, Houghton Mifflin, and Penguin Books.

PAMELA E. KRAMER, ELISSA KOFF, and ZELLA LURIA, "Development of Competence in an Exceptional Language Structure in Older Children and Young Adults," from *Child Development* (1972), *43*, pp. 121–130. © 1972 by the Society for Research in Child Development, Inc. Reprinted by permission of the authors and the Society for Research in Child Development.

A. D. LEIFER, P. H. LEIDERMAN, C. R. BARNETT, and J. A. WILLIAMS, "Effects of Mother-Infant Separation on Maternal Attachment Behavior," from *Child Development* (1972), *43*, pp. 1203–1218. © 1972 by the Society for Research in Child Development, Inc. Reprinted by permission of the authors and the Society for Research in Child Development.

TERESA E. LEVITIN and J. D. CHANANIE, "Responses of Female Primary School Teachers to Sex-Typed Behaviors in Male and Female Children," from *Child Development* (1972), *43*, pp. 1309–1316. © 1972 by the Society for Research in Child Development, Inc. Reprinted by permission of the authors and the Society for Research in Child Development.

ROBERT M. LIEBERT and ROBERT A. BARON, "Some Immediate Effects of Televised Violence on Children's Behavior," from *Developmental Psychology*, *6*, 1972, pp. 469–475. Copyright 1972 by the American Psychological Association and reproduced by permission of the publisher and authors.

ANTON S. MAKARENKO, Excerpts from *The Collective Family: A Handbook for Russian Parents*. Reprinted by permission of the Am-Rus Literary Agency.

DAVID MC CLELLAND, "Why Should Childhood Experience Be So Important?," from *Personality*.

Copyright, 1951, by David C. McClelland. Reprinted by permission of Holt, Rinehart, Winston, Inc. and the author.

TERRY D. MEDDOCK, JOSEPH A. PARSONS, and KENNEDY T. HILL, "Effects of an Adult's Presence and Praise on Young Children's Performance," from *Journal of Experimental Child Psychology* (1971), *12*, pp. 197–211. Reprinted by permission of the authors and Academic Press, Inc.

EDWARD MUELLER, "The Maintenance of Verbal Exchanges Between Young Children," from *Child Development* (1972), *43*, pp. 930–938. © 1972 by the Society for Research in Child Development, Inc. Reprinted by permission of the author and the Society for Research in Child Development.

DAVID S. PALERMO and DENNIS L. MOLFESE, "Language Acquisition from Age Five Onward," from *Psychological Bulletin*, 78, 1972, pp. 409–428. Copyright 1972 by the American Psychological Association and reproduced by permission of the publisher and authors.

FREDA REBELSKY, "Infancy in Two Cultures," from *Nederlands Tijdschrift voor de Psychologie* (1967), pp. 379–385. Reprinted by permission of the author and the North-Holland Publishing Company. "First Discussant's Comments: Cross-Cultural Studies of Mother-Infant Interaction," from *Human Development* (1972), *15*, pp. 128–130. Reprinted by permission of the author and S. Karger AG Basel.

FREDA REBELSKY, CHERYL CONOVER, and PATRICIA CHAFETZ, "The Development of Political Attitudes in Young Children" from *The Journal of Psychology* (1969), pp. 141–146. Reprinted by permission of the authors and The Journal Press.

FREDA REBELSKY and CHERYL HANKS, "Fathers' Verbal Interaction with Infants in the First Three Months of Life," from *Child Development* (1971), *42*, pp. 63–68. © 1971 by the Society for Research in Child Development, Inc. Reprinted by permission of the authors and the Society for Research in Child Development.

HARRIET L. RHEINGOLD and CAROL O. ECKERMAN, "The Infant Separates Himself from His Mother," from *Science, 168*, pp. 73–83, issue 3, April 1970. Copyright 1970 by the American Association for the Advancement of Science. Reprinted by permission of the authors and the publisher.

GAIL C. ROBERTS and KATHRYN NORCROSS BLACK, "The Effect of Naming and Object Permanence on Toy Preferences," from *Child Development* (1972), *43*, pp. 858–868. © 1972 by the Society for Research in Child Development, Inc. Reprinted by permission of the authors and the Society for Research in Child Development.

PAMELA C. RUBOVITS and MARTIN L. MAEHR, "Pygmalion Black and White," from *Journal of Personality and Social Psychology, 23*, 1973, pp. 210–218. Copyright 1973 by the American Psychological Association, and reproduced by permission of the publisher and authors.

ARNOLD J. SAMEROFF, "Can Conditioned Responses Be Established in the Newborn Infant?," from *Developmental Psychology, 5*, 1971, pp. 1–12. Copyright 1971 by the American Psychological Association and reproduced by permission of the publisher and author.

JOHN W. SANTROCK, "Relation of Type and Onset of Father Absence to Cognitive Development," from *Child Development* (1972), *43*, pp. 455–469. © 1972 by the Society for Research in Child Development, Inc. Reprinted by permission of the author and the Society for Research in Child Development.

SANDRA SCARR-SALAPATEK, "Unknowns in the IQ Equation," from *Science, 174*, pp. 1223–1228, issue 17, December 1971. Copyright 1971 by the American Association for the Advancement of Science. Reprinted by permission of the author and the publisher.

DOROTHY Z. SEYMOUR, "Black Children, Black Speech," from *Commonweal* (1971), pp. 175–178. Reprinted by permission of the author and Commonweal Publishing Company.

HAROLD M. SKEELS, "Adult Status of Children with Contrasting Early Life Experiences: A Follow-up Study," from *Monographs of the Society for Research in Child Development* (1966), *31*, Ser. #105, pp. 1–11, 13, 54–59. © 1966 by the Society for Research in Child Development, Inc. Excerpts reprinted by permission of the author and the Society for Research in Child Development.

BENJAMIN SPOCK, Excerpts from *Baby and Child Care.* Copyright © 1945, © 1946, © 1957, © 1968 by Benjamin Spock, M. D. Reprinted by permission of the author and Pocket Books, division of Simon & Schuster, Inc.

L. ALAN SROUFE and JANE PICCARD WUNSCH, "The Development of Laughter in the First Year of Life," from *Child Development* (1972), *43,* pp. 1326–1344. © 1972 by the Society for Research in Child Development, Inc. Reprinted by permission of the authors and the Society for Research in Child Development.

J. M. TANNER, "The Regulation of Human Growth," from *Child Development* (1963), *34,* pp. 817–847. © 1963 by the Society for Research in Child Development, Inc. Reprinted with abridgment by permission of the author and the Society for Research in Child Development.

LEWIS M. TERMAN and MAUDE E. MERRILL, Sample Items from *Stanford-Binet Scale.* Reprinted by permission of the authors and Houghton Mifflin Company.

STEVEN R. TULKIN, "An Analysis of the Concept of Cultural Deprivation," from *Developmental Psychology, 6,* 1972, pp. 326–339. Copyright 1972 by the American Psychological Association and reproduced by permission of the publisher and author.

U.S. DEPARTMENT OF HEALTH, EDUCATION, AND WELFARE, Excerpt from *The Health of Children.* Reprinted by permission of U.S. Department of Health, Education, and Welfare, Health Services and Mental Health Administration, National Center for Health Statistics.

RICHARD N. WALKER, "Body Build and Behavior in Young Children: I. Body Build and Nursery School Teachers' Ratings," from *Monographs of the Society for Research in Child Development* (1962), *27,* Ser. #84, pp. 75–79. © 1962 by the Society for Research in Child Development, Inc. Excerpt reprinted by permission of the author and the Society for Research in Child Development.

JOHN B. WATSON, Excerpts from *Psychological Care of Infant and Child.* Copyright 1928 by W. W. Norton & Company, Inc. Copyright renewed 1955 by John B. Watson. Reprinted by permission of W. W. Norton & Company, Inc.

JOHN S. WATSON, "Smiling, Cooing, and 'The Game,'" from *The Merrill-Palmer Quarterly* (1972), pp. 323–339. Reprinted by permission of the author and the Merrill-Palmer Institute.

preface to the second edition

Four years have passed since we gathered the materials for the first edition of this book. As we continued to read the literature, we have been impressed with some major changes that have occurred in the past few years. Thus, we have restructured the book and replaced most of the readings. The detailed investigation of adult-child interaction and the detailed investigation of children's capabilities are now much more evident.

Our purpose for this edition remains as it was in the first edition. We hope these articles will be understandable stimuli for further thought and provide this generation of students with new ways of looking at developmental issues and new ways to help children live better lives.

We thank our colleagues for the use of their articles in this reader: they are among the group of people who do interesting work and make it clear and accessible to others. Wendy Nevard, Pat Daniel, and Jacqueline Vogel helped search for articles and did much of the drudgery work that goes into a book. Jone Sloman typed the manuscript. Our students and colleagues have been helpful and critical readers, and we appreciate their comments on the first edition and on selections in this edition. The Developmental Psychology Faculty at Boston University, Frank Curcio, George Michel, Gerald Stechler, Ned Mueller, Jean Berko Gleason, Kathleen White, and Margaret Hagen, have been supportive of our intellectual wanderings and make it a real joy to think about developmental issues. We thank all these people for their encouragement and interest.

preface to the first edition

We have collected these readings to give students the opportunity to see some of the issues presently studied in child development, some of the research techniques used to study these issues, and some of the findings in the field. These articles are alive in ways that no summary or textbook reference to them can be: they are written by the people who thought up the questions and who tried to answer them by some research design. Hopefully, students will be stimulated by these readings to delve further into the research literature of the field or a particular area of child development.

A book of readings is truly a collaborative effort. We want to thank our colleagues who have allowed their work to be reprinted in this volume and the journal editors and publishers who gave their permission for these articles. Without them, needless to say, there would be no reader. We also want to thank Lewis Lipsitt who commented on our selections, and the members of our Child Development Journal Group who reviewed our choices with us. We also want to thank Cheryl Conover and Bernice Speiser for their varieties of help and their continued interest. Thanks especially to our past and present students whose critical comments on previous selections of articles prepared the way for this book.

contents

introduction

Child Development

Over the centuries people have been interested in children for both personal and intellectual reasons. Some people are interested in the education of children, and their upbringing. People are also interested because they were once children, and children grow into adults. This somewhat obvious statement has led people into asking certain questions about children: What are they really like? How do they go from being children to being adult? Why do they differ from one another? Developmental psychologists ask these questions, too: What is the nature of the child? What are the processes underlying development? Why do children differ from one another?

Developmental psychology, as other sciences, is still gathering data on the basic nature of its subject matter—the child. Psychology is different from other sciences, though, in one important way—it is the only science where the researcher studies subject matter that is like the researcher. People study people. This is probably why we as psychologists have had a somewhat difficult time getting to understand the basic capacities of the human child. In studying the child, we were apt to "adulterate" the child, attribute adult-like characteristics to the child, and judge the child's responses from an adult's view of right and wrong.

The Nature of the Child

We are still uncertain about the nature of the child; we do not yet know with certainty what capacities or abilities the human child has at various ages. Although some aspects, such as motor development, have been mapped fairly well, there are areas such as intellectual development and the development of self concept that are still poorly understood. The area of motor and physical development is one that we once thought was well known. Physiologists and psychologists had been studying growth and the senses for years. Yet we have just recently learned that babies actually see more than shadows of light and dark in the first few weeks. We have discovered that newborn babies can discriminate between forms a few hours after birth and that babies look longer at one kind of stimulus than at another. These research ideas could not have been presented to a generation who believed that babies were passively waiting around for adults to "teach" them to prefer things.

Language development illustrates another important point; child developmentalists are asking new questions. As we learn more, we can begin to ask questions about what previously seemed obvious. We are now gathering normative data on aspects of development, such as language development, that we previously thought we understood. Now, instead of taking language development as obvious and "natural," we are beginning to ask what the child is capable of saying or understanding at various ages. We have learned that if we ask a young child to repeat sentences too long for him to remember, he will select certain words to repeat, and this behavior is not random. We recognize that many hypotheses we had about language learning are false; we had assumed, without even directly observing, that a child learns his language through correction by parents, especially his mother. Now that real mothers and children have been studied, we discover that a mother rarely corrects her child's linguistic errors. In addition, as we listen to children, we discover that their "errors" are meaningful—the "errors" show us that even very young children are learning the rules of their language and not only the vocabulary. Thus, a child who has never heard "runned" forms such a word from his understanding of the English past tense.

We are like ethologists, trying to understand the human animal in its natural habitat with childhood our unknown culture. As Flavell (1968) has suggested, we are "developmental naturalists," who are interested in exploring the capacities of the organism at various ages in a variety of situations. So in language development, we undertake studies to determine the linguistic competence of the child: What does he say? What can he understand? Does he speak differently to adults than to children?

Such normative data on development can sometimes be gathered by careful observation, but in recent years developmentalists have recognized that what the researcher can see in the organism's normal behavior does not necessarily tell us about his capacities. For example, if we want to study children's language development, we can learn some things by waiting to see what exists after changes in the particular environment of one child. But we can learn aspects by setting up experiments that elicit underlying language competence.

The Processes Underlying Development

Developmental psychologists can at present only speculate about the processes underlying development. Why does a child move from cooing and babbling to talking sentences? What process is operating? Is it the same process by which a child learns which sex he is and what people of that sex are supposed to do?

For years developmentalists have been concerned with the processes underlying growth. For convenience, the field has been grossly categorized into environmentalists and geneticists; that is, those who feel that development is largely the result of events in the environment versus those who see development as stemming largely from biological maturation. It is obviously apparent that the human child changes as he ages. But aging alone is an unsatisfactory explanation.

Probably no one feels that either biological growth or environmental conditions totally explain development. Most developmentalists recognize that the human organism's growth is a combination of biological and environmental influences interacting within the framework of a specific individual of the species. No child would have biological growth without food (an environmental factor), but the way food is given probably depends to some extent on the stage of biological growth (for example, we feed babies differently from school children). Also, environmental conditions can affect biological growth in other ways, such as through lack of good nutrition and through individual differences (for example, some babies from birth may reject a certain food).

Thus, an interaction between biological growth and environment is necessary for development. Many would also agree that for optimal growth there should be an appropriate match between environment and heredity. We don't try to teach manners to three-month-old babies, and we don't expect them to eat steak. Hebb (1953) suggested a congenial way to describe the influences on developmental processes: "Behavior is determined 100 percent by heredity and 100 percent by environment." Development does not proceed through either environment or heredity alone, but through a continuing interaction between the organism and its environment.

As Kohlberg stated, when discussing this issue in relation to cognitive development:

> We have contrasted the maturationist assumption that basic mental structure results from an innate patterning with the learning theory assumption that basic mental structure is the result of the patterning or associations of events in the outside world. In contrast, the cognitive developmental assumption is that basic mental structure is the result of an interaction between certain organismic structuring tendencies and the structure of the outside world, rather than reflecting either one directly. [1968, p. 13.]

In the readings that follow, it will become even more apparent that there is no consensus about the processes underlying child development. Some processes seem to work better at one age than at another, and some processes seem to work better for certain kinds of development than others.

Why Children Differ

Since we do not know (1) the nature of childhood or (2) the processes underlying development, we cannot explain why there are individual differences between children. Why is one child walking at 6 months and another at 16 months? Why is one child responsive and another withdrawn? Why is one baby easily conditioned to a sound and another not? We are aware of marked differences between children. We have seen that the range of "normal" behavior is great, and we have guessed that individuality is both set at birth and developed during life. These three issues: (1) the nature of the child, (2) the nature of the processes underlying development, and (3) the explanation of individual differences, are illuminated by readings in this volume.

It would in one sense be nice to be able to know more, to be studying a field that has "hard facts." But since all sciences are continually changing, the "hard facts" of one time are the open questions of another time. An interesting example of this is the study of dinosaurs. Until about a century ago, anyone who had "seen" dinosaur bones didn't "see" them as different from other bones or else misidentified them as belonging to already existing categories. Once scientists were able to take the leap of imagination required to recognize the large bones as "new," "unknown," and not categorizable, they were able to ask questions about them and to come to think about them. During the next one hundred years, there were more discoveries of concrete evidence of the existence of dinosaurs than had been found in all prior centuries together. Why? Because once scientists became aware of a problem as a problem, they asked more questions (and not always appropriate ones at that). The knowledge that dinosaurs existed, and that they usually lived in certain climates, raised many new questions about our universe. For example, dinosaur bones have been found in Greenland—was it once warm enough there to support the tropical forest needed for dinosaurs, or did dinosaurs migrate to cold regions? Either question leads to a host of others.

In child development, too, we are asking new questions that make us look differently at development and that lead us to ask more questions (also not always appropriate). Developmental psychology, as a field, is thus somewhat like a developing organism. A child of 2 can understand the world and ask questions about it. So can a child of 12 and a college student of 20. But the understanding of the world is different and the questions are of very different natures.

As you read the following articles, it is hoped you will learn that there are as yet unanswered questions. You have come to child psychology after many years of your own growth. This is not the study of distant stars or impersonal plant development. We are interested in child development, and our experiences as children can aid our understanding, but limit our acceptance of data that conflict with our own experiences.

We hope these articles help you learn more about the nature of childhood and what is now thought of as processes of development. We also hope you will become aware of issues related to the scientific study of children—how to pose a research question so that it can be answered, how to devise a research tool that is appropriate for children of a specific age, and how our science moves forward as we accumulate more and more information about child development.

Using This Book

The Written Word Is Not the Final Word

We recognize that readers tend to accept published material written by experts as "truth." We are presenting these articles as examples of the varieties of interest, research design, and findings about children. However, you should be aware that even the best article can only present the data of a specific time as seen by a specific person. And we believe that all observers of data are biased by their interests and training. This does not by any means imply that the articles are not worth reading. A major reason for studying the material in this book is to help you see phenomena in different ways than you did before. We want to open your eyes, not close your mind.

Reading Specific Articles

We think people learn more when they are actively involved in their own learning than when they are passive recipients. Our students have found that outlining an article enables them to summarize it thoroughly and easily, and, in addition, forces them into a critical attitude.

For your own sanity, and to help you to compare articles later, we have found that abstracts should be done with some uniformity. It seems to make little difference what size paper you use, or even how much you write about an article. What does matter is consistency—the same ordering of material and the same size paper.

Many of our students start off thinking that criticism of an article means that they have to tear it apart, to criticize all of its parts. They feel obligated to comment on sample size, statistics used, and so forth. Abstracting and criticism then become frustrating tasks, since most undergraduate students simply do not have the background and working knowledge of the field that are required to do this sort of criticism adequately. On the other hand, even without extensive knowledge of the subject of an article, a thoughtful reading of it will at times allow a reader to see data more clearly than the author did. Research readings are not "hard facts" to be interpreted in only one way. You may disagree with the author's discussion as to WHY the results came out as they did and WHAT the results mean in more general terms. This is fine—that's how new research is generated, by people attempting new or different interpretations of data. But even if you disagree with the interpretations, you should accept the author's actual data or results.

Most research is done carefully and systematically. The results obtained and the results of statistical analyses are, in most cases, acceptable. Results are results. You may certainly question why certain statistical tests are used or why the author thinks some measure is actually measuring the phenomenon, but again, spend some time criticizing other things than the results of the measurement. We suggest this because many students get so involved in questioning the results that they overlook the major problem in many studies, that of interpretation of the results.

By raising questions about the research, you are able to bring your own training and experience to bear on someone else's thinking. You thereby establish a real dialogue on an equal level with the author.

There are articles in this book that when you read them may seem silly, dull, obvious, brilliant, and so on. The above were culled from our own students, but you may have your own words to use! The interesting thing is that an article described as "useless" by one student is often thought of as "brilliant" by another student in the same class.

Each of us, when reading an article, fits it into our current background of information. If you already know much about an area, articles in that area may seem obvious. If you don't like or aren't particularly interested in an area, those articles may seem silly or useless to you. If the article excites you in some way, you may think of it as brilliant. All that can be said is, try to be fair to each article as you read it. Each selection was published because the editors of the journal thought it was important for *some* reason. The reason is not always that it was the first research done in an important area. It might have been that the methodology was unique or the discussion and rationale seemed useful to others. We selected the articles to provide you with a chance to see the breadth of current research interests and methods.

Before reading an article, look at the date when it was originally published. This may help you in your appraisal of the article. Also read the introduction section before reading the articles contained there. You may disagree with us, and you certainly aren't alone in that, but at least you will have some idea of our thinking on the topics and this may give you a point of reference to argue from.

An outline that we find useful for abstracting articles is presented below, though you may find a better way to organize the material you read.

Outline for Abstracting Articles

RESEARCH ARTICLES

Problem: General statement of previous research. Author's hypothesis or hypotheses.
Method: Instruments used (their validity and reliability). Experimental procedure.
Sample: Relevant variables, e.g., age, sex, socio-economic status.
Results: Author's findings and interpretation.

In addition to the abstract of the research article, you should attempt to:

1. Evaluate the article.
2. Offer alternative interpretations.
3. Comment on the implications for classroom and/or parental behavior.

THEORETICAL ARTICLES

Brief summary of major points.
Author's interpretation and implications.

In addition to this abstract of the theoretical article, you should attempt to:

1. Evaluate the theoretical position (or compare to another).
2. Comment on the implications for research and/or parental behavior.

These abstracts need not be long. They are for your own benefit: to encourage you to think about what you read, to help you write better critical papers, and to participate more effectively in class.

Relating Articles Within a Section

After you've read a few articles within a section, you will start to notice several things:

1. that different authors approach the same topic from very different points of view
2. that different conclusions are possible within the same topic
3. that you emotionally, from your own training and biases, tend to accept and reject certain findings.

Imagine what it would be like if all the authors were in a room together. How would they interpret each other's data? Where would they agree or disagree? What would you say? Arguing for the positions of the various authors also helps one to understand that there is no one answer to the questions asked by the authors.

Bring to the articles a sense of intelligent curiosity. Study them, think about them, put yourself into them. Evaluate their conclusions. Do they make sense to you? Do you agree? Consider other research or evidence on the topic.

Relating Articles Across Sections

After you read several sections you will begin to realize that the human child is extremely complex and that the whole child is made up, at least, of the material presented in chapters 1–8 in this book. For example, if you are reading an article on an infant's laughter, depending on which chapters you read before it, you might ask what would happen if the infant came from a situation of maternal deprivation, or a Dutch home, or a large family, or a small family. You may find yourself designing research along new lines, something few of our students think themselves capable of doing. Students are quite capable of designing research, but most of them brush off their ideas with a statement to the effect that if they thought of it, it must obviously have been done already.

We'd like you to reread this section after you finish the book. If we are wrong, we would like to know. From our own experience with students of many types, we find that this development in students is possible.

Use of Supplementary Readings

After reading some of the articles or some of the complete chapters, you may find that you wish to read further on a certain topic. We have suggested some further readings on each topic at the end of the chapters, but this may not be enough for some people. We, therefore, are including the names of some general reference books that might be used for searching for literature on a given topic. Chapters in most of these general references will often tell you what others have thought about the topic, and what others have learned about it. All of this information is useful to you as you read or perhaps design a study on the topic.

Good reviews of the literature in child development can be found in four main sources: review and abstracting services, handbooks, periodicals, and textbooks. You could look in the index of any of these sources under various categories of your interest.

Reviews and abstracting services

Annual review of psychology— contains chapters on various fields in psychology.
Child development abstracts and bibliography— reviews all child-related research.
Mental measurements yearbook— reviews tests, giving reliability, validity, etc.
Psychological abstracts— reviews all psychological literature.
Review of educational research— reviews research related to education.

Handbooks

Brackbill, Y. (Ed.) *Infancy and early childhood.* New York: Free Press, 1967.

Goslin, D. (Ed.) *Handbook of socialization theory and research.* Chicago: Rand McNally, 1969.

Hoffman, M. L., and Hoffman, L. W. (Eds.) *Review of child development research.* New York: Russell Sage. Two volumes.

Lipsitt, L. *et al.* (Eds.) *Advances in development and behavior.* New York: Academic Press. Six Volumes.

Mussen, P. (Ed.) *Carmichael's manual of child psychology.* New York, Wiley, 1970.

Mussen, P. (Ed.) *Handbook of research methods in child development.* New York: Wiley, 1960.

Stevenson, H. (Ed.) *Child psychology.* Chicago: University of Chicago Press, 1963.

Reese, H., and Lipsitt, L. *Experimental child psychology.* New York: Academic Press, 1970.

Periodicals

Child Care Quarterly
Child Development
Developmental Psychobiology
Developmental Psychology
Genetic Psychology Monographs
Human Development (Vita Humana)

Journal of Child Psychology and Psychiatry
Journal of Comparative and Physiological Psychology
Journal of Genetic Psychology
Journal of Experimental Child Psychology
Journal of Youth and Adolescence
Merrill-Palmer Quarterly
Monographs of the Society for Research in Child Development
Psychological Bulletin
Young Children

Statistics

In reading some of the articles, you will probably come across those things that many have come to feel dumb about: numbers, data, statistical tests, and so forth. Don't feel dumb, and don't skip the tables, graphs, and figures, either. They are there to help you understand the research and they are important. Yes, the author might say some of these things in real words, but you must also learn to read them in figure form. For that reason, and because we don't believe in mathematical blocks, especially in college students, we have included a brief section on how to read statistics.

Mean—usually the same as the mathematical average.

Standard deviation—a measure of the variability of the scores. The more spread out, or variable, the scores are, the larger the standard deviation.

Normal curve—represents the distribution of many psychological characteristics in the general population. When the distribution is not normal, the data are sometimes transformed via some procedure to approximate normality.

Correlation—the relationship between variables. When there is a tendency for variable A to always go with variable B, in the same direction, we speak of a positive correlation. An example is height and weight in children. When two variables go together but in opposite directions, we speak of a negative correlation. For example, the relationship between income and family size is negative. Large families tend to have small incomes and small families tend to have larger incomes.

Level of confidence—you will most often read things such as: significant at the .01 level or $p<.05$. These all refer to the "goodness" of the results obtained. A level of .05 means that the results could have happened by chance only 5 times out of 100; .01 means that chance could account for the results only 1 time out of 100. The present level of confidence acceptable to psychologists is .05.

Chi square, t-test, and analysis of variance—the names of various statistical tests that we use for examining our data to see if they answer the questions asked. We aren't going to explain the various tests, but we want to familiarize you with their names. You will come across an assortment of letters, both English and Greek, that are used for naming what one student once called "baroque statistics." Some of the letters you will encounter are X^2, F, r, U. You will also read sentences that have phrases like this in the middle of them: ($t=2.69$, $p<.01$) or ($F=5.32$, $p<.005$). What they mean is that the statistical test, represented by the first letter, yielded a final number (in the above cases these are the 2.69 and the 5.32) which was significant at the given level of confidence (here they were significant at .01 and .005 respectively). The results, thus, are likely not to be due to chance.

Use of Indexes

There are also two indexes in this book: The first is of the authors of the articles in this book and of authors mentioned in all references (boldface type indicates the page on which an author's article begins), the second is an index of concepts. The concept index can be useful in helping you relate articles to each other.

References

FLAVELL, J. H. *et al. The development of role-taking and communication skills in children.* New York: Wiley, 1968.

HEBB, D. O. Heredity and environment in mammalian behavior. *British Journal of Animal Behavior*, 1953, *1*, 43–47.

KOHLBERG, L. Early education: A cognitive-developmental view. *Child Development*, 1968, *39*, 1013–1062.

part one general developmental issues

chapter one
the role of theory

In every field there are theories that attempt to explain events. In developmental psychology many theories and hypotheses exist. Some people suggest that because we do not have an all-encompassing theory, our field is deficient. Either there is no one theory to explain development or perhaps we just do not know enough yet to have developed one theory. We believe that with our present knowledge it is beneficial to child psychology that there be many theories; they serve to keep us actively attempting to reconcile or contradict them.

Theories serve many useful purposes. In developing a theory, the researcher fits together knowledge from different areas. His resultant theory or hypothesis may then serve as an "eye-opener" to others, causing them to "see" things they never saw before. Freud, for example, theorized that events in childhood were anxiety producing and remained with the child affecting his adult personality. This led others to look at young children differently. In the research done by others, Freud's ideas were often not borne out, but new areas of study did become apparent: mother-child interaction, maternal attitudes, child-rearing practices, children's perceptions of events, and so forth.

Thus Freud's theories and the resultant

for the norms of behavioral development which he and his students accumulated over the years, Gesell was nonetheless an important formulator of a theory of child behavior.

Gesell's theory of development is relatively simple yet, in some ways, more global than other more complex theories. The key concept is that of *maturation* or growth. It is a theory of intrinsic development, of an infant's maturation proceeding from both the human and the individual nature of the infant.

Implicit in the concept of maturation is self-regulation of growth. Gesell urged recognition of this principle in every aspect of development from the establishment of infant feeding schedules to the acquisition of moral values. Acceptance of the principle by parents calls for a certain considerateness, an "alert liberalism," to use Gesell's phrase. Infants, as well as older children, are entitled to certain courtesies, to being regarded as "people." A passionate regard for the individual was, Gesell maintained, crucial to a truly democratic orientation to life.

A corollary of this stress on the importance of the individual is the concept of individual differences. Yet, paradoxically, it is here that Gesell seems to have been most generally misinterpreted and, indeed, almost to have courted misinterpretation. This stems from the organization of most of his books in terms of ages and stages of behavior. Indeed, the books' typography—the capitalization of each age period as though personified—conduces to such misinterpretation. For example:

> THREE is a kind of coming-of-age . . . You can bargain with THREE and he can wait his turn . . . FOUR (and half past) tends to go out of bounds . . . FIVE is a SUPER-THREE with a socialized pride in clothes and accomplishments, a lover of praise (Gesell and Ilg, 1943).

About this approach, Gesell and Ilg say:

> We regard the formal concept of chronological age and the functional concept of maturity level as indispensable both for practical common sense and for the science of child development. In the guidance of children it is absolutely necessary to consider the age values of behavior and the behavior values of age. The reader is warned, in advance, however, that *the age norms are not set up as standards and are designed only for orientation and interpretive purposes*. . . . The prevalence and significance of individual variations are recognized at every turn (1943).

Perhaps these occasional warnings do not carry enough weight to counterbalance the continued stress on ages and stages in development throughout childhood and adolescence.

With respect to the timing of the maximum impact of the three major theories we are discussing, Gesell followed Watson and preceded Freud. Nevertheless, many of Gesell's most popular publications came out during the period of popularization of psychoanalytic thought. Gesell did not seem to be a man for polemics, however, and he seldom bothered to take notice of other points of view. His books deal largely with the presentation of his own material. He quotes other researchers only when their studies relate to his interests. In the four Gesell books reviewed for this article, there are only two references to Freud. Gesell was more concerned with developmental congruences than interpersonal conflicts, with eye-hand coordination and prehension than emotional cathexes. Even in the volume "Youth" (Gesell, 1956), "sex" is indexed in terms of "differences" and not of preoccupations and problems.

Watson is quoted once in these four Gesell works, but anonymously as "a distinguished behaviorist" and the source of the quote is not in the reference list. However, in isolated articles, Gesell occasionally opposed certain points important in behavioristic doctrine, as he did when he suggested (1929) that the conditioned reflex theory promised too much and threatened too much, and that maturation protected the infant from certain chance conditionings.

of the basic drives is likely to result in permanent personality distortions remediable only through a kind of regrowth process via the therapeutic relationship.

These formulations have been theoretically enticing and have provided many hypotheses for investigation by workers in the field of child development as well as for child-care workers in various disciplines interested in the prevention of emotional disorders. Many psychoanalytic concepts have been embraced as guides to child rearing by parents concerned with raising "emotionally healthy" children. However, a review of the experimental literature (Richmond and Caldwell, in press) indicates that no specific relationships between early experiences and later development can be established at the present time.

There is growing recognition among psychoanalytic investigators that the application of knowledge gained from psychoanalysis in preventive efforts must be approached cautiously. The objective of psychoanalytic investigation as stated by Erikson (1950) a decade ago remains valid:

> Psychoanalysis today is implementing the study of the ego, the core of the individual. It is shifting its emphasis from the concentrated study of the conditions which blunt and distort the individual ego to the study of the ego's roots in social organization. This we try to understand not in order to offer a rash cure to a rashly diagnosed society, but in order to first complete the blueprint of our method.

To pursue these objectives, psychoanalytic research workers are departing from the predominant use of reconstructive interview or play techniques to the greater use of direct observation of development (as indicated by the current interest in research in mother-infant interaction), experimental approaches (animal and human), and cross-cultural studies. Also, more intensive and objective studies of psychoanalytically oriented interviews are being developed.

Implications for Today

The fact that different theories can flourish contemporaneously validates Knapp's observation (1960) that man is a "recalcitrant and reluctant experimental subject." Yet these theories of child development are not contradictory or mutually exclusive. All are concerned with learning, with the interaction of organism and environment. They all highlight different facets of behavior and use different conceptual systems. And, undoubtedly, they are all a little bit right.

From all of them one can infer that parents wield an awesome degree of power in shaping the lives of their children. Even maturational theory, with its emphasis upon the growth integrity of the young organism, its inherent potential for healthy development, implies that the parent can inhibit or distort this growth potential. With greater awareness of the implications of their caretaking activities, some parents have shown signs of what might be loosely termed a midcentury parental neurosis: an over-determination to seek suggestions for child rearing as insurance of healthy development for their children.

Professional workers in the field of child care (pediatricians and other health workers, psychologists and child welfare workers) have not been immune to these pressures. They have sometimes advocated as universally desirable such programs as "natural childbirth," rooming-in of the newborn with the mother at the hospital, breast feeding, and permissive or self-regulating patterns of child care. To their credit, psychoanalysts have not been in the forefront of these movements. Rather, these movements have often represented misinterpretation or premature application of psychoanalytic principles. Recently they have been placed in a more appropriate perspective, as doctrinaire approaches to "prevention" have been given up in favor of the more traditionally eclectic orientation of child-care professions—except perhaps by social work which has remained heavily committed to psychoanalytic theory.

Guidance in child rearing will probably become increasingly professionalized in the United States in the years to come. The child-care professions, therefore, must face up to the challenge of providing services for parents even with incomplete knowledge. If these services are to be provided for families, adequate professional personnel must be made available. The specific professions to provide this personnel, the appropriate distribution, and the organization of services are issues with which we as a nation have not yet come to terms. The current ferment about the "new pediatrics" and concern with the directions in which this profession should move educationally and in practice suggest the need for planning constructively for all kinds of child-care services.

Since the launching of Sputnik in 1957, we have awakened to our responsibilities to fulfill our potentialities as a democratic nation. The resultant emphasis on academic achievement has the same over-determined emphasis which other child-rearing formulae have had in previous years. While we must strive for full intellectual development of our children, this need not be at the expense of their social and emotional growth. If it is, we may inhibit the learning we seek to foster.

Implications for Future Theories

What thoughts can now be projected about the child-development theories of the future? Undoubtedly they will con- [illegible] both at the scientific

heuristic child development theories of the future:

1. Extrapolation from research data will not be so extreme.

The science of behavior has matured into a more conservative, slightly subdued stage. Professionals in the field have themselves matured somewhat. Also the interdisciplinary origin of many of the reasonably stable parts of child-development knowledge is conducive to conservatism.

The young Watson, with little knowledge of genetics and its constitutional limitations upon adaptability of the organism, could assert that he could take any four healthy infants and make them whatever type of adult he wished. The somewhat provincial Freud, unaware of the nascent body of data from cultural anthropology, could assume that the memories and fantasies of individuals from a fairly narrow sociocultural context represented universal attributes. Today's theorists are no longer permitted the luxury of being uninformed about work in any area of knowledge which might limit the predictions from a given theoretical system. With greater availability of information which might make predictions hazardous, the theories themselves will become more cautious about specific predictions.

2. Future theories of child behavior will be concerned with a broader time spectrum.

The view of the child as a miniature adult is outmoded. But in its place has come with too much finality a view of the child almost as an eternal child. The child *is* a future adult, as he is a future adolescent and a future senescent. The 6-month- [illegible] a certain type

predictions about the [illegible]

predictions which span wide segments of the developmental curve, not just one narrow section.

3. Future theories of child behavior will be related to broader aspects of social theory and philosophy.

A point already stressed in this paper is that each enduring or influential child-development theory [is] related to powerful currents of social history. Within the past few decades even the seemingly remote physical sciences have had to face such a relationship. There is now less talk about a separation of science from values. Certainly in the field of child development no such separation is possible. We rear children to fit into a particular culture, on the basic premise that the culture is somehow "good" or at least acceptable.

The past two decades have seen considerable sniping at Watson for the naïveté of his theories, with an occasional implication that he was heartless and cruel for denouncing mother love and the child-rearing practices of most parents. Such criticism fails to recognize that Watson was far more explicit than most theorists about the behavioral attributes he wished to foster. He concludes one of his books (Watson, 1928) with a formal apologia to critics who have taken him to task for having no "ideals" for bringing up children, commenting perceptively that different programs of care fit different civilizations. Then he describes briefly the kind of child he had in mind when making his child-rearing suggestions, the kind he considered best adapted to the changing America of the late twenties:

> We have tried to sketch in the foregoing chapters a child as free as possible of sensitivities to people and one who, almost from birth, is relatively independent of the family situation . . . Above all, we have tried to create a problem-solving child. We believe that a problem-solving technique (which can be trained) plus boundless absorption in activity (which can also be trained) are behavioristic factors which have worked in many civilizations of the past and which, so far as we can judge, will work equally well in most types of civilizations that are likely to confront us in the future (Watson, 1928).

Undoubtedly, many persons would not agree with Watson's goals, but it is to his credit that he attempted to relate his theory to the social milieu.

4. Future theories of child development will not attempt to answer (or predict) everything about child development for all time. They will modestly relate themselves to one sociocultural group—until something is proven to have universal relevance—and for a finite scientific era.

New discoveries can outmode existing theories overnight. For example, future research on behavioral genetics might drastically modify many of the assumptions underlying research on the effects of specific parent practices on child behavior. Any heuristic theory will be quick to incorporate new data, thus building a more stately theoretical structure. Victor Hugo's tribute to the power of an idea whose time has come might well apply in reverse here, for nothing is more effete than a theory that has outlived its time.

References

ERIKSON, E.: Childhood and society. Norton and Company, New York. 1950.

GESELL, A.: Maturation and infant behavior pattern. *Psychological Review*, July 1929.

GESELL, A.: and others: The first five years of life. Harper and Bros., New York. 1940.

GESELL, A.; and ILG, FRANCES L.: Infant and child in the culture of today. Harper and Bros., New York. 1943.

———. The child from five to ten. Harper and Bros., New York. 1946.

———. Youth—the years from ten to sixteen. Harper and Bros., New York. 1956.

KNAPP, P.: Symposium: expression of emotions in man. Annual meeting, American Association for the Advancement of Science, 1960.

MILLER, N. E.; DOLLARD, J.: Social learning and imitation. Yale University Press, New Haven. 1953.

RICHMOND, J. B.; CALDWELL, BETTYE M.: Child rearing practices and their consequences. In press.

ROTTER, J. B.: Social learning and clinical psychology. Prentice-Hall, New York. 1954.

SKINNER, B. F.: Science and human behavior. Macmillan, New York. 1953.

SPOCK, B. M.: The common sense book of baby and child care. Duell, Sloan, and Pearce, New York. 1946.

WATSON, J. B.: Psychological care of infant and child. Allen and Unwin, London. 1928.

2. RESEARCH IN THE PSYCHOLOGICAL DEVELOPMENT OF INFANTS: AN OVERVIEW

WILLIAM KESSEN

The infant has not always been treated kindly by American psychologists. Although almost all theories—whether in the tradition of Watson, Freud, or Koffka—celebrate the importance of infant behavior, and claim that the baby is striking proof of the validity of their views, systematic empirical study of the child in his crucial first year has been an on-again, off-again affair. And for a number of reasons, not the least of which is the difficulty of seeing young children in the large numbers that we have at our command in studying the pre school child or the ado-

our frustration by constructing theoretical babies instead of observing real ones.

Happily, these disabilities no longer block research. There is evidence, and not only in the United States, that psychologists are studying the infant more closely than ever before. Merely to call the names of investigators and refer to some of their findings would consume many pages. This is not to say, by the way, that the theoretical or constructed child has disappeared. Far from it! Behind each empirical investigation, there is a model, and this model colors and sometimes dominates the interpretation that is given the empirical protocols.

I would like to be able to present a

tion of theoretical subtleties would approach the complexity of a recitation of research findings. In the face of this kind of variety, I cannot hope to lay out a complete or even a fair summary of current research and thought about the behavior of the infant. Rather, I will present for your comment, review, and evaluation, a short set of propositions about babies and studies of babies; under each of these loose-jointed statements, we can examine a part of the research and speculation that has appeared over the last several years.

The first proposition or summary statement that I will propose is that *a comparative psychology of infancy can be anticipated.* Harlow's well-known work (1958) on affectional systems in the monkey, though incomplete, is as stimulating a body of research as has been done on animal development over the last decade. Less widely known, but of at least equal theoretical impact, are T. C. Schneirla's (1959) speculations about approach and avoidance and their relation to stimulus intensity. Hess (1959), among others, has presented data and commentary on the phenomena of imprinting. Seymour Levine (1957) has contributed a number of papers on the effect of infantile stress on later behavior. These names only begin a list of the researchers who are working on developmental problems with infra-human animals.

Two general comments are warranted here. The animal work which is now going on in developmental psychology is not "dry-as-dust" laboratory demonstration. Moreover, little of this work leads to procedures routinely applicable to children, in the way that some current studies of reinforcement are; nor is the current animal work aimed at elaboration of the obvious. The psychologists studying animal development are in advance of their colleagues in human developmental studies, not only in regard to novel empirical techniques, but more important, in their willingness to take an intellectual chance or risk a speculation. The second note to be appended to the work with animals is the classical one, namely, the possibility of experimental manipulation of more than a trivial sort. We have only seen the beginning of work with animals, and particularly with primates, that will permit us to examine experimentally propositions that would otherwise remain available only to limited observational examination. Studies of the relation of infant to parent, for example, can be investigated along all relevant dimensions only by the use of animals. That is not to say that once we have found the rhesus we can abandon the human being, but the thoughtfulness and energy of investigators currently working in animal research will have no small impact on current research in the psychology of development.

But let me put aside the allure of precision and control possible with animal work and confine the rest of my general propositions to those about human behavior.

The first proposition about children to be considered, and perhaps the most obvious, is that *infants are various*—young children are different from one another. I may see a straw man when I speak against the notion that human infants at birth, like well-made cigarettes, cannot be distinguished from one another; but there is still abroad in psychology—at least in the academical variety—the feeling that children at birth are, by and large, pretty much undifferentiated protoplasm or no more than merely randomly varying beings. Whatever the present state is of the pure, undifferentiated position in the sociology of knowledge, evidence is accumulating that parents and nurses were right all along—stable differences in behavior can be detected in the first days of life. Hammond (1957) has shown the stability of physical growth patterns. Richmond and his colleagues at Syracuse (1955) have reported psychophysiological stabilities in the newborn. Thomas, Chess, Birch, and Hertzig (1960), although they have published only preliminary reports, have stated that on nine variables—among them, reactivity and irritability—they have found stability in children followed longitudinally over a period of two years. There are some suggestions in Bell's work (1960), and there are some findings in our work on newborns at Yale (1961), which tend to support a strong generalization that stable individual differences in a large number of behaviors—sucking, general movement, reactivity—exist very early in life. Yet, impressive as it is, the work on the assessment of individual differences among human infants has not, like some of the animal work, been "built out" from novel observations and speculations. Rather, it has come largely from the essential and tedious work of constructing adequate response measures. These advances in technology or method are clear and welcome, but they leave open two larger questions about individual differences.

First, what is the long-range stability or relevance of these differences? It is good to know that the newborn shows stable differences in activity level from his colleague in the next crib, but the importance of this observation is markedly reduced if the difference does not show up in some form later. Among the investigators, other than the Birch group, who have done some interesting speculative work on this score, is the French psychologist Stambak (1956). She has segregated two groups of infants—hypertonic and hypotonic—and has discussed the relation of this tendency to be active or quiet to such important developmental changes as onset of walking. In addition, the Czech group (Papoušek, 1961) is investigating the stability of the infant's behavior during conditioning over the first six months of life. Such studies are [illegible] on the intricate

[illegible]

as active or quiet, [illegible]
crimination in the first five or ten days of life. We can suspect, too, that some mothers like active babies and some mothers like quiet babies. What do you get when you combine an active baby with a mother who wanted a quiet one or a quiet baby with a mother who wanted an active one? We have very little to go on here, not only because of the obvious technical difficulties of longitudinal studies of this kind, and not only because of the fluidity of our ideas about what is important in the home, but also because, until recently, we have not had reliable ways of describing the young child's environment. The technical advance in the methods of describing newborn behavior have not been matched by methods for describing the home. But here, again, there is promise. Schaefer, Bell, and Bayley (1959) have proposed a parent attitude scale. The important interview work of Sears, *et al.* (1957) provides a framework for the description of parents' behavior. Rheingold (1960) has recently specified some of the dimensions of variation between home and institution. These papers point the way toward the time when a genuine analysis can be made of the interaction between mother and child. The word "genuine" reflects the hope that this analysis will not be a contaminated one; that we can make assessments of the status of the newborn, independent of observing the mother, and make assessment of the mother, independent of observing the child.

The next summary proposition that I want to suggest warrants detailed examination. I submit that *the young infant is not incompetent* or, by André-Thomas' (1954) catching phrase, "the neonate is not a neophyte."

[illegible] not so very

[illegible]

the existence of a non [illegible]

in early life, where the newborn does not code inputs at all. In this view of the infant, by no means limited to psychoanalysts, both the baby's sensory capacities and his response capacities are held to be severely limited. The trend of recent research is clearly against this conception of the child. Research on newborn behavior over the last five years has invariably added to the newborn's list of abilities. Peiper (1956) in his encyclopedic treatment, André-Thomas (1954) and his colleagues in Paris, Madame Ste. Anne-Desgassies, and Prechtl (1958) are among the workers who have discussed the extended sensory and response range of the newborn in some detail. Gorman and his associates (1959) have recently found in a study of acuity that the newborn has visual resolving powers which are not markedly inferior to those of the older child. From the research available on the competence of the newborn, let me present three studies in some detail as illustrative and somewhat representative of this newer view of the newborn.

The first study, by Blauvelt (1960), deals with the precision of at least one response the newborn makes. Following up earlier work of Prechtl on head-turning, Blauvelt has studied the baby's response to a very simple stimulation, in which the experimenter moves her finger from the tragus of the baby's ear—the baby lying on its back in the crib—toward the baby's mouth and then away in a flat elliptical course. It turns out that the baby tracks this movement by turning his head at a speed and to a position that will reduce the distance between his mouth and the stimulating finger. He tracks this movement without special tuition; it is, if you like, built-in. The infant can pick up approaching stimulation and reduce the distance to it very quickly; he can "find" the approaching breast or bottle. What is impressive about this response is the precision of it. This is not the response of a wild newborn, flailing around uselessly and without direction; this is an organism making a precise and exact tracking response. It is a limited skill, to be sure, and certainly not widely generalizable to other activities, but it illustrates the responding precision of some newborn.

The second study illustrative of newborn competence may be one of the most important empirical research products of the last decade in infancy work. Bronshtein, Antonova, Kamenetskaya, Luppova, and Sytova (1958) have described a technique for assessing the limits of sensory differentiation in the infant that promises a precision in psychophysical description that has heretofore been possible only for the much older child. Briefly, the procedure is this. You permit or induce the child to suck, and record his rhythmic response. If, during sucking, you sound a brief tone, say of 512 cycles/sec., the baby stops sucking. When the tone stops, the baby begins to suck again. To a second stimulation of the same tone, he will stop sucking. This sequence can be repeated four or five times for sounds and then when you sound your 512-cycle tone he goes on sucking without interruption. He has adapted to that sound. If, however, you now present a different tone, say one of 1,024 cycles, he will stop sucking. If he continues to suck on the application of the second stimulus, this is presumptive evidence that he cannot discriminate the two stimuli. If he does stop sucking on the second stimulus, if it "undoes the adaptation," then there is evidence that he can discriminate these two stimuli. If this technique is as sensitive as the Russians suggest, we will be able to find out more about the sensory capacities of the young infant than we can find out about the sensory capacities of young five- or six-year-olds. Bronshtein presents data to indicate that the infant makes clearly differential responses to variations in pitch, light intensity, and other stimulus changes. Lipsitt, at Brown, has adapted this technique to a study of olfactory stimulation and has found that not only is sucking inhibited and adapted in this fashion but so also is movement. Just as the Blauvelt study illustrates the possible response flexibility of the newborn, so the Bronshtein and Lipsitt studies indicate the remarkable amount of stimulus coding the newborn is capable of. The world of the infant is not a vast confusing "blob."

Consider yet a third study. In our work at Yale (1963), we have found that if you put a nipple in a baby's mouth, he will stop general movement at once, and when you take it out he will start moving again. This effect appears in the absence of nutrient; the nipple does not supply food—it only provides an opportunity to suck. And, this inhibition of movement takes place in the fourth or third or second, or even first day of life. The child is able to deal with a complex and vitally important input—namely, nipple or sucking—by a very regular response. Nor, apparently, does he have to learn either how to suck or how to be quiet. There is of course the argument that he learned the responses in *utero*, but we have hardly advanced beyond Hippocrates' statement of that argument 2,500 years ago.

These studies suggest that the newborn has far greater capacities for sensory discrimination than could have been guessed a decade ago, and though less impressive, the evidence is beginning to indicate that he has surprising response competencies as well. But the evidence for newborn resourcefulness poses a peculiar paradox. To put the question very bluntly, if the human newborn is so capable, why does he not learn more? If he is so capable, why is he so stupid? These questions form the bridge to my next general proposition, [illegible] that I have

[illegible]

days of life. There are many [illegible] let me cite just one.

Peiper maintains that there are three techniques of infantile sucking. One of them is the response that most mammals use to get milk out of a breast; it is a lapping response that involves pressing the nipple against the roof of the mouth with the tongue and squeezing milk out of it. Another one is to reduce pressure inside the mouth so as to pull the milk in by a discrepancy in pressure. This is the way most babies suck from bottles. And the third, fairly infrequent technique—confined to bottle-fed babies for obvious reasons—is to bite hard at the back of the nipple and squirt milk into the mouth. This variation is interesting because babies apparently come to use one of these different patterns very quickly. They learn, if "learn" is appropriate, the kind of sucking to use.

The difficulty with calling this kind of change "learning" arises from our failure to demonstrate early learning in a controlled setting. If the newborn is capable of this natural learning it should be possible for a psychologist to teach him something in a systematic learning study. And yet the evidence, controlled evidence for newborn learning, hardly exists. There is research by Marquis (1931), recently replicated in the USSR, showing that the baby adapts to a feeding rhythm, but the evidence does not support the conclusion that learning according to the usual theoretical models takes place in the period of early infancy. The Russians, with their strong demand for environmental control of behavior, have tried a large number of times to condition young infants. Sometimes they are successful; oftentimes they are not. Russian studies do not report con- [illegible] eight or nine

[illegible]

to his feeding routines on the one [illegible]

and the difficulty that all investigators have had in demonstrating newborn learning on the other?[1]

The following three options seem available to us: First, in spite of my statements about newborn competence, there may be genuine neurological incapacity in the newborn. There is no such thing as early learning, in the usual sense, because the child is not complete. A case for this position can be made. There are data on myelinization, on changes in pattern of EEG, on developments of vision and prehension, on the appearance of smiling—to take the most obvious case—all of which can be used to bolster the view that the young infant is a neurologically deficient organism. Under this reading, how do we account for the changes in behavior that do take place? Perhaps by maintaining that the caretaker becomes more competent. This would be a case of training the parent to adapt more effectively to the child rather than teaching the child to adapt to his environment. And to the data from Bronshtein and Lipsitt on the ability of the young infant to make sensory discriminations, we would have to say, "True infants can make sensory discriminations, but there is no associative coding; there is a deficiency in the hooking of links together."

The second answer, and the one I think that would be given by the learning analysts (Gewirtz, 1961), is that nobody has tackled the problem of early learning. In particular, holders of this position would maintain that the procedures of classical conditioning as used by the Russians are the wrong tactics. What we should do if we want to demonstrate early learning is to use instrumental techniques; that is, to make some effective reinforcement contingent on the occurrence of some response of the infant. For example, let the baby turn his head and then give him something to suck on. This is a testable proposition and it is being tested.

I would like to suggest a third possibility—an unpopular one. In brief, there may be experiential effects that are not learning. To put it another way, not all adaptation of the infant represents either classical conditioning or instrumental learning. I think it is inappropriate to maintain that all changes in behavior that can be related to the child's contact with the environment are the result of reinforcement contingencies. Of course, the instrumental learning position can be made to fit them, but it seems to me that such a forced fit results in theoretical vagueness and a weakening of the instrumental position.

Perhaps in pulling apart the problem of behavioral change in early infancy to exaggerate the variation among options, I have only shown that the resolution of the problem will require revisions in method, new knowledge of infantile neurophysiology, and a reworking of contemporary learning theory.

But consider now another interesting problem which illuminates some theoretical disagreements among students of infancy. Two theoretical positions have occupied this field: the psychoanalytic and the learning theoretical. Justice can be done to neither in a summary presentation. Rapaport (1959) and Wolff (1960) present the psychoanalytic presuppositions in detail and with force; Gewirtz (1961) has prepared a closely reasoned argument for a learning analysis.[2] Now, there is a new entrant into the field of theories of mother attachment. John Bowlby in a series of recent papers (1958) has borrowed from the investigators of instinct in

[1] The argument for early adaptation by the infant can probably be made much more forcefully, but a natural history of the first months of life remains to be written.

[2] It should be noted in passing that a learning analysis is both stronger and in a better position for compromise with other views by virtue of a retreat from the drive-reduction interpretation of reinforcement and by recent animal studies which show stable secondary reinforcement effects.

animals, a notion that sounds very much like imprinting and has suggested that the child's responses of sucking, clinging, and following lead to mother attachment. Just sucking, and just clinging, and just following on the part of the child, without obvious reinforcement or redistribution of cathexis, will result in a union between child and mother; much as the chick will imprint on a blinking light. Not only does Bowlby discuss what ties the child to his mother—namely, these three responses—but he also discusses what links the mother to the child. Not only does the child become attached to the mother because of sucking, clinging, and following, but the mother is drawn or attached —Bowlby does not use the word "imprinting"—to the child by the child's smiling and crying. Smiling and crying are held to be congenital or innate releases of material behavior.

It is difficult to evaluate this position and I am hard pressed to invent a satisfactory test for it. Perhaps we must call on animal research to work out the implications of Bowlby's assertions. But the main value of this new view will probably be the value of all theories of development that they jog thinking, they make people run a study just to see what happens. Certainly Bowlby's ideas have had that effect. His own research with Robertson on separation (1952), the work done by Schaffer (1959) on hospitalization of young children, and an unpublished study by Ainsworth (1961) have demonstrated the provocative effect of these speculations. One of the achievements of the work done by Ainsworth, in Uganda, is that, instead [illegible] attachment as a

[illegible]

have had heretofore.

It is interesting to note, as an adjunct to the problem of mother attachment, that something very curious indeed seems to happen to children near the middle of the first year. Ambrose's (1961) results on smiling indicate that at 17–25 weeks, general social smiling begins to decay and the child begins to smile only at its caretakers. Schaffer's work indicates that children who are hospitalized before they are 28 weeks old, accept hospital routines and separation easily; children hospitalized after 28 weeks-of-age show striking symptom patterns of distress and refusal to accept normal hospital care. Ainsworth finds that almost all of her criteria of mother attachment begin to show transition in the period from 17 to 30 weeks, with much of the change occurring in the narrow band between 25 and 28 weeks. Somewhere in the middle of the first year, the child appears to shift from being attached to human beings at large to being attached to one, or two, or three human beings.

The Ainsworth study is comparable in its impact to Rheingold's (1956) study of caretaking in institutionalized infants—both of these studies represent the payoff for the theoretical positions underlying them. The psychology of infancy undoubtedly profits from being in a state of theoretical dis-equilibrium, and the diversity of ideas about the nature of the child's attachment to his mother will almost certainly be productive of important empirical advances.

Consider one last generalization about infancy. It is one where contention, compromise, and reciprocation among theoretical positions have already resulted in general agreement. *The infant is active,* [illegible] *of infant and caretaker is*

[illegible]

United States, was of a recip[illegible]

—a reactive one. Behavior at any particular time is the function of the current stimulating environment. This remains technically a sound view, but the effect of it on the psychology of the infant was to diminish our appreciation of how complicated and subtle is the child.

Not only can the child be usefully seen as active, rather than merely as reactive, but it may also be useful to think of even the infant as a problem-solver. Certainly the child, like the adult, can be seen as encountering problems in his environment. At least from the age of six months, the child's behavior can be discussed in terms of discrepancy, goal-seeking, means to an end, and so on. One student of children has not deviated from this view of the active searching child. Piaget and his students have seen the child, especially the infant, as being in a constant exchange with the environment, meeting its demands, and what American investigators somehow forgot, making its own demands on that environment.

The shift in point-of-view—to set the antithesis sharply—has been from the child who is a passive receptacle, into which learning and maturation pour knowledge and skills and effects until he is full, to the child as a complex, competent organism who, by acting on the environment and being acted on in turn, develops more elaborated and balanced ways of dealing with discrepancy, conflict, and disequilibrium. This shift, I believe is of incalculable implication and seems to have been accepted to some degree by almost all students of children. Bowlby emphasizes the control by the child in crying and smiling; psychoanalytic theory makes more space for autonomous ego functions; child psychologists dedicated to a learning analysis speak of the child as active; and I suspect Piaget thinks of how he knew it all the time. But this shift only sets the problem for the psychology of the infant; questions abound. What is a "problem" for the infant? What is an environmental discrepancy for the newborn, for the six-month-old, for a walker? Do Piaget's speculations about assimilation, accommodation, and equilibration have more than a metaphorical value? Can child psychologists follow the lead of psychologists of cognition in adults who use computer analogies? Can we build a theory of cognitive development without the use of terms like reinforcement, drive, or dissonance resolution?

Only one thing seems certain. We are better equipped, with attitude and technique, to make a systematic and meaningful analysis of infant behavior than ever before. The current psychology of infant behavior, by and large, is managing to steer skillfully between the Scylla of "Oh, Oh, look what the baby did!" and the Charybdis of "But the theory says thus and so." We are engaging in hot, theoretical debate, but more and more the debate refers back to the child—back to the theory illuminated facts.

References

AINSWORTH, M. D. The development of infant-child interaction among the Ganda. Paper read at Tavistock Study Group on Mother-Infant Interaction, London, 1961.

AMBROSE, J. A. The development of smiling response in early infancy. In Foss, B. M. (Ed.), *Determinants of infant behavior*. New York: Wiley, 1961.

ANDRÉ-THOMAS. Ontogénèse de la vie psychoaffective et de la douleur. *Encéphale,* 1954, *43,* 289–311.

BELL, R. Q. Relations between behavior manifestations in the human neonate. *Child Develpm.,* 1960, *31,* 463–477.

BLAUVELT, H. & MCKENNA, J. Capacity of the human newborn for mother-infant interaction. II. The temporal dimensions of a neonate response. *Psychiat. Res. Rep.*, 1960, *13*, 128–147.

BOWLBY, J. The nature of the child's tie to his mother. *Int. J. Psychoanal.*, 1958, *39*, 1–24.

BRONSHTEIN, A. I., ANTONOVA, T. G., KAMENETSKAYA, A. G., LUPPOVA, N. N. & SYTOVA, V. A. On the development of the functions of analyzers in infants and some animals at the early stage of ontogenesis. In *Problems of evolution of physiological functions.* OTS Report No. 50–61066. Translation obtainable from U.S. Dept. of Commerce. Moscow: Acad. Sci., 1958.

DASHKOVSKAYA, V. S. First conditioned reactions in newly born children in normal state and in certain pathological states. *Zh. vyssh. nervn. Deiatel.*, 1953, *3*(2), 247–259.

GEWIRTZ, J. L. A learning analysis of the effects of normal stimulation, privation, and deprivation on the acquisition of social motivation and attachment. In Foss, B. M. (Ed.), *Determinants of infant behavior.* New York: Wiley, 1961.

GORMAN, J. J., COGAN, D. G. & GELLIS, S. S. A device for testing visual acuity in infants. *Sight-Saving Rev.*, 1959, *29*, 80–84.

HAMMOND, W. H. The constancy of physical types as determined by factorial analysis. *Hum. Biol.*, 1957, *29*, 40–61.

HARLOW, H. F. The nature of love. *Amer. Psychologist*, 1958, *13*, 673–685.

HESS, E. H. Imprinting. *Science*, 1959, *130*, 133–141.

KESSEN, W., WILLIAMS, E. J. & WILLIAMS, J. P. Selection and test of response measures in the study of the human newborn. *Child Develpm.*, 1961, *32*, 7–24.

LEVINE, S. Infantile experience and resistance to psychological stress. *Science*, 1957, *126*, 405.

MARQUIS, D. P. Can conditioned responses be established in the newborn infant? *J. genet. Psychol.*, 1931, *39*, 479–492.

PAPOUŠEK, H. A physiological view of early ontogenesis of so-called voluntary movements. In Sobotka, P. (Ed.), *Functional and metabolic development of the central nervous system.* Prague: State Pedagogic Publ., 1961.

PEIPER, A. *Die Eigenart der Kindlichen Hirntätigkeit* (2nd Ed.). Leipzig: Theme, 1956.

PRECHTL, H. F. R. The directed head turning response and allied movements of the human baby. *Behaviour*, 1958, *13*, 212–242.

RAPAPORT, D. The structure of psychoanalytic theory: A systematizing attempt. In Koch, S. (Ed.), *Psychology: a study of a science, vol. 3.* New York: McGraw-Hill, 1959.

RHEINGOLD, H. L. The modification of social responsiveness in institutional babies. *Monogr. Soc. Res. Child Develpm.*, 1956, *21*(2).

———. The measurement of maternal care. *Child Develpm.*, 1960, *31*, 565–575.

RICHMOND, J. B. & LUSTMAN, S. L. Autonomic function in the neonate: I. Implications for psychosomatic theory. *Psychosom. Med.*, 1955, *17*, 269–275.

ROBERTSON, J. & BOWLBY, J. Responses of young children to separation from their mothers. *Courrier de la Centre Internationale de l'Enfance*, 1952, *2*, 131–142.

[illegible] N. Development of a maternal behavior research

Peterson, 1957.

SPITZ, R. A. *A genetic field theory of ego formation; its implications for pathology.* New York: Internat. Univer. Press, 1959.

STAMBAK, M. Contribution à l'étude du developpement moteur chez le nourrisson. *Enfance,* 1956, 9(4), 49–59.

THOMAS, A., CHESS, S., BIRCH, H. & HERTZIG, M. E. A longitudinal study of primary reaction patterns in children. *Comprehensive Psychiat.,* 1960, *1,* 103–112.

WOLFF, P. H. *The developmental psychologies of Jean Piaget and psychoanalysis.* New York: Internat. Univer. Press, 1960.

CHAPTER 1: SUGGESTED FURTHER READING

BALDWIN, A. *Theories of Child Development.* New York: Wiley, 1967.

———. A cognitive theory of socialization. In Goslin, D. A. (Ed.) *Handbook of Socialization Theory and Research.* Chicago: Rand McNally, 1969. Pp. 325–345.

BANDURA, A. Social-learning theory of identification processes. In Goslin, D. A. (Ed.) *Handbook of Socialization Theory and Research.* Chicago: Rand McNally, 1969. Pp. 213–262.

ERIKSON, E. *Childhood and Society.* (2nd ed.) New York: Norton, 1963. (The Eight Ages of Man, Chapter 7.) (Also available in paperback.)

FLAVELL, J. H. *The Developmental Psychology of Jean Piaget.* New York: Van Nostrand, 1963.

FREUD, S. Infantile sexuality. In J. Strachey (Tr., Ed.), *Three Essays on the Theory of Sexuality. Standard Edition of the Complete Psychological Works of Sigmund Freud.* London: Hogarth Press and the Institute of Psycho-Analysis, Vol. VII, 1953.

GINSBURG, H., and OPPER, S. *Piaget's Theory of Intellectual Development: An Introduction.* Englewood Cliffs, N.J.: Prentice-Hall, 1969.

HARRIS, D. B. (Ed.). *The Concept of Development.* Minneapolis: University of Minnesota Press, 1957.

HUNT, J. MC V. *Intelligence and Experience.* New York: Ronald, 1961.

INHELDER, B., and PIAGET, J. *The Growth of Logical Thinking from Childhood to Adolescence.* New York: Basic Books, 1958.

KOHLBERG, L. Stage and sequence: The cognitive-developmental approach to socialization. In Goslin, D. A. (Ed.) *Handbook of Socialization Theory and Research.* Chicago: Rand McNally, 1969. Pp. 347–480.

LANGER, J. *Theories of Development.* New York: Holt, Rinehart, and Winston, 1969.

———. Werner's theory of development. In Mussen, P. (Ed.) *Carmichael's Manual of Child Psychology, Vol. 1.* New York: Wiley, 1970. Pp. 733–771.

MAIER, H. *Three Theories of Child Development.* (rev. ed.) New York: Harper & Row, 1962.

MILLER, D. Psychoanalytic theory of development: A re-evaluation. In Goslin, D. A. (Ed.) *Handbook of Socialization Theory and Research.* Chicago: Rand McNally, 1969. Pp. 481–502.

PIAGET, J. *The Child's Conception of the World.* New York: Harcourt, Brace & World, 1929.

———. *Six Psychological Studies.* New York: Random House, 1967.

———. Piaget's theory. In Mussen, P. (Ed.) *Carmichael's Manual of Child Psychol-* [illegible] 1970. Pp. 703–732.

chapter two
the organism

Psychology, like other sciences, is still discovering things about the basic nature of its subject matter—the human organism. Much of the current research is focused on the infant in an attempt to discover what capacities and capabilities the organism has early in its existence. Through this research we might also come to understand more about humans in general. For example, if we discover that infants learn through many channels, such as touch, vision, taste, smell, and hearing, we might ask why some of these channels are more important for adult learning than others. We could also ask what would happen if all these channels were kept "open" for communication throughout life, or are some channels better for certain kinds of learning than others?

These are very different questions than we were asking earlier in the history of psychology. Earlier, basic assumptions were made about the organism and were never questioned. For instance, adults once believed (and some still do) that babies could only see shadows until they were a few months old. This assumption was based on data gathered from that notion and was not scientifically questioned until the last quarter century. Such strongly held beliefs do not lead people to ask questions about vision, such as, can babies focus? Do they prefer one thing over another to look at?

We are now in a period where many exciting questions are being asked about the basic nature of the organism. Some questions are being answered; some are not. More recent evidence sometimes negates earlier findings, but this all adds to the excitement and interest in the field.

There are studies in other sections of the reader that also deal with the capabilities of the organism. In effect they all do. We have included the readings in this section at the beginning of this book because they provide a basic understanding of the early capacities of the human organism and also indicate some of the more recent ways in which these capacities are studied.

The excerpt from McClelland, although written much earlier than most of the others, indicates why learning in infancy and early childhood is so important. It also serves as a frame of reference for the articles that follow in this and other sections.

The article by Sameroff on conditioning indicates much of what we have recently studied about learning. This type of research depends on newer methodologies and equipment than we had available earlier. The same is true for the article by Kagan. These articles tell us much about learning processes of the human, at least as much as our current methods allow us to discover.

Watson's article on "the game" is an example of current research that would have been unheard of earlier—the infant having some control over its environment instead of being a passive recipient of knowledge! It demonstrates very clearly that research needs appropriate tools and appropriate attitudes and, with both, new ideas may be tested. Tanner's research on growth tells us much about the capabilities of the human body and, within certain limits, how resilient our bodies are.

We have included as the last article in this section one that describes an ongoing developmental laboratory. Not all labs look like this one, although many wish they did, but aspects of this lab are included in many studies, and the article gives a good idea of what kinds of equipment currently are used to help us learn more about the organism.

3. EXCERPTS FROM *PERSONALITY*

DAVID McCLELLAND

Why Should Childhood Experiences Be So Important?

Psychoanalysts like Kardiner have not been overly concerned with this question. They have been content for the most part to know that in the case of some individuals early traumata have had important effects on adult adjustments. Can we add anything to this bare fact from our general knowledge of the way schemata develop or are acquired? Are there any theoretical reasons why early childhood experiences should be relatively more important than later ones? When the question is put in this way, it is immediately apparent that there are a number of factors which should operate to make early experiences more important than later ones, factors which derive from theories and experiments about how schemata are acquired.

Primacy As long ago as 1897 Jost formulated two hypotheses about associative learning which have subsequently come to be known as Jost's laws: "If two associations are of equal strength but of different age, a new repetition has a greater value for the older one," and "If two associations are of equal strength but of different age, the older diminishes less with time." (McGeoch, 1942, p. 140.) These "laws" have been confirmed by experiments in the laboratory over relatively short intervals of time, but as McGeoch points out, they do not have much explanatory value because of "our ignorance of the effective variables which differential age brings with it." (1942, p. 142.) If we think of age of associations ontogenetically, it is clear that associations formed in childhood all have the benefit of age according to Jost's laws. We can further argue that the reason why age is an advantage in this case is that they are assimilated less to preexisting trace systems. Certainly as far as young children are concerned positive and negative transfer from previous experiences must be relatively much less than with older children or adults. The child has fewer previously formed associations, less "apperceptive mass" into which new experiences are assimilated and modified. In fact, early experiences, simply because they occur first, are probably of greater importance in setting up the frames of reference in terms of which subsequent experiences are classified and modified. In experiments like Bartlett's (1932) on serial reproduction of a story or a perceptual figure, there is considerable evidence to indicate that the first impression is more important in determining the "final" conception than are any subsequent impressions, although data on this point are hard to collect (cf. Asch, 1946; Hanawalt, 1937). Numerous experiments on regression in animals (cf. Mowrer, 1940) have indicated that a response learned first becomes prepotent over subsequent learned responses, especially if frustration is introduced. Finally, experiments on the recognition process (Bruner and Postman, 1949) have demonstrated that the hypotheses brought to a situation tend to shape subsequent perception to a marked extent. From such evidence it seems safe to infer that *part* of the relatively greater importance of childhood events lies in the mere fact that they occur first and therefore can shape rather than be shaped by other conceptions and later experiences.

Underdeveloped symbolic processes A child experiences a great many things during the first eighteen to twenty-four months of his life before he has symbol systems developed to the point where they can adequately represent what he has experienced. What about all those experiences which occur before language or "consciousness" develops? One can either assume that they are of relatively little importance in determining subsequent behavior because they have not been symbolized, or that they go on influencing behavior but in a way which is relatively independent of the symbol systems developed in connection with later experiences. The latter assumption, which certainly seems more reasonable, is essentially the one the psychoanalysts have made in arguing for the importance of the "unconscious." If we read for "unconscious" some such term as "unverbalized" or "unsymbolized," it is easy to see on theoretical grounds why early experiences might continue to exert a disproportionate influence on subsequent behavior because they are not under symbolic control. Not enough experimental attention has been given to this important theoretical problem, but several experiments demonstrate the greater resistance to extinction of unverbalized learning (cf. Hilgard and Marquis, 1940, pp. 267–268). In short, early experiences may assume such great importance in personality because they are not represented by the kinds of symbols, particularly verbal, which facilitate subsequent discrimination, assimilation, extinction, and control.

Repetition Few people have com[illegible]mented on the fact, although it [illegible] apparent to young par[illegible]

[illegible]

of feeding arises around [illegible] times in the first two years of an infant's life. The parent for reasons of economy acquires certain methods of handling the feeding problem and the infant in turn learns to expect certain responses from the parent. Is it then so surprising that reponses and expectations which have been reinforced thousands of times should be of importance in determining the subsequent conception a child develops of the world? Or take the problem of bowel control. The average infant probably soils himself from six to ten times a day, at least in the beginning. In the first year alone the problem of changing his diapers or cleaning him up must arise somewhere around two thousand times. One does not need to assume any extraordinary learning capacity on the infant's part to infer that many expectations and habitual modes of reaction will be acquired during all these repetitions of a problem situation. D. P. Marquis (1941) has shown that newborn infants can learn a certain feeding schedule in a matter of a few days (25–35 paired repetitions). But the habits we are speaking of here would have many thousands of opportunities for a particular association to be formed and strengthened. When one considers how often the Alorese child associates his mother with the pangs of frustration and hunger, it seems reasonable to assume that he might develop the kind of anticipation of frustration from women that Kardiner postulates (1945). The fact is that there are few situations as important to the organism, outside early child training, that give such extensive opportunities through sheer repetition for the learning of attitudes, expectations, and [illegible]

learned during the first year is of imp[illegible]

tance in the second year, the third year, or the twenty-third year? This takes us directly into the problem of unlearning or forgetting. What are the conditions for forgetting? In recent years, the general consensus among learning theorists is that forgetting is not due to *disuse*. McGeoch in particular has argued that forgetting is "not a matter of passive decay." "Decrements in retention are a function of three fundamental conditions: (a) interference by intervening activities; (b) altered stimulating conditions; (c) inadequate set at the time of the measurement of retention." (1942, p. 457.)

How would each of these factors operate to produce forgetting of early experiences? As the child grows older he will learn new responses but under somewhat different stimulating conditions. For one thing, he is simply bigger, and the world looks different to him. Consider for a moment how the world must look to a child of one or two. It must be populated largely with feet and legs, with the underneath surfaces of chairs and tables, with large obstacles such as steps to be crawled over. The context changes radically as he grows bigger. In terms of retroactive inhibition theory, this means that his new responses will be attached to new stimulating conditions and older responses will not necessarily be unlearned or forgotten as a result of this new or "interpolated" activity. In fact, careful consideration of the conditions which McGeoch sets down for forgetting would lead us to expect that the rapid growth of the child would favor the acquisition of new learning without corresponding decrements in old learning. In technical terms, such a state of affairs would show up as reproductive interference making it difficult for the child to *recall* earlier learning, because of new learned responses, while some other method of measuring retention such as a savings score in relearning would demonstrate that earlier experiences were still retained. Actual unlearning is apparently most likely to occur when the same situation gives rise to incompatible responses, one of which may then be extinguished by lack of reinforcement. But such an opportunity for unlearning is not so likely to occur in the rapidly growing infant (a) when stimulus situations change quickly and (b) when similarities among situations are not as great as they are when they can be grouped under a common symbol.

Let us take a concrete example to make the point clear. Suppose for the sake of argument that an infant develops on the basis of earlier experiences with his mother an expectation that she will be harsh and punishing. As he grows older he learns a new expectation based perhaps on the fact that she is no longer harsh and frustrating since he is now toilet-trained, which removes the source of most of her irritation. The new expectation, however, is tied to somewhat different stimulus conditions (he has grown up), and there is no reason for supposing on the basis of contemporary theories of forgetting that the earlier expectation is completely wiped out. It may be difficult to recall, except under conditions of free association and fantasy, as the psychoanalysts have demonstrated, but that is no reason to assume that its influence is entirely lost. As savings scores demonstrate, the influence of past learning persists long beyond the point when recall is reduced to zero. Subsequent learning, to be sure, produces *some* unlearning (cf. Melton and Von Lackum, 1941), but the point that needs emphasis here is that conditions do not seem adequate to account for complete forgetting of early childhood associations.

Furthermore, there are other reasons why early experiences are not as readily forgotten as later ones. Much early learning which occurs before the child has developed the symbol systems discussed above, must be exceedingly generalized and vague. Extinction and forgetting occur most readily when the elements in a stimulus-response-reward sequence are easily discriminated by a rat or a human.

When, however, such sequences are made to be vague or variable through aperiodic reinforcement (Jenkins and Stanley, 1950), or random variation of "correct" cues, correct responses, or time delays to reinforcement (cf. McClelland and McGown, 1950), extinction or unlearning becomes much more difficult to produce. Yet variability of the elements in a learning sequence is probably the rule in early childhood. All Johnny learns is that sometimes "something" painful may happen when he has done "something." In the beginning at least such associations may be so general as to be very hard to extinguish. The isolation of "cue" and "response" and "reward" (cf. Miller and Dollard, 1941) is an achievement of later childhood or of an experimenter who is careful to isolate these elements in a regular and systematic fashion for the animal or child performing in the typical learning experiment. As the apperceptive mass gets more differentiated, as discriminations become easier to make in terms of language and other symbolic systems, what is learned becomes increasingly specific and therefore increasingly easy to forget or unlearn by altered motivation, changed stimulus conditions, etc.

In conclusion, then, it is apparent that many considerations based on our knowledge of the learning and forgetting process would lend support to the psychoanalytic position that early childhood is of very great importance in determining "basic personality structure." Since the reasons derive directly from learning theory, careful reasoning and experimentation along the lines suggested above ought to quiet many theoretical psychologists' doubts about a mysterious "unconscious" which obeys laws of its own. Often psychoanalysts have been right for the wrong reasons. Their lack of training in formal learning psychology has not enabled them to give satisfactory explanations as to why unconscious early learning should be so important and the explanations they have resorted to have seemed so anthropomorphic and strange to other psychologists that many psychoanalytic formulations have been dismissed without the serious consideration they deserve (cf. Sherif and Cantril, 1947).

References

ASCH, S. Forming impressions of persons. *Journal of Abnormal and Social Psychology*, 1946, *41*, 258–290.

BARTLETT, T. C. *Remembering: A study in experimental and social psychology*. Cambridge, Mass.; Cambridge University Press, 1932.

[illegible] of immunity: a paradigm. *Journal of* [illegible]

MC GEOCH, J. A. *The psychology of human learning*. New York: [illegible]

MARQUIS, D. P. Learning in the neonate: The modification of behavior under three feeding schedules. *Journal of Experimental Psychology,* 1941, *29,* 263–282.

MELTON, W. A., and VON LACKUM, W. J. Retroactive and proactive inhibition in retention: Evidence for a two-factor theory of retention intuition. *American Journal of Psychology,* 1941, *54,* 157–173.

MILLER, N. E., and DOLLARD, J. *Social learning and imitation.* New Haven: Yale University Press, 1941.

MOWRER, O. H. An experimental analogue of "regression" with incidental observations on "reaction-formation." *Journal of Abnormal and Social Psychology,* 1940, *35,* 56–87.

SHERIF, M., and CANTRIL, H. *The psychology of ego-involvements.* New York: Wiley, 1947.

4. CAN CONDITIONED RESPONSES BE ESTABLISHED IN THE NEWBORN INFANT: 1971?

ARNOLD J. SAMEROFF

The learning capabilities of the human newborn are evaluated. Classical conditioning is difficult to demonstrate in the newborn, while operant conditioning is possible. Two hypotheses are evaluated as explanations for difficulties in conditioning the newborn: (a) The newborn is unable to respond to stimulus change. (b) The newborn is able to respond to a general change but cannot respond to specific differences in stimulation. It is proposed that classical conditioning may involve the integration of two sensory modalities: that of the CS and that of the US. The newborn infant must first develop cognitive systems, through his experience with various stimuli, to differentiate each modality separately before he can integrate any two modalities in classical conditioning. The roles of the orientating reaction and defensive reaction are discussed.

The title of this article is taken from Dorothy Marquis who asked the same question in 1931. She answered that question in the affirmative, but recent data suggest that her conclusion may have been premature. For the purpose of exploring the issue of newborn learning in detail, the present author has divided the literature into two parts. The section on studies of infant activity focuses on the infant's ability to alter his behavior in experimental situations. The section on studies of infant reactivity deals with the newborn's ability to respond to stimulus change in his environment. In a later section the relation between the infant's ability to react to stimuli and his ability to form new associations to these stimuli is explored. The operational definition of the newborn period used in this article is the length of time that the infant remains in the hospital after birth, currently from 3 to 10 days.

Studies of Activity

In Kessen's (1963) description of infants as active as well as reactive, he suggested that the child is engaged in the process of integrating his experience and thereby constructing his world, and is not atomistically accepting the contingencies of which he finds himself a part. An empirical question that would help in the definition of a theoretical position is, What are the kinds of contingencies to which the newborn can respond; that is, which experimental paradigms will be effective in showing learning, and which paradigms will not show alteration in the performance of the infant? The two major paradigms of consequence for learning studies are the classical or respondent and the instrumental or operant.

There have been many investigations in which attempts were made to show classical conditioning in newborn infants. These studies were uniformly unsuccessful or inconclusive. A prototype of this kind of study is one done by Wickens and Wickens in 1940, who elicited foot withdrawal by using an electrotactual shock as an unconditioned stimulus. In their experimental group, they paired a buzzer with the shock for 36 trials over 3 days. On the third day, they tested for conditioning by presenting the buzzer alone and got, as they had hoped, the foot withdrawal response. However, in a control group which also had 36 trials of electrotactual shock, but without a buzzer, they were also able to get a foot withdrawal response when the infants were stimulated with the buzzer. It appeared that pairing the buzzer with the shock was irrelevant to the [illegible] obtained. They concluded

unsuccessful. Lipsitt and Kaye ([illegible]

1963) worked with a different aversive response. They paired a tone with the presentation of acetic acid vapor to the infant's nose. The unconditioned response was withdrawal from the vapor or heightened activity. They were also unsuccessful in obtaining this response.

There is a second group of studies[1] in which conditioning effects were purportedly found, but a number of important questions were left unanswered about control groups or peculiarities in results. These studies have been criticized by a number of authors including Lipsitt (1963) and Bijou and Baer (1965). Among these are Spelt's (1948) report of fetal conditioning, Marquis's (1931) report of conditioning sucking movements to a buzzer, Marquis's (1941) later report of conditioning infants to their feeding schedules, and Lipsitt and Kaye's (1964) recent attempt to condition sucking movements to a tone.

During the last few years a change in paradigm took place and investigators using operant techniques have been able to find positive evidence of learning abilities in the newborn. Lipsitt, Kaye, and Bosack (1966) were able to increase the infant's sucking rate to a rubber tube by reinforcing the sucking with dextrose solution. They demonstrated both extinction and retraining effects.

Sameroff (1968) was able to differentially alter two components of the sucking

[1] The author has classed all studies in which sucking on a nipple was the UR and anticipatory sucking without a nipple was the CR in

response. Infants had been noted to get milk out of a nipple either by expression, that is, squeezing the nipple between tongue and palate, or by suction, that is, enlarging the oral cavity and creating a vacuum which pulls the milk out of the nipple. When the expression component was reinforced, that is, squeezing the nipple, the suction component was diminished and in many cases disappeared during the training period. When the newborns had to express above certain pressure thresholds to obtain milk, they changed their performance to match the thresholds.

Siqueland (1968) was able to influence the head turning response in newborns by operant training. He succeeded in increasing the rate of head turning in two groups (one of which was put on a 2:1 fixed-ratio schedule), and to decrease head turning in a third group which was reinforced for holding the head still.

Using a modified classical conditioning paradigm, Siqueland and Lipsitt (1966) performed three experiments using Papousek's (1961) head turning method. They stroked the cheeks of newborn infants which under normal conditions elicited ipsilateral head turns about 25% of the time. In their first experiment they paired a buzzer with the stroking and, if the infant turned his head, he received an immediate dextrose solution reinforcement. In their experimental group, the rate of head turning to the tactual stimulus increased to 80%, while in a control group in which the reinforcement was given only 8–10 seconds after the tone-touch stimulation, the rate remained at 25%. However, there was no evidence that the auditory stimulus had any influence on the results, since the head turn did not occur until the stroke was performed.

In the second experiment, Siqueland and Lipsitt investigated differentiation of two auditory stimuli, a buzzer and a tone. The positive stimulus was paired with a tactual stimulus eliciting head turning to one side, while on alternate trials the negative stimulus was paired with tactual stimulation eliciting head turning to the other side. After training by reinforcing the response to the positive stimulus with dextrose solution, they were able to show an increase of head turning to the stroke on the positive side as opposed to no increase of head turning to the stroke on the negative side. Again, however, there was no evidence that the auditory stimuli played any role in the learning since the infants responded only to the differential stroking of the cheek to one side or the other.

In the third experiment, the same authors showed some evidence for differentiation of the auditory stimuli. They used the same buzzer and tone as positive and negative stimuli, presented alternately as in the previous experiment; but, this time both were paired with a tactual perioral stimulus eliciting head turning on only one side. When the positive stimulus sounded, the tactual stimulus was applied and if a head turn occurred the infant was reinforced with dextrose solution. When the negative stimulus sounded, the infant was stroked on the same side, but a head turn did not result in reinforcement. In this situation, the infant increased his responding to the tactual stimulus following the positive auditory stimulus while the stroke associated with the negative stimulus did not increase in effectiveness in eliciting head turns. These results are interesting, both from the point of view of having a differentiation of response associated with the two auditory stimuli, and the failure to demonstrate the infant's ability to be classically conditioned. The auditory signal still did not elicit the head turning response anticipatorily; it was only after the tactual stimulus was presented that the head turn was elicited.

What differentiates those studies in which investigators were able to show learning effects in newborns from those where there was less success? Is there any generalization that can be made which will help to understand the behavior of these newborns better? One clear difference is between the classical and operant conditioning paradigms. The unsuccessful studies have typically been attempts at classical conditioning, attempts to relate a previously neutral stimulus to an unconditioned stimulus and response.

On the other hand, the unsuccessful experiments either have not been in the classical conditioning paradigm or have not yielded classical results. In all cases, a previous relationship has already existed between the stimulus and response in question. No previously neutral stimuli have been associated. The results of the various training procedures have been to strengthen or alter what Kessen (1967) has described as *organized patterns of behavior* in the newborn. In the Lipsitt, Kaye, and Bosack (1966) study, an already existing low sucking rate to an oral stimulus was enhanced. In the Sameroff (1968) study, already existing expression and suction components of the sucking response were modified. In Siqueland's (1968) operant conditioning of head turning, an already existing organized component of the rooting-sucking-feeding complex was modified; and in Siqueland and Lipsitt's (1966) three experiments, an already existing relation between tactual perioral stimulation and head turning was enhanced.

If classical conditioning has not been demonstrated in the newborn, when can it be said to have been reliably shown? Polikanina (1961) paired a tone CS with ammonia vapor as an US eliciting motoric ... She found a con-

work of Lipsitt and Kaye (in Lipsitt, 1963) and Siqueland and Lipsitt (1966) became possible during the third week of life, as seen in the work of Polikanina (1961) and Papousek (1967).

A *caveat* must be included here about considering the Polikanina (1961) or Papousek (1967) studies as evidence for successful classical conditioning. The Polikanina study included no controls for pseudoconditioning. As a result, her findings may be identical in origin to those of Wickens and Wickens (1940). The Papousek head turning paradigm that was also used in the Siqueland and Lipsitt (1966) studies is not true classical conditioning. The milk reinforcement as a consequence of the head turning made the procedure a mixed model during training, and an operant after criterion was reached. Morgan and Morgan (1944), also without controls, claimed no eyeblink conditioning was possible before 45 days of life. Janos (1965) presented the best case for conditional eyeblink, but he got it only after 86 days. He was also able to show differentiation of response to two auditory cues.

The failure to classically condition newborns requires that an attempt be made at some theoretical explanation of the data. A starting point for such an explanation will be an analysis of the task. Since the problem seems to be related to the establishment of an association to a previously neutral stimulus, a first requirement for the subject in the classical conditioning paradigm is that he be able to perceive this neutral stimulus. A starting hypothesis can

onstrated in the first week of life

studies of perception using habituation or eye orientation fall into this class. The main concern, however, is with a group of responses which the Russians, especially Sokolov (1963), have called the orienting reaction.

The function of the orienting reaction is to prepare the organism to deal with novel stimulation (Lynn, 1966). Lynn (1966), following Sokolov (1963), lists five classes of responses in the orienting reaction. They include (*a*) increases in the sensitivity of the sense organs, (*b*) motor orientation of the sense organs toward the source of stimulation, (*c*) changes in general skeletal musculature, (*d*) desynchronization of the EEG with accompanying lowered amplitude and increased frequency, and (*e*) a number of autonomic responses consisting of GSR, vasoconstriction in the limbs and vasodilation in the head, decrease in respiratory frequency with increase in amplitude, and heart-rate deceleration. In the last decade, several studies have produced evidence for the existence of various components of the orienting reaction in the newborn. They are listed below following Lynn's (1966) categorization.

Increase in the sensitivity of the sense organs Stechler, Bradford, and Levy (1966) stimulated newborn infants with an air puff to the abdomen in two conditions while measuring the GSR. In the first condition, the infants were awake with eyes open and fixated on a patterned visual stimulus. In the second condition the infants were awake with eyes open but not fixated on any apparent stimulus. The electrodermal response was much stronger in the fixated condition as compared with the unfixated condition. The existence of the orienting reaction can be inferred from the lower sensory thresholds for GSR elicitation in the fixating group.

Motor orientation of sense organs Motor orientation of head and/or eyes to visual stimuli have been found by Fantz (1963), Hershenson (1964), Wolff (1966), and Salapatek and Kessen (1966). Eye orientation to auditory stimulation has been reported by Wolff (1966) and Turkewitz, Moreau, and Birch (1966). The rooting reflex is an orientation of the head to perioral tactual stimulation.

Changes in general skeletal musculature Motor quieting and cessation of ongoing activity to novel stimuli have been found by Papousek (1967) and Bronshtein and Petrowa (1952).

Desynchronization of the EEG Generalized EEG responses have been reported by Dreyfuss-Brisac and Blanc (1956) and Ellingson (1967) to indicate that the newborn can react to novel stimuli with a change to the low amplitude, fast activity which has been described as part of the orienting reaction.

Autonomic responses Sokolov (1963) used the vasomotor responses as one of his prime indicators for the orienting reaction. However, as yet, vasomotor responses have not been investigated in the newborn, so little can be said about them. More work has been done with other autonomic responses. Until recently there was some question as to whether the GSR could be found in newborns. However, Crowell, David, Chun, and Spellacy (1965) and Stechler, Bradford, and Levy (1966) in a study cited above, both found the GSR by careful experimental preparation. Respiration has not received much attention as an orienting reaction component. Sameroff (1970) has found respiratory slowing to auditory stimulation in some conditions. Steinschneider (1968) reported that white noise stimuli between 55 and 100 decibels increased respiratory rate. However, if only the first respiratory cycle following stimulus change was considered, the low intensity stimuli, 55 and 70 decibels, resulted in respiratory deceleration. The different direction of response to the low intensity stimuli might be interpreted as an orienting reaction component.

The one response that seems to be quite different from what was expected in an orienting reaction is the heart-rate response. Authors working with newborns have consistently shown heart-rate acceleration to novel stimuli. The heart-rate-decelerative response to stimulation does exist in the 4-month-old infant (Kagan & Lewis, 1965). Lipton, Steinschneider, and Richmond (1966) found some heart-rate deceleration before acceleration in infants 2½ months of age, and Lewis, Bartels, and Goldberg (1966) also found initial deceleration before acceleration in a third of their awake subjects between the ages of 2 and 8 weeks. Schulman (1968), in a recent study, was able to find consistent deceleration in awake 1-week-olds, further lowering the age boundary. In newborns, Schachter, Williams, Khachaturian, Tobin, and Druger (1968) found a triphasic response to auditory clicks, the first phase being a short deceleration.

From this survey of the newborn orienting reaction literature, it can be seen that the field has moved in the last 10 years from little or no knowledge to an almost complete outline of newborn reactivity. Apparently, the one component of the orienting reaction about which there is some serious question is the heart-rate response. Is the heart-rate-decelerative component of the orienting reaction undeveloped, or can some other explanation be put forth as to why acceleration seems to be the predominate heart-rate response in the newborn? One hypothesis is related to [illegible]

source of stimulation. The defensive reaction avoids the stimulus source, whereas the orienting reaction approaches the source of stimulation. Perhaps the heart-rate acceleration to stimulation found in newborn infants is part of the defensive reaction rather than a sign of an immature orienting reaction.

A question which immediately arises is, What kind of stimulation gives rise to one reaction over another? Sokolov (1963) defined the defensive reaction as occurring when stimulation increases above a certain limit and threatens the integrity of the body, that is, becomes painful. However, in the case of the newborn there are stimuli which are not painful, but which elicit defensive reactions (Kessen & Mandler, 1961). Loud noises or loss of support evoke obvious defensive reactions in the form of startles or Moro reflexes. Less obvious defensive reactions, expressed only autonomically, can occur to any intense stimulus.

It may be that there are two kinds of defensive reactions, a quantitative one and a qualitative one. The quantitative defensive reaction would be the response to the high intensity stimuli which Sokolov (1963) discussed. The qualitative defensive reaction would be to stimuli for which there is no cognitive or neuronal model. Given the limited experience of the newborn, it would be expected that there would not be a model for most of the stimuli he encounters. Therefore, it can be expected that the newborn's initial reaction to most novel stimulation is defensive

a decrease and a reaction away from the

tion in which defensive reactions have not been found might be thought to contradict this position. However, no study has been performed on the just born newborn, so that it can be hypothesized that the defensive reaction to general low intensity visual stimuli has already been habituated by the time the first experiments were performed, possibly *in utero*. Studies using low-intensity stimuli are different from studies where loud sounds or bright lights, which would seem to be novel for the newborn, lead to clear defensive reactions. The point could be confirmed if heart-rate response to the kinds of low-level visual stimuli that elicit orientation behavior in the newborn were to be studied. A finding of heart-rate deceleration would further support the existence of the full orienting reaction in the newborn.

Another hypothesis explaining the change from accelerative heart-rate responses in the newborn to decelerative responses in the 3-month-old has been proposed by Graham and Jackson (1970). They suggested the difference in findings might be a function of the state of the infant during the experimental sessions, that newborns are typically examined while they are asleep or drowsy, and 3-month-olds are examined while they are awake. The ability of Schulman (1968) and Lewis, Bartels, and Goldberg (1966) to find the decelerative response only in waking infants supports the Graham and Jackson (1970) hypothesis.

The significance of the preceding discussion as to whether or not the orienting reaction exists in the newborn is in the light it throws on the infant's ability to respond to changes in his environment, especially novel ones. Sokolov (1963) maintained that preceding conditioning, there must be an initial orienting reaction to the conditional stimulus. Therefore, if the orienting reaction is incomplete in the newborn, there can be no conditioning until it matures.

For learning to occur, the infant must react to new contingencies in his environment. If he is unable to respond to new situations, it is unlikely that he can show changes in his behavior related to these new situtaions. That the orienting reaction seems to be present in the newborn, boosts the infant one rung up the ladder.

The second rung on the ladder is related to the distinction between a "neutral" stimulus and a "new" stimulus. Classical conditioning is defined as the association of a previously neutral CS with the nonneutral US. An additional problem in newborn conditioning is that a neutral stimulus is also a new stimulus. How many newborns have had previous experience with electric shock or acetic acid vapors or even bells and buzzers? Since, from the studies described in this section, it seems that the newborn can respond to general changes in stimulation, the first hypothesis related to his inability to be classically conditioned seems disconfirmed. The next hypothesis to explain his inability could be that the newborn is unable to respond differentially to the specific stimuli that have been used in studies of early classical conditioning. To elaborate this hypothesis, one must move away from the empirical base of the preceding two sections and explore some theoretical positions in the next section.

Cognitive Schemas

Until now stimuli and responses have been discussed only as observables. The attempt to explain all of behavior on the basis of observables has been a goal of radical behaviorists for a number of decades. A high point in this attempt was Skinner's (1957) explanation of language behavior. However, Skinner's work was judged by Chomsky (1959) to be inadequate for linguistic analysis. Learning theorists of a less fundamentalist bent have dealt with the issue of nonobservables in the explanation of complex human behavior (Kendler, 1963) by inferring covert analogies of overt S-R processes. The use of covert mediation to reinforce the reductionism in the S-R approach to behavior has not resolved the inability of a nonhierarchical model to explain complex thought processes (Scheerer, 1954). Piaget (1960) also believed that the associationist position was inadequate to explain the complexities of logical behavior and language. Instead, Piaget formulated a theory in which the same cognitive *functions* were used to explain both the complex symbolic behavior of the adult and the simple sensory-motor behavior of the infant, while at the same time the cognitive structural elements associated with the two age periods were quite different. The addition that Piaget makes to behaviorism is to fill in the black box with a cognitive organization composed of structural elements called *schemas.* The schema is a cognitive structure which is adapted through the organism's interaction with the environment. The general function of adaptation is composed of two subfunctions: assimilation, the incorporation of a stimulus into a previously organized schema; and accommodation, the process by which a schema alters itself in order to incorporate new inputs. Focusing on the active internal organization that accompanies the adaptation process, Piaget (1960) is able to trace the development from innate sensory-motor schemas to the formal logical operations of the adult human. What for many may seem to be an unnecessary complication in theory for understanding simple behaviors is for Piaget an excellent application of Occam's razor. Piaget has extended accepted prin-

with a set of built-in reflex schemas. These

schemas may have been previously tuned or adapted *in utero* to an optimal input, but almost immediately begin adapting to new inputs. For example, the sucking schema seems optimally fitted to the tactual input of the nipple, but is readily adapted to sucking on a finger, tube, tongue, blanket, or anything else that stimulates the lips. Experiments such as Lipsitt and Kaye (1964), Lipsitt, Kaye, and Bosack (1966), and Sameroff (1968) have shown that the sucking schema is sensitive to many input contingencies and can be readily altered by manipulating variables directly related to food getting. It is through the adaptation of these already existing reflex schemas that any demonstration of learning has been possible in the newborn.

It is when one departs from these built-in schemas that difficulties arise. In the typical classical conditioning problem, there is an attempt to relate two previously unrelated stimuli in different sensory modalities. For adults, both the CS and the US already are part of various schematic hierarchies. In the typical newborn study, only the US is part of the schema, for example, tactual stimulation leading to head turning. The "newness" of the CS for the infant also means that it is unrelated to any of his activity schemas other than through the possibility of generalizing assimilation. As a consequence, there is no place for the CS in the infant's cognitive structure.

The failure of classical conditioning attempts can occur for two possible reasons.

taneous process of differentiation in the sensory systems as various stimuli are related to different activities of the organism, and at the same time these various activities are integrated at higher levels.

The relations to be established in experimental classical conditioning situations might be placed midway in the developmental sequence between (*a*) the differentiation of innate schemas and (*b*) the subsequent integration of these schema systems. In an experiment, an attempt is made to coordinate schemas artificially that are not coordinated in the organism's real world. For control purposes, the experimental association is made between elements different from those which arise in organism's normal environment. As a result of this controlled reliable relationship, the organism might be able to make coordinations which would only appear at a later stage in the more erratic real world.

To return to the initial problem, how would it be possible to obtain classical conditioning in the infant? The answer cannot be found by generalizing from a procedure used with adult dogs. There is no compelling reason to differentiate between the adult dog or rat and the older prelinguistic child. Both can have perceptually differentiated the world, and can have established differentiated modalities of perception.

In contrast, the newborn rat, dog, or infant has not yet achieved this differentiation. It is not even clear that the infant initially differentiates inputs from the auditory, visual, or tactual systems other than at the level of the perceiving organ, the reflex schema. The sensory system in the mouth seems to be highly developed (Jensen, 1932; Sameroff, 1968). The same cannot be said for the visual system, as recent studies by Salapatek (1968) and Salapatek and Kessen (1966) have indicated; nor for the auditory system (Stubbs, 1934). Before a specific auditory input can be related to other response schemas, the auditory schema must itself become differentiated. An interactionist position is called for, since it does not seem appropriate to call a perceptual system immature if its maturity depends on an interaction with the environment. If conditioning is to occur in the classical sense that a specific previously neutral stimulus will now elicit a response, the organism must first be able to differentiate that stimulus from the other stimuli in its environment. For Piaget (1952), the only possibility of recognizing an input is through the subject's response to it, through what has been called motor recognition or recognitory assimilation. Until the response to one specific stimulus is adequately differentiated from responses to other specific stimuli in the auditory schematic hierarchy, there can be no connection of these to other schemas.

For example, it may be that in the typical conditioning study the modality of the CS and the modality of the US are distant on some dimension, thus making their schematic coordination difficult. Using a CS and US in modalities that are less different might lead to more successful results. Ignoring the differentiation problem for the present, the earliest and most stable conditioning should occur if the sensory modalities of the CS and US are identical. There is evidence that this is, indeed, the case. Kasatkin (1948), on the basis of Russian research, ranks the sensory modalities of CSs on the basis of the age at which they can first be used in successful conditioning. Earliest on the list are changes of body position which involve proprioceptive as well as vestibular stimulation. Neurologically, the interrelations between proprioceptive receptors and motor centers are very close, from the gamma efferent fibers through the cerebellum and into cortical areas.

Brackbill, Lintz, and Fitzgerald (1968; Abrahamson, Brackbill, Carpenter, & Fitzgerald, in press) made a more general point in differentiating the conditioning of autonomic versus somatic responses. Rather than accepting a developmental progression from one to the other in conditionability, they have demonstrated in the first months of life that they could obtain an autonomic CR to an autonomic CS (temporal conditioning of the pupillary response) and somatic CR to a sensory CS (tactual stimulus associated with eyeblink), but could not cross-condition between the somatic and autonomic systems, that is, obtain an eyeblink to temporal conditioning or a pupillary response to a tactual stimulus.

Schema Differentiation

There is no reason to believe that the response systems associated with perception are any more differentiated at birth than the response systems associated with motor activity. Researchers from Gesell and Amatruda (1945) to White, Castle, and Held (1964) have spelled out the development from global responses to specific, directed motor functioning in coordination with other response systems. Recent research indicates the same can be said for the perceptual systems.

The case is clearer for the differentiation of stimuli leading to sucking behavior, but a parallel case can be made for audition. Initially, there is an innate global response to suck on anything sensed by the mouth that does not elicit a defensive reaction, such as a hot nipple. Differentiation occurs through accommodation of the response to the specific object sucked upon, and is evidenced by the increase in coordination and stability of sucking in the first days of life found by Halverson [illegible]

[illegible]

swallowing, now makes a difference in the

infant's behavior. There is an integration of new elements into the set of schemas which permits differentiations to be made in the infant's response to his environment.

An analogous case can be made for auditory stimuli. The initial differentiation of auditory inputs found in Siqueland and Lipsitt's (1966) third experiment could not be integrated at that stage with other response schemas. It was only after a period of differentiation and stabilization of the auditory schema that it could be coordinated with other behaviors, as was evidenced by Papousek's (1967) success in obtaining head turning to the tone alone without mediating oral stimulation after 3 weeks of age.

Papousek's (1967) research is a case study of the infant's changing ability to respond to auditory stimuli. When number of trials to a conditioning criterion was compared for groups of newborns, 3-month-old infants, and 5-month-old infants, the data showed an inverse correlation with age: 177, 42, and 28 trials, respectively. The longer experience that the older infants had in responding to differential auditory stimuli in their natural environment was reflected in their faster conditioning in the experimental situation. An alternate hypothesis is that the infants had somehow matured neurologically, thus making faster conditioning possible. However, a maturation hypothesis is weakened by Papousek's extinction data. The three age groups extinguished their responses in almost identical numbers of trials: 27, 25, and 27, respectively.

[illegible]

forced, a [illegible]

turn in the opposite direction would be reinforced. In Papousek's (1967) original work, differentiation training began when the newborn group was an average of 44 days old, because it followed three other procedures—conditioning, extinction, and reconditioning. In the later study, Papousek (1969) investigated the ability of younger infants to learn the differentiation. In one group, he began training at an average age of 31 days when the infants had completed only one previous procedure—conditioning of a head turn to the left. In another group, he began differentiation training with newborns, completely eliminating any previous procedures. The results were suprising in that, while the group that began differentiation at 44 days took 224 trials, reaching criterion at an average age of 72 days, the group that began at 31 days took 278 trials and reached criterion at an average of 71 days of age. Thus, the younger subjects were unable to capitalize on their earlier start.

To support a maturation hypothesis, the newborn group should also have reached criterion at around 72 days of age. However, they provided surprising results. They required an average of 814 trials, and were 128 days old when the differentiation criterion was reached, almost double the age of the other two groups. It thus seems that not only must the auditory schemas become differentiated before conditioning can take place, but also that the infant's experience must be paced or an input overload of the schema can occur with consequent retardation in its development.

Summary

Rather than hypothesize stages of development in the newborn period, the proposed theory has a progression in cognitive structure based on differentiation and hierarchic integration of schemas. On the activity side, the newborn initially can respond with prenatally organized cognitive schemas, which can assimilate, that is, are adapted either genetically or *in utero* to include specific stimuli. Development is through the increasing differentiation and enlargement of the activity schemas by accommodation to a growing number of stimuli. The initial limited range of stimuli to which the reflex was sensitive is expanded as a function of feedback from the infant's experience with differential effects of his responding.

On the reactivity side, suprathreshold novel stimuli, that is, those which are not assimilated by the innate reflex schemas, elicit a defensive reaction. Repeated exposure to novel stimuli builds up the infant's schema repertoire. As the repertoire grows, the likelihood of encountering a stimulus for which there is no differentiated schema declines, reducing the chances for eliciting the qualitative defensive reaction. Subsequently, the response to the novel stimulus will be an orienting reaction. The activity-reactivity dichotomy is more than a division between those stimuli that can be assimilated to existing schemas and those that cannot, because it also includes the dynamic experiential aspect of the qualitative defensive reaction and orienting reaction in the adaptation process. Eventually, sufficient plasticity is achieved within the cognitive framework. Separate schema systems can then be coordinated making possible the association necessary for classical conditioning in the experimental situation.

To conclude, the evidence strongly indicates that before classical conditioning can occur there must be a differentiation of the schema systems related to both the US and CS. For distance receptors, this development seems to take about 3 weeks, after which the infant begins to be able to coordinate his differentiated perceptual response systems with other sensory-motor schemas such as sucking or head turning.

KEEN, R. Effects of auditory stimulation on sucking behavior in the human neonate. *Journal of Experimental Child Psychology,* 1964, *1,* 348–354.

KENDLER, T. S. Development of mediating responses in children. *Monographs of the Society for Research in Child Development,* 1963, *28* (28, Serial No. 86).

KESSEN, W. Research in the psychological development of infants: An overview. *Merrill-Palmer Quarterly of Behavior and Development,* 1963, *9,* 83–94.

———. Sucking and looking: Two organized congenital patterns of behavior in the human newborn. In H. W. Stevenson, E. H. Hess, & H. L. Rheingold (Eds.), *Early behavior.* New York: Wiley, 1967.

KESSEN, W., & MANDLER, G. Anxiety, pain, and the inhibition of distress. *Psychological Review,* 1961, *68,* 396–404.

KRON, R. E., STEIN, M., & GODDARD, K. E. A method of measuring sucking behavior of newborn infants. *Psychosomatic Medicine,* 1963, *25,* 181–191.

LEWIS, M., BARTELS, B., & GOLDBERG, S. State as a determinant of infants' heartrate response to stimulation. *Science,* 1966, *115,* 486–488.

LIPSITT, L. P. Learning in the first year of life. In L. P. Lipsitt & C. C. Spiker (Eds.), *Advances in child development and behavior.* Vol. *1.* New York: Academic Press, 1963.

LIPSITT, L. P., & KAYE, H. Conditioned sucking in the human newborn. *Psychonomic Science,* 1964, *1,* 29–30.

LIPSITT, L. P., KAYE, H., & BOSACK, T. N. Enhancement of neonatal sucking through reinforcement. *Journal of Experimental Child Psychology,* 1966, *4,* 163–168.

LIPTON, E. L., STEINSCHEIDER, A., & RICHMOND, J. B. Autonomic function in the neonate: VII. Maturational changes in cardiac control. *Child Development,* 1966, *37,* 1–16.

LYNN, R. *Attention, arousal and the orientation reaction.* Oxford: Pergamon, 1966.

MARQUIS, D. P. Can conditioned reflexes be established in the new born infant? *Journal of Genetic Psychology,* 1931, *39,* 479–492.

———. Learning in the neonate: The modification of behavior under three feeding schedules. *Journal of Experimental Psychology,* 1941, *29,* 263–282.

MORGAN, J. J. B., & MORGAN, S. S. Infant learning as a developmental index. *Journal of Genetic Psychology,* 1944, *65,* 281–289.

PAPOUSEK, H. Conditioned head rotation reflexes in infants in the first months of life. *Acta Paediatrica,* 1961, *50,* 565–576.

———. Experimental studies of appetitional behavior in human newborns and infants. In H. W. Stevenson, E. H. Hess, & H. L. Rheingold (Eds.), *Early behavior.* New York: Wiley, 1967.

———. Elaborations of conditioned head-turning. Paper presented at the meeting of the XIX International Congress of Psychology, London, 1969.

PIAGET, J. *The origins of intelligence in children.* New York: International Universities Press, 1952.

———. *Psychology of intelligence.* New York: Littlefield, Adams, 1960.

POLIKANINA, R. I. The relation between autonomic and somatic components in the development of the conditioned reflex in premature infants. *Pavlov Journal of Higher Nervous Activity,* 1961, *11,* 51–58.

SALAPATEK, P. Visual scanning of geometric figures by the human newborn. *Journal of Comparative and Physiological Psychology,* 1968, *66,* 247–248.

SALAPATEK, P., & KESSEN, W. Visual scanning of triangles in the human newborn. *Journal of Experimental Child Psychology,* 1966, *3,* 155–167.

SAMEROFF, A. J. Nonnutritive sucking in newborns under visual and auditory stimulation. *Child Development,* 1967, *38,* 443–452.

———. The components of sucking in the human newborn. *Journal of Experimental Child Psychology,* 1968, *6,* 607–623.

———. Respiration and sucking as components of the orienting reaction in newborns. *Psychophysiology,* 1970, *7,* 213–222.

SCHACHTER, J., WILLIAMS, T. A., KHACHATURIAN, Z., TOBIN, M., & DRUGER, R. The multiphasic heart rate response to auditory clicks in neonates. Paper presented at the meeting of the Society for Psychophysiological Research, Washington, D. C., 1968.

SCHEERER, M. Cognitive theory. In G. Lindzey (Ed.), *Handbook of social psychology.* Vol. *1.* Cambridge, Mass.: Addison-Wesley, 1954.

SCHULMAN, C. A. Effects of auditory stimulus on heartrate in high-risk and low-risk premature infants as a function of state. Paper presented at the meeting of the Eastern Psychological Association, Washington, D. C., April 1968.

SELIGMAN, M. E. P. On the generality of the laws of learning. *Psychological Review,* 1970, *77,* 406–418.

SEMB, G., & LIPSITT, L. P. The effects of acoustic stimulation on cessation and initiation of nonnutritive sucking in neonates. *Journal of Experimental Child Psychology,* 1968, *6,* 585–597.

SIQUELAND, E. R. Reinforcement patterns and extinction in human newborns. *Journal of Experimental Child Psychology,* 1968, *6,* 431–442.

SIQUELAND, E. R., & LIPSITT, L. P. Conditioned head-turning behavior in newborns. *Journal of Experimental Child Psychology,* 1966, *3,* 356–376.

SKINNER, B. F. *Verbal behavior.* New York: Appleton, 1957.

SOKOLOV, YE. N. *Perception and the conditioned reflex.* New York: Macmillan, 1963.

SPELT, D. K. The conditioning of the human fetus in utero. *Journal of Experimental Psychology,* 1948, *38,* 338–346.

STECHLER, G., BRADFORD, S., & LEVY, H. Attention in the newborn: Effect on motility and skin potential. *Science,* 1966, *151,* 1246–1248.

STEINSCHNEIDER, A. Sound intensity and respiratory responses in the neonate. *Psychosomatic Medicine,* 1968, *30,* 534–541.

STUBBS, E. M. The effect of the factor of duration, intensity, and pitch of sound stimuli on the responses of newborn infants. *University of Iowa Studies in Child Welfare,* 1934, *9*(4), 75–135.

TURKEWITZ, G., MOREAU, T., & BIRCH, H. G. Head position and receptor organization in the human neonate. *Journal of Experimental Child Psychology,* 1966, *4,* 169–177.

WERNER, H. The concept of development from a comparative and organismic view. In D. B. Harris (Ed.), *The concept of development.* Minneapolis: University of Minnesota Press, 1957.

& HELD, R. Observations on the development of visually-directed

5. ATTENTION AND PSYCHOLOGICAL CHANGE IN THE YOUNG CHILD

JEROME KAGAN

One of the great unanswered psychological questions concerns the mechanisms responsible for the transformations in organization of behavior and cognitive structure that define growth and differentiation. Until recently most of these changes were viewed as the product of learning. The child was presumably born unmarked, and the imposing hand of experience taught him the structures that defined him. Hence, many behavioral scientists agreed that learning was the central mystery to unravel, and conditioning was the fundamental mechanism of learning. There is a growing consensus, however, that conditioning may be too limited a process to explain the breadth and variety of change characteristic of behavioral and psychological structures. What was once a unitary problem has become a set of more manageable and theoretically sounder themes.

Category of Change

It is always desirable to categorize phenomena according to the hypothetical processes that produced them. But since psychology has not discovered these primary mechanisms, it is often limited to descriptive classifications. One category includes alterations in the probability that a stimulus will evoke a given response, which is a brief operational definition of conditioning. Half a century of research on the acquisition of conditioned responses has generated several significant principles, some with developmental implications. It is generally true, for example, that the acquisition of a conditioned response proceeds faster as the child matures (*1*). Although the explanation of this fact is still not settled, it is assumed that, with age, the child becomes more selectively attentive and better able to differentiate the relevant signal from background noise. Thus a newborn requires about 32 trials before he will turn his head to a conditioned auditory stimulus in order to obtain milk; a 3-month-old requires about nine trials (*2, 3*).

A second category of change refers to the delayed appearance of species-specific behaviors after exposure to a narrow band of experience. A bird's ability to produce the song of its species (*4*) or a child's competence with the language of his community (*5*) requires only the processing of particular auditory events, with no overt response necessary at the time of initial exposure. The environment allows an inherited capacity to become manifest. Close analysis indicates that the development of these and related behaviors does not seem to conform to conditioning principles, especially to the assumption that the new response must occur in temporal contiguity with the conditioned stimulus. This class of phenomena suggests, incidentally, the value of differentiating between the acquisition of a disposition to action and the establishment of and successive changes in cognitive structures not tied directly to behavior. This distinction between behavioral performance and cognitive competence is exemplified by the difference between a child's learning to play marbles and his ability to recognize the faces of the children with whom he plays.

A third category of change, and the one to which this essay is primarily devoted, involves the initial establishment and subsequent alteration of representations of experience, called schemata (singular: schema). A schema is a representation of experience that preserves the temporal and spatial relations of the original event, without being necessarily isomorphic with that event. It is similar in meaning to the older term "engram." Like the engram, the construct of schema was invented to explain the organism's capacity to recognize an event encountered in the past. Although the process of recognition is not clearly understood, the neurophysiologist's suggestion that a cortical neuronal model is matched to current experience captures the essential flavor of the concept (*6*). It is important to differentiate between the notion of schema as a representation of a sensory event and the hypothetical process that represents the organism's potential action toward an object. Piaget (*7*) does not make this differentiation as sharply as we do, for his concept of *sensory-motor scheme* includes the internal representation of the object as well as the organized action toward it.

There is some evidence that some form of primitive representation of experience can be established prior to or soon after birth. Grier, Counter, and Shearer (*8*) incubated eggs of White Rock chickens (*Gallus gallus*) from 12 to 18 days under conditions of quiet or patterned sound. Within 6 hours after hatching, each chick was tested for responsiveness to two auditory stimuli, the 200-hertz tone presented prenatally and a novel 2000-hertz sound. The control chicks moved equivalent dis-

characterized by high rate of change (movement, contour contrast, and acoustic shifts). Hence a schema for the human face should develop early, for the face is characterized by an invariant arrangement of eyes, nose, and mouth within a frame that moves and emits intermittent, variable sounds. Experimental observations of young infants suggest that the face is one of the earliest representations to be acquired. Since the establishment of a schema is so dependent upon the selectivity of the infant's attention, understanding of developmental priorities in schema formation should be facilitated by appreciation of the principles governing the distribution of attention. These principles will be considered in the sections that follow.

Contrast, Movement, and Change

Ontogenetically, the earliest determinant of duration of orientation to a visual event is probably inherent in the structure of the central nervous system. The infant naturally attends to events that possess a high rate of change in their physical characteristics. Stimuli that move, have many discrete elements, or possess contour contrast are most likely to attract and hold a newborn's attention. Hence, a 2-day-old infant is more attentive to a moving or intermittent light than to a continuous light source; to a solid black figure on a white background than to a stimulus that is homogeneously gray (*10, 11*). The newborn's visual search behavior seems to

terns that are part of a larger context

optimum amount of contour that maintains attention at a maximum. Four-month-old infants exposed to meaningless achromatic designs with variable contour length were most attentive to those with moderately long contours (*13*). Karmel (*14*) has reported that, among young infants, duration of attention to meaningless achromatic figures is a curvilinear function of the square root of the absolute amount of black-white border in the figure.

The behavioral addiction to contour and movement is in accord with neurophysiological information on ganglion potentials in vertebrate retinas. Some cells respond to movement; others, to onset of illumination, to offset, or to both. Objects with contour edges should function better as onset stimuli than do solid patterns, because the change in stimulation created by a sharp edge elicits specialized firing patterns that may facilitate sustained attention (*15*).

There is some controversy over the question of whether contour or complexity exerts primary control over attention in the early months, where complexity is defined in terms of either redundancy or variety or number of elements in the figure and where contour is defined in terms of the total amount of border contained in the arrangement of figures on a background. Existing data support the more salient role of contour over complexity. McCall and Kagan (*13*) found no direct relation, in 4-month-olds, between fixation time and number of angles in a set of achromatic meaningless designs. Rather, there was an approximate inverted-U relation between attention and total length of contour in the figure. Similarly, fixation time in 5-month-old infants was independent of degree of asymmetry and irregularity in the arrangement of nine squares; however, when these indices of complexity were held constant but area and amount of contour were varied, fixation times were a function of contour (*16*). Finally, the average evoked cortical potentials of infants to checkerboard and random matrix patterns were independent of redundancy of pattern, but they displayed an inverted-U relation with density of contour edge (*17*).

Although indices of attention to auditory events are considerably more ambiguous than those used for vision, it appears that stimuli that have a high rate of change, such as intermittent sounds, produce more quieting and, by inference, more focused attention than continuous sounds (*18*). Nature has apparently equipped the newborn with an initial bias in the processing of experience. He does not, as the 19th-century empiricists believed, have to learn what he should examine. The preferential orientation to change is clearly adaptive, for the locus of change is likely to contain the most information about the presence of his mother or of danger.

Discrepancy from Schema

The initial disposition to attend to events with a high rate of change soon competes with a new determinant based largely on experience. The child's attentional encounters with events result, inevitably, in a schema. Somewhere during the second month, duration of attention comes under the influence of the relation between a class of events and the infant's schema for that class. One form of this relation, called the discrepancy principle, states that stimuli moderately discrepant from the schema elicit longer orientations than do either minimally discrepant (that is, familiar) events or novel events that bear no relation to the schema. The relation between attention and magnitude of discrepancy is assumed to be curvilinear (an inverted U). Although an orientation reflex can be produced by any change in quality or intensity of stimulation, duration of sustained attention is constrained by the degree of discrepancy between the event and the relevant schema. Consider some empirical support for the discrepancy principle.

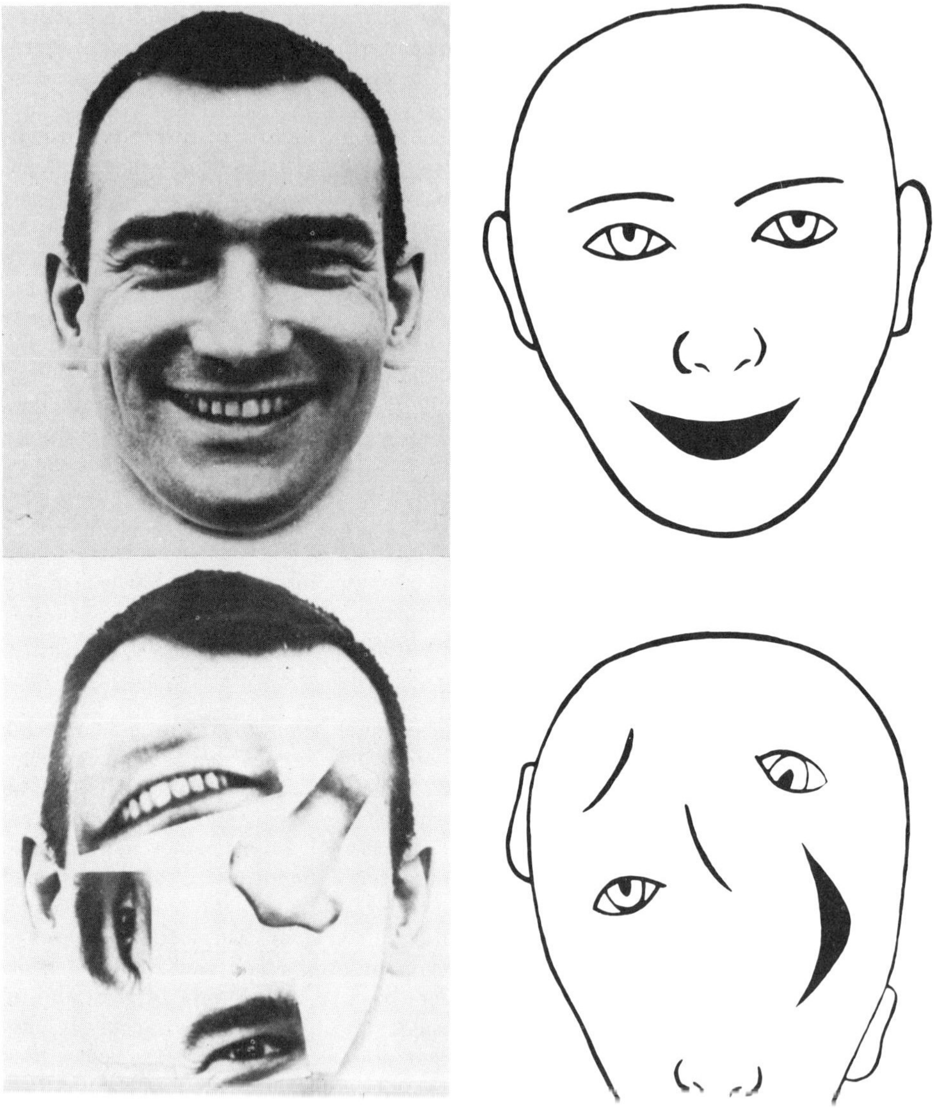

the 8-week-old shows equivalent fixations

schema for a human face and the laboratory representation is moderately discrepant from that schema. If the representation of the face is too discrepant, as when the facial components are rearranged (see Figure 2.1), fixation times are reduced (*20, 21*).

Fixation times to photographic representations of faces drop by over 50 percent after 6 months and are equivalent to both regular and irregular faces during the last half of the first year (*20, 21*). This developmental pattern is in accord with the discrepancy principle. During the opening few weeks of life, before the infant has established a schema for a human face, photographs of either regular or irregular faces are so discrepant from the infant's schema that they elicit equivalent epochs of attention. As the schema for a human face becomes well established, between 2 and 4 months, the photograph of a strange face becomes optimally discrepant from that schema. During the latter half of the first year, the face schema becomes so well established that photographs of regular or irregular faces, though discriminable, are easily assimilated and elicit short and equivalent fixations.

A second source of support for the discrepancy principle comes from research designs in which familiarity and discrepancy are manipulated through repeated presentation of an originally meaningless stimulus, followed by a transformation of the standard. Fixation times are typically longer to the transformation than to the last few presentations of the habituated standard (*22*). For example, 4-month-old infants were shown three objects in a triangular arrangement for five repeated trials. On the sixth trial, infants saw a transformation of the standard in which one, two, or three of the original objects were replaced with new ones. Most infants displayed longer fixations to the transformation than to the preceding standard. When the analysis was restricted to the 42 infants who displayed either rapid habituation or short fixations to the last four presentations of the standard trials (2 through 5), an increasing monotonic relation emerged between amount of change in the standard (one, two, or three elements replaced) and increase in fixation from the last standard to the transformation (*23*).

Although fixation time cannot be used as an index of sustained attention to auditory stimuli, magnitude of cardiac deceleration, which covaries with motor quieting, provides a partial index of focused attention. Melson and McCall (*24*) repeated the same eight-note ascending scale for eight trials to 5-month-old girls; this repetition was followed by transformations, in which the same eight notes were rearranged. The magnitude of cardiac deceleration was larger to the discrepant scale than to the preceding standard. The curvilinear form of the discrepancy principle finds support in an experiment in which 5½-month-old male infants were shown a simple stimulus consisting of five green, three-dimensional elements arranged vertically on a white background (far left in Figure 2.2). The order of stimulus presentation was SSSSSS-SSTSSTSSTS, in which S was the standard and T was one of three transformations of differing discrepancy from the standard. Each infant was shown only one of the three transformations in Figure 2.2. The magnitude of cardiac deceleration was larger to the moderate transformation of the standard (oblique arrangement of the five elements in Figure 2.2, second from left) than to the two more serious transformations (*22*). This finding is partially congruent with an earlier study on younger infants that used the same stimuli but established the schema over a 4-week period. The girls, but not the boys, displayed larger decelerations to the transformation than to the standard (*25*).

The most persuasive confirmation of the curvilinear relation between attention and discrepancy was revealed in an experiment in which firstborn, 4-month-old infants were shown a three-dimensional stimulus

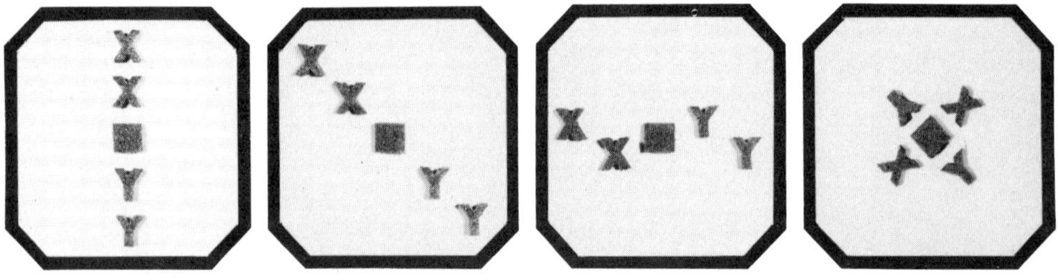

Figure 2.2. Standard (far left) and three transformations shown to infants in study of reaction to discrepancy.

composed of three geometric forms of different shape and hue for 12 half-minute presentations (*26*). Each infant was then randomly assigned to one of seven groups. Six of these groups were exposed to a stimulus at home that was of varying discrepancy from the standard viewed in the laboratory. The seventh was not exposed to any experimental stimulus. The mother showed the stimulus to the infant, in the form of a mobile above his crib, 30 minutes a day for 21 days. The seven experimental groups are summarized in Figure 2.3.

Three weeks later each subject returned to the laboratory and saw exactly the same stimulus he viewed initially at the age of 4 months. The major dependent variable was the *change in fixation time* between the first and second test sessions. Figure 2.4 illustrates these change scores for total fixation time across the first six trials of each session.

The infants who saw no mobile at home

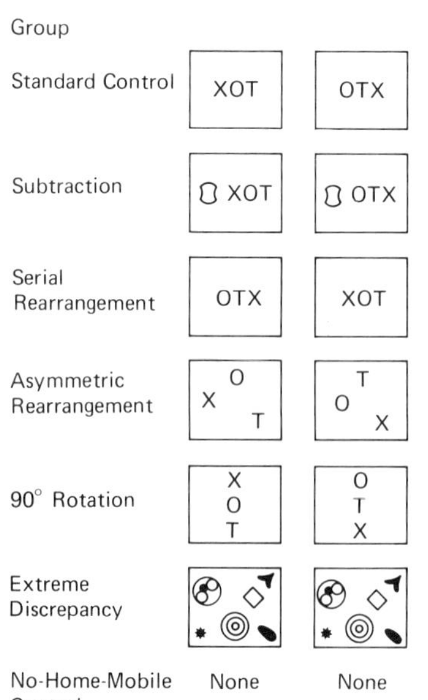

Figure 2.3. Summary of the home mobile conditions of the seven experimental groups. The drawings illustrate in schematic form the stimulus to which each child was exposed at home.

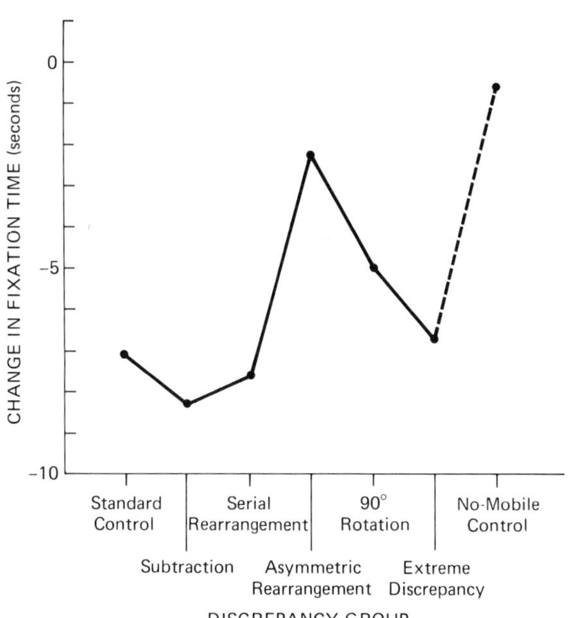

Figure 2.4. Change in mean total fixation time across the two test sessions for each of the seven experimental groups.

showed no change in fixation time across the 3 weeks, which indicates that the laboratory stimulus was as attractive on the second visit as it had been on the first. The infants who had an opportunity to develop a schema for the asymmetric and vertical rotation mobiles and, therefore, could experience a moderate discrepancy on the second visit, showed the smallest drop in attention across the 3 weeks. By contrast, the infants who experienced a minor or major discrepancy showed the greatest drop in interest ($F=5.29$, $P<.05$). There was a curvilinear relation between attention and stimulus-schema discrepancy.

The incidence of smiling to familiar and discrepant stimuli also supports the discrepancy principle. It is assumed that the infant is likely to smile as he assimilates an initally discrepant event (*7*). Hence, very familiar and totally novel stimuli should elicit minimum smiling, whereas moderately discrepant events should elicit maximum smiling. The smile to a human face or a pictorial representation of a face during the first 7 months is most frequent at 4 months of age among infants from varied cultural settings (*27*). It is assumed that, prior to 4 months, the human face is too discrepant to be assimilated, and after this time it is minimally discrepant and easily assimilated. The smile of assimilation is not restricted to human faces. Three different auditory stimuli (bronze bell, toy piano, and nursery rhyme played by a music box) were presented to 13-week-old infants in two trial blocks on each of 2 successive days (*28*). Frequency of smiling was lowest on the first block of trials on day 1, when the sounds were novel, and on the second block on day 2, when they had become very familiar, but highest on the two intermediate blocks, when the infant presumably was able to assimilate them after some effort.

A final illustration of the display of the smile as a sign of assimilation comes from a study in progress in which 60 children, 5½ to 11½ months old, watched a hand slowly move an orange rod clockwise in an arc until it contacted a set of three differently colored light bulbs. As the rod touched one of the lights, all three turned on. This 11-second sequence was repeated eight or ten times (depending upon the age of the child) during which most children remained very attentive. Each child then saw only one of four transformations for five successive trials: (i) the bulbs did not light when the rod touched them, (ii) the hand did not appear, (iii) the rod did not move, or (iv) no hand appeared and no bulbs lit, but the rod moved. After the fifth presentation, the original sequence was repeated three more times. The proportion of infants who smiled was largest on the sixth repetition of the standard and on the third presentation of the transformation. Figure 2.5 illustrates the pattern of smiling to this episode for one 7½-month-old girl who displayed maximum smiling on trials 4 and 5 of the initial familiarization series and trials 3, 4, and 5 of the transformation series, during which the hand did not appear. Thus both duration of fixation and probability of smiling seem to be curvilinearly related to degree of discrepancy between an event and the child's schema for that event. Moreover, the child seems to become most excited by moderately discrepant events that are perceived as transformations of those that produced the original schema. If the infant does not regard a new event as related to a schema, he is much less excited by it. To illustrate, 72 infants, 9½ and 11½ months old, were exposed to one of two different transformations after six repeated presentations of a 2-inch (5-cm) wooden orange cube. The infants exposed to the novel event saw a yellow, rippled, plastic cylinder differing from the standard in color, size, texture, and shape. The infants exposed to the moderate transformation saw a 1-inch (2.54-cm) wooden orange cube, in which only size was altered. Almost half (43 percent) of the females in the moderate group displayed an obvious increase in vocalization when the smaller cube appeared, suggesting they were excited by this transformation. By contrast, only one female exposed to the novel yellow form showed increased vocalization, and most showed no change at all ($P<.05$). There was no comparable difference for boys.

The onset of a special reaction to discrepancy at about 2 months may reflect the fact that structures in the central nervous system have matured enough to permit long-term representation or retrieval of such representations. It is probably not a coincidence that a broad band of physiological and behavioral phenomena also occur at this time. The latency of the

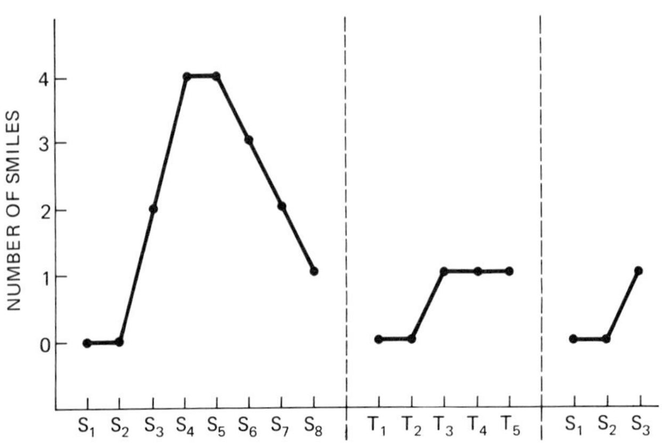

Figure 2.5. Frequency of smiling to the light episode for a 7½-month-old girl (*S*, standard presentation; *T*, transformation).

visual evoked potential begins to approach adult form, growth of occipital neurons levels off, alpha rhythm becomes recognizable (29), the Moro reflex begins to disappear, habituation to repeated presentations of a visual event becomes a reliable phenomenon (*30*), and three-dimensional representations of objects elicit longer fixations than two-dimensional ones (*11*).

Activation of Hypotheses

Two empirical facts require the invention of a third process that influences attention and, subsequently, produces change in cognitive structures. The relation between age and fixation time to masklike representations of a human face (see Figure 2.6) decreases dramatically across the period from 4 to 12 months, but it increases, just as dramatically, from 12 to 36 months (*21*). If discrepancy from schema exerted primary control over attention, increased fixation times after 1 year should not have occurred, for the masks should have become less discrepant with maturity. Furthermore, educational level of the infant's family was independent of fixation time prior to 1 year but was positively correlated with fixation time (correlation coefficient of 0.4) after 1 year (*21*). These data suggest the potential usefulness of positing the emergence of a new cognitive structure toward the end of the first year. This structure, called a *hypothesis*, is the child's interpretation of a discrepant event accomplished by mentally transforming it to a form he is familiar with, where the "familiar form" is the schema. The cognitive structure used in the transformation is the hypothesis. To recognize that a particular sequence of sounds is human speech rather than a series of clarinet tones requires a schema for the quality of the human voice. Interpretation of the meaning of the speech, on the other hand, requires the activation of hypotheses which, in this example, are linguistic rules. The critical difference between a schema and a hypothesis is analogous to the difference between the processes of recognition and interpretation and bears some relation to Piaget's complementary notions of assimilation and accommodation (*7*).

It is assumed that the activation of hypotheses to explain discrepant events is accompanied by sustained attention. The more extensive the repertoire of hypotheses, the longer the child can work at interpretation and the more prolonged is his attention. The interaction between discrepancy and the activation of hypotheses is illustrated in the pattern of fixation times of 2-year-olds to four related stimuli: a doll-like representation of a male figure; the same figure with the head placed between the legs; the same figure with the head, arms, and legs rearranged in an asymmetric pattern; and an amorphous free form of the same color, size, and texture as the other three. Duration of fixation was significantly longer to the two moderately discrepant forms (8.5 seconds) than to the regular figure (7 seconds) or to the free form (5.5 seconds) (*21*).

In sum, events that possess a high rate of change, that are discrepant from established schemata, and that activate hypotheses in the service of interpretation elicit the longest epochs of attention. These events are most likely to produce changes in cognitive structures, for the attempt to assimilate a transformation of a familiar event inevitably leads to alterations in the original schema.

Summary

This article began by suggesting that different processes are likely to mediate alterations in behavior and cognitive structure and that conditioning principles do not seem sufficient to explain all the classes of change. Although the acquisition of conditioned responses, the potentiation of inborn capacities, and the establishment of schemata probably implicate different processes, all three involve selective attention to sensory events, whether these events function as conditioned stimuli,

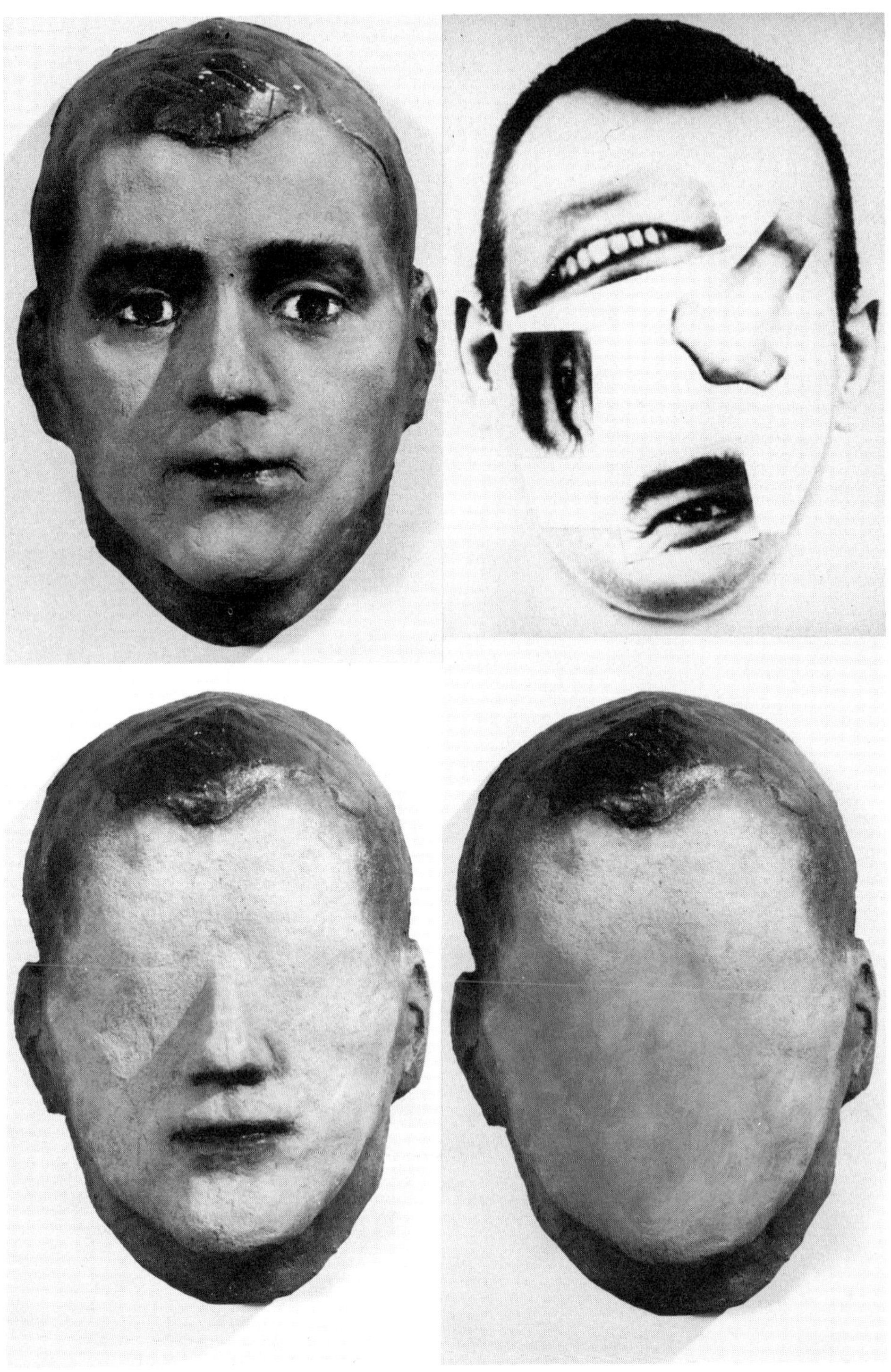

Figure 2.6. Facelike masks shown to infants from 4 to 36 months of age.

releasers of innate response dispositions, or the bases for mental representations. Hence, better understanding of the forces that control selectivity and duration of attention should provide insights into the nature of psychological growth, especially the lawful alterations in cognitive structure that seem to occur continually as a function of the child's encounter with discrepant events. The heart of this article was devoted to this theme. It was argued that events that possessed a high rate of change in their physical characteristics, that were moderately discrepant from established schemata, and that activated hypotheses in the service of assimilation had the greatest power to recruit and maintain attention in the young child.

Unfortunately, quantification of the fragile process of attention is still inelegant, for an infant displays a small set of relatively simple reactions to an interesting event. The infant can look at it, vocalize, be quiet, thrash, smile, or display changes in heart rate, respiration, or pattern of electrocortical discharge. Each of these variables reflects a different aspect of the attention process. Fixation time provides the clearest view and seems controlled by movement, contour, discrepancy, and the activation of hypotheses. Smiling seems to reflect the state that follows effortful assimilation. Cardiac deceleration occasionally accompanies attention to discrepant events, but not always, and vocalization can index, among other things, the excitement generated by a stimulus that engages a schema. It is important to realize, however, that a specific magnitude for any of these responses serves many different forces. The future mapping of these magnitudes on a set of determinants will require a delicate orchestration of rigorous method, ingenious theory, and a keen sensitivity to nature's subtle messages.

References

1. L. P. LIPSITT, in *Advances in Child Development and Behavior,* L. P. Lipsitt and C. C. Spiker, Eds. (Academic Press, New York, 1963), p. 147.
2. H. PAPOUSEK in *Early Behavior,* H. W. Stevenson, E. H. Hess, H. L. Rheingold, Eds. (Wiley, New York, 1967), p. 249.
3. Infants over 3 months old who had learned the conditioned response continued to turn their heads to the auditory stimulus even though they were completely satiated for milk and did not drink. This phenomenon replicates similar observations with pigeons and rats who, after having acquired a conditioned response to obtain food, continued to respond even though ample food was available without any effort [see B. Carder and K. Berkowitz, *Science 167,* 1273 (1970); A. J. Neuringer, *ibid. 166,* 399 (1969)]. One interpretation of this phenomenon assumes that when an organism is alerted or aroused, for whatever reason, he issues those responses that are prepotent in that context. This view is congruent with the demonstration that intracranial stimulation of the hypothalamus elicits behaviors appropriate to the immediate situation [E. S. Valenstein, V. C. Cox, J. W. Kakolewski, *Psychol. Rev. 77,* 16 (1970)]. If food is available, the rat eats; if water, he drinks; if wood chips, he gnaws. Intracranial stimulation, like transfer from the home to the experimental chamber, alerts the animal, and prepotent behavior is activated.
4. E. NOTTEBOHM, *Science 167,* 950 (1970).
5. R. W. BROWN, and U. BELLUGI, *Harvard Educ. Rev. 34,* 135 (1964).
6. H. W. MAGOUN, in *On the Biology of Learning,* K. H. Pribram, Ed. (Harcourt, Brace & World, New York, 1969), p. 171.

7. J. PIAGET, *The Origins of Intelligence in Children* (International Universities Press, New York, 1952).
8. J. B. GRIER, S. A. COUNTER, and W. M. SHEARER, *Science 155*, 1692 (1967).
9. C. G. BEER, *ibid. 166*, 1030 (1969).
10. P. SALAPETEK, and W. KESSEN, *J. Exp. Child Psychol. 3*, 113 (1966); R. L. Fantz and S. Nevis, *Merrill-Palmer Quart. 13*, 77 (1967); M. M. Haith, *J. Exp. Child Psychol. 3*, 235 (1966).
11. R. L. FANTZ, in *Perceptual Development in Children*, A. H. Kidd and J. L. Rivoire, Eds. (International Universities Press, New York, 1966), p. 143.
12. M. M. HAITH, paper presented at the regional meeting of the Society for Research in Child Development, Clark University, Worcester, Massachusetts, March 1968.
13. R. B. MC CALL, and J. KAGAN, *Child Develop. 38*, 939 (1967).
14. B. Z. KARMEL, *J. Comp. Physiol. Psychol. 69*, 649 (1969).
15. S. W. KUFFLER, *Cold Spring Harbor Symp. Quant. Biol. 17*, 281 (1952); *J. Physiol. London, 16*, 37 (1953).
16. R. B. MC CALL, and W. H. MELSON, *Develop. Psychol.*, in press.
17. B. Z. KARMEL, C. T. WHITE, W. T. CLEAVES, and K. J. STEINSIEK, paper presented at the meeting of the Eastern Psychological Association, Atlantic City, New Jersey, April 1970.
18. R. B. EISENBERG, E. J. GRIFFIN, D. B. COURSIN, and M. A. HUNTER, *J. Speech Hear. Res. 7*, 245 (1964); Y. Brackbill, G. Adams, D. H. Crowell, M. C. Gray, *J. Exp. Child Psychol. 3*, 176 (1966).
19. G. C. CARPENTER, paper presented at the Merrill-Palmer Infancy Conference, Detroit, Michigan, February 1969.
20. R. A. HAAF, and R. Q. BELL, *Child Develop. 38*, 893 (1967); M. Lewis, *Develop. Psychol. 1*, 75 (1969).
21. J. KAGAN, *Change and Continuity in Infancy* (Wiley, New York, in press).
22. R. B. MC CALL, and W. H. MELSON, *Psychonomic Sci. 17*, 317 (1969).
23. R. B. MC CALL, and J. KAGAN, *Develop. Psychol. 2*, 90 (1970).
24. W. H. MELSON, and R. B. MC CALL, *Child Develop.*, in press.
25. R. B. MC CALL, and J. KAGAN, *J. Exp. Child Psychol. 5*, 381 (1967).
26. C. SUPER, J. KAGAN, F. MORRISON, M. HAITH, and J. WEIFFENBACH, unpublished manuscript.
27. J. L. GEWIRTZ, in *Determinants of Infant Behaviour*, B. M. Foss, Ed. (Methuen, London, 1965), vol. 3, p. 205.
28. P. R. ZELAZO, and J. M. CHANDLER, unpublished manuscript.
29. R. J. ELLINGSON, in *Advances in Child Development and Behavior*, L. P. Lipsitt and C. C. Spiker, Eds. (Academic Press, New York, 1963), p. 53.
30. C. DREYFUS-BRISAC, D. SAMSON, C. BLANC, and N. MONOD, *Etud. Neo-natales 7*, 143 (1958).

6. THE REGULATION OF HUMAN GROWTH

J. M. TANNER

The most striking and perhaps most fundamental characteristic of the growth of an animal is that it is self-stabilizing, or, to take another analogy, "target-seeking." Children, no less than rockets, have their trajectories, governed by the control systems of their genetical constitution and powered by energy absorbed from the natural environment. Deflect the child from its natural growth trajectory by acute malnutrition or a sudden lack of a hormone and a restoring force develops so that as soon as the missing food or hormone is supplied again the child catches up towards its original curve. When it gets there it slows down to adjust its path onto the old trajectory once more.

There was a time when this self-correcting and goal-seeking capacity was thought to be a very special property of living things, but now that we understand more about the dynamics of complex systems consisting of many interacting substances we realize that it is not, after all, such an exceptional phenomenon. Many complex systems, even of quite simple lifeless substances, show such internal regulation simply as a property consequent on their organization. Indeed the activity of the rocketeers has made us all too dismally familiar with the general notions of cybernetics and equifinality. Animal geneticists and auxologists, in particular Waddington and his colleagues at Edinburgh (see Waddington, 1957), have in the last decade introduced this approach into their ways of thinking, and amongst developmental psychologists Piaget at least (see Piaget in Tanner and Inhelder, 1960) has endeavoured to do the same. But though new models and a new mathematical symbolism are powerful aids to thought they do not of themselves tell us anything about the mechanisms of regulation that are at work. We know very little as yet about how these intricate growth patterns are organized. It is to this ignorance that I wish to draw your attention.

Let me begin by illustrating how regular is the growth of a healthy, well-nourished child. The upper section of Figure 2.7 shows the measurements of height of a boy in the Harpenden Growth Study taken every six months from age 4 to 10 by a single observer, Mr. R. H. Whitehouse. The circles represent the measurements, and the solid line is a simple mathematical curve of the form $h = a + bt + c \log t$ (where h is height and t age) fitted to them. None of the measurements deviates more than 4 mm from this line, although the experimental error of measuring height may be 3 mm even in experienced hands. The lower section of Figure 2.7 shows the same data plotted as six-monthly velocities; the continuous curve is the first derivative of the fitted curve in the upper section. This child shows a slightly better fit than average, but is by no means exceptional; the curves of many others in the Harpenden Growth Study are very similar. A curve of this form fits height data very well from about six months to around 10 years. If there were any periods of acceleration common to most children during this time, then they would be shown by the deviations of velocity from the fitted curves being mostly positive at that age, and negative before and after. When we

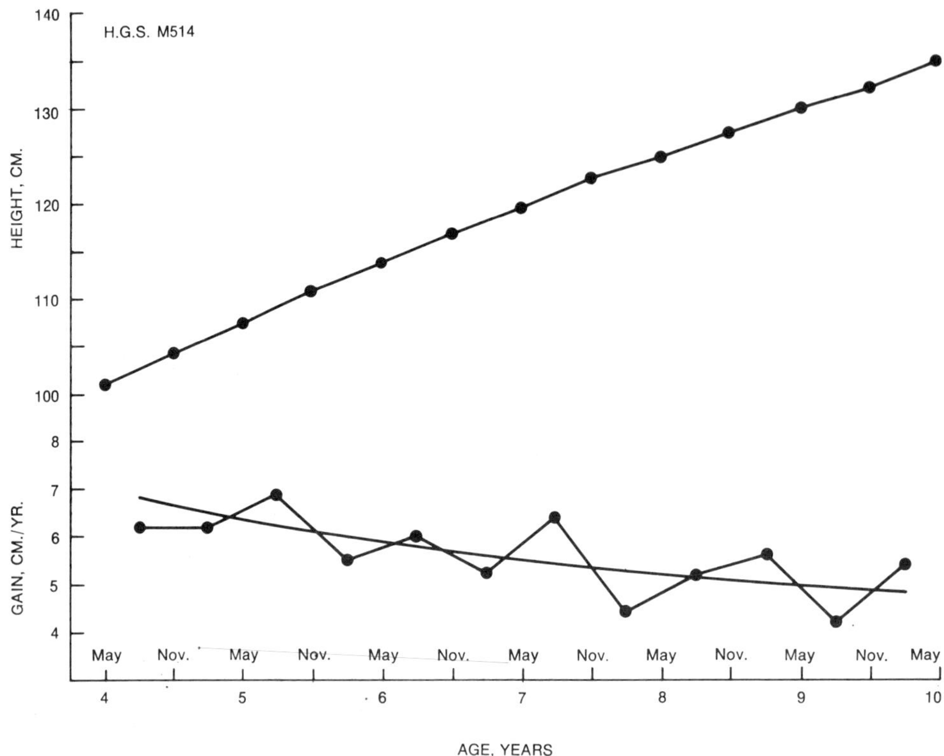

Figure 2.7. Growth of a boy in the Harpenden Growth Study measured every six months by R. H. Whitehouse.

Above: "distance" plot of height achieved at each age.
Below: velocity plot of average velocities each six months.
Solid lines: above, curve of form *Height*=*a*+*bt*+*c* log *t* (*t*=age) fitted to individual's height-achieved points; below, the derivative of the fitted curve.
(From Tanner, in F. Gross (Ed.), *Protein metabolism.* Berlin: Springer, 1962.)

average the deviations for 19 boys and 13 girls each fitted from 4½ years to 9 years we find no age at which these averages depart significantly from zero (see Table 2.1). In others words we can find no satisfactory evidence of a midgrowth or juvenile spurt in height occurring at 6 or 7 to 8.

At adolescence a different curve is needed, but Deming (1957) has shown and we have confirmed that the Gompertz function, which is a sigmoid curve with four parameters, fits just as well at that time as the simple curve does earlier (Figure 2.8).

There is no magic in these curves, which are simply graduation devices. The parameters, so far as we know, represent no particular physiological entities. They could be replaced by other equally well-fitting equations with equally few parameters. But the fact that 16 to 20 measurements taken at intervals of three to six months can be so accurately fitted by curves with only three or four parameters shows that growth, both before and during adolescence, is a very regular process.

Seasonal effect A number of children show greater deviations from the fitted

Table 2.1. Deviations from velocity predicted by individual's fitted curve for height measurements, for each year or half-year of age (i.e., "excess velocity" over that predicted)

A. 19 boys and 13 girls, H.G.S., one measurer; curves fitted for minimum of age 5 to 9 years at half-year intervals, maximum age 3 to 10 years. Mean excess velocity in cm/year.

Age Period	5–5½	5½–6	6–6½	6½–7
19 boys	−0.17	−0.14	0.05	−0.16
13 girls	−0.11	−0.18	−0.15	+0.24[2]
Age Period	7–7½	7½–8	8–8½	8½–9
19 boys	+0.37[1]	−0.07	−0.11	+0.04
13 girls	+0.08	+0.05	−0.24	+0.07

[1] S.E. 0.21.
[2] S.E. 0.47.

B. 36 boys and 31 girls, C.S.C.; curves fitted for period six months to 8 years at one-year intervals after 2. Mean excess velocity in cm/year.

Age Period	4–5	5–6	6–7	7–8
36 boys	+0.11	+0.09	−0.12[1]	+0.08
31 girls	+0.02	−0.05	−0.05	+0.07

[1] S.E. 0.14.

curve than does the child in Figure 2.7, but when they are investigated most of the deviations turn out to be regular, as in Figure 2.9. The fluctuations of velocity from 6½ onwards represent the effect that season of the year has on growth in height of many, but not all, children. (Small and irregular six-monthly fluctuations could be caused by measuring error: a low value on one occasion causing a low velocity, followed by a compensatory high one.) In Figure 2.9 deviations from the distance curve amount to 5 mm above and below it and the velocity of April to October growth averages no less than 1.6 cm/yr more than growth from October to April. But this seasonal rhythm is only superimposed on the basic regularity. In fact a small seasonal effect can be seen also in Figure 2.7 where the average May to November growth rate is 0.2 cm/yr more than the rate from November to May.

The cause of the seasonal effect is not known. Presumably the endocrine system is affected by light or temperature or some other climatic or just possibly some nutritional factor. The most likely endocrine mediators are probably the thyroid and the adrenal cortex, with thyroxine possibly accelerating growth and increased cortisol secretion possibly decelerating. We have no sure evidence however that a seasonal change in rate of secretion of either of these hormones takes place in man. Growth hormone could be another possibility and perhaps insulin a fourth. All we can say for certain is that there are marked individual differences in this response to seasonal change.

Illness This is a simple example of the regulation of growth. Similar individual differences in the ability to regulate growth seem to occur in response to illness. We have fitted curves to six-monthly height measurements of children who have suffered relatively minor illness, but omitted the first measurement following the illness. We then tested whether the post-illness measurement was significantly below the fitted non-illness curve. In the great majority of cases it was not; either the illness had had no effect or the catch-up had been complete within a few months. But in a few children the post-illness point was depressed, and these children were not apparently any sicker than the others, nor were they apparently eating less or behaving in any obviously different way in the uniform environment of the children's home where all were resident. Some children seem to be less well regulated, or canalized, in Waddington's terminology, than others.

Catch-up Growth

More severe diseases, or acute malnutrition, cause a retardation in growth. In

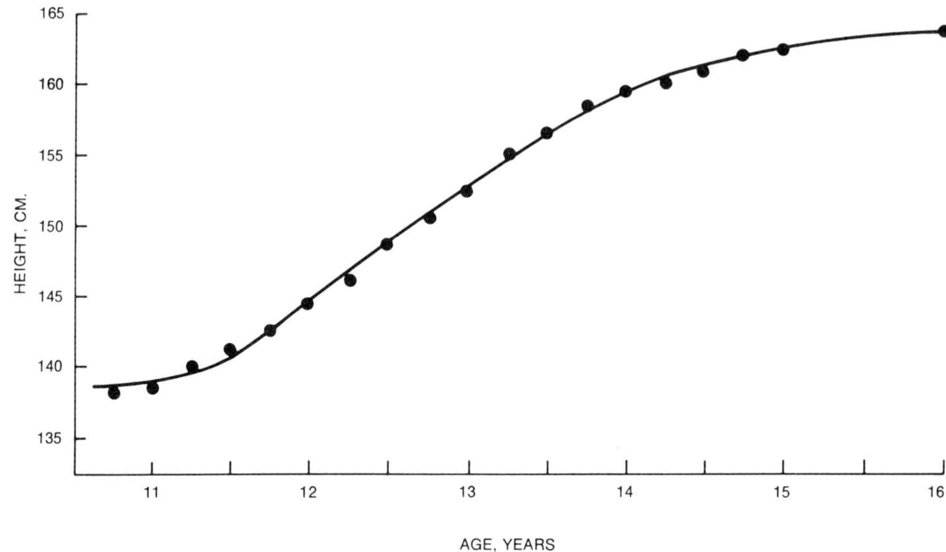

Figure 2.8. Growth of a girl in the Harpenden Growth Study measured at three-monthly intervals during adolescence by R. H. Whitehouse.

"Distance" plot of height achieved at each age.
Solid line: Gompertz curve fitted by maximum likelihood to individual's height-achieved points.
(From Tanner, in F. Gross (Ed.), *Protein metabolism.* Berlin: Springer, 1962.)

Figures 2.10 through 2.13, two instances of this are illustrated; three are from studies recently published with my paediatric colleagues Professor Prader and Dr. von Harnack (Prader, Tanner, and von Harnack, 1963). In each case a period of what we call catch-up growth follows restoration of the child's physiological state towards normal.

Figure 2.10 shows the effect on growth of a young child of two periods in which food intake was much reduced for psychological reasons. On the left is the curve of body length at successive ages ("distance" curve) and on the right are the average rates of growth at successive periods, plotted against the 50th percentile lines for length growth velocity (for details see Prader *et al.*, 1963). The velocity during each period of catch-up reached more than twice the average velocity for the chronological age; it was nearly twice average for the skeletal age, which was retarded in parallel with the retardation in length and caught up as the length caught up. The catch-up is apparently complete in that the child is quite normal in both length and velocity of length growth by age 5.

Figure 2.12 concerns a boy who was hypothyroid from his seventh year or before up to the age of 12 years, when thyroid administration was begun. In early childhood height velocity had been average, but from 7 to 10 it dropped and from 10 to 12 actually became zero. During the first eight months after thyroid hormone was given the height velocity reached over twice average for chronological age. The boy's growth soon moved back to the normal pattern and he underwent an adolescent growth spurt which was average in intensity and took place at the nearly average skeletal age of 14 years. His chronological age was nearer 16, however. It seems that some of the years of hypothyroid arrest had been eliminated from his biological calendar so

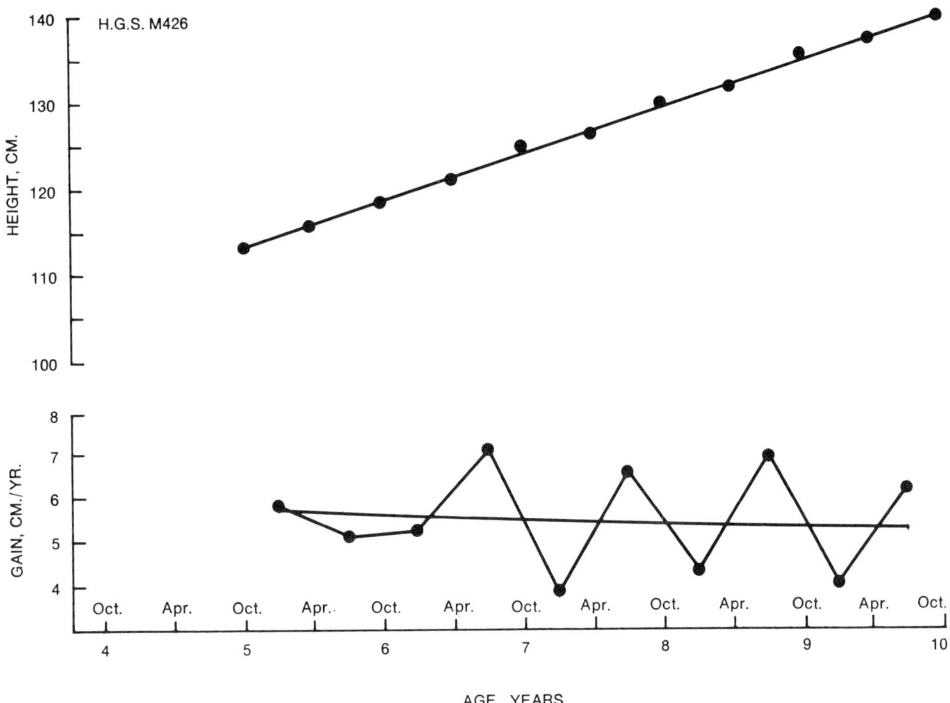

Figure 2.9. Growth of a boy in the Harpenden Growth Study measured every six months by R. H. Whitehouse.

Above: "distance" plot of height achieved at each age.
Below: velocity plot of average velocities each six months.
Solid lines: above, curve of form *Height*=*a*+*bt*+*c* log *t* (*t*=age) fitted to individual's height-achieved points; below, the derivative of the fitted curve. Note the regular seasonal variation, Apr–Oct having a greater velocity than Oct–Apr.
(From Tanner, in F. Gross (Ed.), *Protein metabolism.* Berlin: Springer, 1962.)

that he was still two years behind, but by 20, when his skeletal maturation was practically complete, he had caught up (presumably completely) in height.

. . .

Birth catch-up This capacity to catch up in growth seems to be used normally around the time of birth in man. There is evidence that the growth rate of the foetus, at least in weight, slows down during the last four weeks of pregnancy, as illustrated in Figure 2.14. The prenatal values are calculated from McKeown and Record's (1952) data on birth weights of live children born after a shorter gestation than average. In using them we are assuming that these early-delivered children's weights are the same as the weights of foetuses of the same age as yet still in the uterus; in other words, that amongst healthy singletons the early-born are not specially big or small children for their gestational age. Such an assumption may be challenged. But there is good evidence also of a catch-up occurring after birth, particularly in small babies. Figure 2.15, taken from the Ministry of Health (1959) partially longitudinal survey of some sev-

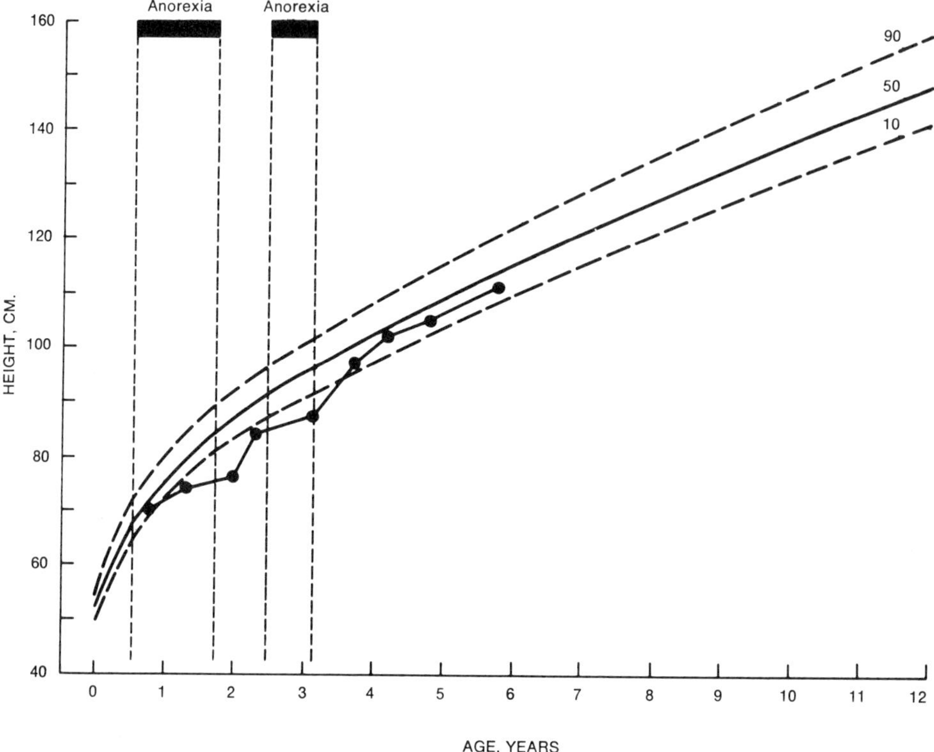

Figure 2.10. Two periods of catch-up growth following episodes of anorexia nervosa in a young child. For explanation of charts see text.
(From Prader, Tanner, & von Harnack, 1963.)

enteen thousand babies, shows this well. Babies below the average weight gained more than the others, thus reducing the range of weight in the whole group. The catch-up finishes by about five months in this data and is distinctly more marked in boys than in girls (see Ministry of Health, 1959, Fig. III). Thus there is a negative correlation between birth weight and weight gain from birth to three months, or from birth to six months of the order of about −0.15 (Thompson, 1955). The negative correlation is still present, though lower, by the time one year is reached. Norval, Kennedy, and Berkson (1951) give figures for the correlation of birth weight with the birth-to-one-year increment of −0.15 in boys and −0.05 in girls. The catch-up occurs also in length, indeed, probably to a greater extent than in weight. Simmons and Todd (1938) found it in the longitudinal data of the Brush Foundation and in 1938 remarked that

> of particular interest are the negative coefficients between birth length and the birth to one year increment in length (boys −0.46, girls −0.01) and of the three month length with the three month to one year increment in length (boys −0.20, girls −0.05). It appears that during the first post-natal year our short babies gain in length more than our long babies and that this reversal occurs to a greater extent in the male than in the female.

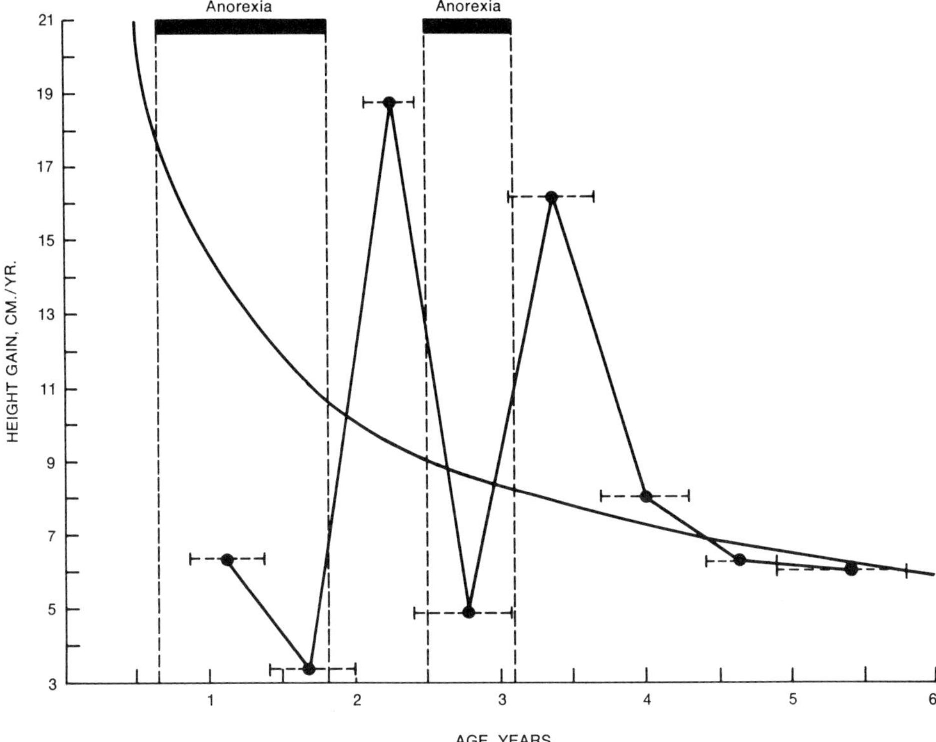

Figure 2.11

Thompson (1956) found correlations of the order of −0.4 in both sexes between birth length and the length increment from birth to six months in some 4,500 babies in Edinburgh. By one year the correlation had somewhat dropped, but was still appreciable (average correlation −0.35).

The catch-up mechanism at birth is of much genetical importance. It seems to be the chief means by which variability in adult size is maintained in the population. Most of the adult size variability is established by two years after birth, since by then the individual's adult size is to a large extent fixed (presuming adequate environmental conditions). The correlation coefficient between length of child at 2 years and length of the same child when adult, is nearly 0.8; it approaches 0.7 even at age 1. (Genetical differences in the time and intensity of the adolescent spurt account for the remainder of the adult variability.) Thus there would be many genetically large children developing in the uteri of small mothers and constituting a problem at the time of birth unless selection for assortative mating were very strong, a solution which would produce other genetically undesirable effects. The problem is solved by birth size being controlled almost entirely by uterine factors (Penrose, 1961), the correlation of birth length and adult length being only

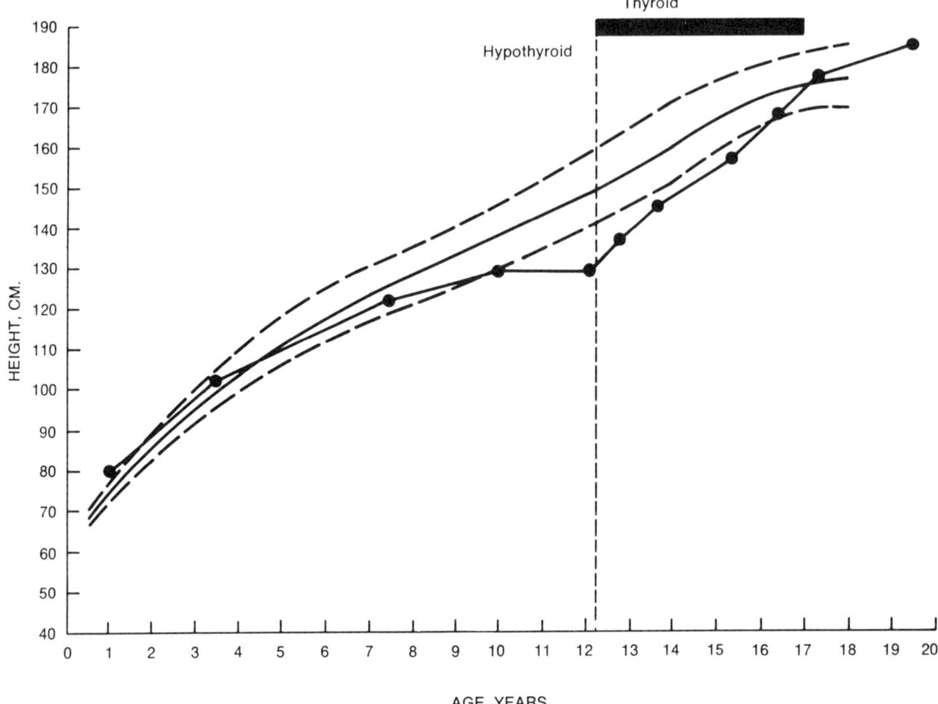

Figure 2.12. Catch-up in a hypothyroid boy following treatment at 12 years old. For explanation of charts see text.
(From Prader, Tanner, & von Harnack, 1963.)

about 0.2. The catch-up after birth does the rest. Note that this is a true regulatory problem, for the form of Figure 2.15 makes it clear that only some of the small babies catch up. A proportion of them need little or no catch-up to reach and continue on their natural growth curves since they are genetically small; it it those aimed, so to speak, at largeness, who catch up to their proper track. The same phenomenon appears particularly clearly in cattle, where the size at birth of a calf born to a small-breed mother mated with a large-breed father is considerably smaller than a calf of a large-breed mother and small-breed father. The two calves grow at different rates after birth so that by the time adult size is reached there is no longer any difference (Dickinson, 1960).

Control of Catch-up

In all the examples of catch-up growth the velocity of growth was rapid at first, became less as the child approached what we can reasonably assume was its pre-illness curve, and finally settled down to a normal value as the child regained the trajectory of his natural curve. A major problem that remains quite unsolved at present is the manner in which the organism knows when to stop the catch-up phase.

During a typical catch-up the whole organism grows rapidly and in at least approximately its proportionate manner. . . . It is difficult (though not impossible) to see how this could happen unless the

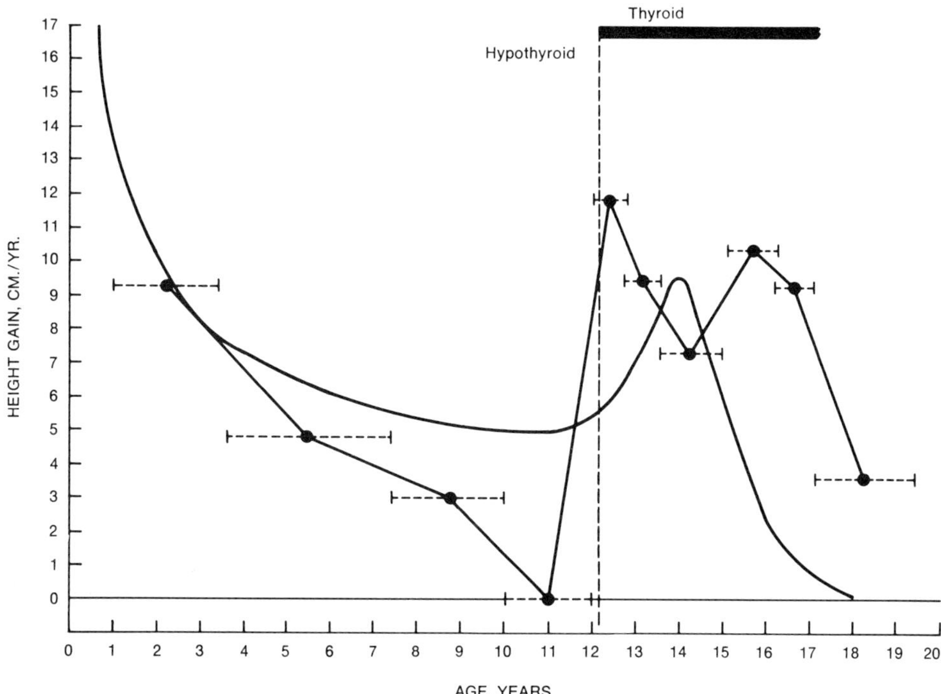

Figure 2.13
For explanation of charts see text.
(From Prader, Tanner & von Harnack, 1963.)

stimulus to catch up is a systemic one circulating with the blood to all parts of the body. In everything that follows it must be remembered that we are dealing with growth in *size* and not in *shape*. So far as our present data goes shape in the human is little affected by a slow-down and subsequent catch-up of growth. Differential effects of malnutrition on limbs and trunk, for example, have never been proved to occur, though they have been suggested by analogy with some results on cattle. Growth in shape must clearly be regulated by peripheral mechanisms rather than the central mechanism for size postulated here.

We do not know what the catch-up stimulus is: growth hormone alone is not it, for one of the features of the catch-up is that skeletal maturity, retarded along with size, catches up also. Human growth hormone does not cause an increase in skeletal maturity when administered to hypophysectomized children (at least to those with bone ages of about 12), although it causes growth. Given to bone-age-delayed, insulin-sensitive dwarfs however (with bone ages of 4 to 10), it does cause advancement in bone age along with growth (personal observations). These dwarfs have apparently normal functioning of their ACTH and TSH mechanisms, and we must attribute the bone age result to an increase in one of these secretions (of a degree not detectable on present tests), or else to an unknown pituitary factor. We

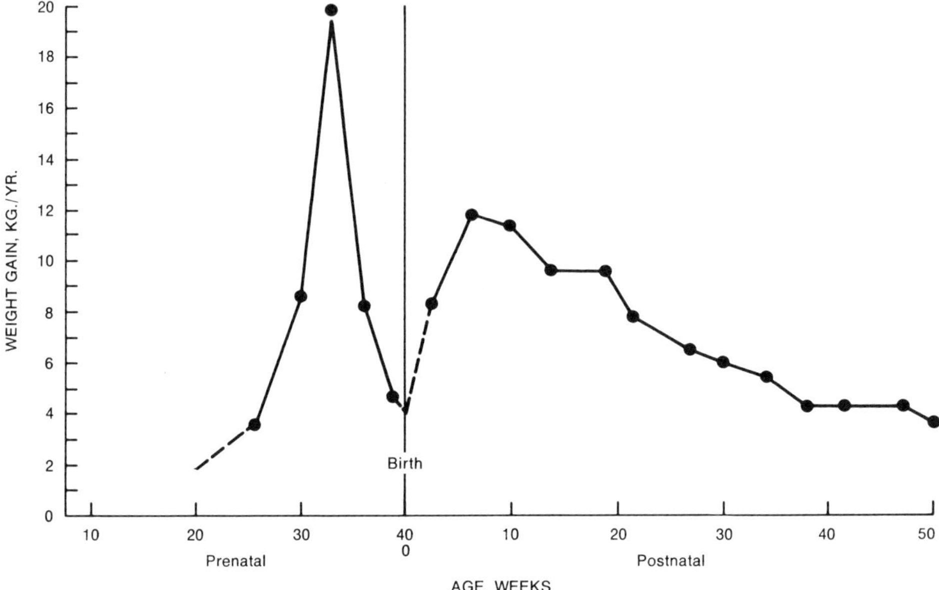

Figure 2.14. Velocity of growth in weight of singleton children.

Prenatal care is derived from the data of McKeown and Record (1952) on birth weights of live-born children delivered before 40 weeks of gestation. Postnatal data is from the Ministry of Health (1959) mixed longitudinal data (their table VII).
Dotted line indicates the estimate of velocity immediately before and after birth, showing catch-up.

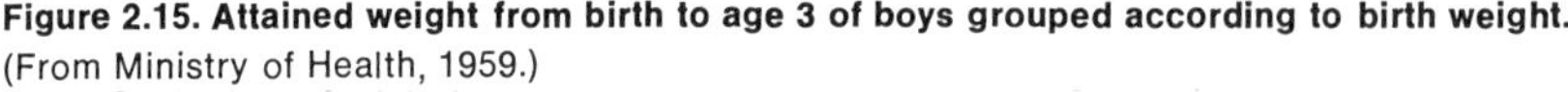

Figure 2.15. Attained weight from birth to age 3 of boys grouped according to birth weight.
(From Ministry of Health, 1959.)

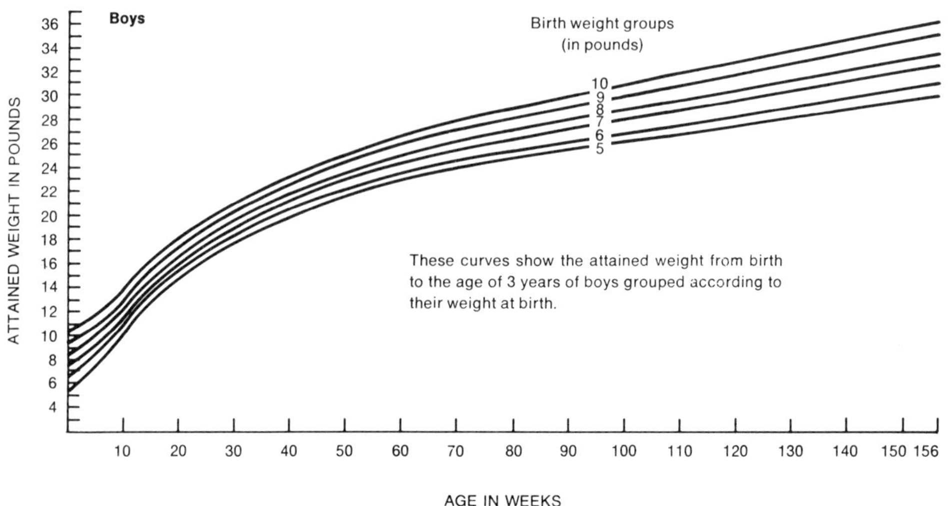

cannot identify ACTH with the catch-up factor because it does not cause growth in preadolescent children; indeed, in dwarfed children with evidence of ACTH deficiency, administration of ACTH to restore normal 17-hydroxycorticoid values does not result in either growth or skeletal age catch-up (Tanner and Clayton, unpublished). Thyroid hormone might possibly be the catch-up stimulus, but we cannot detect any increase in protein-bound iodine during growth hormone-dependent catch-up, and administration of thyroid causes only a transient effect on growth unless there is a definite thyroid deficiency. On the whole it seems more likely that the catch-up factor is not a single substance, but a balanced response involving several hormones, all dependent on the pituitary.

The factor or factors must be released in response to a signal, and it seems likely that this signal acts either on the brain or the pituitary since its mode of operation is to cause a whole-body catch-up in response to a whole-body delay. Lack of growth of a limb, as in poliomyelitis, or hypertrophy of a limb, as in arteriovenous aneurysm, does not cause any catch-up or slow-down of the body as a whole (though in certain organs, such as the liver and kindney, local factors are additionally operative, causing hypertrophy of the corresponding organ alone following removal or disease of part of it).

The characteristics of catch-up require, it seems to me, that this signal represents the degree of mis-match between the actual size (or, for the sake of clarity, actual height) of the organism and the size (or height) required at that age by the hypothetical built-in or "target" growth curve. As the target curve is approached, the mis-match diminishes and the catch-up slows down. For the mis-match to be read both actual size and target size must somehow be represented in the organism. At present we do not know how either representation is made. It is possible that the mis-match is a peripheral phenomenon and occurs in all cells in all tissues, the cells themselves each carrying the code for their own maturity. The catch-up in treated hypothyroidism might indeed be explicable on this basis. But it seems an unlikely hypothesis for explaining most catch-ups and for explaining the normal control of growth in size, which is our ultimate objective. I should like to suggest a possible and, I believe, more plausible hypothesis for investigation.

Consider "target" size. Suppose that somewhere in the brain a tally is kept of the time passed since conception, or rather since the age (perhaps about three months after conception), when the mechanism of the tally begins to function. This tally can represent the target curve, for both are fundamentally series of signals made against a continuing time base. Suppose, purely for simplicity's sake, that the tally consists of a steady increase in the amount of a substance in certain nerve cells; then the form of the growth curve may be represented at any time by (some function of) the concentration of this substance (see Figure 2.16).

Now as to actual size—it is scarcely conceivable that the body can represent its actual extension in space. Suppose, instead, that the organism measures its actual height or size by the concentration of some form of circulating substance produced by cells as an inevitable accompaniment to the process of growth or protein synthesis. In this supposition I follow the most provocative and stimulating ideas of Paul Weiss (see Weiss and Kavanau, 1957), except that he envisages these substances—which he calls anti-templates—as numerous, tissue-specific, and acting directly on peripheral cells, whereas I prefer to think primarily of a single substance acting at the brain level. In the simplest model then, the concentration of this substance (which we will call the "inhibitor") would be proportional to the size of the organism. Its actual concentration can be measured against the concentration expected on the basis of the time tally and the dis-

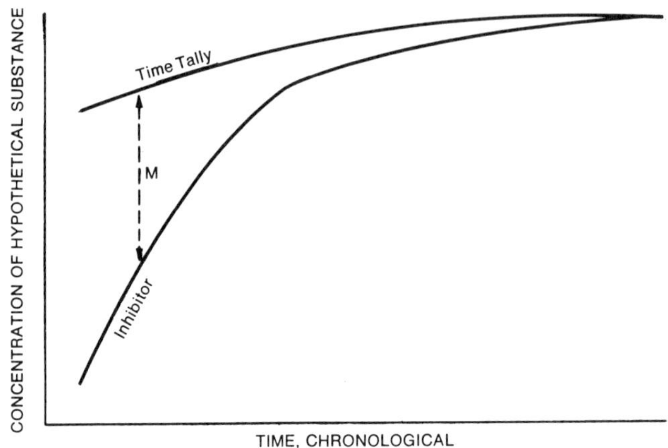

Figure 2.16. Hypothetical relations underlying supposed growth-controlling agents (see text).

The quality *m* represents the mis-match signal.

crepancy can be used as the mis-match signal for release of the growth-stimulating factor. If, for simplicity's sake, we suppose that the time tally consists of a steady increase in the number of receptive sites for the growth-inhibitor substance, then the mis-match signal would consist of the number of unoccupied sites.

The tally need not, of course, represent clock time; on the contrary, it will represent the maturation rate for each individual organism. The rate of tally, and rate of change of that rate, will be an individual, presumably inherited characteristic.

The growth inhibitors are purely hypothetical substances. Neither their origin nor their site of action is known. Weiss supposes that each type of tissue produces inhibitors as it grows and that these diffuse out into the blood and inhibit the growth of the same tissue elsewhere in the body by local action at the cellular level. This is doubtless a valid model for lower animals. It may also be valid for certain aspects of shape in mammals. One might even suppose, at least a priori, that the general correspondence of development throughout the whole body of a given individual of a tissue such as muscle or bone (see Tanner, 1964) might be brought about in this way. But in the control of mammalian growth, certainly in size and probably even in bone and muscle, it seems more likely that the inhibitors act centrally. Furthermore it seems unlikely that many tissues produce tissue-specific inhibitors (though the kidney and liver may). Clearly the limbs contribute nothing important, for children with poliomyelitis, or even limbs entirely missing, grow perfectly normally in the rest of their bodies: they do not hypertrophy due to lack of inhibitors. Thus bone muscle and fat do not seem to be the source of inhibitor production. The liver is the obvious choice, but it is very difficult to provide evidence for this since damage to the liver diminishes the ability to metabolize substances essential for growth and hence may result in a slowing down of growth, even if inhibitor production is also diminished. Teng, Daeschner, Singleton, Rosenberg, Cole, Hill, and Brennan (1961) have reported that in childhood hepatomas growth slows down and on their removal a catch-up occurs. Though it is not the most obvious and likely explanation, the hepatoma *could* have been producing excess inhibitors. A case has recently been reported by Davis (1962) of a girl who had a liver disorder of unknown origin and suffered from lipodystrophy and much accelerated growth. This could be interpreted as lack of inhibitor, but of course other explanations are also available. The kidney seems an unlikely but possible site, and the thymus and lymph nodes are an attractive possibility on immunological grounds, but thymectomized mice in fact grow less and not more than normal.

We may reasonably think that the same mechanism underlies the form of the normal velocity curve of growth, wherein a baby grows faster than a 9-year-old. Suppose, again for simplicity, that the tally accumulates at a constantly decreasing rate as illustrated in Figure 2.16. Suppose also that the inhibitors develop in proportion to the sites of synthesis used up in the cells as they pack in more protein, each turn of the RNA wheel, as it were, throwing off a molecule of inhibitor. Then the inhibitor concentration would rise in an exponential fashion, fast at first and slowly later. The mis-match (m) between these two concentrations would be large at first and decrease after the manner of the growth velocity curve. In this simple model the concentration of growth-stimulating factor is directly proportional to the mis-match, and the velocity of catch-up is supposed to be directly proportional to the concentration of growth-stimulating factor. (Really one or other of these relationships might well be logarithmic.)

As Figure 2.17 shows, the model represents the chief feature of catch-up correctly. The catch-up velocity seems usually to be not only greater than the velocity expected at the age of catch-up, but also greater than the velocity expected at the age at which growth stopped (see Prader *et al.*, 1963). The model predicts that the mis-match and hence the catch-up velocity will be the velocity appropriate to a younger age than this, how much younger depending on the relative curvatures of the time tally and inhibitor lines. The model also predicts that catch-up growth, following a given time of growth arrest, will be more intense at young ages than at older ones. This is generally thought to be the case, although our own data give no direct evidence for it.

We should not press such a crude model too far, but one cannot help noticing that the relation between the time tally curve and the inhibitor curve resembles that between the growth of the central nervous system and the growth of the rest of the body. Perhaps one of the reasons that the central nervous system develops ahead of the remainder of most of the body is that the time tally is located there. It would be logical if the earliest developing part of the organism carried the programme for the growth of the remainder.

Of course, this model may be quite wrong and, if not quite wrong, is certainly much oversimplified. The true situation is without doubt more complex; for example, we have assumed that the tally continues

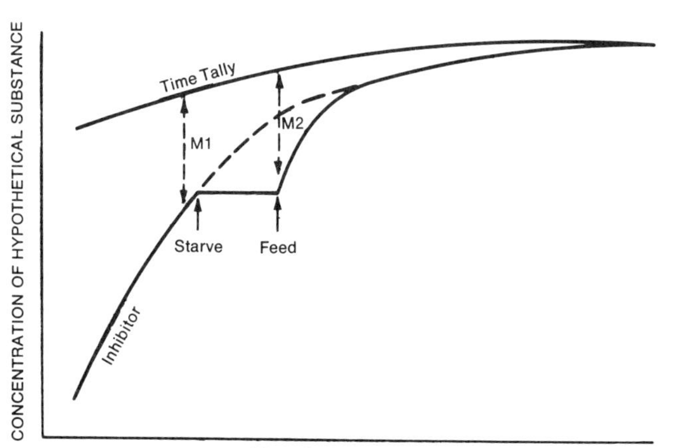

Figure 2.17. Velocity expected in catch-up growth, assuming control system of Figure 2.16.

Catch-up velocity is proportional to the mis-match m_2, which is greater than the mis-match when starvation began and equal to the mis-match at an earlier age, as represented by $m_1 = m_2$.

unaltered, even under circumstances which stop the rest of the organism from growing altogether. This is somewhat unrealistic. Catch-up is probably incomplete if the period of growth arrest by starvation, say, is prolonged. To explain this we may assume that the time tally is somewhat affected by the starvation, though to a much lesser extent than the rest of the body. It may fail to resume its old rate at refeeding, or it may return to its old rate but without a catch-up. Alternatively we can assume that catch-up depends not only on mis-match but also in the time tally's velocity (or its integral or total amount).

On purely cybernetical grounds we may expect at least two complications. To combat sluggishness in the response to the mis-match (under normal conditions) it is likely that the rate of change of the mis-match, rather than its absolute amount, would be taken as the signal for release of the growth-stimulating factor. Secondly we may expect multiple feedback pathways from tissues to centre, rather than a single feedback, in order to ensure stability of the system. This is what cyberneticists call reliability through redundancy, and we may expect it to complicate our physiological analysis here as elsewhere in analyses of feedback in the body.

We have so far ignored the existence of the adolescent spurt and dealt with growth as though it gradually ceased at the end of its exponential preadolescent curve, as it does in fishes and reptiles. In primates, particularly, there is a secondary growth system superimposed on this basic one, causing a new increase of growth rate to occur just when the impetus of the basic system is nearing its end. This secondary system, be it noted, is not a necessary condition for growth to cease, even in man. Children who suffer gonadal or gonadotrophic failure at adolescence may not close their epiphyses, but their growth gradually ceases all the same (see e.g., cases C X and C XII of Bayer & Bayley, 1959). Rats never close their epiphyses and reptiles do not have epiphyses to close. Evidently it is the dwindling of the mis-match signal which causes growth to slow down; finally the signal becomes vanishingly small, and the organism remains in a steady state of equilibrium. There is no reason to suppose that the adolescent growth cycle is organized in a different manner from the basic cycle, but it uses different substances. Its time tally and its inhibitors must be distinct from those of the basic cycle, just as its growth-stimulating factor is also distinct. But it is linked to the basic cycle in that its beginning occurs when the basic cycle has reached a certain point in its evolution.

Linkages such as these occur between many systems during growth and we must try to form some idea of how they may work. We know that adolescence is initiated when a restraining influence from the hypothalamus on the pituitary is removed We think that under normal circumstances certain cells in the hypothalamus mature and that when they reach a certain stage of maturity they cease sending inhibitory impulses to the pituitary. This may be because they themselves no longer respond to the small amount of sex hormones or similar substances thought to be circulating in the blood even before puberty. Control over the hypothalamic cells is only reasserted when sex hormone levels rise much higher following adolescence (see Werff ten Bosch, 1959). It is tempting to identify the hypothalamus as the site of the time tally. Harris and Jacobsohn (1952) showed that when the pituitary gland of an adult rat was replaced by grafted pituitaries of newborn rats of the same strain, these newborn pituitaries assumed adult function and secreted gonadotrophins as soon as the vascular connection of the graft was complete. This is long before the donor rat would have reached puberty. It is therefore the hypothalamus which carries the information as to maturity.

. . .

Simple linkage alone does not seem able

to account for the postponement of puberty after starvation. Though the facts here may be a little questionable, it seems that if a period of starvation occurs at the normal time of puberty, puberty is delayed, and that on refeeding puberty does not occur at once (as demanded by the simple linkage model), but only after a certain amount of catch-up growth has occurred. We could account for this by assuming that the switch mechanism is dependent not only on the velocity of the tally reaching a critical value L, but also on the mis-match reaching a certain value m_1. (See Figure 2.18.) In this case ordinary catch-up would occur until the mismatch reached m_2 equal to m_1. As the scanty experimental and clinical data make it seem probable that in fact puberty occurs before the catch-up velocity has actually fallen the whole way to the usual preadolescent velocity, we may think that the relationships are quantitative and that a further lowering of the tally velocity after L is passed makes possible a higher mis-match, the combination of the two being the quantity required to reach a threshold value. A two-factor linkage such as this seems more typical of events in growth than a single-factor one, in that it permits greater variability amongst a number of individuals. In this sense it is a "looser" coupling. Actually the recent results of McCance (1962) on starvation and refeeding in pigs agree with a fairly simple direct linkage, for puberty occurred in the starved and then fed pigs much before the body had caught up to its usual puberty size.

The model must be capable of explaining the disorder of precocious puberty. In some cases pubertal changes occur early, at a nearly normal size for chronological age; the children then finish their growth as very small adults. Essentially the same can be brought about in rats by destruction of an area in the hypothalamus; in an experiment of Donovan and Werff ten Bosch (1959), vaginal opening occurred at 33 days instead of 40, but the growth in body size was not accelerated. In this case we may suppose that L has been drastically moved back along the tally curve, that is, that the linkage takes place at a higher tally velocity than normal. Physiologically, it may be that the inhibitory impulses to the pituitary are steadily diminishing as the velocity of the time tally diminishes (i.e., as the maturity of the cells increases). If some of the inhibitory cells are destroyed, then the total effective inhibition diminishes, and the threshold is

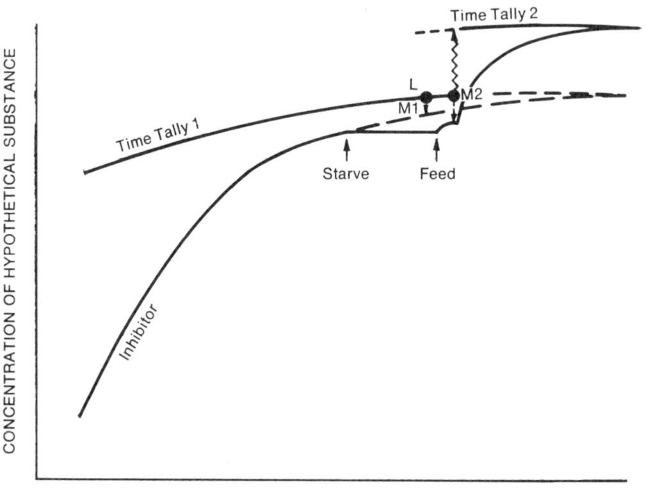

Figure 2.18. Hypothetical linkage of two systems under conditions of temporary starvation.

The distances marked m_1 and m_2 are supposed equal. See text.

reached at an earlier point on the tally curve.

Other cases occur in which the child grows excessively fast from an early age, at first without any signs of puberty. He reaches puberty early however—very early as regards chronological age and somewhat early as regards size. The simplest supposition about the growth regulation of such a child is that the form of the tally curve is distorted so that its velocity is at first abnormally large. This would give rise to an abnormally large mis-match at the beginning of growth and hence to the accelerated growth. The point L would occur early in chronological time, if it reflects the same critical velocity as usual in the time tally. In this form of precocious puberty, therefore, puberty would occur early without any shift in time tally threshold. The disorder could equally be explained by underproduction of inhibitors, except that then, if we follow the linkage hypothesis above, we would not expect to get puberty till after the normal time and at a very large size.

Factors Affecting the Regulatory System

The regulatory system is evidently built into the organism and we would expect its characteristics, such as precision, speed of response, and so forth to be mainly genetically determined. Such indeed is the case. Two factors are known which affect the system: heterozygosity and sex. In animals hybrids seem to be better regulated, or canalized, than inbred strains, at least in a number of instances. Hybrid mice for example vary less than inbred in weight and in tail length either in a normal or a hot environment (Harrison, Morton, & Weiner, 1959). Nothing is as yet known about this in the human. The effect of sex however is becoming well documented in man (see Tanner, 1962, p. 127). Girls are apparently less easily thrown off their growth curves by adverse circumstances than boys. Greulich (1951) first drew attention to this, after studying the effects on growth of wartime hardships in Guam and of the atomic bombing in Hiroshima and Nagasaki. The same sex difference seems to occur in response to malnutrition in rats.

Conclusion

We have apparently ended rather far into physiological and genetic technology, but I think this an appearance only. One reason that I chose to speak about regulation in growth was because it is a general problem. By this I mean that formal, model solutions may be applicable not only to the problems of physical growth but in several different fields. It is an old and entirely justified complaint that the great majority of so-called interdisciplinary studies of child growth fail in their endeavour to link the psychology and physiology of development. The mistake was to suppose that the child was the integrating factor; that when psychologists and physiologists applied their techniques not to different children but to the *same* child, that integration would follow. An integral view can be obtained only when both groups use a common, and because common, more fundamental language than their present ones, and I have a feeling that that language insofar as child development is concerned will be cybernetics.

Summary

An animal's growth is self-stabilizing, or "target-seeking," in the sense that the animal has a strong tendency to return to its natural growth curve after being deflected from it by disease or starvation. Illustrations of the regularity of growth in height of children are given, showing the excellent fit of simple curves to longitudinal data before and during adolescence. Seasonal variation in growth rate about these curves is also illustrated.

Examples are given of "catch-up" or compensatory growth occurring in children at the end of periods of starvation, hypothyroidism, Cushing's syndrome, and growth-hormone-responsive dwarfism. It is pointed out that in healthy children a catch-up occurs frequently during the first six months after birth; genetically large babies are thus able to reach their growth curves after having been restrained when developing in the uterus of a small mother.

A hypothesis concerning the regulation of catch-up growth and of the normal velocity of growth is then presented. Since during the catch-up the whole organism grows in a proportional manner, it is thought likely that the control of size resides in a central mechanism. To explain how the organism "knows" when to stop the rapid catch-up velocity, it is supposed that in the brain there is a time tally mechanism which represents the normal growth curve by means of maturation changes occurring in certain nerve cells. The actual size of the organism is supposed to be monitored by means of an inhibitor substance produced proportionately to the increase of material in body cells. The mis-match between the time tally and the inhibitor concentration is then read and the velocity of growth is adjusted to be proportional to this mismatch. It is thought that this mechanism may underlie the normal velocity curve of growth (high velocity at first, low later) as well as catch-up growth.

Examples of how this simple model represents the known events of catch-up growth, of chronic starvation, and of precocious puberty are given. A second cycle is supposed to occur at adolescence, and the manner in which the linkage between the first and second cycles may be made definite, but relatively loose, is discussed. Work on the regulation of sex and maturity in experimental animals is quoted, indicating that the location of the time tally and of the reading of the mis-match may well be in the hypothalamus. It is stressed that this model is hypothetical only; if correct at all, it is certainly oversimplified. Nevertheless it might serve as a necessary basis for investigation in this neglected field.

References

BAYER, LEONA M., & BAYLEY, NANCY. *Growth diagnosis.* Chicago: Univer. Chicago Press, 1959.

DAVIS, J. Paper given at the International Congress on Paediatrics, Lisbon, 1962. (Unpublished.)

DEMING, J. Application of the Gompertz curve to the observed pattern of growth in length of 48 individual boys and girls during the adolescent cycle of growth. *Hum. Biol.,* 1957, *29,* 83–122.

DICKINSON, A. G. Some genetic implications of maternal effects: an hypothesis of mammalian growth. *J. agric. Sci.,* 1960, *54,* 379–390.

DONOVAN, B. T., & WERFF TEN BOSCH, J. J. VAN DER. The hypothalamus and sexual maturation in the rat. *J. Physiol.,* 1959, *147,* 78–92.

GREULICH, W. W. The growth and developmental status of Guamanian school children in 1947. *Amer. J. phys. Anthrop.,* N.S., 1951, *9,* 55–70.

HARRIS, G. W., & JACOBSOHN, D. Functional grafts of the anterior pituitary gland. *Proc. Royal Soc.* (Series B), 1952, *139,* 263–276.

HARRISON, G. A., MORTON, R. J., & WEINER, J. S. The growth in weight and tail length of inbred and hybrid mice reared at two different temperatures. *Philos. Trans.* (Series B), 1959, *242,* 479–516.

MCCANCE, R. A. Food, growth and time. *Lancet,* 1962, *2,* 621–626; 671–676.

MCKEOWN, T., & RECORD, R. G. Observations on foetal growth in multiple pregnancy in man. *J. Endocrin.*, 1952, *8*, 386–401.

MINISTRY OF HEALTH (Great Britain). Standards of normal weight in infancy. *Min. Hlth. Rep. Publ. Hlth. No. 99.* London: H.M.S.O., 1959.

NORVAL, M. A., KENNEDY, R. L. J., & BERKSON, J. Biometric studies of the growth of children of Rochester, Minnesota. The first year of life. *Hum. Biol.*, 1951, *23*, 274–301.

PENROSE, L. S. *Recent advances in human genetics.* London: Churchill, 1961.

PRADER, A., TANNER, J. M., & VON HARNACK, G. A. Catch-up growth following illness or starvation; an example of developmental canalization in man. *J. Pediat.*, 1963, *62*, 646–659.

SIMMONS, K., & TODD, T. W. Growth of well children: Analysis of stature and weight, 3 months to 13 years. *Growth*, 1938, *2*, 93–134.

TANNER, J. M. *Growth at adolescence* (2nd ed.). Oxford: Blackwell, 1962.

———. Growth and constitution. In G. A. Harrison, J. M. Tanner, J. S. Weiner, & N. A. Barnicot, *Human biology.* Oxford: Clarendon Press, 1964.

TANNER, J. M., & INHELDER, BÄRBEL (Eds.). *Discussions on child development.* Vol. 4. London: Tavistock Publications and New York: International Universities Press, 1960.

TENG, C. T., DAESCHNER, C. W., SINGLETON, E. B., ROSENBERG, H. S., COLE, V. W., HILL, L. L., & BRENNAN, J. C. Liver disease and osteoporosis in children: I. Clinical observations. *J. Pediat.*, 1961, *59*, 684–702.

THOMPSON, J. Observations on weight gain in infants. *Arch. Dis. Childh.*, 1955, *30*, 322–327.

———. Infant Growth. *Arch. Dis. Childh.*, 1956, *31*, 382–389.

WADDINGTON, C. H. *The strategy of the genes. A discussion of some aspects of theoretical biology.* London: Allen & Unwin, 1957.

WEISS, P., & KAVANAU, J. L. A model of growth and growth control in mathematical terms. *J. gen. Physiol.*, 1957, *41*, 1–47.

WERFF TEN BOSCH, J. J. VAN DER. *Normale en abnormale Geslachstrijping.* Leiden: Univer. Leiden Press, 1959.

7. SMILING, COOING, AND "THE GAME"

JOHN S. WATSON

Two separate lines of my research with infants have recently merged in their implications for the meaning of smiling and cooing in early infancy. One line began as a study of the development of the perception of object orientation, and the other began as a study of early instrumental learning. Recently, data from these two research directions have suggested what might be called an ethological-social-cognitive hypothesis concerning the onset of vigorous smiling and cooing in early infancy. This hypothesis is less simple than one might desire, but those who would focus on the limited parsimony rather than the presumed heuristic and explanatory breadth of this hypothesis will at least be pleased that it has been given a short name, "The Game."

"The Game" Hypothesis

The hypothesis of "The Game" proposes that when an infant perceives the occurrence of a neutral or positive stimulus, a process termed "contingency analysis" begins (Watson, 1966b, 1967a). If, across successive exposures of the stimulus, this analysis confirms the existence of a contingency between the stimulus and a response, then this contingent stimulus and eventually the stimuli which mark this contingency situation gain new meaning for the infant. The new meaning is that the stimuli become the releasing stimuli for vigorous smiling and cooing. In essence, the stimuli begin functioning as "social stimuli." It is assumed that this process of defining what shall be viewed as social is limited to some set of initial contingency experiences.

In most situations in which the average infant finds himself during the first 2–3 months, the combination of slow response recovery and short contingency memory prohibits his becoming aware of contingencies between his behavior and its stimulus effects in the physical environment because by the time he is able to repeat an effective response, he has usually forgotten why it was selected for repetition.[1] Then one day someone begins playing a game with the infant. They touch his nose each time he widens his eyes, or they bounce him on their knee each time he bobs his head, or they blow on his belly each time he jiggles his legs, or they make sounds after he makes a sound. These games are variants of "The Game." There are many other potential variants, but what makes them a special and singular class is that they share the features of presenting a clear stimulus contingent upon a response which is small or mature enough to have a relatively quick recovery time. As the specific game is played more times, the infant experiences an increasing awareness of a clear contingency, and with that, vigorous smiling and cooing begins.

The infant is committed to making very precise discriminations about the context of his initial contingency experiences. If the situation or contingency is unclear, the releasing of vigorous smiling and cooing will not occur, and indeed if the situation is an ambiguous mixture of sometimes times contingent, sometimes not contingent, then negative emotional responses may occur.

To begin viewing the empirical background of this hypothesis we need to consider some studies of the uncontested champion stimulus for eliciting vigorous smiling and cooing within the first 6 months of infancy.

Studies of the Face Stimulus

While there is little doubt that infants smile at many things, the quickest, longest, and most vigorous smiling in the first 16 months occurs to the face stimulus. The many studies which have assessed the infant's smiling reaction to a silent human face are in agreement on a number of points. Vigorous smiling to the face stimulus increases rapidly during the second and third months of life, reaching a peak at approximately 14 weeks in home-reared infants (Ambrose, 1961; Watson, 1966a), and reaching a peak at about 20 weeks for institutionalized infants (Spitz & Wolf,

---

[1] These are two major natural constraints on the process whereby the human infant first encounters a situation in which he can become aware of contingencies between his responses and stimuli which follow them. One natural constraint is the infant's immature motor system, with the relatively long recovery times for responses which have salient stimulus consequences in his physical environment (see Watson, 1966b, for more discussion). The second major constraint is the infant's relatively short memory span for contingencies. In the so-called "free operant" situation this span appears to be approximately 5–7 seconds in length (Watson, 1967a).

1946; Ambrose, 1961). A number of competing proposals have been put forth to explain the infant's vigorous response to the face stimulus. These have ranged from the proposal of an innate responsiveness to the facial pattern (Gibson, 1950; Bowlby, 1958; Fantz, 1961), to the proposal of a responsiveness to its particular level of complexity (Rheingold, 1961), to the proproposal of a responsiveness to its particular level of familiarity (Piaget, 1952; Kagan et al., 1966; Lewis, 1969; Walters & Parke, 1965; Zelazo, in press), and to the proposal that the face becomes established as a secondary reward and/or a discriminative stimulus during primary rewarding, caretaking activities (Spitz & Wolf, 1946; Gewirtz, 1961; Ambrose, 1961).

It is important to note, however, that this rapid rise of vigorous smiling to the face during the second month is a phenomenon which is dependent on proper alignment of the facial stimulus with the face of the infant. That is, during the third and fourth months of life the face stimulus can be shown to be an elicitor of vigorous smiling only if it is aligned with the infant's face as in the 0° orientation of Figure 2.19, but not so if aligned in the 90° or 180° orientation. In home-reared infants at the 14-week, peak period of smiling to a silent face, the 0° face (real face of mother or stranger) elicits approximately twice as much smiling as the 90° face (Watson, 1966a). This finding has important and immediate implications. It is sufficient in itself to eliminate stimulus complexity as the explanation of the special significance of the face stimulus for the 14-week-old infant. There is no existent definition of stimulus complexity which would determine a difference in the level of complexity between a 0° and a 90° face.[2]

The finding of differential potency of the face stimulus in different orientations also raises strong doubts as to the potency of the variables of familiarity and reward association as explanations of "face power" when the differential effect of orientation

[2] While the logic of this analysis should be compelling, it is worth noting that it has the empirical support of a study by Haaf and Bell (1967) where, in a specially constructed series of stimuli, infants distinguished the variable of faceness from the variable of stimulus complexity.

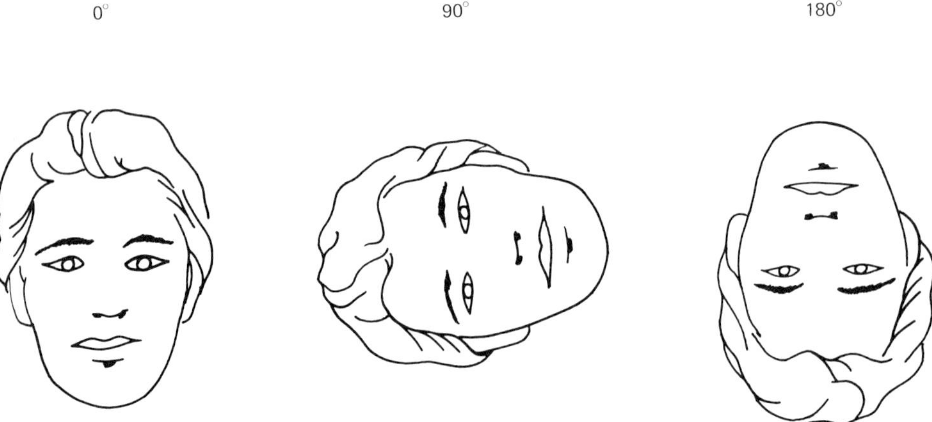

Figure 2.19. Illustration of 0°, 90°, and 180° facial orientations.

is combined with observations of mother-infant interaction. There is evidence that the primary rewards in caretaking activities such as feeding and diaper-changing are more commonly associated with the 90° face or even the profile position of the face than they are with 0° presentation (Watson, 1967b). On the basis of available evidence, then, it does not seem that the 0° face acquires its special significance for the infant due to its association with primary rewarding, caretaking activities.

Likewise, the familiarity hypothesis does not appear compatible with these data. Familiarity is presumably based on the frequency and duration of past exposures of a stimulus, yet it seems clear that the previously mentioned exposure differences in caretaking situations would not support any proposal of the 0° face being a more familiar exposure pattern. Although we have no data concerning the relative exposure frequencies of the various orientations of the face in situations other than caretaking, it does not seem likely that the 0° face is especially more frequent during the rest of the infant's day. In addition, the familiarity hypothesis must have great difficulty accounting for the following fact. We know the 90° face does occur with some frequency for the infant, but we have yet to see, and find it hard to imagine, many 180° facial presentations. Yet our data indicate that the 180° (e.g., upside down) face and the 90° face are not differentially effective in eliciting responses from the infant.

It would seem then that the major contenders for understanding the special responsiveness to the face stimulus are, on the one hand, an hypothesis of an innate responsiveness to the 0° face or, on the other hand, some experiential hypothesis which provides for the association of the 0° face with some special experience. I would now propose an experiential hypothesis with the provision that the special experience associated with the 0° face is "The Game." It is proposed that in those situations in which a caretaker begins playing his game with his infant, he looks at his infant's face; and when he looks at his infant's face, he aligns himself so that he is making a 0° facial presentation. We do have some evidence that mothers will make special effort to align themselves in 0° when being asked to check the face of their baby (Watson, 1967b). Thus, the 0° face becomes the special marker of the situation in which the infant first becomes aware of a clear contingency between his behavior and a stimulus occurrence in the environment. With the experience of "The Game" the infant emits vigorous smiling and cooing, and these in turn are very likely received by the caretaker as inspiration for new games both with other responses and with the smile and coo themselves.

Studies of Response-Contingent Stimulation

One might ask why "The Game" hypothesis proposes that "The Game" initially elicits vigorous smiling and cooing, rather than proposing that initial games are taken up with and progressively reward the smiling and cooing responses themselves. This proposal arises from a set of studies which has presented the possibility of instrumental learning over a period of days in early infancy. The first research to take special note of the apparent release of vigorous smiling and cooing to response-contingent stimulation was that of Hunt and Uzgiris (1964). In that study some infants had a mobile which was fixed to their cribs so that if they jiggled, the mobile would move. Other infants had a mobile attached outside the crib, which prevented control of the mobile's movement. The authors report that a few infants, whose mobiles jiggled neither too little nor too much, were able to establish clear control of their mobiles and showed smiling and cooing when doing so. They interpreted their results as indicating the pleasure in the process of assimilating responsive stimulation. In some recent studies by my colleagues and myself many infants have been observed to blossom into vigorous smiling and cooing during our attempts to provide early beneficial learning experiences. Before our data which corroborate Hunt and Uzgiris' finding are described, however, an important difference in interpretation of the smiling and cooing reaction should be noted.

Hunt and Uzgiris' interpretation of smiling and cooing, indeed the interpretation of many of the proponents of familiarity hypotheses, is one in which the responses serve two functions, one to release the emotional energy of pleasure and the other to serve as a behavioral basis for the recognition process in a manner similar to Piaget's proposal of "recognitive assimilation" (Piaget, 1952). While it may be true that smiling and cooing do indeed serve as aids to recognition and as avenues of emotional release, it seems unlikely that they would have survived behavioral evolution within our species as so distinct and so external a set of responses were it not for their social functions. Why should the offspring of our species be so vigorously expressive of their pleasure in recognizing their control of the environment? The young of other species seem to gain com-

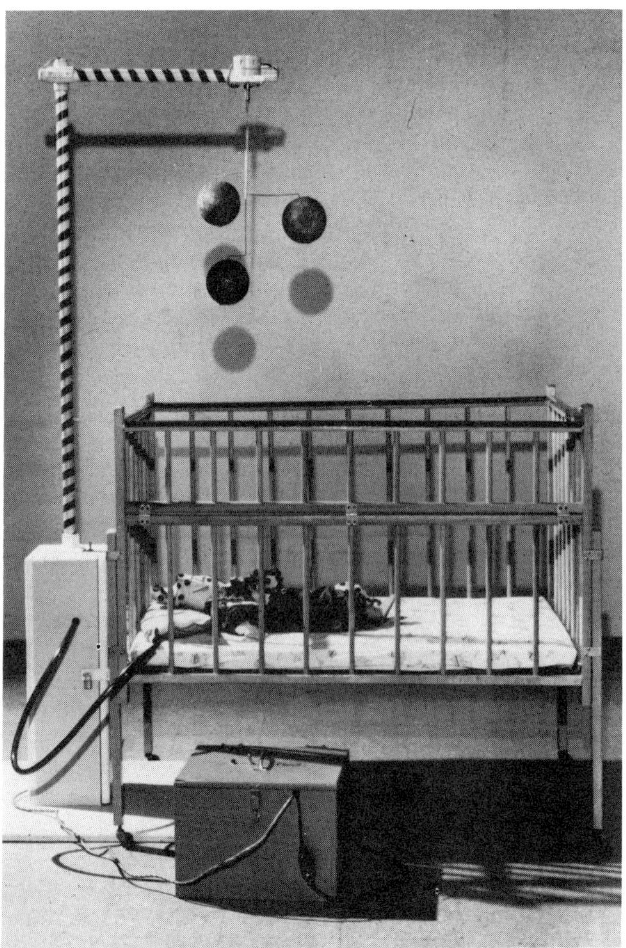

Figure 2.20. Machine used for stimulus display and recording of pillow responses.

parable control without a similar display of emotion. The recognition hypothesis appears to say we do so simply because we are what we are, while "The Game" hypothesis proposes that we do so because in this way we are normally guaranteed to begin vigorous smiling and cooing at fellow species members.

Our data come from a series of studies aimed at stimulating the development of contingency awareness in early infancy. Encouraging the arrival of contingency awareness before its normally expected appearance in the natural environment was intended to have beneficial effects in accord with certain theoretical proposals made elsewhere (Watson, 1966a) and which need not be restated here. Special machines were constructed for these studies. A picture of a machine is shown in Figure 2.20 and it will be seen that the essential feature of the system is a very sensitive pillow which is designed to allow very small and quick recovery responses to have discrete and clear contingent effects on a visual display hanging over the infant.

Experiment I The initial study was carried out by Craig Ramey and myself (Watson & Ramey, 1969). The machines were placed in the homes of 18 infants who were exposed to them for 10 min. a day for 2 weeks starting when they were 8 weeks old. For these 18 infants a mobile hanging over them turned for 1 second after each time they pressed their head on the pillow. Experiment I also had two control groups, each composed of 11 infants. In one group the infants saw a stabile that did not move, and in the other control group the infants saw a noncontingent mobile which turned periodically and unrelated to their head movements. These infants and those of the following three experiments were children of college-educated fathers, and virtually all were Caucasian. The machines accumulated the daily records of the infants, and these are shown in Figure 2.21. The infants of Experiment I who had contingent mobiles showed a significant increase in daily activity across the 2 weeks (change in pillow response rate from days 1–2 to 13–14, $t = 3.72$, $p < .01$). The two control groups did not change appreciably in their activity. In short, these 8-week-old infants showed they could learn in this situation. But more dramatically for us at the time, and more importantly for this paper at this time, the mothers of the infants with contingent mobiles almost unanimously reported the appearance of vigorous smiling and cooing in their infants on approximately the third or fourth day of exposure. Considering the fact that the machines were not rewarding smiling and cooing, it seems reasonable to assume that the contingency experience was releasing these responses. The mothers of control infants reported that they saw some smiling among their infants, but at a much lower degree of vigor and duration than that observed among infants with contingent mobiles.

At about this time a study by Rovee and Rovee (1969) was reported in which infants were attached to a mobile by a string from their feet and were able to make it move by kicking. These infants showed a rapid increase in kicking responses to what was here termed "conjugate reinforcement." The term refers to a relational connection wherein the intensity of the reinforcement stimulus is related contingently to the frequency of responses, but no discrete stimulus is made contingent on a discrete response. The infants were seen only for one day. The fact that Rovee and Rovee apparently did not observe the release of vigorous smiling and cooing is possibly due to either the limitation of experience to a single day or to the fact that conjugate reinforcement is not as effective a releaser as discrete contingent stimulation. This latter possibility is consistent with the fact that in Hunt and Uzgiris' study the infants

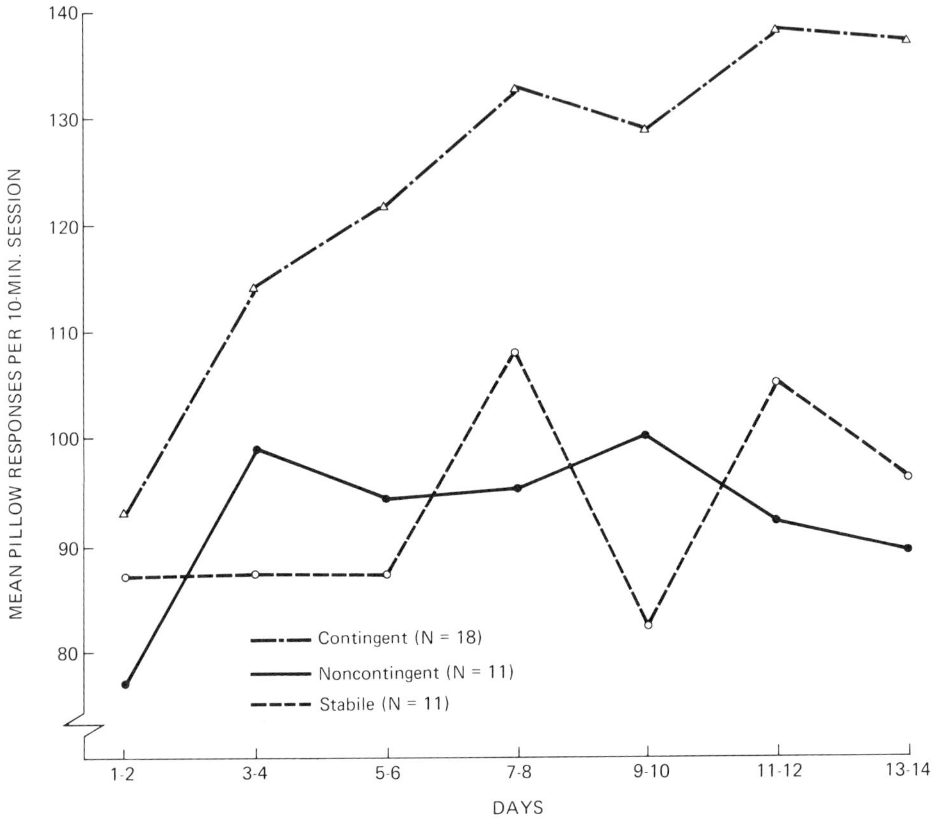

Figure 2.21. Pillow responses across two weeks by the three groups in Experiment I.

who had very responsive cribs also did not blossom into smiling and cooing.[3]

[3] It seems reasonable to speculate that from the perspective of selective evolution there may well be a significant difference to the infant between stimulation which is contemporaneous with his response and stimulation which is slightly but clearly postcedent to his response. For example, discrete contingent stimulation should be easily discriminated from proprioceptive feedback stimulation, but discrimination should be more difficult between conjugate reinforcement and proprioceptive feedback since these are both contemporaneous with responding. Put simply, perhaps stimulation which is clearly postcedent to the response upon which it is contingent has evolved to be more salient to the infant because in such instances the odds are the stimulation is coming from outside and not from within.

Experiment II The second, third, and fourth experiments of our series were carried out by Peter Vietze, Lynn Dorman, and myself. In the second experiment, fourteen 8-week-old infants were exposed to the machine for two 10-minute periods each day for 2 weeks. In one 10-minute session a contingent stimulus was presented, and in the other 10-minute session a different stimulus was presented noncontingently. For the first four of these subjects the two stimulus events were different visual displays which turned. One was a cluster of three balls, and the other was a large square. We hoped to obtain learning and a release of smiling and cooing with the contingent stimulus, and passive responsiveness to the noncontingent stimulus. As it turned out, the rate of responding from day to day rose initially for both contingent and noncontingent conditions and then progressively declined; and none of the infants showed the characteristic release of vigorous smiling and cooing. We guessed that the visual stimuli were not distinct enough and that the infants were becoming confused, so we replaced the large square mobile with a stabile upside-down umbrella which had a light behind it. When the stimulus light came on, the translucent umbrella glowed for 1 second. For half the subjects this lighted umbrella was the contingent stimulus, and for the other half it was the noncontingent stimulus. We now felt sure the infants would discriminate clearly the contingent and noncontingent situations. We were, however, clearly wrong in this prediction. These remaining 10 infants showed the same pattern as the initial four. Figure 2.22 summarizes the performance of all 14 subjects of Experiment II, showing the initial rise in both contingent and noncontingent sessions and then the decline in response rate on the pillow.

Experiment III At the same time as Experiment II was being conducted, Peter Vietze initiated Experiment III to assess the initial reactions and eventual adaptation to two different ratios of reinforcement. In one group the mobile turned 40%

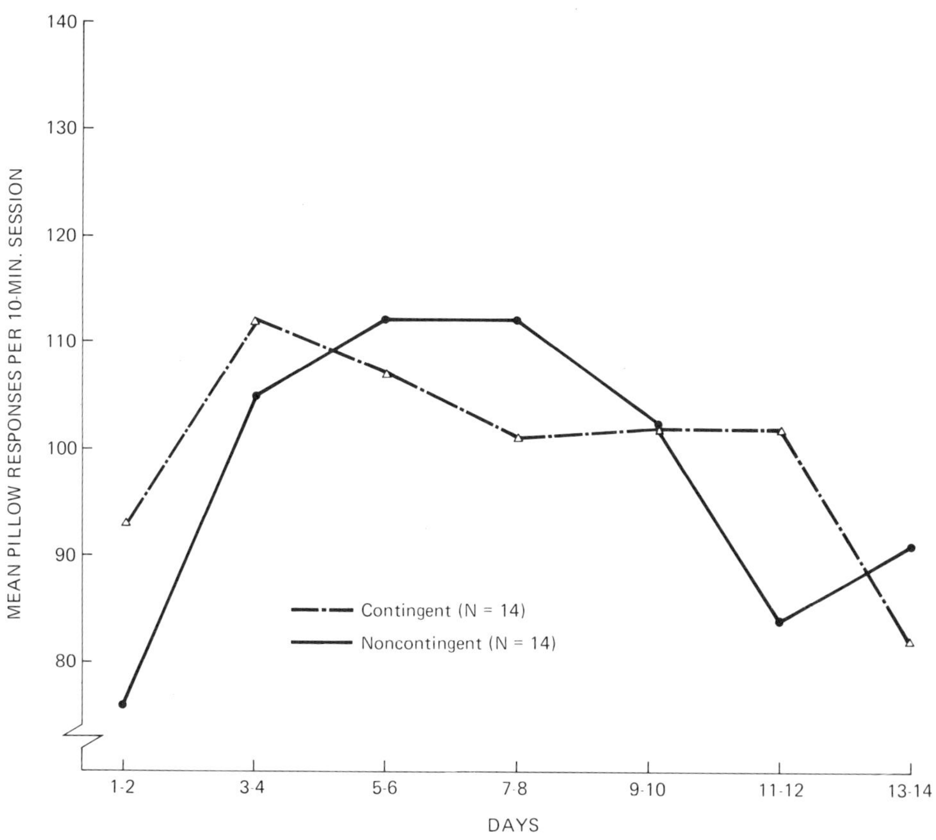

Figure 2.22. Pillow responses across two weeks for the contingent and noncontingent sessions of the 14 subjects in Experiment II.

of the time that the infant pressed his head on the pillow. In the other group the mobile turned 60% of the time the pillow was pressed. Both groups, then, were partially noncontingent in the special sense that some of the times the infants pressed their heads on the pillows the mobiles would not turn. Twelve 8-week-old infants were involved in Experiment III, and they did not learn to increase the rate of their behavior, nor did they show an increase in vigorous smiling and cooing.

One can view partial reinforcement as having a similarity both to noncontingent and to contingent stimulation, so the results of Experiment III are presented in both contexts. Figure 2.23 shows the two-week response record in the context of the noncontingent stimulation group of Experiment I and the noncontingent sessions of Experiment II. The contrast between Experiment III and Experiment II would seem to suggest that while the infants of Experiment II initially generalized a sense of potential contingency to these noncontingent sessions, the infants in Experiment III sensed confusion from the start. Figure 2.24 shows the response record of Experiment III in the context of the contingency group of Experiment I and the contingency sessions of Experiment II. The contrasts of records are quite convincing that the infants of Experiment III were confused or at least uninspired from the

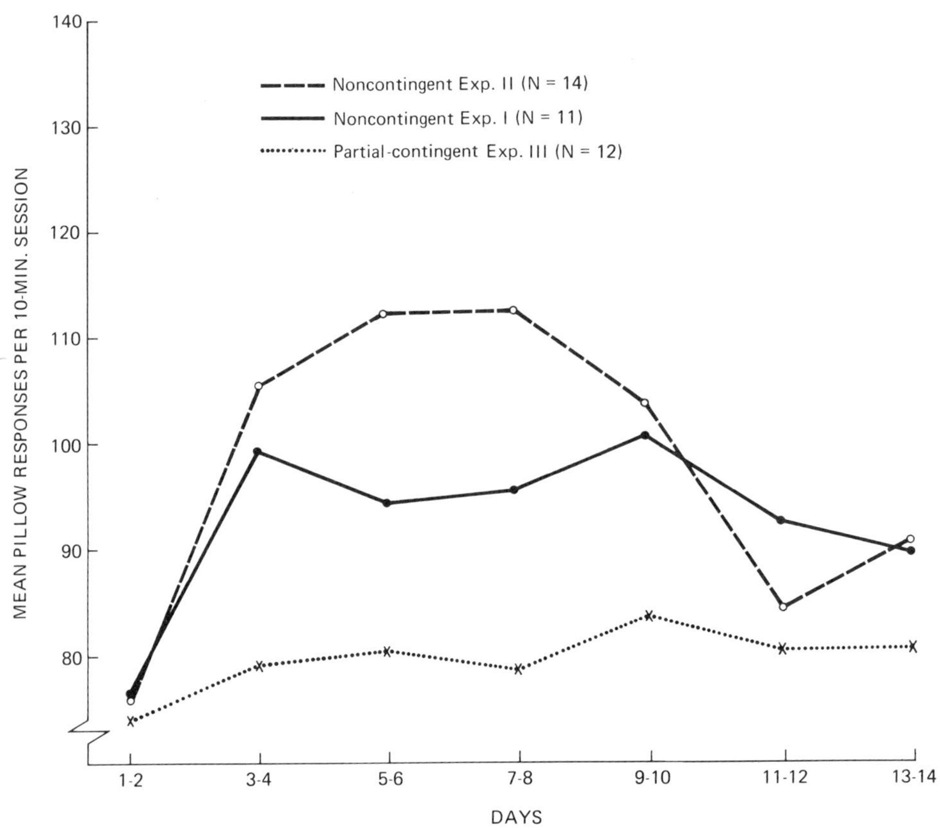

Figure 2.23. Pillow responses across two weeks for partial-contingent group of Experiment III, noncontingent group of Experiment I, and noncontingent sessions of Experiment II.

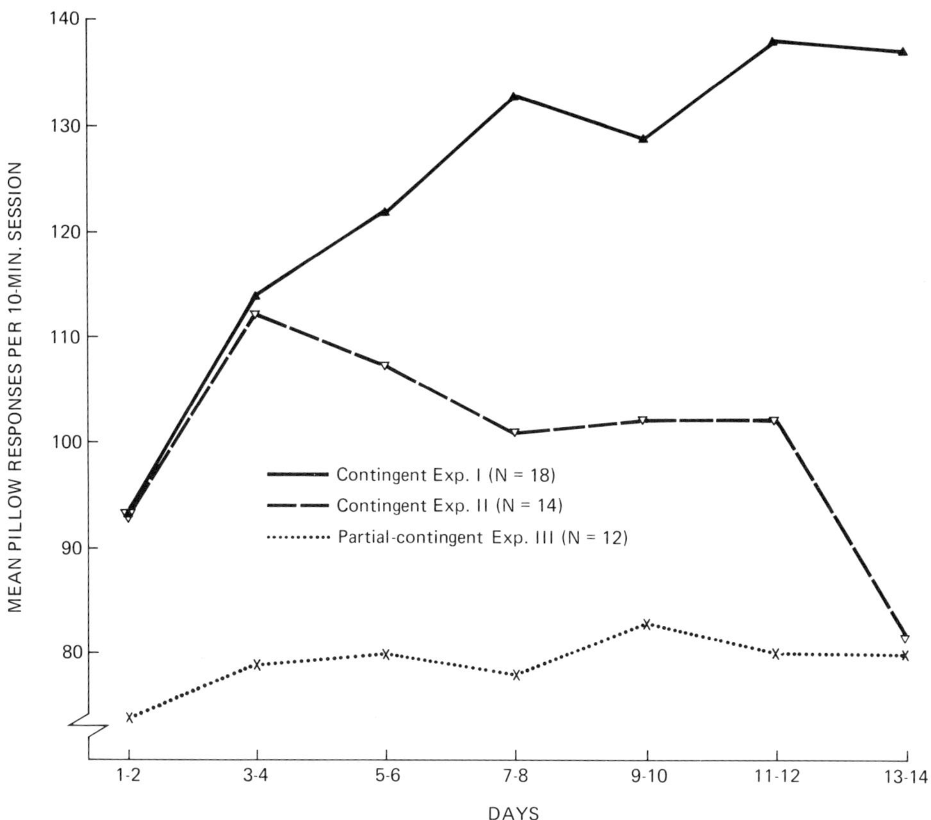

Figure 2.24. Pillow responses across two weeks for partial-contingent group of Experiment III, contingent group of Experiment I, and contingent sessions of Experiment II.

beginning by their partial contingency experience. Figure 2.24 also highlights the initial similarity of Experiments I and II and the succeeding decline in response rate by infants in Experiment II presumably as an effect of generalized confusion with their noncontingency sessions.

Experiment IV At this point we began to doubt the findings of Experiment I. We had observed 26 infants in Experiments II and III for whom we had had reasonable expectancies of seeing both learning and the associated release of social responses, yet we had seen essentially none of either. We then speculated that if an infant is committed to making a clear discrimination between contingent and noncontingent situations, he may be very sensitive to situations which are ambiguous. This hypothesis seemed more probable once we realized there was a potential stimulus basis for confusion in Experiment II, where infants experienced both contingent and noncontingent sessions. In both sessions the infant was placed in the unique position of having his head on the pillow. With this in mind we conducted Experiment IV in which we presented nineteen 8-week-old infants the opportunity to experience only a clear contingency. This was thus a return to the condition experienced by the 18 infants in the contingency group of Experiment I. Across subjects in Experiment IV we did vary the specific nature of the contingency, but for any given subject his experience was a particular contingency for 10 minutes each day for 2 weeks. For approximately half the subjects the contingent stimulus was a lighted umbrella, and for the other half the event was a turning mobile. Half the infants controlled their contingent stimulus with head movement and half with feet movement. As Figure 2.25 shows, the infants of this study increased in their daily activity rates across the 2 weeks (change in pillow response rate from days 1–2 to 13–14, $t=2.21$, $p<.05$) just as the contingency group of Experiment I had, and we again received almost unanimous reports of vigorous smiling and cooing arising after about 3 to 5 days.

One additional piece of data worth mentioning at least briefly concerns our recent work with a severely retarded 8-month-old infant who had a developmental quotient of a month and a half. The baby was termed a "developmental failure" and reportedly had never shown any instrumental activity or any appreciable smiling or cooing at anyone or anything. Within 11 days of exposure to a contingent mobile for 10 min. a day her leg activity increased four-fold from 3 to 12 per minute, and she evidenced vigorous and prolonged smiling and cooing in the contingency situation.

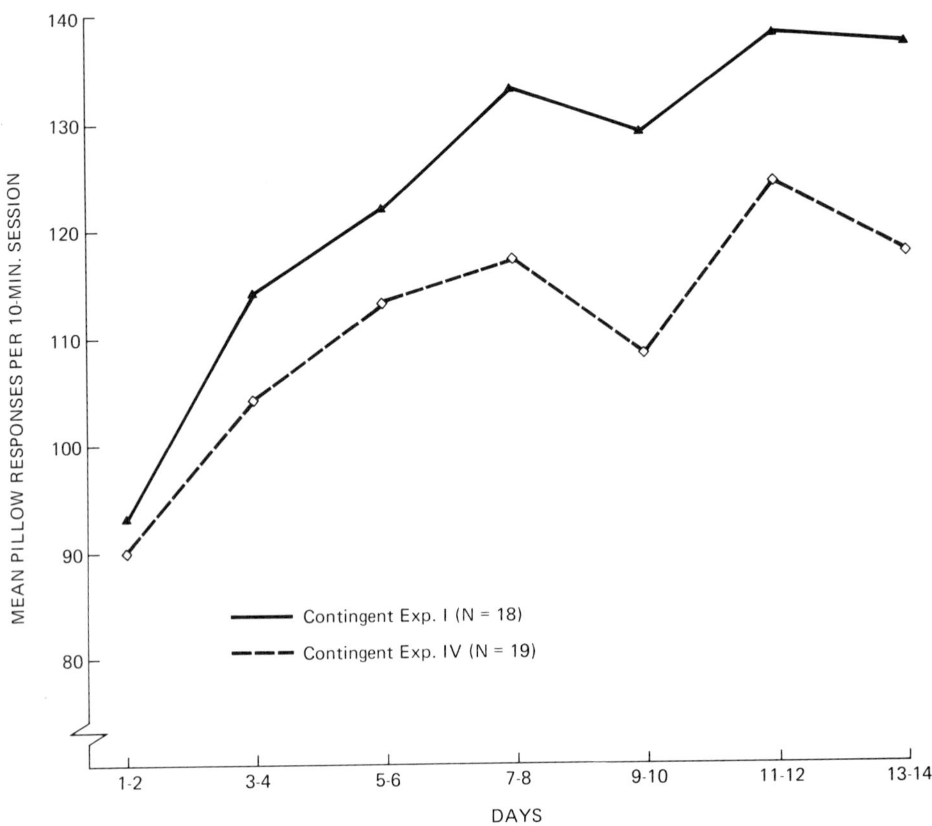

Figure 2.25. Pillow responses across two weeks for contingent group of Experiment IV and contingent group of Experiment I.

The simultaneous arrival of instrumental behavior and vigorous smiling for this retarded infant is not likely a coincidence. Nor is it likely a coincidence that the average normal infant is expected to show peak vigorous smiling to a human face at about the third or fourth month, which is also the time he is expected to show active instrumental behavior. If the proposal made here is correct, both developments arise from an infant's initial experience of a clear contingency.

Overview of "The Game" Hypothesis

Taken as a whole, then, these studies of reactions to facial orientation and response-contingent stimulation have led us to the hypothesis of "The Game." Let us consider the hypothesis one more time in graphic form prior to relating it to some alternative proposals in the attachment literature. Figure 2.26 shows the graphic form of the hypothesis. The graph indicates that as a stimulus initially becomes more familiar, it increasingly becomes a candidate for classification as contingent. At this point one of three things can occur. First, if contingency analysis through successive exposures of the stimulus indicates that the stimulus is indeed a clearly contingent one, then the smiling and cooing and attention of the infant is expected to sharply increase to an asymtote of vigorous responding. Secondly, if the continuing contingency analysis indicates that the stimulus is clearly noncontingent, then the modest level of smiling and cooing is expected to decline back to the base rate elicited by completely novel stimuli. Thirdly, if, through continuing exposure, the contingency analysis of the stimulus is

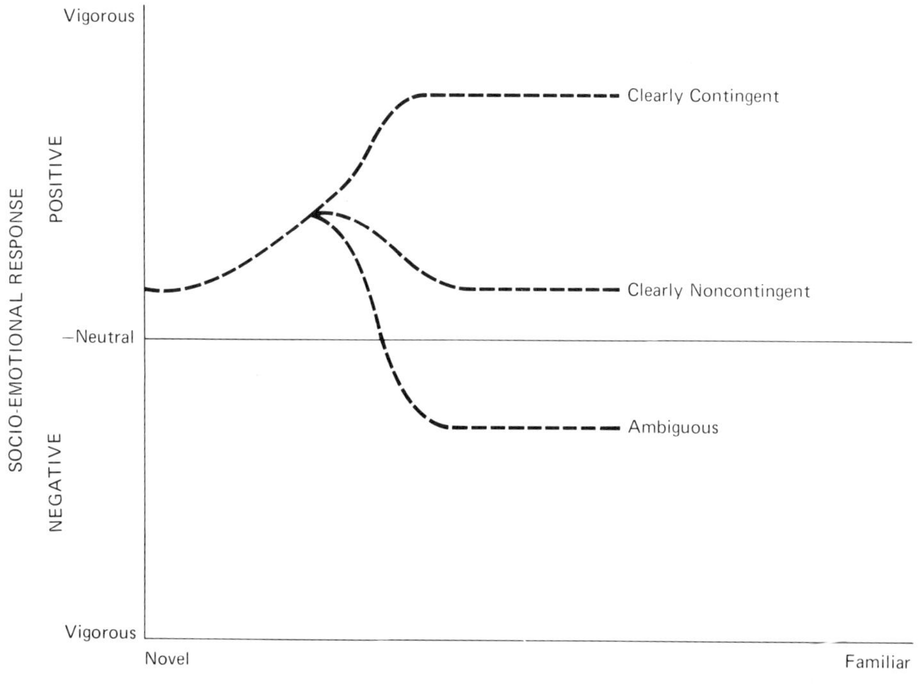

Figure 2.26. Theoretical relationship between stimulus familiarity and socio-emotional response for three types of stimulation.

continuously indeterminate due either to ambiguous aspects of the contingency itself or to confusing situational characteristics, then the response to the stimulus is expected to become progressively less positive and eventually to begin eliciting negative emotional responses.[4]

That, then, is "The Game" hypothesis. Its name is derived from the game-like interactions which are assumed to normally generate the infant's first awareness of a clear contingency. Most adults probably view these occasional interaction games as casual and insignificant episodes in their infant's life. The infant, however, appears to engage in these episodes with a commitment far greater than casual. The refined discrimination of facial orientation by 3-month-olds is possibly but one example of the infant's commitment to learn the specific context of his game. Another example is very likely provided by Zelazo's recent discovery that 3-month-old girls vocalize more to male than to female faces (Zelazo, 1967, 1969). From the perspective of "The Game" hypothesis one would ask if fathers are more likely to play talking games with their infant girls than with their boys. The likelihood of this interesting sex-linked game is supported by recent findings of Rebelsky and Hanks (1971) wherein the average father of an infant girl engaged in twice the number of talking interactions with his infant during the first 3 months than did the average father of an infant boy. If these examples of refined facial discrimination are testimony to the infants' attentional commitment to "The Game," then there seems little doubt that infants take their initial games most seriously.

[4] If one now adds a proposal that familiarity of a previously exposed stimulus may be diminished through distortion of the stimulus, then a number of additional predictions can be made. For instance, if a stimulus has a history which has established it as clearly noncontingent (or a marker of a situation which is clearly noncontingent), then it would be responded to with a minimal level of smiling and cooing. However, if the stimulus were distorted and therewith reduced in its familiar characteristics, then a backward movement on the graph would be called for; and a concomitant rise in smiling and cooing would be predicted for certain moderate distortions. By contrast, if a stimulus which had been established as clearly contingent (or as a marker of a contingency situation) were to be distorted, then a backward movement on the graph would lead one to predict a decline in smiling and cooing for the stimulus. Finally, if a stimulus were presented to an infant which was similar to both a previously established clearly contingent stimulus and a previously established noncontingent stimulus, the infant's response would be predicted by the line indexing negative responsiveness toward an ambiguous stimulus.

Some Competing Hypotheses

Before closing it should be acknowledged that there are some hypotheses about the origin of social responsiveness which are quite similar to "The Game" hypothesis proposed here. Notable are the recent proposals of Rheingold (1961), Ainsworth and Wittig (1969), and Bowlby (1969). Also relevant are some writings by Schaffer and Emerson (1964), Walters and Parke (1965), and Bettelheim (1967). These theorists have emphasized to a greater or lesser extent that a significant aspect of the infant's caretaker, which makes him an arousing stimulus and a candidate for attachment, is his responsiveness to the social behavior initiated by the infant. Clearly, then, these theorists have noted the infant's need to sense a contingency between his behavior and resulting stimulus events. In this regard "The Game" hypothesis adds nothing especially new. However, it is my belief that all of these proposals have centered their attention on the social nature of the infant's behavior or on the social nature of the contingent stimulation from the caretaker. That is, these previous hypotheses appear to have implicitly, and at times explicitly, assigned special significance to the type of responses an infant normally makes when interacting with infants. If these previous proposals are correct, then one could state in summary that *"The Game" is important to the infant because people play it.*

On the other hand, if "The Game" hypothesis does add something new to the speculations of early social responsiveness, it does so in denying special significance for one type of stimulation as opposed to another or one type of response as opposed to another. The hypothesis states that what is important is the perception of the relationship of contingency between a specific stimulus and a specific response. With this proposal, in contrast to previous proposals, an infant can be expected to release smiling and cooing and perhaps even begin the initial stages of attachment with innumerable artificial or even mechanical situations if they should happen to be correctly arranged. Thus, if "The Game" hypothesis adds anything, it is that it states *"The Game" is NOT important to the infant because people play it, but rather people become important to the infant because they play "The Game."*

References

AINSWORTH, M., & WITTIG, B. Attachment and exploratory behavior of one-year-olds in a strange situation. In B. Foss (Ed.), *Determinants of infant behavior.* Vol. *4.* New York: Barnes and Noble, 1969.

AMBROSE, J. A. The development of the smiling response in early infancy. In B. Foss (Ed.), *Determinants of infant behavior.* New York: Wiley, 1961.

BETTELHEIM, B. *The empty fortress: Infantile autism and the birth of the self.* New York: The Free Press, 1967.

BOWLBY, J. The nature of the child's tie to his mother. *International Journal of Psychoanalysis.* 1958, Vol. *39,* 350–373.

———. *Attachment and loss.* Vol. *1. Attachment.* London: The Hogarth Press, 1969.

FANTZ, R. The origin of form perception. *Scientific American,* 1961, Vol. *204,* 66–72.

GEWIRTZ, J. A learning analysis of the effects of normal stimulation, privation, and deprivation on the acquisition of social motivation and attachment. In B. Foss (Ed.), *Determinants of infant behavior.* New York: Wiley, 1961.

GIBSON, J. J. *The perception of the visual world.* Boston: Houghton Mifflin, 1950.

HAAF, R., & BELL, R. A social dimension in visual discrimination by human infants. *Child Development,* 1967, Vol. *38,* 893–899.

HUNT, J., & UZGIRIS, I. Cathexis from recognitive familiarity: An exploratory study. Paper presented at the 1964 Convention of the American Psychological Association, Los Angeles, California, September, 1964.

KAGAN, J., HENKER, B., HEN-TOV, A., LEVINE, J., & LEWIS, M. Infants' differential reactions to familiar and distorted faces. *Child Development,* 1966, Vol. *37,* 519–532.

LEWIS, M. Infants' responses to facial stimuli during the first year of life. *Developmental Psychology,* 1969, Vol. *1,* 75–86.

PIAGET, J. *The origins of intelligence in children.* (Trans. by Margaret Cook.) New York: International Universities Press, 1952.

REBELSKY, F., & HANKS, C. Fathers' verbal interactions with infants in the first three months of life. *Child Development,* 1971.

RHEINGOLD, H. The effect of environmental stimulation upon social and exploratory behavior in the human infant. In B. Foss (Ed.), *Determinants of infant behavior.* New York: Wiley, 1961.

ROVEE, K., & ROVEE, D. Conjugate reinforcement of infant exploratory behavior. *Journal of Experimental Child Psychology,* 1969, Vol. *8,* 33–39.

SCHAFFER, H., & EMERSON, P. The development of social attachments in infancy. *Mono-*

graphs of the Society for Research in Child Development, 1964, Vol. *29* (Whole No. 94).

SPITZ, R., & WOLF, K. The smiling response: A contribution to the ontogenesis of social relations. *Genetic Psychology Monographs,* 1946, Vol. *34,* 57–125.

WALTERS, R., & PARKE, R. The role of the distance receptors in the development of social responsiveness. In L. Lipsitt & C. Spiker (Eds.), *Advances in child development and behavior.* Vol. 2. New York: Academic Press, 1965.

WATSON, J. Perception of object orientation in infants. *Merrill-Palmer Quarterly,* 1966a, Vol. *12,* 73–94.

———. The development and generalization of "contingency awareness" in early infancy: Some hypotheses. *Merrill-Palmer Quarterly,* 1966b, Vol. *12,* 123–135.

———. Memory and "contingency analysis" in infant learning. *Merrill-Palmer Quarterly,* 1967a, Vol. *13,* 55–76.

———. Why is a smile? *Trans-action,* 1967b (May), 36–39.

WATSON, J., & RAMEY, C. Reactions to response-contingent stimulation in early infancy, Revision of paper presented at biennial meeting of the Society for Research in Child Development, Santa Monica, California, March, 1969.

ZELAZO, P. Social reinforcement of vocalizations and smiling of three-month-old infants. Unpublished doctoral dissertation, University of Waterloo, 1967.

———. Differential three-month-old infant vocalizations to sex-of-strangers. Paper presented at the International Congress of Psychology, London, England, July, 1969.

———. Smiling to social stimuli: Eliciting and conditioning effects. *Developmental Psychology,* in press.

8. A LABORATORY FOR DEVELOPMENTAL PSYCHOLOGISTS

CAROL O. ECKERMAN, HARRIET L. RHEINGOLD, and RICHARD A. HELWIG

The laboratories for the study of the behavior of young organisms at Chapel Hill have proved so useful for research and the training of students that a description of their main features may be helpful to investigators planning similar laboratories. These features include adaptability of the rooms to many experimental procedures and to subjects of different ages and a number of different species; central apparatus that controls the stimulating and recording equipment and permits the simultaneous conduct of two studies, as well as the quick transition from one study to another; and observation through one-way vision windows of almost all experimental rooms, many from a common space.

The laboratories are housed in Davie Hall, a new building erected for the Psychology Department in the fall of 1967. The laboratories are part of the wing on the second floor devoted to developmental psychology. They occupy the central core of the wing, and are surrounded on three sides by a corridor. (The fourth side is bounded by rooms that can eventually be incorporated into the developmental laboratories but now are classrooms and laboratories for students of other programs.)

The corridor separates the laboratories from the offices of faculty, graduate students, laboratory personnel, and secretaries. The offices are outside rooms, ringing the corridor. This arrangement of laboratories, corridor, and offices possesses several advantages. The laboratories are shielded from street noises by the corridor and offices, and from the visual distractions of outside windows. The corridor provides access at many points to the experimental space, and its noises, moderate as they are, are controlled by cautionary signs when experiments are run. Then, too, experimenters and other laboratory personnel are but a step from the laboratories.

Spatial Arrangements of the Laboratory

The experimental rooms are organized around two main observation areas, A and H (Figure 2.27); from each area, several experimental rooms can be viewed, successively or simultaneously.

The larger observation area (A) is also the control room for the laboratories; it contains the major controlling apparatus for the entire research space. Cables connect the second observation area and each experimental room to this controlling apparatus. The controlling apparatus and cables will be described later. Note here that controlling apparatus refers to only the electronic programming apparatus; equipment, in distinction, refers to the instruments or devices, such as tape recorders, event recorders, and projectors, that are controlled by the apparatus. Equip-

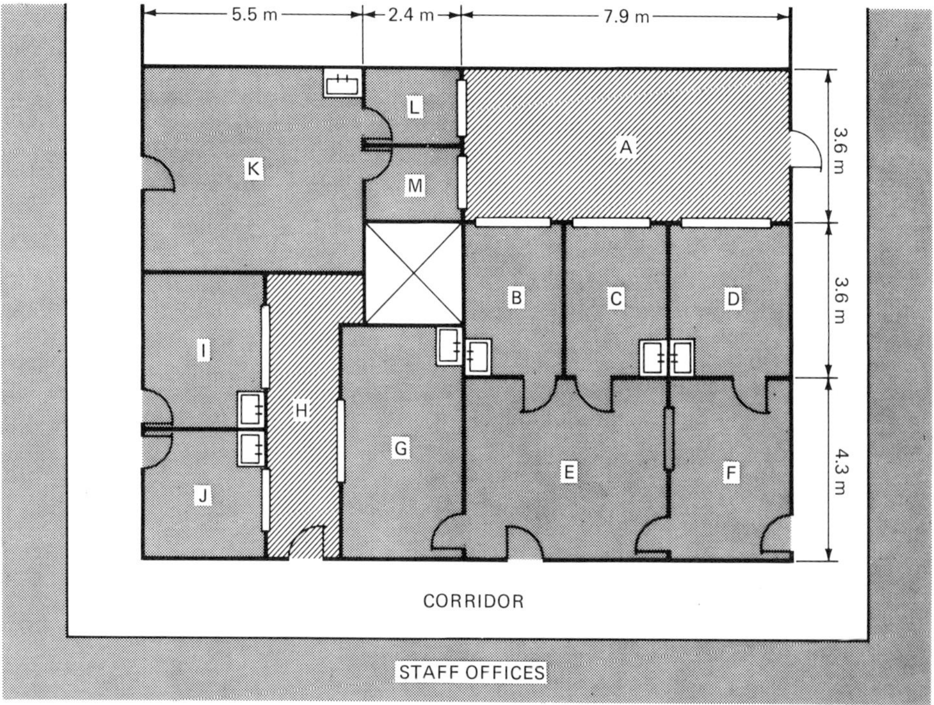

Figure 2.27. Spatial arrangement of the laboratories.

ment for monitoring the operation of the controlling apparatus, as well as additional recording or stimulating equipment, may be located in the second observation area (H) or in any room, according to the dictates of a study.

From either main observation area, then, laboratory personnel can set the stimulating conditions for a study, observe and record the behavior occurring in a number of rooms, and monitor the apparatus. Costly duplication of apparatus is avoided, and the potential for simultaneous viewing of a number of experimental rooms is gained.

The experimental rooms together with the observation areas form three relatively independent research units. Rooms B, C, D, E, and F with the control and observation area (A) form Unit 1; Rooms G, I, and J and the second observation area (H) form Unit 2; and Rooms K, L, and M with A form Unit 3. Room G can function as part of Unit 1 or 2. And the one-way window between Rooms E and F allows either room to be used as an experimental room, and the other room as an observation room.

The independence of these units provides facilities for three concurrent sets of research projects and, even, for projects using different species. At the present time, for example, Unit 1 is used for studies of the human infant's social and exploratory behavior; Unit 2, for studies of adult-child interaction; and Unit 3, for studies of the effects of early experience on rats. A later section will describe how the controlling apparatus facilitates both simultaneous research projects within a research unit and the consecutive use of the same space for different studies.

Two further characteristics of the organization of the research space contribute to its flexibility: the connecting rooms within Units 1 and 3; and the similar rooms within each unit. The connecting rooms greatly expand the number of spatial arrangements available; up to six rooms can be joined together. The pairs of similar rooms can be furnished to duplicate an experimental setting for the simultaneous study of two subjects (Ss), or to provide two different settings for the study of one S.

Control of General Stimulating Conditions

In this and the following sections we present the broad outline of a workable laboratory. Hence, the provisions for presenting stimuli and recording responses are described in only general terms and technical specifications are omitted. The latter are available on request, but it is likely that the experimenter's choice will depend on local conditions and his particular research needs.

The experimental rooms are constructed of cinderblock and plasterboard walls painted in light shades, ceilings of poured concrete, and floors of white vinyl-asbestos tiles. Their general appearance can be modified according to the study; furniture, rugs, or drapes can be added, and false ceilings or walls constructed.

Fluorescent light fixtures provide general-purpose illumination for the experimental rooms. Additional incandescent cove lights in Rooms B, C, and D provide a continuously adjustable source of illumination when needed. Silicon Controlled Rectifier dimmers in Room A govern the illumination of the incandescent bulbs mounted behind sheets of white, translucent plastic. With the cove lights, illumination at the floor can range up to 398 lm/m^2; the addition of the fluorescent lights provides a maximum illumination of 1109 lm/m^2. In the absence of exterior windows, these two systems of artificial light allow adequate control of the lighting.

A central heating and air-conditioning system provides a fairly constant level of temperature and humidity, which can be altered as required.

The sinks in some of the experimental rooms provide for caretaking of the human infant and animal Ss, as well as for the cleaning of test materials.

Visual Communication

Windows in the walls of all but one of the experimental rooms allow observation of behavior occurring in the rooms as well as the delivery of visual stimuli into them. The windows, approximately 1.6 m wide, extend from 1.0 to 1.8 m above the floor of the experimental rooms. Their width, roughly equivalent to the entire wall of the smaller research rooms, provides an unobstructed view of all sections of the room.

All windows consist of two sheets of plate glass, separated by an air space to reduce sound transmission. For most windows, one sheet of glass has a single silvered surface (one-way glass); the second is clear glass. The windows of Rooms B, C, and D, however, contain instead of the sheet of one-way glass a sheet composed of three equal-sized vertical panels, the two side panels of one-way glass and the middle panel of clear glass. The one-way portion allows observers (*O*s) and stimulating equipment to be hidden from the S's view; the clear portion allows the delivery of visual stimuli into the experimental rooms and the filming of behavior within them. Masks can be affixed to the clear glass panel to cover all but that portion necessary for filming or stimulating; a sliding wood panel covers the clear panel when not in use.

A sheet of drafting film affixed to either the clear glass or one-way glass portion of the window makes an effective screen for the rear projection of visual stimuli. Projection, however, need not be limited to the surface of the window; visual stimuli can be positioned anywhere in the rooms by a system of mirrors. And visual stimuli need not even be projected; a lighted stimulus box, for example, could be placed behind the clear glass and objects positioned within it.

Opaque curtains are hung on both sides of the one-way windows. On the side of the observation spaces they are drawn to restrict a S's view of the control room when increased illumination is needed there; on the side of the experimental rooms, when a degree of privacy for the S is desired.

Although the windows allow direct observation of the experimental rooms, visual access, of course, need not be direct. Cameras can be mounted anywhere in the rooms and their output monitored either immediately on a TV monitor or at a later time from slides, movies, or video tape.

Auditory Communication

The laboratories are equipped for the transmission of sound between experimental and observation rooms. A lavalier microphone with a cardioid reception pattern hangs from the center of the ceiling of the experimental rooms. The microphones are connected to amplifiers in the control and observation area (A); the amplifiers are connected through the controlling apparatus to a loudspeaker in the observation room and (or) to one channel of a two-channel tape recorder. In this way the sounds of the experimental rooms —the S's vocal productions, the experimenter's (*E*'s)instructions to the S, and any programmed auditory stimuli—are detected and recorded.

Loudspeakers are mounted at the ceilings of experimental rooms. The controlling apparatus selectively distributes the auditory input, whether pure tones, noise, music, or human speech, to the loudspeakers. A lavalier microphone is plugged into cable outlets in the observation rooms to connect with the controlling apparatus; this arrangement allows the *E* or *O* to give directions through the microphone to the mother, S, or another *E* in the experimental rooms. One could also thus direct the performance of students learning research procedures. With the same microphone the *O* can dictate accounts of behavior and procedures to be recorded on one channel of a tape recorder, while the auditory input from the experimental rooms is recorded on the other; the *O*'s comments thus correspond exactly in time to the S's vocalizations. The *O* determines with a push-to-talk switch what portion of his speech will be transmitted to the experimental room.

Sound in fact can be transmitted between any two rooms, not just between experimental rooms and the two main observation rooms. An *O* stationed in Room F, for example, can listen to or talk to the S in Room E, as well as to another *O* in the control and observation room. This flexibility results from the connecting of the microphones and speakers of all rooms to equipment in the control room. Thus, with a system of switches, the *E* decides which rooms to listen to, which rooms to record from, which rooms to deliver auditory stimuli to, and which rooms to talk into.

The Controlling Apparatus

The controlling apparatus, located in the control and observation area, is composed of two units of solid-state electronic equipment. The two units allow two experiments to proceed simultaneously without interference.

Each unit consists of digital components (logic functions, time bases, flip-flop memories, lamp drivers, and reed-relay drivers) wired to a program-receiver panel having 1632 contacts arranged in a 48-column by 34-row array. Connections to the stimulating and recording equipment, to manipulanda, and to the observer's recording instruments (described in the next section) appear on the receiver panel. A prewired program patch-board, inserted into the receiver panel, makes all connections of the logic for an experiment.

The program patch-boards add to the flexibility of the laboratories because different types of experimental sessions can be preprogrammed, each on a separate board. By inserting the appropriate board, the same set of controlling apparatus and peripheral equipment can serve successively different experimental purposes. Since no rewiring is necessary, switching from one experiment to another is not only practically instantaneous, but error free.

The controlling apparatus can also transform responses into other measures: in current work, for example, analog levels of the physical activity of an infant seated in a high chair, fitted with strain gauges, are quantized into one of five ranges.

The primary recording device is a digital data-acquisition system which encodes information about the onset and offset of events (up to 64 events are possible) and their time of occurrence (1-msec resolution) on IBM System/360 compatible, magnetic tape. Computers then produce detailed reports of the events of each experimental session. Other recording devices, such as event recorders, yield an immediate "picture" of the session.

The controlling apparatus, audio system, event recorders, and data-acquisition system are mounted together in four racks that utilize a total of 1.4 m^2 of floor space in the control and observation room. The compactness of the apparatus provides ample space for several *O*s at any of the five observation windows and for the storage of research supplies.

Observer's Recording Instrument

Since many of the responses of interest to developmental psychologists still require the use of the human observer, the laboratories are equipped with portable recording instruments. They are metal boxes (18 × 23 × 5 cm) containing a toggle switch, eight silent push-button switches, an indicator light, and a jack for attaching headphones. With the toggle switch the *O* (or the *E*) can start the trial and the necessary equipment and apparatus. By depressing the buttons he records the occurrence and duration of up to eight behavioral or stimulus events; the button switches record on both the event recorder and the magnetic tape of the data-acquisition system. Illumination of the light indicates the passage of time during a study and can be differentially programmed for separate studies. The headphones isolate the *O* from the sounds of the observation room and allow selective auditory input—*S*'s vocalizations or an auditory time signal.

The instruments are plugged into outlets beneath the observation windows and are thus connected by cables to the controlling apparatus. Provisions for two instruments at each window allow checks of the amount of agreement between two *O*s.

Although the outlets for cables connect the observer's recording instruments with the controlling apparatus in current work, they could instead connect other response-detecting systems with the controlling apparatus. Similarly, a device containing a number of manipulanda and stimulus display panels, placed in an experimental room and connected to the controlling apparatus, could record an *S*'s responses automatically, as well as program antecedent and consequent stimulus changes.

Research in the Laboratories

Some recent uses of the laboratories will demonstrate their suitability for a variety of research projects.

Studies of the human infant's social and exploratory behavior are carried out in Unit 1. Room F serves as a reception room for mother and infant and Room D as a place for adapting the infant to the laboratory setting and the *E*. Rooms B, C, and E are used for the tests. For example, a mother and her creeping infant are placed in Room E, and Rooms B and C are furnished with different stimulating objects (the doors are left open); the objects may be strange or familiar persons or toys, or toys varying in complexity or sensory feedback. The level of illumination can differ from room to room, and Room G can be incorporated in the design.

Apparatus in the control room automatically times the duration of trials. Photocells at the doorways record entries and exits, and yield measures of durations of time spent in the different rooms. The *O*s behind the one-way windows record the frequency and duration of such infant responses as visual regard, smiling, and manipulating of objects. The infant's vocalizations are recorded on audio tape.

In Unit 2, Dr. Brian Coates studied how adults of both sexes use verbal statements to train black and white school-age children on a discrimination problem. Here in Room J the child and adult sit at opposite sides of a table with a low barrier between them. The child responds to the problem by depressing keys. The adult does not see the child's response but is "told" it by the illumination of one of a series of lights before him. Which light is illuminated is determined not by the child's response, but by an *O* in observation area H who follows some prearranged schedule. The adult in turn responds with one of a number of specified verbal statements.

Unit 3 provides both housing and testing space for studies by Dr. Robert T. Brown of the effects of differential early rearing of rats. Rats are reared from birth in different environments, and the effects are analyzed by learning tasks. Most testing requires the presence of an *O* within the test rooms. At other times, the unit is used to study the object-approach behavior of precocial birds as the result of differential rearing.

In the past, litters of kittens with their mothers were reared in Rooms L and M of Unit 3. The kittens' development was charted by means of checklists and by daily observation from behind the one-way glass. At different ages, a kitten's behavior was recorded in a strange environment—alone, with his mother, or a littermate; or in the home environment without mother or littermates. The home environment was the room in which the kitten was reared from birth, either Room L or M; the strange environment was the other room, similar in size and physical arrangement to the home room but emptied of furnishings and cleaned with a disinfectant. A microphone transmitted the kitten's vocalizations to a tape recorder; an *O* behind one-way glass measured locomotor activity by marking the kitten's position within the grid formed by the floor tiles; a second *O* dictated additional observations of the kitten's behavior.

Other uses of the laboratories come to mind. The smaller rooms, for example, would be suitable for studies of infant perception and learning. They are large enough to include the mother, and so provide a setting for studies of mother–infant interaction. With children of all ages the smaller rooms are suitable for normative studies, as well as for many kinds of learning studies. The larger rooms make possible the study of social interplay between two or more children. The sets of similar rooms present interesting possibilities, as do the connecting doors. And, although one unit is here set aside for the study of small animals, other units can be similarly used; alternatively, all units could be used for the study of children.

The addition of specialized equipment would also expand the uses of the laboratories. Physiological recording devices could monitor a S's respiration, heart rate, and EEG. Pressure-sensitive floors could monitor a subject's movements in space. Sound-deadening materials would aid studies of audition and baffles, studies of vision. The possibility of recording by telemetry could also be considered.

In short, the flexibility of the spatial arrangements and the capabilities of the controlling apparatus—with the possibility of adding further stimulating, recording, or reinforcing equipment—make the laboratories suitable for many types of studies.

CHAPTER 2: SUGGESTED FURTHER READING

EICHORN, D. H. Biological correlates of behavior. In Stevenson, H. (Ed.) *Child Psychology*. Chicago: University of Chicago Press, 1963. Pp. 4–61.

———. Physiological development. In Mussen, P. (Ed.) *Carmichael's Manual of Child Psychology*, Vol. 1. New York: Wiley, 1970. Pp. 157–283.

GARN, S. M. Body size and its implications. In Hoffman, L. W. and Hoffman, M. L. (Eds.) *Review of Child Development Research*, Vol. 2. New York: Russell Sage Foundation, 1966. Pp. 529–561.

HESS, E. H. Ethology and developmental psychology. In Mussen, P. (Ed.) *Carmichael's Manual of Child Psychology*, Vol. 1. New York: Wiley, 1970. Pp. 1–38.

KESSEN, W., HAITH, M., and SALAPATEK, P. Infancy. In Mussen, P. (Ed.) *Carmichael's Manual of Child Psychology*, Vol. 1. New York: Wiley, 1970. Pp. 287–446.

MC CLEARN, G. E. Genetic influences on behavior and development. In Mussen, P. (Ed.). *Carmichael's Manual of Child Psychology*, Vol. 1. New York: Wiley, 1970. Pp. 39–76.

TANNER, J. M. Physical growth. In Mussen, P. (Ed.) *Carmichael's Manual of Child Psychology*, Vol. 1. New York: Wiley, 1970. Pp. 77–156.

WHITE, S. H. Evidence for a hierarchical arrangement of learning processes. In Lipsitt, L. P., and Spiker, C. C. *Advances in Child Development and Behavior*, Vol. 2. New York: Academic Press, 1965. Pp. 187–220.

chapter three
the effects of early experience

In the last chapter we presented some basic data on the human organism and indicated that, for various reasons, early experiences are important. (See the article by McClelland.) Before the egg is fertilized, it is already subject to experiences. Developmentalists have recently been looking at the effects of prenatal experiences on development. It appears that the mother's nutrition, general mental and physical health, drug taking, and smoking all affect the developing organism.

Not all fetuses make it through to birth, and not all live after delivery. We have included infant and fetal mortality statistics to indicate some basic differences in the organism's ability to live after birth. The experiences of those that do survive differ—both prenatally, and postnatally. Even the birth process itself can yield different experiences, since drugs used during labor also affect the child. Stechler (1964) found that infants whose mothers were heavily drugged during labor and delivery were less attentive than infants whose mothers had been lightly drugged. The infant who is attentive is very different certainly from the infant who is incapable of attending to its environment, and both are going to have very different early experiences. There is also evidence that the drugs taken by the mother during labor and delivery have an effect on the child for several weeks (Brazelton, 1962).

Many of the studies concerning early experiences deal with the effects of mother-child interaction or the lack of such (maternal deprivation). Studies on the effect of maternal deprivation are usually done with subjects other than human subjects. Not having a mother around leads not only to social deprivation but to a general lack of all stimulation. Monkeys raised without real mothers (Harlow et al., 1966) did not develop normal sexual behavior as adults; they refused to mate. If and when females so raised had offspring, they handled their first-borns in an abusive manner. Puppies raised in isolation respond "abnormally" to pain for most of their lives. For example, months after the isolation experience, such dogs will move toward a flame or a fearful object (Thomson and Heron, 1954; Thomson and Melzack, 1956).

Positive early experiences are also studied, usually in the form of stimulation or enrichment. Rats that are stimulated by handling or by shocking in their early days are generally "brighter" and "healthier" than rat pups that are left untouched. Certainly we wouldn't want to shock or isolate human babies, but we can use animal data to provide further hypotheses about the effects of various amounts and types of stimulation and deprivation. There are also some data on human deprivation and stimulation seen through various cultural behaviors and through situations such as institutionalization, which indicate that such generalizations are warranted. Infants that are raised in institutions or in cultures that are minimally stimulating have very different early experiences from infants raised in homes or in maximally stimulating cultures. How these may affect later behavior and growth is not yet clear, but as we learn to better identify what is stimulation and deprivation to young organisms, we will know better how to ask about the effects.

References

BRAZELTON, T. B. Observations of the neonate. *Journal of the American Academy of Child Psychiatry*, 1962, *1*, 38–58.

HARLOW, H. F., HARLOW, M. K., DODSWORTH, R. O., and ARLING, G. L. Maternal behavior of rhesus monkeys deprived of mother and peer association in infancy. *Proceedings of the American Philosophical Society*, 1966, *110*, 58–66.

STECHLER, J. Newborn attention as affected by medication during labor. *Science*, 1964, *144*, 315–317.

THOMSON, W. R., and HERON, W. The effects of restricting early experiences on the problem-solving capacity of dogs. *Canadian Journal of Psychology*, 1954, *8*, 17–31.

THOMSON, W. R., and MELZACK, R. Early environment. *Scientific American*, 1956, *194*, 38–42.

9. EXCERPT FROM *THE HEALTH OF CHILDREN—1970:* PART I. THE WORLD THAT GREETS THE INFANT

The Infant Deaths

Some children today are born into hopeful circumstances, some into circumstances that lessen their chance to live. In the United States in 1969, infant deaths totaled about 74,000. Large differences in infant mortality are found by the color, the income, the education of the child's parents, and the age of the mother.

In spite of the decline in infant mortality in recent years, the United States ranks 13th in the world.

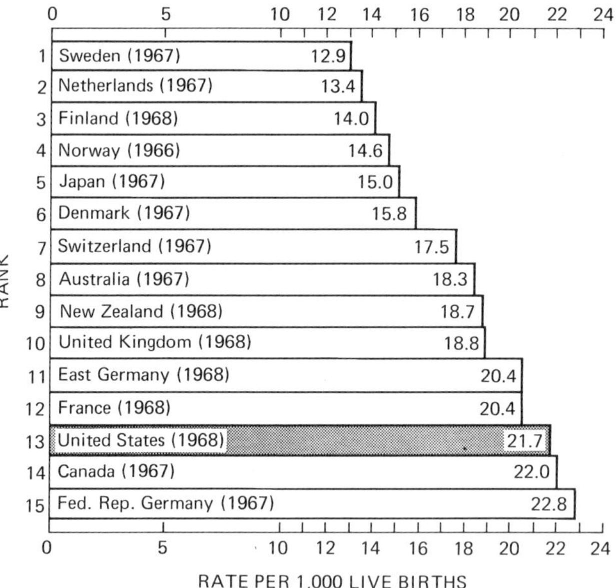

Figure 3.1. Infant mortality rates: selected countries in rank order
Source: United Nations, 1968 Demographic Yearbook.

Table 3.1. Legitimate live births and infant mortality rates, by age of mother: United States, 1946–66

Age of mother	*Legitimate live births (1000's)*	*Infant mortality rate per 1,000 live births*
All ages	3,480	22.8
Under 20 years	475	29.5
20–24 years	1,257	20.3
25–29 years	892	21.2
30–34 years	506	22.7
35–39 years	270	23.8
40 years and over	80	36.4

Infant mortality rates vary greatly among the States and between the white and other than white races by State. If the infant mortality rate of each State had been as low as that of the best State in 1967, 20,579 babies would not have died during their first year.

But all the children born today have a greatly increased chance of reaching adulthood compared with those at the begining of the century.

If a child is male and other than white, he can expect to live several years less than the national average.

Figure 3.2. Infant mortality rates by color: United States, 1940–68

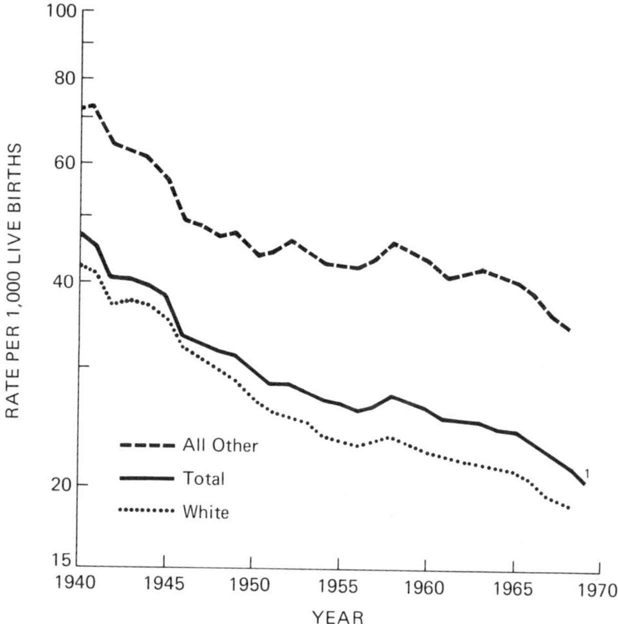

[1] Provisional figure

Figure 3.3. Infant mortality rates by color, family income, and education of the parents: United States, 1964–66

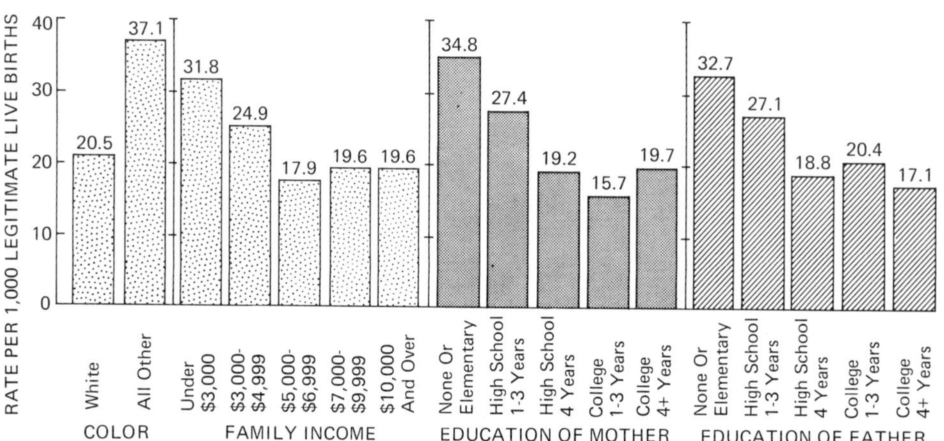

Table 3.2. Infant mortality rates by color, for the United States, and for each State in rank order of total infant mortality rate: 1967 (Rates are deaths under 1 year per 1,000 live births in specified group)

State	*Total*	*White*	*All other*	*State*	*Total*	*White*	*All other*
United States	22.4	19.7	35.9				
Utah	16.6	16.2	28.8[1]	Indiana	22.3	21.0	35.0
Hawaii	16.7	14.9	17.5	Pennsylvania	22.3	19.9	39.2
Connecticut	19.2	17.9	30.9	South Dakota	22.4	20.8	35.3
Iowa	19.2	18.9	32.4	Missouri	22.7	19.1	42.1
Washington	19.2	18.3	31.1	Arizona	22.8	20.2	35.8
Idaho	19.4	19.5	11.0[1]	Colorado	22.8	22.3	33.6
Oregon	19.4	18.9	32.0	Maine	22.9	22.8	32.1[1]
Rhode Island	19.4	18.2	43.5	Wyoming	23.1	23.8	8.7[1]
Wisconsin	19.4	18.4	36.5	Texas	23.3	21.1	34.9
Kansas	19.5	18.4	34.4	Illinois	23.6	20.3	36.9
California	19.6	18.8	24.9	Florida	23.8	18.8	37.2
Nevada	19.6	18.6	25.7	Montana	23.8	22.9	33.0
Minnesota	19.8	19.5	29.9	Kentucky	24.1	22.9	36.1
Nebraska	19.8	19.0	36.2	Arkansas	24.3	20.5	34.2
Massachusetts	20.0	19.2	34.6	Virginia	24.3	20.1	37.4
Delaware	20.5	15.9	39.3	Tennessee	24.4	21.0	36.4
New Hampshire	20.6	20.1	150.0[1]	New Mexico	24.8	22.5	37.9
Ohio	20.7	19.0	33.8	West Virginia	25.2	24.8	33.1
Oklahoma	20.8	19.0	31.3	Louisiana	26.4	19.1	37.4
Vermont	20.9	21.0	[2]	Georgia	26.5	19.8	39.4
North Dakota	21.0	21.0	21.4[1]	North Carolina	26.8	20.0	42.0
New Jersey	21.9	18.5	38.2	Alabama	26.9	20.7	38.2
Michigan	22.0	19.8	35.2	District of Columbia	27.3	20.5	28.7
Maryland	22.1	19.0	32.5	South Carolina	27.7	21.0	37.8
New York	22.1	19.1	36.8	Alaska	29.2	19.1	51.2
				Mississippi	33.5	22.8	47.4

[1] Figure does not meet standard of reliability and precision.
[2] Rate is 0.

Table 3.3. Percentage of infants who could expect to reach age 20, by color and sex: United States, 1900 and 1967

Color and sex	*Percentage who could expect to reach 20*	
	1967	*1900*
White, male	96.3	76.4
White, female	97.5	79.0
All other, male	94.0	56.7
All other, female	95.5	59.1

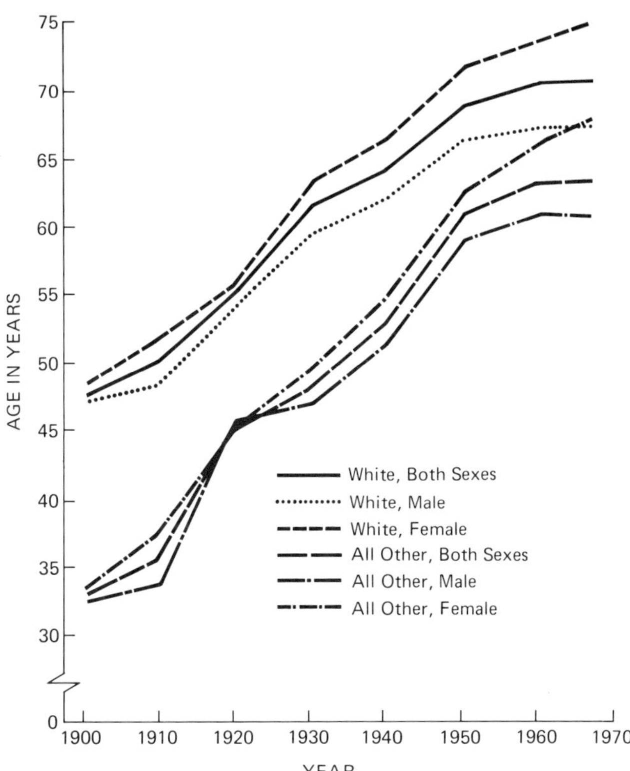

Figure 3.4. Estimated average length of life in years, by color and sex: United States, 1900–67

10. MALNUTRITION AND MENTAL DEFICIENCY

BONNIE J. KAPLAN

This review examines the interaction of malnutrition and mental deficiency. Although the evidence on nonhuman species shows fairly conclusively that malnutrition retards mental development, no definitive study on humans has yet been done. The ethical and methodological difficulties involved in studying the malnutrition of humans are several: We cannot intentionally subject an experimental group of children to a low-protein diet and thereby risk the possibility of retarding the child for life; we cannot be certain to what extent a child has been malnourished in his home environment since diets can fluctuate daily; and we cannot even be certain that a relatively undernourished and mentally subnormal child is, in fact, subnormal because of his malnutrition.

Although a causal connection has not been directly demonstrated, the research reviewed contains compelling evidence that early malnutrition is a contributing factor in the incidence of mental deficiency. First, malnutrition is discussed as a physiological entity, affecting physical health and the development of the central nervous system. Next, the evidence relating malnutrition and mental deficiency is analyzed, comparing existing research to six criteria that should be fulfilled in an adequate research design. Finally, the problem is discussed in relation to social factors and relevance for psychologists.

Malnutrition as a Physiological Entity

Specific Vitamin and Mineral Deficiencies

A great deal is known about the role of specific nutrients in affecting physical development. Beriberi is the disease that results from an insufficient supply of thiamine; pellagra results from insufficient nicotinic acid; rickets results from insufficient vitamin D; and scurvy results from a deficient supply of vitamin C (Crome & Stern, 1967). In terms of psychological effects, insufficient iodine in a pregnant woman's diet can cause her to give birth to a child suffering from endemic cretinism, which involves extreme mental deficiency (Robinson & Robinson, 1965).

It is not surprising to find that nutritional anemias, such as those caused by a lack of folic acid or vitamin B_{12}, are significantly more common in low-income groups than in other classes (Klipstein, 1968). This unequal distribution of anemias is obviously due to the unequal distribution of nutritious food. This type of deficiency is one example of a common phenomenon: Deficiencies in a woman's diet may have a minimal observable effect on her own physical health, but the deficiency can severely affect her offspring. Some anemias, such as iron deficiency anemia in infants, can be the direct result of iron deficiency in the mother's diet, specifically during her pregnancy (Strauss, 1953). There is also evidence, however, that iron deficiency in the pregnant woman's diet can have a much more deleterious effect than the production of anemia. McGanity, Bridgforth, and Darby (1958) found a significantly higher rate of serious congenital abnormalities in babies of mothers suffering from iron deficiency anemia than in nonanemic mothers.

Marasmus and Kwashiorkor: Two Types of Protein-Calorie Malnutrition

Marasmus is a disease resulting from a diet insufficient in both calories and proteins. It usually occurs in children between the ages of 6 and 18 months (Gopalan, 1967). Its two major characteristics are severe weight loss in all body organs and subcutaneous fat, plus mental apathy (Chatterjee & Mukherjee, 1968).

Kwashiorkor has been interpreted both as a disease entirely separate from marasmus and as a more severe form of marasmus that occurs later in life. Kwashiorkor results from "prolonged subsistence on diets which [are] . . . moderately poor in calories but very poor in protein [Chatterjee & Mukherjee, 1968, p. 145]." It usually occurs between the ages of 12 and 36 months, though it can appear later. Although the severe wasting found with marasmus is not apparent, there is some loss of weight, especially involving muscle tissue. Kwashiorkor's major characteristics are severe skin disorders, excessive infiltration of fat into the liver (thus enlarging the liver and causing the commonly seen protruberant belly), low plasma proteins (and consequent edema, which is the subcutaneous fluid often noted), mental apathy, and the discoloration and loss of hair.

In both these diseases the child's condition is usually worsened by infectious diseases. The death rates of children aged 1–4 years in countries such as Mexico, Guatemala, and Peru are often 40 times the rate for the same age group in the United States. This difference reflects mainly the problems of malnutrition and subsequent vulnerability to infectious disease and parasites (Jelliffe, 1968). In cases where children are inadequately spaced, the difficulties are exacerbated. Each child must be separated from the breast, usually the most reliable source of nutrition for the newborn, in order to make room for the next child. In fact, the name "kwashiorkor" actually comes from a word in the Ga language of West Africa that means "disease that occurs when displaced from the breast by another child [Jelliffe, 1968, p. 76]."

Mental apathy is characteristic of both marasmus and kwashiorkor. The return of interest in the environment and responsivity to external stimuli are often used as indexes of the effectiveness of treatment for the diseases.

Physiological Changes Attributed to Nutritional Deficiencies

Some of the most interesting, although necessarily less rigorous, studies of undernutrition are those that examine the effects of wars and depression. Montagu (1962) summarized 29 studies of malnutrition during World Wars I and II, all of which showed that the average birth weights of infants born during and immediately after the war periods were significantly lower than during nonwar years.

Antonov's (1947) study of the German siege of Leningrad was one of the most complete reports. The siege lasted from August 1941 to January 1943. The food supply was extremely low for most of that time, and there was no heat for most homes, even during the coldest winter months. There were also the added stresses of daily air raids and shelling. During the worst part of the siege, the prematurity rate was 41.2%; the mortality rate of full-term births was 9% and of premature births was 30.8%. All of these figures are extraordinarily high. Antonov, minimizing the role of stress, attributed these problems—high rate of premature births, high mortality rates of full-term and premature births—to intrauterine undernutrition of the fetus.

Laporte (1946) studied the heights and weights of Paris grade school children in 1944 and compared the data to those of the same age groups in 1938. He found there was a significant decrease corresponding to the war years. Again, the results were attributed to inadequate nutrition.

Palmer (1935) did a longitudinal analysis of three groups of Americans who experienced the depression: children who were not poor and whose families did not suffer from the depression, children who were poor and who remained poor, and children whose families experienced extreme economic losses due to the depression. He found that the first group remained above average in height and weight; the second group remained below average; but the third group dropped from above average to below average. Once again, the author attributed the changes to decreased nutrition.

The fact that Antonov, Laporte, and Palmer attributed their results to decreased nutrition does not rule out the possibility that stress was the crucial factor. Montagu (1962), in reviewing a series of German studies done following World War II, concluded that the general wartime decrease in birth weights and increase in congenital malformations were due to malnutrition and stress. That stress does increase during wars and depression is obvious. Perhaps the results of these studies cannot be interpreted entirely in terms of nutrition.

Since there is no direct evidence to determine which variable is more important —malnutrition or stress—we might turn to a different type of research for an indirect answer. There are many studies in the literature that compare different socioeconomic groups (Anderson, Baird, & Thomson, 1958; McCance, Widdowson, & Verdon-Roe, 1938; Montagu, 1962; Walker, 1955). In virtually all such studies the following relationship seems to hold:

Relatively poorer women, when compared to women of higher economic classes, have less nutritious diets and give birth to babies who are more often of low birth weight or perhaps premature, are less healthy, are more likely to have congenital malformations or serious diseases, and have a somewhat lower probability of living beyond a few months. It can be argued that women of lower classes are also under more stress than women of higher economic classes, but a series of experiments has proven that dietary supplements given to pregnant women of low socioeconomic groups have a significant effect in improving the health of their babies (Dieckmann, Turner, Meiller, Savage, Hill, Straube, Pottinger, & Rynkiewicz, 1951; Ebbs, Brown, Tisdall, Moyle, & Bell, 1942; Toverud, Stearns, & Macy, 1950). In these experiments the economic and social problems presumably creating the stresses in their lives were not treated. Ebbs et al. (1942), in a Toronto prenatal clinic, studied 120 pregnant women on low protein-calorie diets (their normal diets) and 90 women on the same diet who were given supplements. All the women were of low economic status. The authors concluded that on every physical measure the babies of mothers given the supplements were superior to the babies of the other group.

This line of argument leads one to the conclusion that the role of stress within the intrauterine environment is not known, but that intrauterine nutrition seems to be very important.

The relationship between social class and nutrition seems clear. Now what of the relationship between nutrition and problems of pregnancy and birth? Toverud et al. (1950) reviewed a large number of studies in which vitamin and mineral intakes of pregnant women were controlled. The overall results were that the control of vitamins and minerals led to significant decreases of stillbirth and neonatal mortality rates. McCance et al. (1938) compared pregnant wives of unemployed English miners to pregnant wives of professionals. They concluded that the intake of vitamins and minerals was related to the economic income and social class of the women. Consumption of calories, fats, and carbohydrates was not at all related to income, but protein consumption was definitely associated with economic status. This finding is important because Burke, Harding, and Stuart (1943) then found a consistent parallel between protein intake of mothers during the last 6 months of pregnancy and the heights and weights of the infants. Dieckmann et al. (1951) also noted a significant increase in the physical health of babies as the consumption of protein was increased during the mother's pregnancy.

The Harvard School of Public Health along with two Boston hospitals conducted a longitudinal study of 200 women and their pregnancies (Kirkwood, 1955). After following the women for 20 years, the researchers concluded that a good prenatal diet produced the best chance of insuring the good physical condition of the child. Nutrition of the mother was considered important not only during pregnancy but also when she herself was a child. As Kirkwood summarized: "Good obstetrical care [including good diet] is a very broad type of care that must start with the birth of the future mother, or even before that, with her mother who is the grandmother of the baby we are discussing [1955, p. 31]."

Birch[1] has discussed the intergenerational aspects of this problem. Citing data from a series of studies in Aberdeen, Scotland (Baird, Thomson, & Duncan, 1953; Baird, Walker, & Thomson, 1954), Birch claimed that low birth weights of infants were highly correlated with mothers' heights, which were in turn correlated with the mothers' socioeconomic status

[1] H. G. Birch. Nutritional risk and learning disabilities: An epidemiological view. Symposium presented at the meeting of the American Association for the Advancement of Science, Boston, December 1969.

when the mothers were born, not with the mothers' socioeconomic status at the time of pregnancy. (In Aberdeen all women receive comparable health care because of the national health care system, and complete records are kept on all individuals throughout their lives. These records permitted accurate assessment of social class.)

One mechanism by which the intergenerational influences of socioeconomic status might affect pregnancy and childbirth was suggested by Walker (1955). He pointed out that in the Aberdeen studies perinatal mortality (which includes stillbirths and babies who die in the first week after birth) was more frequent in the lower social classes, and even more frequent in small women. He attributed the role of stature to the structure of the pelvic region:

> Good environment and adequate nutrition during childhood should prevent flattening of the bony pelvis. Full nutrition during prepuberty and puberty phases should allow the child to attain full potential height and physique, and the pelvis its maximal capacity [p. 30].

Thomson (1959) studied what he termed the "reproductive efficiency" of women. He found that there was an inverse relationship between the mother's stature and (presumably pelvic size) and problems of pregnancy such as fetal malformations, hemorrhage, and perinatal deaths.

Jeans, Smith, and Stearns (1955) collected data on 400 pregnant, low-income women in Iowa, whose diets were commonly deficient in calcium and protein. Besides the relationship between mothers' nutrition and birth weight of babies, as also reported by Burke et al. (1943), there were significant relationships between poor diet and prematurity rates (more than twice as high as the prematurity rate of the control group with good diets) and also between poor diet and multiple congenital anomalies. Again referring to data from the Aberdeen research, we can conclude that women from the lower social classes (especially those of small stature) tend to have the least nutritious diets and the highest rates of congenital malformations, especially those malformations affecting the central nervous system (anencephaly, hydrocephaly, spina bifida, and so forth) (Montagu, 1962).

The data that have been reported in this subsection suggest more than a relationship between undernutrition and physical deficiencies. They suggest also a mechanism by which undernutrition may cause difficulties in pregnancy and birth (viz., reduced pelvic development), and they also demonstrate that the central nervous system is frequently the part of the body that is damaged.

Brain Growth and Myelination

In the previous subsection evidence was presented that links prematurity rates, perinatal deaths, low birth weights, and congenital malformations to nutritional deficiencies in the mother's diet during pregnancy and even earlier. The congenital anomalies, as pointed out by Jeans et al. (1955), are mainly those that involve the central nervous system. Since the main concern in this review is with the psychological effects of malnutrition, the literature on brain and spinal cord defects is discussed in detail.

A number of studies have been done on dogs (Platt, Heard, & Stewart, 1964), pigs (Dickerson, Dobbing, & McCance, 1967), and rats (Davison & Dobbing, 1966; Winick & Noble, 1966), in which the animals have been fed diets that were deficient in some of the basic nutrients. When the animals were sacrificed and their brain tissue analyzed, in all cases the experimenters reported significantly retarded brain development.

It appears that brain growth may be retarded through a number of different mechanisms. Davison and Dobbing (1966) noted that when the undernutrition occurred during the myelination period of development of the rat's brain, they obtained the most severe growth retardation. These researchers believed that inadequate myelination in humans might be a significant factor in mental deficiency, and they emphasized that the impaired intellectual development of children suffering from phenylketonuria is associated with (though not necessarily caused by) defective myelination in the brain.

Another mechanism by which brain growth is retarded in the rat is through insufficient cell division. Winick and Noble (1966) found that the effects of malnutrition on brain cells depended on the phase of growth of the animal at the time of the dietary insufficiencies. For rats, very early malnutrition obstructed cell division; even when the rats were subsequently fed on nutritious diets, they did not recover fully. In general, Winick and Noble found that the later the period of malnutrition occurred, the more likely it was the cell division was unimpeded; later malnutrition did produce decreased cell size, but with subsequent nutritious diets the animals could recover.

The animal studies clearly support the view that the earlier the malnutrition occurs, the more deleterious is the effect on brain growth. There are very few reports in the literature of attempts to verify this conclusion in humans. Although it is not ethical to induce experimentally severe malnutrition in newborn babies, it is possible to do autopsies on children who die of malnutrition. Winick, Rosso, and Waterlow (1970) have reported on the autopsies of 16 Chilean and Jamaican babies who died of malnutrition before 2 years of age. All the children had a subnormal number of brain cells; three of them had less than 40% of the normal number. According to Winick (1968, 1970), the human brain grows mainly by cell division during gestation and the first 6 months of life; after 6 months of age the brain grows mainly by taking in proteins and fats, without increasing the cell number. He concluded:

> Severe undernutrition in the neonatal period will curtail cell division in all organs including brain. Recovery will occur only if adequate feeding is resumed early, presumably while cell division is still occurring [1968, p. 197].

Verification for Winick's results can be found in several other autopsy studies. Brown's (1966) autopsy report on organ weight in 1,094 Ugandan children, who died while suffering from various degrees of malnutrition, demonstrated that brain weight was low for malnourished children. Naeye, Diener, and Dellinger (1969) chose an urban American sample of 252 babies either stillborn or dead within 48 hours of birth. Autopsy results showed that those from poor families were 15% smaller than those from nonpoor environments. All the body organs and the brain weighed significantly less in the infants from poor families. Parekh, Pherwani, Udani, and Mukherjee (1970) found a 28%–36% weight deficit in the autopsied brains of 357 malnourished Indian children. The greater the nutritional deficiency, the greater was the weight deficit, especially if the malnutrition occurred in the last 3 months of gestation or the first 3 months after birth.

Since the present interest is mainly the psychological effects of nutritional deficiencies, the obvious question arises: What parts of the brain seem to be most traumatized in the autopsied tissue? This issue was discussed briefly following one of the American Association for the Advancement of Science symposia on malnutrition and behavior, December 1969. The evidence seems to be inconclusive. Winick and others have found a general reduction in brain weight, with no particular area more significantly affected than any other.

Relationship Between Malnutrition and Mental Deficiency

Some of the research reported in the previous section demonstrated that malnutrition can affect not only prematurity, perinatal deaths, and birth size but also congenital anomalies of the central nervous system and brain weight. Early malnutrition appears to affect cell number in the brain and is not easily overcome; later malnutrition (after approximately 6 months of age in humans) affects brain cell size and is more easily reversed.

What are the behavioral and mental effects of malnutrition? The question is most easily answered in terms of nonhuman species. Changes in the postures, gaits, brain weights, electroencephalographic records, exploratory activity, and learning ability of rats, pigs, dogs, and other animals have been well documented (Scrimshaw & Gordon, 1968). Typical are the results of Caldwell and Churchill (1967); protein-deficient rats had lower birth weights, had a higher preweaning mortality rate, and performed less well on the Lashley III water maze than well-nourished rats.

Mental apathy and psychological deficiency can be the results of insufficiencies of specific vitamins, proteins, and calories, and also of congenital malformations. Having demonstrated that malnutrition is also related to birth weight and prematurity rates, can we show that birth weight and prematurity rates are related to mental deficiency?

Prematurity, Birth Weight, and Mental Development

Knobloch, Rider, Harper, and Pasamanick (1956) studied a variety of factors related to physical and mental development in premature infants. They defined a "continuum of casualty" which ranged from more severe problems such as spontaneous abortion and stillbirths to less severe results like cerebral palsy, epilepsy, and mental deficiency. Comparing 500 premature births with 492 full-term controls, matched for socioeconomic status, season of birth, and parity of the mother, the authors then administered physical and Gesell developmental examinations at about 40 weeks after birth. In general, they found that the incidence of physical and mental abnormalities increased as birth weight decreased. With regard to intellectual potential, they found that whereas 21.8% of the controls were above average, only 16.3% of the moderately low birth weight babies (1,500–2,500 grams) and only 5.3% of the very low birth weight babies (less than 1,500 grams) were above average. Judged as mentally defective or borderline defective were 1.6% of the controls, 1.8% of the moderately small babies, and 17.6% of the very small group. In sum, the probability of a very small baby being completely normal was only 50.9%, compared to 88.4% for the controls. Knobloch et al. (1956) did not control for several variables that might have influenced their data (e.g., the intellectual potential of parents), but the study as a whole was quite complete and the evidence is dramatically clear: babies of low birth weights have significantly lower probability of being entirely physically and psychologically healthy than babies of normal birth weights.

Using the Gesell schedule, Cravioto, DeLicardie, Montiel, and Birch (1967) tested motor and adaptive development of 95 premature Guatemalan babies. They excluded from their sample any baby with physiological complications, yet the tests still showed a significant lag in performance when compared to babies born at full term. There was apparently no follow-up study to determine the permanency of the lag. Churchill (1965) used IQ as a measure of the development of a sample of American babies and found a significant negative correlation in twins between IQ and birth weight. Churchill's sample consisted of full-term, low birth weight babies; his results are consistent with Cravioto's.

Cravioto and DeLicardie (1968) were interested in the role of social variables in the relationship between size and intelligence. They compared a group of rural

Guatemalan children with a sample of upper-class urban Guatemalans. Height of the children was highly correlated with intelligence in the former group, but not in the latter. The implication of this research, which has been verified in several countries, is that where malnutrition is not a problem, a child's size is determined mainly by genetic factors. In rural areas where malnutrition is more common, however, children who are malnourished never achieve their full height potential, and this stunting of growth is accompanied by mental deficits. Consequently, smaller children also tend to have lower IQs. This type of research is strong confirmation that good nutrition enables a child to reach his maximum genetic potential.

This relationship between birth weight and intelligence has been examined extensively in twins. Willerman and Churchill (1967) administered intelligence tests to 27 sets of identical twins, aged 5 to 15 years. In all cases the twin member who was the smaller of the pair at birth achieved lower scores in verbal and performance IQ. All the twins had normal, full-term deliveries with no complications. In other words, no twin member would have been defined as premature, low birth weight, or physically "at risk." Yet the differences in IQ were statistically significant, and the results were consistent across all pairs studied.

One interpretation of Willerman and Churchill's data is that unequal prenatal sharing may occur such that one twin receives more nutrients than the other. There is evidence for this theory in the "twin transfusion syndrome" (Driscoll, 1964). Because of the sharing of vasculature common among identical twins, one twin sometimes receives more blood (and, consequently, nutrients) than the other. The smaller twin may suffer to the extent of becoming anemic, while the larger fetus frequently has an abundance of blood.

Babson, Kangas, Young, and Bramhall (1964) confirmed Willerman and Churchill's findings: In twins born with widely disparate birth weights, but with no apparent physiological disorders, the smaller twin member consistently had a lower IQ than the larger twin.

Several research teams have done retrospective studies of mentally subnormal children. Pasamanick and Lilienfeld (1955) collected data on mentally defective children born in Baltimore between 1935 and 1952. They compared them with mentally normal children born during the same period. There were significantly more complications of pregnancy and significantly higher rates of prematurity and neonatal anomalies in the mentally defective children. As previously noted, these latter factors are linked with nutritional deficiencies. Birch (1968) reported similar data on prematurity rates.

Churchill, Neff, and Caldwell (1966) pursued the issue of the relationship between birth weight and intelligence. Comparing 51 normal and 51 moderately retarded children, they concluded that the retarded group had significantly lower birth weights than the normal children. All the children were of comparable socioeconomic status. The results could have been attributed to differential prematurity rates, since there is a high prematurity rate among mentally retarded children. When premature births were excluded from the analysis, however, there was still a significant relationship between mental retardation and low birth weight. Churchill et al. (1966) suggested that their results were probably due to intrauterine nutritional variations.

Direct Evidence Linking Malnutrition and Mental Deficiency

What this author considers "direct evidence" are studies that examine and/or manipulate nutrition and assess mental development or IQ in humans. This group of experiments differs from those that are concerned with related or intervening variables (prematurity rates, birth weight, and so forth).

An adequate model for a research design to answer the question, "What is the effect of malnutrition on mental development?" should strive to fulfill the following criteria:

1. Both the duration of malnutrition and the extent of physiological and psychological effects should be assessed.
2. The approximate period in life during which the malnutrition was experienced should be consistent across subjects.
3. All other physiological variables—prematurity, chronic disease, congenital malformations—should be carefully controlled.
4. Environmental factors—family income, socioeconomic class, diet, parents' education—should be carefully controlled.
5. Mental development should be assessed with a variety of measures: tests for IQ, for cognitive development, for perceptual and motor skills, and perhaps for emotional and personality development.
6. Tests of psychological development should be given periodically over a decade or more, to examine the permanency of the effects.

All of the studies reviewed in this section fail in some way to meet these criteria. This statement does not justify ignoring the research. Several of the studies —notably Chase and Martin (1970), Cabak and Najdanvic (1965), Pollitt and Granoff (1967), and Stoch and Smythe (1967)—present relatively thorough methodologies and very convincing results.

One of the earliest attempts in the United States was the Harrell, Woodyard, and Gates study reported in 1955 (for discussions, see Masland, 1958; Montagu, 1962; Robinson & Robinson, 1965). Harrell et al. chose two samples of pregnant women and administered four types of dietary supplements. The Kentucky sample consisted of 1,200 white women, most of whom were already on fairly adequate diets. The Virginia sample consisted of 1,200 women, both black and white, of poor economic status. The four daily dietary supplements were as follows: (*a*) ascorbic acid; (*b*) thiamine, riboflavin, niacin, and iron; (*c*) inert material; and (*d*) thiamine. Each sample was divided into four groups to receive the four supplements. In the Virginia sample, 518 of the offspring were tested at age 3; 811 of the Kentucky offspring were tested. There were no significant differences in the Kentucky children's IQs, perhaps due to the generally adequate diets of the mothers even without the supplements. In Virginia, however, the group receiving Supplement *b* had a significantly higher average IQ than the group receiving Supplement *c*.

The conclusions drawn from this research are limited, yet still significant. The dietary control was restricted to the supplements, so we are unsure whether the women's normal diets were exactly comparable. The reasons for testing less than half of the Kentucky children are unclear, and there might be some contaminating factors that contributed to the selection of these 518 out of the 1,200. And as Harrell et al. (1955) admitted, the best conclusion that can be drawn from their research is that vitamin supplements can yield a higher IQ until age 4. Children were not followed beyond that age to test the stability of the results. Thus, this experiment did not control for socioeconomic factors in the Kentucky sample, and they failed to examine the permanency of the effects.

Another study that fails to provide complete control of diet is the Christakis, Miridjanian, Nath, Khurana, Cowell, Archer, Frank, Ziffer, Baker, and James (1968) investigation of 642 New York City fifth- and sixth-grade children from the Lower East Side of Manhattan. Each child's nutritional status was determined from subjective reports, while reading test scores provided the index of mental ability. In the entire sample only 6.4% were judged to have excellent dietary histories. In general there was a positive correlation between relatively high reading scores and excellent diet patterns, with Chinese children at the high end on both variables and Puerto Ricans at the low end. Although there were few clinical signs of malnutrition, the researchers did identify a cluster of Puerto Rican children with "suboptimal" nutrition and very low reading scores. This research does not attempt to fulfill any of the six criteria outlined above. It is an epidemiologic survey that depends entirely on subjective reports of dietary habits and on reading ability as a measure of intellectual capacity.

One American study of severe malnutrition was reported by Chase and Martin (1970). Choosing 19 children who had been hospitalized for malnutrition before the age of 1, they tested the children from 2 to 5 years after treatment. Height, weight, head circumference, and developmental quotients were all significantly low for these children. Chase and Martin fulfilled all the criteria outlined above for physiological and environmental controls. Perhaps in a few years they will be able to report further follow-up data.

Cabak and Najdanvic (1965) were concerned about the depression of IQ that they felt followed in severe cases of infant malnutrition. They chose a sample of 36 children in Sarajevo, Yugoslavia, who had been hospitalized between the ages of 4 months and 24 months for treatment of marasmus. At the time of the study, all the children seemed to be physically normal; those with chronic diseases and other defects were excluded from the sample. About two-thirds of the children were the offspring of unskilled laborers; the remaining one-third represented families of higher economic status. When the children were tested with a modified Binet test, only 18 of them scored in the normal range (91–110); 12 scored between 71 and 90; the remaining 6 scored below 70. In other words, not one had an IQ above average, and exactly one-half of them were mentally deficient. The results were significantly lower than Serbian norms. Unfortunately, Cabak and Najdanvic failed to use a control group matched for environmental variables. Birch and Cravioto (1968) obtained similar results with Guatemalan children who had experienced malnutrition. There was an increased tendency for the children to fall in the borderline or subnormal IQ range.

Pollitt and Granoff (1967) conducted a study very similar to Cabak's, using 27 children from the slum section of Lima, Peru. All the children, aged 11–32 months, had been hospitalized for severe protein-calorie malnutrition. When they had apparently recovered from the malnutrition (judged by physiological measures), they were given the Bayley Infant Scales of Mental and Motor Development. Only two of the children scored above the basal levels of the scales; there was severe mental deficiency apparent despite the physiological recovery. To exclude the effects of social and economic factors, Pollitt and Granoff used siblings of the subjects as controls. In all cases, the siblings scored within the normal range. The retardation of the malnourished children seems to be explained best in terms of dietary deficiencies.

One fault in the preceding studies—Chase and Martin, Cabak and Najdanvic, Pollitt and Granoff—is the lack of long-term follow-up data. Are the impairments irreversible? With subsequent adequate nutrition and education for 10 years or so, could the mental deficiencies of these children disappear? This is a crucial question, and so far it has not been answered satisfactorily. Cravioto and Robles (1965) believe that the possibilities for complete recovery from severe protein-calorie malnutrition are slim if the malnutrition occurs before the child is 6 months old. This estimate coincides well with Winick's (1968) research, which showed that total recovery from early malnutrition can occur only if rehabilitation begins during the first 6 months of life, while cell division is still taking place in the brain. Thus, if malnutrition does occur before 6 months of age, and is not treated during the period of cell division, it seems that the brain will be irreparably damaged. Presumably, later malnutrition interferes with protein synthesis, which is easier to correct.

There is one major study in the literature that reports the only significant attempt so far in the world to collect long-term follow-up data. Since the long-term effects of malnutrition seem to comprise a major gap in our knowledge, this research deserves detailed consideration.

Stoch and Smythe (1967) began their South African study in 1955. Twenty black infants who had suffered from extreme protein-calorie malnutrition were matched for sex and age with controls. A large variety of tests were used for the children: Gesell infant scales, electroencephalographic evaluations, and perceptual tasks. An IQ score was estimated from these tests every 2 years.

As might be expected, the heights and weights of the malnourished group were significantly less than the controls. Head circumference was also significantly less; this is an important finding, because there is generally a very high correlation between head circumference and brain weight. Thus, the experimental children seem to have had much smaller brains than the controls. Stoch and Smythe (1967) estimated that the average intracranial volume of the experimental group was 13.7% less than that of the controls.

The majority of the experimental infants (12 of the 20) had lower IQs than the very lowest child from the control group. All the experimental children scored significantly lower than the average control score.

It is worth noting that the control group was itself not above average. They were from the lowest socioeconomic class (as were the experimental children) and their mean weight at age 1 year was below normal. The living conditions of the two groups in the beginning of the study did differ, however, with the experimental children more commonly living in broken homes, with a higher rate of alcoholism and unemployment. By 1967 most of the experimental group's home environments had improved. The initial differences, however, indicate poor control of environmental factors. Stoch and Smythe considered the environmental effect in one possible explanation of their data. They suggested that the inactivity and lack of energy associated with malnutrition, plus an inadequate home environment, could have combined to decrease the receptiveness of the malnourished children to stimuli and therefore have impaired the learning process. Their alternative hypothesis was that early malnutrition causes brain damage by retarding brain growth.

There are a number of reasons why Stoch and Smythe favor the second explanation. Many of the results from the nonverbal tests (e.g., visual-motor and pattern perception) were very similar to the tests of children suffering from brain damage. The abnormal electroencephalograms and the decreased head circumferences also led them to favor the organic damage interpretation. And finally, the children had experienced undernutrition during the period of maximum brain growth and development, namely, before the age of 2 years. They concluded that the first 2 years of life are crucial.

These 2 years are the years of maximum brain growth; they are also the years during which malnutrition occurs most frequently in all countries of the world. According to Thomson (1968), the situation is worsening in many countries because of an increasing tendency to wean children from the breast at an earlier age. Breast feeding is entirely adequate for children for many months, especially in underdeveloped nations where there is often no other adequately nutritious food available. If the child is deprived of the breast after only 3 or 4 months, and if no other adequate food source is available, malnutrition is very likely to occur.

Conclusions

Continuum of Casualty

The information in the preceding pages provides compelling evidence that malnutrition can prevent the expression of the full genetic potential for mental development. The definitive study to prove causality and to study the significance of timing, environmental compensation, and so on, has not been done; it cannot be done because of the ethical restrictions on experimentation with human subjects.

Nutrition begins to affect the life of a baby long before it is born. The intergenerational data from the Aberdeen studies (Baird et al., 1953; Baird et al., 1954) demonstrated that the nutrition of the baby's mother, grandmother, and perhaps other ancestors can influence his own chances for unimpeded physical and mental development. One mechanism by which the intergenerational factor expresses its influence appears to be via the mother's stature, particularly the structure of her pelvis. Smaller women have an increased risk of giving birth to injured or low birth weight babies.

Another way in which nutrition affects a child prenatally is through intrauterine environment. In multiple births it may be the case that one fetus receives less arterial nourishment than the other. The deprived fetus may be stunted in physical or mental growth. In single births a fetus can still suffer from intrauterine malnutrition. An obvious factor that can affect the mother's consumption of crucial nutrients is income. Clearly, it is more difficult to provide adequately nutritious diets on poverty-level incomes than on middle-class incomes.

The extent of malnutrition in this country is directly correlated with income level (Citizens' Board, 1968). This relationship is easy to understand. In Massachusetts, as one example, welfare recipients receive approximately 30¢ per person, per meal (Massachusetts Welfare Rights Organization, 1969). Neither this amount nor the surplus commodity food available can provide adequate amounts of essential nutrients, especially since high protein foods are always more expensive than starches and other carbohydrates.

After a baby is born he is still vulnerable to the effects of nutritional deficiencies, some of which are reversible. Kugelmass, Poull, and Samuel (1944) found they were able to increase the average IQ score of a group of malnourished children by 18 points, by increasing their intake of nutrients. The IQs of mentally retarded children increased by an average of 10 points with the same treatment. The timing of the rehabilitation was crucial: the earlier the treatment, the greater was its effect.

With regard to the factor of timing, perhaps it is most helpful to imagine a continuum of casualty, to borrow the term used by Knobloch and Pasamanick. Beginning 6 months before birth and lasting until 6 months after birth, cell division is providing rapid growth of brain tissue. Nutritional deprivation during this period can severely retard psychological development, and it is probably irreversible unless treatment begins before cell division ends (Cravioto & Robles, 1965; Winick, 1968). From 6 months through the first or second year of life the rate of brain growth is still very rapid, mainly by protein synthesis, but nutritional rehabilitation still can be partially effective (Stoch & Smythe, 1967). Beyond this point, the rate of brain growth is significantly slower, and Kugelmass et al. (1944) found negligible effects of treatment on IQ scores beyond the age of 4 years.

The Cravioto-Birch Model: Interaction of Organic and Social Factors

The preceding discussion has considered only the organic effects of malnutrition, and how organic changes might retard mental development. Social factors are also important. As usual, the question should not be phrased in terms of one or the other type of influence, but rather the interaction of both. Figure 3.5 is a model of the effects of nutritional stress, as proposed by Cravioto and Birch (Birch, 1968; see Footnote 1; Cravioto, 1966), which

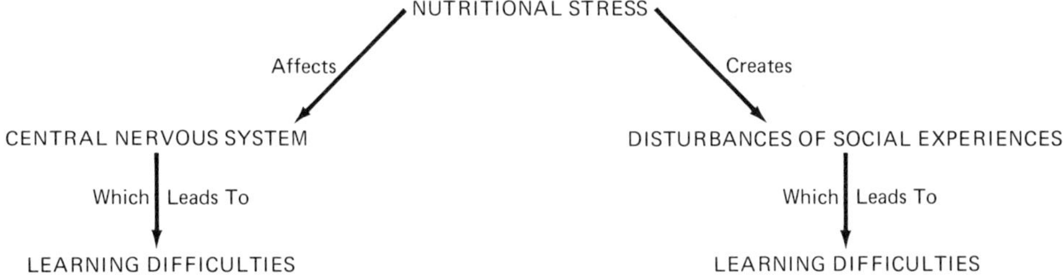

Figure 3.5. Model of the effects of nutritional stress.

illustrates the ways in which social learning factors and organic changes probably interact. The left-hand chain illustrates the sequence of events this paper has emphasized. Nutritional deprivation (either pre- or postnatal) leads to changes in the brain and impedes mental development. Learning difficulties, or, in the extreme case, mental deficiency, result.

The other chain illustrates the fact that nutritional deprivation can work indirectly on mental capacity. As Cravioto[2] explained, malnutrition can interfere with learning by three indirect mechanisms:

Loss of learning time. Children who receive insufficient nutrients are more vulnerable to illness and consequently miss more school days than healthy children.

Changes in concentration or motivation. Especially for children who are not only malnourished, but also hungry, continual distraction by the discomforts of an empty stomach can seriously interfere with the child's efforts in school.

Loss of the social interaction involved in meal times. As Cravioto pointed out, we do not often think of the amount of learning that occurs at most family dinner tables: learning of symbolic and social systems, learning of cultural norms, and exposure perhaps to adult interests. With poverty and lack of food, this social learning setting may break down, and the malnourished child is deprived of still another type of educational experience.

This model illustrates the complexity of the problem of malnutrition and mental development. Birch (1968) summarized:

> Children who are ill-nourished are reduced in their responsiveness to the environment, distracted by their visceral state, and reduced in their ability to progress and endure in learning conditions. . . . Consequently . . . [there is] a reduction in the profit which a child may derive from exposure to opportunities for experience [p. 596].

Urgency of the Problem

Preschool children appear to be the major at-risk group all over the world. According to Béhar (1968), approximately 75% of preschool children in South America, Asia, and Africa are underweight for their age. Since about 400 million children under 5 years of age live in these areas, he suggested that there are approximately 300 million preschool children—60% of the total preschool population of the world—suffering from mild to moderate protein-calorie malnutrition.

Malnutrition is also an urgent problem in the United States. In April 1968 the Citizens' Board of Inquiry into Hunger and Malnutrition in the United States published its report, which claimed that more than 10 million Americans were affected by hunger and malnutrition. Congress, in the "Partnership for Health" Bill, charged the Secretary of Health, Education and Welfare (HEW) to conduct a

[2] J. Cravioto. Symposium presented at the meeting of the American Association for the Advancement of Science, Boston, December 1969.

survey of the "prevalence and location of serious hunger and malnutrition, and the health problems incident thereto, in the U.S. [Schaffer, 1968, p. 1130]." The survey was conducted by the Nutrition Program of the Public Health Service. In the spring of 1968 HEW published its report, which stated:

> children are smaller, they suffer from anemia and the effects of substandard protein and vitamin dietary intake. There is reason to believe that the continuing levels of inadequacy in dietary intake are associated with physical and mental damage . . . [Nelson, 1968, p. 1434].

In 1969 the White House Conference on Food, Nutrition and Health presented the President with a 625-page report. The priority list for target groups reflects some of the issues discussed in this paper: preschool children, pregnant women, primary school children, and then other specific deprived groups, such as American Indians and migrant workers. The recommendations of the conference, if implemented immediately, would apparently eliminate hunger and malnutrition within 3 years. When Senate subcommittee hearings were held in February 1971, it became obvious that in reality little progress had been made since the White House Conference.

The issue of malnutrition has traditionally been considered the province of medical and public health experts, as demonstrated by the bibliographic references for this review. It is puzzling that psychologists have shown so little interest in the psychological effects of malnutrition. (A notable exception is the Bay Area Psychologists and Social Scientists for Social Action; see Opton, Margen, Neilands, Pilisuk, & Sanford.[3]) There is much yet to be learned about motor deficits, personality development, and learning defects and their possible relationships to malnutrition.[4]

---

[3] E. M. Opton, S. Margen, J. B. Neilands, M. Pilisuk, & N. Sanford. Hunger causes mental retardation: A Report to the California Assembly Committee on Health and Welfare, 1969. (Mimeo)

[4] Research published since this review was submitted (Kotch, 1970; Kotz, 1969; Levitsky & Barnes, 1972; Rosso, Hormazábel, & Winick, 1970; Van Marthens & Zamenhof, 1969; Winick, 1970; Zamenhof, Van Marthens, & Grauel, 1971) includes several excellent review articles, new evidence on the intergenerational effect and on environmental interaction, and also a thorough analysis of the political obstacles to eliminating hunger in the United States.

References

ANDERSON, W. J., BAIRD, D., & THOMSON, A. M. Epidemiology of stillbirths and infant deaths due to congenital malformation. *Lancet*, 1958, *1*, 1304–1306.

ANTONOV, A. N. Children born during the siege of Leningrad in 1942. *Journal of Pediatrics*, 1947, *30*, 250–259.

BABSON, S., KANGAS, J., YOUNG, N., & BRAMHALL, J. Growth and development of twins of dissimilar size at birth. *Pediatrics*, 1964, *33*, 327–333.

BAIRD, D., THOMSON, A. M., & DUNCAN, E. H. L. Causes and prevention of stillbirths and first week deaths, II: Evidence from Aberdeen clinical records. *Journal of Obstetrics and Gynaecology of the British Empire*, 1953, *60*, 17–30.

BAIRD, D., WALKER, J., & THOMSON, A. M. Causes and prevention of stillbirths and first week deaths, III: Classification of deaths by clinical cause: Effect of age, parity, and length of gestation on death rates by causes. *Journal of Obstetrics and Gynaecology of the British Empire*, 1954, *61*, 433–448.

BÉHAR, M. Prevalence of malnutrition among preschool children of developing countries.

In N. W. Scrimshaw & J. E. Gordon (Eds.), *Malnutrition, learning and behavior.* Cambridge, Mass.: M.I.T. Press, 1968.

BIRCH, H. G. Health and education of socially disadvantaged children. *Developmental Medicine and Child Neurology,* 1968, *10,* 580–599.

BIRCH, H. G., & CRAVIOTO, J. Infection, nutrition and environment in mental development. In H. F. Eichenwald (Ed.), *The prevention of mental retardation through control of infectious diseases.* (Public Health Service Pub. No. 1692) Washington, D. C.: United States Government Printing Office, 1968.

BROWN, R. E. Organ weight in malnutrition with special reference to brain weight. *Developmental Medicine and Child Neurology,* 1966, *8,* 512–522.

BURKE, B. S., HARDING, V. V., & STUART, H. C. Nutrition studies during pregnancy: 4. Relation of protein content of mother's diet during pregnancy to birth length, birth weight, and condition of infant at birth. *Journal of Pediatrics,* 1943, *23,* 506.

CABAK, V., & NAJDANVIC, R. Effect of undernutrition in early life on physical and mental development. *Archives of Disease in Childhood,* 1965, *40,* 532–534.

CALDWELL, D. F., & CHURCHILL, J. A. Learning ability in the progeny of rats administered a protein-deficient diet during the second half of gestation. *Neurology,* 1967, *17,* 95–99.

CHASE, H. P., & MARTIN, H. P. Undernutrition and child development. *New England Journal of Medicine,* 1970, *282,* 933–939.

CHATTERJEE, K. K., & MUKHERJEE, K. L. Phospholipids of the liver in children suffering from protein-calorie undernutrition. *British Journal of Nutrition,* 1968, *22,* 145–151.

CHRISTAKIS, G., MIRIDJANIAN, A., NATH, L., KHURANA, H., COWELL, C., ARCHER, M., FRANK, O., ZIFFER, H., BAKER, H., & JAMES, G. A nutritional epidemiologic investigation of 642 New York City children. *American Journal of Clinical Nutrition,* 1968, *21,* 107–126.

CHURCHILL, J. A. The relationship between intelligence and birth weight in twins. *Neurology,* 1965, *15,* 341–347.

CHURCHILL, J. A., NEFF, J. W., & CALDWELL, D. F. Birth weight and intelligence. *Obstetrics and Gynecology,* 1966, 28, 425–429.

CITIZEN'S BOARD OF INQUIRY INTO HUNGER AND MALNUTRITION IN THE UNITED STATES. *Hunger, U.S.A.* Boston: Beacon Press, 1968.

CRAVIOTO, J. Malnutrition and behavioral development in the pre-school child. In *Pre-school child malnutrition.* (Publ. No. 1282) Washington, D. C.: National Academy of Science-National Research Council, 1966.

CRAVIOTO, J., & DE LICARDIE, E. R. Intersensory development of school-age children. In N. W. Scrimshaw & J. E. Gordon (Eds.), *Malnutrition, learning and behavior.* Cambridge, Mass.: M.I.T. Press, 1968.

CRAVIOTO, J., DE LICARDIE, E. R., MONTIEL, R., & BIRCH, H. G. Motor and adaptive development of premature infants from a preindustrial setting during the first year of life. *Biologia Neonatorum,* 1967, *11,* 151–158.

CRAVIOTO, J., & ROBLES, B. Evolution of adaptive and motor behavior during rehabilitation from kwashiorkor. *American Journal of Orthopsychiatry,* 1965, *35,* 449–464.

CROME, L. C., & STERN, J. *The pathology of mental retardation.* London: Churchill, 1967.

DAVISON, A. N., & DOBBING, J. Myelination as a vulnerable period in brain development. *British Medical Bulletin,* 1966, *22,* 40–44.

DICKERSON, J. W., DOBBING, J., & MCCANCE, R. A. The effect of undernutrition on the postnatal development of the brain and cord in pigs. *Proceedings of the Royal Society of London,* 1967, *166,* 396.

DIECKMANN, W. J., TURNER, D. F., MEILLER, E. J., SAVAGE, L. J., HILL, A. J., STRAUBE, M. T., POTTINGER, R. E., & RYNKIEWICZ, L. M. Observations on protein intake and the health of the mother and baby: I. Clinical and laboratory findings. *Journal of the American Dietetic Association,* 1951, *27,* 1046.

DRISCOLL, S. G. Why are twins dissimilar? *Pediatrics*, 1964, *33*, 325–326.

EBBS, J. H., BROWN, A., TISDALL, F. F., MOYLE, W. J., & BELL, M. The influence of improved prenatal nutrition upon the infant. *Canadian Medical Association Journal*, 1942, *46*, 6–8.

GOPALAN, C. Malnutrition in childhood in the tropics. *British Medical Journal*, 1967, *4*, 603–607.

HARRELL, R. F., WOODYARD, E., & GATES, A. I. *The effects of mothers' diets on the intelligence of offspring*. New York: Teachers College, 1955.

JEANS, P. C., SMITH, M. B., & STEARNS, G. Incidence of prematurity in relation to maternal nutrition. *Journal of the American Dietetic Association*, 1955, *31*, 576–581.

JELLIFFE, D. B. *Child nutrition in developing countries*. Washington, D. C.: United States Government Printing Office, 1968.

KIRKWOOD, W. Aspects of fetal environment. In H. Wolff (Ed.), *Mechanisms of congenital malformation*. New York: Association for the Aid of Crippled Children, 1955.

KLIPSTEIN, F. A. Nutritional anemia among America's poor. *Annals of Internal Medicine*, 1968, *68*, 1125–1127.

KNOBLOCH, H., RIDER, R., HARPER, P., & PASAMANICK, B. Neuropsychiatric sequelae of prematurity: A longitudinal study. *Journal of the American Medical Association*, 1956, *161*, 581–585.

KOTCH, J. Protein-calorie malnutrition and mental retardation. *Social Science and Medicine*, 1970, *4*, 629–644.

KOTZ, N. *Let them eat promises: The politics of hunger in America*. New York: Doubleday & Co., 1969.

KUGELMASS, J. N., POULL, L. E., & SAMUEL, E. L. Nutritional improvement of child mentality. *American Journal of Medical Sciences*, 1944, *208*, 631–633.

LAPORTE, M. The effect of war imposed dietary limitations on growth of Paris school children. *American Journal of Disease in Children*, 1946, *71*, 244.

LEVITSKY, D. A., & BARNES, R. H. Nutritional and environmental interactions in the behavioral development of the rat: Long-term effects. *Science*, 1972, *176*, 68–71.

MASLAND, R. L. The prevention of mental subnormality. In R. L. Masland, S. B. Sarason, & T. Gladwin, *Mental subnormality*. New York: Basic Books, 1958.

MASSACHUSETTS WELFARE RIGHTS ORGANIZATION. Five lies about welfare. Cambridge, Mass.: Author, 1969.

MCCANCE, R. A., WIDDOWSON, E. M., & VERDON-ROE, C. M. A study of English diets by the individual method: III. Pregnant women at different economic levels. *Journal of Hygiene*, 1938, *38*, 596.

MCGANITY, W. J., BRIDGFORTH, E. B., & DARBY, W. J. Effect of reproductive cycle on nutritional status and requirements. *Journal of the American Medical Association*, 1958, *168*, 2138–2145.

MONTAGU, M. F. A. *Prenatal influences*. Springfield, Ill.: Charles C Thomas, 1962.

NAEYE, R. L., DIENER, M. M., & DELLINGER, W. S. Urban poverty: Effects on prenatal nutrition. *Science*, 1969, *166*, 1206.

NELSON, B. Hunger and malnutrition: HEW says nation must know more and do more. *Science*, 1968, *160*, 1433–1436.

PALMER, C. E. Height and weight of children of the depression poor. *Public Health Reports*, 1935, *59*, 33.

PAREKH, U. C., PHERWANI, A., UDANI, P. M., & MUKHERJEE, S. Brain weight and head circumference in fetus, infant and children of different nutritional and socio-economic groups. *Indian Pediatrics*, 1970, 7, 347–358.

PASAMANICK, B., & LILIENFELD, A. Association of maternal and fetal factors with the development of mental deficiency: I. Abnormalities in the prenatal and paranatal periods. *Journal of the American Medical Association,* 1955, *159,* 155–160.

PLATT, B. S., HEARD, R. C., & STEWART, R. J. Experimental protein-calorie deficiency. In H. N. Munro & J. B. Allison (Eds.), *Mammalian protein metabolism.* New York: Academic Press, 1964.

POLLITT, E., & GRANOFF, D. Mental and motor development of Peruvian children treated for severe malnutrition. *Revista Interamericana de Psicologia,* 1967, *1,* 93–102. (*Psychological Abstracts,* 1967, *41,* No. 1169)

ROBINSON, H. B., & ROBINSON, N. M. *The mentally retarded child.* New York: McGraw-Hill, 1965.

ROSSO, P., HORMAZÁBEL, J., & WINICK, M. Changes in brain weight, cholesterol, phospholipid, and DNA content in marasmic children. *American Journal of Clinical Nutrition,* 1970, *23,* 1275–1279.

SCHAFFER, A. E. The national nutrition survey. *Annals of Internal Medicine,* 1968, *68,* 1130–1131.

SCRIMSHAW, N. W., & GORDON, J. E. (Eds.) *Malnutrition, learning and behavior.* Cambridge, Mass.: M.I.T. Press, 1968.

STOCH, M. B., & SMYTHE, P. M. The effect of undernutrition during infancy on subsequent brain growth and intellectual development. *South African Medical Journal,* 1967, *41,* 1027.

STRAUSS, M. B. Anemia of infancy from maternal iron deficiency in pregnancy. *Journal of Clinical Investigation,* 1953, *12,* 345–353.

THOMSON, A. M. Maternal stature and reproductive efficiency. *Eugenics Review,* 1959, *51,* 157–162.

———. Historical perspectives of nutrition, reproduction, and growth. In N. W. Scrimshaw & J. E. Gordon (Eds.), *Malnutrition, learning and behavior.* Cambridge, Mass.: M. I. T. Press, 1968.

TOVERUD, K. U., STEARNS, G., & MACY, I. G. *Maternal nutrition and child health: An interpretive review.* (Bulletin No. 123) Washington, D. C.: National Research Council, 1950.

VAN MARTHENS, E., & ZAMENHOF, S. Deoxyribonucleic acid of neonatal rat cerebrum increased by operative restriction of litter size. *Experimental Neurology,* 1969, *23,* 214–219.

WALKER, J. Aspects of fetal environment. In H. Wolff (Ed.), *Mechanisms of congenital malformation.* New York: Association for the Aid of Crippled Children, 1955.

WILLERMAN, L., & CHURCHILL, J. A. Intelligence and birth weight in identical twins. *Child Development,* 1967, *38,* 623–629.

WINICK, M. Nutrition and cell growth. *Nutrition Reviews,* 1968, *26,* 195–197.

———. Nutrition and mental development. *Medical Clinics of North America,* 1970, *54,* 1413–1428. (a)

———. Nutrition and nerve cell growth. *Federation Proceedings,* 1970, *29,* 1510–1515. (b)

WINICK, M., & NOBLE, A. Cellular response in rats during malnutrition at various ages. *Journal of Nutrition,* 1966, *89,* 300–306.

WINICK, M., ROSSO, P., & WATERLOW, J. Cellular growth of cerebrum, cerebellum, and brain stem in normal and marasmic children. *Experimental Neurology,* 1970, *26,* 393–400.

ZAMENHOF, S., VAN MARTHENS, E., & GRAUEL, L. DNA (cell number) in neonatal brain: Second generation (F_2) alteration by maternal (F_0) dietary protein restriction. *Science,* 1971, *172,* 850–851.

11. EFFECTS OF MOTHER-INFANT SEPARATION ON MATERNAL ATTACHMENT BEHAVIOR

A. D. LEIFER, P. H. LEIDERMAN, C. R. BARNETT, and J. A. WILLIAMS

Attachment behaviors recorded in time-sampled observations of 3 groups of mothers were compared prior to, and 1 and 4 weeks after, infants' hospital discharge. There were no differences between 2 groups separated by their premature infants' 3–12 week hospitalization, although 1 group aperiodically had nearly full sensory contact with their infants and the other only visual contact. Mothers of full-term infants, who experienced periodic full contact during 2–3 days hospitalization, smiled at them and held them close to their bodies more than mothers of prematures. The 3 groups differed in the incidence of divorce and mother's relinquishment of infant's custody. Mechanisms involved in establishing maternal attachment are considered.

Because of concern for the physical and social development of human infants, much effort has been devoted to studying the effects of variations in maternal caretaking on infant and child development. However, the variables that promote maternal caretaking of and attraction to a human infant or child have not been elucidated. Such variables have been explored among numerous animal species, including monkeys, goats, sheep, rats, hamsters, mice, and chickens. The results of these studies will be briefly reviewed here.

A short separation of mother and infant in the neonatal period has been found to impair permanently, or even eliminate, maternal caretaking upon reunion of mother and offspring among rats (Rosenblatt, 1965) and among goats and sheep (Hersher, Moore, & Richmond, 1958; Hersher, Richmond, & Moore, 1963; Moore, 1968).

There is also evidence that a reduction in the sensory modes of contact available between an animal mother and infant will impair maternal behavior. Maier (1963) reported that visual and auditory cues from chicks were not sufficient to elicit maternal behavior nor to maintain it once established, nor was physical presence sufficient if the contact part of the hen's ventral surface had been anesthetized. Citing the lack of ventral contact and cradling of infants by inadequate monkey mothers (Seay, Alexander, & Harlow, 1964), Harlow and his colleagues (Harlow & Harlow, 1965; Harlow, Harlow, & Hansen, 1963) have suggested that contact clinging in monkeys is the primary variable that binds the mother to her infant and the infant to his mother.

A young animal infant is also likely to elicit more maternal caretaking than an older infant. Maternal behavior decreases significantly among naïve females as the age of test pups increases for mice (Noirot, 1964), hamsters (Noirot & Richards, 1966; Richards, 1966a), and rats (Rosenblatt, 1965). Five to 6 days of continuous exposure to newborn pups results in maternal behavior in 75%–100% of test populations of naïve female or male rats (Rosenblatt, 1967, 1969). Field studies report that an infant primate is very attractive to the female members of a group (DeVore, 1963; Jay, 1965).

Although the exact mechanisms have not been worked out, there is clear evidence that hormonal changes that occur both before and after parturition predispose the female to care for newborn infants. In the hamster, maternal behavior toward test pups increases from virgin to pregnant to lactating females (Richards, 1966b). In the rat, the length of time required for newborn test pups to elicit maternal behavior is shorter for a pregnant female than a nonpregnant female, with the latency decreasing the closer the pregnant rat is to parturition (Rosenblatt, 1969). Termination of pregnancy by hysterectomy or Cesarean further decreases the latency, with the effect greater the closer to parturition the surgery occurs (Rosenblatt, 1969). Injection of blood plasma taken from females who have recently given birth decreases the latency of maternal behavior to test pups among naïve females (Rosenblatt, 1969). Finally, Cross and Harlow (1963) reported that after parturition there was a sharp increase in females' preferences for looking at an infant monkey.

All of this work with infrahuman mammals and other animals suggests that a temporary separation of a human mother from her infant in the immediate postpartum period might deleteriously affect her subsequent maternal behavior. The work reported here sought to examine this hypothesis with respect to patterns of maternal caretaking and attachment behavior. This paper will present the results for maternal attachment behavior, which we have defined as the degree to which a mother is attentive to and maintains physical contact with her infant. A theoretical formulation of separation among humans and a detailed description of the experimental manipulations imposed upon a hospital nursery in order to carry out this study have been presented elsewhere (Barnett, Leiderman, Grobstein, & Klaus, 1970). An abbreviated description of the experimental manipulations will be presented here.

Method

Experimental Manipulation

Mothers and infants who constitute the "separated" group experienced the standard hospital procedure for care of a premature infant. Chronologically, these procedures involved: (1) separation of mother and infant at birth; (2) placement of infant in an incubator in an intensive care nursery, allowing the parents only visual contact with the infant (3–12 weeks duration); (3) placement of infant, at a weight of 2,100 grams, in a bassinet in a discharge nursery, allowing the parents all modes of contact as often as they chose to enter the nursery and attend to the infant (7–10 days duration); (4) discharge of infant, at a weight of 2,500 grams, to his parents' care at home.

Conditions for the "contact" group were identical, except for (2). Mothers in the contact group were allowed to enter the intensive care nursery, beginning 2–3 days after the birth of their infants, to handle them in the incubator and, when possible, participate in normal caretaking procedures.

Assignment of Ss [Subjects] to the separation and contact conditions was random, and Ss remained unaware of the existence of the other group. Except for the different mother-infant contact possible while the infant was in an incubator, the premature nursery routine, staff, and general environment were similar for both groups of mothers and infants. While separated infants resided in the intensive care nursery, they were given additional handling several times a week by nurses to avoid possible differences in the two groups due to differential amounts of early stimulation of the infants.

A comparison group of full-term mothers was also studied. These women all delivered without complications, bottle-fed their infants, experienced full sensory contact only during four or five feedings per day of the infant while in the hospital, and were discharged to their home within 3 days after parturition. An attempt was made to match the full-term mothers and infants to the prematures with respect to parity of the mother, sex of the infant, and social class.

All three groups of mothers were separated from their infants at parturition and continued to experience some separation until the infants were discharged from the hospital. However, the groups differed in the sensory modes of contact initially available to them, the length of time some sensory deprivation persisted, and the age and maturity of the infant and the physiological and hormonal status of the mother upon restoration of full contact. In animals, longer separation, fewer sensory modes of contact during separation, a more mature infant, and a mother less influenced by hormonal conditions during and immediately following pregnancy are predictive of less adequate maternal caretaking and attachment upon reunion of mother and infant.

Subjects

Twenty-two separated, 22 contact, and 24 full-term mother-infant dyads were observed. Multiparous and primiparous mothers of male and female infants were included in each of the three groups, although they are not quite equally distributed among them, as is apparent in Table 3.4. Infants in all three groups came from intact families who lived within a 20-mile radius of the Stanford University Hospital. At birth for full-terms and within 72 hours of birth for prematures, infants were judged free of abnormalities and illnesses. Infants were the result of a single birth, and no mother had had a previous premature infant. Premature infants weighed between 2 and 4 pounds at birth.

The characteristics of the separated and contact mothers are substantially different from the normative picture of a mother of a premature infant in the United States (e.g., Rider, Taback, & Knobloch, 1955),

Table 3.4. Number of subjects in the separated, contact, and full-term groups by parity of mother and sex of infant

	Subjects Available at Each Observation Point											
	Obs. 1			*Obs. 2*			*Obs. 3*			*Total Sample*		
	F	*M*	*Total*	*F*	*M*	*Total*	*F*	*M*	*Total*	*F*	*M*	*Total*
Separated:												
Primipara	4	7	11	4	7	11	4	8	12	4	8	12
Multipara	6	4	10	5	4	9	6	2	8	6	4	10
Total	10	11	21	9	11	20	10	10	20	10	12	22
Contact:												
Primipara	3	10	13	3	8	11	2	10	12	3	10	13
Multipara	2	7	9	1	7	8	2	6	8	2	7	9
Total	5	17	22	4	15	19	4	16	20	5	17	22
Full-term:												
Primipara	4	8	12	4	8	12	4	8	12	4	8	12
Multipara	6	6	12	6	6	12	6	6	12	6	6	12
Total	10	14	24	10	14	24	10	14	24	10	14	24

and considerably more like those of an average middle-class mother (e.g., for parents of prematures in this study median education is completion of high school for mothers and some college education for fathers, median social class by Hollingshead's index is III, median age of both mothers and fathers is 25–29 years, and 80% of the mothers are white). This is due to the population of the area surrounding the hospital and to our requirement that the family of the infant be intact, rather than to our selecting Ss by these social criteria.

Procedure

Each mother-infant dyad was observed six times over a period of nearly 2 years while the mother engaged in normal caretaking activities such as feeding, bathing, and diapering her infant (for a complete description, see Leifer, 1971). The time, place, activities, and persons present for the first three observations, for which data will be presented, are outlined in Table 3.5. The second and third observations were the same for all three groups, but the activities of the mothers of full-terms were curtailed in contrast to those of the mothers of prematures at the first observation.

Mother and infant behaviors were recorded using a point-sampling technique, with behavior observed for about 5 seconds at the beginning of each 15-second interval and recorded during the rest of that interval. A checklist was devised for frequently occurring, important behaviors, while those occurring less frequently were written down in abbreviated form. All recorded behaviors and behavior units were selected prior to the study, with emphasis upon relevant, easily observed behaviors. The technique is similar to ones devised by Hansen (1966) and by Jensen and his colleagues (Jensen & Bobbitt, 1965) for observations of monkeys, and to Moss's (1967) modification of Hansen's techniques for use with human Ss. Observations were carried out by two female *Es* [Experimenters], one of whom was naïve as to the hypotheses and experimental manipulation of the study.

Data Reduction

Each observation interval was coded as to the behavior unit occurring, persons within the environment, and the presence of specified maternal and infant behaviors. The total number of intervals each behavior unit and behavior occurred was then calculated as was the average number of consecutive intervals for each behavior unit. Most of the individual behaviors

Table 3.5. Observation plan

Observation	*Time*	*Place*	*Persons Present*	*Activities*
1:				
P	Mother's fifth visit to discharge nursery	Discharge nursery	Mother, infant, nurses, doctors, observer	Feed, diaper, change clothes, bathe
F	Mother's fifth feeding of infant	Maternity ward	Mother, infant, nurses, doctors, observer	Feed
2:				
P and F	1 week after discharge	Home	Mother, infant, siblings, observer	Feed, diaper, change clothes, bathe
3:				
P and F	1 month after discharge	Pediatrics clinic	Mother, infant, observer behind one-way mirror	10 minutes of idle time with infant, feed

Note.—P=premature infants and their mothers, F=full-term infants and their mothers.

were converted to percentage scores using either the total number of observation intervals, the number of intervals coded as some specific behavior unit (e.g., feeding, bathing), or the number of intervals some other behavior occurred (e.g., infant silent or crying, bottle in infant's mouth).

Two separate interobserver reliability estimates were made upon the data in this form. One included 19 Ss observed jointly by the first author and a naïve observer in the pediatrics clinic at 1 and 6 months postdischarge, and the other included 16 Ss observed jointly by the first author and a second naïve observer in the discharge nursery prior to discharge to the home and in the pediatrics clinic at 1 and 6 months postdischarge. Of the 114 measures considered, 19 in the first study and 20 in the second were either not observed, showed no range, or scored yes-no. Of the reliability coefficients for the remaining 95 measures in the first study, 47% were greater than .90, 68% greater than .70, and their median was .89. The comparable figures for the reliability coefficients for the 94 measures in the second study are 42%, 68%, and .84. Measures with both reliability coefficients less than .70 were excluded from further analyses.

An attempt was made to combine behaviors into single summary scores representative of such concepts as maternal caretaking skill, maternal attachment behavior, and infant activity. However, behaviors thought to represent any one such concept did not correlate well at any observation (median correlations were very near zero in all instances), and factor analysis of all behaviors did not load the same behaviors on the same factors at any two observations, nor did it load together on one factor behaviors that were easily interpreted as unidimensional. Therefore, all behaviors were analyzed separately.

Analysis of the data was complex. Repeated measures ANOVA using the three factors of primary interest (condition, parity, and time) was not feasible due to the fact that many Ss were not observed at all three scheduled observations, as may be seen in Table 3.4. Instead 3 × 2 ANOVAs (condition by parity) were performed separately for each of the three observations, using all Ss observed at that time. Two such analyses were carried out for observation 1: (1) all observed activities for separated and contact Ss, and (2) all observed activities except those associated with bathing, dressing, undressing, diapering, and putting to bed for separated, contact, and full-term Ss. A subsidiary set of analyses combined all available Ss for all three observations in regression analyses in which the independent variables were condition, parity, sex, time (observation day), and individual mothers (accounting for the repeated measurement of the same Ss and individual differences). In these analyses, observation 1 scores for full-term Ss, and the adjusted observation 1 scores for separated and contact Ss were included rather than the full observation 1 scores for the two groups of premature Ss. Arcsine transformation of the data produced little difference in the significance of the results, hence only raw data and the analyses of them will be reported here.

Results

The data were first examined to see that the three groups were observed at comparable points in time relative to the mothers' experiences caring for their infants. Two-way ANOVAs (condition by parity) of the number of times a mother had fed her infant when the first observation occurred and the number of days postdischarge the second and third observations occurred revealed no significant main or interaction effects. All three groups were observed on the average at the mother's fourth feeding of her infant either in the discharge nursery or the maternity ward (3–4 days prior to discharge for premature infants and 1 day for full-term infants), and at 7 and 31–34 days after the infant's hospital discharge.

The mean duration of the three observations combined was somewhat greater for the separated group than for the other two groups, with the separated group observed for an average of 169 intervals and the other two for 149 each, $F(2,57) = 4.8$, $p < .05$, in regression analysis. This is a total difference of about 5 minutes observation time. However, analysis of each observation separately revealed no significant difference among the three groups in the duration of any one observation. Hence, any differences in observed attachment behavior should probably not be attributed to differences in the length of the observation.

Three categories of overt maternal attachment behavior were examined: that involving close bodily contact between mother and infant, that involving more distal contact, and the amount of time devoted solely to interaction with the infant, excluding caretaking interaction.

There were three maternal attachment behaviors that involved proximal contact: holding the infant, affectionate touching of the infant (patting, rubbing, kissing, etc.), and ventral contact with the infant when holding him. The mean percentage of the total intervals each group devoted to holding and touching the infant and the mean percentage of all holding intervals that involved ventral contact are presented in Figure 3.6. Two-way ANOVAs of the holding measure at each observation revealed a significant difference only at the second observation, during which contact mothers held their infants 73.6% of the time, separated mothers 69.9% of the time, and full-term mothers 64.0% of the time, $F(2,57) = 3.46$, $p < .05$.

At this observation, there was also a nearly significant interaction between condition and parity with primiparous mothers holding their infants less than multiparous mothers in the separated and full-term groups and more in the contact group, $F(2,57) = 3.32$, $p < .10$. The t tests between the separated and contact groups at each observation revealed no significant differences between them.

Similar ANOVAs of the affectionate touching measure revealed only one significant effect for condition, with full-term mothers caressing their infants 18.9% of the time at the first observation, separated mothers 12.1% of the time, and contact mothers 11.7% of the time, $F(2,61) = 3.24$, $p < .05$. There were no significant effects of condition at the other two observations nor at the first observation when only the data for the two groups of premature infants were analyzed, nor was there any significant interaction between condition and parity. There were no significant differences, by t test, between the separated and contact groups at any of the three observations.

The most consistent and striking finding is the group differences in the amount of ventral contact the mothers maintained between themselves and their infants. At all three observations the effect is strong. At the first observation full-term mothers hold their infants close to the ventral surface of their body 77.2% of the time, contact 59.4%, and separated 55.2%, $F(2.61) = 5.20$, $p. < .01$; at the second the percentages are 70.3%, 48.8%, and 41.0%, respectively, $F(2,57) = 10.44$, $p < .01$; and at the third they are 71.8%, 52.2%, and 51.6%, $F(2,58) = 4.60$, $p < .05$. There was no interaction with parity in any of these three ANOVAs. Analysis of the data for all observation 1 activities of the separated and contact mothers revealed a significant interaction between condition and parity with contact multiparas holding their infants close to their bodies 68.3% of the time, separated primiparas 56.0%, contact primiparas 49.7% and separated multiparas 43.4%, $F(1,39) = 4.86$, $p < .05$. Separated and contact mothers did not differ, by t test, at any of the three observations.

Regression analyses of these three measures for all Ss at all three observations revealed no significant effect of condition

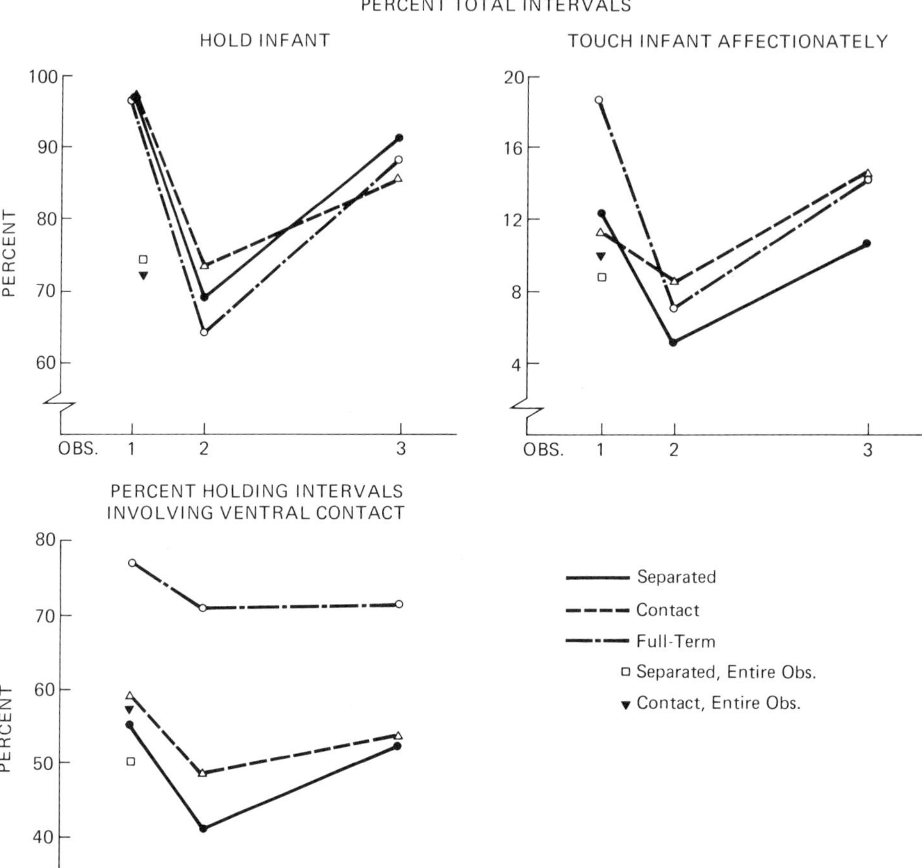

Figure 3.6. Attachment behaviors involving proximal contact by condition and observation.

on how much the infant was held. Condition was a significant predictor of the amount of affectionate touching that occurred with full-term mothers on the average caressing their infants 13.6% of the time, contact mothers 11.6%, and separated mothers 9.2%, $F(1,188) = 5.6$, $p < .05$. Condition also predicted the amount of ventral contact between mother and infant, with full-term mothers on the average maintaining ventral contact 73.1% of the time they held their infant, contact mothers 53.7%, and separated mothers 49.4%, $F(1,188) = 27.6$, $p < .01$.

There were four maternal attachment behaviors that involved distal contact: looking at the infant, smiling at him, talking to him, and laughing at or singing to him. The mean percentage of the total intervals devoted to these activities is presented in Figure 3.7. Two-way ANOVAs of the data for looking, talking, and laughing-singing revealed no significant effect of condition nor any significant interaction between condition and parity at any of the three observations. For the smiling measures, there was a significant effect for condition at each of the three

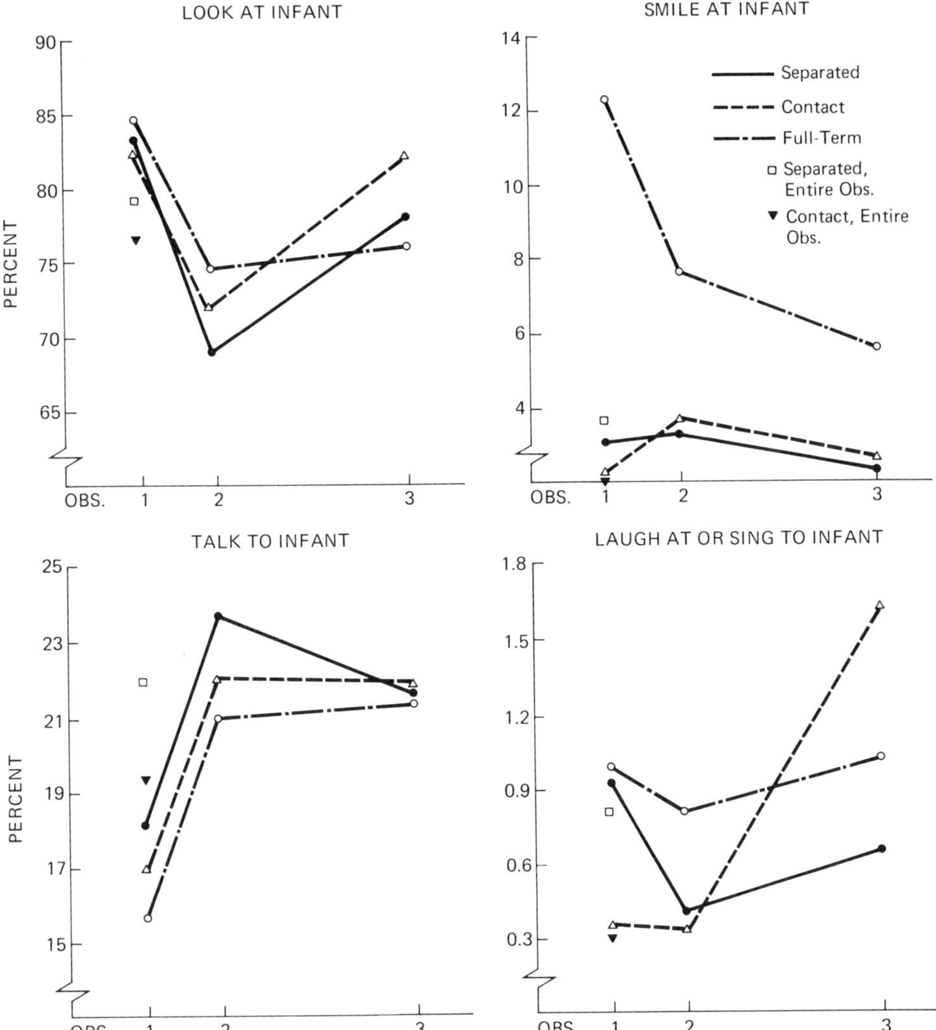

Figure 3.7. Attachment behaviors involving distal contact by condition and observation.

observations. At the first observation, full-term mothers smiled at their infants 12.3% of the time, separated mothers 3.0% of the time, and contact mothers 2.2% of the time, $F(2,61) = 9.92$, $p<.01$. These percentages are not due to the fact that most separated and contact mothers wore masks during the first observation, while only one full-term mother wore a mask, since similar percentages occur at the second and third observations when no one wore a mask. At the second observation, the full-term mothers smiled 7.7% of the time, contact 3.5%, and separated 3.2%, $F(2,57) = 5.56$ $p < .01$; and at the third, the percentages are 5.8%, 2.6%, and 2.5%, respectively, $F(2,58) = 5.05$, $p < .01$. The t tests of these four measures for the separated and contact groups revealed only one significant difference: separated mothers laughed at or sang to their infants more than contact mothers did in the adjusted data for the first observation, $t(41) = 3.24$, $p < .01$. However, this result should not be emphasized since ANOVA of laughing-singing for the entire first observation of these two groups of Ss revealed no significant difference between them.

When the data for all Ss were combined over the three observations and subjected to regression analyses, there was again no significant effect of condition on looking, talking, and laughing-singing. There was, however, a significant effect for smiling, with full-term mothers smiling 8.6% of the time, separated mothers smiling 2.9%, and contact mothers smiling 2.7%, $F(1,188) = 13.0$, $p < .01$.

The three groups did not differ in the third type of attachment behavior assessed in this study. There was no significant difference in the number of intervals devoted solely to interaction with the infant or in the percentage of the total number of observation intervals devoted to such interaction in either the two-way ANOVAs at each observation or in the aggression analyses combining all Ss at all three observations.

The results thus far have indicated that condition has minimal effect upon the amount of time spent with an infant, the amount of time devoted solely to noncaretaking interaction with him, or specific attachment behaviors, other than smiling, involving distal contact. It has a greater effect upon specific attachment behaviors involving proximal contact, the usual mode of contact among primates with newly born infants. These results showed little change over the three observations; what change there was (i.e., total number of intervals, number of interaction intervals) could be attributed to differences in the observational environment and tasks rather than to maturation of the infant or changes in the mother-infant interaction pattern.

There are other differences between the groups that are not reflected in the observational data presented here and are probably outcomes of their separation experience. For instance, within the sample of 26 separated and 23 contact mothers of prematures who participated in any phase of the study, two relinquished custody of their infants sometime after hospital discharge. Both of these mothers were in the separated group. Also, there have been six instances of divorce among the parents in this study, five of them in the separated group. Divorce, serious emotional disturbance, and poor adjustment have been reported to be unusually common in families stressed by a child's fatal illness (Binger, Ablin, Feuerstein, Kushner, Zoger, & Mikkelsen, 1969; Hamovitch, 1964). Finally, there were four mothers of premature infants who attempted to breast-feed their infants. Two of these mothers were in the contact group and two in the separated group; one mother in each group was a primipara and the other a multipara who had successfully breast-fed at least one previous child. The only mother to succeed was the multiparous contact mother.

Discussion

The work just reported sought to assess the effects of mother-infant separation on maternal behavior. One evaluation of these effects would come from a comparison of the maternal behavior of the separated and contact mothers. These mothers all had prematurely born infants who were required to reside within an incubator in the same hospital setting for at least 3 weeks. The mothers were randomly selected for each group and were not demonstrably different when their infants entered the intensive care unit. However, our manipulation, while difficult to carry out, resulted in only minimal differences in the amount of separation these two groups of mothers experienced. Even the contact mothers could only handle their infants through the portholes of the incubator, preventing most close bodily contact between mother and infant. Moreover, the frequency of such visits by the contact mothers was relatively low due, undoubtedly, to such factors as distance, home responsibilities, strength of the mother, and distaste for the hospital atmosphere within which the infant resided. Indeed, rough estimates of visiting patterns indicate that contact mothers entered the intensive care nursery only about once every 6 days to handle and/or feed their infants.

The lack of observed behavioral differences between the separated and contact mothers must be evaluated in light of these considerations and other available data on the two groups. We did not find differences in the observed attachment behavior of the separated and contact mothers during the first month of full contact. Yet there were some notable differences in other behavior of the two groups of mothers. Two separated mothers chose to relinquish custody of their infants, and five of the marriages in this group ended in divorce. These actions represent severe disturbance of normal maternal and marital behavior, and, with the exception of one divorce, they do not occur among the families in the contact group. The existence of these cases, while few in number, suggests that early separation of mother and infant may seriously disrupt normal behavior. Moreover, other data collected in the course of the full project indicate that mothers in the separated group, especially primiparas, are not as confident of their caretaking ability as are contact mothers until the infant has been home for more than 1 month (Seashore, Leifer, Barnett, & Leiderman, in press). Examination of other areas of maternal and infant behavior and sequelae occurring more than 1 month after assumption of full-time responsibility may clarify the areas in which, and times at which, early separation of mother and infant influences maternal behavior among these two groups of mothers of prematures.

In contrast to the mothers of premature infants, mothers of full-terms experienced very little separation from their infants. Thus, it is interesting to note that mothers of full-terms smile at their infants much more often and hold them close to their bodies much more frequently than do mothers of prematures, while the two groups of mothers of prematures differ little on these measures. No mother of a full-term relinquished custody of her infant, nor did one institute divorce proceedings. The mothers of full-terms and of prematures do not differ in attachment behaviors involving the amount of time spent with the infant, the amount of noncaretaking interaction with him, or attending to him without close bodily contact. Such an effect in the last area may become visible when the infant has become more independent and such modes of contact are more appropriate.

These differences in the attachment behavior of mothers of full-terms and of prematures may be due to the amount of separation from their infants they have experienced; yet, the reported results may be due to some factor other than separation or to some combination of factors including separation since there are at least seven ways in which the experiences of these mothers differ. For five of these factors the experience of the separated and contact mothers is the same and different from that of the full-term mothers, while for the remaining two factors the experience of each of the groups is different from that of the other two. Examination of all seven factors may clarify the possible role of each in facilitating maternal attachment behavior.

Separation of a mother and her premature infant lasts considerably longer than separation of a mother and her full-term infant. For the mothers studied here it is 3–12 weeks versus 2–3 days. Separations as short as ½ hour immediately after birth have been found to influence adversely the maternal behavior of goats and sheep, yet it takes 4 days of separation beginning immediately after birth to eliminate all maternal responses of rats to newborn pups. Thus, it is certain that the mothers of prematures experienced severe separation in comparison to the mothers of full-terms, while it is also conceivable that all mothers in our study experienced some separation that might be detrimental to adequate maternal behavior.

When mothers of full-terms and prematures did assume full responsibility for their infants, they differed in their hormonal and physiological status and in the characteristics of their infants. Mothers of prematures were 3–12 weeks postpartum, and all but four of them were not lactating. Thus, the hormonal factors, apparently operant in infrahuman mammals during the immediate postpartum period, that predispose females to care for infants should not be present when mothers finally assume caretaking responsibility, but they should be present in mothers of full-terms. Moreover, full-term infants are all neonates when their mothers assume full caretaking responsibility, while premature infants are at least 3 weeks old, show bodily evidence of various hospital tests and procedures, and yet are quite immature. Since work with animals indicates that newborn infants elicit more maternal behavior than older infants, perhaps the different ages of the premature and full-term infants influenced maternal behavior, although the immaturity of the premature infant complicates such an assumption.

Mothers of prematures and full-terms also differ in the mothers' status at birth and their cognitive and affective experiences during separation. Mothers of prematures give birth 1–3 months early. More than half of them had some indication the birth would be premature, but more than half also stated they did not believe the baby would actually arrive early. It is also conceivable that they are not as physiologically ready to care for an infant as they would be if they carried the infant to term. This is suggested by the finding that early surgical termination of pregnancy in rats results in increases in maternal behavior to newborn pups, with the effect greater the closer to term the surgery is performed. Whatever the hormonal status of mothers of full-terms and prematures at the infants' births, the cognitive expectations of the two groups of mothers differ considerably after the birth. Many mothers of prematures, even in this study where infants were nearly certain to survive and were without obvious defects, expect their infants to die or perhaps be permanently damaged by their early birth. These feelings may be reinforced by the medical setting within which the infant resides and the intensive care he receives. This setting and care may also communicate to the mother that she is incompetent to care for her own infant. Such experiences did not occur for the mothers of full-terms in this study.

These then are the five areas in which the experiences of the full-term and premature mothers differed. There are two additional areas in which the experience of each group differed from that of the other two. These are the time after birth at which the first contact between mother and infant occurred and the types of contact available during separation. All mothers of full-term infants were wheeled from the delivery room holding their infants, while only some of the mothers of prematures even touched their infants after delivery. The infants were then removed to a regular or intensive care nursery. Full-term mothers next handled their infants within 12–24 hours, contact mothers within 3–7 days, and separated mothers within 3–12 weeks. While infants resided in the hospital, full-term mothers experienced visual, auditory, olfactory, and tactile, including ventral, contact 4–6 times a day, contact mothers experienced all the same kinds of contact—except ventral—at least once a week, and separated mothers experienced only visual, and perhaps some auditory, contact at least once a week.

This review of the separation experiences and physiological statuses of the full-term, contact, and separated mothers and the group differences in subsequent maternal attachment behavior suggests something of the factors involved in the elicitation and maintenance or maternal attachment behavior. It is suggested that the hormonal condition of the mother at the time of first contacting her infant and/or the time of assumption of full caretaking responsibility influences the quality of maternal attachment, with mothers most ready to accept their infants soon after they have given birth. Periodic contact with an infant through all sensory modalities during a period of separation apparently also facilitates maternal attachment. Ethologically speaking, such contact would present an infant as a usual eliciting stimulus for maternal behavior, while more limited modes of contact would not. Cognitive expectations and evaluations undoubtedly influence human maternal behavior and are operative in the mothers reported here. Their role should diminish with time as premature and full-term infants become more similar in their developmental status. Moreover, as all mothers return to normal nonpregnant status and, at the same time, all experience the pleasures associated with infant care, differences between full-term, contact, and separated mothers should diminish and disappear.

This project hoped to specify the role of early, mother-infant separation in determining later maternal behavior. Clinically, the results suggest that such a separation should be avoided whenever possible and should be minimized when separation is unavoidable. Theoretically, the results neither isolate nor specify the role of any one variable in determining subsequent maternal behavior. Rather they suggest that maternal behavior is the result of a confluence of factors and that these factors are not all equally influential at any one point in time or over time. Specification of the role of any one variable has proceeded with animals; it is to be hoped that more similar work with humans will be forthcoming.

References

BARNETT, C. R.; LEIDERMAN, P. H.; GROBSTEIN, R.; & KLAUS, M. Neonatal separation: the maternal side of interactional deprivation. *Pediatrics,* 1970, *54,* 197–205.

BINGER, C. M.; ABLIN, A. R.; FEUERSTEIN, R. C.; KUSHNER, J. H.; ZOGER, S.; & MIKKELSEN, C. Childhood leukemia: emotional impact on patient and family. *New England Journal of Medicine,* 1969, *280,* 414–418.

CROSS, H. A., & HARLOW, H. F. Observation of infant monkeys by female monkeys. *Perceptual Motor Skills,* 1963, *16,* 11–15.

DE VORE, I. Mother-infant relations in free-ranging baboons. In H. I. Rheingold (Ed.), *Maternal behavior in mammals.* New York: Wiley, 1963.

HAMOVITCH, M. B. *The parent and the fatally ill child.* Duarte, Calif.: City of Hope Medical Center, 1964.

HANSEN, E. W. The development of maternal and infant behavior in the rhesus monkey. *Behavior,* 1966, *27,* 107–149.

HARLOW, H. F., & HARLOW, M. K. The affectional systems. In A. M. Schrier, H. F. Harlow, & F. Stollnitz (Eds.), *Behavior of nonhuman primates.* New York: Academic Press, 1965.

HARLOW, H. F.; HARLOW, M. K.; & HANSEN, E. W. The maternal affectional system of rhesus monkeys. In H. L. Rheingold (Ed.), *Maternal behavior in mammals.* New York: Wiley, 1963.

HERSHER, L.; MOORE, A. U.; & RICHMOND, J. B. Effect of postpartum separation of mother and kid on maternal care in the domestic goat. *Science*, 1958, *128*, 1342–1343.

HERSHER, L.; RICHMOND, J. B.; & MOORE, A. U. Maternal behavior in sheep and goats. In H. L. Rheingold (Ed.), *Maternal behavior in mammals*. New York: Wiley, 1963.

JAY, P. Field studies. In A. M. Schrier, H. F. Harlow, & F. Stollnitz (Eds.), *Behavior of nonhuman primates*. New York: Academic Press, 1965.

JENSEN, G. D., & BOBBITT, R. A. On observational methodology and preliminary studies of mother-infant interaction in monkeys. In B. M. Foss (Ed.), *Determinants of infant behavior*. Vol. 3. London: Methuen, 1965.

LEIFER, A. D. *Effects of early, temporary mother-infant separation on later maternal behavior in humans*. (Doctoral dissertation, Stanford University.) Ann Arbor, Mich.: University Microfilms, 1971. No. 71–2792.

MAIER, R. A. Maternal behavior in the domestic hen: the role of physical contact. *Journal of Comparative and Physiological Psychology*, 1963, *56*, 357–361.

MOORE, A. U. Effects of modified maternal care in the sheep and goat. In G. Newton & S. Levine (Eds), *Early experience and behavior*. Springfield, Ill.: Thomas, 1968.

MOSS, H. A. Sex, age, and state as determinants of mother-infant interaction. *Merrill-Palmer Quarterly*, 1967, *13*, 19–36.

NOIROT, E. Changes in responsiveness to young in the adult mouse: the effect of external stimuli. *Journal of Comparative and Physiological Psychology*, 1964, *57*, 97–99.

NOIROT, E., & RICHARDS, M. P. M. Maternal behavior in virgin female gold hamsters: changes consequent upon initial contact with pups. *Animal Behavior*, 1966, *14*, 7–10.

RICHARDS, M. P. M. Maternal behavior in virgin female golden hamsters (*Mesocricetus auratus* Waterhouse): the role of the age of the test pups. *Animal Behavior*, 1966, *14*, 303–309. (a)

———. Maternal behavior in the golden hamster: responsiveness to young in virgin, pregnant, and lactating females. *Animal Behavior*, 1966, *14*, 310–313. (b)

RIDER, R., TABACK, M., & KNOBLOCH, H. Association between premature birth and socio-economic status. *American Journal of Public Health*, 1955, *45*, 1022–1028.

ROSENBLATT, J. S. The basis of synchrony in the behavioral interaction between the mother and her offspring in the laboratory rat. In B. M. Foss (Ed.), *Determinants of infant behaviour*. Vol. 3. London: Methuen, 1965.

———. Nonhormonal basis of maternal behavior in the rat. *Science*, 1967, *156*, 1512–1514.

———. The development of maternal responsiveness in the rat. *American Journal of Orthopsychiatry*, 1969, *39*, 36–56.

SEASHORE, M. J.; LEIFER, A. D.; BARNETT, C. R.; & LEIDERMAN, P. H. The effects of denial of early mother-infant interaction on maternal self-confidence. *Journal of Personality and Social Psychology*, in press.

SEAY, B.; ALEXANDER, B. K.; & HARLOW, H. F. Maternal behavior of socially deprived rhesus monkeys. *Journal of Abnormal and Social Psychology*, 1964, *69*, 345–354.

12. INFANT CRYING AND MATERNAL RESPONSIVENESS

SILVIA M. BELL and MARY D. SALTER AINSWORTH

This naturalistic, longitudinal study of 26 infant-mother pairs shows that consistency and promptness of maternal response is associated with decline in frequency and duration of infant crying. By the end of the first year individual differences in crying reflect the history of maternal responsiveness rather than constitutional differences in infant irritability. Close physical contact is the most frequent maternal intervention and the most effective in terminating crying. Nevertheless, maternal effectiveness in terminating crying was found to be less powerful than promptness of response in reducing crying in subsequent months. Evidence suggests that whereas crying is expressive at first, it can later be a mode of communication directed specifically toward the mother. The development of noncrying modes of communication, as well as a decline in crying, is associated with maternal responsiveness to infant signals. The findings are discussed in an evolutionary context, and with reference to the popular belief that to respond to his cries "spoils" a baby.

Like infants of many mammalian and avian species, a human infant is equipped with a number of behaviors that promote proximity to or contact with his mother figure. Such behaviors have been termed "attachment behaviors" by Ainsworth (1967) and Bowlby (1958, 1969). Attachment behaviors are of two main classes: active behaviors through which an infant himself achieves proximity or maintains contact once it has been attained, and signaling behaviors that stimulate his mother to come into closer proximity or contact with him. Unlike infants of precocial species, a human newborn lacks active proximity-promoting behaviors such as approaching and following, and he is slower than nonhuman primates to develop active clinging. He resembles newborns of many other species, however, in his ability to emit vocal signals that activate maternal behavior. His crying signals are gradually supplemented with other signals–vocalization, smiling, gesture—until by the last quarter of his first year a child can bridge the distance to his mother, not only through active approach, but also through a complex repertoire of nonverbal communications.

Crying is the most conspicuous of early attachment behaviors. Unlike smiling, which gratifies a caretaker, crying arouses displeasure or alarm and elicits interventions aimed at terminating it and discouraging its recurrence. Herein lies the power of crying to promote proximity more effectively than other early signaling behavior.

Because it is disagreeable to adults, however, crying is generally considered a changeworthy behavior. The issue of infant crying and the effect of maternal responsiveness to it has prompted pronouncements on infant care and is at the center of the controversy between "strict" versus "permissive" practices. A review of U.S. Children's Bureau *Infant Care* pamphlets shows that, in the period between 1920 and 1940, mothers were admonished not to pick up a baby between feedings, lest he learn "that crying will get him what he wants, sufficient to make a spoiled, fussy baby, and a household tyrant whose continual demands make a slave of the mother" (1924, p. 44). Although more recent advice of the bureau encourages mothers to follow their natural impulse to respond to crying, the belief that this may result in increased crying persists, supported by untested or perhaps naïve extrapolations from learning theory which assume that to respond to a cry will reinforce crying behavior. Significant though this isssue may be for infant-care practices, there has been relatively little research pertinent to it.

One set of experimental studies was based on the hypothesis that crying behavior, even though it might begin as a "respondent" behavior elicited by painful stimuli, could become an "operant" behavior, and as such could be reduced either by an extinction procedure or by this in combination with social reinforcement of other behaviors, such as smiling, that are incompatible with cyring. Williams (1959) treated temper tantrums in a 21-month-old subject at home through an extinction procedure. Hart, Allen, Buel, Harris, and Wolf (1964) treated two 4-year-olds in nursery school, and Wolf, Risley, and Mees (1964) dealt with the temper tantrums of one 3½-year-old autistic child using a combination of extinction and reinforcement procedures. These three studies demonstrated that crying in preschool children could be reduced by such experimental treatment. Etzel and Gewirtz (1967) conducted an experiment, including both reinforcement and extinction phases, on two well babies in a hospital nursery, for six 2-minute periods a day for 7 days in one case and 25 days in the other, and demonstrated that the incidence of crying could be controlled by such procedures.

The only relevant study based on observation in the home environment without experimental intervention dealt with fussing rather than crying. Moss and Robson (1968) observed 54 primiparous mothers and their infants during two 6-hour visits at 1 month, and again during one 6-hour visit at 3 months. They focused on fussing behavior because although positively correlated with crying, it was more frequent and more strongly associated with maternal behavior. They found a low negative correlation between the latency of maternal response to fussing at 1 month and the frequency of fussing at 3 months ($r = -.29$, $p < .05$).

Although these findings lend apparent support to the popular belief that maternal responsiveness to crying strengthens a baby's tendency to cry, the investigations that yielded them span too little time to throw direct light upon the developmental and interactive processes through which child and mother affect each other throughout the infancy period. Despite the fact that mothers tend on the whole to respond to a large percentage of an infant's cries, crying nevertheless decreases with age as more effective modes of communication are required. Both Gewirtz (1969) and Moss (1967) have theorized about the ways in which learning in both mother and infant could facilitate such an outcome, but past research has not yielded sufficient longitudinal data to elucidate the developmental issues implicit in the interaction between infant crying and maternal responsiveness.

As part of an investigation of the development of infant-mother attachment in the first year of life, data were collected on infant crying and maternal responsiveness to it. In the analysis of these data specific attention was devoted to: developmental changes in crying (a term used here to connote all vocal protests, from unhappy noises to fusses to full-blown cries); individual differences in both infant crying and maternal responsiveness, and the stability of these differences throughout the first year; the effect of maternal responsiveness on developmental changes in infant crying and vice versa; the nature of maternal interventions and their relative effectiveness in terminating crying; and the relationship of an infant's degree of proximity to his mother and the onset of crying.

Method

Subjects

The Ss were 26 white, middle-class, infant-mother pairs in intact families who were contacted through pediatricians in private practice, usually before the baby's birth. Sixteen of the babies were boys; 10 were girls. Six were firstborn; 20 were not.

Data-collection Procedure

Observations were undertaken during visits to the home lasting approximately 4 hours. The first 15 Ss were visited at 3-week intervals from 3 to 54 weeks. The 11 Ss were visited for 2 hours at each of 1, 2, 3, and 4 weeks, and for 4 hours at 6 weeks and every third week thereafter. Thus the usual amount of observation per S was 64 hours, or 16 for each of the 4 quarters of the first year.

Except for joint visits made by two observers and for the occasional visit by an alternate for the purposes of reliability checks, each family was visited by one regular visitor. Four visitors were required to cover the 26 cases. In order to sustain rapport over the long period encompassed by the study, observers were obliged to play a semiparticipant but noninterventive role. Insofar as this role permitted, the observer made continuous notes, having been instructed to note all infant behavior and mother-infant interaction, as well as to record the mother's spontaneous comments and responses to open-ended interview. Observers were instructed to mark off 5-minute time intervals in their records and to pay particular attention to the timing of episodes of crying as well as to all circumstances pertaining to a cry. The raw data consist of narrative reports transcribed from accounts subsequently dictated by observers from their notes.

Data-analysis Procedure

Using the typed narrative report, six coders, working in ignorance of any of our hypotheses or other findings, coded each instance of crying that occurred in a visit. Reliability of coding was forwarded by careful initial training and subsequent spot checks.

The particulars of coding relevant to this present report are as follows: the duration of the cry; the time lag between the end of one cry and the onset of the next one; the baby's location relative to his mother at the time of the onset of each crying episode; the latency of the mother's intervention to the cry, its nature, and its success in terminating the cry. Since observers in their participant roles sometimes found it impossible to time precisely, and hence resorted to estimates, it was necessary for one of the coders to check all estimates (using all the clues provided by a narrative report, and if necessary, an acted-out replication of infant-care procedures) in order to ensure that estimates had a consistent basis in all cases.

Three measures of infant crying were utilized in the analyses: frequency of crying episodes, frequency of crying clusters, and duration of crying. A crying episode refers, as stated earlier, to any instance of a vocal distress signal—whether protest, fuss, or full-blown cry. A new episode was considered to have started when there was more than a momentary pause separating two instances of crying. A crying cluster is defined as a group of crying episodes taking place less than 2 minutes apart. The frequency of crying episodes refers to the number of episodes per infant's waking hour, and frequency of clusters to the number of clusters occurring per waking hour. Duration of crying refers to the combined length of all crying episodes (excluding those too brief to be timed), expressed in minutes per waking hour. This measure reflects prolonged crying; thus it is possible for an infant to have a high score on the frequency measure but a low score on the duration measure if he produces many cries of a short duration.

In addition, for each infant was found the proportion of total cries emitted under three conditions of proximity to the mother: no proximity, in which a baby cannot see or hear his mother; proximity, in which he can see and hear her, and perhaps also touch or be touched by her; close proximity, in which a baby is in close physical contact with his mother, usually being held by her. Since the proportion of total observation time that babies spent in three conditions of proximity to the mother was unequal, most babies spending far more time away from her than either in proximity or close contact, the percentage of cries emitted under the three conditions was equalized for sampling time by expressing it as a ratio of the percentage of time babies were actually observed in each condition. For the purposes of this analysis, cries were excluded from consideration when a baby was clearly protesting a routine or a maternal intervention such as washing, changing, interruption of a feeding, and the like. Otherwise all cries were considered, regardless of their apparent cause.

The following measures of maternal behavior were obtained: the number of crying episodes that a mother ignored; the duration of maternal unresponsiveness, as measured by the length of time that a baby cried without obtaining a response from her; the types of interventions produced by the mother and the degree of effectiveness of each type; and, finally, the effectiveness of the mother in terminating crying. Maternal interventions were classified as follows: picks up, holds; vocalizes, interacts; feeds; approaches, touches; offers pacifier or toy; removes noxious stimulus; enters room; and other. A crying episode was considered to have been terminated successfully when the baby remained quiet for more than 2 minutes thereafter. Whereas the maternal unresponsiveness measure reflects the promptness with which the mother intervened, the measure of maternal effectiveness reflects the mother's perceptiveness and willingness to give the type of intervention that will serve to terminate the cry. Maternal effectiveness was measured by the mean number of interventions a mother undertook before the cry was properly terminated.

The information obtained for each 1/4 year was averaged, in order to obtain a stable measure of the behaviors characteristic of each 3-month period. The measures were subsequently converted to ranks and nonparametric statistics used in the analyses.

When comparing infant and maternal behavior in the *same* quarter there is a problem of confounding of measures. The number of episodes which a mother ignores is comprehended in the total number of infant crying episodes—that is, for a mother to ignore any number of cries, an infant must produce at least that many episodes. Because a correlation between two such measures would be spuriously high, the measure of infant crying was corrected when used for within-quarter comparisons. The correction involved excluding from the infant measure all episodes ignored by the mother (that is, all episodes which comprise the measure of maternal ignoring). Thus, the corrected infant measure can vary independently of the maternal measure, since it includes only cries produced in addition to those ignored by the mother. It is possible, for example, for the mother to obtain a score of 4 and the infant a score of 0 in the same quarter.

A similar correction was used for within-quarter comparisons of the duration of maternal unresponsiveness and the duration of infant crying, given the fact that the length of time a mother takes prior to responding to the cry is included in the total duration of crying for the same quarter. The measure was corrected by excluding from the infant's score the length of time that it took for mother to respond, for those episodes when the baby continued crying until she responded. Consequently, the measure used in this analysis is the duration of crying after maternal intervention, a measure which hypothetically can vary independently of the maternal measure.

It was decided to correct the infant measures rather than to convert the maternal measures to percentages of the infant crying measures because percentages would not reflect accurately the infant's experience. An infant who produces 100 cries in a given period and whose mother ignores 50 of these would have experienced many more actual instances of being ignored than one whose mother ignored one of his two cries; the use of a measure based on percentages, however, would have given the mothers a tied rank.

For interquarter comparisons of infant crying and maternal responsiveness no correction of the measures is necessary, since the measures are independent of each other. The maternal measure of unresponsiveness in one quarter refers to infant cries emitted in the same quarter, and not to those emitted in any other quarter.

Two other analyses to which reference is made in this report are those of infant activity level and infant communication. Each employed a three-point rating scale. Each infant was assessed in the first 6 weeks of life either as inactive, moderately active, or active and vigorous. The communication scale took into account the subtlety, clarity, and variety of facial expression, bodily gesture, and noncrying vocalization characteristic of infants in the fourth quarter of the first year.

Results

Developmental Changes in Infant Crying

Figure 3.8 shows changes in the duration of crying throughout the first year. There is an overall reduction in duration of crying from a median of 7.7 minutes per hour in the first quarter to 4.4 minutes per hour in the fourth quarter. The range is very wide in the first quarter, from 21 minutes per hour to almost no crying at all, but narrows considerably toward the end of the first year. No comparable decline was observed in frequency of crying. Episodes occur at a median frequency of four per hour throughout the first year, with a stable range of from slightly less than 2 to 10 episodes per hour. The average 1-year-old, then, is found to cry as frequently, but for briefer periods, than the tiny infant.

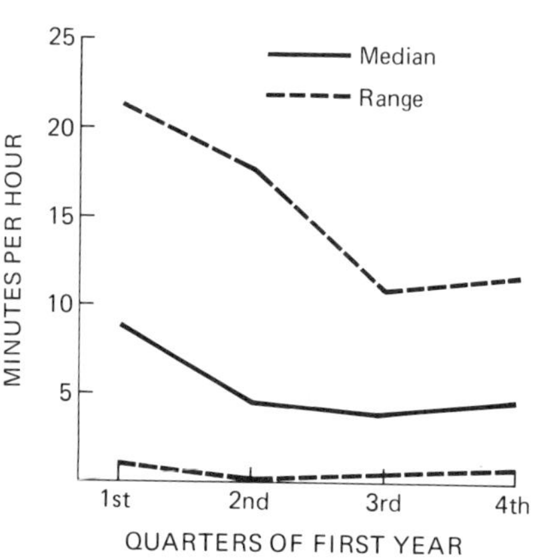

Figure 3.8. Duration of crying in minutes per hour throughout the first year of life.

Possible Constitutional Correlates

The wide ranges of the two measures reflect substantial individual differences in infant crying. Several factors were explored which might influence amount of crying, either directly or through affecting maternal behavior, namely, sex, birth order, and general activity level. No correlation between either sex or activity level and crying in the first quarter was found. There was a tendency, however, for firstborns (who in this sample happen all to be male) to cry more than later borns in the first quarter ($\rho = .41$, $p < .05$). Since no sex differences were found when birth order was disregarded, these findings suggest that firstborn boys, but not boys in general, tend to cry more in the first quarter, although not in subsequent quarters of the first year. These findings are congruent with those of Moss and Robson (1968); in their sample of firstborns, during the first 3 months boys significantly exceeded girls in frequency of fussing.

Stability of Infant Crying

In view of the range of individual differences in crying, it was of interest to examine their stability throughout the first year. Are those babies who cry most at first the same who still head the list later on? Correlations of crying frequencies among different quarters of the first year were undertaken. All correlations, except that between the third and fourth quarters ($\rho = .43$, $p < .05$), were not significant. This finding, which is similar to that reported by Bayley (1932), suggests that initial individual differences in frequency of crying do not persist to a significant extent throughout the first year, but that infants tend to stabilize in regard to frequency of crying during the second half of the year.

A similar finding was obtained when duration of crying was compared for different quarters of the first year. Only the correlation between third and fourth quarters achieved significance ($\rho = .39$, $p < .05$), suggesting that there is no significant persistence of individual differences in duration of crying, but rather a tendency to stabilize in the second half of the first year.

These findings do not support a hypothesis that constitutionally determined physiological differences give rise to individual differences in degree of irritability that are consistent throughout the first year. Rather, they suggest that it is only toward the end of the first year that babies tend to develop consistent, idiosyncratic crying characteristics.

Differences in Maternal Responsiveness

The median percentage of crying episodes ignored by the mother was 46 in the first quarter, but the range was very wide; the most-responsive mother ignored only 4% of cries, while the least-responsive mother ignored 97%. The median percentage of episodes ignored declined somewhat through the baby's first year to 37 in the fourth quarter. The range also narrowed somewhat, with the most-responsive mother ignoring 13% of cries and the least-responsive mother 63% in the fourth quarter.

The duration of maternal unresponsiveness to crying also decreased in the first year from a median of 3.83 minutes per hour in the first quarter to 2.13 minutes per hour in the fourth. The range of the measure was also wide—from 2 minutes to more than 9 minutes in the first quarter and from 1 to over 4 minutes in the fourth quarter.

Stability of Maternal Responsiveness

In contrast to infant differences, individual differences in maternal responsiveness to crying are more stable. Table 3.6 shows that mothers who fail to respond to crying episodes in the first quarter tend to ignore them in the second and third quarters as well. Those who ignore them in the third

Table 3.6. Consistency of maternal responsiveness to crying throughout first year: episodes of crying ignored by mother

Quarters of First Year	Quarters of First Year		
	Second	Third	Fourth
First	.54**	.40*	.15
Second	...	.42*	.29
Third	...	...	.40*

* $p<.05$.
** $p<.01$.

quarter tend to ignore them in the fourth. The evidence of maternal consistency is even stronger in regard to the measure of duration of the mother's unresponsiveness —that is, how long her infant cries without a response from her. In table 3.7 the coefficients tend to be higher than in the preceding table, and all but one is significant at least at the 5% level. In particular it is noteworthy that mothers who are unresponsive in the fourth quarter tend to have been so throughout the first year of the baby's life. Maternal tendencies to respond to crying with more or less delay, or to ignore crying altogether, therefore, seem to be relatively stable characteristics, probably influenced strongly by the mother's personality.

Relation of Infant Crying to Maternal Responsiveness

Here we are concerned not only with the question of whether infants who cry more tend to have mothers who are more or less responsive to crying, but also with direction of effects. Is the amount that a baby cries influenced by the degree of responsiveness of his mother to crying? Or, conversely, is a mother's responsiveness influenced by the frequency and duration of her baby's cries? Table 3.8 shows the interrelations between episodes of crying ignored by the mother and the frequency of infant crying. There are three parts of the table upon which to focus. The first is the diagonal, which shows the correlation of maternal and infant behavior in the same quarter and which cannot show direction of effects. The second is the six-celled lower left portion of the matrix, which gives the correlation of maternal behavior in each quarter with infant behavior in subsequent quarters. It is this portion of the matrix that is relevant to the effect of maternal behavior on subsequent infant crying. Finally, the upper right portion shows the correlation of infant behavior in each quarter with maternal behavior in later quarters, and thus it is this portion that is relevant to the effect of infant crying on subsequent maternal behavior.

Let us consider first the diagonal (in which corrected measures have been used). These findings show that there is no relationship between episodes ignored and frequency of crying in the first quarter. In the second quarter there is a positive relationship somewhat short of significance, but in each of the third and fourth quarters there is a significant positive relationship. Except at the beginning, thus, there is a tendency for babies who cry more frequently to have mothers who more frequently ignore their cries.

The lower left portion of the matrix of table 3.8 indicates that, from the beginning of the first year, maternal ignoring in one quarter is correlated significantly with a higher frequency of infant crying in the following quarter. Thus, although tiny babies do not respond immediately to maternal ignoring by crying

Table 3.7. Consistency of maternal responsiveness to crying throughout first year: duration of mother's unresponsiveness to crying

Quarters of First Year	Quarters of First Year		
	Second	Third	Fourth
First	.39*	.33	.49**
Second	...	.58**	.69**
Third	...	...	.49**

* $p<.05$.
** $p<.01$.

Table 3.8. Episodes of crying ignored by mother and frequency of crying

	Episodes Ignored by Mother			
Frequency of Crying	*First Quarter*	*Second Quarter*	*Third Quarter*	*Fourth Quarter*
First quarter	*−.04*	.34	.48*	.21
Second quarter	.56**	*.35*	.32	.29
Third quarter	.21	.39*	*.42**	.40*
Fourth quarter	.20	.36	.52**	*.45**

Note.—Italic figures have been corrected to avoid confounding.
* $p<.05$.
** $p<.01$.

more frequently (as shown by the zero within-first-quarter coefficient), from the beginning of the fourth month on they tend to be more insistent in their crying as a consequence of the past history of mother's ignoring tactics.

Looking, finally, at the upper right portion of the table, it is evident that (except for one significant correlation between first-quarter crying and third-quarter ignoring) the frequency of infant crying does not seem significantly to affect maternal ignoring until the fourth quarter. Thus, a longitudinal inspection of these findings for the first year of life suggests that maternal ignoring increases the likelihood that a baby will cry more frequently from the fourth month of life on, whereas the frequency of infant crying has no consistent influence on the number of episodes the mother is inclined to ignore.

Table 3.9 shows the results of a comparable analysis of the relation between duration of maternal unresponsiveness and the duration of infant crying. The within-quarter findings support those reported for frequency in Table 3.7; babies who cry longer have mothers who are relatively unresponsive, except within the first quarter when the amount of infant crying is not significantly related to maternal unresponsiveness. From the second quarter on, maternal failure to respond to the cry is associated with persistent crying.

The lower left portion of the matrix also shows findings congruent with those in table 3.8, although here the suggestion of effects of maternal behavior on infant crying is even stronger. Babies seem to be responding to the past history of maternal unresponsiveness, so that in each quarter the maternal measure is highly correlated with duration of infant crying in the following two quarters.

The upper right portion of table 3.8 suggests a complication of effects, how-

Table 3.9. Duration of mother's unresponsiveness to crying and duration of crying

	Duration of Mother's Unresponsiveness			
Duration of Crying	*First Quarter*	*Second Quarter*	*Third Quarter*	*Fourth Quarter*
First quarter	*.19*	.37	.12	.41*
Second quarter	.45*	*.67***	.51**	.69**
Third quarter	.40*	.42*	*.39**	.52**
Fourth quarter	.32	.65**	.51**	*.61***

Note.—Italic figures have been corrected to avoid confounding.
* $p<.05$.
** $p<.01$.

ever. By the second half of the first year, an infant's persistence in crying seems to affect the mother, making her more reluctant to respond promptly. In conjunction with the above-mentioned findings that suggest a strong effect of maternal on infant behavior, the implication is that a vicious spiral has been established. Mothers who ignore and delay in responding to the crying of an infant when he is tiny have babies who cry more frequently and persistently later on, which in turn further discourages the mother from responding promptly and results in a further increase of infant irritability.

Nature and Effectiveness of Maternal Interventions

Figure 3.9 shows the relative frequency of various maternal interventions occurring in response to infant crying in the first and fourth quarters of the first year. The most common response in each quarter was to pick the baby up for no purpose other than to institute contact with him. Other fairly frequent interventions were: to talk to him or interact with him without touching him; to feed him, which also usually implied physical contact; and to approcah the baby, perhaps touching him. Rarely was it necessary to remove a noxious stimulus which presumably caused the cry. This analysis shows that most of the interventions, including vocalizing and interacting with the baby, imply that a mother bridges the distance, and usually actively decreases the distance, between herself and her baby. Infant crying thus is demonstrated to promote proximity.

Figure 3.10 shows that, both at the beginning and still at the end of the first year,

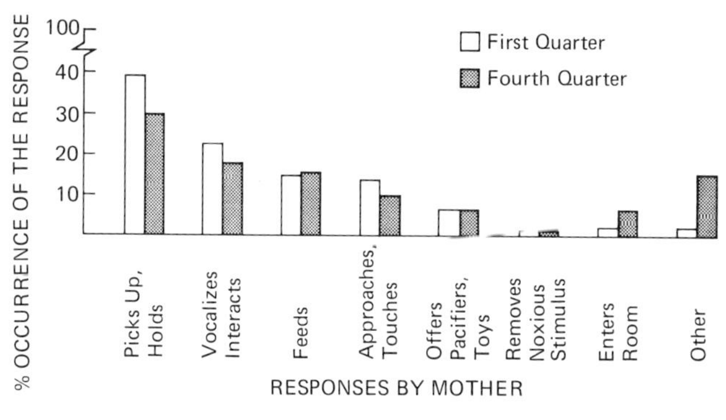

Figure 3.9. Behaviors performed by the mother in response to crying in the first and fourth quarters of the first year.

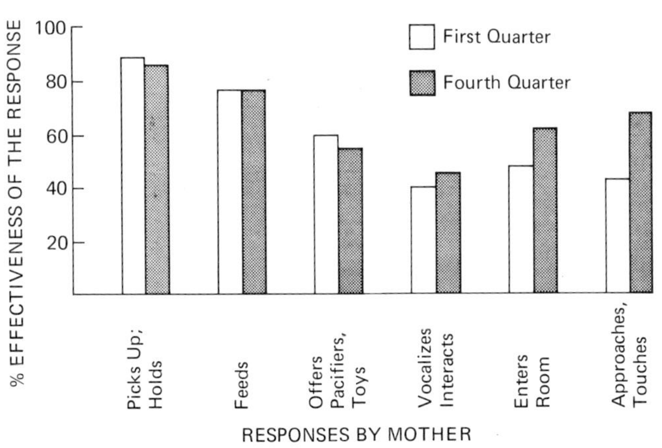

Figure 3.10. Effectiveness of various maternal responses to crying in the first and fourth quarters

to pick a baby up and hold him is the intervention most effective in terminating crying—effective in more than 80% of the instances in which it occurs. Feeding, which usually implies physical contact as well, was almost equally effective. The least effective of the interventions was merely to talk to or interact with the baby without coming any closer to him. Toward the end of the first year, however, responses which merely decrease the distance between mother and baby—entering the room, approaching, and/or touching —without bringing them into close physical contact become increasingly effective as terminators. Thus, whereas a tiny baby tends to require holding if he is to be soothed, the 1-year-old is sometimes content with increased proximity to his mother. Despite the fact that physical contact is the most effective terminator of crying, it is evident from Figure 3.5 that even the least-effective intervention is successful in terminating crying in 40%–50% of its occurrences, and this was found irrespective of the specific circumstances under which the cry arose.

Some mothers were more sensitive than others in gearing their particular intervention to the circumstances which were judged to activate the cry, and hence were more effective in terminating crying. Thus it was of interest to determine whether maternal effectiveness in producing appropriate intervention is related to a baby's tendency to cry. Since a baby may produce a series of brief cries in rapid succession until his mother responds with the most appropriate intervention, the frequency of crying clusters rather than the frequency of crying episodes was chosen as the infant measure for this analysis. Since this measure collapses into one cluster all cries which were not successfully terminated, it is not confounded with the measure of maternal effectiveness.

Table 3.10 shows that the frequency of crying clusters is negatively and substantially related to maternal effectiveness within each of the four quarters of the first year. Although direction of effects cannot be judged from these correlations alone, the overall effectiveness of several interventions in terminating cries (shown in Figure 3.9) inclines us to conclude that these relations are attributable to maternal ineptness in finding an appropriate way of soothing the baby rather than to characteristic infant differences in irritability. Irrespective of which partner is more potent in the failure to soothe, however, the relationship between the two measures is confined to the same quarter. Maternal effectiveness in one quarter does not significantly affect the infant's tendency to cry less frequently in later quarters, nor does frequent infant crying decrease the likelihood that the mother will be effective subsequently.

In conjunction with the findings shown in tables 3.7 and 3.8, the present findings point to the conclusion that, although some maternal responses to crying are more effective terminators of crying than others, the single most important factor associated with a decrease in frequency

Table 3.10. Maternal effectiveness and crying clusters

	Maternal Effectiveness			
Crying Clusters	*First Quarter*	*Second Quarter*	*Third Quarter*	*Fourth Quarter*
First quarter	−.45*	−.18	−.21	−.35
Second quarter	−.11	−.46*	−.34	−.20
Third quarter	.25	−.27	−.58**	−.14
Fourth quarter	−.10	−.25	−.32	−.60**

* $p<.05$.
** $p<.01$.

and duration of crying throughout the first year is the promptness with which a mother responds to cries.

Crying and Proximity

Crying is classed as an attachment behavior because it serves to bring mother and baby in proximity with each other. Our data show that this indeed tends to be the outcome of crying. It seems equally interesting to examine the conditions of proximity to the mother most commonly associated with the onset of crying. Figure 3.11 shows the proportion of total cries emitted under the three conditions described earlier: no proximity, proximity, and close proximity. In the first quarter babies cried almost three times as frequently when not in proximity to the mother than when in close contact with her. Of all cries in the first quarter, 74% have their onset when a baby is not in proximity or contact, and only 45% of these seemed clearly to be associated with hunger. In the fourth quarter, when a baby is mobile, he seems equally likely to cry when he is in contact with his mother as when he is not in proximity at all. He is most likely to cry, however, when he is in proximity but not in contact with her.

These findings suggest that crying is at first expressive and indiscriminate. It is activated by states such as hunger, but it also seems likely to be activated by the condition of being alone and out of visual, auditory, and physical contact with others. Toward the end of the first year, however, it appears that crying may often be a mode of communication that is directed specifically toward the mother, and thus is emitted most frequently when in proximity to her. Crying is no longer exclusively an expressive signal emitted without intent to influence the behavior of others.

Crying and Communication

Crying is only one of the various ways in which a 1-year-old infant communicates with his mother. Since those babies whose mothers have been responsive to crying cry less frequently, we were interested in determining the extent to which other modes of communication had developed to replace crying. For this purpose we utilized the three-point rating scale to assess the subtlety, clarity, and variety of infants' facial expression, bodily gesture, and vocalization as signals and communications. Table 3.11 shows that infant communication has a substantial negative correlation with crying in the fourth quarter; those babies who cry a great deal seem to lack other modes of communication, whereas

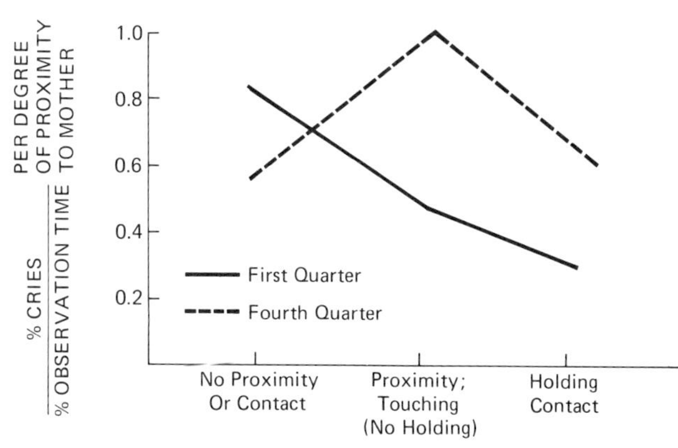

Figure 3.11. Incidence of crying relative to the proportion of time spent in varying degrees of proximity to the mother.

infants who cry little tend to use a variety of other more subtle modes which nevertheless clearly convey their feelings and wishes and which are effective in inviting and sustaining interaction. Table 3.11 shows also that the degree of mother's unresponsiveness to crying as well as the ineffectiveness of her interventions in terminating crying are negatively correlated with the adequacy of the infant's noncrying signals and communications. Those babies who, by the end of the first year, have well-developed channels of communication tend to be the same who cry little, and, as has been shown previously, these are the ones whose cries were promptly heeded throughout the first year of life.

Discussion

Our data suggest that, in the first ¼ year, crying is a signal that promotes proximity and contact with the mother by activating her behavior. Tiny babies tend to cry more frequently when out of visual, auditory, and physical contact with others and to be soothed most effectively by close physical contact. Mothers, in turn, tend to pick their crying babies up more frequently than they intervene in any other way. Thus infant and maternal behavior are basically well adapted to each other.

By the fourth quarter a change has taken place. Crying occurs more frequently when an infant is in proximity to his mother than when she is wholly out of sight and earshot. Like other attachment behaviors, crying has become focused on a specific figure and has become "goal corrected" (Bowlby, 1969). This implies that an infant's attachment behavior is not only directed toward an attachment figure, but is constantly being "corrected" in accordance with the changing location and behavior of that figure. Furthermore, the desired degree of proximity to or contact with the attachment figure provides the conditions for termination of the attachment behavior.

Table 3.11. Infant communication in fourth quarter, crying and maternal responsiveness

	Fourth-Quarter Infant Communication
Duration of crying	−.71**
Frequency of crying	−.65**
Mother's unresponsiveness	−.63**
Episodes ignored by mother	−.54**
Mother's effectiveness	.53**

** $p<.01$.

Crying is the earliest of a repertoire of proximity-promoting, signaling behaviors. Maternal response to the crying signal tends to terminate an episode of crying. Reasonably consistent promptness of response tends to decrease an infant's readiness to use crying as a signal, this effect following not immediately but by the second quarter of the first year. Concomitant with this decrease, there is a development of other social signals and, later, communications which also become focused on the mother as a major attachment figure. Although the data reported here did not deal directly with maternal responsiveness to signals other than crying, our observations yield the unequivocal impression that mothers who promptly heed an infant's cries are sensitively responsive to other signals as well. Mother and infant form an interactional dyad: the more responsive she is the less likely he is to cry and the more likely he is to develop more varied modes of communication.

It is useful to view these findings in the light of an ethologically oriented paradigm advanced by Ainsworth (1967, 1969, and in press, a and b; Ainsworth & Bell, 1970) and Bowlby (1958, 1969). A basic assumption of this approach is that species-characteristic behaviors, including attachment behaviors such as crying, have become part of the genetically programmed repertoire of the species through performing a significant survival-promoting function for individual, population, and/or species in the environment in which the species evolved—and indeed continue to perform such a function in the present environments occupied by the species. Bowlby has argued that the biological function of infant-mother attachment, and of both infant attachment behaviors and reciprocal maternal behaviors, is protection from danger; and in the original environment of evolutionary adaptedness it was likely that predators were the most conspicuous danger. Attachment behaviors protect an infant by bringing him close to his mother, who can defend him from danger or help him escape from it. In a species in which an infant is as helpless as the human, attachment behavior could not effectively perform its protective function were it not dovetailed with reciprocal maternal behavior, activated either by the infant's signals or directly by danger or by both in combination. Infant and maternal behaviors are adapted to each other, and thus the environment to which an infant's attachment behaviors are adapted includes a mother who responds to his signals without undue delay.

From what is known of ground-living nonhuman primates and present-day human communities of hunters and gatherers, it is believed that in the original environment of evolutionary adaptedness mother and infant, usually with companions, moved about frequently through open country where predators presented an ever-possible danger. In a wide variety of mammalian species that currently occupy such environments, the victims of predation tend to be limited to the very young, the very old, and those disabled through illness or injury—especially when they become separated from their companions. Under such circumstances it is of obvious survival advantage for an infant who has somehow lost proximity to his mother to emit a vocal signal perceptible across a distance; it is equally of advantage for his mother to respond to such a signal promptly. Since a vocal signal might also attract a predator, it is of advantage also that it be terminated promptly once infant and mother are together again, but at the same time it seems adaptive for an infant to continue and perhaps intensify his signals should his mother not respond quickly. Nevertheless it is advantageous for an infant to learn to reserve crying for the more alarming situations he encounters, and to use other modes of communication, provided, of course, that his mother is close enough to perceive them.

Our argument is thus that babies are programmed to cry when out of contact or otherwise distressed, behaving as though it were a matter of life or death, even though such behavior may not be necessary to ensure protecton under the conditions that commonly (although not invariably) prevail in the present-day Western world. Although mothers may be influenced by a realistic perception of the improbability of danger, a baby's behavior is nevertheless adapted to the prototype of a responsive mother.

Many contemporary mothers are promptly responsive to infant crying, but many are not. Some are deliberately unresponsive, in the belief that to respond will make a baby demanding, dependent, and "spoiled." Our data suggest the contrary—that those infants who are conspicuous for fussing and crying after the first few months of life, and who fit the stereotype of the "spoiled child," are those whose mothers have ignored their cries or have delayed long in responding to them.

Other aspects of our analysis of mother-infant interaction in the first year (Ainsworth, Bell, & Stayton, in press) confirm the conclusion that maternal responsiveness promotes desirable behavior rather than "spoiling" a child. Infants whose mothers have given them relatively much tender and affectionate holding in the earliest months of life are content with surprisingly little physical contact by the end of the first year; although they enjoy being held, when put down they are happy to move off into independent exploratory play. In contrast, those held for relatively brief periods during the early months tend to be ambivalent about contact by the end of the first year; they do not respond positively when held, but yet protest when put down and do not turn readily to independent activity.

When in the familiar home environment, those babies who tolerate without distress mother's leaving the room briefly tend to have mothers who have been responsive to crying and other signals, while those who more frequently cry when she leaves and do not want to let her out of sight tend to have mothers who have been unresponsive. Finally Stayton, Hogan, and Ainsworth (1971) found that disciplinary practices, such as frequent commands and physical interventions intended to restrict and modify a baby's behavior, do not foster infant obedience. Those infants who can be controlled by their mothers across a distance and who comply with maternal commands are those whose signals have been promptly and sensitively heeded by their mothers. In short, those infants in our sample who are fussy, demanding, and difficult to control are those whose mothers have been unresponsive to signals and generally insensitive or interfering in their efforts to mold their babies to their routines, wishes, and expectations.

It has commonly been assumed that what terminates crying—picking up, feeding, etc.—constitutes a reward which necessarily reinforces the behavior. Furthermore, according to popular belief, crying should decrease through maternal failure to respond contingently to it. Such an "extinction" mechanism may operate under conditions of extreme lack of contingent responsiveness, as, for example, in typical institutional environments where babies soon become quiet and cry little and also become apathetic and retarded in overall development (Provence & Lipton, 1962; Schaffer & Callender, 1959). There is no evidence of an extinction process in our sample of home-reared infants. It has sometimes been suggested that the crying of babies with unresponsive mothers does not decrease because it has been partially or intermittently reinforced, thus making it resistant to extinction. Such an explanation cannot account for individual differences in our sample, since all infants experienced intermittent interventions; not even the most responsive mother can over time respond to all cries promptly. Our findings clearly indicate that the processes implicit in a decrease of crying must be more complex than these popular extrapolations from learning theory would suggest.

In the first part of the first year, crying may be viewed as a fixed-action pattern, activated by a variety of conditions in which intraorganismic components are often conspicuous but which include environmental components as well. Crying is terminated by various other conditions, but it seems most likely to remain deactivated for long periods if the terminating conditions substantially alter the activating conditions. A responsive mother, our data suggest, not only provides the conditions that terminate a cry, thus reducing its duration, but also is likely to provide conditions that tend to prevent crying from being activated or reactivated. Thus, for example, we found that mothers who are sensitively responsive to infant signals in regard to the onset, termination, and pacing of feeding in the first quarter have babies who cry less than the infants of mothers who are relatively unresponsive (Ainsworth & Bell, 1969). From other findings (Ainsworth et al., in press) we may also infer that tiny infants who have relatively long periods of physical contact in nonroutine contexts would less frequently than other infants have crying activated by being alone and out of contact. Thus, infants whose mothers are responsive to their signals have less occasion to cry—not only in the first few months but throughout infancy.

Nevertheless, in the latter part of the first year, crying loses some of its fixed-action quality in that it can be directed specifically toward the mother and thus can be used intentionally as a means to an end, as a mode of communication. According to Piaget's (1952) observations, it is not until about 8 months of age that a baby can differentiate means from ends and flexibly uses a variety of "schemata" as means with intent to achieve an end. It is our hypothesis that in responding to a baby's signaling behavior a mother provides feedback, which, since it is contingent upon his signals, fosters the development of flexible, means-end communicative behavior. The child of a responsive mother comes to anticipate her responsiveness. Although some of his communications may be cries, the predictability of his mother's responsiveness tends to reduce the intensity of the conditions that might otherwise activate a cry, if only because he does not feel alone and out of contact. Thus a mother who is responsive to the signals implicit in a wide range of her baby's behavior creates an atmosphere in which he can signal through varied means less urgent than crying.

An infant whose mother's responsiveness helps him to achieve his ends develops confidence in his own ability to control what happens to him. It seems likely that toward the end of his first year he begins to distinguish between what he can effect directly through his own actions and what he can accomplish through eliciting his mother's cooperation. Although before this his confidence rests in part on a "magical" control of others, nonetheless it fosters increased initiative in the acquisition of other means-ends activities through which he can achieve his own goals without requesting the intervention of adults. Even before a baby can differentiate between means and ends, there is an inverse relation between crying and competence. A baby who is unable to roll over from a supine to a prone position may fuss when his efforts to do so are in vain; when he is yet unable to reach out and grasp an attractive object he may "cry for it"; when he has mastered rolling over, reaching, and grasping, he has fewer occasions to cry. There is no reason to suppose that to turn him over or to give him the attractive object will deter the development of these basic abilities. A baby is so eager to explore his world and to practice his developing manipulative and locomotor skills that there is no basis for fear that to respond to his signals will hamper the development of competence and self-reliance.

Thus two central concepts have been brought to bear on an understanding of the processes implicit in the decrease of crying and the relations of the decrement to maternal responsiveness. First, crying is not viewed as a behavior to be reinforced or extinguished in isolation from other signaling behaviors, but as one manifestation of an emergent communicative system. Second, a baby, although helpless and dependent at the beginning, not only learns to affect the behavior of others in his environment through his signals and communications, but is also biased from the beginning toward the development of abilities that will make him increasingly competent and self-reliant so that he is increasingly able to act on his own behalf without requiring others to do so much for him. Maternal responsiveness to signals fosters the development of communication. It does not interfere with the early development of increased competence, and through giving a child confidence, it positively encourages the later development of means-ends activities.

References

AINSWORTH, M. D. S. *Infancy in Uganda: infant care and the growth of love.* Baltimore: Johns Hopkins University Press, 1967.

———. Object relations, dependency, and attachment: a theoretical review of the infant-mother relationship. *Child Development,* 1969, *40,* 969–1025.

———. The development of infant-mother attachment. In B. M. Caldwell & H. N. Ricciuti (Eds.), *Review of child development research.* Vol. 3. Chicago: University of Chicago Press, in press. (a)

———. Attachment and dependency: a comparison. In J. L. Gewirtz (Ed.), *Attachment and dependence.* New York: Academic Press, in press. (b)

AINSWORTH, M. D. S., & BELL, S. M. Some contemporary patterns of mother-infant interaction in the feeding situation. In J. A. Ambrose (Ed.), *Stimulation in early infancy.* London: Academic Press, 1969, pp. 133–170.

———. Attachment, exploration and separation: illustrated by the behavior of one-year-olds in a strange situation. *Child Development,* 1970, *41,* 49–67.

AINSWORTH, M. D. S.; BELL, S. M.; & STAYTON, D. J. Individual differences in the development of some attachment behaviors. *Merrill-Palmer Quarterly,* in press.

BAYLEY, N. A study of the crying of infants during mental and physical tests. *Journal of Genetic Psychology,* 1932, *40,* 306–329.

BOWLBY, J. The nature of the child's tie to his mother. *International Journal of Psychoanalysis,* 1958, *39,* 350–373.

———. *Attachment and loss.* Vol. *1. Attachment.* London: Hogarth (New York: Basic), 1969.

ETZEL, B. C., & GEWIRTZ, J. L. Experimental modification of caretaker-maintained high-rate operant crying in a 6- and a 20-week old infant (*Infans Tyrannotearus*): extinction of crying with reinforcement of eye contact and smiling. *Journal of Experimental Child Psychology,* 1967, *5,* 303–317.

GEWIRTZ, J. L. Mechanisms of social learning: some roles of stimulation and behavior in early human development. In D. A. Goslin (Ed.), *Handbook of socialization theory and research.* Chicago: Rand McNally, 1969, pp. 57–212.

HART, B. M.; ALLEN, E. K.; BUEL, J. S.; HARRIS, F. R.; & WOLF, M. M. Effects of social reinforcement on operant crying. *Journal of Experimental Child Psychology,* 1964, *1,* 145–153.

MOSS, H. A. Sex, age and state as determinants of mother-infant interaction. *Merrill-Palmer Quarterly,* 1967, *13,* 19–37.

MOSS, H. A., & ROBSON, K. S. The role of protest behavior in the development of the mother-infant attachment. Symposium presented at the annual meeting of the American Psychological Association, San Francisco, 1968.

PIAGET, J. *The origins of intelligence in children.* 1936. 2d ed. New York: International Universities Press, 1952.

PROVENCE, S., & LIPTON, R. C. *Infants in institutions.* New York: International Universities Press, 1962.

SCHAFFER, H. R., & CALLENDER, W. M. Psychological effects of hospitalization in infancy. *Pediatrics,* 1959, *24,* 528–539.

STAYTON, D. J.; HOGAN, R.; & AINSWORTH, M. D. S. Infant obedience and maternal behavior: the origins of socialization reconsidered. *Child Development,* 1971, *42,* 1057–1069.

U. S. CHILDREN'S BUREAU. *Infant care.* Care of Children Series No. 2. Bureau Publication No. 8 (Revised), 1924.

WILLIAMS, C. D. The elimination of tantrum behavior by extinction procedures. *Journal of Abnormal and Social Psychology,* 1959, *59,* 269.

WOLF, M. M.; RISLEY, T. R.; & MEES, H. I. Application of operant conditioning procedures to the behavior problems of an autistic child. *Behavior Research and Therapy*, 1964, *1*, 305–312.

13. FATHERS' VERBAL INTERACTION WITH INFANTS IN THE FIRST THREE MONTHS OF LIFE

FREDA REBELSKY and CHERYL HANKS

Fathers' verbal interactions with their infants were gathered by means of a microphone attached to the infant for a 24-hour period every 2 weeks, from the time the infant was 2 weeks of age to the time he was 3 months old. The data show that fathers spend little time vocalizing to their infants and that the number of interactions varies by time of day, age and sex of infant, and the kind of activity occurring during the interaction.

In his review of the psychological literature on the father, John Nash (1965) suggests that most American psychologists regard the United States as a matriocentric child-rearing society. In support of this statement, Nash cites numerous publications dealing with child-rearing practices and parent-child relations which make no mention of the father, thereby equating parent with mother, and child-rearing practices with mothers' child-rearing practices.

The dearth of studies that deal with fathers may be partially explained by the fact that fathers are not as available for study as mothers. It may also be due to the fact that psychologists consider fathers unimportant to child rearing and, therefore, make less of an effort to study them. In the light of recent studies of the effects of father absence, this assumption does not seem tenable: the absence (or presence) of a father does seem to have important effects, especially on the male child (Carlsmith 1964; Lynn & Sawrey 1959). Carlsmith's (1964) study of the relationship between father absence and the aptitude patterns of male college students showed that the effects were greatest if a father left when his son was 0–6 months old. Thus it appears that, especially in infancy, the presence or absence of a father is important to the subsequent development of male children. It is difficult to explain many of the data that we do have because there have been no studies on fathers' interactions with infants. The present study, part of a larger study of infant vocalization (Lenneberg, Rebelsky, & Nichols 1965), was designed to supply some basic descriptive data on fathers' verbal interactions with their infants.

Method

Subjects

The sample consisted of 10 normal, full-term, white, winter-born babies, seven males and three females. They were born into lower-middle- to upper-middle-class families who lived in Boston suburbs. Only two of the babies were firstborn. The sample was obtained through professional contacts with pediatricians. The research was presented to the parents as a general study of how infants live, what they do, etc., with the explanation that such basic data are not as yet known. The experimenter [*E*] explained that she did not want to interfere in any way with the household schedule and that no changes in the babies' normal environment or routine should be made for *E*'s convenience.

Procedure

Beginning in the second week of life, 24-hour tape recordings were made approximately every 2 weeks for a 3-month period. Thus, there were six 24-hour observation periods for each infant. A microphone approximately the shape of a half-dollar, with a cord of about 27 feet, was attached to the infant's shirt such that the infant could be moved around without removing him from the sound field. The microphone picked up both the noises emitted by the infant and the noises to which he was exposed. In order to eliminate silent periods on the tapes, a recording instrument (described more fully in Chan, Lenneberg, & Rebelsky 1964) was operated by a voice key which turned the recorder off if there was a silence of more than 20 seconds, and turned it on if there was noise in the sound field.

Coding the tape recordings Two coders listened to the tapes for the 10 infants and recorded the duration, time of day, and activity occurring each time a father vocalized to his infant. Ten percent of the tapes were coded by both coders, with an interjudge reliability of over .90 for each of the items scored. An interaction began with a father vocalizing to his infant and ended if there was an interval of silence longer than 30 seconds. The silent period was not included in the interaction time.

Results

The data indicate that fathers spend relatively little time interacting with their infants. The mean number of interactions per day was 2.7, and the average number of seconds per day was 37.7. While there were large individual differences, even the father with the most interactions spent an average of only 10 minutes, 26 seconds interacting with his infant each day. This is low when compared with the Moss data on mothers' verbal interactions with their infants (Moss 1967). Table 3.12 summarizes the group data on fathers' daily interactions with their infants. In addition, there was a Spearman rank correlation of +.72 between the number of interactions per father and the mean length of each father's interaction. This is significant at the .05 level ($p<.05$).

As might be expected, fathers talked to their babies most often in the morning hours before going to work (41 percent of all interactions) and in the evening hours after work (33 percent of all interactions).

The amount of fathers' interactions varied by the age and sex of their infants. Unlike mothers, who increase their vocalization time during the first 3 months of life (Moss 1967; Rebelsky 1967), seven out of ten of the fathers spent less time vocaliz-

Table 3.12. Means and ranges of fathers' daily interactions with their infants

	Number of seconds per day	*Number of interactions per day*	*Length of interactions in seconds*
Mean	37.7	2.7	13.9
Range	0–1,370	0–17	4–220

ing to their infants during the last half of the study (8–12 weeks) than in the first half (2–6 weeks). This decrease of vocalization over time is more marked among the fathers of female infants. While all three of the fathers of female infants decreased their number of vocalizations during the last 6 weeks, only four out of seven fathers of male infants decreased their number of vocalizations in the same time period. None of these interactions reached significance.

Of the 164 verbal interactions of these fathers with their infants, about half (54 percent) were during caretaking activities (e.g., diapering, feeding) and 46 percent were not during caretaking (see Table 3.13).

When the data are analyzed in terms of the kinds of activities that were occurring while the father was vocalizing to his infant, the decrease of vocalization during caretaking activities is largely responsible for the overall decrease in vocalization over time. With only one exception, all fathers decreased their number of vocalizations during caretaking activities during the second three observations. On the other hand, the number of vocalizations during noncaretaking activities remained about the same for the fathers of male infants, but decreased somewhat for the fathers of female infants.

Discussion

Fathers talk infrequently and for short periods of time to their infants in the first 3 months of life. When compared with similar data on mothers' verbalizations to infants (Moss 1967; Rebelsky 1967), the data suggest that fathers do some things differently from mothers. For example, whereas mothers increase their vocalization time during their infants' first 3 months, seven of the ten fathers in this study spent less time verbalizing to their infants during the last month and a half compared with the first month and a half of life.

Like mothers, fathers seem to behave differently toward male and female infants; however, the differential behavior of fathers toward their infants is opposite from the differential behavior of mothers. While the fathers of female infants verbalized more than did the fathers of male infants at 2 weeks and 4 weeks of age, Moss's data show that mothers of male infants vocalized more than mothers of female infants at 3 weeks of age (Moss 1967, p. 23). By the time infants reach 3 months of age, these patterns are reversed. Fathers of male infants vocalize somewhat more than do fathers of female infants at 12 weeks; by 12 weeks, mothers of female infants vocalize more than mothers of male infants (Moss 1967). To account for his data, Moss suggests that mothers initially respond more to male infants because the infants are awake more and are generally more irritable than female infants. He suggests that the shift in behavior at 3 months is due to the more reinforcing nature of the mother's interactions with her less-irritable female infant (Moss 1967).

Table 3.13. Sex differences in developmental trends in the number of fathers' verbal interactions during caretaking and noncaretaking activities

	Weeks 2, 4, 6			*Weeks 8, 10, 12*		
	Male	*Female*	*Total*	*Male*	*Female*	*Total*
Vocalization during caretaking	24(52%)	34(64%)	58(59%)	13(34%)	17(62%)	30(46%)
Vocalization not during caretaking	22(48%)	19(36%)	41(41%)	25(66%)	10(38%)	33(54%)
Total	46(100%)	53(100%)	99(100%)	38(100%)	27(100%)	65(100%)

While this explanation is reasonable, it cannot be extended to apply to the data which show a shift in the opposite direction on the part of fathers. However, it may easily be that mothers and fathers are responding to different things in their infants. For example, the mother may be responding to the sex-related behavior of her infant, whereas the father may be initially responding more to his role of father-of-daughter or father-of-son. That is, fathers may perceive the role of father-of-daughter as a more nurturant, verbal role than the role of father-of-son. This suggestion receives some support from our finding that fathers of female infants verbalize more during caretaking activities than do fathers of male infants. If this is true, it may be that father absence has greater effects on males than on females because fathers of female infants define their role as more similar to the maternal role (i.e., nurturant) than do fathers of male infants. This is at best a tentative hypothesis; moreover, it does not clarify the father's definition of his role as father-of-son.

This study has raised some interesting questions. We now know that the patterns of mothers' and fathers' vocalizations to infants differ, but we do not know about other than vocal interactions of the fathers. It may be that fathers are more physical than verbal with their infants; it may be that fathers interact more physically with sons and more verbally with daughters. We do know that the presence or absence of a father has effects on the subsequent development of his children. What we now need are more comprehensive observations of fathers' interactions with their children to determine how they do interact so that we can hypothesize more clearly about how the effects we have seen might occur.

References

CARLSMITH, L. Effect of early father absence on scholastic aptitude. *Harvard Educational Review,* 1964, *34,* 3–21.

CHAN, C. H.; LENNEBERG, E. H.; & REBELSKY, F. G. Apparatus for reducing play-back time of tape recorded, intermittent vocalization. In U. Bellugi & R. Brown (Eds.) The acquisition of language. *Monographs of the Society for Research in Child Development,* 1964, *29,* (1, Serial No. 92), 127–130.

LENNEBERG, E. H.; REBELSKY, F. G.; & NICHOLS, I. A. The vocalizations of infants born to deaf and to hearing parents. *Human Development,* 1965, *8,* 23–37.

LYNN, D. B., & SAWREY, W. L. The effects of father absence on Norwegian boys and girls. *Journal of Abnormal and Social Psychology,* 1959, *59,* 258–262.

MOSS, H. A. Sex, age and state as determinants of mother-infant interaction. *Merrill-Palmer Quarterly,* 1967, *13,* 19–36.

NASH, J. The father in contemporary culture and current psychological literature. *Child Development,* 1965, *36,* 261–297.

REBELSKY, F. G. Infancy in two cultures. *Nederlands Tijdschrift voor de Psychologie,* 1967, *22,* 379–385.

14. THE INFANT SEPARATES HIMSELF FROM HIS MOTHER

HARRIET L. RHEINGOLD and
CAROL O. ECKERMAN

At some point in time an infant leaves its mother. It is our purpose to call attention to this behavior in man and animal, to examine its biological and psychological consequences, and to relate the behavior to current principles of behavior theory. The argument is first presented very generally. The general presentation is followed by a review of the literature on nonhuman primates, and then by an outline of some procedures for experimental analysis of this behavior, based upon recent work in our laboratory.

The infant's leaving the mother is well-nigh universal behavior throughout the animal kingdom. Here, however, we limit the presentation to species of the class Mammalia. And within that class the focus is the human infant, although the discussion moves freely between him and infants of other species. Recent studies of nonhuman primates (see, for example, *1–5*) offer some data on the infant's separating himself from his mother, but the behavior has not often been precisely documented in other mammals, even in the human infant (*6*). With only a few exceptions, the behavior has seldom been the primary subject of study.

Let us consider this behavior. At some point in his life the mammalian infant leaves his mother's side. The first excursion is typically short in extent, and brief. In many species the mother promptly retrieves the infant making his first excursions, but the excursions are not thereby suppressed; they occur again and again. With time, and experience, the distance traveled increases, and so does the time spent away from the mother.

The infant's separating himself from his mother depends, of course, on his ability to move his body by his own efforts. As soon as the human infant is able to move thus—it takes him all of 7 months—he does so, even if he can progress only by inching along on his belly. Later he creeps, and then walks away from his mother. He goes out the door and enters another room. In time he walks out of the house, plays in the yard all morning, goes to school, goes still farther away to high school, then to college and to work. He crosses the country, and now he may go even to the moon. Eventually he sets up his own home and produces infants who, in turn, repeat the process.

Biological and Psychological Significance

The infant's separating himself from his mother is of biologic importance. It is of consequence for the preservation of both the individual and the species—of the individual, since it confers the advantage of greater familiarity with the environment and thus increases the likelihood of adaptation to the environment; of the species, since it allows the mother to care for the next offspring and leads eventually to the formation of breeding pairs.

The infant's separating himself from his mother is also of psychological importance for it enormously increases his opportunities to interact with the environment and thus to learn its nature. For, while he is in physical contact with his mother, his universe is confined to her person and the environment near her. There are limits to what the most attentive mother can bring to him. Even when he is carried about, his contacts with the universe are necessarily circumscribed. When, however, he leaves her side by himself, many new kinds of learning can occur.

The infant comes in contact with an increasing number and variety of objects. Through touching them he learns their shapes, dimensions, slopes, edges, and textures. He also fingers, grasps, pushes, and pulls, and thus learns the material variables of heaviness, mass, and rigidity, as well as the changes in visual and auditory stimuli that some objects provide. He moves from place to place within a room, and from one room to another. From the consequent changes in visual experience, coupled with his own kinesthetic sensations, he learns the position of objects relative to other objects (*7*). He also learns the invariant nature of many sources of stimulation. In a word, he learns the properties of the physical world, including the principles of object constancy and the conservation of matter.

Although in considering what can be learned by the infant as he moves away from his mother we have been speaking of the human infant, parallels can be drawn for the infant of other species. Similarly, although we have been considering what can be learned about the *physical* environment, parallels can be drawn for the *social* environment.

Relation to Attachment

Up to this point we have presented a class of behavior rather generally; now its relations with some other classes of behavior can be considered.

The first of these other classes of behavior is the infant's attachment to his mother, and of course for some species this also includes attachment to the nest and the littermates. It is clear that mammals of necessity stay with their mothers for some time; that at an early age they distinguish their mothers from other individuals; that they often respond more positively to their mothers and to other familiar individuals than to less familiar individuals; and that they are upset by the departure of these familiar social objects. Attachment, furthermore, persists throughout the life of some species, although the form of the behavior changes.

We use the term *detachment* for the behavior of interest here, for balance with *attachment*, and for contrast (*8*). Detachment occurs later in the life of some infant mammals than the first evidence of attachment. This is the case with the rodents, carnivores, and primates. But detachment does not signal the end of attachment, nor is it simply the opposite of attachment. Attachment and detachment should be viewed as an interplay of classes of behavior, developing side by side and coexisting for the life of the individual.

Finally, the kind of separation we are talking about is not to be confused with the separation of "separation anxiety" (*9*). We know from observation and from our laboratory studies that the infant who *separates himself* does so without anxiety.

Relation to Exploratory Behavior

When an infant leaves his mother, moves toward objects, and touches and fingers them, his behavior may be characterized as exploratory. Exploratory behavior has proved a troublesome class of behavior to handle conceptually (*10*) (Is the organism exploring or just active?). But exploratory behavior is so obvious in the young animal that the concept cannot be ignored just because it does not yet fit easily into traditional behavior theory.

The psychological advantages proposed as resulting from the child's leaving his mother's side are those very products assumed to result from exploratory behavior—an increase in a store of perceptions; new opportunities to learn what can be done with an object and what results from manipulating it; and an increase in new techniques for controlling external events. Furthermore, in our early attempts to study the infant's leaving his mother, we see that some of his behavior appears to be under the control of those same factors that control exploratory behavior—among them, novelty, complexity, and change.

Mother's Role in the First Separations

What is the human mother's role in the infant's leaving her side? In our culture, even from the beginning, the mother often physically separates herself from the infant, in contrast to some other mammals who seldom leave when the infants are young, or to the primates, whose young maintain physical contact with them. The mother's leaving cannot be responsible for the infant's leaving her, because even in cultures where the mother separates herself less often, the infant also leaves at some point in time. The human mother *permits* the infant to leave. Although she is watchful, she nevertheless appears to retrieve the infant less often than many other mammals do. Later, as the human infant progresses farther and faster, the mother does restrain and retrieve him more often, but she is generally ingenious in constructing an environment where restraining and retrieving are less necessary, since such foresight reduces her caretaking duties.

Primate Studies

In the last decade or so, many investigators of nonhuman primate behavior have followed the lead of Harlow and Zimmermann (*11*) in studying the interaction between mother and infant. We have drawn data from the reports of field and laboratory studies of several primate species to support the thesis that the infant does separate himself from his mother. These studies supply information on when the infant leaves, how far he goes from his mother, how long he stays away, how often he leaves, and how the mother responds to his first departures.

Measures of separation Several investigators have reported that, as the primate infant matures, he goes farther and farther from his mother. Kaufmann (*12*) provides explicit data concerning the rhesus monkey (*Macaca mulatta*) on Cayo Santiago, Puerto Rico. The distance infants *walked away* from their mothers increased rapidly over the first 2 months of age (Figure 3.12). In Figure 3.12 the data points for the curve labeled "first seen" are the lower limits of the age range Kaufmann reported at each distance, and those for the curve labeled "commonly seen" are the midpoints of the age range, for a sample of 30 infants observed from birth.

Vessey (*13*) provides additional data for rhesus monkeys; he found that the *average* distance between mother and infant increased linearly after the first 8

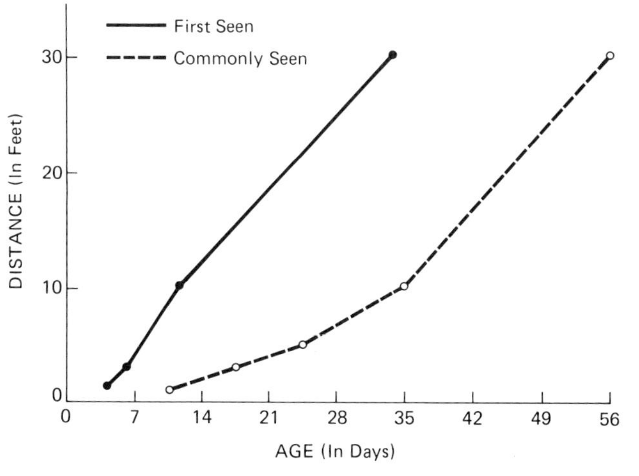

Figure 3.12. Distance traveled from mothers by infant rhesus monkeys of different ages (see text).

weeks to 30 feet (9 meters) at the end of the first year. The measures were based on minute-by-minute observations, averaging 1 hour per week, of nine rhesus infants born into the colony at La Parguera, Puerto Rico. Six of the infants were male and three were female; no difference by sex was found.

Data for some other primates are shown in Figure 3.13. The curves are based on the distances between mother and infant reported by Jay (*14*) for langur monkeys (*Presbytis entellus*), by DeVore (*15*) for the baboon (*Papio*, olive and yellow), and by Schaller (*16*) for the gorilla (*Gorilla gorilla beringei*). We have used the exact ages and distances reported by the investigators, but it should be pointed out that these observations were not the subject of their main interest. In general, the text of the reports implies that the distances resulted from the infant's movement away from his mother, rather than from the mother's movements. The first point of the curve for human infants in Figure 3.13 is based on Nancy Bayley's (*17*) age placement for forward progression; the second point is based on the distance that 10-month-old infants traveled from their mothers in our laboratory. This point differs from the other distances in that, given the dimensions and arrangement of the particular rooms used, it is the farthest the infant could travel. Informal observation of infants in their own homes suggests that the distance can be much greater.

The *time* a primate infant spends away from his mother at one time also increases with age. Altmann (*18*) recorded in the field that the howling monkey (*Alouatta palliata*) at the age of 15 days stayed away from his mother for 10 seconds; at 26 days, for 1 minute; and at 1 month (only 5 days later), for as long as 4 minutes. Infant langurs in the field, according to Jay (*14*), also separated themselves from their mothers for 4 minutes at the age of 1 month, but at 1 year they stayed away, playing, for more than 20 minutes at a time. In the laboratory, Kaufman and Rosenblum (*4*) found that, in the case of both bonnet (*Macaca radiata*) and pig-tailed (*M. nemestrina*) infants, the mean duration of their vertical separations from the mother (separations involving progress to a different level of the cage) increased up to the fourth and fifth month; that the duration was stable thereafter may be attrib-

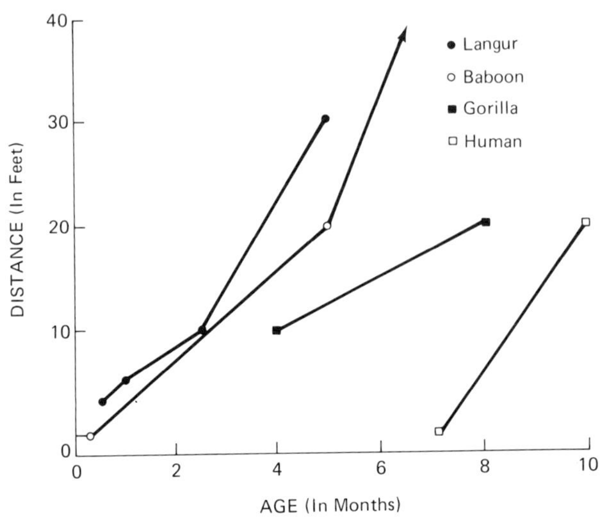

Figure 3.13. Distances between infants and mothers of some primate species. The data points represent the earliest ages and the maximum distances reported. (The curve for the baboon reaches 90 feet at the end of 10 months.)

uted to the space limitations of their living quarters.

As he grows older, not only does the nonhuman primate infant go farther from his mother and stay away longer, he also leaves more frequently. Kaufman and Rosenblum (*4*) reported that the *frequency* of the bonnet infants' moving away from their mothers, while remaining on the same level of the cage (horizontal departures), increased from 4.5 departures at the age of 1 month to 9 departures at 4 months, per 1000 seconds of continuous observation. Concurrently, the frequency of going to another level of the cage (vertical departures) increased from 0 at the age of 1 month to 16 at 15 months. Similar changes in the pig-tailed infants' behavior also occurred; horizontal departures increased over the first 6 months, while vertical departures increased from 0 to 6 over the first 11 months. Furthermore, throughout the 15 months of observation, both bonnet and pig-tailed infants left their mothers more frequently than their mothers left them (*19*).

The data summarized so far show that the nonhuman primate infant leaves his mother, and that, as he grows older (and more experienced), he leaves more frequently, goes farther, and stays away longer.

The mother's response As the primate infant matures, the mother is not passive. Her behavior undoubtedly contributes to the changes seen in her infant's departures. It has been shown by various investigators that she restrains him from departing and retrieves him once he has left. Her thwarting of his attempts to suckle and her punishing him when he approaches occur much later; although they affect his subsequent behavior, they are not relevant to the central issue of this article.

Data on the mother's restraining and retrieving are shown in Figure 3.14. Curve A, derived from the data of Doyle, Andersson, and Bearder (*20*), shows the frequency with which the galago mother (*Galago senegalensis moholi*) retrieved an infant that had left the nest. Curves B and C are based on data for the rhesus monkey. (Because of the differences in the measures and time-sampling procedures of the investigators, the scores for the various sets of data are expressed as percentages of the maximum score reported, a procedure that permits comparisons of events over time but not, of course, comparisons of actual frequencies.) Curve B is based on the data of Harlow, Harlow, and Hansen (*1*) for the rhesus monkey and combines frequencies for the mother's restraint and retrieval of the infant. Curve C, from the work of Hinde and Spencer-Booth (*2*), represents the percentage of rhesus infants restrained by their mothers. Curves D, E, and F are derived from the work of Rosenblum and Kaufman (*21*) with bonnet and

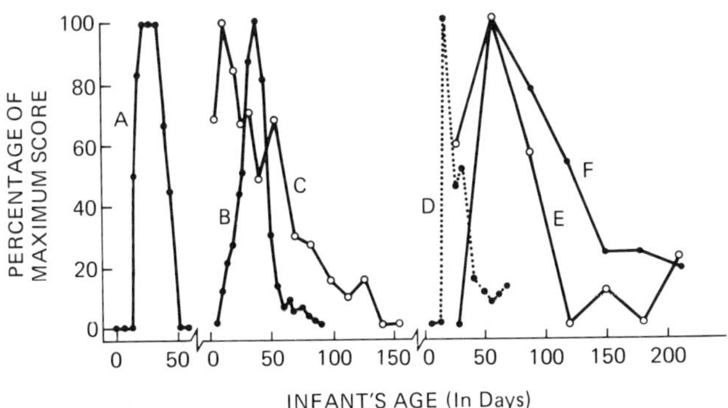

Figure 3.14. Frequency with which primate mothers restrained and retrieved their infants (see text).

pig-tailed macaques. Curve D shows the percentages of time the pig-tailed mother prevented her infant from leaving; curves E and F give the frequency of retrieval by bonnet and pig-tailed mothers.

The data of Jensen, Bobbitt, and Gordon (22) on this subject are not presented in Figure 3.14 because they are given not as actual frequencies but as frequencies *relative* to other classes of behavior. Still, the data of these workers also show that the mother's "retaining" of the infant relative to all her manipulations increased over the first few weeks, and then decreased.

Despite the differences in procedures of observation and in classes of behavior reported, the data show (i) that these nonhuman primate mothers restrain their infants from leaving and retrieve them once they have left, and (ii) that the frequency of the behavior increases over the early days of the infant's life and then decreases. It is clear that the mother's behavior reflects the increasing frequency of the infant's attempts to leave—the topic of central concern here—and that, over time, he gets his way.

Studies of Human Children

In the past 2 years we have studied children in the process of separating themselves from their mothers. Two studies are reviewed here to show that the behavior can be subjected to experimental analysis. The first was carried out in a seminaturalistic setting with children between 1 and 5 years of age, the other in the laboratory with 10-month-old infants.

Relationship between age and distance To measure the relationship between a child's age and the distance he will travel from his mother, 48 children were studied, three boys and three girls at each half-year of age between 12 and 60 months. We placed a mother and child at one end of an unfenced lawn, with the mother sitting in a chair and the child starting at the mother's knee but left free to roam for the 15 minutes of the study. The mother was instructed to remain in her chair but was encouraged to respond otherwise to the child in her usual manner. Neither mother nor child had been in the yard before. The yard contained a couple of trees, two birdbaths, a set of planted terraces to one side, and a small paved patio and the house to the other. Aside from these usual objects, no lures were provided. The yard was L-shaped, running along the back of the house and around its corner to the road. The first leg of the L, in front of the child, was 27.4 meters long and 12.2 meters wide; the second leg began 15.2 meters from the child's starting position and extended 39.6 meters to the road; it too was 12.2 meters wide. Thus the child could get out of range of the mother's vision; the trial was ended, however, for any child who went 15.2 meters past the corner, a precaution taken to guard against his getting into the road.

Observers stationed at windows in the house traced the child's path on a map of the yard. Small rods were inserted at the borders of the lawn, inconspicuous in the tall grasses, to mark off 10-foot (3.05-meter) squares for the use of the observers in plotting the child's course. Distance was calculated as the midpoint of each square the child entered. In 25 of a sample of 26 records, the two observers, working independently, agreed exactly on the farthest square the child entered.

The mean farthest distance traveled from the mother by 1-year-olds was 6.9 meters; by 2-year-olds, 15.1 meters; by 3-year-olds, 17.3 meters; and by 4-year-olds, 20.6 meters. Figure 3.15 shows that variability after the second year of life was considerable; for example, one 2½-year-old boy went 31.5 meters but another went only 7.5 meters. Nevertheless a linear regression of distance relative to age was significant at P less than .01. The equation for the estimated regression line was

$$\hat{Y} = 2.43 + 0.35X$$

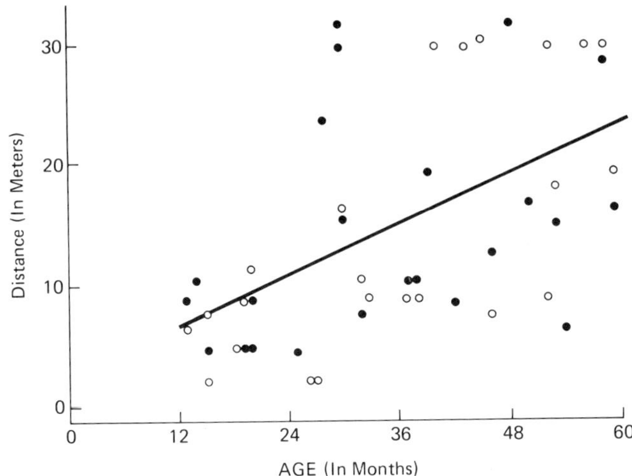

Figure 3.15. Distance traveled from mothers by children of different ages. (Solid circles) males; (open circles) females.

This suggests that, for each added month of age, the children went about a third of a meter farther.

Clearly this relationship cannot be linear for ages much below 1 year; the predicted average of 4.9 meters at 7 months (the average age of first forward progression) would be too great. Furthermore, the boundaries imposed not only by the topography of the lawn but also by the experimenter's stopping a child at an arbitrary point appear to have restricted the distance the older children might have gone.

No evidence of a difference by sex appeared in these small samples. The regression for each sex was significant, and the two regressions did not differ reliably (F = 0.37, 2 and 44 d.f.). Of the ten children who went out of sight of their mothers, it is interesting to note, two were males and eight were females. Unlike rhesus infants, as reported by Kaufmann (*12*), the human child, according to the regression equation, would not attain a distance of 30 feet until the age of 19 months, a distance reached by rhesus monkeys at 2 months. But the comparison can be only suggestive because the children were placed in an environment with which they were unfamiliar; the mothers reported that at home children went much farther (*23*). One could of course use a longer session or repeated sessions to increase familiarity. Interesting objects could be placed at varying distances from the mother to lure the child farther, or another child could be present, as a means of measuring the effect of social facilitation.

Environmental stimuli and the infant's leaving his mother In the laboratory we have investigated some properties of the environment that lead the 10-month-old human infant away from his mother (*24*). A simple situation composed of mother, infant, two adjacent rooms, and a few toys provided the laboratory setting. The mother placed the infant beside her in one of the rooms, and the door to the second room was left open. The properties of the environment were altered by varying the number and location of toys within the second room, and by having the toys sometimes present from the start and sometimes added later.

Two observers behind windows fitted with one-way glass independently recorded how long an infant took to enter the second room, how long he stayed there, how far he went, what he touched and manipulated, how often he returned to his mother, and how much time he spent in contact with her. Vocal behavior was tape-recorded and subsequently analyzed as either distress or nondistress sounds. The agreement between observers was substantial, product-moment correlations being in the neighborhood of .95 for the duration of actual events.

The subjects were normal, home-reared infants, 10 months of age, an age that insured that most of them could locomote by some means. In fact, about two-thirds of the infants could creep proficiently on their hands and knees. Of the other third, half were still crawling on their bellies and the other half were already toddling. The infants were selected by age alone from the register of births at the University Hospital at Chapel Hill, North Carolina, and thus reflected the socioeconomic characteristics of a small university town.

The experimental area consisted of two rooms—a small room in which the test was started, called the "starting room," and a larger room, called the "open field"; both were unfurnished (Figure 3.16). The small room measured 2.7 by 2.7 meters; the large room, 2.7 by 5.5 meters. The floor of the large room was divided, by narrow masking tape, into cells approximately 0.9 meter (1 yard) square. Neither the mother nor the infant had seen the rooms prior to the test.

To start the test, the mother sat on the floor of the starting room and placed the infant facing herself. She had been told that she could look at and smile at her infant, and that she could talk softly to him in short phrases when he was near her, but that she should allow him to leave or to stay.

Twenty-four infants were studied. In experiment 1 the open field was empty for 12 of the subjects (group 0); for the other 12 (group 1) it contained a toy—a plastic pull toy—in the cell just outside the starting room (the cell that the infant has reached in Figure 3.16). The experiment lasted for 10 minutes.

All 24 infants left their mothers and, without fussing or crying, crept out of the room in which the mother sat and entered the larger room, whether it was empty or contained a toy.

The two groups, group 0 and group 1, spent similar amounts of time in the larger room (Figure 3.17A). (This statement, and

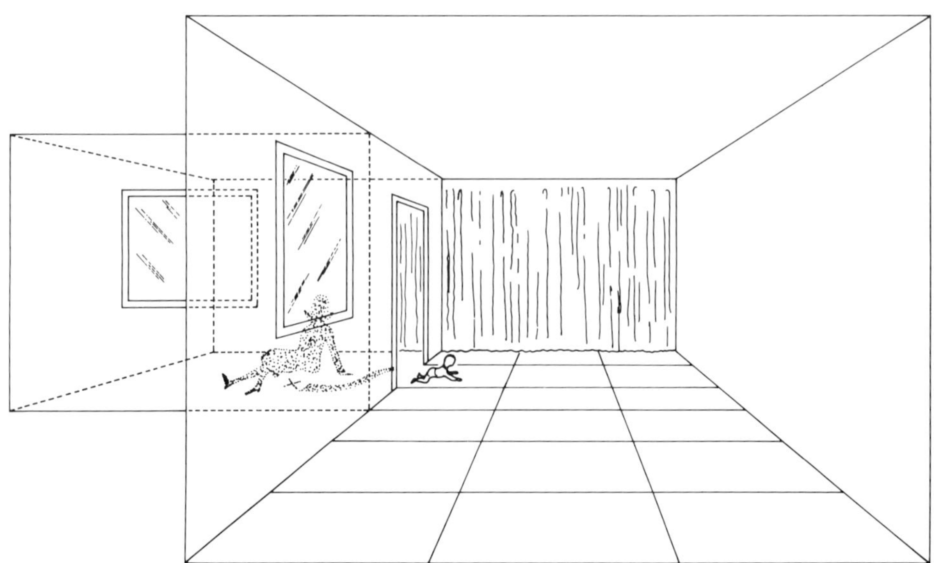

Figure 3.16. The experimental situation for studying the human infant's departure from his mother.

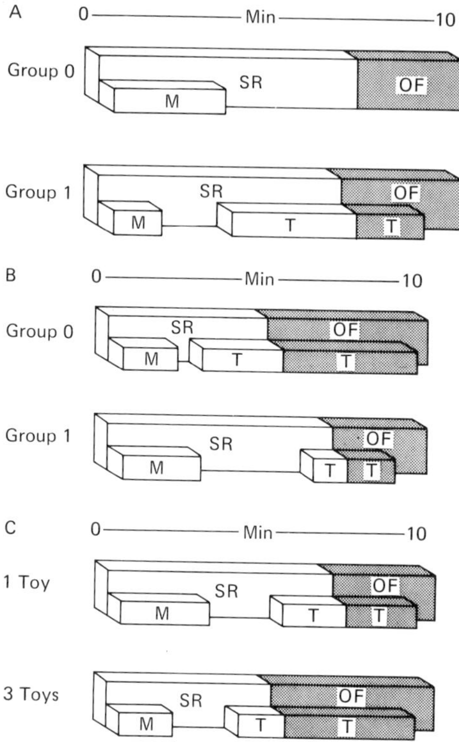

Figure 3.17. (A) Experiment 1: effect of a toy. (B) Experiment 2: effect of previous experience. (C) Experiment 2: effect of number of toys. *SR*, Starting room; *OF*, open field; *M*, mother; *T*, toy or toys. The sizes of *SR* and of *OF* denote time spent in each; the sizes of *M* and *T* denote time spent in contact with that object in each environment.

all succeeding statements of difference, are supported by *P* values of less than .05, obtained in Wilcoxon two-tailed matched-pairs signed-ranks tests.) The presence of the toy did not keep group 1 infants in the open field longer than group 0 infants. This result may be attributed to an unanticipated response of group 1 infants: they brought the toy *into* the starting room.

The major difference between the two groups was difference in the amount of time spent with the mother. When group 0 infants were in the starting room they spent more time with the mother than group 1 infants did; group 1 infants spent at least half the time playing with the toy.

Of interest, also, was the observation that infants did not go out, come back, and stay in the starting room; rather they went out again and returned again, some infants alternating many times whether or not the environment contained a toy. One infant went out of the starting room 13 times.

Experiment 2 followed directly after experiment 1. The same infants were now exposed to essentially the same environment but with certain changes in the toys. Half the infants who had no toy in experiment 1 now had one toy, and the other half had three toys, arranged diagonally across the larger room from upper left to lower right. Similarly, half of those who previously had the toy in experiment 1 now had the same single toy in the same place, and half now had the three toys, also spaced across the larger room.

Group 0 infants now entered the open field sooner and spent more time there than group 1 infants did (Figure 3.17B). They also made contact with a toy more quickly and spent more time playing with it.

An independent analysis of the effect of three toys as compared with one toy for both groups of infants showed that three toys drew them farther from the mother. Three toys also kept them out of the mother's room longer and elicited more play in the open field than one toy did (Figure 3.17C).

The results, in summary, showed that infants left their mothers and entered a new environment. How quickly they entered it, how far they went, and how long they stayed away were responses controlled by the number and location of the stimulating objects and by whether the objects were part of the new environment from the beginning of the test or were added later.

That infants leave their mothers and, with no distress, go from one room to another is a matter of everyday observation. But the findings that infants crept into the experimental environment of this study and moved freely about with no distress contrasts sharply with the marked distress and almost complete inhibition of locomotion shown, in an earlier study (25), by infants *placed* alone in that same environment.

An infant's entering a room that contains a toy would seem to demand no explanation. But an infant's entering a room that does not contain a toy, or any other prominent object, raises the question of what evokes entry. Devoid though the room was of any prominent object, it nevertheless was brighter than the starting room, and it contained many visual stimuli —a doorstop, curtains, lines and angles. If an infant can creep at all, creeping into a new environment must often have been reinforced previously by such changes in visual stimulation.

The infant's return to the starting room and his reentry into the large room may be considered illustrative of Ainsworth's (6, p. 78) "exploration from the mother as a secure base," and is reminiscent of the report by Harlow and Zimmermann (*11*) of infant rhesus monkeys that, after several sessions in an open field, used the cloth cylinder on which they had been raised "as a base of operations," moving away and returning to it between contacts with stimuli in the environment. But if the mother is considered a base, the data of our study show that the infants did not always *touch* base; on one-third of the returns, to *see* seemed sufficient. Furthermore, Ainsworth's term *secure* implies the affording of safety, and would be more appropriate here if the return to the mother were a flight from the larger environment. Of this there was no evidence. Quite the contrary; the return was often accompanied by facial and vocal expressions of pleasure and not by signs of fear or of relief from fear.

Problems for Further Study

Many questions about the process by which the infant separates himself from his mother still await investigation. Questions about the role of environmental stimuli in effecting his departure lend themselves most easily to experimental analysis. We propose that the visual properties of objects, both social and nonsocial, control the infant's leaving the mother and making contact with the objects. As we have shown, such properties also determine how long it takes him to leave, how far he goes, and whether he gets out of sight of his mother. The feedback properties of objects determine the duration of contact, the nature and extent of manipulation, and hence the time spent away from the mother; they may also control the child's subsequent return to the objects. The properties of the ambient environment may similarly affect the infant's leaving his mother. For example, we have noticed in the laboratory that the infant is more likely to enter a brightly illuminated room than a dimly lighted one. The mother's behavior in laboratory studies will certainly be a determinant of the infant's behavior. Her talking, caressing, or playing games may keep him at her side. If she moves to a new position or leaves the room, will he follow?

So far we have been reporting laboratory studies. Naturalistic studies in the child's own home can supply complementary information. As in the primate studies, the frequency of contacts, approaches, and departures by both infant and mother can be charted at different ages, and charted in a given child over a period of time. Which behaviors of the infant evoke maternal restraining and retrieving behavior? Alternatively, how does the mother foster or encourage his departures? These questions specify variables of maternal behavior that should be viewed as a set of environmental stimuli modifying the infant's leaving her side. Although the first movement away from her side is his, her response may alter its subsequent occurrence. Similarly, the behavior of other members of the family deserves attention (*26*).

Once again, the details of study have been outlined for the human infant. It is clear, however, that the same questions and the same procedures, with minor variations, apply to other mammals. Although many accounts of the development of behavior in young mammals contain some information on the infant's leaving the mother and nest (see, for example, *27*), we found no substantial body of data on this topic for mammals other than the primates.

The lines of inquiry proposed up to this point seem straightforward and clear. One sees how the stimulating conditions can be varied and the behaviors measured. Less clear are the procedures for demonstrating the psychological advantages that moving away from the mother may confer on the infant. Reasonable and likely as these advantages seemed when proposed earlier in this article, they nevertheless await confirmation in tests on the young, developing organism.

If we look beyond the period of infancy, the full significance of the child's separating himself from his mother comes into view. Leaving her side is but the first step in the continuous process of achieving psychological independence.

Summary

In this article we have defined a class of behavior which has not often been the subject of formal study. Its universality among infants of all species is not basis enough for its engaging scientific attention. Far more important are its biological and psychological consequences; we propose that among these consequences are increased opportunities for learning on the part of the infant. Primarily by his own physical contacts with objects, near and distant, he learns the structural arrangements of objects in space and the tactual and other feedback properties of objects, both social and nonsocial.

The human infant, unlike many other mammals, separates himself from his mother at the first moment any mode of locomotion is possible. He does not wait until he can creep or walk efficiently. The separation, once effected, increases in distance and duration over the life of the individual.

The behavior is patent, it can be measured, it need not be inferred, and, as we have demonstrated, it can be experimentally manipulated. Further, it lends itself nicely to comparisons among species.

We do not propose that the infant's detachment from his mother is a negation of attachment to his mother, but current preoccupation with the attachment of the young to the mother should not obscure the importance of detachment. Its study can present the same challenge that the infant seems to find in going forth on his own.

References

1. H. F. HARLOW, M. K. HARLOW, and E. W. HANSEN, in *Maternal Behavior in Mammals*, H. L. Rheingold, Ed. (Wiley, New York, 1963), pp. 254–281.
2. R. A. HINDE, and Y. SPENCER-BOOTH, *Anim. Behav. 15*, 169 (1967).
3. G. D. JENSEN, R. A. BOBBITT, and B. N. GORDON, in *Social Communication among Primates*, S. A. Altmann, Ed. (Univ. of Chicago Press, Chicago, 1967).
4. I. C. KAUFMAN, and L. A. ROSENBLUM, in *Determinants of Infant Behavior IV*. B. M. Foss, Ed. (Methuen, London, 1969).
5. J. VAN LAWICK-GOODALL, *Anim. Behav. Monogr. 1*, 161 (1968).
6. M. AINSWORTH, in *Determinants of Infant Behavior II*, B. M. Foss, Ed. (Methuen, London, 1963). In this report Ainsworth describes the Ganda infant's separating himself from his mother.
7. R. HELD, and A. HEIN [*J. Comp. Physiol. Psychol. 65*, 872 (1963)] showed the importance of active, rather than passive, movement for the development of visually guided behavior in kittens.
8. In the psychoanalytic literature, the term *detachment* means the suppressing of emotions and has been used by J. Bowlby [*Attachment and Loss:* vol. 1, *Attachment* (Hogarth, London, 1969)] to describe a phase in the child's response to his mother after extended separation.
9. J. BOWLBY, *Int. J. Psycho-Anal. 41*, 1 (1960); *J. Child Psychol. Psychiat. 1*, 251 (1961).
10. C. N. COFER, and M. H. APPLEY, *Motivation: Theory and Research* (Wiley, New York, 1964); H. Fowler, *Curiosity and Exploratory Behavior* (Macmillan, New York, 1965).
11. H. E. HARLOW, and R. R. ZIMMERMANN, *Science 130*, 421 (1959).
12. I. H. KAUFMANN, *Zoologica (New York) 51*, 17 (1966).
13. S. VESSEY, *Amer. Zool. 8*, 740 (1968); personal communication.
14. P. JAY, in *Maternal Behavior in Mammals*, H. L. RHEINGOLD, Ed. (Wiley, New York, 1963), pp. 282–304.
15. I. DEVORE, ibid., pp. 305–335.
16. G. B. SCHALLER, *The Mountain Gorilla, Ecology and Behavior* (Univ. of Chicago Press, Chicago, 1963), pp. 265–266.
17. N. BAYLEY, *Bayley Scales of Infant Development* (Psychological Corp., New York, 1969).
18. S. A. ALTMANN, *J. Mammalogy 40*, 317 (1959).
19. JENSEN *et al.* (3), for the pig-tailed macaque, and R. A. Hinde and Y. Spencer-Booth [in *Primate Ethology*, D. Morris, Ed. (Aldine, Chicago, 1967), pp. 267–286], for the rhesus macaque, also reported the movements of mother and infant toward and away from each other; the data are given in terms of relative and not absolute frequencies. Both sets of data, do, however, show that the frequency of the infant's departures relative to the sum of the infant's and the mother's departures increased as the infant grew older. That the data also show similar increases in the relative frequency of the infant's approaches and that his approaches outnumber his departures are findings that offer additional information about the behavior of young animals but in no way detract from the main thesis of this article.
20. G. A. DOYLE, A. ANDERSSON, and S. K. BEARDER, *Folia Primatol. 11*, 215 (1969).
21. L. A. ROSENBLUM, and I. C. KAUFMAN, in *Social Communication among Primates*, S. A. Altmann, Ed. (Univ. of Chicago Press, Chicago, 1967), pp. 38–39.
22. G. D. JENSEN, R. A. BOBBITT, and B. N. GORDON, *Behaviour 30*, 6 (1968).
23. J. W. ANDERSON, according to J. Bowlby [*Attachment and Loss:* vol. 1, *Attachment*

Hogarth, London, 1969), p. 253] observed the behavior of children with their mothers in a park, but the findings as reported do not lend themselves to direct comparison with ours.

24. H. L. RHEINGOLD, and C. O. ECKERMAN, *J. Exp. Child Psychol.* 8, 271 (1969).

25. H. L. RHEINGOLD, in *Determinants of Infant Behavior IV*, B. M. Foss, Ed. (Methuen, London, 1969), pp. 137–166.

26. JENSEN *et al.* (*3*), Hinde and Spencer-Booth [in *Primate Ethology*, D. Morris, Ed. (Aldine, Chicago, 1967)], and Kaufman and Rosenblum (*4*) describe the effect of the rearing environment upon the infant macaque's departure from the mother.

27. R. C. BOLLES, and P. J. WOODS, *Anim. Behav.* *12*, 427 (1964).

15. ADULT STATUS OF CHILDREN WITH CONTRASTING EARLY LIFE EXPERIENCES: A FOLLOW-UP STUDY

HAROLD M. SKEELS

Introduction

A follow-up study that covers a span of some 30 years will inevitably bracket changes in psychological concepts and practices. In the early 1930s when the subjects of this report were identified as infants, the prevailing concept of intelligence held by psychologists, social workers, and educators was that intelligence is a fixed individual characteristic. It was believed to be related to parental genetic traits that were inferred from the parents' occupational and educational achievements, to show little fluctuation from early childhood to maturity, and to be relatively uninfluenced by the impact of environment. Assessment of the intelligence of young children, while difficult, was regarded as not impossible. It was believed that knowing a child's mental level facilitated planning for his future, since the developmental quotient was considered to be an acceptably stable predictor of his future development. In the absence of reliable measures for an infant, for example, the parents' educational achievement, occupational classification, and general sociocultural status were considered to be predictive of the child's potentialities.

In developing plans for dependent children, social workers in the more sophisticated agencies placed considerable emphasis on details of family history. The resulting assessment of potential was used as a basis for matching children and prospective adoptive parents or for making other plans for the child. When such information was not available, or was unfavorable, the child was held for observation until his development could be assessed. For some children this meant several years of observation. Since foster homes were relatively scarce, most children in this category were detained in orphanages during the observation period.

At the same time, some agencies were not influenced by the prevailing, academically accepted concepts of intelligence and of prediction of future development. In these agencies, a variety of practices was found ranging from indiscriminate placements in adoptive homes to early diagnosis of retardation.

The validity of what were then regarded as desirable practices had never been empirically tested, nor was there evidence to contradict them. Conducting planned and carefully designed research in the area was out of the question for both financial and humanitarian reasons. However, the possibility of observing and studying the results of existing practices was completely feasible. The natural-history approach of observing, measuring, recording, and interpreting data without intervention in the practices that produced them was basic to the initial reports in the so-called Iowa Studies. Included among them were the follow-up studies of the mental development of children who had been placed in adoptive homes in infancy and in later childhood (Skeels, 1936, 1938; Skodak, 1939; Skodak & Skeels, 1945, 1949), and the study of the mental growth of children who had been in inadequate homes for varying periods (Skeels & Fillmore, 1937). Later, studies were made of the effects of specific intervention, such as the influence of language training (Dawe, 1942) and the effect of a nursery-school program (Skeels, Updegraff, Wellman, & Williams, 1938; Wellman, 1938).

The present study is a report on the status as adults of two groups of children originally encountered in the Iowa institutions. One group experienced what was then regarded as the normal course of events in a childcaring institution, while the other experienced a specifically designed and implemented intervention program. Reports on the development of these children have appeared in two previous publications. The first (Skeels & Dye, 1939) described the original experimental period, and the second (Skeels, 1942) reported a follow-up some two years later. The study was not planned nor the data gathered in a way to form the basis for studies of personality structure in depth. The findings reported here, therefore, are concerned with the question of whether and for how long a time mental development is affected by major changes in early environment and, specifically, with the factors significantly associated with deflections in mental development. It is hoped that these findings will contribute to the growing body of evidence on the effects of deprivation and poverty on the young child's ability to learn.

Mention may be made that this report summarizes one unit of a series of studies that were the center of much controversy over the years. In addition to its historical interest, it is hoped that it will have contemporary value and support for workers in the applied fields of child development. Comparisons with the growing body of literature on early childhood development and on the impact of environment on children are left to the reader.

The Original Study

All the children in this study had become wards of the orphanage through established court procedures after no next of kin was found able to provide either support or suitable guardianship. Of the 25 children, 20 were illegitimate and the remainder had been separated from their parents because of evidence of severe neglect and/or abuse. Then as now, the courts were reluctant to sever the ties between child and parents and did so only when clearly presented with no other alternative. All the children were white and of north-European background.

The orphanage in which the children were placed occupied, with a few exceptions, buildings that had first served as a hospital and barracks during the Civil War. The institution was overcrowded and understaffed. By present standards, diet, sanitation, general care, and basic philosophy of operation were censurable. At the time of the study, however, the discrepancies between conditions in the institution and in the general community were not so great and were not always to the disadvantage of the institution. Over the past 30 years, administrative and physical changes have occurred that reflect the economic and social gains of our society. The description of conditions in the institution in the 1930s, therefore, does not apply to the present.

At the time the original study was begun, infants up to the age of 2 years were housed in the hospital, then a relatively new building. Until about 6 months, they were cared for in the infant nursery. The babies were kept in standard hospital cribs that often had protective sheeting on the sides, thus effectively limiting visual stimulations; no toys or other objects were hung in the infants' line of vision. Human interactions were limited to baby nurses who, with the speed born of practice and necessity, changed diapers or bedding, bathed and medicated the infants, and fed them efficiently with propped bottles.

Older infants, from about 6 to 24 months, were moved into small dormitories containing two to five large cribs. This arrangement permitted the infants to move about a little and to interact somewhat with those in neighboring cribs. The children were cared for by two nurses with some assistance from one or two girls, 10 to 15 years old, who regarded the assignment as an unwelcome chore. The children had good physical and medical care, but little can be said beyond this. Interactions with adults were largely limited to feeding, dressing, and toilet details. Few play materials were available, and there was little time for the teaching of play techniques. Most of the children had a brief play period on the floor; a few toys were available at the beginning of such periods, but if any rolled out of reach there was no one to retrieve it. Except for short walks out of doors, the children were seldom out of the nursery room.

At 2 years of age these children were graduated to the cottages, which had been built around 1860. A rather complete description of "cottage" life is reported by Skeels et al. (1938) from which the following excerpts are taken:

> Overcrowding of living facilities was characteristic. Too many children had to be accommodated in the available space and there were too few adults to guide them. . . . Thirty to thirty-five children of the same sex under six years of age lived in a "cottage" in charge of one matron and three or four entirely untrained and often reluctant girls of thirteen to fifteen years of age. The waking and sleeping hours of these children were spent (except during meal times and a little time on a grass plot) in an average-sized room (approximately fifteen feet square), a sunporch of similar size, a cloakroom, . . . and a single dormitory. The latter was occupied only during sleeping hours. The meals for all children in the orphanage were served in a central building in a single large dining room. . . .
>
> The duties falling to the lot of the matron were not only those involved in the care of the children but those related to clothing and cottage maintenance, in other words, cleaning, mending, and so forth. . . . With so much responsibility centered in one adult the result was a necessary regimentation. The children sat down, stood up, and did many things in rows and in unison. They spent considerable time sitting on chairs, for in addition to the number of children and the matron's limited time there was the misfortune of inadequate equipment. . . .
>
> No child had any property which belonged exclusively to him except, perhaps, his toothbrush. Even his clothing, including shoes, was selected and put on him according to size [pp. 10–11].

After a child reached the age of 6 years, he began school. His associates were his cottage mates and the children of the same age and opposite sex who lived on the other side of the institution grounds. Although the curriculum was ostensibly the same as that in the local public school, it was generally agreed that the standards were adjusted to the capabilities of the orphanage children. Few of those who had their entire elementary-school experience in the institution's school were able to make the transition to the public junior high school.

The orphanage was designed for mentally normal children. It was perpetually overcrowded, although every opportunity to relieve this pressure was exploited. One such relief occurred periodically when new buildings were opened at other institutions, such as at the schools for the mentally retarded. It was not uncommon for a busload of children to be transferred on such occasions. A valued contribution of the psychologists was the maintenance of lists of children who, on the basis of test scores and observable behavior, were regarded as eligible for transfers.

The environmental conditions in the two state institutions for the mentally retarded were not identical but they had many things in common. Patient-inmates were grouped by sex, age, and general ability. Within any one ward, the patients were highly similar. The youngest children tended to be the most severely disabled and were frequently "hospital" patients. The older, more competent inmates had work assignments throughout the institution and constituted a somewhat self-conscious elite with recognized status.

Personnel at that time included no resident social workers or psychologists. Physicians were resident at the schools for the mentally retarded and were on call at the orphanage. Administrative and matron and caretaking staffs were essentially untrained and nonprofessional. Psychological services were introduced in the orphanage in 1932 when the author, on the staff of the Iowa Child Welfare Research Station, State University of Iowa, became the first psychologist to be employed by the Iowa Board of Control of State Institutions. Over the years this proved to be a happy marriage of service and research related to the care of dependent children.

Identification of Cases

Early in the service aspects of the program, two baby girls, neglected by their feebleminded mothers, ignored by their inadequate relatives, malnourished and frail, were legally committed to the orphanage. The youngsters were pitiful little creatures. They were tearful, had runny noses, and sparse, stringy, and colorless hair; they were emaciated, undersized, and lacked muscle tonus or responsiveness. Sad and inactive, the two spent their days rocking and whining.

The psychological examinations showed developmental levels of 6 and 7 months respectively, for the two girls, although they were 13 and 16 months old chronologically. This serious delay in mental growth was confirmed by observations of their behavior in the nursery and by reports of the superintendent of nurses, as well as by the pediatrician's examination. There was no evidence of physiological or organic defect, or of birth injury or glandular dysfunction.

The two children were considered unplaceable, and transfer to a school for the mentally retarded was recommended with a high degree of confidence. Accordingly, they were transferred to an institution for the mentally retarded at the next available vacancy, when they were aged 15 and 18 months, respectively.

In the meantime, the author's professional responsibilities had been increased to include itinerant psychological services to the two state institutions for the mentally retarded. Six months after the transfer of the two children, he was visiting the wards at an institution for the mentally retarded and noticed two outstanding little girls. They were alert, smiling, running about, responding to the playful attention of adults, and generally behaving and looking like any other toddlers. He scarcely recognized them as the two little girls with the hopeless prognosis, and thereupon tested them again. Although the results indicated that the two were approaching normal mental development for age, the author was skeptical of the validity or permanence of the improvement and no change was instituted in the lives of the children. Twelve months later they were re-examined, and then again when they were 40 and 43 months old. Each examination gave unmistakable evidence of mental development well within the normal range for age.

There was no question that the initial evaluations gave a true picture of the children's functioning level at the time they were tested. It appeared equally evident that later appraisals showed normal mental growth accompanied by parallel changes in social growth, emotional maturity, communication skills, and general behavior. In order to find a possible explanation for the changes that had occurred, the nature of the children's life space was reviewed.

The two girls had been placed on one of the wards of older, brighter girls and women, ranging in age from 18 to 50 years and in mental age from 5 to 9 years, where they were the only children of preschool age, except for a few hopeless bed patients with gross physical defects. An older girl on the ward had "adopted" each of the two girls, and other older girls served as adoring aunts. Attendants and nurses also showed affection to the two, spending time with them, taking them along on their days off for automobile rides and shopping excursions, and purchasing toys, picture books, and play materials for them in great abundance. The setting seemed to be a homelike one, abundant in affection, rich in wholesome and interesting experiences, and geared to a preschool level of development.

It was recognized that as the children grew older their developmental needs would be less adequately met in the institution for the mentally retarded. Furthermore, they were now normal and the need for care in such an institution no longer existed. Consequently, they were transferred back to the orphanage and shortly thereafter were placed in adoptive homes.

At this point, evidence on the effects of environment on intelligence had been acmumulated from a number of studies. Skeels and Fillmore (1937) had found that older children who came from inadequate non-nurturant homes were mentally retarded or borderline but that their younger siblings were generally of normal ability, which suggested that longer residence in such homes had a cumulatively depressing effect on intelligence. Children also became retarded if they remained for long periods in an institution (1930-style) supposedly designed for normal children (Skeels, 1940). However, if children were placed in adoptive homes as infants, or even as young preschoolers, their development surpassed expectations, and improvement continued for long periods following placement (Skodak, 1939). In even more extreme cases, seriously retarded children were able to attain normal levels of functioning when placed in a setting officially designed for the mentally retarded (Skeels & Dye, 1939). The consistent element seemed to be the existence of a one-to-one relationship with an adult who was generous with love and affection, together with an abundance of attention and experiential stimulation from many sources. Children who had little of these did not show progress; those who had a great deal, did.

Since study homes or temporary care homes were not available to the state agency at that time, the choice for children who were not suitable for immediate placement in adoptive homes was between, on the one hand, an unstimulating, large nursery with predictable mental retardation or, on the other hand, a radical, iconoclastic solution, that is, placement in institutions for the mentally retarded in a bold experiment to see whether retardation in infancy was reversible.

By the time these observations were organized into a meaningful whole and their implications were recognized, individual psychological tests were available for all children in the orphanage. As part of a continuing program of observation and evaluation, all infants over 3 months of age were given the then available tests (Kuhlmann-Binet and Iowa Test for Young Children), and were retested as often as changes seemed to occur. Retests at bimonthly intervals were not uncommon. Older preschoolers were re-examined at 6-

to 12-month intervals; school-aged children, annually or biennially. Children who were showing marked delay in development were kept under special observation.

Children whose development was so delayed that adoptive placement was out of the question remained in the orphanage. The only foreseeable alternative for them was eventual transfer to an institution for the mentally retarded. In the light of the experiences with the two little girls, the possibility was raised that early transfer to such an institution might have therapeutic effects. If not all, then at least some of the children might be able to attain normal mental functioning. In the event they did not, no significant change in life pattern would have occurred, and the child would remain in the situation for which he would have been destined in any case.

This radical proposal was accepted with understandable misgivings by the administrators involved. It was finally agreed that, in order to avoid the stigma of commitment to a state school for the retarded, children would be accepted as "house guests" in such institutions but would remain on the official roster of the orphanage. Periodic re-evaluations were built into the plan; if no improvement was observed in the child, commitment would follow. Insofar as possible, the children were to be placed on wards as "only" children.

In the course of time, in addition to the two little girls who have been described and another transferred to the second of the two institutions at about the same time, 10 more children became "house guests." The transfers were spaced over a year's span in groups of 3, 3, and 4. All went to one institution for the mentally handicapped, the Glenwood State School. Unfortunately, the number of "house guests" exceeded the number of "elite" wards of older girls and necessitated the use of some environments that were less desirable. Consequently, in some wards there were more children, or fewer capable older girls, or less opportunity for extra stimulation, with a resulting variation in developmental patterns.

Experimental group The experimental group consisted of the 13 children who were transferred from an orphanage for mentally normal children to an institution for the mentally retarded, as "house guests." All were under 3 years of age at the time of transfer. Their development had been reliably established as seriously retarded by tests and observation before transfer was considered.

The identification and selection of the children who constituted the experimental group can perhaps be best explained by a description of the procedures that were normally followed. County or welfare agencies, faced with the problem of care for an illegitimate or ward-of-the-court child, applied to the Board of Control and/or the Iowa Soldiers' Orphans' Home, as it was then known. When accepted (rejections occurred rarely and only under most unusual circumstances, such as obvious multiple handicaps identifiable at birth), the child was brought to the institution and placed in the hospital for observation. During the first few days he was given routine medical examinations and was observed for abnormalities or infections, etc. Within 2 to 4 weeks after admission he was also given a psychological examination. The legal commitment, available social history, and other information were collated and at the monthly assignment conferences decisions were made regarding the child. These conferences were attended by the superintendent of the institution, the Director of the Children's Division of the State Board of Control, and the psychologist. On call also were the head nurse or the pediatrician and any other staff member who could supply pertinent information. If no legal, medical or developmental impediments to adoptive placement were found, the child was assigned to an adoptive home, largely on the basis of requested sex, coloring, and religious background.

Decisions on the children who were unplaceable for legal, medical, or developmental reasons were reviewed at each subsequent monthly conference until a resolution was attained. Consequently, the children who remained in the pool of unplaced infants or toddlers became very well known to the conference participants.

As the evidence from the research studies accumulated, concern about the future of these children increased and led to the decision that some radical measure was justified. Coincidentally, a change had occurred in the administration of the state institution for the mentally handicapped which created a favorable climate for social experimentation. Those children who happened to be in the infant to 3-year-old age range, were not ineligible for placement for legal reasons, were not acutely ill, but who were mentally retarded, became members of the experimental group. The entire project covered a span of some three years and was terminated when a change in the administration of the state school reduced the tolerance for such untidy procedures as having "house guests" in an institution. The onset of World War II and the departure of the principal investigator for military service effectively closed the project.

A project such as this could not be replicated in later years because infants were no longer kept exclusively in the orphanage. Temporary boarding homes came to be utilized prior to adoptive placement or for long-term observation and care.

The experimental group consisted of 10 girls and 3 boys, none with gross physical handicaps. Prior to their placement as "house guests," the examinations were routinely administrated to them without any indication that they would or would not be involved in the unusual experience.

At the time of transfer the mean chronological age of the group was 19.4 months (SD 7.4) and the median was 17.1 months, with a range of from 7.1 to 35.9 months. The range of IQ's was from 35 to 89 with a mean of 64.3 (SD 16.4) and a median of 65.0. Additional tests were made of 11 of the 13 children shortly before or in conjunction with the pretransfer tests reported in Table 3.14, using the Kuhlmann-Binet again or the Iowa Test for Young Children, and the results corroborated the reported scores.

The children were considered unsuitable for adoption because of evident mental retardation. For example, in Case 1, although the IQ was 89, it was felt that actual retardation was much greater, as the child at 7 months could scarcely hold up his head without support and showed little general bodily activity in comparision with other infants of the same age. In Case 3, at 12 months, very little activity was observed, and the child was very unsteady when sitting up without support. She could not pull herself to a standing position and did not creep. Case 11 was not only retarded but showed perseverative patterns of behavior, particularly incessant rocking back and forth. Cases 5, 8, and 13 were classified at the imbecile level. In present-day terms, they would have been labeled "trainable mentally retarded children."

Table 3.14 lists for each child the pretransfer test findings and ages at time of transfer; also shown are posttransfer test results, length of experimental period, and changes in IQ from first to last test.

Contrast group Since the original purpose of the experiment was to rescue for normalcy, if possible, those children showing delayed or retarded development, no plans had been made for a control or comparison group. It was only after the data had been analyzed that it was found that such a contrast group was available because of the tests that were routinely given to all children in the orphanage. To select such a contrast group, therefore, records were scrutinized for children who met the following criteria:

1. Had been given intelligence tests under 2 years of age.

Table 3.14. Experimental group: mental development of children as measured by Kuhlmann-Binet Intelligence Tests before and after transfer

		Before Transfer			After Transfer							
		Test 1			Test 2		Test 3		Test Last			
Case Number[a]	Sex	Chronological Age, Months	IQ	Chronological Age, Months, at Transfer	Chronological Age, Months	IQ	Chronological Age, Months	IQ	Chronological Age, Months	IQ	Length of Experimental Period, Months	Change in IQ, First to Last Test
1.	M	7.0	89	7.1	12.8	113	...	...	12.8	113	5.7	+24
2.	F	12.7	57	13.1	20.5	94	29.4	83	36.8	77	23.7	+20
3.	F	12.7	85	13.3	25.2	107	...	...	25.2	107	11.9	+22
4.	F	14.7	73	15.0	23.1	100	...	...	23.1	100	8.1	+27
5.	F	13.4	46	15.2	21.7	77	32.9	100	40.0	95[b]	24.8	+49
6.	F	15.5	77	15.6	21.3	96	30.1	100	30.1	100	14.5	+23
7.	F	16.6	65	17.1	27.5	104	...	...	27.5	104	10.4	+39
8.	F	16.6	35	18.4	24.8	87	36.0	88	43.0	93	24.6	+58
9.	F	21.8	61	22.0	34.3	80	...	...	34.3	80	12.3	+19
10.	M	23.3	72	23.4	29.1	88	37.9	71	45.4	79	22.0	+ 7
11.	M	25.7	75	27.4	42.5	78	51.0	82[b]	51.0	82[b]	23.6	+ 7
12.	F	27.9	65	28.4	40.4	82	...	...	40.4	82	12.0	+17
13.	F	30.0	36	35.9	51.7	70	81.0	74[b]	89.0	81[b]	52.1	+45

[a] Arranged according to age at time of transfer.
[b] Stanford-Binet IQ.
Source: Adapted from H. M. Skeels & H. B. Dye (1939, Table 1).

2. Were still in residence in the orphanage at approximately 4 years of age.
3. Were in the control group of the orphanage preschool study (Skeels et al., 1938).
4. Had not attended preschool.

The Skeels et al. (1938) study had included two groups of children matched in chronological age, mental age, IQ, and length of residence in the institution, of which one group had the advantages of the more stimulating environment of preschool attendance while the other group, the controls, experienced the less stimulating environment of cottage life. Since the purpose of the contrast group in the present study was to provide data on children in a relatively nonstimulating environment, those who had attended preschool were not included. Such limitations, however, did not constitute a selective factor as far as the characteristics of the children were concerned.

A total of 12 children were selected on the basis of the criteria and became the contrast group. The mean chronological age of the group at the time of first examination was 16.6 months (SD 2.9), with a median at 16.3 months. The range was from 11.9 to 21.8 months. The mean IQ of the group was 86.7 (SD 14.3) and the median IQ was 90. With the exception of two cases (16 and 24) the children had IQ's ranging from 81 to 103; the IQ's for the two exceptions were 71 and 50, respectively. When the children were examined, it was not known that they were or would become members of any study group. The re-examinations were merely routine retests that were given to all children.

At the ages when adoptive placement usually occurred, nine of the children in the contrast group had been considered normal in mental development. All 12 were not placed, however, because of different circumstances: 5 were withheld from placement simply because of poor family histories, 2 because of improper commitments, 2 because of luetic conditions, 2 because of other health problems, and one because of possible mental retardation.

The subsequent progress of the children in both the experimental and the contrast groups was influenced by individual circumstances. The groups were never identified as such in the resident institution; the members of each group were considered together only in a statistical sense. A child in the experimental group remained in the institution for the mentally retarded until it was felt that he had attained the maximum benefit from residence there. At that point, he was placed directly into an adoptive home or returned to the orphanage in transit to an adoptive home. If he did not attain a level of intelligence that warranted adoptive plans, he remained in the institution for the mentally retarded.

The contrast-group members remained in the orphanage until placement. One was returned to relatives, but in most instances the children were eventually transferred to an institution for the mentally retarded as long-term protected residents. A few of the contrast group had been briefly approved for adoptive placement, and two had been placed for short periods. None was successful, however, and the children's decline in mental level removed them from the list of those eligible for adoption.

Table 3.15 lists the chronological ages and test findings for the children in the contrast group over the experimental period and the changes in IQ that occurred.

Summary and Implications

In the original study, the 13 children in the experimental group, all mentally retarded at the beginning of the study, experienced the effects of early intervention, which consisted of a radical shift from one institutional environment to another. The major difference between the two institutions, as experienced by the children, was in the amount of developmental stimulation and the intensity of relationships between the children and mother-surrogates.

Table 3.15. Contrast group: mental development of children as measured by repeated Kuhlmann-Binet Intelligence Tests over an average experimental period of two and one-half years.

		Test									
		1		2		3		Last			
Case Number[a]	Sex	Chronological Age, Months	IQ	Chronological Age, Months	IQ	Chronological Age, Months	IQ	Chronological Age, Months	IQ	Length of Experimental Period, Months	Change in IQ, First to Last Test
14.	F	11.9	91	24.8	73	37.5	65	55.0	62	43.1	−29
15.	F	13.0	92	20.1	54	38.3	56	38.3	56	25.3	−36
16.	F	13.6	71	20.6	76	40.9	56	40.9	56	27.3	−15
17.	M	13.8	96	37.2	58	53.2	54	53.2	54	39.4	−42
18.	M	14.5	99	21.6	67	41.9	54	41.9	54	27.4	−45
19.	M	15.2	87	22.5	80	35.5	74	44.5	67	29.3	−20
20.	M	17.3	81	43.0	77	52.9	83[b]	52.9	83[b]	35.6	+ 2
21.	M	17.5	103	26.8	72	38.0	63	50.3	60	32.8	−43
22.	M	18.3	98	24.8	93	30.7	80	39.7	61	21.4	−37
23.	F	20.2	89	27.0	71	39.4	66	48.4	71	28.2	−18
24.	M	21.5	50	34.9	57	51.6	42	51.6	42	30.1	− 8
25.	M	21.8	83	28.7	75	37.8	63	50.1	60	28.3	−23

[a] Arranged according to age at first test.
[b] Stanford-Binet IQ.
Source: Adapted from H. M. Skeels & H. B. Dye (1939, Table 2).

Following a variable period in the second institution, 11 of the 13 children were placed in adoptive homes.

The contrast group of 12 children, initially higher in intelligence than the experimental group, were exposed to a relatively nonstimulating orphanage environment over a prolonged period of time.

Over a period of two years, the children in the experimental group showed a marked increase in rate of mental growth, whereas the children in the contrast group showed progressive mental retardation. The experimental group made an average gain of 28.5 IQ points; the contrast group showed an average loss of 26.2 IQ points.

The first follow-up study was made 2½ years after the termination of the original study. The 11 children in the experimental group that had been placed in adoptive homes had maintained and increased their earlier gains in intelligence, whereas the two not so placed had declined in rate of mental growth. Over the three-year post-experimental period, the children in the contrast group showed a slight mean gain in IQ but were still mentally retarded to a marked degree. In those children that showed gains in intelligence, the gains appeared to be associated with improved environmental experiences that occurred subsequent to the original study.

In the adult follow-up study, all cases were located and information obtained on them, after a lapse of 21 years.

The two groups had maintained their divergent patterns of competency into adulthood. All 13 children in the experimental group were self-supporting, and none was a ward of any institution, public or private. In the contrast group of 12 children, one had died in adolescence following continued residence in a state institution for the mentally retarded, and 4 were still wards of institutions, one in a mental hospital, and the other 3 in institutions for the mentally retarded.

In education, disparity between the two groups was striking. The contrast group completed a median of less than the third grade. The experimental group completed a median of the twelfth grade. Four of the subjects had one or more years of college work, one received a B.A. degree and took some graduate training.

Marked differences in occupational levels were seen in the two groups. In the experimental group all were self-supporting or married and functioning as housewives. The range was from professional and business occupations to domestic service, the latter the occupations of two girls who had never been placed in adoptive homes. In the contrast group, four (36%) of the subjects were institutionalized and unemployed. Those who were employed, with one exception (Case 19), were characterized as "hewers of wood and drawers of water." Using the *t* test, the difference between the status means of the two groups (based on the Warner Index of Status Characteristics applied to heads of households) was statistically significant ($p < .01$).

Educational and occupational achievement and income for the 11 adopted subjects in the experimental group compared favorably with the 1960 U.S. Census figures for Iowa and for the United States in general. Their adult status was equivalent to what might have been expected of children living with natural parents in homes of comparable sociocultural levels. Those subjects that married had marriage partners of comparable sociocultural levels.

Eleven of the 13 children in the experimental group were married; 9 of the 11 had a total of 28 children, an average of three children per family. On intelligence tests, these second-generation children had IQ's ranging from 86 to 125, with a mean and median IQ of 104. In no instance was there any indication of mental retardation or demonstrable abnormality. Those of school age were in appropriate grades for age.

In the contrast group, only two of the subjects had married. One had one child and subsequently was divorced. Psychological examination of the child revealed marked mental retardation with indications of probable brain damage. Another male subject (Case 19) had a nice home and family of four children, all of average intelligence.

The cost to the state for the contrast group, for whom intervention was essentially limited to custodial care, was approximately five times that of the cost for the experimental group. It seems safe to predict that for at least four of the cases in the contrast group costs to the state will continue at a rate in excess of $200.00 per month each for another 20 to 40 years.

Implications of Study

At the beginning of the study, the 11 children in the experimental group evidenced marked mental retardation. The developmental trend was reversed through planned intervention during the experimental period. The program of nurturance and cognitive stimulation was followed by placement in adoptive homes that provided love and affection and normal life experiences. The normal, average intellectual level attained by the subjects in early or middle childhood was maintained into adulthood.

It can be postulated that if the children in the contrast group had been placed in suitable adoptive homes or given some other appropriate equivalent in early infancy, most or all of them would have achieved within the normal range of development, as did the experimental subjects.

It seems obvious that under present-day conditions there are still countless infants born with sound biological constitutions and potentialities for development well within the normal range who will become mentally retarded and noncontributing members of society unless appropriate intervention occurs. It is suggested by the findings of this study and others published in the past 20 years that sufficient knowledge is available to design programs of intervention to counteract the devasting effects of poverty, sociocultural deprivation, and maternal deprivation.

Since the study was a pioneering and descriptive one involving only a small number of cases, it would be presumptuous to attempt to identify the specific influences that produced the changes observed. However, the contrasting outcome between children who experienced enriched environmental opportunities and close emotional relationships with affectionate adults, on the one hand, and those children who were in deprived, indifferent, and unresponsive environments, on the other, leaves little doubt that the area is a fruitful one for further study.

It has become increasingly evident that the prediction of later intelligence cannot be based on the child's first observed developmental status. Account must be taken of his experiences between test and retest. Hunt (1964, p. 212) has succinctly stated that,

> . . . In fact, trying to predict what the IQ of an individual child will be at age 18 from a D.Q. obtained during his first or second year is much like trying to predict how fast a feather might fall in a hurricane. The law of falling bodies holds only under the specified and controlled conditions of a vacuum. Similarly, any laws concerning the rate of intellectual growth must take into account the series of environmental encounters which constitute the conditions of that growth.

The divergence in mental-growth patterns between children in the experimental and contrast groups is a striking illustration of this concept.

The right of every child to be well born, well nurtured, well brought up, and well educated was enunciated in the Children's Charter of the 1930 White House Conference on Child Health and Protection (White House Conference, 1931). Though society strives to insure this right, for many years to come there will be children to whom it has been denied and for whom society must provide both intervention and restitution. There is need for further research to determine the optimum modes of such intervention and the most appro-

BOWLBY, J. *Maternal Care and Mental Health.* New York: Schocken Books, 1951.

BRONFENBRENNER, U. When is infant stimulation effective? In Glass, D. (Ed.) *Environmental Influences.* New York: Rockefeller University Press and Russell Sage Foundation, 1968. Pp. 251–265.

CARMICHAEL, L. Onset and early development of behavior. In Mussen, P. (Ed.) *Carmichael's Manual of Child Psychology,* Vol. 1. New York: Wiley, 1970. Pp. 447–564.

MARLER, P., and GORDON, A. The social environment of infant macaques. In Glass, D. (Ed.) *Environmental Influences.* New York: Rockefeller University Press and Russell Sage Foundation, 1968. Pp. 113–129.

MASON, W. A. Early social deprivation in the nonhuman primates: Implications for human behavior. In Glass, D. (Ed.) *Environmental Influences.* New York: Rockefeller University Press and Russell Sage Foundation, 1968. Pp. 70–101.

NEWTON, G., and LEVINE, S. *Early Experience and Behavior.* Springfield, Ill.: Thomas, 1968.

SCOTT, J. P. *Early Experience and the Organization of Behavior.* Belmont, California: Wadsworth Publishing, 1968.

STEVENSON, H., HESS, E. H., and RHEINGOLD, H. (Eds.) *Early Behavior: Comparative and Developmental Approaches.* New York: Wiley, 1967.

THOMPSON, W. R., and GRUSEC, J. Studies of early experience. In Mussen, P. (Ed.) *Carmichael's Manual of Child Psychology,* Vol. 1. New York: Wiley, 1970. Pp. 565–654.

YARROW, L. J. Separation from parents during early childhood. In Hoffman, M. L. and Hoffman, L. W. (Eds.) *Review of Child Development Research,* Vol. 1. New York: Russell Sage Foundation, 1964. Pp. 89–136.

———. The crucial nature of early experience. In Glass, D. (Ed.) *Environmental Influences.* New York: Rockefeller University Press and Russell Sage Foundation, 1968. Pp. 101–113.

chapter four
cultural influences on development

All children grow up within the context of some culture, but there are many cultural variations in the world. Behavior appropriate in one place would be frowned upon in another. For example, a child who asks many questions would be a delight among some peoples and a horror elsewhere. In some cultures a mother is acting appropriately if she prechews her baby's food and spits it into its mouth; the idea of such behavior is unpleasant to most Americans.

What we see every day is what we think of as normal; normal therefore varies between cultures. Each cultural group has its own behaviors and beliefs that it tries to inculcate in its children. It is often very difficult to look at what another culture does and accept it as appropriate when it is very different from what one is accustomed to.

Even within one country, such as the United States, patterns of behavior change with the generations, as can be clearly seen in dress styles, language usage, and, more deeply, in the patterns of interaction at home, at school, and at work. And, as we are well aware, patterns of usage within the United States also can differ within regions, subcultures, class levels, and so forth.

If we are to understand child development, and not only present day American child development, we must look at the varieties of growth patterns and behaviors found across several cultures and within the same culture over a time. The readings that follow should encourage you to recognize the variability in human beings, and should help you understand more about child development.

Readings in other sections of this book are also about children growing up within a specific society and the relationships found there may also tell you something about that society. In addition, all researchers are members of a society and what they study reflects, to some extent, the interests of their own society.

The selections from Watson, Spock, and Makarenko show that training techniques differ when goals differ. What happens when children are trained in these three different ways is not easy to state. We do not know the effects of training techniques on later development, but we can speculate on the types of behaviors each fosters and, if similar training continues through life, the types of people who might develop.

Rebelsky shows two cultures with very different beliefs about appropriate baby behavior and the different amounts of care that infants receive. The comparison with Goldberg's article points out variations across cultures in what is considered appropriate behavior.

We believe, with Tulkin, that differences in development are just that—and should not be labeled better or worse. It is apparent, as we look at what is appropriate behavior in another culture, that cultures approve of varieties of behaviors and, as stated above, what is desirable in one culture is disliked in another. At this stage of our knowledge, cultural "relativism" is a position that leads to increased insight into developmental processes.

Cross-cultural research provides additional descriptive information about the varieties of child development. Moreover, it serves to stimulate new hypotheses about development. If a baby walks at six months in Uganda, at about twelve months in the United States, and at about sixteen months in Holland, we can begin to try to understand the environmental forces that influence motor development. Cross-cultural research, by exposing more variation than exists within any single culture, helps us to notice behaviors and processes that we fail to notice within our own culture.

16. EXCERPTS FROM *PSYCHOLOGICAL CARE OF INFANT AND CHILD*

JOHN B. WATSON

Since the behaviorists find little that corresponds to instincts in children, since children are made not born, failure to bring up a happy child, a well adjusted child—assuming bodily health—falls upon the parents' shoulders. The acceptance of this view makes child-rearing the most important of all social obligations.

Since the most serious faults in the rearing of children are to be found on the emotional side I have put especial emphasis upon the growth of emotional habits. The other two phases taken up are day and night time care and the kind and amount of sex instruction that should be given.

One of the many criticisms which may be argued against the book is the fact that I have written principally to mothers who have leisure to devote to the study of their children. The reason I have chosen these more fortunate mothers as my audience, grows out of the hope I have that some day the importance of the first two years of infancy will be fully realized. When it is faced, every woman will seriously question whether she is in a proper situation to have a child. Today we debate whether we can buy a motor car—whether the house or apartment is big enough to keep a dog—whether we can afford to belong to a club. But the young mother rarely questions whether her home can house a child or whether her husband's salary or weekly wage will stretch far enough to feed another incessantly hungry body. No, she has the child and we all rush to congratulate the pair and smile and smirk over an occurrence which takes place two and a half million times each year in the United States of America. The having of a child should be a carefully thought out operation. No mother has a right to have a child who cannot give it a room to itself for the first two years of infancy. I would make this a *conditio sine qua non*.

. . .

This doctrine is almost the opposite of what is taught in the schools at the present time. Professor John Dewey and many other educators have been insisting for the last twenty years upon a method of training which allows the child to develop from within. This is really a doctrine of mystery. It teaches that there are hidden springs of activity, hidden possibilities of unfolding within the child which must be waited for until they appear and then be fostered and tended. I think this doctrine has done serious harm. It has made us lose our opportunity to implant and then to encourage a real eagerness for vocations at an early age.

. . .

The mother coddles the child for two reasons. One, she admits; the other, she doesn't admit because she doesn't know that it is true. The one she admits is that she wants the child to be happy, she wants it to be surrounded by love in order that it may grow up to be a kindly, good-natured child. The other is that her own whole being cries out for the expression of love. Her mother before her has trained her to give and receive love. She is starved for love—affection, as she prefers to call it. It is at bottom a sex-seeking response in her, else she would never kiss the child on the lips. Certainly, to satisfy her professed reason for coddling, kissing the youngster on the forehead, on the back of the hand, patting it on the head once in a while, would be all the petting needed for a baby to learn that it is growing up in a kindly home.

But even granting that the mother thinks she kisses the child for the perfectly logical reason of implanting the proper amount of affection and kindliness in it, does she succeed? The fact I brought out before, that we rarely see a happy child, is proof to the contrary. The fact that our children are always crying and always whining shows the unhappy, unwholesome state they are in. Their digestion is interfered with and probably their whole glandular system is deranged.

Should the Mother Never Kiss the Baby?

There is a sensible way of treating children. Treat them as though they were young adults. Dress them, bathe them with care and circumspection. Let your behavior always be objective and kindly firm. Never hug and kiss them, never let them sit in your lap. If you must, kiss them once on the forehead when they say good night. Shake hands with them in the morning. Give them a pat on the head if they have made an extraordinarily good job of a difficult task. Try it out. In a week's time you will find how easy it is to be perfectly objective with your child and at the same time kindly. You will be utterly ashamed of the mawkish, sentimental way you have been handling it.

If you expected a dog to grow up and be useful as a watch dog, a bird dog, a fox hound, useful for anything except a lap dog, you wouldn't dare treat it the way you treat your child. When I hear a mother say "Bless its little heart" when it falls down, or stubs its toe, or suffers some other ill, I usually have to walk a block or two to let off steam. Can't the mother train herself when something happens to the child to look at its hurt without saying anything, and if there is a wound to dress it in a matter of fact way? And then as the child grows older, can she not train it to go and find the boracic acid and the bandages and treat its own wounds? Can't she train herself to substitute a kindly word, a smile, in all of her dealings with the child, for the kiss and the hug, the pickup and coddling? Above all, can't she learn to keep away from the child a large part of the day since love conditioning must grow up anyway, even when scrupulously guarded against, through feeding and bathing? I sometimes wish that we could live in a community of homes where each home is supplied with a well-trained nurse so that we could have the babies fed and bathed each week by a different nurse.

. . .

Certainly a mother, when necessary, ought to leave her child for a long enough period for over-conditioning to die down. If you haven't a nurse and cannot leave the child, put it out in the backyard a large part of the day. Build a fence around the yard so that you are sure no harm can come to it. Do this from the time it is born. When the child can crawl, give it a sandpile and be sure to dig some small holes in the yard so it has to crawl in and out of them. Let it learn to overcome difficulties almost from the moment of birth. The child should learn to conquer difficulties away from your watchful eye.

. . .

Waking Up Time

Morning and bedlam?—No. Modern training calls always for an orderly life. Usually from 1 year of age to 3 pediatricians specify that orange juice shall be given when the child wakes up in the morning. Children who sleep properly awaken on a schedule. The waking time can easily be set for 6:30. The orange juice should then be given regularly at that hour every morning, the child put on the toilet for the relief of the bladder (only). Put the child back to bed and allow it to sit up in bed and play quietly alone with one or two chosen toys. It should be taken up at 7 o'clock, sponged lightly, dressed and given its breakfast at 7:30; then allowed to romp until 8, then put upon the toilet for 20 minutes or less (until the bowel movement is complete). The infant from 8 months of age onward should have a special toilet seat into which he can be safely strapped. *The child should be left in the bathroom without toys and with the door closed.* Under no circumstances should the door be left open or the mother or nurse stay with the child. This is a rule which seems to be almost universally broken. When broken it leads to dawdling, loud conversation, in general to unsocial and dependent behavior.

. . .

Is the End Result Worth the Struggle?

Is is worth all this stuggle—won't the child get along anyway—haven't millions got along before busy-bodies stepped in to tell us how to rear our youngsters? If all of these things have to be done doesn't it mean that motherhood is becoming almost a profession? I believe the struggle is worth while even if the mother does have to turn professional. The end result is *a happy child free as air* because he has mastered the stupidly simple demands society makes upon him. *An independent child* because all during his training you have made him play and work alone a part of the time, and you have made him get out of difficulties by his own efforts. *A child that meets and plays with other children* frankly, openly, untroubled by shyness and inferiority. *An original child* because his perfect adjustment to his environment gives him leisure to experiment. Don't believe anyone who tells you that such insistence on routine tends to steam roller the child and to reduce the growth of his own "inward life and powers." "Spontaneity," "inward development," and the like are phrases used by those too lazy or too stupid or too prejudiced to study children in the actual making.

The only person in life who is effectively original is the person who has a routine and has mastered a technique. The person who has not these is a slave—his life is taken up in trying to keep up with the procession of those struggling to obtain just bread, meat, and a roof for shelter.

17. EXCERPTS FROM *BABY AND CHILD CARE*

BENJAMIN SPOCK

The Parents' Part

Trust Yourself

You know more than you think you do Soon you're going to have a baby. Maybe you have him already. You're happy and excited, but if you haven't had much experience, you wonder whether you are going to know how to do a good job. Lately you have been listening more carefully to your friends and relatives when they talk about bringing up a child. You've begun to read articles by experts in the magazines and newspapers. After the baby is born, the doctor and nurses will begin to give you instructions, too. Sometimes it sounds like a very complicated business. You find out all the vitamins a baby needs and all the inoculations. One mother tells you that egg should be given early because of its iron, and another says that egg should be delayed to avoid allergy. You hear that a baby is easily spoiled by being picked up too much but also that a baby must be cuddled plenty; that fairy tales make children nervous, and that fairy tales are a wholesome outlet.

Don't take too seriously all that the neighbors say. Don't be overawed by what the experts say. Don't be afraid to trust your own common sense. Bringing up your child won't be a complicated job if you take it easy, trust your own instincts, and follow the directions that your doctor gives you. We know for a fact that the natural loving care that kindly parents give their children is a hundred times more valuable than their knowing how to pin a diaper on just right or how to make a formula expertly. Every time you pick your baby up, even if you do it a little awkwardly at first, every time you change him, bathe him, feed him, smile at him, he's getting a feeling that he belongs to you and that you belong to him. Nobody else in the world, no matter how skillful, can give that to him.

. . .

Your Baby

Enjoy Him

Don't be afraid of him You'd think from what some people say about babies' demanding attention that they come into the world determined to get their parents under their thumb by hook or by crook. This isn't true. Your baby is born to be a reasonable, friendly human being.

Don't be afraid to feed him when you think he's really hungry. If you are mistaken, he'll merely refuse to take much.

Don't be afraid to love him and enjoy him. Every baby needs to be smiled at, talked to, played with, fondled—gently and lovingly—just as much as he needs vitamins and calories. That's what will make him a person who loves people and enjoys life. The baby who doesn't get any loving will grow up cold and unresponsive.

Don't be afraid to respond to other desires of his as long as they seem sensible to you and as long as you don't become a slave to him. When he cries in the early weeks, it's because he's uncomfortable for some reason or other—maybe it's hunger or indigestion, or fatigue, or tension. The uneasy feeling you have when you hear him cry, the feeling that you want to comfort him, is meant to be part of your nature, too. Being held, rocked, or walked may be what he needs.

Spoiling doesn't come from being good to a baby in a sensible way, and it doesn't come all of a sudden. Spoiling comes on gradually when a mother is too afraid to use her common sense or when she really wants to be a slave and encourages her baby to become a slave driver.

Everyone wants his child to turn out to be healthy in his habits and easy to live with. But each child himself wants to eat at sensible hours and later to learn good table manners. His bowels (as long as the movements don't become too hard) will move according to their own healthy pattern, which may or may not be regular; and when he's a lot older and wiser, you can show him where to sit to move them. He will develop his own pattern of sleep according to his own needs. In all these habits he will sooner or later want to fit into the family's way of doing things, with only a minimum of guidance from you. Read *Babies Are Human Beings*, by C. Anderson Aldrich and Mary M. Aldrich.[1]

. . .

Play Periods

Being companionable with your baby Be quietly friendly with your baby whenever you are with him. He's getting a sense of how much you mean to each other all the time you're feeding him, bubbling him, bathing him, dressing him, changing his diapers, holding him, or just sitting in the room with him. When you hug him or make noises at him, when you show him that you think he's the most wonderful

[1] New York: Macmillan, 1954, $2.95.

baby in the world, it makes his spirit grow, just the way milk makes his bones grow. That must be why we grownups instinctively talk baby talk and waggle our heads when we greet a baby, even grownups who are otherwise dignified or unsociable.

One trouble with being an inexperienced parent is that part of the time you take the job so seriously that you forget to enjoy it. Then you and the baby are both missing something.

Naturally I don't mean that you should be talking a blue streak at him all the time he's awake, or constantly joggling him or tickling him. That would tire him out, and in the long run would make him tense and spoiled. You can be quiet nine tenths of the time you are with him. It's the gentle, easygoing kind of companionship that 's good for him and good for you. It's the comfortable feeling that goes into your arms when you hold him, the fond, peaceful expression on your face when you look at him, and the gentle tone in your voice.

Companionship without spoiling
Though it's good for a baby during his play periods to be somewhere near his mother (and brothers and sisters, if any) so that he can see her, make noises at her, hear her speak to him, have her show him a way to play with something occasionally, it isn't necessary or sensible for him to be in her lap or arms or to have her amusing him much of the time. He can be enjoying her company, profiting from it, and still be learning how to occupy himself. If a new mother is so delighted with her baby that she is holding him or making games for him a good part of his wakeful period, he may become quite dependent on these attentions and demand more and more of them.

Things to watch and things to play with
Young babies begin waking earlier and earlier, especially at the end of the afternoon. At such times they want something to do and they want **some** companionship. At 2, 3, and 4 months, they enjoy looking at bright-colored things and things that move. Outdoors, they are delighted to watch leaves and shadows. Indoors, they study their hands, pictures on the wall. There are bright-colored plastic shapes on strings that you can suspend between the top rails of the crib. Place them just within arm's reach—not right on top of a baby's nose—for the time when he begins reaching. You can make mobiles yourself —cardboard shapes covered with colored paper that hang from the ceiling or from a lighting fixture and rotate in slight drafts (they aren't strong enough for playing with or healthful for chewing)—or you can hang suitable household objects within reach—spoons, plastic cups, for instance. Remember that eventually everything goes into the mouth. As a baby gets toward the middle of his first year, his greatest joy is handling and mouthing objects: collections of plastic objects linked together (made for this age), rattles, teething rings, animals and dolls of cloth, household objects that are safe in the mouth. Don't let a baby or small child have objects or furniture that has been repainted with outdoor paint that contains lead, or thin celluloid toys that can be chewed into small, sharp pieces, or small glass beads and other small objects that can be choked on. Take the metal whistles out of rubber animals.

Each afternoon when the baby becomes bored with his crib, put him in the play pen near where you are working or sitting. If you are going to use a pen, the baby should become accustomed to it at 3 or 4 months, before he has learned to sit and crawl and before he has had the freedom of the floor. Otherwise he considers it a prison from the start. By the time he can sit and crawl, he has fun going after things that are a few feet away, handling larger objects like cooking spoons, saucepans, strainers. When he becomes bored with the play pen, he can sit in a bouncing chair or a chair-table arrangement. It's good for him to end up with some free creeping.

. . .

Duties

Let him enjoy his duties How does a child learn to perform various duties? By his very nature, he starts out feeling that dressing himself, brushing his teeth, sweeping, putting things away, are exciting and grown-up things to do. If his parents succeed in keeping on good terms with him as he grows older, he enjoys going on errands, carrying wood, beating rugs, because he still wants to have a part in important jobs and to please his mother and father. Most of us (including the author) aren't able to bring up our children so well that we get cooperation all the time, but if we realize that children prefer to be helpful, we are less likely to make household tasks sound like unpleasant duties or to assign them when we're irritable.

A child can't be expected to continue indefinitely to be responsible about his duties—even at 15 years. (Most adults lapse into irresponsibility at times, too.) He has to be reminded. If you can find the patience, try to make the reminder matter-of-fact, polite, as if you were speaking to an adult. It's the nagging, belittling tone that kills all pride in a job. It also helps a lot to assign a child tasks that he can do in the company of other members of the family, whether it's dish-drying or lawn-mowing. Then the grown-upness of the task and the fun of helping spur the child on.

18. EXCERPTS FROM *THE COLLECTIVE FAMILY: A HANDBOOK FOR RUSSIAN PARENTS*

ANTON S. MAKARENKO

No, tricks in family upbringing must be firmly discarded. The care and upbringing of children is a big, a serious, and a terribly responsible task, and it is, of course, also a difficult task. No easy tricks can help you out here. Once you have a child, it means that for many years to come you must give him all your power of concentration, all your attention and all your strength of character. You must be not only father and guardian of your children, you must also be organizer of your own life, because your quality as an educator is entirely bound up with your activities as a citizen and your feelings as an individual.

. . .

What is authority? Many people stumble over this problem, but are generally inclined to think that authority is a gift from nature. But since everyone in the family needs authority, a considerable number of parents forgo real "natural" authority and employ substitutes of their own concoction. These substitutes are often to be observed in our families. Their common characteristic is that they are concocted especially for educational ends.

It is considered that children need authority and, according to various points of view about children, various substitutes are concocted.

Such parents' main fault lies in a failure of perspective in educational matters. Authority made specially for children cannot exist. Such authority will always be a substitute and will always be useless.

Authority must be embodied in the parents themselves, irrespective of their relations to children, but authority is by no means a special talent. Its roots are always to be found in one place: in the parents' conduct, including all aspects of conduct—in other words, the whole lives of both father and mother, their work, thoughts, habits, feelings and endeavors.

A pattern for such conduct cannot be given in short form, but what it amounts to is that parents themselves must live the full, conscious, moral life of a citizen of the Soviet land. And this means that in relation to children they should stand on a certain plane, but a natural, human plane, and not a pedestal created especially for dealing with children.

Thus no problems of authority, freedom and discipline in the family collective can be solved by any artificially devised tricks or methods. The process of upbringing is a constant process, and its separate details find their solution in the *general tone* of the family, and general tone cannot be invented and artificially maintained. General tone, dear parents, is created by your own lives and your own conduct. The most correct, reasonable, well-thought-out methods of upbringing will be of no use if the general tone of your life is bad. And, on the contrary, only correct general tone will suggest to you both correct methods of training a child and, above all, correct forms of discipline, work, freedom, play and . . . authority.

. . .

A child is a living person. He is by no means a mere ornament to our lives; his is a separate, rich, full-blooded life in itself. Judged by its strength of emotion, its deep impressionability, the purity and beauty of its efforts of will, a child's life is incomparably richer than that of an adult. And therefore its variations are not only magnificent but dangerous. The dramas and joys of the child's life shake the personality more deeply and are sooner able to create both the positive characters among the members of the collective, and its vicious, distrustful, lonely characters.

It is only if you observe and know this full, vivid and tender life, if you meditate upon it, if you participate in it, only then does your parental authority become effective and useful, your parental authority being the power that you have stored up earlier in your own personal and social life.

But if your authority, like a lifeless painted doll, only stands on the outskirts of the child's life, if the child's face, his gestures, his smiles, his thoughtfulness, his tears pass by you unheeded, if your conduct as a father bears no resemblance to your conduct as a citizen—your authority is worth less than nothing, whatever anger or strap it is armed with.

If you beat your child it is for him, in any case, a tragedy, either a tragedy of pain and injury, or a tragedy of habitual indifference and stubborn childish endurance.

But that tragedy is the child's. You yourself, a strong grown-up man, an individual and a citizen, a being with brains and muscle—you who strike blows on the weak tender body of a growing child, what are you? In the first place you are unbearably comic, and if one were not sorry for your child, one might laugh oneself to tears at the sight of your pedagogical barbarity. At the very best, at the *very* best, you resemble an ape bringing up its offspring.

You think it is necessary for the sake of discipline?

Such parents never command discipline. Their children are simply afraid of them and try to live out of range of their authority and power.

. . .

Calm and business-like instructions and not petty tyranny, anger, shouting, prayers, persuasion—this should be the outward expression of the technique of family upbringing. Neither you nor your children should have any doubts as to whether you, as one of the senior, authorized members of the collective, have the right to give such instructions. Every parent should learn to give instructions and should be able to keep to them and not take refuge in parental idleness or domestic pacifism. And then the instructions will become the usual, accepted, traditional form, and then you will learn to add to them the faintest shades of tone, beginning with the tone of direction and going on to tones of advice, guidance, irony, sarcasm, request and allusion. And if you learn further how to distinguish between real and fictitious needs of your children, then you yourself will not even notice your parental instructions becoming the dearest and most pleasant form of friendship between yourself and your child.

19. AN ANALYSIS OF THE CONCEPT OF CULTURAL DEPRIVATION

STEVEN R. TULKIN

Those who advance the concept of cultural deprivation limit the understanding of developmental processes because (a) they do not focus attention on the effects of specific experiences, (b) they ignore cultural relativism, and (c) they fail to recognize that the majority culture has contributed to the development of many of the "problems" evidenced in "deprived" populations. Social scientists have been missionaries when they needed to be social change agents, and the result is that many programs have met with very minimal success. Suggestions are presented for specific changes in social scientists' approaches to minority group problems.

The term "cultural deprivation" is commonly used to summarize the presumed reasons why lower-class and minority group children show deficits in the development of "intellectual skills." However, there are serious limitations to the validity of the concept of cultural deprivation, and psychologists and educators should reevaluate their roles in programs which attempt to "enrich" the lives of "deprived" populations. The cultural deprivation concept is limited in that (*a*) it does not advance psychology as a science because it does not focus attention on how specific experiences affect developmental processes; (*b*) it ignores cultural relativism; and (*c*) it neglects political realities, which are likely to be primarily responsible for many of the traits observed in deprived populations. The limitations described under *a* are discussed only briefly, since they are likely to be most familiar to social scientists.

The Importance of Psychological Processes

The concept of cultural deprivation has often made it easy for social scientists to overlook the importance of the processes by which environmental experiences influence development. Jessor and Richardson (1968) stated:

> To speak, for example, of maternal deprivation as an explanation is to attempt to account for certain characteristics of infant development by the absence of the mother rather than by the presence of some specifiable set of environmental conditions. While mother absence may be a useful and convenient way to summarize or symbolize the conditions which will likely be present, the important point is that development is likely to be invariant with or related to the conditions which are present, not with those which are absent [p. 3].

Research concluding that social class or racial differences are found on particular developmental or intellectual tasks does not further understanding of development, unless we examine the actual processes that contributed to the differences. Wolf (1964) urged researchers to distinguish between status variables (class, race, etc.) and process variables (the actual *experiences* of children which contribute to their cognitive growth). He rated parents on 13 process variables descriptive of interactions between parent and child. The items fell under the headings of parental press for academic achievement and language development, as well as provision for general learning. He found a correlation of .76 between these process variables and IQ measures of fifth-grade students. Similarly, Davé (1963) obtained a multiple correlation of .80 between process variables and school achievement. These are substantially higher than the correlations of .40 to .50 which are typically reported between socioeconomic status and measures of intelligence or school achievement.

Need for Cultural Relativism

Many authors who discuss deprived populations appear to disregard cultural relativism, despite the attempts—predominantly from anthropologists—to emphasize the importance of cultural relativism in understanding minority subcultures in the United States. Writers have enumerated certain characteristics of black American culture, for example, which can be traced to the cultural patterns of its African origin (Herskovits, 1958). Other authors have argued that particular minority groups possess cultures of their own, which have "developed out of coping with a difficult environment" here in the United States (Riessman, 1962). Despite the recognition of the need for relativism, middle-class Americans, including professionals, have difficulty remaining relativistic with regard to minority cultures. Gans (1962) discussed the difficulties encountered by middle-class "missionaries" in understanding the Italian-American subculture he studied in Boston's West End. He observed that West End parents made frequent use of verbal and physical punishment, and commented that "to a middle-class observer, the parents' treatment often seems extremely strict, and sometimes brutal." Gans, however, felt that

> the torrents of threat and cajolery neither impinge on the feelings of parental affection, nor are meant as signs of rejection. As one mother explained to her child, "We hit you because we love you." People believe that discipline is needed constantly to keep the child in line with and respectful of adult rules, and without it he would run amok [pp. 59–60].

Another example of a subcultural pattern which is foreign to middle-class observers was reported by Lehmer (1969). She noted that Navajo children would not compete for good grades in school, and explained that Navajo customs emphasized cooperation, not competition: "In Navajo tradition, a person who stands out at the expense of his brother may be considered a 'witch' [p. D-4]." Does this low need for achievement reflect cultural deprivation or cultural difference?

Why is it so difficult for outsiders to acknowledge subcultural behavior patterns? Gans (1962) believed that the difficulty stemmed from the observers' missionary outlook:

> [They] had to believe that the West Enders' refusal to follow object-oriented middle-class ways was pathological, resulting from deprivations imposed on them by living in the West End. They could not admit that the West Enders acted as they did because they lived within a social structure and culture of their own [pp. 151–152].

In fact, Gans had earlier stated that one of the tenets of West End life was a rejection of "middle-class forms of status and culture." In other words, it was culturally valued to be culturally deprived.

The difficulty of achieving a relativistic approach to the study of subcultures has made research difficult, because minority group children are constantly evaluated by middle-class standards. One issue of current interest to psychologists is whether black ghetto residents are less able to communicate verbally, or are simply less proficient in "standard English." It is claimed by many researchers that lower-class subjects are verbally deficient, and the deficits are "not entirely attributable to implicit 'middle-class' orientations [Krauss & Rotter, 1968]." Other experts have argued that black English is a fully formed linguistic system in its own right, with its own grammatical rules and unique history (Baratz & Shuy, 1969; Labov, 1967; Stewart, 1967, 1969a). These critics have stated that black language is "different from standard American English, but no less complex, communicative, rich, or sophisticated [Sroufe, 1970]"; and argued that research reporting language "deficits" among black children reflects only the middle-class orientation of the research instruments and procedures. Supporting this argument, Birren and Hess (1968) concluded that

> studies of peer groups in spontaneous interaction in Northern ghetto areas show that there is a rich verbal culture in constant use. Negro children in the vernacular culture cannot be considered "verbally deprived" if one observes them in a favorable environment—on the contrary, their daily life is a pattern of continual verbal stimulation, contest, and imitation [p. 137].

Similarly, Chandler and Erikson (1968) observed *naturally occurring* group interaction and reported data which disputed the findings of Bernstein (1960, 1961) and others that middle-class children more commonly used "elaborated" linguistic codes while lower classes typically spoke with "restricted" codes. Chandler and Erickson found that the use of restricted or elaborated linguistic codes was not as closely related to the social class of speakers as had been suggested by other researchers.

> Both inner-city and suburban groups . . . were found to shift back and forth between use of relatively "restricted" linguistic codes and relatively "elaborated" codes. These shifts were closely related to apparent changes in the degree of shared context between group members. Examples of extremely abstract and sophisticated inquiry among inner-city Negro young people were found in which a highly "restricted" linguistic code was employed [p. 2].

If black English and standard English are simply different languages, one cannot be seen as more deficient than the other (Sroufe, 1970). Most schools, however, demand that students use standard English, and frequently black children who have been classified by their schools as "slow learners" are able to read passages of black English with amazing speed and accuracy (Stewart, 1969b). Similarly, Foster (1969) found that the introduction of nonstandard English dialect increased the ability of tenth-grade disadvantaged students "to comprehend, to recall, and to be fluent and flexible in providing titles for verbal materials." Black students ($N = 90$) also scored higher than white students ($N = 400$) on Foster's (1970) Jive Analogy Test (H. L. Foster, personal communication, 1970).

This argument does not imply that the teaching of standard English is an infringement of the rights of minority cultures. It is necessary that students learn standard English, but there is a difference between emphasizing the development of positive skills which may facilitate a successful adaptation to a particular majority culture versus devaluating a group of people who may not emphasize the development of these particular skills. As Baratz and Baratz (1970) suggested, research should be undertaken to discover the *different* but not pathological forms of minority group behavior. "Then and only then can programs be created that utilize the child's differences as a means of helping him acculturate to the mainstream while maintaining his individual identity and cultural heritage [p. 47]."

An Objective Look at the Middle Class

The cultural bias of middle-class America has not only hindered an appreciation of the attributes of minority cultures, but it has also prevented an objective evaluation of middle-class culture. Psychologists do not write about the "deficiencies" of the middle class, but the cultural relativist might find a great deal to write about. Coles (1968) suggested that it may be appropriate to label middle-class children deprived, because

> they're so nervous and worried about everything they say—what it will mean, or what it will cost them, or how it will be interpreted. That's what they've learned at home, and that's why a lot of them are tense kids, and, even worse, stale kids with frowns on their faces at age 6 or 7 [p. 277].

Similarly, Kagan (1968) hypothesized that middle-class children were more anxious about failing than lower-class children. He noted that lower-class children may be less anxious about making a mistake and, therefore, more likely to answer questions and make decisions "impulsively." Most people would agree that an impulsive style could be a hindrance to the development of abstract analytical thinking, but researchers have paid little attention to the possible virtues of an impulsive (or "spontaneous," "nonanalytical") style, and have not considered the consequences of attempting to discourage this style. Maccoby and Modiano (1966) spoke to this point in their discussion of differences among children in Mexico City, Boston, and a rural Mexican village. They noted that people socialized into the modern industrialized world often lose the ability to experience. "They are," the authors suggested, "like people who see a painting immediately in terms of its style, period, and influences, but with no sense of its uniqueness [p. 268]." Maccoby and Modiano concluded by cautioning that

> as the city child grows older, he may end by exchanging a spontaneous, less alienated relationship to the world for a more sophisticated outlook which concentrates on using, exchanging, or cataloguing. What industrialized man gains in an increased ability to formulate, to reason, and to code the ever more numerous bits of complex information he acquires, he may lose in decreased sensitivity to people and events [p. 269].

But it is quite doubtful if psychologists would call him culturally deprived.

Relativism Toward Other Cultures

Psychologists frequently label American minority groups as culturally deprived, but they are less likely to make value judgments about other cultures. In fact, social scientists are reasonably tolerant of child-rearing practices observed in other cultures which would be devaluated if they were found in a minority group in the United States. Rebelsky and Abeles (1969), for example, observed American and Dutch mothers with their 0–3-month-old infants. They found that a Dutch baby typically slept in a low closed bed with a canopy overhead. Dutch mothers kept the infant's room cool—"for health reasons"—necessitating infants being "tightly covered under blankets, often tied into the crib with strings from their sheets." Further, the authors reported comparisons showing that "American mothers looked at, held, fed, talked to, smiled at, patted, and showed more affection to their babies more often than did Dutch mothers." These findings, however, were not used to condemn Dutch mothers. The authors related the differences in parental behavior to cultural variations in the parents' conceptions of infancy. For example, they noted that

> Even if a [Dutch] parent sees a child awake and wanting to play or look around, . . . he is not likely to respond to this wish or to the behavior which implies this wish because of fear of "spoiling" the baby (stated by 9 of the 11 mothers in Holland), or because of the belief that a baby in this age range should sleep and not play or stay awake [pp. 16–17].

Observations also revealed that Dutch infants had fewer toys with which to play. By 3 months of age, almost half of the Dutch babies still had no toys within sight or touch. The authors explained that Dutch mothers were concerned that "toys might keep the babies awake, or overstimulate them." There were also cultural differences in the mothers' reactions to their infants crying.

> Crying meant a call for help to U. S. mothers; they often reported lactating when they heard the cry. In Holland, crying was considered a part of a baby's behavior, good for the lungs and not always something to stop. In addition, though a mother might hear the cry in Holland and interpret it as a hunger cry, she still would not respond if it was not time for the scheduled feeding [pp. 7–8].

Rebelsky and Abeles did not suggest that Dutch mothres were rejecting or depriving their infants. They did not argue that intervention was necessary to change the patterns of mother-infant interaction. They concluded, instead, that both United States and Dutch cultures "may be training very different kinds of people, yet with each culture wanting the ones they produce." Such data reported for a group of lower-income American mothers might be followed by a call for a massive intervention program, or possibly the removal of the infants from their homes.

A similar cultural comparison was reported by Caudill and Weinstein (1966, 1969) who investigated maternal behavior in Japan and in the United States. The authors reported that American mothers talked more to their infants, while Japanese mothers more frequently lulled and rocked their infants. These differences were seen as reflecting different styles of mothering:

> The style of the American mother seems to be in the direction of stimulating her baby to respond . . . whereas the style of the Japanese mother seems to be more in the direction of soothing and quieting her baby [1966, p. 18].

In both cultures, the "style" of mothering was influenced by the prevailing conception of infancy. Caudill and Weinstein (1969) reported that in Japan

> the infant is seen more as a separate biological organism who from the beginning, in order to develop, needs to be drawn into increasingly interdependent relations with others. In America, the infant is seen more as a dependent biological organism who, in order to develop, needs to be made increasingly independent of others [p. 15].

American mothers, following their conception of infancy, pushed their infants to respond and to be active; Japanese mothers, also following their conception of infancy, attempted to foster reduced independent activity and greater reliance on others. As a part of this pattern, the Japanese tended to place less emphasis on clear verbal communication. Caudill and Weinstein reasoned that "such communinication implies self-assertion and the separate identity and independence of the person," which would be contrary to the personality which Japanese mothers were attempting to build into their children. Thus, in Japan, as in Holland, mothers related to their infants in a manner consistent with their beliefs and values.

Caudill and Weinstein (1966) also reported data showing that according to American "standards," the Japanese infants might be considered "deficient." They engaged in less positive vocalization and spent less time with toys and other objects: "The Japanese infant," they said, "seems passive—he spends much more time simply lying awake in his crib or on a *zabuton* (a flat cushion) on the floor [p. 16]." The authors further reported that a study by Arai, Ishikawa, and Toshima (1958) found that—compared to American norms—Japanese infants showed a steady decline on tests of language and motor development from 4 to 36 months of age. Caudill and Weinstein, however, remained relativistic. They commented that although Arai, Ishikawa, and Toshima seemed somewhat distressed that the "Japanese mothers were so bound up in the lives of their infants that they interfered with the development of their infants in ways which made it difficult to meet the American norms," Caudill and Weinstein (1969) did not share the Japanese authors' concern over the lack of matching the American norms: "We do not believe that the differences we find are necessarily indications of a better or a worse approach to human life, but rather that such differences are a part of an individual's adjustment to his culture [p. 41.]" Again, it is doubtful if the same conclusion would have been reached had the data been collected from a minority subculture in the United States.

A final example of the need for cultural relativism involves a study of Ashkenazic and Sephardic Jews in Brooklyn (Gross, 1967). Both groups were solidly middle class, and lived only two blocks apart. Both had been long established in this country and spoke English in their homes. On entering school, however, the Ashkenazic children averaged 17 points higher on a standard IQ test, a disparity similar in magnitude to that often reported between children of white suburbs and black slums.

Gross pointed out that it is generally assumed that inferior performance in school necessarily reflects deprivation and lack of opportunity. He argued, on the contrary, that each culture has its own ideas of what is important–some emphasize one skill, some another. Despite their children's lower IQ scores the Sephardic mothers were not deprived, however one defines the term: "In many cases they had minks, maids, and country homes." The Sephardic mothers were all native born, high school graduates, and none worked. The children "were blessed with privilege, money and comfort, but their level of academic readiness was similar to that of their underprivileged Israeli counterparts."

Gross explained that the difference was related to cultural tradition: The two communities represented different routes into the middle class–the Ashkenazim through success in school and the Sephardim through success in the marketplace. The author concluded that educational unpreparedness could be found among the "financially well-to-do" as well as among the lower classes, and suggested that this finding should be a "caution signal to social engineers." Gross questioned those who advocate changing lower-class blacks to conform to the life styles and values of middle-class whites, and suggested that there was an element of "white colonialism" in the attempt to "reshape the economically underprivileged in the image of the education-minded intellectually oriented academicians."

Gross's final point merits expansion, because intervention is becoming a big business in the United States today. The federal government is spending large amounts of money on intervention programs, and some social scientists fear that the interventionists will totally disregard subcultural systems in their attempts to "save" the "deprived" children.

> When we force people of another culture to make an adjustment to ours, by that much we are destroying the integrity of their personalities. When too many adjustments of this sort are required too fast, the personality disintegrates and the result is an alienated, dissociated individual who cannot feel really at home in either culture [Lehmer, 1969, p. D-4].

Why is it so common for researchers to remain relativistic in their discussions of socialization practices in other nations, while being intolerant of subcultural differences among lower-income and minority groups in this country? One could propose that each nation socializes its children according to prevailing cultural values so that regardless of the fact that practices in other nations are different, children in each country develop the personalities and intellectual skills needed for success in their own particular social systems. This theory would agree that it is inappropriate to apply cultural relativism to subcultures because a person's success remains defined by the majority culture. Keller (1963), for example, argued that "cultural relativism ignores the fact that schools and industry are middle class in organization and outlook."

Cultural relativism and success in "schools and industry," however, are *not* mutually exclusive. It is possible to teach children the skills needed for articulation with the majority culture, while encouraging them to develop a pride in their own family or cultural heritage, and to utilize the particular skills which their own socialization has strengthened. A majority culture can, however, promote a narrow definition of success in order to ensure that the power of the society remains in the hands of a relatively select group within the society. Thus, by maintaining that any deviation from the white middle-class norm represents cultural deprivation, the white middle class is guarding its position as *the* source of culture—and power—in this nation. Cultural deprivation, then, is not just a psychological or educational issue; it is also very much a political issue.

Politics and Cultural Deprivation

Subcultural influences may represent a legitimate explanation for some of the behavior observed in particular lower-income or minority populations, but these influences should not be regarded as the sole determinant of life styles in these groups. Social scientists must also consider the way in which the majority culture, by its tolerance for social, political, and economic inequality, actually contributes to the development, in some subgroups, of the very characteristics which it considers "depriving." Responsibility, then, lies not with the subpopulations—for being "deprived"—but rather with the "total environmental structure that disenfranchises, alienates [and] disaffects [Hillson, 1970]." Fatini (1969) echoed this argument when he suggested that the "problem" of disadvantaged school children may not be rooted in the learner's "environmental and cultural deficiencies" but rather with the system—"the school and its educational process." He suggested the need for reorientation "from our present 'student-fault' to a stronger 'system-fault' position."

One of the most obvious system faults—and one that is quite relevant to child development—is inadequate medical care for the poor. Social scientists investigating cultural deprivation have paid insufficient attention to the ways in which poor physical health, both of mothers during pregnancy and of infants early in life, can influence the child's developmental progress. The incidences of inadequate prenatal nutrition, premature births, and complications of delivery which can lead to brain injuries, are all greater among lower-income and non-white groups (Abramowicz & Kass, 1966; Knoblock & Pasamanick, 1962). The effects of these medical differences are not unknown. Kagan (1965), for example, noted that one of the possible consequences of minimal brain damage during the perinatal and early postnatal periods is "increased restlessness and distractability, and inability to inhibit inappropriate responses during the pre- and early school years." The effects of malnutrition on developing cognitive skills have also been reported (Brockman & Ricciuti, 1971). We do not know the extent to which developmental "deficits" of lower-income- and minority-group children can be traced to these differences in their *medical* histories. This is a clear-cut case where responsibility for deprivation falls mainly on the *majority* culture.

Society as a whole is also responsible for other behavior patterns observed in deprived groups. Liebow (1967) argued that many of the behavior patterns he observed among lower-class blacks were "a direct response to the conditions of lower-class Negro life. . . ." His most cogent example involved the "delay of gratification" variable. The frequent finding that lower-class (usually black) children prefer a smaller reward given immediately rather than a larger reward given later is often cited as a serious handicap to their schoolwork. It is often hypothesized that the child-rearing practices employed by lower-class parents lead children to prefer immediate gratification; and attempts are being made to change these practices and to teach the children to defer gratification. Liebow demonstrated that, although socialization patterns may encourage behaviors which are seen as reflecting a preference for immediate gratification, the socialization patterns do not represent the primary determinant of this pattern. He argued that the so-called preference for immediate gratification derives from the conditions of life encountered in this population. The *realities of life* represent the causal agent; the child-rearing patterns are only intermediary variables. The importance of Liebow's argument merits thorough examination.

> What appears as a "present-time" orientation to the outside observer is, to the man experiencing it, as much a future orientation as that of his middle-class counterpart. The difference between the two men lies not so much in their different orientations to time as in their different orientations to future time or more specifically, to their different futures.
>
> As for the future, the young streetcorner man has a fairly good picture of it. . . . It is a future in which everything is uncertain except the ultimate destruction of his hopes and the eventual realization of his fears. The most he can reasonably look forward to is that these things do not come too soon. Thus when Richard squanders a week's pay in two days it is not because, like an animal or a child, he is "present-time oriented," unaware of or unconcerned with his future. He does so precisely because he is aware of the future and the hopelessness of it all.
>
> Thus, apparent present-time concerns with consumption and indulgences—material and emotional—reflect a future-time orientation. "I want mine right now" is ultimately a cry of despair, a direct response to the future as he sees it [pp. 64–68].[1]

---

[1] Liebow also pointed out that there is no intrinsic connection between "present-time" orientation and lower-class persons:

> Whenever people of whatever class have been uncertain, skeptical or downright pessimistic about the future, "I want mine right now" has been one of the characteristic responses. . . . In wartime, especially, all classes tend to slough off conventional restraints on sexual and other behavior (i. e., become less able or less willing to defer gratification). And when inflation threatens, darkening the future, persons who formerly husbanded their resources with commendable restraint almost stampede one another rushing to spend their money. . . . [Thus] present-time orientation appears to be a situation-specific phenomenon rather than a part of the standard psychic equipment of cognitive lower-class man [pp. 68–69].

To encourage greater delay of gratification, interventionists should focus on the conditions causing the "hopelessness" and "despair" in lower-income populations, rather than emphasizing the necessity of changing child-rearing patterns. Other researchers have also noted that "conditions of life" represented major causal factors contributing to parental practices and child development. Minturn and Lambert (1964) interviewed mothers in six cultural settings (New England, Mexico, Philippines, Okinawa, India, and Kenya) and found that situational constraints in the mother's immediate life space were primary determinants of their responses. Hess and Shipman (1966) analyzed situational constraints among lower-income Americans and noted that

> a family in an urban ghetto has few choices to make with respect to such basic things as residence, occupation, and condition of housing, and on the minor points of choice that come with adequate discretionary income. A family with few opportunities to make choices among events that affect it is not likely to encourage the children to think of life as consisting of a wide range of behavioral options among which they must learn to discriminate [p. 4].

The same authors (Shipman & Hess, 1966) spoke specifically about language development:

> The lower-class mother's narrow range of alternatives is being conveyed to the child through language styles which convey her attitudes of few options and little individual power, and this is now being reflected in the child's cognitive development [p. 17].

Gordon (1969) reported specific data. He found that within the "poverty group" the amount of verbal interaction directed toward an infant was related to the "mother's view of her control of her destiny." The extent to which an individual feels he has some control over his destiny is also related to a whole myriad of variables associated with educational achievement. Coleman, Campbell, Hobson, McPartland, Mood, Weinfeld, and York (1966) found that, among minority group students, this factor was the best predictor of academic success. Similarly, Rotter (1966) argued that

> the individual who has a strong belief that he can control his own destiny is likely to (*a*) be more alert to those aspects of the environment which provide useful information for his future behaviors; (*b*) take steps to improve his environmental position; (*c*) place greater value on skill or achievement reinforcements and be generally more concerned with his ability, particularly his failures; and (*d*) be resistive to subtle attempts to influence him [p. 25].

There is little doubt that the realistic perception of the poor that they have little control over their lives leads not only to the "hopelessness" and "despair" observed by Liebow, but also to less concern with education, and reduced academic success.

Interventionists must concern themselves with these social, economic and political realities of lower-class life and see the relations between these realities and indexes of parental behavior and intellectual development. Several interventionists have moved in this direction. Schaefer (1969) reported that "current stresses and the absence of social support influence maternal hostility, abuse and neglect of the child." He suggested that intervention programs hoping to change a mother's behavior toward her child needed to "alleviate the stress and increase the support of mothers at the time the initial mother-child relationship is developed."

Similarly, Kagan (1969) spoke of the "need for ecological change" to improve the conditions of life among lower-class populations. He emphasized that the interventionists needed to be sensitive to "the communities' belief as to what arrangements will help them," and that the changes should be directed toward facilitating the development of a "sense of control over the future."

Other researchers have come to the same conclusion. Pavenstedt (1967) reported that every member of her staff concurred "in the conviction that far-reaching social and economic change must take place in order to fundamentally alter the lives of the families" they observed. Stodolsky and Lesser (1968) suggested that intervention programs "would probably be a lot more successful if we were to modify the conditions which probably lead to many of these [parental] behaviors; namely, lack of money and of access to jobs." Liebow (1967) presented the most convincing argument:

> We do not have to see the problem in terms of breaking into a puncture proof circle, of trying to change values, of disrupting the lines of communication between parent and child so that parents cannot make children in their own image, thereby transmitting their culture inexorably, ad infinitum. No doubt, each generation does provide role models for each succeeding one. Of much greater importance for the possibilities of change, however, is the fact that many similarities between the lower-class Negro father and son (or mother and daughter) do not result from "cultural transmission" but from the fact that the son goes out and independently experiences the same failures, in the same areas, and for much the same reasons as his father. What appears as a dynamic, self-sustaining cultural process is, in part at least, a relatively simple piece of social machinery which turns out, in rather mechanical fashion, independently produced look-alikes. The problem is how to change the conditions which, by guaranteeing failure, cause the son to be made in the image of the father [p. 223].

Intervention programs must effect changes in the conditions of life, and not ignore these issues by merely attempting to change behavior patterns. Intervention programs which do attempt to change the "conditions of life," however, may encounter political opposition, simply because to change the conditions of life necessitates a wider distribution of power and wealth. While it is beyond the scope of the present discussion to closely examine the politics of poverty, it is necessary to understand why poverty may be difficult to eliminate.

All poor peoples do not share the characteristics which Lewis (1965) calls the "culture of poverty" or which researchers have labeled "deprived." Lewis reported that these characteristics are found only among the poor people who occupy a "marginal position in a class-stratified, highly individuated, capitalistic society" in which there is a "lack of effective participation and integration of the poor in the major institutions of the larger society." He reported, for example, that

> many of the primitive or preliterate peoples studied by anthropologists suffer from dire poverty which is the result of poor technology and/or poor natural resources, or of both, but they do not have the traits of the subculture of poverty. Indeed, they do not constitute a subculture because their societies are not highly stratified. In spite of their poverty they have a relatively integrated, satisfying and self-sufficient culture [p. xlviii].

Where a "culture of poverty" exists, however, the poor are less than poor: They are poor while others are rich, and they do not have the power to demand their "fair share." Thus, Lewis aptly characterized the fight for equality in this country as a "political power struggle" and pointed out that, rather than allowing poor people to participate effectively in society, many of those currently holding power "emphasize the need for guidance and control to remain in the hands of the middle class. . . ." The culture of poverty will not be obliterated, however, until power is shared. The elimination of physical poverty per se may not be enough to eliminate the culture of poverty; more basic political changes may be necessary. Some might even argue that a political revolution is the only means of redistributing power and wealth, thus eliminating the culture of poverty. Lewis noted that

> by creating basic structural changes in society, by redistributing wealth, by organizing

the poor and giving them a sense of belonging, of power and of leadership, revolutions frequently succeed in abolishing some of the basic characteristics of the culture of poverty even when they do not succeed in abolishing poverty itself [p. liii].

To illustrate, Lewis went on to report:

> On the basis of my limited experience in one socialist country—Cuba—and on the basis of my reading, I am inclined to believe that the culture of poverty does not exist in the socialist countries. After the Castro Revolution I found much less of the despair, apathy and hopelessness which are so diagnostic of urban slums in the culture of poverty. The people had a new sense of power and importance. They were armed and were given a doctrine which glorified the lower class as the hope of humanity [p. xlix].

The purpose of this discussion is not to encourage political revolution,[2] but rather to point out the complexities of attempting to understand the behavior of people who differ from us—culturally, financially, or any way. It is easier to think of these other people as "groups," and more difficult to think of them as individuals who differ a great deal among themselves—just as members of our own group do. It is easier to think of them as wanting to be like us and needing us to help them; it is more difficult to reject the philosophy of the "white man's burden" and allow people the freedom to retain life styles which differ from the ones we know. It is easy to blame people for what we have defined as their "deficits," but more difficult to consider how we as a society might have contributed to the problems we have defined as "theirs."

Implications for Research[3]

The present author has conducted research on social class differences in maternal behavior and cognitive development (Tulkin, 1968, 1970). He does not advocate that scientists abandon or censor this type of research. However, social scientists need to reevaluate their role in research affecting minority groups (including poor white); and possibly establish a set of guidelines or recommendations to prevent the misuse of research. There are precedents for such guidelines in that psychotherapists ascribe to a set of "ethical standards," and experiments involving human subjects are also regulated. The proposed guidelines could be established by a panel consisting of minority group educators and community leaders, along with those members of the scientific community who have an interest in this type of research. These recommendations might not be binding, but instead would represent an attempt to make research more valid, and hopefully more relevant to the needs of the community. There are several areas in which guidelines might be helpful.

Understanding the Culture

Anthropologists continue to point out the inappropriateness of examining another culture through the experimental framework of one's own (Conklin, 1962; Frake, 1962). The psychologists investigating developmental patterns among minority group children should attempt to understand the "realities of life" in these populations, and how these realities affect life styles. These insights could be developed

---

[2] Nor does the author wish to imply that political and economic changes would provide an automatic panacea for all of our nation's ills. We do need to broaden our perspective, however, and understand that some of the problems which we spend time and money fighting are, in reality, our own creations.

[3] Various colleagues who have read the present article suggested that there is only one implication of the above discussion with regard to research with minority populations: Don't do any. This conclusion may be justified, but it is unlikely to be adopted. Therefore, the following "compromises" are presented.

in several ways: (*a*) living in the minority group community; (*b*) holding meetings with community people—not just professionals from the same minority group as the subjects—to discuss any proposed research; and, most important, (*c*) including minority group (or community) members on the research team at every level of responsibility, from the initial planning of the project through the analysis and interpretation of data. Some effort in this area is sorely needed if research involving human behavior in minority group populations hopes to yield valid conclusions.

Methodological Improvements

Recommendations are also needed in the area of employing more rigorous controls in studies comparing various population groups. Research designs which compare lower-income-minority children to middle-income white children are so confounded that no clear conclusions can be reached. Controlling for social class does not even equate experiential patterns among various populations (Tulkin, 1968). If social scientists hope to understand the processes by which differences develop they must use designs which employ strict controls for economic level (family income, crowded housing conditions, etc.), family milieux (broken homes, family size, birth order, maternal employment, etc.), health of child (prematurity, nutrition, complications of delivery, etc.), and possibly various aspects of the parents' own histories (e.g., birth order and family size). Without these controls, the experiences which contribute to developmental differences cannot be properly investigated.

Finally, we need to reduce the error variance introduced by our testing procedures. Sroufe (1970) criticized researchers who report differences in the performance of white and minority group subjects in laboratory testing situations, because the facilities themselves may "provide different stimuli for the lower-class mother than for the faculty wife." Sroufe questioned, for example, whether "a university waiting room [was] a suitable place for observing restrictions placed by lower-class mothers on their children." Lore (1969) reported the results of a series of animal experiments that supported Sroufe's argument. Lore noted that many experimenters who compared restricted and nonrestricted animals attributed the differences they found to "deficits" in experientially deprived animals; but, upon further study, the differences appeared to reflect only "an exaggerated fear reaction" elicited by the testing procedure.

> For normally reared subjects, the test setting includes many stimulus elements that have been encountered previously. . . . However, for restricted animals, the totally unfamiliar test setting apparently elicits a severe emotional reaction that is incompatible with any form of adaptive behavior [p. 482].

Lore's own data revealed that when tests were conducted in the "home-cage" the behavior of the deprived animals was "entirely comparable to that of subjects exposed to far richer environments." The author's conclusion—which should be heeded by researchers examining the behaviors of minority group populations—is that one cannot infer that "deficits" exist when his test procedures have a different stimulus value to the groups he is attempting to compare.

Community Relevance

The proposed guidelines must also make research more relevant to the needs of minority group communities. The need for change in this area is evidenced by the statement of Whitney Young, National Director of the Urban League, who in 1968 called for a "moratorium" on studies of the Negro (Young, 1968). Similarly, Robert Williams, Past Chairman of the Association of Black Psychologists, asked his white colleagues to stay out of black neighborhoods (Williams, 1969). These statements reflect the feeling among minority group leaders that their communities are being "exploited" by white professionals. Just as white businessmen came into the ghettos, made their money, and retreated to the suburbs, white professionals are applying for federal funds, going into the ghettos, testing subjects, and returning to their universities to write papers describing the "deprivations" they encountered; in both cases the community has gained nothing. If researchers are going to use minority communities to advance the science of child development (and their own reputations), they should be willing to compensate the communities by structuring their research programs to be relevant to the needs of the people they are using. As was pointed out above, the *real* needs of the community are likely to be the *primary* determinants of many of the behavior patterns which have been labeled as "depriving" anyway.

Community needs vary, but some are universal: The need for jobs, job training, and vocational counseling; and the need for health care and legal services. Perhaps the greatest need is for the community to become self-sufficient. Thus, an intervention program initiated by a noncommunity agency should have as its goal turning the program over to the community itself, with the outside agency acting as a consultant as long as its services were requested. Interventionists would then be social change agents, and not missionaries. The "missionary" approach which is common among interventionists, is illustrated by Pavenstedt's (1967) stated goals:

> It is our tenet that *in order to lead out of misery, as well as out of intellectual dearth, intervention must begin very early and must be concerned with total personality development.* We set ourselves the task of bettering their early upbringing, we wanted to prepare them for the competitive struggle with which their parents were incapable of coping [pp. 4–5].

A different type of program was reported by Karnes, Studley, Wright, and Hodgins (1968), who attempted at least minimal social change by relying heavily on the participation of low-income mothers in their intervention program. They found that

> mothers of low educational and low income levels can learn to prepare inexpensive educational materials and to acquire skills for using such materials to foster the intellectual and linguistic development of their children at home [p. 182].

Karnes et al. attributed the success of their program to the participation of the mothers. Similarly, Gilmer (1969) reported that "the effectiveness of programs in stimulating younger children in the home is attributable to the variable of maternal involvement."

Effective involvement of parents, however, is related to the role which parents are asked to play. Chilman (1968) noted that in most intervention programs "lip service" is given to parental involvement, but parents are usually "seen as minor auxiliaries to the major effort." Karnes et al., in contrast, emphasized that mothers were "fully recognized as important members of the educational team," and were actively involved in developing materials to be used with their children.

> Because the mothers had made many of the instructional materials and understood their use, they could approach the teaching of their children with confidence. They could readily observe the progress of their children and were immediately rewarded for their mutual efforts [pp. 182–183].

Finally, the mothers were paid for attending meetings and participating in the program.

Karnes's program did not actually effect major structural changes in the *community*, and thus does not illustrate the ideal model for intervention work which has been proposed; but the program did more than most to enable participants to change themselves as a result of the program, rather than assuming that the community would continue to rely on the professionals to "lead (them) out of misery" (Pavenstedt, 1967). The question now is whether the mothers trained by Karnes et al. are eligible to apply for federal funds to expand the intervention work to other families; and whether Karnes et al. will assist the mothers in this venture and be available to consult with them, and to help them evaluate the success of their intervention. If this type of program could be developed then nobody would be exploited: Karnes et al. would have their data—and publications; the mothers in the study would have learned something about child development and would have more confidence in themselves; and the community would have federal funds, new jobs, and a sense of pride that community members were helping each other. It may finally be the end of the "white man's burden."

References

ABRAMOWICZ, M., & KASS, E. H. Pathogenesis and prognosis of prematurity. *New England Journal of Medicine*, 1966, *275*, 878.

ARAI, S., ISHIKAWA, J., & TOSHIMA, K. Developpement psychomoteur des enfants Japonais. *La Revue de Neuropsychiatrie Infantile et d'Hygiène Mentale de l'Enfance*, 1958, *6*, 262–269. Cited by W. Caudill & H. Weinstein, Maternal care and infant behavior in Japan and America. *Psychiatry*, 1969, *32*, p. 41.

BARATZ, J. C. & SHUY, R. W. (Eds.) *Teaching black children to read.* Washington, D. C.: Center for Applied Linguistics, 1969.

BARATZ, S. S., & BARATZ, J. C. Early childhood intervention: The social science base of institutional racism. *Harvard Educational Review*, 1970, *40*, 29–50.

BERNSTEIN, B. Language and social class. *British Journal of Sociology*, 1960, *11*, 271–276.

———. Social class and linguistic development: A theory of social learning. In A. H. Halsey, H. Floud, & C. A. Anderson (Eds.), *Education, economy and society.* Glencoe, Ill.: Free Press, 1961.

BIRREN, J. E., & HESS, R. Influences of biological, psychological, and social deprivations on learning and performance. In *Perspectives on human deprivation.* Washington, D. C.: Department of Health, Education, and Welfare, United States Government Printing Office, 1968.

BROCKMAN, L. M., & RICCIUTI, H. N. Severe protein-calorie malnutrition and cognitive development in infancy and early childhood. *Developmental Psychology*, 1971, *4*, 312–319.

CAUDILL, W., & WEINSTEIN, H. Maternal care and infant behavior in Japanese and American urban middle class families. Bethesda, Md.: National Institute of Mental Health, 1966. (Mimeo)

———. Maternal care and infant behavior in Japan and America. *Psychiatry*, 1969, *32*, 12–43.

CHANDLER, B. J., & ERICKSON, F. D. *Sounds of society: A demonstration program in group inquiry.* (Final Rep. No. 6-2044) Washington, D. C.: United States Government Printing Office, 1968.

CHILMAN, C. S. Poor families and their patterns of child care: Some implications for service programs. In L. L. Dittman (Ed.), *Early child care.* New York: Atherton Press, 1968.

COLEMAN, J. S., CAMPBELL, E. Q., HOBSON, C. J., MC PARTLAND, J., MOOD, A. M., WEINFELD, F. D., & YORK, R. L. *Equality of educational opportunity.* Washington, D. C.: United States Government Printing Office, 1966.

COLES, R. Violence in ghetto children. In S. Chess & A. Thomas (Eds.), *Annual progress in child psychiatry and child development.* New York: Brunner/Mazel, 1968.

CONKLIN, H. C. The ethnographic study of cognitive systems. In *Anthropology and human behavior.* Washington, D. C.: Anthropological Society of Washington, 1962.

DAVÉ, R. H. The identification and measurement of environmental variables that are related to educational achievement. Unpublished doctoral dissertation, University of Chicago, 1963.

FANTINI, M. D. Beyond cultural deprivation and compensatory education. *Psychiatry and Social Science Review,* 1969, *3,* 6–13.

FOSTER, H. L. Dialect-lexicon and listening comprehension. Unpublished doctoral dissertation, Teachers College, Columbia University, 1969.

———. Foster's Jive Lexicon Analogies Test. Series II. Buffalo: Office of Teacher Education, State University of New York, 1970. (Mimeo)

FRAKE, C. O. The ethnographic study of cognitive systems. In, *Anthropology and human behavior.* Washington, D. C.: Anthropological Society of Washington, 1962.

GANS, H. J. *The urban villagers: Group and class in the life of Italian-Americans.* New York: Free Press of Glencoe, 1962.

GILMER, B. Intra-family diffusion of selected cognitive skills as a function of educational stimulation. *George Peabody College DARCEE Papers.* Vol. 3. Nashville, Tenn.: George Peabody College, 1969.

GORDON, I. J. *Early child stimulation through parent education.* (Final Rep. No. PH5-R-306) Washington, D. C.: Department of Health, Education, and Welfare, United States Government Printing Office, 1969.

GROSS, M. *Learning readiness in two Jewish groups.* New York: Center for Urban Education, 1967.

HERSKOVITS, M. *The myth of the Negro past.* Boston: Beacon Press, 1958.

HESS, R. D., & SHIPMAN, V. C. Maternal attitude toward the school and the role of pupil: Some social class comparisons. Paper presented at the Conference on Curriculum and Teaching in Depressed Urban Areas, Columbia University, June 1966.

HILLSON, M. The disadvantaged child. *Community Mental Health Journal,* 1970, *6,* 81–83.

JESSOR, R., & RICHARDSON, S. Psychosocial deprivation and personality development. In *Perspectives on human deprivation.* Washington, D. C.: United States Government Printing Office, 1968.

KAGAN, J. Information processing in the child. In P. H. Mussen, J. J. Conger, & J. Kagan (Eds.), *Readings in child development and personality.* New York: Harper & Row, 1965.

———. On cultural deprivation. In D. C. Glass (Ed.), *Environmental influences.* New York: Rockefeller University Press, 1968.

———. Social class and academic progress: An analysis and suggested solution strategies. Paper presented at the meeting of the American Association for the Advancement of Science, Boston, December 1969.

KARNES, M. B., STUDLEY, W. M., WRIGHT, W. R., & HODGINS, A. S. An approach for working with mothers of disadvantaged preschool children. *Merrill-Palmer Quarterly,* 1968, *14,* 173–184.

KELLER, S. The social world of the urban slum child: Some early findings. *American Journal of Orthopsychiatry,* 1963, *33,* 823–834.

KNOBLOCK, H., & PASAMANICK, B. Mental subnormality. *New England Journal of Medicine,* 1962, *266,* 1092–1097.

KRAUSS, R. M., & ROTTER, G. S. Communication abilities of children as a function of status and age. *Merrill-Palmer Quarterly,* 1968, *14,* 161–174.

LABOV, W. Some sources of reading problems for Negro speakers of nonstandard English. In A. Frazier (Ed.), *New directions in elementary English*. Champaign, Ill: National Council of Teachers of English, 1967.

LEHMER, M. Navajos want their own schools. *San Francisco Examiner and Chronicle*, December 14, 1969.

LEWIS, O. *La Vida: A Puerto Rican family in the culture of poverty*. New York: Random House, 1965.

LIEBOW, E. *Tally's corner: A study of Negro streetcorner men*. Boston: Little, Brown, 1967.

LORE, R. K. Pain avoidance behavior of rats reared in restricted and enriched environments. *Developmental Psychology*, 1969, *5*, 482–484.

MACCOBY, M., & MODIANO, N. On culture and equivalence. I. In J. S. Bruner, R. R. Olver, & P. M. Greenfield (Eds.), *Studies in cognitive growth*. New York: Wiley, 1966.

MINTURN, L., & LAMBERT, W. W. *Mothers of six cultures*. New York: Wiley, 1964.

PAVENSTEDT, E. (Ed.) *The drifters*. Boston: Little, Brown, 1967.

REBELSKY, F., & ABELES, G. Infancy in Holland and in the United States. Paper presented at the meeting of the Society for Research in Child Development, Santa Monica, March 1969.

RIESSMAN, F. *The culturally deprived child*. New York: Harper & Row, 1962.

ROTTER, J. B. Generalized expectancies for internal versus external control of reinforcement. *Psychological Monographs*, 1966, *80* (1, Whole No. 609).

SCHAEFER, E. S. Need for early and continuing education. Paper presented at the meeting of the American Association for the Advancement of Science, Boston, December 1969.

SHIPMAN, V. C., & HESS, R. D. Early experiences in the socialization of cognitive modes in children: A study of urban Negro families. Paper presented at the meeting of the Conference of Family and Society, Merrill-Palmer Institute, April 1966.

SROUFE, L. A. A methodological and philosophical critique of intervention-oriented research. *Developmental Psychology*, 1970, *2*, 140–145.

STEWART, W. A. Sociolinguistic factors in the history of American Negro dialects. *The Florida FL Reporter*, 1967, *5*(2).

———. Linguistic and conceptual deprivation—fact or fancy? Paper presented at the meeting of the Society for Research in Child Development, Santa Monica, March 1969. (a)

———. On the use of Negro dialect in the teaching of reading. In J. C. Baratz & R. W. Shuy (Eds.), *Teaching black children to read*. Washington, D. C.: Center for Applied Linguistics, 1969. (b)

STODOLSKY, S., & LESSER, G. Learning patterns in the disadvantaged. In S. Chess & A. Thomas (Eds.), *Annual progress in child psychiatry and child development*. New York: Brunner/Mazel, 1968.

TULKIN, S. R. Race, class, family and school achievement. *Journal of Personality and Social Psychology*, 1968, *9*, 31–37.

———. Mother-infant interaction in the first year of life: An inquiry into the influences of social class. Unpublished doctoral dissertation, Harvard University, 1970.

WILLIAMS, R. L. The changing image of the black American: A socio-psychological appraisal. Paper presented at the meeting of the American Psychological Association, Washington, D. C., September 1969.

WOLF, R. M. The identification and measurement of environmental process variables related to intelligence. Unpublished doctoral dissertation, University of Chicago, 1964.

YOUNG, W. Invited address presented at the meeting of the American Association on Mental Deficiency, Boston, May 1968.

20. INFANT CARE AND GROWTH IN URBAN ZAMBIA

SUSAN GOLDBERG

Infants were observed in 38 homes in a high-density suburb in Zambia over the period from 4 months through 12 months. The major focus is upon the mother-infant relationship and the way in which it structures the infant's world. A major difference between Zambian infancy and infancy in the United States is that the Zambian infant spends most of his time in close physical contact with the mother, since he is carried on her back in a sling. The effects of this practice on motor, cognitive and social development are discussed.

The research endeavors of psychology, perhaps more than those of other social sciences, have been limited primarily to Western cultures. This is understandable when we consider the particular importance in psychology of making judgments about the psychological meaning of behavior in social contexts. The moment one enters a strange culture, the meaning of the social context itself is unclear and interpretations of behavior even more shaky. Thus, it is necessary to give special attention to the meaning of behavior in the relevant context at every stage of the research process in a way not necessary on 'home ground'. When I arrived in Zambia in September 1968, there had been no previous work with infants. I was overwhelmed, on the one hand, by my extreme ignorance and, on the other, by the discovery that the act of coming to Zambia with the intention of collecting data on infant development had made me an instant expert, whose papers would be the only ones on the subject: 'classics' regardless of quality. I spent a good deal of time in the early months agonizing over the responsibility of that situation and trying to set up a research program that would be both feasible and genuinely productive. At the end of two years, I realized that I was only beginning to see what the interesting questions were. A major function of this paper is to highlight those questions.

The project itself took the form of a short longitudinal study of a group of 38 infants whose families were first contacted when they were 2 months old and who were last seen in their 13th month. In that time-period, several assessments were made. These included coded observations of mother-infant interaction, the Bayley Motor Scale, the Albert Einstein Scales of Sensorimotor Development (Escalona *et al.*, 1967) and Caldwell's Home Stimulation Inventory (Caldwell, 1969), as well as information collected by interview from the mothers. Some of the data have been presented in reports published by the University of Zambia (Goldberg, 1970a, b). In this paper, I will try to present an overview of Zambian mother-infant relationships in urban life as I saw it, and to examine the consequent structure of the infants' world.

To put things somewhat in context, Zambia is the country formerly known as Northern Rhodesia (independent since October 1964). With the exception of Botswana (a relatively powerless nation) and Tanzania, its neighbors, which entirely surround it, are hostile or indifferent. (These neighbors include South Africa, Southwest Africa, Rhodesia, Mozambique, Malawi, Angola and Congo [Kinshasa].)

It is an area roughly the size of Texas, Georgia and Louisiana and is sparsely populated (total population 4 million).

Most of the town-dwelling population is clustered along the 'line of rail' which runs from the Copperbelt, near the Congolese border, through Livingstone on the Rhodesian border. Lusaka is midway between these two points. Its population in 1968 was 200,000 and it is growing rapidly as Zambians continue to flock to towns and cities at an alarming rate, i.e. faster than jobs or housing can be provided. As a result, in 1968, an estimated 50% of the population in the capital city of Lusaka lived in shantytowns and squatter compounds. The high income groups (Europeans, Asians and a few elite Zambians) live in 'low density' suburbs in comfortable homes with modern conveniences. The majority of the remaining Zambians live in 'high density' city-built housing estates or suburbs of varying modernity. In Lusaka, as in most of the larger towns, the population is tribally mixed and 16 different tribes were represented in our sample. The families I visited lived in a high density suburb called Matero. This is an area north of Lusaka, bordering on its heavy industrial area; the houses of stucco and cement-block with corrugated metal roofs are close together along unpaved streets. Houses vary in size, but most are two or three rooms. Our families ranged in size from 3–17 persons ($\bar{x} = 7.2$), so that living quarters are usually overcrowded. None of the houses has inside plumbing or electricity. Those who are lucky have a nearby watertap and outhouse. Those less fortunate use watertaps and pit latrines at some distance. (Mothers understandably make little effort at early toilet training of infants and consider night trips to distant pit latrines too dangerous for small children to undertake alone.) Most family activities take place out-of-doors. Cooking (on a wood or charcoal fire), washing of clothes and utensils, eating and family socializing take place on a small veranda or on mats in the yard. Grass is rare, but some yards have decorative plants or flowers. Most women grow some vegetables and corn in nearby fields during the rains (November to March). Corn is the staple crop and the traditional diet is based on cornmeal porridge (nsima) eaten with a selection of meat, vegetables, peanuts or a small fish called kapenta. This is a nourishing diet, but lack of money and know-how, availability of beer and soft drinks, and the custom of adults being served first at meals make malnutrition a major problem and probably the basic cause of high infant mortality. The immediate cause of death is usually gastroenteritis or respiratory infection. Measles and resultant complications are a frequent cause of death and most Zambians are surprised to be told that in the US deaths from measles are rare. Medical care is widely available in free clinics, but lack of transportation and lack of understanding about the use of services combine to make medical care inadequate.

Roughly half of the 38 infants who were our basic sample were born in Lusaka Central Hospital. The rest were born at home, with a female relative assisting. Children are highly valued by Zambians for the status they confer on parents. Failure to have children can be grounds for divorce under customary law. When we first visited these families, the infants were 2 months old, were being breast fed and, from mothers' reports and our observations, seemed to be in good health. This did not continue to be true. Serious illness plagued a number of infants and we had four deaths among them. The testing of infants and interviewing of mothers was done in homes or yards by two female Zambian research assistants. I participated as an observer-recorder and was present at most, but not all, visits.

There have been few studies of infant development in Africa, but among existent studies (see Warren, 1971 for a comprehensive review), infant precocity in all areas of development is frequently reported (Geber & Dean, 1957; Geber, 1958; Falade, 1955; Ramarasona, 1959; Ainsworth, 1967; Lusk and Lewis, 1972). A few studies report little or no consistent difference between African and European infants (Falmagne, 1962; Parkin and Warren, 1969). In the first group of studies, a great deal of emphasis is placed on the close and highly stimulating mother-infant relationship and its beneficial effects on development. A common feature of traditional African child care is that the nursing infant spends most of his time being carried in a cloth sling, is nursed on demand and sleeps with his mother at night. This was characteristic of traditional care in many of Zambia's 72 tribes (Doke, 1931; Ritchie, 1943; Read 1959; Stefaniszyn, 1964). It was also, for the Western observer, the most striking feature of infant care in the city. In what ways does this structure the infant's experience? In the following discussion, I will try to analyze the kinds of stimulation available to Zambian infants as they relate to motor, cognitive and social development.

Motor Development

The usual way of carrying an infant in the sling is for the infant to sit in an upright position facing the mother's back, resting in a cloth which is passed over one shoulder and knotted in front. For the first few months, the baby is in this position throughout the day and is horizontal only at night. Konner (1971) has pointed out that, whereas few of the reflexes in the neonatal repertoire (besides sucking and rooting) have survival value for infants in cribs, many reflexes such as stepping movements, head lifting and crawling motions do serve a specific function for infants in a sling. They enable the infant to adjust his posture as his mother moves and to free his face from positions in which he has difficulty breathing. Thus, from birth onwards, the Zambian infant is making use of movement and postural control to a degree rarely required of American infants. In this context, grasping also serves a specific purpose. When the infant is placed in the sling the mother bends forward, with the infant lying on her back. Since she uses both hands to wrap the cloth, the infant must support himself and usually grabs her clothing to keep his position. When he is fed, his mother moves him into a position from which he can nurse; but he may get no further attention. One can see women walking down the street with nursing infants clinging to the breast. Although the sling provides some support, a mother in motion may require that the infant exert some effort to maintain his position and hold on to the breast. These infants are constantly receiving kinesthetic and tactile stimulation, and this is a background for all their experience. In the early months, then, the Zambian infant generally receives more physical stimulation than most American infants and has more opportunities to make use of muscular control than the infant in a crib. In addition, Zambian infants are generally handled in a very vigorous, energetic manner. The usual procedure for positioning an infant on the back is to grip him around one elbow or under one armpit and swing him over the shoulder. He may be bounced or shaken vigorously as a form of play or greeting and mothers sometimes try to quiet a fretful infant by bouncing him up and down vigorously in the sling (although a more frequent response is to offer the breast). So, in addition to greater variety and amount of physical stimulation, the intensity of stimulation for Zambian infants is probably greater than that experienced by American infants. This kind of handling does not reflect the 'fragile baby' image which is often impressed on American mothers. Is it possible that Zambian neonates are physically more mature and able to 'take it' from birth. Or would American babies handled in the same way be able to respond like the Zambian infants? We did not test our infants at birth, but Brazelton *et al.* (1971) reported that their sample of hospital-born Zambian infants were less active and responsive than American infants on day 1, more alert and responsive on day 5 and, by day 10, clearly more advanced than American samples on the Brazelton Newborn Assessment. Thus, they concluded that the Zambian infants they saw were not more mature at birth than American infants and that their subsequent rapid development in the first few days of life might well be attributed to the kind of mothering they received. We first tested motor development in our sample at 4 months on the Bayley Motor Scale. Our sample showed more advanced development than Bayley's standardization sample, obtaining a mean Psychomotor Development Index of 125.7, 1.5 standard deviations above Bayley's mean (Bayley, 1969). The mean raw score of 24 for our subjects was equivalent to the score for American infants three weeks older. The most noticeable advantage of the Zambian infant was better ability to sit without support and pull to standing position. This might be a consequence of continual practice of muscular control.

Once the child was able to sit well, he was left on a mat near his mother part of the day, but would usually nap in the sling. By the age of a year, the sling is primarily a mode of transportation. Only a third of our mothers said that they still carried their one-year-olds for long periods of time. There is little deliberate stimulation of motor development. Only six mothers said that they encourage new behavior, and we did not observe any encouragement of this kind. On the other hand, there are few restrictions. Clothing is minimal and equipment such as playpens and swings are unknown (one does occasionally see a carriage). Except for what might endanger his safety, the child, when he is not in the sling, can move about freely. In fact, the sling may be his main physical restriction.

Cognitive Development

In recent years, the role of stimulation in cognitive development has received considerable attention. In addition to the mother's role as caretaker, we have begun to view her as a source of stimulation for the infant and as a mediator of environmental stimuli. Different theoretical views emphasize different aspects of this role, some pointing to frequency and variation of stimulation as the crucial variable (Hunt, 1961), and some to the mother as a source of reinforcement (Gewirtz, 1966; Watson, 1966). Lewis and Goldberg (1969) have argued that an important characteristic of maternal behavior is the extent to which it is contingent upon infant behavior. It is important because, in addition to reinforcing specific behaviors, the mother's response to the infant enables him to learn that his behavior has consequences. The expectation of consequences is a motive underlying exploratory behavior and practice of skills. The mother first serves as the contingency producer and later, when the motive has been learned, the kind of environment she provides determines the infant's opportunities for self-reinforcement. I would argue that the Zambian mother is highly effective as a contingency producer, but relatively ineffective in providing subsequent opportunities for self-reinforcement.

The physical closeness between Zambian mother and infants makes it possible for the mother to respond immediately to the infant's needs. It also enables her to be constantly aware of the infant's state and needs in ways that the mother at a distance cannot be.

Since the infant is, at first, inseparable from his mother, he shares her life. In addition to participating in her daily routine of housework, trips to market, cultivation of crops and social exchange with neighbors, infants are found in bars and cinemas, at football matches and political meetings. His contacts with the world are wide and varied.

Child-centered activities, however, are rare. On the Home Stimulation Inventory, our families often scored low on stimulation of development and play contact. Mothers said they did not attempt to structure the environment or play activities or have a daily routine for the child. Only four children had toys; none of these mothers thought of toys as a stimulus to development. During interviews, few mothers tried to occupy the infant in any way. Thus, although the Zambian infant encounters a great range of environmental stimuli, his exposure is frequently inadvertent rather than intentional on the part of the mother.

Even more important, his exposure is often passive in nature. Except for what he can see and reach from his position at the moment, the infant in the sling has little control over his experiences. In fact, his visual field is quite limited, since his mother's body presents a major obstacle to viewing what is directly in front of him. On the other hand, given his mother's movements and the ability to turn his head, he has a more extensive view of his surroundings than the infant in the crib in the early months when mobility is limited. The Zambian baby views things from the beginning in what adults consider 'natural' orientation. This is not necessarily an advantage, since it can be argued that seeing the same object in different orientations is a necessary experience for the learning of orientation. Korner and Grobstein (1966) found that lifting a crying neonate to the shoulder was not only effective in soothing the infant, but increased visual alertness and scanning behavor over the control conditions of sitting him up or leaving him horizontal. They argued that this position, because it increases visual alertness, is optimal for early learning; the authors speculated about the advantages of infants who are constantly carried. The normal Zambian sling position has some, but not all, of the characteristics of the shoulder position. It would be interesting to ask whether the change from sling to shoulder (a position rarely used by Zambian mothers) would have the same effect as the change from the lying-down position to shoulder.

When the infant is able to sit alone, he spends his time seated on a mat in the yard. From here, he has a relatively unobstructed view of the street-scene, since there are no fences, although sometimes vegetation serves this purpose. He may have very little in the way of objects to manipulate. When we asked mothers what children played with, they mentioned objects found in homes and yards: old cans, pots and dishes, sand and water, sticks and stones, pieces of cloth, bottle-tops and boxes. However, we rarely saw infants playing with any of these objects. Since mothers said they did not structure children's play, it is likely that opportunities for manipulaiton of objects were limited to happenstance. As the infant learned to crawl, his ability to reach such materials theoretically increased; but, as will be pointed out later, there may have been concurrent social learning which tended to depress exploratory behavior.

At 6, 9, and 12 months, we administered the Albert Einstein Scales of Sensorimotor Development. These scales reflect Piaget's observations and theoretical ideas about sensorimotor development and include three scales designed to assess prehension (hand-eye-mouth coordination), object permanence (the idea that objects exist independent of immediate sensory contact with them) and spatial concepts. At the 6 month visit, all but 5 subjects were capable of performing at the most advanced levels on the prehension scale, while the remainder completed the scale by the 9 month visit. At 6 months, performance on the object and space scales was slightly in advance of the American validation sample (Corman and Escalona, 1969), while at 9 and 12 months, their performance was less advanced. Another difference was that while American subjects had generally moved into more advanced stages on the object scale earlier than on the space scale, the reverse was true for our Zambian subjects. We found more advanced performance on the space scale at every age level (6 months, $p < 0.02$; 9 months, $p < 0.04$; 12 months, $p < 0.001$).

At these visits, particularly at 9 and 12 months, we experienced extreme difficulty in eliciting responses to test items, especially those involving retrieval of hidden objects. Our results can be interpreted as arising from this difficulty: As testing difficulty increased, performance scores were depressed. Since the space scale had fewer items calling for finding hidden objects, the difference in performance level for the object permanence-and-space scales could also be explained in this way. Early performance was slightly superior to that of the American sample. This is congruent with the notion that Zambian mothers excel in early contingency-producing but later fail to provide opportunities for self-reinforcement. However, this interpretation assumes that the 9 and 12 month test scores are accurate reflections of the infants' abilities. I am not convinced that this is so. These infants struck me as remarkably passive and unresponsive in a way that was disturbing. While the few European infants we tested spent a great deal of time crawling away from the tester and attempting to play with the toys not in use, this was not true of the Zambian babies. They were unbelievably 'good'. Perhaps this general lack of responsiveness and activity does indicate some retardation of development as a result of lack of stimulation. It may also reflect decreased alertness and activity as a result of subclinical malnutrition. It may also indicate early learning of obedience and conformity in the presence of adults, a highly valued behavior pattern for Zambian children. It is not unreasonable to assume that in ordinary daily life the objects most frequently removed from these infants are things they are told not to play with. In the test situation, it is possible that removing objects is interpreted as meaning 'don't play with that', and that Zambian infants have learned not to disobey such prohibitions.

Social Development

The constant physical contact between the Zambian infant and his mother, as well as the position in which he is carried, makes his early relationship with the mother basically a tactile kinesthetic one. This is true of the mother's experience of the infant as well. She determines the state of the infant and his needs by the 'feel' of what is happening on her back. There is no need for her to go and look or listen the way American mothers do when the baby is at a distance or in another room.

Clearly, these babies experience a great deal of contact-comfort; it underlies all their experience and is not specific to feeding as it often is for American infants. It is interesting to note that Zambian mothers do not seem to attach any specific importance to the feeding situation as a social event. They may take feeding-time to look at and talk to the baby; but this is just as often not the case. A great deal of sucking is non-nutritive, since the breast is offered for comfort as well as food. Thus, the nursing situation is important for the infant in fulfilling his need for food and sucking, but does not add physical comfort and may or may not add the sight of the mother's face and the sound of her voice to his normal background.

In many respects, the early mother-infant relationship has few of the characteristics of what we normally consider a 'social' relationship. Robson and Moss explored subjective aspects of attachment for 54 primiparous mothers and found that face-to-face contacts, particularly eye-contact and smiling, played an important role in the mother's sense of the baby as a person and as a social being and in the arousal of her positive feelings for him. Robson (1967) has emphasized the importance of mutual gazing in the formation of mother-infant attachment bonds. Clearly, the Zambian infant's opportunities for face-to-face contact with his mother are minimal. Assuming that the face-to-face position is the natural one for exchanging speech, it is tempting to explain lack of maternal vocalizing to Zambian infants as a direct consequence of the 'front-to-back' position normal to mother-infant pairs. At our 4 month observations, vocalization occurred less frequently than any of the other maternal behaviors we coded (looking, holding, touching, smiling, feeding and playing). At the same time, it is important to realize that those experiences which we consider to be central to the mother-infant relationship may have different meanings in another culture. Similarly, there may be other patterns (such as physical contact) which serve the same functions in Zambian mother-infant pairs that mutual gaze and vocalization fulfill for American pairs. Given that in the early months the experience of physical separation from his mother is an infrequent one for the Zambian infant, it is possible that he takes longer to learn the self-other distinction which we consider a necessary pre-condition for social learning than an infant for whom separation is the norm and contact is more occasional.

In general, Zambian infants experience greater exposure to a variety of people earlier in life than American infants. Families are large and most women and school children are at home during some part of the day. Given the high unemployment rate in Lusaka, it is not unusual for adult males to be at home during some part of the day. Although the mother is usually the primary caretaker in the early months, there are many other people who are a constant part of the infants' daily life. It is also common for women and children in the family to assist the mother in caring for the infant, so that multiple-mothering is the rule rather than the exception. One may ask whether this familiarity with so many people at an early age does not preclude stranger-anxiety. This is not at all true. During the time we were visiting, most infants, especially at the 9 month visits, showed extreme anxiety both to me and the research assistants. Most infants had to be visited repeatedly at this age to complete testing, and with some we were never successful. Konner (1971) has had similar experiences with Bushman infants who have equally wide social contacts, but probably more face-to-face contact, since mothers carry their infants in front. By 12 months, stranger-anxiety had abated considerably and we were better able to test infants. Benjamin (1959) has shown that those infants who are dependent on the visual mode develop earlier and more-intense stranger-anxiety than is usual. Both the Bushman and Zambian infants may illustrate this principle if we assume that being in the sling tends to encourage dependence on the visual mode. Since the sling does restrict many kinds of physical activity, it is not unreasonable to assume that even though the Zambian infant's visual field is also limited, he is highly dependent on vision.

Weaning for the Zambian infant signals the end of infancy. Not only does the mother stop giving the breast (and this is usually abrupt and total stoppage), but she may also smear the nipple with irritating substances to discourage nursing-attempts. In some tribes, the child was traditionally sent to stay with another relative, but nowadays this is rare. Only four of our mothers had weaned their infants at a year and these were all unusual circumstances (such as maternal illness or absence). Thus we were not able to obtain information on current urban patterns of weaning. Once the child is weaned, he is expected to be fairly independent and to spend his time in the company of the older children who are responsible for him. In particular, he is not supposed to demand any special attention from his mother who is often occupied with a younger child. Weaning thus takes away not only the comfort and nourishment of the breast, but the right to the mother's attention.

I hope that this description has brought

into question the common description of African mother-infant relationships as 'highly stimulating, close and indulgent'. I cannot make any claims about the applicability of my comments to African groups other than the urban Zambian. But, clearly, physical closeness does not necessarily entail emotional or social closeness as we define it in the West. Likewise, exposure to a variety of experiments may provide a high level of stimulation. However, it is important to evaluate the extent to which it is relevant to the infant and available to a variety of modalities for control.

Most of what we know about infancy is derived from studies of the most easily accessible subject: The American middle-class infant. If the infant population of the world is the group about which we ultimately hope to make generalizations, we have chosen a highly atypical subject population. Whereas most infants of the world are carried by their caretakers, he is not. While most infants share sleeping quarters with other relatives and continue to do so most of their lives, the American middle-class infant frequently has his own room and always his own bed. I do not mean to imply that what we learned from our studies thus far is necessarily wrong or inapplicable to other populations. But it is important to verify the extent to which our 'general principles' hold for other populations. This may appear to be trivial in those cases where we find no difference from our standard population; but it is far from trivial when the results are otherwise. The repeated finding is that African infants from families living in poverty with inadequate nutrition, sanitation and medical care initially are developmentally advanced in comparison to more privileged Western infants. It suggests that, in some important way, our understanding of the complex factors which influence development is inadequate.

A second important function of studies of unusual populations is that they offer opportunities to observe effects that we predict, but would not ordinarily find in our standard population because the range of behavioral variation is too narrow. Thus, to verify some of Robson's hypotheses about the role of eye-to-eye contact in mother-infant relations, the Zambian infant, with few opportunities for early contacts of this kind, and the Bushman infant, with almost constant opportunities (Konner, 1971), are important cases on the extremes of the continuum.

The third, and perhaps most important, function of such studies is the clarification of some of the limitations and unquestioned assumptions of more conventional work. Had we all grown up in Matero, we would have begun with the assumption that contact-comfort is the primary ingredient in mother-infant attachment bonds, and would have only recently learned about drive-reduction in the feeding situation. Implicit in the description above is the questioning of a number of assumptions: (a) that the horizontal position is the 'normal' one for young infants; (b) that neonatal reflexes are interesting but largely without function; and (c) that infants are inherently fragile. It would be difficult for me to fully understand Zambian mother-infant relationships even with many more years of work, as well as a Zambian psychologist could. The primary value of having worked two years in Zambia with mothers and infants was the gaining of a different view of American infancy, an awareness of possibilities I formerly could not envisage—and a new range of questions to ask.

References

AINSWORTH, M. D. *Infancy in Uganda: infant care and the growth of love.* (Johns Hopkins Press, Baltimore 1967).

BAYLEY, N. *Manual for the Bayley scales of infant development.* (Psychological Corp., New York 1969).

BENJAMIN, J. D. Prediction and psychopathological theory. In Jessner and Pavenstadt *Dynamic psychopathology in childhood,* pp. 6–77 (Grune & Stratton, New York 1959).

BRAZELTON, T. B., KOSLOWSKY, B., and TRONEK, E. Neonatal evaluation of urbanizing blacks in Lusaka. Meet. Soc. for Research in Child Development, Minneapolis, Minn. 1971.

CALDWELL, B. Inventory of home stimulation. Children's Center, Syracuse University (Unpublished manual, 1969).

CORMAN, H. H., and ESCALONA, S. K. Stages of sensorimotor development; a replication study. *Merrill-Palmer Quart., 15,* 351–362 (1969).

DOKE, C. M. *The Lambas of Northern Rhodesia; a study of their customs and beliefs.* (G. Harrap, London 1931).

ESCALONA, S. K., CORMAN, H. H., *et al.* Albert Einstein scales of sensorimotor development. Department of Psychiatry, Albert Einstein School of Med. (Unpublished test manual, 1967).

FALADE, S. *Le développement psychomoteur du jeune africain du Sénégal au cours de sa première année* (Foulon, Paris 1955).

FALMAGNE, J. C. Etude comparative du développement psychomoteur pendant les six premiers mois de 105 nourissons blancs et de 73 nourissons noirs. Mém. Acad. roy. Sci. d'outre-mer. Cl. Sci. nat. méd., *13,* 5, (1962).

GEBER, M. The psychomotor development of African children in their first year and the influence of mother behavior. *J. soc. Psychol., 47,* 185–195 (1958).

GEBER, M. and DEAN, R. F. A. The state of development of newborn African children. *Lancet, i:* 1216–1219 (1957).

GEWIRTZ, J. L. On conceptualizing the functional environment; the roles of stimulation and change in stimulus conditions in effecting behavior outcomes. Nat. Inst. ment. Hlth. (Unpublished manuscript, 1966).

GOLDBERG, S. Infant care in Zambia, measuring maternal behavior. *Human Develop. Res. Unit.* (University of Zambia, Institute for Social Research, Lusaka 1970a).

———. Infant care, stimulation and sensory-motor development in a high density urban area of Zambia. *Human Develop. Res. Unit,* report No. 15. (University of Zambia, Institute for Social Research, Lusaka 1970b).

HUNT, J. MC. V. *Intelligence and experience.* (Ronald Press, New York 1961).

KONNER, M. Aspects of the developmental ethology of a foraging people. In Blurton-Jones, *Ethological Studies of child behavior,* 1973.

KORNER, A. F. and GROBSTEIN, R. Visual alertness as related to soothing in neonates: implications for maternal stimulation and early deprivation. *Child Develop., 37,* 867–876 (1966).

LEWIS, M. and GOLDBERG, S. Perceptual-cognitive development in infancy; a generalized expectancy model as a function of mother-infant interaction. *Merrill-Palmer Quart., 15,* 81–100 (1969).

LUSK, D. and LEWIS, M. Mother-infant interaction and infant development among the Wolof of Senegal. *Human Develop.,* 1973.

PARKIN, J. M. and WARREN, N. A comparative study of neonate behavior and development; differences at birth between Europeans and Africans and between Africans from widely differing social levels. University Soc. Sci. Counc. Conf., Nairobi, Kenya 1969.

RAMARASONA, A. Psychomotor development in the Tananarive region. Working paper of the CSA Meet. on the Basic Psychology of African and Madagascan populations, Tananarive, Madagascar 1959.

READ, M. *Children of their fathers; growing up among the Ngoni of Nyasaland.* (Methuen, London 1959).

RITCHIE, J. F. The African as suckling and as adult. Paper No. 9. (Rhodes-Livingstone Institute, Lusaka 1943).

ROBSON, K. S. The role of eye-to-eye contact in maternal-infant attachment. *J. Child Psychol. and Psychiat.*, *8*, 13–25 (1967).

ROBSON, K. S. and MOSS, H. A. Subjective aspects of maternal attachment in man. Nat. Inst. ment. Hlth. (Unpublished report).

STEFANISZYN, B. *Social and ritual life of the Ambos of Northern Rhodesia.* (Oxford University Press, London 1964).

WARREN, N. African infant precocity. University of Sussex (Unpublished report 1971).

WATSON, J. S. The development and generalization of contingency awareness in early infancy; some hypotheses. *Merrill-Palmer Quart.*, *12*, 123–135 (1966).

21. INFANCY IN TWO CULTURES

FREDA GOULD REBELSKY

Introductory Statement

This preliminary report of a study of the lives of Dutch and American babies in the first 3 months of life is presented with the hope that it will interest Dutch students or colleagues to gather some additional data.

Problem

In recent years there has been an increased interest in infancy and in the relationship between infantile experiences and later development. Freud, Erikson and others have suggested that certain personality development is set in the first few months. Piaget, Hunt and a large group of American experimenters believe that perceptual and intellectual development may have important roots in early infant experiences.

Although many theorists posit the importance of infancy, very few studies of the environment of babies have been attempted. Most data on infancy come from data gathered in unusual situations (e.g., hospitals or laboratories), from data gathered in parental interviews, or from records kept by interested parents. All of these three types of data have been frequently criticized.

A baby in the first 3 months is usually confined to its home. In order to talk realistically about the effects of early experience on a variety of later behaviors, it is important to assess of what the home environment of a baby consists.

Method

In both the United States and the Netherlands babies were seen in their homes during the first 3 months of life. Each baby was seen for 3 hours every 2 weeks for the first 3 months after birth. Thus each baby was observed 6 times, for a total of 18 hours.

All observations were done on a standard observation form, calling for one observation approximately every 5 minutes. The form contained categories for the baby's behavior and for the behavior of any caretaker. In addition, a variety of items, such as type of bed, temperature of room, time out of bed, types of toys and distance from baby, were noted. High reliability was easily obtained between two trained observers, both in the United States and in the Netherlands (see Rheingold, 1960, for a precursor of the form used, and Lenneberg, Rebelsky, & Nichols, 1965, for the use of the form in a larger study of infant vocalizations).

Sample

The sample consisted of 10 normal, full-term, white, winter-born babies in each culture. They were born into lower-middle to upper-middle class families with existing children. American babies were from environs of Boston; Dutch babies from Enschede and Hengelo. The samples were as closely matched as possible for family size, sex of child and occupation of father. There were some differences, such as the greater education of American mothers and the fact that Dutch babies tend to be born at home and American babies are born in hospitals, which could not be controlled.

In both cultures the sample was obtained through professional contacts. Pregnant mothers were asked to participate if they already had other children. The research was presented to the mothers as a general study of how babies live, what they do, how they sleep, etc., with the explanation that such basic data are not yet known. *E* explained that she did not want to interfere in any way and that no changes in the baby's normal environment should be made for *E*'s convenience (for example, many Dutch mothers felt pity for *E* sitting 3 hours in a cold room and wanted to put on a heater. Since this might have affected the baby in unknown ways, it was not done). The mothers were very cooperative and even tried to recruit other mothers for the study. Mothers were not paid, but *E* promised to inform them of the results of the study and a small gift was given to the baby at the last visit.

Results and Conclusions

The results presented below are tentative: not only are the data in preliminary form, without statistical analysis, but the study itself was on a small sample.

In general, Dutch and American babies seem to have very different experiences in the first 3 months of life. Not only are the two environments physically dissimilar, but there are also differences between the amounts, though not the kinds, of maternal care. Both of these differences, in physical environment and in caretaking, will be described separately.

The Physical Environment

A Dutch baby sleeps in his own bed in his own room, and so does an American baby, though these sleeping arrangements are rare among the world's cultures. However, a Dutch baby's bed is usually a low, closed one, with a canopy overhead and the U.S. crib is usually higher and open on the sides and above. Dutch rooms are kept cool for the babies, American rooms are kept warm (in each instance, for health!). Therefore, Dutch babies are tightly covered under blankets and American babies have few, if any, blankets and have more opportunity for movement.

American children have toys in their crib from the first weeks; Dutch babies usually do not have them within sight or touch until the third month or later (at 3 months, 3 Dutch babies and 9 U.S. babies had toys within sight or touch).

Since the baby's room is cold in Holland, Dutch babies are often fed or bathed in other rooms than where they sleep. In

America babies were more often fed and bathed in their bedrooms. Dutch babies were in their beds more of the time than U.S. babies, who often spent time after feeding propped up or sitting on a reclining chair.

Caretaking

In both cultures, there is one main caretaker, the mother. Most of the mothers breast fed for some time (8 in Holland; 7 in the U.S.), though American mothers tended to breast feed for more months (7 out of the 8 Dutch breast-fed babies and 2 out of the 7 American breast-fed babies were on the bottle by 5 weeks). Regardless of feeding method, feeding time for a Dutch baby averaged 13 minutes, while the U.S. average was 30 minutes. Length of feeding was often prescribed by a doctor in Holland, while in the American sample the mothers were told to judge by the baby's behavior.

Every Dutch baby was fed on a schedule, 3 hours apart at the start, moving to 4 hour feedings generally by the end of the first month. Most American babies (8) were not on a pre-set schedule, and were fed "on demand," though by the second month the babies were asking to be fed at regular times, though the interval between feedings varied. The two U.S. mothers who scheduled feedings were not as regular as the Dutch mothers tended to be. Some Dutch mothers varied as little as ±5 minutes around the prescribed feeding times. Pre-set feeding times meant that Dutch babies were more frequently woken from sleep for a feeding than were American children and more frequently fell asleep while feeding.

U.S. mothers tended to hear their babies crying and responded to the cry, whereas in Holland mothers often couldn't hear the crying (since the bedroom door was shut and the mother was in another room with the door shut) or didn't respond if the crying was heard. The cultural views differ: crying meant a call for help for U.S. mothers, they often reported lactating when they heard the cry. In Holland crying was considered a part of a baby's behavior, good for the lungs and not always something to stop. In addition, though a mother might hear the cry in Holland and interpret it as hunger cry she still would not respond if it was not time for the scheduled feeding.

American mothers looked at, held, fed, talked to, smiled at, patted and showed more affection to their babies more often than did Dutch mothers. U.S. and Dutch mothers did not differ in amount of time spent adjusting, rocking, nodding or playing with the baby. The rank order of the behaviors was similar across cultures, though the frequencies differed. For example, all mothers tended to look at a baby more than they held it. The behaviors where Dutch and American mothers differed the most in frequency were also the behaviors which occurred most often in each culture. In general, U.S. mothers spent more time with their babies than did Dutch mothers. In addition, Dutch mothers spent less time in interaction with their babies at 3 months than at 2 weeks, unlike the American mothers who spent more time with their baby, especially increasing in talking to the baby, at 3 months than at 2 weeks.

As one would expect comparing a stable European country to one with a variety of immigrant strains, there were bigger differences between U.S. mothers than between Dutch mothers, that is, the range of behavior was greater in the U.S. than in the Netherlands.

The Babies

These twenty babies were all normal, healthy infants. Despite the differences in stimulation from the environment, both groups of babies slept about the same amount of time. When Dutch babies were awake, they often played with their hands, gazed at the meeting point of crib and canopy or slats and material, or cried. American babies, when awake, played with their toys (e.g., banged their feet to make a mobile move), looked through the slats of the crib or at its contours or played with their mothers. In both cultures, when a baby had a toy, he tended to "talk to it" by 2–2½ months. U.S. babies made more pleasant vocalization than Dutch babies, but whether this is due to the presence of more objects to vocalize to (such as people or toys) or to the greater amount of vocal stimulation from the mother is unknown.

American babies cried less than Dutch babies by the second month and fewer sucked their fingers (all 10 Dutch babies sucked fingers; 2 out of the 10 U.S. babies did). Laughing, or smiling, emerged about the same time in both cultures, 6–8 weeks, though this was more frequently seen in American than Dutch babies. The babies cooed by 3 months, though again this was heard more frequently in the U.S.

Both cultures produced scheduled babies by 2–3 months. Near feeding times most babies could wait until the mothers were ready, but were also clearly ready to begin feeding promptly.

By 2 months most U.S. babies tended not to look at their mothers but at other things. Only half of the Dutch babies did this. In Holland one possible reason for this phenomenon became apparent. Half of the Dutch babies at 3 months looked only at the mother if she was within sight, and these were all babies whose mothers were with them least frequently. This was not seen in all the U.S., because no American mother was with her child as infrequently as any Dutch mother.

Discussion

U.S. research suggests that stimulation is important in early infancy. Visual search (Fantz, 1966; Hunt, 1961; Piaget, 1952; White, 1964), vocalization (Rheingold *et al.*, 1959; Weisberg, 1963), smiling (Brackbill, 1958) and other forms of social behavior (Rheingold, 1966) are thought to be improved or facilitated by stimulation and responsiveness.

In addition it has been suggested that interaction with the baby is most effective if it is contingent upon the baby's behavior (Weisberg, 1963; Bettelheim, 1967). Both European and American theorists suggest that scheduled interaction, stemming mainly from the parents, can lead to passivity (Bettelheim, 1967) and a general lack of basic trust (Erikson, 1960).

As has been demonstrated, Dutch parents schedule much of their interaction with their infants, and most interaction begins with the parent. Even if a parent sees a child awake and wanting to play or look around, and Dutch parents do see this, he is not likely to respond to this wish or to the behavior which implies this wish, because of fear of "spoiling" the baby (stated by 9 out of the 10 mothers in Holland) or because of the belief that a baby in this age range should sleep and not play or stay awake.

The question raised by this research has been answered only slightly: are there differences between Dutch and American babies? It is clear that there are differences in their environments. Yes, there are some differences between the babies, as outlined above. However, what are clearly needed are some general measures on many Dutch children, especially in 3 areas thought to be affected by stimulation. Helpful to obtain would be (1) a general development quotient (e.g., Griffiths or other baby tests which measure vocalization, motor development, social responsiveness, etc.), (2) a measure of visual acuity and visual search, and (3) a measure of exploratory behavior.

Are there any Dutch students or colleagues willing to undertake this work? It would provide completely new normative data for Holland, perhaps useful for other studies of development, as well as helping to answer the questions raised by this research. As is apparent, this research is not meant to be evaluative. Both cultures may be training very different kinds of people, yet with each culture wanting the ones they produce.

References

BETTELHEIM, B. 1967. *The empty fortress.* N.Y., Free Press.

BRACKBILL, Y., 1958. Extinction of the smiling response in infants as a function of reinforcement schedule. *Child Development 29,* 115–124.

ERIKSON, E., 1960. *Childhood and society.* N.Y., Norton.

FANTZ, R. L., 1966. Pattern discrimination and selective attention as determinants of perceptual development from birth. In: Kidd, A. H. and Rivoire, J. L. (Eds.), *Perceptual development in children.* N.Y., Int. Univ. Press, pp. 143–173.

HUNT, J. MC V., 1961. *Intelligence and experience.* N.Y., Ronald.

LENNEBERG, E., F. REBELSKY and I. NICHOLS, 1965. The vocalizations of infants born to deaf and hearing parents. *Human Development* 8, 23–37.

PIAGET, J., 1952. *The origins of intelligence in children.* N.Y., Int. Univ. Press.

RHEINGOLD, H., 1960. The measurement of maternal care. *Child Development 31,* 565–575.

———, 1966. The development of social behavior in the human infant. In: Stevenson, H. (Ed.), *Concept of Development.* Monogr. Soc. Res. Child Development serial no. 107, *31,* No. 5, 1–17.

———, J. L. GEWIRTZ and H. ROSS, 1959. Social conditioning of vocalizations in the infant. *J. comp. and physiol. Psychol., 52,* 68–73.

WEISBERG, P., 1963. Social and nonsocial conditioning of infant vocalizations. *Child Development 34,* 377–388.

WHITE, B. L. and P. W. CASTLE, 1964. Visual exploratory behavior following postnatal handling of human infants. *Percept. Mot. Skills 18,* 497–502.

22. FIRST DISCUSSANT'S COMMENTS: CROSS-CULTURAL STUDIES OF MOTHER-INFANT INTERACTION

FREDA REBELSKY

Environmental influences on social behavior, intelligence and language have been an increasingly large part of developmental research—not only in the United States, but in Israel, the USSR and other countries as well. Most of this research is conducted within the psychologist's own culture, using the variations found within that one culture. For example, in the US, institutionalized infants are often compared to home-reared American babies. Recently, researchers interested in the impact of stimulation and deprivation on children have been led to study children across cultures because the large observed variation in behavior allows for greater insight into psychological processes. This is likely to be fruitful, just as it was in the area of perception when visual illusions were examined cross-culturally and found to be related to cultural experiences.

As Goldberg put it so well, 'in some important way, our understanding of the interweaving of the complex factors that influence development is incomplete or inadequate.' The three presentations today help us again understand that we do not yet know a great deal about human development. But the data they present should help psychologists emerge from their cultural cocoons.

I have recently completed a study of the development of Dutch infants during the first two years of life, using the Cattell Test of Infant Development. I find very different scores, compared to US norms (table 4.1).

As can be seen, the means at 3 and 6 months are lower than the US means of 100. Even at age 12, 18, and 24 months, when the means were not significantly different from those of the US, there were no babies at the upper-end of the continuum.

Eighteen of the 19 babies tested longitudinally went up in score in the later test; the one exception scored 95 at 12 months and 92 at 24 months. The mean change score was + 9.6 from 3 months to 6 months test (n = 9); + 17.4 from 3 months to 18 months test (n = 8) and + 12.4 from 12 to 24 months tests (n = 8). One baby increased 37 points (from 60 at age 3 months to 97 at age 6 months).

Six months is the time when playpens are often introduced in Holland. Of the 10 babies tested at 6 months, 7 had playpens and 3 did not. The mean DQ for 6 month babies with playpens was 83.4 and for those without, 69.0.

Item analysis of the Cattell revealed that there was no item in the first year which was passed by 50% of the babies. Some items, such as No. 3 at 3 months, regarding cube, and No. 4 at 6 months, unilateral reaching, were passed by only 1 out of the 10 babies of that age.

What shall we make of this? I find myself frequently saying, as I did in my first study of Dutch infant-rearing, 'This research is not meant to be evaluative. Both cultures may be training very different kinds of people, yet with each culture wanting the ones they produce' [Rebelsky, 1967]. Brazelton also holds a similar position when he states about Zinacanteco Indian-rearing, 'This different, but nurturing environment produces strong, adequate, imitative children who may show subtle differences from North American children in cognitive tasks, but who seem well-adapted to their society's emphasis on conformity.'

Ainsworth [personal communication] has suggested that such a culture-relative discussion 'tends to discredit the value of cross-cultural studies as a substitute for experimentation in finding out more about

Table 4.1. Cattell DQ's of Dutch infants

Age months	*n*	*Means*	*Standard deviations*	*Range*	*Number of cases within scores of 100±16*	*Number of cases above scores of 100*
3	10	70.3	16.0	55–109	2	1
6	10	79.1	17.2	59–118	3	1
12	11	92.5	10.8	75–116	8	2
18	9	91.6	10.3	74–110	6	1
24	11	101.7	6.0	91–109	11	7

the relative effect of different rearing conditions upon development.' I think all the participants in this symposium would agree with Ainsworth.

The resolution to me is simple: People are different in important ways around the world; different societies need different types of children and adults; societies differ from each other. A developmental psychologist can only be enriched by learning about these differences and how the rearing develops different adequacies. We are impoverished, as human beings, even within our own culture, when we call differences in development 'worse.' If we assume that in all societies and in all children development occurs, we shall begin to look for the strands that lead to our understanding of developmental processes. When we stopped looking at children's performance on tests compared to adults and started looking at children's so-called 'errors,' a la Piaget, we began to learn about how children think, talk, perceive. This stance is needed even more cross-culturally. Kids are different, not worse—or better. As we notice the differences and ask where they come from and what they lead to, we discover, as is evident in the papers of this symposium, that our present understanding of development does not explain the phenomena we find cross-culturally.

References

AINSWORTH, M. Personal communication.

BRAZELTON, T. B. Implications of infant development among the Mayan Indians of Mexico. *Human Development,* 1972, *15,* 90–111.

GOLDBERG, S. Infant care and growth in urban Zambia. *Human Development,* 1972, *15,* 77–89.

REBELSKY, F. G. Infancy in two cultures. *Ned. T. Psychol.,* 1967, *22,* 379–385.

CHAPTER 4: SUGGESTED FURTHER READING

AINSWORTH, M. *Infancy in Uganda.* Baltimore: Johns Hopkins Press, 1967.

BETTLEHEIM, B. *The Children of the Dream.* Toronto, Ontario: Collier-Macmillan Ltd., 1969.

BRONFENBRENNER, U. *Two Worlds of Childhood.* New York: Russell Sage Foundation, 1970.

CHILD, I. L. Personality in culture. In Borgatta, E. F., and Lambert, W. W. *Handbook of Personality Theory and Research.* Chicago: Rand McNally, 1968.

ERIKSON, E. *Childhood and Society.* New York: Norton, 1950.

GREENFIELD, P. M., and BRUNER, J. S. Culture and cognitive growth. In Goslin, D. A. (Ed.) *Handbook of Socialization Theory and Research.* Chicago: Rand McNally, 1969. Pp. 633–657.

HESS, R. D. Social class and ethnic influences on socialization. In Mussen, P. (Ed.) *Carmichael's Manual of Child Psychology,* Vol. 2. New York: Wiley, 1970. Pp. 457–557.

LEVINE, R. A. Cross-cultural study in child psychology. In Mussen, P. (Ed.) *Carmichael's Manual of Child Psychology,* Vol. 2. New York: Wiley, 1970. Pp. 559–612.

chapter five
socialization: the family

All children are born into a "family" of some sort. It may be a family as we know it, consisting of a mother, father, and siblings, or it may have grandparents, uncles, in-laws, etc., or it may be an institution in which the infant is cared for by various caretakers. All of these situations could be defined as "family," since one of the definitions of a family is a "group of persons living together in one household" (English and English, 1958).

The type of living arrangement or family in which a child grows up influences his or her development in several possible ways. The presence or absence of a mother, father, or siblings will affect the child, as will the number of people included in the household, the number of different caretakers, and so on.

The most common family arrangement in our North American culture is that of the nuclear family—mother, father, and offspring—all living under one roof. It may come as a surprise to you, it did to us, to discover that this accounts for only 25 percent of the families in the world. There is some research on the effects of other types of family arrangements but they are mainly cultural studies. They do indicate that the family arrangement itself has a great effect on the child's development (Whiting and Whiting, 1960). Since most of our research is concerned with ourselves, the studies on family influences are largely about the nuclear family.

One of the questions asked about family structure is whether the presence or absence of a father has an effect on different psychological functions in the child. Many children are without fathers, for a variety of reasons. A man who has lost his wife may hire a housekeeper to care for the children, thus providing them with a surrogate mother, but a surrogate father is rare in our society. Hence, more children are fatherless than are motherless and are the subjects of many studies.

The article by Santrock raises the issue of the effect of and onset of father absence on cognitive development in both boys and girls. Hoffman studies children of both sexes in looking at the relationship between father absence and conscience development. As should be clear, father absence is not a simple variable. The reasons for father absence may vary: divorce, death, military service, occupation (such as seaman), and so on. The length of absence may vary (was the child an infant or older?) and, of course, the reactions of the mother and others to the absence could influence the child too.

One of the reasons we study the effects of a missing parent is to obtain some clue as to what the function of parenting is. If we discover that children without a father behave or respond differently from children with fathers, we may gain some insight into the role or effect of the father within the home.

There have been many studies on maternal deprivation, but they mostly concern children who are raised in institutions where the issue of not having a parent is often combined with the problems of lack of general stimulation of all kinds. The Skeels study in the section on early experiences shows what the effects of institutionalization could be versus being cared for in a familial way. From that we know that having some sort of family experience is important for all development.

The effects of parents' presence and behaviors are studied in many ways. Most of the studies are concerned with the specific effects of home atmosphere and parental discipline techniques. Home studies are difficult, as one can imagine. Most families are two parents who interact, not only with each other but with their children. Several studies in this volume, such as Rebelsky and Hank's study on father verbalization to infants, demonstrate the usefulness and possibilities inherent in home observations. But most of these studies in the home have been with infants, where the multiple interactions of parents and children are somewhat more comprehensible than they would be with older children.

A recent approach to the study of the family is the study of the child's effects on the parents. It makes good biological sense that the child should influence his parents' behavior. In the Halverson article, mothers behave differently to children who are their "own" than they do to strange children, partly in response to the children's behavior. Harper reviews many articles that indicate the child elicits and structures parental behavior. If, in the future, all aspects of the family structure are taken into account in any one study, we shall have an overwhelmingly multifactor study. However, it is still useful to look at the effects in smaller groupings, in an effort to understand more about the impact of family members on each other.

References

ENGLISH, H., and ENGLISH, A. C. *A Comprehensive Dictionary of Psychological and Psychoanalytical Terms.* New York: Longmans, Green and Co., 1968. P. 202.

WHITING, J. W. M., and WHITING, B. B. Contributions of anthropology to the methods of studying child rearing. In Museum, P. (Ed.). *Handbook of Research Methods in Child Development.* New York: Wiley, 1960. Pp. 918–944.

23. RELATION OF TYPE AND ONSET OF FATHER ABSENCE TO COGNITIVE DEVELOPMENT

JOHN W. SANTROCK

Third- and sixth-grade IQ and achievement scores were compared for 286 father-absent and 57 father-present white, predominantly lower-class boys and girls. Father absence was analyzed by onset, whether at 0–2, 3–5, 6–9, 10–11, or 12–13 years of the child's age, and by type, whether (a) death, (b) divorce, desertion, or separation, or (c) presence of a stepfather. While father absence due to divorce, desertion, or separation had the most negative influence in the initial 2 years of the child's life for boys and girls, father absence due to death was the most detrimental when it occurred in the 6–9 period of the boy's life. Father-absent boys consistently performed more poorly than father-absent girls and father-present boys. Remarriage of boys' mothers who were divorced from, deserted by, or separated from their previous husband in the initial 5 years of the son's life had a positive influence.

On many occasions researchers have demonstrated that the father-absent child performs more poorly than the father-present child on intellectual and achievement measures (Bronfenbrenner 1967; Deutsch 1960; Deutsch & Brown 1964; Landy, Rosenberg, & Sutton-Smith 1967; Sutherland 1930; Sutton-Smith, Rosenberg, & Landy 1968). The Sutton-Smith et al. (1968) study also evaluated the effect of the age at which father absence occurred —whether at 0–4, 5–9, or 10+ years of the child's age—on the ACT scores of entering college freshmen. The only effect on males was lower ACT scores by males whose fathers left in the 0–4 and 5–9 periods combined than by males whose fathers left in the 0–4 period. A number of significant effects occurred for the father-absent females, with the most intellectual deficits resulting when the father left in the early or middle period. A limitation on these data was the use of overlapping age categories and a lack of control for type of father absence, which for the 0–4 period was predominantly war service, and for all other groups, divorce, desertion, or separation. In a similar study, Deutsch and Brown (1964) found that father-absent first and fifth graders scored significantly lower than their father-present counterparts on the Lorge-Thorndike Intelligence Test. Blacks scored significantly lower than whites, but no interactions with age were significant. Father absence seemed to have a cumulative effect, since father-absent fifth graders generally performed more poorly than first graders. A limitation on the Deutsch and Brown data was their lack of knowledge of when the father became absent.

The recent study by Blanchard and Biller (1971) overcame some of the methodological problems of prior father-absence studies by matching early father-absent (before the age of 5), later father-absent (after the age of 5), low father-present (spends less than 6 hours per week with son), and high father-present (more than 2 hours per day) boys. Matching was carried out for age, IQ, SES, and the presence or absence of male siblings. However, these researchers did not control for the type of father absence, which was predominantly divorce or separation. Early father absence had the most detrimental effect on third-grade achievement test scores and high father presence had the most positive effect. Other recent studies concerned with personality have supported the contention that the effects of father absence should not be considered in isolation from the onset of the absence (Biller & Bahm 1971; Hetherington 1966; Santrock 1970; Santrock & Wohlford 1970) and the type of absence (Santrock 1970; Santrock & Wohlford 1970).

What kind of predictions can be made about the relation of onset and type of father absence to cognitive development? If the absence of the father predisposes the child to miss certain cognitive experiences, then it seems logical to hypothesize that earlier father absence disrupts cognitive development more than later absence. In the preadolescent years, the child likely has established many peer ties. Thus, the disruption during the 6–11 period of the child's life may be cushioned by his reliance on peer attachment. The trauma of father absence in later years may not be as negative as in earlier years of the child's life when the father plays a more substantial role than peers do in the child's psychological development. However, the consciousness of the father's death or marital disharmony should be greater for the child in the preadolescent period than in the earlier years of his life. Anderson and Anderson's (1954) comments about the child's preoccupation with the concept of death around the ages of 8 and 9 provide further support for predicting that the father's death is most disruptive when it occurs in preadolescence. In comparing the effects of death and divorce or separation, Despert (1961) pointed out that death should be more disruptive for the child following father separation, whereas living in a family after actual divorce or separation may provide a more beneficial setting for the child than the conflicted and ambiguous atmosphere in the predivorce, albeit structurally intact, family. Due to the significance of the same-sex parent in the child's psychological development, the boy's cognitive development should be influenced by the father's absence more than the girl's. A possible exception to this hypothesis is the exit of the father in the 3–5 period of the girl's life when her Oedipal, or romantic, attachment to the father supposedly is strongest.

On these theoretical bases, the following hypotheses were tendered with respect to the child's performance on IQ and achievement tests in the third and sixth grades:

1. Father-absent children score lower than father-present children.
2. When father absence is due to divorce, desertion, or separation, earlier absence, at 0–2, 3–5, or 0–5 years of the child's age, is more detrimental than later father absence, at 6–9, 10–11, or 6–11 years.
3. However, when father absence due to divorce, desertion, or separation occurs at 12–13 years of the child's age, he shows more disruption on sixth-grade IQ and achievement tests than when divorce, desertion, or separation occurs at 10–11 years.
4. Children whose fathers have died show more disruption when the father died at 6–9, 10–11, or 6–11 years of the child's age than at 0–2, 3–5, or 0–5 years of age.
5. Boys are influenced more negatively than girls by father absence.
6. However, when the father departs in the 3–5 period of the girl's life, she is more influenced negatively than the boy is when the father leaves in the 3–5 period of his life.
7. Originally father-absent children who now have a stepfather score higher than father-absent children with no stepfather.

Method

Four high schools and five junior high schools permitted their students to fill out a group questionnaire about their fathers in their classroom. The teacher informed the children that a teacher from the local college was interested in the types of events which happen in children's lives as they grow up. They were told that the information they were asked to provide would remain confidential. The questions were very simple. The child was asked if he had a father present in his home. If he responded that he did not have a father living in his home, he was asked when the father left the home, and the reason for his absence. Both children with fathers and without fathers were asked if a stepfather was present in their home. Eighteen children did not want to fill out the information requested. Several mothers of father-absent children called and wanted to know why their children were being asked this information. On three occasions, mothers were so persistent and uncooperative that their children's scores were not included in the study. Certain information was available on the child's permanent record card. If the child's father had died, that fact was listed along with the year in which he died. Most instances of divorce were listed. A further check on the accuracy of information about father absence in the first 5 years involved looking to see whether a father was listed on the card when the child entered the first grade. The parents' names and occupations also were listed for elementary school, junior high, and high school. If a stepfather was present, his name was entered on the card below the name of the real father. In instances where the information on the questionnaire and on the permanent record card clearly was discrepant, the guidance counselor of the school was requested to clarify the difference. If this could not be done, the child was excluded from the study. Forty-two children were not included in the study because of these discrepancies in background information.

Following elimination of children whose information was inconsistent with permanent record-card data and whose mothers requested their exclusion from the study, 286 white, father-absent subjects remained. A random sample of 65 father-present subjects was obtained by including every twenty-seventh student from the nine schools. If the twenty-seventh student was not white or not father-present, the twenty-eighth student was used. The occupation of the father as listed on the permanent record became the SES index. In cases where the father was not listed on the card, the occupation of the mother became the SES index. Social-class ratings were from 1 to 6, 1 being highest and 6 lowest. For example, a welfare recipient was rated 6, a construction worker 5, an electrician 4, an insurance salesman 3, a doctor 2, and there were no 1 ratings.

As might have been expected based on prior studies, the random sample of father-present children included a greater number of higher SES families than the father-absent sample. Thus, the eight father-present children with the highest SES ratings were removed from the sample. Analyses by t tests indicated no significant SES differences for any of the intergroup comparisons of IQ and achievement-test data discussed in the results section below. All samples characteristically were lower class. For instance, the means of several important groups were: father absence due to divorce, desertion, or separation, $\overline{X} = 4.9$; father absence due to death, $\overline{X} = 4.9$; father presence, $\overline{X} = 4.9$; father absence due to divorce, desertion, or separation at 0–2 years of the child's life, $\overline{X} = 5.1$; and father absence due to death at 0–2 years of the child's life, $\overline{X} = 5.0$.

Third- and sixth-grade Otis Quick Scoring IQ and Stanford Achievement Test scores were obtained from permanent record card files. Although group testing of IQ has been criticized on a number of grounds, group IQ scores, nevertheless, are free of biasing experimenter influences.

Results and Discussion

Hypothesis 1 *Father-absent children score lower than father-present children.*— Father-absent children, boys and girls combined, scored lower than father-present children on third-grade achievement, $t(221) = 4.29$, $p < .001$. The results were similar in the separate analysis for boys, $t(103) = 2.00$, $p < .05$, and for girls, $t(116) = 2.41$, $p < .02$. Boys whose fathers were absent because of divorce, desertion, or separation scored lower than father-present boys on third-grade achievement, $t(74) = 2.17$, $p < .05$. The corresponding difference for girls also was significant, $t(79) = 3.55$, $p < .001$. Boys whose fathers died scored lower than father-present boys on third-grade achievement, $t(52) = 2.95$, $p < .01$, and results were similar for girls, $t(103) = 2.00$, $p < .05$. A trend in most other global comparisons of father absence and father presence favored higher scores for father-present children. For instance, father-present children scored slightly higher than father-absent children on sixth-grade achievement, $t(261) = 1.84$, $p < .10$.

In later portions of the results section, more specific comparisons of father-absent categories and father presence show that the same pattern of findings evolves in practically all comparisons of father-absent and father-present children on cognitive measures. On some occasions, no differences are found when father-absent and father-present children are compared, but, when significant differences between the two groups do occur, they invariably favor the father-present child. The lone exception in the many comparisons of this study was the trend for boys whose father died in the first 2 years of the boy's life to score higher than father-present boys on sixth-grade IQ. For the more generic comparisons of father absence and father presence, differences were found on the achievement measures but did not occur on the IQ measures. Perhaps this reflects a greater impact of environmental influence on achievement compared with a greater genetic component of intelligence.

Hypothesis 2 *When father absence is due to divorce, desertion, or separation, earlier absence, at 0–2, 3–5, or 0–5 years of the child's age, is more detrimental than later absence, at 6–9, 10–11, or 6–11 years.* —The mean scores on the Otis IQ and Stanford Achievement Tests, categorized by onset and type of father absence and more specific father-present samples, are presented in Table 5.1.

The most debilitating age for father-absence onset due to divorce, desertion, or separation for boys was the initial 2 years of the boy's life. In all four instances, boys whose fathers were absent due to divorce, desertion, or separation in the first 2 years of the son's life scored lower than father-present boys—third-grade IQ, $t(44) = 2.12$, $p < .05$; sixth-grade IQ, $t(43) = 2.97$, $p < .01$; third-grade achievement, $t(42) = 2.90$, $p < .01$; sixth-grade achievement, $t(44) = 2.36$, $p < .05$. Achievement scores frequently were related to the onset of father absence for boys, and particularly were depressed in the third grade. In most cases, IQ scores were not influenced strongly in comparisons of onset of father absence with father presence.

For females, onset of father absence due to divorce, desertion, or separation during the 0–2 or 3–5 periods was detrimental to achievement, but was not in the 6–9, 10–11, or 12–13 periods when comparisons were made with father-present girls—0–2 period, third-grade achievement, $t(38) = 2.50$, $p < .01$; 3–5 period, sixth-grade achievement, $t(38) = 2.16$, $p < .05$; 0–5 period, third-grade achievement, $t(54) = 3.53$, $p < .001$, and sixth-grade achievement, $t(57) = 3.64$, $p < .001$. Further evidence that the 0–2 age period is the most disruptive age for divorce, desertion, or separation was found in the specific comparisons of father-absent onset categories. When the father left because of divorce, desertion, or separation in the first 2 years of the son's life, the boys scored lower than boys whose fathers departed in the third through fifth years on third-grade IQ, $t(30) = 2.19$, $p < .05$; sixth-grade IQ, $t(30) = 2.12$, $p < .05$; and sixth-grade achievement, $t(30) = 2.24$, $p < .05$. Similarly, when divorce, desertion, or separation happened in the first 2 years of the

Table 5.1. Mean scores on the Otis IQ and Stanford Achievement Tests for onset and type of father-absent and father-present samples

Onset of Father Absence	*Male*				*Female*			
	IQ		*Achievement*		*IQ*		*Achievement*	
	3d	*6th*	*3d*	*6th*	*3d*	*6th*	*3d*	*6th*
				Divorce, Desertion, or Separation				
0–2	92.95	88.75	3.0	5.5	101.2	96.1	2.9	5.7
	(20)	(20)	(18)	(20)	(11)	(14)	(12)	(13)
3–5	106.3	103.2	3.3	6.9	100.8	101.5	3.2	5.9
	(12)	(12)	(12)	(12)	(15)	(15)	(14)	(17)
0–5	97.3	94.5	3.2	5.9	100.9	99.3	3.0	5.8
	(32)	(32)	(30)	(32)	(26)	(29)	(26)	(30)
6–9	100.1	102.4	3.0	6.6	105.7	102.7	3.4	6.6
	(13)	(12)	(10)	(13)	(16)	(17)	(17)	(17)
10–11.........	99.1	99.1	3.1	6.3	109.2	109.0	3.3	7.6
	(15)	(11)	(10)	(15)	(10)	(12)	(10)	(12)
6–11.........	101.3	100.2	3.3	6.3	106.2	105.4	3.45	6.7
	(28)	(23)	(20)	(28)	(26)	(29)	(27)	(29)
12–13.........	101.7	96.1	2.9	6.3	105.9	108.8	3.2	6.1
	(9)	(8)	(9)	(8)	(9)	(8)	(8)	(9)
				Death				
0–2	109.5	114.0	3.7	6.9	107.3	109.0	3.6	6.9
	(6)	(6)	(6)	(6)	(5)	(5)	(4)	(5)
3–5	106.0	109.4	3.3	5 8	99.1	102.4	3.8	7.3
	(9)	(8)	(8)	(9)	(7)	(9)	(9)	(10)
0–5	107.8	104.0	3.5	6.3	102.8	109.8	3.8	7.2
	(15)	(14)	(14)	(15)	(12)	(14)	(13)	(15)
6–9	96.1	93.9	3.0	5.8	100.1	101.4	3.7	6.6
	(13)	(14)	(12)	(14)	(15)	(17)	(15)	(17)
10–11.........	96.7	98.8	3.2	5.8	107.3	101.7	3.3	6.2
	(3)	(4)	(3)	(4)	(8)	(10)	(9)	(9)
6–11.........	96.3	94.1	3.1	5.8	103.1	101.5	3.4	6.5
	(16)	(18)	(15)	(18)	(23)	(27)	(24)	(26)
				Father Present				
	101.4	102.6	3.8	6.5	105.2	103.2	4.0	6.8
	(26)	(26)	(27)	(26)	(29)	(27)	(28)	(27)

Note.—Numbers in the parentheses refer to the number in each category.

son's life, he had lower sixth-grade IQ, $t(33) = 2.48$, $p < .05$, and sixth-grade achievement, $t(33) = 3.06$, $p < .01$, than boys whose fathers left in the 6–9 age period because of divorce, desertion, or separation. Boys whose fathers became absent due to divorce, desertion, or separation in the first 5 years of the son's life scored lower on sixth-grade achievement than boys whose fathers left in the 6–11 period because of these reasons, $t(58) = 2.44$, $p < .05$.

Specific comparisons of onset of father-absence categories for girls did not reveal as many significant differences as were found for boys. However, when father absence occurred because of divorce, desertion, or separation in the first 2 years of the daughter's life, she scored lower on third-grade IQ, $t(19) = 2.84$, $p < .05$, and sixth-grade achievement, $t(23) = 2.15$, $p < .05$, than girls whose father left in the 10–11 period because of these reasons. Furthermore, when divorce, desertion, or separation happened in the 0–5 period of the daughter's life, she performed less well than girls whose fathers departed in the 6–11 period on sixth-grade achievement, $t(57) = 2.44$, $p < .05$.

Based on these analyses, a clear pattern of the negative influence of father absence due to divorce, desertion, or separation in the first 2 years of the child's life on the child's cognitive development evolved. Although the comparisons of onset of father absence with father presence indicated that third-grade achievement scores were depressed the most, comparisons of specific onset categories with each other did not lead to a loading of significant differences on any particular instrument or grade level.

Before going further, attention should be directed to the combining of divorce, desertion, and separation into a single category. Logically, the effects of a father's desertion of the home are different from a planned, mutually arranged divorce or separation. In the case of desertion, the mother likely feels more anger at being left by the child's father than in the case where she has more choice in the separation. The mother's psychological situation, then, would seem to be influenced more negatively by desertion. Many father desertions occur very early in the child's life, the most probably coming before the child is born. Thus, the more negative influence of the 0–2 period for father absence due to divorce, desertion, or separation may be a consequence of including a greater number of children whose fathers deserted the home in the 0–2 period, compared with relatively fewer children whose fathers deserted the home in later periods. The different dynamics involved in a divorced, deserted, or separated home certainly would prove an interesting area of investigation. For instance, would the mother who has been deserted by the child's father punish male sex-typed behaviors in her child more than the divorced or separated mother?

Hypothesis 3 *When father absence due to divorce, desertion, or separation occurs at 12–13 years of the child's life, he scores lower on sixth-grade IQ and achievement tests than when divorce, desertion, or separation happens at 10–11 years.*—For achievement only, girls whose fathers became absent in the 10–11 year period scored higher than girls whose fathers became absent in the 12–13 period because of divorce, desertion, or separation, $t(19) = 2.64$, $p < .05$. Comparisons of the third-grade achievement scores of girls whose fathers became absent in the 12–13 period, $\overline{X} = 3.2$, with girls whose fathers became absent in the 10–11 period, $\overline{X} = 3.3$, indicates that the significant difference between these two groups at the sixth grade is not an artifact of an earlier inflated achievement level. It is interesting to note that the IQs of boys whose fathers became absent because of divorce, desertion, or separation in the 12–13 period dropped an average of 5 points from the third to the sixth grades, whereas the IQs of boys whose fathers became absent in the 10–11 period had the same means over the same period of comparison, although the differences were not significant. The number of subjects for these comparisons was relatively small, but the results do indicate that Despert's concept (1961) of a "psychological divorce" may be more damaging to the child's cognitive development than the actual divorce or separation. A more concentrated study of children in these particular circumstances, before and after divorce, desertion, or separation, as well as assessment of the mediating effects of the mother's psychological situation in such circumstances, would be helpful in advancing our knowledge of the effects of father absence.

Hypothesis 4 *Children whose fathers are dead show more disruption when the father died at 6–9, 10–11, or 6–11 years of the child's life than at 0–2, 3–5, or 0–5 years.*—Consistent differences were found between boys whose fathers died in the first 2 years and in the sixth through ninth years of the boy's life. When the father died in the first 2 years of the son's life the son scored higher on third-grade IQ, $t(17) = 2.69$, $p < .05$, sixth-grade IQ, $t(18) = 3.58$, $p < .01$, and sixth-grade achievement, $t(18) = 2.16$, $p < .05$, than when the father died in the sixth through ninth years. Similarly, when the father died in the initial 5 years of the son's life, the son scored higher on sixth-grade IQ than when the father died in the sixth through eleventh years, $t(30) = 3.29$, $p < .01$. In one comparison there was even a trend for boys whose fathers died in the first 2 years of the son's life to score higher on sixth-grade IQ than boys with a father present, $t(29) = 1.84$, $p < .10$. No significant differences were found for any of the comparisons of girls whose fathers died at different times in their lives.

These findings call attention to the importance of looking at the age of the child when the father becomes absent. If the onset of father absence had not been demarcated into a number of specific time periods, the conclusion from earlier reported results would be that the death of the father is detrimental to the child's cognitive development. However, when the onset of father absence was analyzed, it was shown that when the father died in the sixth through ninth years of the boy's life the boy's cognitive growth was depressed, but when the father died in the initial 2 years, it was not. Although the findings for onset of father absence due to death seem fairly consistent, it should be noted that there is an unusually high IQ at both the third- and sixth-grade levels for boys whose father died in the 0–2 period. Nevertheless, the social-class difference, the only, and unfortunately crude, indicator of "matching" on intellectual stimulation possibilities, does not reveal a difference that might make the IQ finding artifactual.

The developmental sequence which seems to unfold is that the death of the father in the 6–11-year period predisposes the boy to experience less cognitive growth than death in the 0–5 period of the boy's life. Based on the comparison of categories in which the father died at different times in the son's life with father-present boys, very early father absence due to death in some way provided an avenue for increased cognitive growth. Possibly the mother perceives the situation as one in which it is all the more necessary that the young son grow up to be someone her husband would have been proud of. Consequently, the mother then rewards the son's educational achievements more consciously than she usually would. An alternative explanation focuses on the increased responsibility and independence the lack of a father creates in the young son's life. Consistent with this explanation, Santrock (1971) found that the boys whose fathers died were rated by their teachers as more independent than boys whose fathers were present. A third explanation centers on the greater consciousness of the older boy about the event. Obviously, the child who is 0–2 years old will not remember the events surrounding the father's death, whereas when the boy is 6 to 11 years old the trauma of the father's death undoubtedly is more vivid. Two other hypotheses may provide clues to the uncommonly high IQs of boys whose fathers died in the 0–2 period. First, the N for this category was extremely small and probably was among the most unrepresentative samples of the study. Second, the SES ratings of boys whose fathers died in the initial 2 years of the boy's life typically were derived from the mother's occupation. Thus, for instance, the widowed mother may have inherited a substantial insurance policy which allowed her not to work and to remain a housewife, perhaps even to receive public assistance. Such circumstances may have led to a deflated SES rating for the boys from homes in which the father died, particularly in the early onset period.

In search of further validation of the differential effects of the reason for father absence, comparisons of divorce, desertion, and separation categories with death categories at each of the onset levels were carried out. On three of the four measures of IQ and achievement for the 0–2 onset period, boys whose fathers were absent because of divorce, desertion, or separation scored lower than boys whose fathers died —third-grade IQ, $t(24) = 2.09$, $p < .05$; sixth-grade IQ, $t(24) = 3.47$, $p < .01$; sixth-grade achievement, $t(24) = 2.50$, $p < .05$. On the fourth measure, third-grade achievement, a strong trend in the same direction occurred, $t(22) = 2.03$, $p < .10$. In contrast, there was a trend for boys whose fathers died in the 6–9 age period to attain lower IQ scores in the sixth grade than boys whose fathers were absent due to divorce, desertion, or separation in the same period, $t(24) = 1.73$, $p < .10$.

For females, the significant differences among categories of reason for father absence were confined to the 0–5 onset period. Girls whose fathers became absent during the 0–2 period because of divorce, desertion, or separation scored lower on sixth-grade IQ than girls whose fathers died in the same period, $t(25) = 3.17$, $p < .05$, and the same pattern of differences was observed for the 3–5 onset period on sixth-grade achievement, $t(25) = 2.28$, $p < .05$.

These results support the belief that divorce, desertion, separation, and death differentially affect the child's cognitive development. As mentioned previously, research needs to be conducted to discover the possible, and probable, differences among the effects of divorce, desertion, and separation, which were combined for this study. One suspects that the mother who has been divorced, deserted, or separated from her husband might communicate "maleness" to her son or daughter as a worthless or disparaged role. This hypothesis would seem particularly valid for the mother who has been deserted by the child's father and marital situations in which the husband decided on the divorce or separation. In contrast, the widowed mother may communicate an entirely different image of "maleness" to her son or daughter, particularly when the spouse was loved deeply and esteemed highly by the mother. Furthermore, when divorce, desertion, or separation occurs in the first 2 years of the child's life, the mother possibly never has experienced stability, trust, and other positive psychological characteristics in her marital and interpersonal relationships, whereas there is no reason to assume that psychological imbalance and mistrust are as frequent and as intense in the mother before the death of her husband. Further support for the differential effect of divorce and death on the child's psychological development was reported by Tuckman and Regan (1966). Personality problems of children referred to an outpatient psychiatric clinic were related to the type of home the children came from. Children from widowed homes were more likely to show anxiety and neurotic symptoms, whereas children from divorced homes most often displayed abnormally high aggression and antisocial behaviors. Thus, both the child's cognitive and affective development are related to the type of father absence the child experiences.

Hypothesis 5 *Boys are influenced more negatively than girls by father absence.*— In a number of comparisons, father-absent boys scored significantly lower on cognitive measures than father-absent girls, and in no comparisons did they score significantly higher than father-absent girls. Father-absent boys scored lower on sixth-grade IQ, $t(201) = 2.86$, $p < .01$, than father-absent girls. Furthermore, boys whose fathers were absent because of divorce, desertion, or separation had lower sixth-grade IQs than girls whose fathers were absent for the same reason, $t(125) = 2.13$, $p < .05$. Similarly, boys whose fathers died scored lower on sixth-grade achievement than girls whose fathers died, $t(54) = 2.73$, $p < .01$. Also, when father absence due to divorce, desertion, or separation occurred in the 12–13 age period, girls scored higher on sixth-grade IQ than boys, $t(13) = 2.49$, $p < .05$. When the father died in the 3–5 age period, girls attained higher sixth-grade achievement scores than boys, $t(22) = 2.22$, $p < .05$. There also was a trend for girls whose fathers became absent because of divorce, desertion, or separation in the 10–11 period to score higher on sixth-grade IQ than boys from the same background, $t(25) = 1.87$, $p < .10$. The more negative influence of father absence on boys than on girls is logical and adds support to the assumption that the same-sex parent's presence is important for optimal psychological development in the child.

Hypothesis 6 *When the father departs in the 3–5 age period, the girl is influenced more negatively than the boy.*—The trend of lower sixth-grade achievement scores for girls whose father left when the girl was 3–5 years old, when compared with boys whose fathers departed in the same period, because of divorce, desertation, or separation, is intriguing in view of the girl's supposed Oedipal, or romantic, attachment to the father during this period, $t(42) = 1.93$, $p < .10$. However, as mentioned in the analysis of the preceding hypothesis, when the father died in the 3–5 period, boys performed more poorly than girls on sixth-grade IQ tests. Thus, no conclusive support of hypothesis 6 was found.

Hypothesis 7 *Originally father-absent children who now have a stepfather score higher than father-absent children with no stepfather.*—In support of hypothesis 7, most father-absent categories with a stepfather were higher than father-absent categories with no stepfather, although only one significant difference occurred. Boys who had no stepfather present and whose fathers became absent because of divorce, desertion, or separation in the first 5 years of the boy's life scored lower on third-grade IQ, $t(51) = 2.10$, $p < .05$, than boys whose real fathers became absent for the same reason and in the same period but who now have a stepfather present. Trends in the same direction resulted for the same onset and type categories on sixth-grade IQ, $t(52) = 1.83$, $p < .10$, and sixth-grade achievement, $t(52) = 1.90$, $p < .10$. Entrance of a stepfather into the home of a boy whose real father left in the first 5 years of the boy's life apparently has a positive effect on the boy's cognitive development. Again, the psychological status of the mother may be an important mediating influence. Those mothers who do remarry likely are more concerned about the necessity of an adult male in the son's life than the mother who does not remarry. The mother who remarries probably holds less of a grudge against males, as a consequence of her previous experience with marriage, than the mother who does not remarry.

Further evaluation of the effects of a stepfather on the child's cognitive development was accomplished by comparing children from originally father-absent homes now with a stepfather present with children from father-present homes. Whereas most comparisons of father-absent categories with father presence have shown significant differences, the presence of a stepfather in the boy's home brought the previously father-absent boy more in line with boys from father-present homes on cognitive measures. However, the entrance of a stepfather into a previously father-absent girl's home did not have a positive influence on the girl's cognitive development. Father-absent girls with a stepfather present performed significantly lower than father-present girls on third-grade achievement, $t(51) = 3.50$, $p < .01$. Also, comparison of the third-grade achievement means of father-absent girls, $\overline{X} = 3.4$, with the mean of father-absent girls with a stepfather, $\overline{X} = 3.4$, further indicates that the presence of a stepfather appears to relate differently to the cognitive development of boys and girls. There seems to be greater conflict for the girl surrounding the remarriage of the mother than for the boy. Perhaps the girl sees the stepfather as taking the mother away from her, while the boy welcomes the presence of a "new" father whom he can brag about to his peers and who can play ball with him and take him places.

More precise assessment of the influence of a stepfather in the child's cognitive development could be accomplished by focusing on a comparison of widowed homes and divorced, deserted, or separated homes. The *N*'s of the widowed, father-absent categories were very small and thus were not included in the stepfather analyses. A major mediating variable likely is the way the mother handles the development of the "new" father's relationship with the previously father-absent child. Possibly in the interim of the absence of a father in the home, the divorced, deserted, or separated mother has disparaged the male role in her communication with the child, and the entrance of a stepfather into such homes may cause more conflict than when a stepfather enters the widowed home. This line of reasoning would seem more valid for girls than boys, since the boy so eagerly seeks adult male attention in the preadolescent period. Also, the widowed mother may be more stable and positive in her presentation of the male role to the child. Further increments in our knowledge about the father-absent child would be accomplished by assessing the child's reaction to the stepfather, the stepfather's reaction to the child, the child's tie to his mother, and so on into the dynamics of the newly arranged home.

The findings of the present study strengthen the contention that cognitive changes are affected strongly by social influence. The hypothesis that the effects of father absence frequently are different for both the onset and type of father absence was supported firmly. The descriptive data reported here, based on large numbers of subjects in most comparisons, point to a number of areas toward which future research should be targeted. Focus should be on the mediating processes involved in father separation, particularly the dynamics of the father-son and mother-son relationships, both before and after father separation. For instance, the father may still be available in the community in the case of the divorced or separated home, and assessment of the quality, as well as frequency, of the father-son relationship following father separation would augment our knowledge of the father-absent child. Attention should be given to the possibility of parental cooperation in the breakdown of the family when divorce or separation is the reason for the absence. Hopefully, more researchers firmly grounded in experimental child psychology will answer the challenge to enter an area of investigation which should reap many benefits in advancing our knowledge of how the child develops and the reason for that development.

References

ANDERSON, H. H., & ANDERSON, G. L. Social development. In L. Carmichael (Ed.), *Manual of child psychology.* (2d ed.) New York: Wiley, 1954.

BILLER, H. B., & BAHM, R. M. Father absence, perceived maternal behavior, and masculinity of self-concept among junior high school boys. *Developmental Psychology,* 1971, *4,* 178–181.

BLANCHARD, R. W., & BILLER, H. B. Father availability and academic performance among third grade boys. *Developmental Psychology,* 1971, *4,* 301–305.

BRONFENBRENNER, U. The psychological costs of quality and equality in education. *Child Development,* 1967, *38,* 909–925.

DESPERT, J. L. *Children of divorce.* Garden City, N.Y.: Doubleday, 1961.

DEUTSCH, M. Minority group and class status as related to social and personality factors in scholastic achievement. *Society for Applied Anthropology,* 1960, No. 2.

DEUTSCH, M. & BROWN, B. Social influences in Negro-white intelligence differences. *Journal of Social Issues,* 1964, *20,* 24–35.

HETHERINGTON, E. M. Effects of paternal absence on sex-typed behaviors in Negro and white preadolescent males. *Journal of Personality and Social Psychology,* 1966, *4,* 87–91.

LANDY, F.; ROSENBERG, B. G.; & SUTTON-SMITH, B. The effect of limited father absence on the cognitive and emotional development of children. Paper presented at the meeting of the Midwestern Psychological Association, Chicago, May 1967.

SANTROCK, J. W. Influence on onset and type of paternal absence on the first four Eriksonian crises. *Developmental Psychology,* 1970, *3,* 273–274.

———. The relation of onset and type of father absence to personality development. Unpublished manuscript. University of Minnesota, 1971.

SANTROCK, J. W., & WOHLFORD, P. Effects of father absence: reason for the absence, and onset of the absence. *Proceedings of the 78th Annual Convention of the American Psychological Association,* 1970, 265–266.

SUTHERLAND, H. E. G. The relationship between IQ and size of family in the case of fatherless families. *Journal of Genetic Psychology,* 1930, *38,* 161–170.

SUTTON-SMITH, B.; ROSENBERG, B. G., & LANDY, F. Father absence effects in families of different sibling compositions. *Child Development,* 1968, *39,* 1213–1221.

TUCKMAN, J., & REGAN, R. A. Intactness of the home and behavioural problems in children. *Journal of Child Psychology and Psychiatry,* 1966, *7,* 225–233.

24. FATHER ABSENCE AND CONSCIENCE DEVELOPMENT

MARTIN L. HOFFMAN

A father-absent and a father-present group—controlled for sex, IQ and social class—were compared concerning seven moral attributes and overt aggression. All subjects were seventh-grade white children. The data were based on structured and semiprojective items and ratings by parents, teachers, and peers. Father-absent boys obtained lower scores for all the moral indexes—significantly lower for internal moral judgment, maximum guilt following transgressions, acceptance of blame, moral values, and rule conformity. They were also rated by teachers as significantly more aggressive than father-present boys. No differences between father absence and father presence were obtained for girls. Evidence is presented that the effects of father absence on boys are similar but somewhat more pronounced than the effects of nonidentification with a father who is present, which suggests that some but not all of the effects of father absence are attributable to the lack of a paternal model. Evidence is also presented which suggests that the effects of father absence on boys may be partly mediated by the resulting changes in the mother's child-rearing practices.

There are many reasons for expecting the absence of a father to have an adverse effect on the child's conscience development. At the theoretical level, the father is one of the child's two major socialization agents, and for this reason alone his absence must create an enormous gap in the child's experience. The father's special role in moral development, furthermore, is suggested in both the Parsonian view that the father brings the larger society's normative standards into the home, and the Freudian view that by identifying with the father the child—at least the boy—acquires the moral standards of society as well as the motivational and control systems needed to assure adherence to them.

The empirical research is less clear in its implications. There is a growing body of evidence that the father's absence has important effects on personality development, especially for boys (see Biller, 1970, for most recent review of this research) but while some of the findings seem relevant to moral development, they do not provide a consistent picture. Thus, although father absence appears to be associated with a relative absence of doll-play aggression in young boys (Bach, 1946; Sears, 1951; Sears, Pintler, & Sears, 1946), it has also been found—primarily in lower-class samples—to relate positively to frequency of overt aggression and other antisocial behaviors in older boys (Glueck & Glueck, 1950; Gregory, 1965; Miller, 1958; Siegman, 1966). The explanation for the first set of findings has typically been that in the father's absence the child is likely to lack an aggressive role model; and the second set has typically been accounted for in terms of the compensatory or reactive masculinity of males whose primary identification is feminine because they lack a father. A more parsimonious interpretation of both sets of findings might be that fathers more typically provide models of self-control and in their discipline tend to discourage rather than encourage the expression of aggression. When such experiences are lacking, the boy develops less effective controls and is thus more likely to express aggression overtly; he need not express it in fantasy. Boys who have fathers, on the other hand, are more apt to control aggression in real life but express it in fantasy. Father absence has also been found to be associated with inability to delay gratification (Mischel, 1961), but the relevance of the delay measure to morality may be limited, since it considered only greater gains for the self in the future and did not contrast immediate gains with altruistic or prosocial future gains.

Further complicating the picture is the research on child-rearing practices and moral development in intact families. A recent study by Hoffman (in press) indicates that the boy's conscious identification with his father contributes to the acquisition of certain moral attributes; this suggests the absence of the father will have adverse effects on the son's moral development. The findings in the discipline research, however, indicate that the mother's, but not the father's, discipline is important in the child's moral internalization (Hoffman, 1970); this suggests that father's absence may have little or no effect on moral development. The notion that the effect might even be positive has been advanced by Moulton, Burnstein, Liberty, and Altucher (1966). Their view is based on the theory advanced by Henry and Short (1954) and extended by Rosen, Hoffman, and Lippitt (1957) and Hoffman (1961) that internalization of parental characteristics, as evidenced in guilt and aggression against the self, is most likely to occur when the same parent is the major source of both frustration and affection. Under these circumstances, the child is likely to inhibit aggression against the source of frustration—turning it inward—because not to do so would jeopardize the gratifications received in this affectionate relationship. In support of this view, Moulton et al. found that the affection level of the parent reported as the dominant disciplinarian relates more closely to the son's self-report of guilt than the affection level of the other parent. Extrapolating from these findings, they suggest that the absence of the father might tend to increase the extent to which affection and discipline will be focused in one parent; and when this occurs, low aggression and high guilt should be expected in the sons.

The upshot of these theories, conjectures, and research findings is that it is difficult to predict the effects of father absence on moral development, although it seems clear that any effects that do occur are likely to be more pronounced in boys than girls. The aim of this study was to throw light on these matters by making a direct comparison of the moral orientation of children with and without fathers.

Method

Sample

This is part of a larger study of the effects of discipline and identification on moral development in intact families. The subjects were all seventh-grade white children in the Detroit metropolitan area. This age group was chosen because it is old enough to show the needed variation in moral orientation, yet young enough for parental influences to be still salient. The total pool consisted of 262 boys and 235 girls. In this group 25 boys and 28 girls were found to have no adult male living in the home for at least 6 months prior to the study. These children constituted the father-absent sample. Since this was not initially planned as a study of father absence, data about the nature of the absence, including its duration, were unfortunately not obtained.

Control group A control group of children from intact families, equal in size and matched closely to the father-absent group on IQ and social class, was selected from the larger pool. These controls were deemed necessary, since the previous research has reported father absence to be associated with low IQ and low socioeconomic status (Deutsch, 1960; Deutsch

& Brown, 1964; Landy, Rosenberg, & Sutton-Smith, 1967; Maxwell, 1961; Sutton-Smith, Rosenberg, & Landy, 1968; Miller, 1958). Scores from either the California Test of Mental Maturity or Iowa Test of Basic Skills were available for all the children. Social class was determined on the basis of the child's responses to questions about the parent's occupation and education. The distinction was basically between white-collar and blue-collar.[1] The control groups were formed by matching each child in the father-absent group with one from an intact family who was in the same social class, attended the same school, and had the same IQ decile score. Though no effort was made to control for sibling distribution, the two groups finally selected turned out to be closely matched on both sibling order and number of siblings. This was fortunate, since there is evidence (Landy et al., 1967; Sutton-Smith et al., 1968) that sibling distribution can influence the effects of father absence on the child's cognitive development.

Morality Indexes

Several moral indexes, each tapping a different aspect of the child's moral structure, were used. Three pertain to the degree to which the child's moral orientation is internalized: intensity of guilt following transgressions; use of moral judgments about others which are based on moral principles rather than external considerations; and tendency to accept responsibility for one's misdeeds. The other indexes pertain to the extent to which the subject shows consideration for others, conforms to rules, verbally accepts moral values, and expresses anger. In intact families, all but the last three have previously been found to be associated with a maternal discipline pattern which includes frequent induction (techniques pointing out the consequences of the child's behavior for others), infrequent power assertion, and frequent expressions of affection in nondiscipline situations (Hoffman & Saltzstein, 1967). The indexes of internal moral judgments, conformity to rules, and acceptance of moral values have also been found to relate positively to father identification in boys from intact families (Hoffman, in press).

Guilt Two semiprojective story-completion items were used to assess the intensity of the child's guilt reaction to transgression. The child is presented with a story beginning which focuses on a basically sympathetic child of the same sex and age who has committed a transgression under conditions in which detection is unlikely. The subject's instructions are to complete the story and tell what the protagonist thinks and feels and "what happens afterwards." The assumption made is that the child identifies with the protagonist and therefore reveals his own internal (although not necessarily his overt) reactions through his completion of the story.

One story (adapted from Allinsmith, 1960) was about a child who cheats in a swimming race and wins. The other was concerned with a child who through negligence contributes to the death of a younger child. In rating the intensity of guilt, care was taken to assess first that the subject identified with the central character. If such identification was dubious, the story was not coded for guilt, nor were stories involving only external detection or concern with detection coded for guilt. All others were. For a story to receive a guilt score higher than zero there had to be evidence of a conscious self-initiated and self-critical reaction. Given this evidence, guilt

[1] The middle class was defined in terms of father's occupation being white-collar and both parents having at least a high school education; the lower class in terms of father's occupation being blue-collar and neither parent having more than a high school education. It should be noted that occupation and education data for fathers were provided by all but nine of the father-absent subjects—four boys and five girls. In these cases, the mother's occupation and education were used as the index of class.

intensity was rated on a scale ranging from 1 to 6. At the extreme high end were stories involving personality change in the hero, suicide, etc. In coding the stories the attempt was made to ignore differences in sheer writing style and to infer the feeling of the subject as he completed the story.

Two guilt scores were assigned to each story—one for the maximum guilt experienced by the hero, usually occurring early in the story, and the other for terminal guilt. The scores for the two stories were added to obtain an overall score for maximum guilt and one for terminal guilt.

Internal moral judgments The moral judgment items consisted of several hypothetical transgressions which the children were asked to judge. These were of the type used by Kohlberg (1958) including moral judgments about persons committing various crimes, for example, stealing; choosing which of two crimes was worse, for example, one involving simple theft and the other a breach of trust; and judgments of crimes with extenuating circumstances, for example, a man who steals in order to procure a drug which he cannot afford and which is needed to save his wife's life. The subjects were first asked to indicate whether the act was right or wrong, or which was worse, and then give the reason for their choice. In coding, the reasons given were more important than the direction of the choices, and perfunctory responses were not coded at all. Rseponses were coded as external (e.g., "you can get put in jail for that"), internal (e.g., "Joe was worse because the man trusted him"), or indeterminate. The internal scores were summed for all items to obtain the child's internal moral judgment score.

Moral values Moral values were assessed by a measure in which the child rates the importance "in boys [girls] your age" of 21 personal attributes, some of which were moral, for example, consideration for others and obedience to rules; and some of which were nonmoral, for example, leadership, popularity, achievement, and sense of humor. The child was asked first to rate the importance of each item and then to indicate which three were most important. Only the three top-ranked items were counted and these were assigned weights of 3, 2, and 1.[2] The subject's moral value score was simply the weighted sum for the moral items.

Acceptance of blame The measure of acceptance of blame is based on the teacher's report. The teacher is asked to check which of the following characterizes the child's reactions when he is caught doing something wrong: (*a*) denies he did it, (*b*) looks for someone else to blame or makes excuses, (*c*) cries, looks sad, or seems to feel bad, (*d*) accepts responsibility for what he has done, (*e*) where possible, tries on own initiative to rectify situation. In the scoring, *a* and *b* are treated as low, *c* as intermediate, and *d* and *e* as high on acceptance of blame. The scores range from 1 to 5.[3]

Conformity to rules and consideration for others Conformity to rules was assessed in terms of the teacher's reports of the extent to which the child (*a*) "behaves according to the rules . . . or breaks them" and (*b*) copies his classmates' answers to tests. The class was divided into quartiles, and scores of 1–4 for Item *a* and 4–1 for Item *b* were assigned depending on the quartile in which the child was placed. The two were summed to obtain an overall score for rule conformity.

Data about consideration for others were

[2] The initial ratings of each item were included primarily to make sure the respondent thought about all the items in the list before ranking them.

[3] Where the teacher checked two or more reactions for a child, she also indicated which was most typical for him. The final scoring takes into account the reactions checked alone and those specified as most typical when two or more were checked. Hence a range of 1–5 is possible.

obtained from sociometric ratings by the children in the same classroom. Each child made three nominations for the child first, second, and third most "likely to care about the other children's feelings" and "to defend a child being made fun of by the group." The usual weights were assigned and the two scores summed.

These two indexes were deemed relevant to morality but not necessarily internalization, since they could pertain to instrumental acts for gaining approval from authority or peers.

Overt aggression Data about the child's aggression were based on the teacher's report of how the child "expresses anger toward other children." The categories include (*a*) physically attacks or threatens to . . . , (*b*) expresses anger verbally, (*c*) looks angry or sulks but says or does nothing, (*d*) acts nervous, (*e*) turns to new constructive activity, (*f*) never seems to get angry. In the scoring, *a* and *b* are treated as high, *c* and *d* as intermediate, and *e* and *f* as low on aggression. The scoring procedure is the same as that used for "acceptance of blame," and the scores range from 1 to 5.

Data Analysis

Coding To avoid contamination in the story-completion and moral-judgment coding, the responses of all the children in the larger pool were coded for one variable at a time. This made it impossible for the coder to build up a picture of a subject that might influence his subsequent coding of that subject's record for other variables. The intercoder reliabilities were 77% for maximum guilt, 69% for terminal guilt, and 91% for internal moral judgment. The final coding was done independently by two coders, and discrepancies were resolved in conference.

Statistics The data were analyzed separately for boys and girls and the test of significance used throughout was the median test.

Results and Discussion

The results (Table 5.2) provide strong support for the expectation that father absence has adverse effects on moral development in boys. Thus, father-absent boys obtained relatively low scores on all the moral indexes. The differences were significant for internal moral judgment, maximum guilt, acceptance of blame, moral values, and rule conformity. They were also rated by their teachers as more aggressive than father-present boys, which replicates the findings obtained in previous research with boys this age and older (Glueck & Glueck, 1950; Gregory, 1965; Miller, 1958; Siegman, 1966). In contrast to the clear-cut findings for boys, there was no consistent pattern for girls, and only one finding approached significance, that involving moral values ($p < .10$).

The next question we may ask is: What aspect of the father's absence is respon-

Table 5.2. Median differences between father-absent and father-present subject on moral indexes

	Boys		*Girls*	
Moral index	*Father absent*	*Father present*	*Father absent*	*Father present*
Maximum guilt	3.70	4.65*	4.50	5.26
Terminal guilt	2.47	2.66	2.66	3.16
Internal moral judgment	2.95	3.82**	3.65	3.54
Acceptance of blame	0.35	3.65**	3.83	3.71
Moral values	4.00	4.95*	3.60	4.50
Consideration for others	1.63	1.80	1.90	1.75
Conformity to rules	2.33	3.72**	3.83	3.93
Overt aggression	3.55*	2.65	2.65	2.45

Note.—Asterisk denoting significance level is placed in higher cell (e.g., father-present boys are higher on maximum guilt than father-absent boys).
* $p<.05$.
** $p<.01$.

sible for these effects? The possible influence of the intellectual deficit or low socioeconomic status often associated with father absence can be ruled out, since the two groups of subjects were closely equated for these variables. Another explanation which immediately comes to mind is related to the sheer absence of a paternal model as the significant factor. This seems like a reasonable explanation which might not only account for the effects of father absence on boys but also for the lack of effects on girls, since in the earlier mentioned study of intact families (Hoffman, in press) boys were overwhelmingly more likely than girls to identify with fathers ($p < .0001$), and father identification related to a number of moral indexes among boys but not girls.

Assuming that the absence of a paternal model is important, a further question is whether it is a complete answer. One way to assess this is to compare the effects of father absence with the effects of nonidentification with fathers who are present. For this purpose, we selected two groups from our larger sample of boys from intact families—one which obtained very high and another which obtained very low scores on a measure of conscious father identification. (This was the number of times father was mentioned in response to these items: "Which person do you admire or look up to the most?" "Which person do you want to be like when you grow up?" and "Which person do you take after mostly?") The two groups were the same size as the father-absent and father-present groups and controlled for IQ and social class in the same manner. The differences between the high- and low-father-identification groups on our moral indexes are presented in Table 5.3. Comparing this to Table 5.2, it appears that the effects of low identification with fathers who are present are quite similar though somewhat less pronounced than the effects of father absence (Table 5.3).[4] The main difference is that father absence is associated with low scores for maximum guilt and acceptance of blame, whereas low father identification is not (although its relation to acceptance of blame is in the same direction—$p < .15$). Maximum guilt and acceptance of blame, despite their limitations, are very likely our best indexes of moral internalization (which may in essence be defined as the application of standards to one's own behavior without regard to sanctions by authority) for the following reasons. First, it seems reasonable to assume that the guilt measure reflects the subject's own response to transgression, since a prerequisite for coding guilt was evidence that the subject identified with the story hero. The moral judgment measure, on the other hand, pertains to judgments of transgressions of others, and while one may "sincerely," and in that sense internally, hold the beliefs that one applies to the conduct of others, this may

Table 5.3. Median differences between high- and low-father-identification on moral indexes

Moral index	*High father identification*	*Low father identification*
Maximum guilt	4.38	4.86
Terminal guilt	2.88	3.15
Internal moral judgment	3.96*	3.30
Acceptance of blame	3.53	2.80
Moral values	5.20**	3.50
Consideration for others	1.72	1.62
Conformity to rules	3.80*	3.14
Overt aggression	2.44	3.25*

* $p<.05$.
** $p<.01$.

[4] The fact that rejecting a father who is present appears to be virtually as detrimental to moral development as not having a father, may at first seem difficult to accept. Bearing in mind the temporal limitation of our father-absence index, however, it is entirely possible that some of the boys in the father-absent group had extended and satisfactory relationships with their fathers before separation—an experience which may have been denied the low identification group.

not indicate the reaction to one's own transgression. Similarly, the moral values index pertains to surface acceptance of moral standards and may therefore be irrelevant to internalization. Finally, the scores for aggression and rule-conformity are based on teacher ratings of behaviors which have obvious relevance to "social desirability" and may therefore reflect a pro-authority orientation rather than an internally based self-control. This is apt to be less true of acceptance of blame which, though also based on teacher ratings, involves acknowledging to authority that one has behaved in a disapproved fashion. If our argument is correct, we may tentatively conclude that whether or not the boy identifies with his father influences the degree to which he accepts moral standards, uses them as a basis for judging right and wrong, and behaves in accord with them in the presence of authority. The presence or absence of a father also bears on these matters, but in addition influences the extent to which the boy applies moral standards to his own behavior.

These differences suggest that the lack of a paternal model is not the only significant aspect of the father's absence. Another obvious factor that may be operating is the pressure the father's absence puts on the mother, which may affect her behavior toward the child. Not having a husband, for example, may result in her becoming busier and more harassed, hence impatient with the child and oriented toward immediate compliance rather than long-range character goals. As a result, she may express affection less frequently, and in her discipline use more power assertion and less induction—the pattern found in previous research to be associated with weak moral internalization (Hoffman, 1970). Furthermore, we might expect this pattern to be more pronounced with boys, who are normally more aggressive and resistant to influence than girls and may even be more so when they have no father. To test this hypothesis, we used available data for the subjects' reports of their mother's expression of affection and the discipline techniques used in several situations. These measures are described in detail elsewhere (Hoffman & Saltzstein, 1967). The findings provide partial support for the hypothesis. The boys without fathers reported that their mothers expressed less affection than boys with fathers ($p < .05$). There was no difference in the type of discipline reported, but it seems reasonable to assume that the paucity of affection would have an adverse effect on the boys' reactions in the discipline encounter. For girls, the findings were the reverse of those obtained for boys: The girls without fathers reported that their mothers express affection *more* frequently ($p < .10$). They also report less power assertion and more induction, although these findings are nonsignificant. Should this pattern of findings be replicated, it would suggest that the mother may compensate for the father's absence, but only with girls. Perhaps it is more difficult to do this with boys because of their more abrasive qualities. This stands especially if what the mother wants is ease in running the household in contrast to the girl who is more likely to help with household chores rather than make additional trouble. It is also likely that the reason for the father's absence is frequently divorce, and in these cases the mothers may carry a residue of resentment which is expressed toward their sons. As a result, a greater proportion of mother-son interactions, when there is no father, may revolve around discipline encounters, that is, there is more discipline, although the discipline is not of a different sort, and correspondingly less time is spent in affectionate interchange.

Conclusions

The findings clearly indicate that the absence of the father has adverse effects on the boy's conscience development. We have also presented evidence that these effects may be somewhat greater than the effects of nonidentification with a father who is present, which suggests that some but not all of the effects of father absence are attributable to the lack of a paternal model. That the effects may also be mediated in part by changes in the mother's child-rearing pattern is suggested by the finding that women without husbands appear to express less affection to their sons than women with husbands.

The absence of the father appears to have no discernible effect on the conscience development of girls. This is probably due mainly to the fact that girls usually identify with their mothers and not their fathers, although we have also presented evidence that mothers may compensate for their husband's absence by expressing additional affection to their daughters.

These conclusions must be qualified because of the limitations of our index of father absence, that is, we do not know its duration or how old the child was when it began. Further research, in which duration and age of child vary, is needed to find out if the effects of father absence are greater with younger than older boys, as seems to be true, for example, with respect to masculine sex-role identity (Biller, 1970). Such research may also tell us if our findings have a bearing on the origins of conscience development, or if they pertain only to the reduction in strength of an already developed conscience.

References

ALLINSMITH, W. Moral standards: II. The learning of moral standards. In D. R. Miller & G. E. Swanson (Eds.), *Inner conflict and defense.* New York: Holt, 1960.

BACH, G. R. Father-fantasies and father typing in father-separated children. *Child Development,* 1946, *17,* 63–80.

BILLER, H. B. Father absence and the personality development of the male child. *Developmental Psychology,* 1970, *2,* 181–201.

DEUTSCH, M. Minority group and class status as related to social and personality factors in scholastic achievement. *Monograph of the Society for Applied Anthropology,* 1960, *2,* 1–32.

DEUTSCH, M., & BROWN, B. Social influences in Negro-white intelligence differences. *Journal of Social Issues,* 1964, *20,* 24–35.

GLUECK, S., & GLUECK, E. *Unravelling juvenile delinquency.* New York: Commonwealth Fund, 1950.

GREGORY, I. Anterospective data following childhood loss of a parent: I. Delinquency and high school dropout. *Archives of General Psychiatry,* 1965, *13,* 99–109.

HENRY, A. F., & SHORT, J. F. *Suicide and homicide.* Glencoe, Ill.: Free Press, 1954.

HOFFMAN, L. W. The father's role in the family and the child's peer-group adjustment. *Merrill-Palmer Quarterly,* 1961, *7,* 97–105.

HOFFMAN, M. L. Moral development. In P. Mussen (Ed.), *Handbook of child psychology.* New York: Wiley, 1970.

———. Identification and conscience development. *Child Development,* in press.

HOFFMAN, M. L., & SALTZSTEIN, H. D. Parent discipline and the child's moral development. *Journal of Personality and Social Psychology,* 1967, *5,* 45–57.

KOHLBERG, L. The development of modes of moral thinking and choice in the years 10 to 16. Unpublished doctoral dissertation, University of Chicago, 1958.

LANDY, F., ROSENBERG, B. G., & SUTTON-SMITH, B. The effect of limited father absence on the cognitive and emotional development of children. Paper presented at the meeting of the Midwestern Psychological Association, Chicago, May 1967.

MAXWELL, A. E. Discrepancies between the pattern of abilities for normal and neurotic children. *Journal of Mental Science,* 1961, *107,* 300–307.

MILLER, W. B. Lower-class culture as a generating milieu of gang delinquency. *Journal of Social Issues,* 1958, *14,* 5–19.

MISCHEL, W. Delay of gratification, need for achievement, and acquiescence in another culture. *Journal of Abnormal and Social Psychology,* 1961, *62,* 543–552.

MOULTON, R. W., BURNSTEIN, E., LIBERTY, P. G., & ALTUCHER, N. Patterning of parental affection and disciplinary dominance as a determinant of guilt and sex typing. *Journal of Personality and Social Psychology,* 1966, *4,* 356–363.

ROSEN, S., HOFFMAN, L. W., & LIPPITT, R. Some effects of role reversal between parents in their relations with children. Paper presented at the Midwestern Psychological Association, Chciago, May 1957.

SEARS, P. S. Doll play aggression in normal young children: Influence of sex, age, sibling status, father's absence. *Psychological Monographs,* 1951, *65*(6, Whole No. 323).

SEARS, R. R., PINTLER, M. H., & SEARS, P. S. Effect of father separation on preschool children's doll play aggression. *Child Development,* 1946, *17,* 219–243.

SIEGMAN, A. W. Father-absence during childhood and antisocial behavior. *Journal of Abnormal Psychology,* 1966, *71,* 71–74.

SUTTON-SMITH, B., ROSENBERG, B. G., & LANDY, F. Father-absence effects in families of different sibling compositions. *Child Development,* 1968, *39,* 1213–1221.

25. EFFECTS OF AN ADULT'S PRESENCE AND PRAISE ON YOUNG CHILDREN'S PERFORMANCE

TERRY D. MEDDOCK, JOSEPH A. PARSONS, and KENNEDY T. HILL

The separate effects of praise from an adult and the presence of that adult on preschool children's performance rate change at a simple motor task were studied for 32 4-year-old children of each sex. Following a base-line minute during which the experimenter was present but nonresponsive to the subject, the child was assigned to one of four experimental groups for the next 5 min in which the experimenter: (a) either made supportive comments or remained nonresponsive, and (b) either remained present or was absent behind a screen. The session was completed by a 5-min extinction phase in which the base-line conditions were reinstituted. The major finding was that performance increased under both adult praise and adult presence, with the effects being additive: performance increase was highest when the adult was present and praising the child, and lowest (actually decreasing) when the adult was absent and nonresponsive to the child. The reintroduction of the experimenter during extinction also facilitated performance. The results were related to previous research on both social reinforcement and imitation, and several developmental changes were hypothesized for the effects of both adult reactions and an adult's presence.

The major goal of the present study was to separate out and compare the effects of an adult's presence and of positive reactions from an adult on young children's performance at a simple operant task.

The interest in demonstrating that praise from an adult raises children's performance level at a simple motor task dates back to a number of earlier studies of social reinforcement effects with children. Social reinforcement conditions often failed to produce significant differences in performance compared to nonreinforcement control conditions, although there was a consistent tendency across studies for performance to be higher under praise than nonreaction, at least for normal children (see Parton & Ross, 1965; Stevenson & Hill, 1966).

More direct evidence for social reinforcement effects of adult praise for preschool and young elementary-school-age children comes from several recent studies. Allen (1966), e.g., found that kindergarten children performed longest at a simple peg-sorting task under praise, stayed an intermediate length of time under nonreaction, and left the task soonest under criticism. Hill and Moely (1969) also found performance significantly higher under adult praise than adult nonreaction for first- and second-grade children in a study assessing rate change at a marble-dropping task. Both Allen (1966) and Hill and Moely (1969) found complex or opposite "reinforcement" effects for older elementary-school-age children and attributed performance of such older children to cognitive rather than motivational factors (see Rosenbaum & Hill, 1969).

On the basis of the Allen (1966) and Hill and Moely (1969) results, it was expected that the 4-year-old children in the present study would show higher performance (measured by rate change at a simple motor task) under adult praise than adult nonreaction when the experimenter was present with the child. The present design also included conditions in which the experimenter praised the child or failed to react to the child's performance while the experimenter was in the testing room but not visible to the child, making it possible to analyze whether the expected facilitating effect of adult praise was operative and as strong when the adult was absent as when the adult was present.

The interest in determining the effects of the adult's presence on young children's performance level also dates back to earlier research on social reinforcement with children. Many early studies included a single social reinforcement condition, and it is not possible to ascertain the specific effects of the experimenter's making positive (or negative) comments in the absence of control conditions in which the adult is nonresponsive. It is possible, e.g., that in many such studies the presence of the adult was as or more important than the adult's reaction in determining performance (Parton & Ross, 1965; Stevenson & Hill, 1966).

Evidence for the potential importance of an adult's presence compared to his evaluative reactions comes from a recent study by Leventhal and Fischer (1970) of the performance of older elementary-school-age children on a two-choice learning task. In two conditions, an adult was present and either praised the subject or was nonreactive. In a third condition, the adult removed himself from the experimental task to the corner of the testing room, busied himself at a task, and did not interact with the child. Leventhal and Fischer found greater increases in performance rate in the social reinforcement condition than the other two conditions in which the adult was nonreactive (and either present or removed from the child). Since this "social reinforcement" effect emerged during base line, however, it was attributed to expressive cues rather than the praise from the adult. In addition, marked learning was shown by both groups in which the experimenter was present regardless of whether or not he praised the child for the correct response but not by the group in which the experimenter was removed. Again, it would have to be assumed that expressive cues such as eye movements produced the response preference change of subjects in the condition in which the adult was present but not talking to the subject and possibly also when the adult was praising the subject. Leventhal and Fischer concluded from their results that praise was far less important than the presence of the experimenter and expressive, nonverbal cues from the experimenter in determining performance of their elementary-school-age children.

It was expected in the present study that children's performance would be higher when a nonreactive adult was present than when the adult was in the testing room but not visible to the child. It was seen as an empirical question as to whether such an effect of the experimenter's presence might recede in importance if the experimenter was praising the subject; that is, whether there might be an interaction between the Social Reinforcement and Experimenter Presence variables or whether their effects were additive.

The present study included an extinction phase not usually included in previous group studies of social reinforcement. This phase, in which the experimenter was present but nonreactive to the subject's performance, was intended to further clarify the effects of both praise and the presence of the experimenter. For example, it was expected that if performance was lower when the adult was absent than present during the experimental period, then performance should increase more during the extinction phase for children for whom the adult returned to the experimental task than for subjects for whom the adult was present throughout the task. It was also of interest to ascertain whether any obtained results for performance to be higher under praise than nonreaction during the experimental period would be maintained during the extinction period.

The design and procedure of the present study was developed in such a way so as to control for a potentially important problem in much of the social reinforcement literature, the possibility of experimenter bias (Dusek, 1971; Gewirtz, 1969; see Rosenthal, 1969). In the present study attempts were made to avoid the possibility of experimenter bias by tape-recording both the task instructions and the praise statements used in the social reinforcement condition (see Allen, 1966; Baer & Sherman, 1964). Facial cues from the experimenter were minimized by having the experimenter "talk" to the subject over a microphone he held in front of his mouth.

The present study, then, investigated the separate effects of praise from an adult and the presence of that adult on preschool children's performance rate change in a research paradigm in which controls were introduced to minimize the possibility of experimenter bias, and an extinction period was added to clarify effects of the experimental variables.

Method

Subjects

The 32 girls and 32 boys in the experimental design were obtained from 70 4–5-year-old children from the Children's Research Center Nursery School at the University of Illinois, Urbana. Of the original 70 children, five potential subjects were dropped from the experiment due to apparatus malfunction and one subject was dropped because of a very discrepant low rate of response at the experimental task which would preclude matching of experimental groups on base rate.

Apparatus and Equipment

The experimental space was a 24 × 27-dm, well-illuminated, sound-attenuated room. An adjoining observation room contained all recording equipment. Observation was possible through a small one-way-vision window. The experimental apparatus was a 5-hole marble-dropping task similar to that described by Stevenson and Fahel (1961). Briefly, it consisted of a table with two bins, a 10.2-cm vertical partition separating the experimenter and the subject's side of the table, and a 15.3 × 15.3 × 10.2-cm box housing the session light. The left bin contained approximately 1500 marbles all of the same size and color. An event recorder was used to measure the rate at which marbles were dropped.

Instructions and praise comments were prerecorded and presented through the speaker box (15.3 × 10.2 × 3.8 cm). The subject's chair was located facing the task with the marbles on the left. The experimenter's chair was on the opposite side of the table facing the task. In addition, the experimenter had a second chair located behind a 21 × 15-dm curtain placed diagonally across one corner of the room, 15 dm from the subject's chair.

Procedure

Each subject was individually escorted to the experimental room by the experimenter and was seated at the game table facing the adult. The experimenter then picked the speaker up and held it in front of his mouth for the duration of the testing session in all conditions. The recorded instructions were simultaneously activated by the observer in the adjoining observation room.

As in previous research, the experimenter introduced the experimental task as a marble game and instructed the child to pick up the marbles one at a time, with one hand, and drop them through the holes. The experimenter said that he would tell the subject when to stop. It was found in pilot testing, however, that the specific instructions used in previous research with children several years older (Hill & Moely, 1969) were inadequate for preschool children. The pilot subjects often failed to perform correctly at the task and sometimes stopped performing after the first praise statement. The present instructions, then, were developed to include several repetitions of critical portions of the procedure, a carefully standardized demonstration of how to perform at the task, and the addition of a light to signal completion of the task. Brief portions of the instructions were repeated if the child did not follow the instructions correctly. If the child asked any questions during the task, the adult said "We can talk about that later." Such comments were necessary for 29 of the 64 subjects in the final sample and usually just once in these cases.

Most studies of social reinforcement with children have assessed change in response rate from a short base-line period using difference scores in an attempt to provide some control over individual differences. Problems arise in the use of difference scores, however, if the groups differ in their base-line performance and base-line performance is correlated with change (Parton & Ross, 1965, 1967; Stevenson & Hill, 1966; see also Cronbach & Furby, 1970). Stevenson and Hill (1966) suggested that one way to treat these base-line effects in analyses of difference scores would be to block subjects on base-line level in the design. The present blocking procedure improved upon previous *post hoc* procedures (Hill & Moely, 1969; Montanelli & Hill, 1969) by randomly assigning subjects *a priori* to experimental conditions on the basis of the subject's base rate of response and the median base rate for each sex. Without any sample loss, then, it was possible to test for interactions between the subject's base-line level and all other variables with which base line was crossed in the design.

The experimental design called for an equal number of boys and girls in each of the four experimental cells with base rates above and below the median performance for each sex. An effort was made to match extreme as well as near-median base-rate subjects in each experimental grouping. The observer was able to assign subjects to experimental conditions at the end of the 1-min base-line period and signal the experimenter as to the subject's condition without pause in the task. The base-line period, similar to previous studies (see Stevenson & Hill, 1966), had the experimenter present and attending to the task but nonreactive to the child's performance (Present–Nonreaction). Then during the immediately subsequent 5-min experimental period, the Presence–Absence and Praise–Nonreaction manipulations were both introduced in an orthogonal design, with subjects assigned to the four possible combinations of Presence–Absence and Praise–Nonreaction at random within the restrictions of matching on base rate mentioned above. For the Presence–Absence Condition, the experimenter either remained seated across the table from the child (Presence) or moved to the chair behind the curtain out of the child's view (Absence). The Praise–Nonreaction Condition was introduced during this same 5-min experimental period, in which the child either received verbal praise comments from the adult (Praise) or no comments from the adult (Nonreaction). The prerecorded praise statements were activated by the observer in the next room contingent upon the subject's first response following a 20-sec interval, fixed-interval 20 sec (see Stevenson & Hill, 1966). Praise statements were randomized without replacement within blocks of five. Three such randomizations were taped from the following comments: "You're playing well," "You're playing very well," "You're doing well," "You're doing very well," and "You're doing a good job." The Praise–Nonreaction social reinforcement condition procedure was thus similar to those of many previous studies except that praise comments were prerecorded (see Allen, 1966) and possible effects of the experimenter's facial cues were minimized by the experimenter holding the speaker box in front of his mouth.

In the 5-min extinction period, which followed immediately after the experimental period, the procedure was identical to that of base line; that is, for all subjects the experimenter was both present and nonreactive (Present–Nonreaction). Following the extinction period the adult praised the child for his help, illuminated the session light, and terminated the task.

Design

The procedures resulted in a 2 (Presence–Absence) × 2 (Praise–Nonreaction) × 2 (Sex of Subject) factorial arrangement with 8 subjects in each cell. Differences between boys and girls in median base rate necessitated nesting Base-Rate Level of Subject within Sex. Separately by sex, then, and on the basis of the median base rate for each sex, 4 subjects with low-base rate and 4 with high-base rate were assigned to each of four experimental groupings, yielding a total sample of 64 children.

Results

Base Line

The dependent variable used in the analysis of base-line performance was the total number of responses emitted during the 1-min base-line period, the sample mean for which was 17.3. As noted earlier, it was intended to block on Base-Rate Level of subject in the analyses of difference scores. A 2 (Presence–Absence) × 2 (Praise–Nonreaction) × 2 (Sex of Subject) × 2 (Base-Rate Level) analysis of variance, with Base-Rate Level nested within Sex, of the base-line scores revealed a significant sex effect ($F(1,48) = 7.54$, $p < .01$) reflecting the higher mean performance of girls ($M = 18.2$) than of boys ($M = 16.5$). This difference necessitated entering Base-Rate Level as a nested factor within Sex in this initial analysis as well as all further analyses. The highly significant Base-Rate-Level effect ($F(2,48) = 58.2$, $p < .001$) was a necessary result of blocking on the Base-Rate-Level variable, and held ($p < .001$) for both sexes. The mean base rate was 19.9 and 21.5 for high-base-rate boys and girls, respectively, and 13.2 and 15.1 for low-base-rate boys and girls, respectively. Of greater importance, no other main effects or their interactions were reliable or approached significance for either sex in the analysis of base-rate scores, indicating that the sampling procedures were successful in matching experimental groups on base rate.

Experimental Period

The scores used in the data analysis for the 5-min experimental period were difference scores obtained separately for each subject by subtracting his base-line score from each of the five experimental minute scores.

A 2 (Presence–Absence) × 2 (Praise–Nonreaction) × 2 (Sex of Subject) × 2 (Base-Rate Level) × 5 (Minutes) mixed analysis of variance with Base-Rate Level nested within Sex yielded significant main order effects for Base-Rate Level, Presence–Absence, Praise–Nonreaction, and Minutes. The effect for Base-Rate Level nested within Sex ($F(2,48) = 7.08$, $p < .01$) was significant for boys ($p < .01$) but not for girls ($p > .05$). As has been found in previous studies (Stevenson, 1965; Hill & Moely, 1969), subjects with low-base rates had higher mean difference scores (boys, $M = 2.76$; girls, $M = 2.13$) than subjects with high-base rates (boys, $M = -1.05$; girls, $M = 0.83$).

The major results of the present study are the significant main-order effects for the two experimental variables, which were similar in strength. The significant effect for Presence–Absence ($F(1,48) = 4.86$, $p < .05$) revealed greater mean increases in rates for subjects in the Present Condition ($M = 2.00$) than for subjects in the Absent Condition ($M = 0.33$). The significant effect for Praise–Nonreaction ($F(1,48) = 5.46$, $p < .05$) indicated greater mean rate increases for those subjects receiving praise ($M = 2.05$) than for those subjects not receiving praise ($M = 0.28$). The interaction of Presence–Absence × Praise–Nonreaction was not significant ($F(1,48) = 2.81$, $p > .05$), indicating that the effects of presence and praise tended to be additive. Thus, performance increased the most for the Praise–Present subjects ($M = 2.25$), and the least (an actual decrease) for the Nonreaction–Absent subjects ($M = -1.20$). Performance of the other two experimental groups, Nonreaction–Present ($M = 1.75$) and Praise–Absent ($M = 1.85$), was intermediate and similar, again suggesting that the effects of praise and presence were similar in strength. It should be noted that there was no tendency for the Presence–Absence or Praise–Nonreaction variables to interact with Base-Rate Level separately or together in a 3-way interaction ($F < 1$).

The overall main effect for minutes ($F(2,48) = 7.08$, $p < .01$) reflected a slight inverted *U* function, which was present in most significant within-subject functions. The means, for successive minutes were: 0.56, 1.56, 1.58, 1.63, 0.50. The Praise–Nonreaction × Minutes interaction ($F(4,192) = 3.14$, $p < .05$) indicated that subjects receiving praise generally increased in mean rate over minutes (from 1.19 to 2.19), while those subjects not receiving praise decreased in mean rate (from 0.06 to −1.20) across the 5 min of the experimental period. The significant Base-Rate Level × Minutes interaction ($F(8,192) - 4.07$, $p < .01$) was significant for boys ($p < .001$) but not for girls ($p > .05$); for both sexes, subjects with low base rates generally increased in mean rate over the experimental period (boys, from 1.25 to 3.88; girls, from 0.81 to 1.69) while subjects of both sexes with high base rates generally decreased in mean rate over minutes (boys, from −0.44 to −3.00; girls, from 0.63 to −0.56). The Praise–Nonreaction × Sex of Subject × Minutes ($F(4,192) = 3.33$, $p < .05$) and the Presence–Absence × Praise–Nonreaction × Sex of Subject × Minutes ($F(4,192) = 2.84$, $p < .05$) interactions were the other two significant effects. The group means contributing to these higher order interactions were not systematically related to the main effects of Presence–Absence or Praise–Nonreaction but rather varied unsystematically across minutes, making these effects difficult to interpret.

Extinction Period

A major analysis of extinction data incorporated difference scores, calculated in the same manner as those used in the experimental period, into a 2 (Presence–Absence) × 2 (Praise–Nonreaction) × 2 (Sex of Subject) × 2 (Base-Rate Level nested within Sex) × 5 (Minutes) mixed analysis of variance. The two significant main order effects were Base-Rate Level and Praise–Nonreaction. The effect for Base-Rate Level ($F(2,48) = 15.70$, $p < .001$) was significant for both boys ($p < .001$) and girls ($p < .01$) and indicated that subjects with low base rates, regardless of sex, continued to have higher mean difference scores (boys, $M = 3.29$; girls, $M = 2.54$) than subjects with high original base rates (boys, $M = -1.86$; girls, $M = -1.05$). The Praise–Nonreaction effect ($F(1,48) = 5.42$, $p < .05$) reflected a tendency for the subjects previously receiving praise to continue to have higher mean difference scores ($M = 1.65$) during the extinction period than subjects not receiving praise ($M = -0.19$).

To further explore effects during the extinction period, the extinction data were subjected to additional analysis using the last minute of the experimental period as a base line for the extinction period. This value was subtracted from each successive minute of extinction to obtain second difference scores. It was felt that the effects of the experimenter's return to the nonreaction role of base-line condition on rate change might better be assessed using an index of response rate immediately preceding initiation of the extinction phase.

A 2 (Presence–Absence) × 2 (Praise–Nonreaction) × 2 (Sex of Subject) × 2 (Base-Rate Level nested within Sex) × 5 (Minutes) mixed analysis of variance of these second difference scores yielded two significant main order effects and one significant interaction. The effect for Praise–Nonreaction ($F(1,48) = 5.38$, $p < .05$) showed a tendency for subjects perviously being praised to decrease in rate ($M = -0.53$) when the experimenter returned to the nonreaction role, while subjects previously not receiving praise showed a mean increase in rate ($M = 1.00$). The significant main order effect for Presence–Absence ($F(1,48) = 4.78$, $p < .05$) reflected the fact that subjects in the Absent Condition increased in rate upon the return of the experimenter ($M = 0.96$), while subjects in the Present Condition decreased in rate under the continued presence of the experimenter ($M = -0.49$). The Praise–Nonreaction × Sex of Subject × Minutes interaction was the only other significant effect in the analysis of the second difference scores from the extinction period. The mean differences accounting for this higher order interaction varied unsystematically across minutes and were difficult to interpret.

Discussion

The present study produced a strong, consistent set of results. Performance was enhanced by both praise from an adult and the presence of that adult, and their effects tended to be additive: the strongest performance increase was found when the adult was present and delivering praise and the weakest performance, actually a rate decrement, was obtained when the adult was absent and nonresponsive during the experimental period. The differences for the praise manipulation increased across minutes, with performance increasing in general under praise and decreasing in general under nonreaction across the five experimental minutes. In addition, the reappearance of the experimenter during the extinction period in which the experimenter was nonreactive increased performance in general for subjects for whom the experimenter had been absent, compared to subjects for whom the experimenter had been present throughout the session. It was also found that using the initial baseline minute to assess change, the social reinforcement effect from the experimental period was maintained as a significant difference during the extinction period. Evidence that the social reinforcement effect weakened during extinction, however, came from the finding that when the last minute of the experimental period was used to assess change, performance tended to decrease for subjects in the Praise Condition and to increase for subjects in the Nonreaction Condition.

All of the present results, then, indicate that both praise and the adult's presence served to facilitate performance rate for the 4-year-old children studied. Task instructions and praise statements were precisely standardized through the use of a tape recorder, so that the possibility of unintended vocal and other expressive cues from the experimenter were minimized. It is encouraging that where comparisons are possible, the results of the present study closely parallel those of previous studies, e.g., the findings for the first and second graders in the Hill and Moely (1969) study. Conclusions from the present study must still be drawn cautiously, however, because of several questions that arise in interpreting certain aspects of the effects under study. It would be desirable, e.g., to have more information on the effect of having the experimenter present during base line on the subsequent effects of his presence vs absence during the experimental period. It is possible that some subjects had high base rates because of their responsiveness to the adult being present. It might then be expected that the later effects of adult presence would be different for High- than for Low-Base-Rate subjects. The failure for base-rate level to interact with the Presence–Absence variable, however, suggests that the adult's presence during base line did not modify the later effects of his presence. It would be of interest in future investigations, however, to manipulate the adult's presence during base line if such periods are used.

A second question that arises concerns how the children interpreted the adult's reactions in the Praise–Absent Condition which was included to achieve an orthogonal design for the Praise–Nonreaction and Presence–Absence variables. If praise statements are to retain face validity, they presumably carry the implication that the adult experimenter is monitoring the child's performance and is giving reactions on the basis of that performance. In the present task, the marbles make a noise as they drop through the holes and are counted by the event recorder. It is possible that most children interpreted the adult's evaluation as being contingent upon their performance but responded less to that reaction when the adult was out of sight behind the screen than when the adult was present. Another possibility is that children in the Praise–Absent Condition responded to the adult's reaction either as strongly as if he were present or not at all. Examination of the distribution of scores in this condition failed to reveal support for this latter possibility, however, there being no tendency toward a bi-model distribution in this cell or for greater variability in general than in other cells. It would be of interest to interview children in such conditions in future studies. It is also clear that the adult's "presence vs absence" is a complex dimension whose multiple components need to be systematically investigated. Factors studied might include whether the adult is perceived as being able to evaluate the child's performance, the physical proximity of the adult, and to what degree the adults is attending to (e.g., through eye contact) and appears to be evaluating the child's performance (e.g., through recording his response choices).

The results of the present study taken together with the findings of Leventhal and Fischer (1970) and other social reinforcement studies cited earlier suggest two related developmental changes. First, it is possible that in simple operant tasks and perhaps other behavior domains, praise and criticism function as positive and negative reinforcers, respectively, for young preschool children but with increasing age either change in their effects or become less important, being subordinated to other factors operating in the experimental situation, such as the adult's presence and currently unidentified reinforcers. There is evidence (e.g., V. C. Crandall, 1963), that with increasing age children due to more diverse reinforcement histories, rely more on their own evaluation of their task performance and less on adult reactions. It appears that with the simple learning and performance paradigms used in the social reinforcement literature, young children do not attempt to assess the adequacy of their performance, which is controlled instead simply by whether the adult responds positively or negatively. Older children, in contrast, may respond to these tasks by applying their own standards of evaluation developed during their long history of evaluative interactions with adults in problem solving situations. The effects of the adult's reactions may then be modified by the older child's self-evaluation of his performance and discrepancies between his and the adult's evaluations (Allen, 1966), or by the child's motivation to avoid failure and negative evaluations from adults (Hill, 1971a).

Second, it appears that the presence of an adult serves to enhance performance throughout the age range under consideration with the possibility that the influence of the experimenter's presence becomes stronger with age relative to the effect of praise. In the present study with preschool children, praise from the adult enhanced performance rate and was as effective as the adult's presence in doing so. The Leventhal and Fischer (1970) study cited earlier, in contrast, suggests that for older elementary-school-age children the adult's presence and expressive cues are not only important determinants of performance rate and learning but more effective than praise. Evidence for facilitating effects of the adult's presence throughout the preschool and elementary-school-age range under consideration comes not only from the social reinforcement literature but also from recent research on generalized imitation in children (Baer & Sherman, 1964; Bandura, 1969; Gewirtz & Stingle, 1968; Peterson, 1968). It has been found in this literature that children will continue to perform both reinforced and nonreinforced imitative responses across repeated testing sessions. Steinman (Steinman, 1970a, 1970b; Steinman & Boyce, 1971) has recently demonstrated that children of age 4–8 years are able to discriminate between the reinforced and nonreinforced imitative responses when called upon to do so and has concluded that the experimenter's presence and instructions from the experimenter rather than contingent praise from the experimenter are what control performance of children in the often used generalized imitation research paradigm. Peterson and Whitehurst (1971) with subjects of age 5–7 have produced more direct evidence suggesting that subjects' performance of nonreinforced imitative responses is controlled in good part by whether the experimenter remains present or not.

Steinman (1970a) has noted that a child may perform at a high level when an adult is present either to obtain approval from the adult or to avoid disapproval from the adult depending on the child's previous reinforcement history with adults in similar situations. High performance with the experimenter present could, then, be a conditioned response, with the experimenter having a discriminative function due to previous pairings of positive social and nonsocial reinforcers from adults in the presence of adults. Or, high performance with an experimenter present could be a conditioned avoidance response where the experimenter is a conditioned discriminative stimulus for negative reinforcers. For example, due to a history of criticism or punishment from adults when the child had failed to perform satisfactorily when adults were present, the child might perform with an adult present to avoid negative reactions. Hill (1971b) has suggested also that the effects of adult presence on performance may not be unidirectional. Present research in the social reinforcement and imitation literatures suggests that the adult's presence facilitates performance for behaviors and objects with which the child has likely had a positive or neutral social interaction history. It is possible that the adult's presence will actually suppress performance if he has had a negative social interaction history for the behaviors (e.g., aggressive responses) or objects (e.g., sex-inappropriate toys). Both the basis for and the direction of the effects of an adult's presence on children's performance, then, may be more complex than suggested by research to date (see Hill, 1971b).

It would be important to determine which components of naturally occurring social reinforcement from adults to children were critical in determining its effects (see Leventhal & Fischer, 1970). There is already some research bearing on this question. Several recent studies with middle-class children similar to the present sample, e.g., have suggested that verbal content is more important than tonal inflection or facial expression in determining the effects of social reinforcement on children's learning or perception of the adult's reactions (Brooks, Brandt, & Wiener, 1969; Bugental, Kaswan, Love, & Fox, 1970; Solomon & Yaeger, 1969). In addition, such children appear to discount or make minimal use of adult evaluations involving contradictory combinations of verbal content and tonal inflection (Brooks *et al.*, 1969; Solomon & Yaeger, 1969). There is also evidence that each new (congruent) component of an adult's reaction produces a smaller increment in the child's report of the evaluative meaning of that reaction, so that effects of verbal content, tonal inflection, and facial expressions are not additive (Bugental *et al.*, 1970). It would also be expected that, in general, as children become older, increasingly subtle and complex combinations of cues would determine the effectiveness of an adult's evaluative reactions in modifying children's behavior. There is evidence, e.g., suggesting that in order to reverse the initial effects of praise (or criticism) on children's achievement expectancies, an adult must switch to a reaction of the opposite kind (e.g., from praise to criticism) with elementary-school-age children (Montanelli & Hill, 1969) but need only switch to a neutral reaction with junior-high-school-age children (V. C. Crandall, 1963; V. C. Crandall, Good, & V. J. Crandall, 1964). It is hypothesized that older children would be more likely than younger children to respond to small changes in an adult's tonal inflection, facial expressions, and other expressive cues in delivering social reinforcement of a given evaluative meaning.

Research clarifying the motivational and cognitive components of children's social interaction history with adults in evaluative settings and how these factors underlie age changes in the effects of various components of an adult's "presence" and his reactions to the child would appear to be a fruitful area for future investigation.

References

ALLEN, S. The effects of verbal reinforcement on children's performance as a function of type of task. *Journal of Experimental Child Psychology*, 1966, *3*, 57–73.

BAER, D. M., & SHERMAN, J. A. Reinforcement control of generalized imitation. *Journal of Experimental Child Psychology*, 1964, *1*, 37–49.

BANDURA, A. Social-learning theory of identificatory processes. In D. A. Goslin (Ed.), *Handbook of Socialization Theory and Research.* Chicago: Rand McNally, 1969, pp. 213–262.

BROOKS R., BRANDT, L., & WEINER, M. Differential response to two communication channels: Socioeconomic class differences in response to verbal reinforcers communicated with and without tonal inflection. *Child Development*, 1969, *40*, 453–470.

BUGENTAL, D. E., KASWAN, J. W., LOVE, L. R., & FOX, F. N. Child versus adult perception of evaluative messages in verbal, vocal, and visual channels. *Developmental Psychology*, 1970, *2*, 367–375.

CRANDALL, V. C. Reinforcement effects of adult reactions and non-reactions on children's achievement expectations. *Child Development*, 1963, *34*, 335–354.

CRANDALL, V. C., GOOD, S., & CRANDALL, V. J. Reinforcement effects of adult reactions and non-reactions on children's achievement expectations: A replication study. *Child Development*, 1964, *35*, 485–497.

CRONBACH, L. J., & FURBY, L. How we should measure "change"—or should we? *Psychological Bulletin*, 1970, *74*, 68–80.

DUSEK, J. B. Experimenter bias in performance of children at a simple motor task. *Developmental Psychology*, 1971, in press.

GEWIRTZ, J. L. Mechanisms of social learning: Some roles of stimulation and behavior in early human development. In D. A. Goslin (Ed.), *Handbook of Socialization Theory and Research.* Chicago: Rand McNally, 1969, pp. 57–212.

GEWIRTZ, J. L., & STINGLE, K. G. Learning of generalized imitation as the basis for identification. *Psychological Review*, 1968, *75*, 374–397.

HILL, K. T. Anxiety in the evaluative context. In W. W. Hartup (Ed.), *The Young Child*, Vol. II. Washington, D. C.: National Association for the Education of Young Children, 1971, in press. (a)

———. Social determinants of imitation: The questions of direction and generality of effects. Paper presented at the biennial meeting of the Society for Research in Child Development, Minneapolis, April, 1971. (b)

HILL, K. T., & MOELY, B. E. Social reinforcement as a function of task instructions, sex of S, age of S, and base-line performance. *Journal of Experimental Child Psychology,* 1969, *7,* 153–165.

LEVENTHAL, H., & FISCHER, K. What reinforces in a social reinforcement situation—words or expressions. *Journal of Personality and Social Psychology,* 1970, *14,* 83–94.

MONTANELLI, D. S., & HILL, K. T. Children's achievement expectations and performance as a function of two consecutive reinforcement experiences, sex of subject, and sex of experimenter. *Journal of Personality and Social Psychology,* 1969, *13,* 115–128.

PARTON, D. A., & ROSS, A. O. Social reinforcement of children's motor behavior: A review. *Psychological Bulletin,* 1965, *64,* 65–73.

———. A reply to "the use of rate as a measure of response in studies of social reinforcement." *Psychological Bulletin,* 1967, *67,* 323–325.

PETERSON, R. F. Imitation: A basic behavioral mechanism. In H. N. Sloane, Jr. & Barbara MacAulay (Eds.), *Operant Procedures in Remedial Speech and Language Training.* Boston: Houghton, 1968, pp. 61–74.

PETERSON, R. F., & WHITEHURST, G. J. A variable influencing the performance of nonreinforced imitative behaviors. *Journal of Applied Behavior Analysis,* 1971, in press.

ROSENBAUM, M., & HILL, K. T. Effects of success-failure and praise-criticism on retardates' persistence and performance. *Journal of Experimental Research in Personality,* 1969, *3,* 253–263.

ROSENTHAL. R. Interpersonal expectations: Effects of the experimenter's hypothesis. In R. Rosenthal & R. L. Rosnow (Eds.), *Artifact in Behavioral Research.* New York: Academic Press, 1969, pp. 181–277.

SOLOMON, D., & YAEGER, J. Determinants of boy's perceptions of verbal reinforcers. *Developmental Psychology,* 1969, *1,* 637–645.

STEINMAN, W. Generalized imitation and the discrimination hypothesis. *Journal of Experimental Child Psychology,* 1970, *10,* 79–99. (a)

———. The social control of generalized imitation. *Journal of Applied Behavior Analysis,* 1970, *3,* 159–167. (b)

STEINMAN, W. M., & BOYCE, K. D. Generalized imitation as a function of discrimination difficulty and choice. *Journal of Experimental Child Psychology,* 1971, *11,* 251–265.

STEVENSON, H. W. Social reinforcement of children's behavior. In L. P. Lipsitt & C. C. Spiker (Eds.), *Advances in Child Development and Behavior,* Vol. 2, New York: Academic Press, 1965, pp. 97–126.

STEVENSON, H. W., & FAHEL, L. S. The effect of social reinforcement on the performance of institutionalized and noninstitutionalized normal and feeble-minded children. *Journal of Personality,* 1961, *29,* 136–147.

STEVENSON, H. W., & HILL, K. T. The use of rate as a measure of response in studies of social reinforcement. *Psychological Bulletin,* 1966, *66,* 321–326.

26. MATERNAL BEHAVIOR TOWARD OWN AND OTHER PRESCHOOL CHILDREN: THE PROBLEM OF "OWNNESS"

CHARLES F. HALVERSON, JR., and
MARY F. WALDROP

The interactions between mothers and their own and other 2½-year-olds were explored to identify maternal behaviors which were consistent across children and those which were closely tied to individual children. A structured interaction session was designed to obtain data on mother-child interactions for male and female preschool children. Results indicate that while maternal behavior tended to be consistent with both children, mothers used significantly more positive, encouraging statements with other children and significantly more negative sanctions with their own children. Mothers of girls talked more than mothers of boys. Also, boys rated as aggressive in the nursery school had mothers who gave more negative, controlling statements to their sons than they did to the other children.

Traditional socialization theory has assumed that the mother is the major and consistent agent in shaping her child's behavior. In socialization studies the methodology most typically employed to test various propositions has been correlational. Investigators have selected parent-child pairs from a population and intercorrelated parent and child characteristics, usually interpreting significant correlations across parent-child pairs as evidence that parent characteristics influence child characteristics. Bell (1968), however, after pointing out that the interpretation of the correlation coefficient is necessarily circular, argued that it is just as plausible to interpret major findings from studies of socialization as indicating the effects of children on parents. Given the problem of circularity of inference in correlational studies, the manipulational-experimental mode of research would appear to be a likely solution. It can be shown, however, that the experimental mode also suffers from possibly serious difficulties of generalization due to the problem of subject selection. One demonstrable aspect of this problem is the issue of "ownness." For example, when a mother is brought together experimentally with a child who is not her own, she may not behave in the same way as she does with her own child. Likewise, a child with a strange mother may behave differently than with his own. Both participants lack the cumulative effects of interactions as well as the mutual involvement of parents and their own children. When parents and their own children are studied together, another potentially serious problem is created by the "ownness" factor. Parents and children have a past history together, and much of their behavior could be interpreted idiosyncratically on the basis of expectancies which stem from a knowledge of each other. One way to investigate the importance of the issue of "ownness" in experimental research is to have mothers interact with their own children and with other children, noting the changes in maternal behavior.

In the present paper, the importance of "ownness" for maternal verbal interaction styles was investigated. The purpose was to uncover the consistencies and inconsistencies that emerge when mothers interact separately with their own and other children of the same sex. It was hypothesized that mothers would behave in some ways which were unique to their own children and in other ways which might reflect maternal interaction patterns which are general across children. The expectation was that when a mother was interacting with her own child in an achievement situation, she would display more verbal control behavior and make more negative, performance-oriented statements than when interacting with someone else's child. In addition, it was hypothesized that mothers would behave with their own children partly on the basis of expectancies about their performances which would not be operative with other children. Specifically, mothers of fast-moving, aggressive children would give more negative, controlling statements to their own children than they would to other children. A structured, achievement-oriented interaction situation was designed to produce verbal interaction which could be analyzed to determine the amount and quality of the interchange between each mother and her own child as well as between each mother and a child not her own.

Method

Subjects

Data were obtained for mothers of 42 2½-year-olds, 23 males and 19 females. The children were participants in the preschool phase of a longitudinal study.

Interaction Task and Procedure

The children attended the nursery school in same-sexed groups of five for approximately 5-week periods. In the final week of the nursery school the mothers came in separately for a day to observe their children in the various nursery school settings. During this visit each mother was asked if she would like to "assist in the administration of some developmental tests" to her child and to one other child.

The interaction situation consisted of having each mother administer six different tasks to each of the two children. Four of the tasks were taken from the Stanford-Binet: the form board, block stacking, bead stringing, and picture vocabulary. For the other two tasks, the mothers attempted to get the children to tell a story (impossible for most children at this age) and to place yellow and red marbles in designated holes of a box. They were told that some of the items would be easy and others hard and that none of the children could do them all. The examiner and the testing room were familiar to the children, and during the testing the examiner was present but remained minimally responsive to both mothers and children.

In half the sample, each mother administered the items first to her own child and then to another same-sexed child; for the other half of the sample, the order was reversed. The focus of the present study was not on the child's performance per se but rather on the nature of the verbal exchanges between mother and child.

Interaction Analysis

The verbal exchanges between mothers and the children were tape recorded. Two coders using a modified system of Bales Interaction Analysis (Bales, 1950) categorized maternal verbalizations into four categories: (*a*) positive, encouraging statements, (*b*) negative, controlling statements, (*c*) total words, and (*d*) total statements. Maternal statements were defined as utterances which communicated an idea or thought to the child.

In coding the children's verbal behavior, it was found that understanding their speech from tape recordings was not always possible because their articulation was often quite poor. Therefore, the time the children spent vocalizing was used as an index of their verbal performance instead of the number of statements. Data were analyzed separately for the sexes to investigate the possible influence that the sex of the children might have had on the interactions. Intercoder agreements were satisfactory for all the categories, ranging from 88 percent to 94 percent agreement. The disagreements were resolved by discussion.

Results

The major results are summarized in Table 5.4. Data were corrected for the length of the interaction sessions by equating all the interaction codes on the basis of the shortest session. This procedure resulted in very minor adjustments in a few instances, as the lengths of the sessions were generally quite comparable. Significance levels for mean differences in the four categories were assessed by *t* tests.

In examining the changes in the mothers' behavior as a function of interacting with their own or other like-sexed children, it was found that mothers used significantly more positive encouragement with the other children than with their own. In fact, 41 out of 42 mothers gave more positive statements to the other children. "Ownness" apparently determined a highly reliable effect in this sample. The mothers also, as a group, made significantly more negative, controlling statements to their own children than to the other children.

Table 5.4. Differences in maternal behavior between own and other children[a]

	Maternal Statements				
		Mean Positive		Mean Negative	
Relation of Child	*Mean Total*	N	%	N	%
Own	180	36	20.0	8	4.2*
Other	198	55	28.0*	2	0.8

[a] Combines male and female samples.
* Own vs. other contrast, $p<.01$.

Table 5.5. Sex differences in maternal and child verbalization[a]

	Sex of Child	
Measure	*Male*	*Female*
Mean total words spoken (mother)	614	846**
Mean total statements (mother)	172	199*
Mean total time talking in seconds (child)	145	190**

[a] Data for own and other child combined.
* Difference significant at $p<.05$.
** Difference significant at $p<.001$.

It is also interesting to note that for both own and other children of both sexes, there were significant positive correlations between how long the children talked and how much the mothers talked (total words). That is, the more time the children talked, the more the mothers said. The average *r* for males and females, own and other, was .68.[1]

In Table 5.5, it can be seen that for both own and other children mothers talked more with the girls, and the girls spent more time talking than the boys. Thus, it seems likely that there was more verbal interchange between girls and mothers.

Maternal consistencies are summarized in Table 5.6. For both mothers of girls and boys, there are significant consistencies in maternal behavior between own and other children in terms of both the number of positive and negative statements made and in the total number of words the mothers spoke.

Impulsive child behavior as measured in the nursery school was significantly related to maternal performance in the mother-child interactions. Boys who were rated by two teachers during the 5-week session as more uncontrolled, fast-moving, and impulsive tended to have mothers

[1] There were no significant differences among the four correlations.

Table 5.6. Maternal consistencies between own and other child

	Mothers of Males	Mothers of Females
r between proportion positive statements, own vs. other	.63*	.59*
r between proportion negative statements, own vs. other	.52*	.48*
r between total words, own vs. other	.57*	.52*

* $p < .01$.

who employed more negative, controlling statements during the interaction, *only* with their *own* sons ($r = + .41$, $p = .05$). Two facts make this correlation interesting: First, the more impulsive boys did not seem to differ from the less impulsive boys in performance during the mother-child tests. Second, the relation between impulsive behavior in the nursery school and maternal negative statements held only for mothers and their own sons. The direction of this correlation is the same for mothers and daughters but does not reach significance. For boys, it seems that the mothers' past interactions with the children may have led to some expectancies about their children's potential performance in the experimental situation. The mothers of the more impulsive boys seemed to be "set for trouble" and instituted more negative, controlling behavior, even in the apparent absence of behavior which would promote this sort of response.

Discussion

The results indicate that there are important and significant differences, as well as consistencies, in the interactions between mothers and their own and other children. These findings, of course, represent only some of the important complexities encountered in experimental studies of mother-child interactions. It is clear that mothers do change their behavior as a function of "ownness." That is, they are more negative with their own and more positive with other children.

The fact that mothers tend to be more negative and controlling with their own children probably reflects the operation of several situational pressures on the mother: First, the interaction situation was, no doubt, perceived by a majority of the mothers as an achievement situation in which it was important for their own children to do well. Second, mothers when out "in public" with their own children generally tend to assume responsibility for their children's performance. As a result of these pressures, mothers might have been more task-oriented with their own children, as evidenced by the more negative and controlling environments which they provided. With other children, maternal involvement in child performance was probably lower, and the most socially desirable behavior with a strange child may often be a positive and friendly searching for "nice" ways to get the child to perform.

That mothers and girls seem to have a higher rate of verbal interchange is consonant with other literature on mother-child relations. For example, Moss (1967) found that mothers imitated vocalizations of female infants more than those of males; and Goldberg, Godfrey, and Lewis (1967) have observed that 1-year-old infant girls vocalized more than boys and that mothers of girls talked significantly more than did mothers of boys.

The results of the present study have implications for socialization research, particularly when each parent or an adult is studied with only one child in an interaction situation. In some ways, mothers are consistent with different children, probably reflecting to some extent underlying maternal dispositions. But, just as importantly, mothers behave very differently with different children, or different sexes, reflecting the complex interaction of the behavior and sex of the children and maternal expectancies and personality.

In the present investigation there were both consistencies and differences in maternal behavior as a function of the "ownness." It is clear that future investigators who experimentally manipulate the behavior of parents, adults, or children need to take "ownness" into account in making generalizations. The study of parents with their own and other children should aid in the goal of clarifying the parental behaviors that are consistent across children and those that remain specific to their own children.

References

BALES, R. F. *Interaction process analysis*. Cambridge, Mass.: Addison-Wesley, 1950.

BELL, R. Q. A reinterpretation of the direction of effects in studies of socialization. *Psychological Review*, 1968, *75*, 81–95.

GOLDBERG, S.; GODFREY, L.; & LEWIS, M. Play behavior in the year-old infant: Early sex differences. Paper presented at the Society for Research in Child Development meeting, New York, March 1967.

MOSS, H. A. Sex, age and state as determinants of mother-infant interaction. *Merrill-Palmer Quarterly*, 1967, *13*, 19–36.

27. THE YOUNG AS A SOURCE OF STIMULI CONTROLLING CARETAKER BEHAVIOR

LAWRENCE V. HARPER

The effects of mammalian offspring on their caretakers are reviewed, following a general classification system in which the offspring are seen as providing exogenous stimuli which facilitate (trigger, sensitize, orient) or inhibit (check, desensitize, disorient) caretaker behavior. Comparative studies provide well-documented examples of general offspring stimulus effects. Evidence suggests that it would be fruitful to apply the same behavior analysis to parent-offspring relations in man.

Traditional concepts of the parent-child relationship in humans emphasize the ways in which adults shape the behavior of the young (e.g., Baumrind, 1966; Becker, 1964). Relatively little attention has been devoted to the possibility that the influence may be reciprocal despite the fact that Bell (1968) has shown that many of the "demonstrations" of caretaker effects can readily be reinterpreted as effects of the young upon their parents. Sociologists (e.g., Brim, 1957) and psychoanalysts (e.g., Brody, 1956) have long recognized the interactive nature of the parent-child relationship. However, the former have limited themselves to rather general formulations concerning reciprocity of role expectations while the latter have focused upon the interplay between the child's developing "instinctual needs" and the intrapsychic conflicts they arouse in the parents. Neither the sociological nor the psychoanalytic approach has led to systematic behavioral analyses of caretaker-young interactions (see Bell, 1971, for a review and discussion). To date, only a few studies have attempted to specify any of the ways in which human offspring modify their parents' behavior (e.g., Bell, 1968, 1971; Gewirtz & Gewirtz, 1969; Robson & Moss, 1969).

In the comparative literature, a substantial number of reports are directly concerned with the effects of infrahuman offspring on their caretakers. The details concerning the ways in which young mammals influence their parents' behavior are often species and even response specific. However, when the young are viewed simply as a source of stimulation, the data provide well-documented examples of rather general offspring effects. It is these stimulus *functions* to which this review is addressed. Once these "phenotypic" effects of the young of a given species are identified, analysis of underlying processes can proceed.

The purposes of this article are to bring together studies from the comparative literature which demonstrate that young mammals provide stimuli which affect the behavior of their caretakers, and to point out evidence that suggests the fruitfulness of adopting a similar approach in the behavioral analysis of parent-offspring relations in man. In the following discussion, the effects of mammalian offspring on their caretakers are organized according to Marler and Hamilton's (1966) general classification of the effects of exogenous stimuli on behavior: Stimuli are viewed as functioning to either increase (facilitate) or reduce (inhibit) the probability of any given behavior—from highly complex action patterns to specific responses. Response facilitation is subdivided into "triggering," "sensitizing," and "orienting"; response inhibition is discussed in terms of the "checking," "desensitizing," and "disorienting" of behavior. As they are used here, these rubrics are concerned only with classifying effects and not with the mechanisms by which they are achieved.

Response Facilitation[1]

Triggering

To be considered as the trigger for a response, a stimulus must be related to the occurrence of that act in at least one of the following ways: (*a*) The response occurs only in the presence of the stimulus; (*b*) it has a high probability of occurrence in the presence of the stimulus regardless of setting; (*c*) the response has a high probability of occurring in a particular setting in the presence of the stimulus.

Eliciting unique responses or patterns In some species particular response patterns are directed only toward the young. In domestic dogs (Scott & Fuller, 1965) and mountain gorillas (Schaller, 1963), observation suggests that social grooming behavior is almost entirely limited to caretaker-young interactions. In captive groups of rhesus monkeys, adults do not play among themselves; however, several instances of play with infants have been recorded (Hinde, Rowell, & Spencer-Booth, 1964). In each of the examples, the young appear to constitute the necessary stimulus for the observed responses.

In some species that bear several offspring at a time, various aspects of the caretaking cycle may be prolonged well beyond the "normal" duration by re-

[1] The attempts at definition presented here and the organization of the empirical data represent the present author's understanding and interpretations of Marler and Hamilton's categories.

peatedly fostering litters of younger animals when the current young reach a given age. In mice (Selye & McKeown, 1934) and rats (Bruce, 1961; Nicoll & Meites, 1959; Wiesner & Sheard, 1933), lactation has been prolonged for as long as twice the usual period by this technique. It appears that stimuli emitted by a certain age class are necessary for maintaining lactation in females of these species.

In addition, behaviors different from the adult-directed patterns observed in otherwise similar situations may occur in response to immatures. Calhoun (1962) noted that wild adult Norway rats either walked over juveniles or crowded them off trails in encounters—low-status adults were chased. Mature rats never bit juveniles under the age of 50 days; when dominance was displayed, it took the form of "trouncing" them using all four feet. King (1955) reported a similar offspring-directed pattern of assertion in adult black-tailed prairie dogs which he called "front-paw drubbing." Among barren ground caribou (Lent, 1966) and captive baboons (Rowell, 1966b), the threat displays and attacks directed toward immatures differed from those characterizing interadult encounters. Thus, animal young appear to provide the stimuli for a specific repertoire of behavior.

There is evidence that the human infant, like the young of infrahuman mammals, may evoke particular responses from caretakers. Rheingold (1961) measured the nature and amount of stimulation provided to 3–4-month-old infants in an orphanage and to "only" infants in well-to-do homes. Despite the facts that the degree of caretaker investment in the infants and the nature of the overall environments were strikingly different in the two settings, each of the caretaking activities found in the homes was also seen in the institution, although less often. More importantly, the *relative* frequency of occurrence for these activities was similar in the two environments. Similarly, in a study of the mothering behavior of women whose infants were 4, 12, 20, or 28 weeks old, Brody (1956) found that the patterns of responses displayed by the mothers varied according to their infants' ages. The 4-week-old infants elicited a distinctive set of behaviors when compared to the other babies, and overall, the mothers' behavior was considered remarkably similar in view of their apparently great differences in personality.

The most pervasive triggering effects of offspring characteristics are those elicited by the apparent gender of the young. Hampson (1965) has summarized the findings of several investigations that indicate quite clearly that the external morphology of an infant can elicit a complex of attitudes and practices that will persist throughout the entire child-rearing process, and perhaps throughout the individual's life. The strength of this phenomenon is demonstrated by the cases of infants whose external genital morphology was incongruous with their genetic sex, and who were subsequently reared according to their apparent gender.

Thus, like infrahuman young, the attributes of the human offspring may serve as eliciting stimuli for uniquely patterned behavior on the part of caretakers.

Transsituational efficacy Certain qualities of animal young appear to be effective in eliciting caretaking in a rather wide variety of situations. According to Kummer (1968), female and young adult male hamadryas baboons are highly attracted toward, and frequently attempt to touch, groom, or carry infants in the natal coat. In subadult and young adult males, this tendency was so pronounced that even during the outbreak of hostilities attendant upon the introduction of a group of animals from a "foreign" troop, the alien infants were "adopted" by members of this class.

In those forms that defend their offspring, the distress calls of the young are often sufficient to elicit protective behavior. For instance, in a captive colony of Patas monkeys, Hall and Mayer (1967) reported that the distress call of an infant was likely to result in the nearest adult individual—including even the dominant male—being attacked by the infant's mother. Similar observations have been reported in ground squirrels (McCarley, 1966). The calls of infant bushbabies (Sauer, 1967), domestic cats (Schneirla, Rosenblatt, & Tobach, 1963), rats (Noirot, 1968), and mice (Noirot, 1966) have been reported to release maternal retrieving behavior. In all these cases, it can be shown that although similar motor responses may be elicited by stimuli besides those emitted by the young, such behavior has a high probability of occurrence whenever the appropriate offspring stimuli are encountered.

Comparable data exist at the human level. At the first meeting of the Tavistock study group on mother-infant interaction, Gunther (1961) showed a film of an infant attempting to fight its way free from being smothered by the mother's breast. While the mothers in the film were reported to have become exceedingly distraught in the situation, even a number of those viewing the film reported feeling discomfort upon observing the struggling infant (Gunther, 1961).

The baby's cry provides a more familiar example of the way in which an infant may elicit responses from a caretaker. Moss and Robson (1968) recorded the behavioral exchanges between mothers and their infants in the home during the first and third months postpartum. Over 2,000 episodes of protest ("fussing") were recorded; of these, 77% were followed by a maternal response, while only 17% of the episodes terminated without maternal intervention. The remaining 6% occurred during interactions. The same eliciting effect of the infant's cry has been observed in other settings. David and Appell (1961) found that the crying of infants in a residential nursery hospital was related to the amount of contact they received. Although crying only accounted for about 14% of the infants' activity, the nurses spent 15 times more time with them when they were crying than when they were not.

Other behavior of the young appears to be able to regularly elicit caretaker responses. Gewirtz and Gewirtz (1969) studied patterns of caretaker-infant interaction in an Israeli orphanage, a kibbutz, urban single-child homes, and urban multichild homes. They found that, across all these settings, the probability that a 6-month-old child's vocalization would be followed by an adult's talking ranged from .52 to .82 and that the probabilities that a child's smile would be followed by an adult's ranged from .46 to .88.

A determinant of response in a specific setting In a number of forms, the nature of a response to a given situation may be uniquely modified by the presence of young. For example, when fleeing from wolves, pairs of adult moose usually split up and fled in different directions; in contrast, cows with calves maintained a position close behind their offspring (Mech, 1966). Booth (1962) reported that adults in wild troops of Vervet, Brazza, and Sykes monkeys, became exceptionally bold and aggressive when they saw a hand-reared infant in the natal coat in human possession. No threatening behavior was observed when juveniles, whose pelage resembled that of adults, accompanied a human.

A variety of behaviors may be elicited by the human young in particular settings. Hilton (1967) studied the responses of mothers of first born, only, and later-born 4-year-old children to their offspring's apparent success or failure in a task of "independent thinking." She found that the mothers of first born and only children exhibited a higher incidence of "demonstrative love" when led to believe that their offspring had done well. In a film of mother-infant interaction in a feeding situation (Blauvelt & McKenna, 1961), it was noted that the mothers seemed to follow physically the movements of their children, including opening their mouths as the babies did so. With regard to the latter, B. Jacobs (personal communication, 1967) has observed that when feeding infants solid food, the majority of mothers (among nearly 100 observed in the home), and even her 11-year-old daughter, opened their mouths with each spoonful. Recently, O'Toole and Durbin (1968) reported observing over 1,000 feeding episodes (spoonfuls) in 26 mother-infant pairs. In 59% of these bouts, the mothers were seen to open their mouths—usually *after* the infant had opened his. Only 2 of the 26 mothers displayed no obvious mouth opening at any time during the observation period.

In summary, there is experimental and observational evidence that in certain contexts the young may predictably determine the nature of the behavior of caretakers.

Orienting

Much caretaker activity is directed in space by, or toward the young.

In the physical environment Among those species that rear their offspring in nests, dens, or sheltered hiding places, the location of the young may become a focal point about which the caretaker's activity centers (e.g., Eisenberg, 1963; Joslin, 1967; Kaufmann, 1962; McCarley, 1966). According to Lockley (1961), the site in which the European rabbit first litters tends to be used during later caretaking cycles despite the subsequent availability of "more suitable" areas elsewhere in her range. In some precocial forms that move about with their offspring, such as goats (Collias, 1956) and moose (Altmann, 1958), the young select their own hiding spot in which to rest after nursing. Thus, in these species, the offspring directly determine the area to which the mother's activity is confined.

The young of a number of species utter "lost calls" when separated from their parents. The effectiveness of offspring vocalizations in orienting caretaker approach has been demonstrated by playing tape-recorded calls over a loudspeaker. When a captive mother bushbaby was out of the nest, Sauer (1967) found that playing a recording of her infant's calls would immediately bring her to the source. Among marmosets, all adult members of the group care for the young. In a captive group, recorded distress calls of an infant elicited an "excited" approach from every adult in the pen (Epple, 1968).

Although little experimental evidence is available on this point, it is clear that a human parent's knowledge of his child's location can influence his orientation in space. Moss and Robson (1968) interviewed mothers of 3½-month-old infants in one room while their offspring were being studied in another part of the laboratory. During one phase of the interview, as a test of maternal response to a knowledge of the baby's state, as opposed to the cry itself, they told the mother that her infant was crying and that she could go to it if she wished. Under these circumstances, 13 of 54 mothers responded by leaving the interviewer and going to the test room. The infant's cry may also "move" nonparents. Ostwald (1963) reported that when he played tape recordings of infants' cries in his office, "secretaries busy in other rooms often would drop their work and come running. They had to know what was wrong 'with the baby' . . . [p. 39]."

From common experience, other examples of children's influence on the locus of caretaker activity would include the increased time spent in playgrounds, contacts with public schools, and so forth.

In the social environment Stimuli from the young may also direct the behavior of the caretaker with respect to others in the group. The triggering effects on maternal attack behavior by the distress calls of infant patas monkeys have already been mentioned. Parental response to other young may be affected as well. Rhesus monkey mothers were observed to threaten or attempt to "punish" other infants who played "too roughly" with their own offspring (Arling & Harlow, 1967). Hinde et al. (1964) also observed that mothers of this species would discourage the approaches of other infants when their own were either sucking or sleeping. Like the mother moose under attack by wolves (aforementioned), barren ground caribou cows have been observed to maintain a position alongside or slightly behind their calves when steadily pursued by man (Lent, 1966). Thus, the presence, behavior, and/or state of the young may direct parental defensive responses to either conspecifics or predators.

Another form of orientation is that which is related to the recognition of individual offspring. This is most apparent in species such as sheep and goats in which the parent-offspring bond is highly exclusive (Hersher, Richmond, & Moore, 1963). However, even in such forms as laboratory rats, where lactating females will usually accept and "mother" very young infants from another litter, Beach and Jaynes (1956) have shown that mothers tend to retrieve their own offspring before alien young.

Among human beings, the identification of an infant as "one's own" certainly can be considered as an orientation to the young. There is evidence that such discriminations can develop early. Valanne, Vuorenkoski, Partanen, Lind, and Wasz-Hockert (1967) found that within 1 week of birth, about one-third of a group of 35 multiparous mothers could distinguish the hunger cries of their own offspring from those of other infants.

Gender can also orient caretaker attention and sensitivity toward certain offspring characteristics. Moss (1967) observed that mothers of 1- to 3-month-old girls were more likely to repeat their offspring's vocalizations than were the mothers of 1- to 3-month-old boys. Similarly, Goldberg, Godfrey, and Lewis (1967) rated the mothers of female infants as vocalizing to their offspring more often than mothers of male infants. No sex difference in the infants' vocalizations was found in either of these studies. Further, Moss (1964) found that when mothers and fathers were requested to get their 7-week-old infants to vocalize or smile, the parents spent more time with female babies than with males, despite the fact that the infant girls responded no better than did the boys. These data suggest that the parents' differential efforts were a function of their offspring's sex rather than their performance.

Within the individual Not only do the young orient caretakers to them as individuals or as groups but specific portions of the infant's anatomy may be the objects of particular attention. For instance, parental grooming is not random. Goswell and Gartlan (1965) reported that the head and face of the neonatal patas monkey received the most maternal cleaning at parturition. In pigtail and bonnet macaque monkeys, mothers of male infants were observed to spend more time inspecting the genitals of their offspring than were mothers of females (Rosenblum & Kaufman, 1967). In a wide variety of species, the anal and/or umbilical regions of the young receive a great deal of grooming relative to other portions of their anatomy (e.g., Haskell & Reynolds, 1947; Rosenblatt & Lehrman, 1963), which indicates that stimuli peculiar to these regions orient caretaker behavior.

In man, Wasz-Hockert, Partanen, Vuorenkoski, Valanne, and Michelson (1964) have shown that caretakers can distinguish between the crying of uncomfortable and hungry infants. To the extent that a caretaker can make such discriminations, the infant's cry may orient a parent's activity with respect to the child's physiological needs.

In summary, there is evidence which indicates that the stimuli emitted by the young can serve to orient parental activity within the physical and social environments and with respect to the infant itself.

Sensitizing

Sensitization refers to the increase in the probability of responding to a stimulus as a result of prior or increased exposure to it or to some related stimulus.

Parent-offspring bonds The development of an exclusive parent-offspring relationship could be considered a type of sensitization. In sheep and goats (Collias, 1956; Klopfer & Gamble, 1966; Smith, van Toller, & Boyes, 1966), there is a "sensitive period" in the puerperium for the development of the mother-young bond. If mother and offspring are separated at birth and the young are not returned within an hour or less, the offspring will subsequently be driven away when they attempt to approach their mother. However, during the sensitive period, it is even possible to cross-foster sheep and goat young (Hersher et al., 1963).

Although there seems to be no involvement of a sensitive period, the development of a highly specific mother-infant relationship has been observed in rhesus monkeys. Hansen (1966) reported that during their first 3 months postpartum, mothers rearing their offspring in the Wisconsin playpen apparatus made more "positive" than "negative" responses to other infants the same age as their own. However, in the following 6 months, the mothers became increasingly intolerant of their offspring's peers while the former continued to enjoy a preponderance of positive responses. In pigtail monkeys, Jensen (1965) found that immediately after parturition, mothers could discriminate their own from older infants. By the end of 1 week, four of five subjects could distinguish their own from another infant of the same age; in each case they showed more responsiveness to their own young.

As indicated by Wasz-Hockert et al. (1964), the necessary precursors of the specific parent-offspring bond in human beings may develop quite early in the postpartum period. The role of experience in developing discriminations between own and other infants was demonstrated by Formby (1967) who found that within the first 48 hours postpartum only 12 of 22 mothers who were rooming-in could distinguish their offsprings' cries from those of four other infants. However, after 48 hours, every one of 8 mothers tested was successful in making the discrimination. Further, mothers in three- or four-bed wards reported that, in the first 3 postpartum nights, 15 of 26 wakings were in response to the crying of their babies, while from the fourth night on, 22 of the 23 wakings were to their own infants' cries.

That parents in the American culture are likely to react differentially to their own offspring is a common observation which has recently gained experimental confirmation. Halverson (1969) had mothers of nursery school children assist in the administration of a number of simple tasks to their own and to another child. It was found that, in terms of a proportion of their total verbal output, mothers made more positive, encouraging statements to strange children than to their own. However, including negative statements, they made more performance-oriented, contingent responses to their offspring than to another's child. Thus, the existence of a particular relationship between caretaker and offspring served to color the nature of an adult's reactions to a child.

Inducing responsiveness As mentioned earlier, under normal conditions, if mother sheep or goats are denied contact with their offspring in the early postpartum period, they will not allow the young to nurse. However, experiments in which mothers were physically prevented from discouraging the young indicated that acceptance could be induced. Collias (1956) locked a rejecting ewe in a stanchion so that she could not butt away her offspring. In this situation, the mother gradually accepted her lamb. Hersher et al. (1963) found that lactating sheep and goats could even be induced to accept the young of the other species if they were restrained so that the foster infant had repeated opportunities to nurse.

In rats, caretaking usually is limited to lactating females; under standard laboratory conditions only a few nulliparous females retrieve pups in a testing situation. However, as a result of prolonged exposure to young, responsiveness has been induced in some unresponsive virgin females (Wiesner & Sheard, 1933) and even in a few males (Riddle, Lahr, & Bates, 1942). In a more recent experiment, Rosenblatt (1967) caged naïve nulliparous females and naïve males individually with a group of five 5–10-day-old pups for periods lasting up to 15 days. Under these conditions, almost all of the animals—males included—retrieved, licked, and assumed a nursing posture over the test young at some time during the course of daily trials.

Sensitizing effects of preexposure to young can even be demonstrated in laboratory mice, a species in which caretaking is spontaneously shown by both naïve males and females (Beniest-Noirot, 1958). Animals were individually allowed 5 mintes' contact with either a live or a drowned 1-day-old infant and tested 2–8 days later with a pup from the alternative exposure condition. It was found that prior exposure to a live pup markedly increased the likelihood that a drowned pup would be retrieved, licked, and crouched over. Prior enactment could not account for the increase in retrieving. Allowing females 5 minutes' contact with a live pup placed in the nest, thus precluding the necessity for retrieving, followed by a test with a drowned infant placed on the floor resulted in every one of the subjects' retrieving the dead pup, whereas only 3 of 20 retrieved a drowned pup upon their initial exposure to it (Noirot, 1964b).

As the phenomenon of specific mother-offspring relations suggests, even in human beings, a certain amount of exposure to the infant is required to consolidate, or at least orient, responsiveness. Robson and Moss (1969) interviewed mothers before term and in the early postpartum period. They found that strong, "personal," affective bonds were not evident from maternal reports until the infant appeared to be "looking at" its mother or "smiling at" her. From behavioral observations on a different sample, Moss (1967) reported an increment in maternal affectionate behavior around the third month—the time at which the child's rates of looking at its mother, smiling, and vocalization increased.

A blood relationship to an infant is not required for relatively continuous contact to lead to the arousal of a caretaker's affectionate feelings toward him. David and Appell (1961) studied the effects of intensive personalized nursing care on babies who were separated from their tubercular parents for 2 months. They found that nurses could only develop and enjoy affective interactions with the infants if they had given them a considerably greater amount and continuity of care than that resulting from the usual caretaking routine in the hospital.

Specific responses may also be facilitated as a result of repeated or increased contacts with one's child. Newton and Newton (1950) studied the milk "let down" reflex in 127 parturient mothers who had elected to breast feed their offspring. They found that the proportion of the group that reported dripping of the opposite breast during suckling, and milk flow before suckling, increased during the first 6 days of postpartum—presumably as a result of experience.

Effects of parity In the aforementioned experiments, changes in responsiveness were demonstrated after relatively short periods of time; comparable effects can be observed when the responsiveness of primipara and multipara is compared. In feral-born, captive rhesus monkeys, multiparous females spent more time viewing a neonate in a multiple-choice apparatus than did primiparous animals (Sackett, Griffin, Pratt, Joslyn, & Ruppenthal, 1967). In domestic cats, during the intervals between kitten births, experienced mothers spent more time cleaning their neonates and less time licking themselves than did inexperienced females (Schneirla et al., 1963). Multiparous mice were more likely than primipara to respond with caretaking to pups which were older than their own (Richards, 1967). The efficiency of response may be enhanced, presumably representing a sensitization to relevant cues. Mother rats retrieved their second litters "more efficiently" (dropped fewer pups) than they had when tested while caring for their first litters (Carlier & Noirot, 1965).

Enhancement of a more general nature has also been reported. In a series of careful experiments with rats, Moltz and his co-workers demonstrated that prior caretaking experience may be sufficient to overcome the debilitating effects of endocrine disturbances. Moltz and Wiener (1966) found that among Caesarean-delivered ovariectomized females, almost all the multiparous subjects accepted foster litters of six pups upon recovery from the operation, while only half the primipara did so. Similarly, Moltz, Levin, and Leon (1969) found that when injected with progesterone before Caesarean delivery, experienced females were more likely to care for foster litters than were inexperienced mothers.

Parity has been shown to affect parental responsiveness even in isolation-reared rhesus monkeys. Seay, Alexander, and Harlow (1964) and Arling and Harlow (1967) found that females who were separated from their mothers at birth and reared in individual cages during infancy displayed quantitatively less caretaking, and, in some cases, violent rejection of their first offspring (Seay et al., 1964). However, among seven of these animals which gave birth to a second infant, only one failed to be responsive to her second-born young (Harlow, Harlow, Dodsworth, & Arling, 1966). An interesting finding was that among the six mothers who responded adequately to their second born, there was one female who had displayed *no* caretaking in response to her first offspring, even though at that time the infant had presented sufficiently attractive stimuli to be adopted by a feral-born animal (Seay et al., 1964). These data suggest that prior parity or exposure to a newborn may sensitize isolated rhesus monkey mothers to the care-eliciting cues provided by subsequent offspring.

Thus, the evidence indicates that, in a number of mammals, prior or prolonged exposure to young conspecifics may function to facilitate "parental" impulses in a (potential) caretaker. The same may be true in man. A study of the nature and effects of the infant's cry provides an example of how prior experience may affect responsiveness (e.g., the increased efficiency in recognition of own infants' cries). Michelson, Vuorenkoski, Partanen, Valanne, and Wasz-Hockert (1965) found that experienced adults (parents, nurses, pediatricians) were better able to distinguish pain, hunger, and "contentment" crying than were inexperienced adults. In an earlier experiment they had obtained similar results, although significant only with respect to the identification of the hunger cry (Wasz-Hockert et al., 1964). Thus, in human beings, as in animals, prior caretaking experience may enhance an individual's sensitivity in that role.

In summary, the data presented in this section have shown that stimuli emanating from the young may serve to elicit caretaker responses, to control their direction in space, either toward others or the offspring, and to increase the likelihood or efficiency of parental behavior.

Response Inhibition

Checking

To be considered as a check to behavior, the presence of a stimulus must be shown to reduce the probability of a response which would otherwise occur in that situation.

Failure to respond A number of observers of social relations in mammals have remarked on the fact that adults often appear to "ignore" certain acts of immatures which, if performed by an older individual, would trigger a response.

Adults of a number of species have been reported to be more tolerant of the activities of the young than of older individuals. Among howler monkeys, it is rare for adults to share food with subordinate peers, yet mother howlers were observed to allow their offspring to take food from them (Carpenter, 1965). Similar findings have been reported in the marmoset (Hampton, Hampton, & Landwher, 1966), and even the highly aggressive savannah baboon (Rowell, 1966a). The contact-seeking activity of young waterbuck (Kiley-Worthington, 1965) and goats (Blauvelt, 1956) was reported to be tolerated much more by adult males than was the same activity from other animals. In vicunas, it was observed that while adults and yearlings were attacked when they strayed into an alien territory, young under the age of 6 months were not (Koford, 1957). While copulating, adult male chimpanzees tolerated the attempts of infants to push them off females; the same response from older young was met by blows (van Lawick-Goodall, 1967). Thus, some (unspecified) attributes of the young of a number of species apparently check adults' tendencies to aggressively defend feeding, individual distance, territorial, and sexual prerogatives.

Often what appear to be properly executed communicative displays fail to elicit a response or evoke one different from that directed toward adults. While chital generally follow any moving ungulate, they appeared to be indifferent to the movements of yearlings and fawns (Schaller, 1967), and adult elk did not respond to the flight and threat signals of calves, although the same signals from juveniles did elicit appropriate behavior (Altmann, 1960). Among adult squirrel monkeys, a stereotyped genital display is frequently directed by dominants toward subordinates; the reverse is seldom seen, and when it is, it triggers threat or attack by the higher ranking individual. Nevertheless, Ploog (1966) observed that infants may even address this response to the dominant male without fear of attack.

In human beings, there are no systematic studies of this phenomenon known to the writer. However, it is a common observation that children are frequently ignored, particularly when, in a fit of pique, they announce "I hate you," "bad mommy," etc. Likewise, their more or less fantastic statements or "egocentric speech" are indulged or at least not taken seriously, whereas such behavior, if performed by an adult, might cause some concern (cf. Vygotsky, 1962). The quiet inactivity of an infant may also serve to check the caretaker's impulse to handle it. In David and Appell's (1961) study, the amount of attention paid to crying infants was far greater than that paid to quiet infants. It is common knowledge that a harried mother will avoid disturbing an infant when it is asleep.

It was noted in the foregoing sections that the apparent gender of an infant triggers and orients an entire complex of caretaking activities in western culture (Hampson, 1965). To the extent that such selective responsivity represents an inhibition of behaviors "appropritae" to the opposite sex, this offspring stimulus quality may be considered to cause caretakers to *fail* to respond in certain ways. Thus, the physical appearance as well as the activity (including sleep) of the child may be responsible for a caretaker's not responding.

Blocking an ongoing activity A few reports have indicated that characteristics or responses typical of the young may serve to stop an adult's ongoing activity or inhibit its complete expression. Bushbabies are one of the few primate species in which the young are carried in the caretaker's mouth. Sauer (1967) observed that when an adult and a juvenile male bushbaby fought and the adult male secured a grip on the back of the juvenile's neck, the adult male's aggression terminated whenever the juvenile adopted the relaxed posture characteristic of the infant during transport. In golden hamsters, Rowell (1960) suggested that the tendency of pups to crawl under an adult inhibited the attacking tendency of virgin females, and Richards (1966) described a "puffing" call which appeared to have the same effect. Such blocking need not be limited to the execution of aggression. DeVore (1963) observed that female baboons tended to stop their movement when their offspring released or lost their grip on their mothers' fur. In bushbabies, Sauer (1967) reported that an infant's clinging appeared to inhibit the mother's leaving the nest.

In the foregoing discussion, a number of the examples cited could be interpreted as representing the facilitation of incompatible caretaking-related responses. Whatever the mechanisms by which the effect is obtained, however, it seems clear that the behavior or other aspects of the presence of young animals may act as a block to certain classes of activity in adult conspecifics.

In human beings, just as the infant's rapidity or efficiency of sucking may determine the duration of a feeding bout (Moss, 1964), observations of the effects of an infant's rejecting the nipple (Gunther, 1961) indicate clearly that the young can effectively terminate particular interaction sequences. Likewise, fussing or crying may block one activity such as feeding and lead to "burping" or some other pacifying behavior.

These observations, while far from substantial or definitive, indicate that the human child, like infrahuman young, can provide stimuli which check caretaker response.

Disorienting

To be considered disoriented, a response must be directed toward some object other than the one eliciting it or be more appropriate to a different class of consummatory stimulus objects.

Redirection In a number of gregarious species, it is frequently observed that when an adult appears to be about equally torn between tendencies to flee from or to attack another mature individual, a juvenile bystander may become the object of aggression. Espmark (1964) observed that equally matched, rutting bull reindeer often attacked calves, and Klopfer and Gilbert (1966) reported that in groups of elephant seals, the incidence of mothers' nipping calves increased both when a human approached and when females became involved in disputes. Jay (1965) reported that when threatened by a more dominant individual, adult female langurs may, in turn, threaten a small subadult male. Thus the young may become the object of responses aroused by other individuals.

Again, there are no systematic studies documenting the frequency of occurrence of the phenomenon in man, but the fact that a small child may become the object of "displaced" impulses—either of a "loving" or "hostile" nature—has been reported frequently in the clinical literature (e.g., Mandler, 1963; Shainess, 1963).

Deception In some species in which adult males are mutually intolerant, juveniles of either sex physically resemble adult females. Several authors have suggested that this phenomenon may function to protect young males from adult sexual competition in that they are able to avoid conflict with mature males by virtue of their eliciting responses appropriate to the opposite sex (Geist, 1968; van Hooff, 1967).

In man, the term deception, in itself, probably provides sufficient cues to bring examples to mind. The most obvious example is the falsehood of the verbal child. The importance of deceptive behavior such as lying and cheating is suggested by the emphasis placed upon studying the antecedents and correlates of "moral development" (e.g., Kohlberg, 1964).

Although there is a serious dearth of systematic study in this area, there seem to be sufficient grounds from clinical and common experience for asserting that the young human may disorient caretaker behavior. This fact also raises the intriguing possibility of studying the conditions under which caretakers may be misled, as well as the antecedents of the human child's proclivities in that direction.

Desensitizing

Desensitization may be defined as the converse of sensitization: the reduction in the probability of a response to a stimulus as a result of exposure to it or to a related stimulus.

Stimulus satiation Continuous or repeated exposure to young may result in a progressive decrement in responsivity. In mice, virgin females that were given 20 daily exposures to a litter of six pups were more likely to lick and crouch over the infants than were primipara that were concurrently rearing litters of six young (Noirot, 1964a). In addition, when naïve females were given 10 successive 5-minute presentations of the same infant pup, the number of animals licking or assuming a lactation posture over the test infant declined progressively. The latter finding could not be attributed to motor fatigue, because in a replication of the same experiment, it was found that responsiveness returned to the level of the first trial when, instead of a newborn, a 10-day-old test pup was presented on the last trial (Noirot, 1965). In rats, Rosenblatt and Lehrman (1963) found that during a series of daily tests of retrieving and nest building in response to 5–10-day-old test pups, the performance of lactating females that were concurrently rearing their own litters declined at the same rate as it did to their own offspring. Since 5–10-day-old young can induce retrieving in both lactating or nonlactating female rats (mentioned previously), Rosenblatt and Lehrman concluded that exposure to their own young must have caused a progressive response decrement in these mothers.

Decrements in responsivity may also be observed when different intensities of stimulation, as represented by litter size, are compared. Fuchs and Wagner (1963) found that mother rabbits would allow single pups to nurse for longer durations than entire litters. Using a composite score of maternal behavior, Seitz (1958) found that female rats which were rearing litters of 3 or 6 offspring displayed more solicitude for their young than did those whose litters numbered 8 or 12 pups.

In man, relatively brief encounters between parent and young may also have lasting decremental effects. Gunther (1961) observed that some infants developed a pattern of rejecting the breast as a result of being held so that they had difficulty in breathing. In such cases, most of the mothers were reported to lose any desire to continue breast feeding within the span of 2 or 3 days, stating that they could not bear to be rejected by their infants. Prechtl (1963) followed longitudinally the development of 8 neurologically damaged, "hyperexcitable" infants and a matched normal group. He found that by the end of 3 months, the mothers of 7 of these children were either rejecting or overanxious toward their offspring as compared to only 1 of the 10 control mothers. He noted that when he and his assistants attempted to examine the brain-damaged children, even they became "annoyed by these infants because of their exaggerated reactions and their sudden changes in state . . . [Prechtl,

1963, p. 56]." Similar decrements in solicitude have been observed in response to the behavior of older foster children. Provence and Lipton (1962) followed the foster-home adjustments of fourteen 1- to 2-year-old infants whose first 8–28 months had been spent in an orphanage. They found that when the children entered a stage of aggressive, provocative, and negativistic behavior, some of the foster parents appeared to reduce their emotional investment in their charges, and a few actually requested the child's removal.

The foregoing examples indicate that unusual offspring behavior may produce a rather rapid decline in caretaker responsiveness. However, this phenomenon need not be limited to cases of pathology or unusual circumstances; in the normal course of caretaking with healthy infants, decrements can be observed. Moss (1967) found that at the age of 1 month, the amount of contact that mothers made with both male and female infants was positively related to the amount of fussing and crying of the offspring. However, by 3 months, for the more irritable male babies, the correlation between maternal contact and infant crying was negative; the same positive relation held for females. Moss concluded that while the females could be pacified, the failure of the male babies to become quieted by their mothers' ministrations had actually led to a reduction in maternal responsiveness to crying. Thus, it appeared that continued exposure to the same offspring stimulus, if maintained at a relatively high intensity, may lead to a decrement in responsiveness.

Effects of parity In addition to facilitating the expression or efficacy of certain caretaking responses, prior parental experience may reduce the incidence or duration of other aspects of maternal behavior. Seay (1966) found that "positive" maternal acts were replaced by "rejecting" behavior earlier in multiparous rhesus monkeys than in primipara. In mice, Noirot (1964a) found that mothers consistently attempted to retrieve young from their first litter over the first 18 days; however, with their second litters, this response declined by Day 14. Further, at the end of a retrieving bout, the young of the second litter were less likely to elicit licking or the lactation posture.

Similarly, in human parents, desensitizing effects of prior exposure to offspring stimuli may be manifest when the responses of new parents are compared with those of experienced individuals. Moss (1964) studied the methods used by both the mothers and fathers of fifty 7-week-old infants to get their children to perform a number of different tasks. He found that fathers of first children tended to spend more time in administering tasks than did fathers of second children; likewise, primiparous mothers remained by the crib longer than did multipara. The effects of parity can be observed at later periods. In her study of the responses of mothers of firstborn and later-born children, Hilton (1967) found that the more experienced mothers were less demonstrative of affection toward their offspring and appeared to be less affected by their children's performances, both in terms of their expression of affect and their expectancies for their children's success. Further, despite instruction to the contrary, mothers of firstborns were significantly more likely to get their offspring started on the tasks and to make task-oriented suggestions, or to give direct help.

Thus there are sufficient data in both man and animals to support the view that caretaker responsiveness to offspring stimuli may be subject to both long- and short-term decrements as a result of prior exposure. As in many of the other examples cited, the specification of the precise mechanism underlying these phenomena awaits further experimentation.

In summary, the evidence reviewed above indicates that in infrahuman mammals the stimuli emitted by the young may affect caretakers in any of the several ways in which Marler and Hamilton (1966) have shown that other classes of exogenous events influence the behavior of animals. Evidence has been presented which demonstrates that the appearance and/or behavior of the young can facilitate caretaking by triggering, orienting, and sensitizing parental responses. Likewise, offspring stimuli can also inhibit such behavior by checking, disorienting, and desensitizing caretaking activities. Furthermore, when the data are taken together, they indicate that *Homo sapiens* does not differ qualitatively from other mammals in this respect.

Discussion and Conclusions

The studies reviewed in this article clearly indicate that the young of infrahuman mammals direct and regulate the course of caretaking interactions. Although the evidence from observations of human parent-child relationships is neither as extensive nor detailed as the comparative work, the data do support the contention (Bell, 1968, 1971) that human offspring play an active role in determining the form and patterning of child rearing. While such phenomena as the recognition of one's own offspring seem self-evident, they have not been the subject of controlled study by students of socialization. Yet, in order to understand fully the parent-offspring relationship, the human infant, like any other immature mammal, will have to be viewed as a stimulus object which can affect the behavior of its caretakers. When offspring stimuli are evaluated in these terms, more detailed and sensitive analyses will be possible. Until such time, the bases for many aspects of parental behavior will remain obscure.

Although there are limits to the nature and amount of manipulation that are permissible in the study of human behavior, the difficulties involved in obtaining clear and meaningful results are not insurmountable. The value of naturalistic as well as controlled observations is amply demonstrated by the work of Moss (1964, 1967). Bell (1968, 1971) has outlined a number of ways in which parent and child effects can be separated. The Swedish investigators' work with the infant's cry, and Brooks and Hochberg's (1960) studies of the stimuli controlling adults' judgments of "infant's cuteness" indicate the feasibility of fine-grained analyses of offspring stimuli.

Given that the child does affect the behavior of his parents in identifiable ways and that the stimuli provided by the child can be analyzed in measurable terms, the caretaker-young relationship in human beings may be approached as a process of stimulus interchange. As emphasized by Schneirla and Rosenblatt (1961, 1963), the parent-offspring relationship in mammals can most fruitfully be analyzed in terms of a mosaic of mutually stimulative interactions. At any point, in each stage of the relationship, the state of the actors—and thus their responses in a given exchange—are both products of previous exchanges and determinants of future stages of the interaction. Although any particular attempt to intrude upon such an ongoing cycle may be arbitrary and inadequate to capture the complexity of the whole, in animals there already exists ample evidence that by a number of such interventions one can characterize the processes affecting the caretaking cycle (e.g., Rosenblatt & Lehrman, 1963; Schneirla et al., 1963). Bell (1971) has presented a persuasive argument for the view that the same can be done in man. By investigating the ways in which the child's behavior influences that of the parents, we may not only be able to overcome some of the problems of interpretation encountered in the analysis of the effects of socialization practices, but we may also be able to ascertain some of the situational determinants of these practices.

References

ALTMANN, M. Social integration of the moose calf. *Animal Behaviour*, 1958, *6*, 155–159.

———. The role of juvenile elk and moose in the social dynamics of their species. *Zoologica*, 1960, *45*, 35–39.

ARLING, G. L., & HARLOW, H. F. Effects of social deprivation on maternal behavior of rhesus monkeys. *Journal of Comparative and Physiological Psychology*, 1967, *64*, 371–377.

BAUMRIND, D. Effects of authoritative parental control on child behavior. *Child Development*, 1966, *37*, 887–908.

BEACH, F. A., & JAYNES, J. Studies of maternal retrieving in rats. I. Recognition of young. *Journal of Mammalogy*, 1956, *37*, 177–180.

BECKER, W. C. Consequences of different kinds of parental discipline. In M. L. Hoffman & L. W. Hoffman (Eds.), *Review of child development research*. Vol. *1*. New York: Russell Sage Foundation, 1964.

BELL, R. Q. A reinterpretation of the direction of effects in studies of socialization. *Psychological Review*, 1968, *75*, 81–95.

———. Stimulus control of parent or caretaker behavior by offspring. *Developmental Psychology*, 1971, *4*, 63–72.

BENIEST-NOIROT, E. Analyse du comportement dit maternal chez la souris. *Monographies Francaises de Psychologie*, Vol. *1*. Paris: Centre de la Recherche Scientifique, 1958.

BLAUVELT, H. Neonate-mother relationship in goat and man. In B. Schaffner (Ed.), *Group processes. Transactions of the second conference*. Madison, N.J.: Josiah Macy Foundation, 1956.

BLAUVELT, H., & MC KENNA, J. Mother-neonate interaction: Capacity of the human newborn for orientation. In B. M. Foss (Ed.), *Determinants of infant behavior. I*. New York: Wiley, 1961.

BOOTH, C. Some observations on behavior of *Cercopithecus* monkeys. *Annals of the New York Academy of Sciences*, 1962, *102*, 477–487.

BRIM, O. G., JR. The parent-child relation as a social system: I. Parent and child roles. *Child Development*, 1957, *28*, 343–364.

BRODY, S. *Patterns of mothering*. New York: International Universities Press, 1956.

BROOKS, V., & HOCHBERG, J. A psychophysical study of "cuteness." *Perceptual and Motor Skills*, 1960, *11*, 205.

BRUCE, H. M. Observations of the suckling stimulus and lacation in the rat. *Journal of Reproduction and Fertility*, 1961, *2*, 17–34.

CALHOUN, J. B. *The ecology and sociology of the norway rat*. (Publication No. 1008) Bethesda, Md.: United States Department of Health, Education, and Welfare, Public Health Service, 1962.

CARLIER, C., & NOIROT, E. Effects of previous experience on maternal retrieving in rats. *Animal Behaviour*, 1965, *13*, 423–426.

CARPENTER, C. R. The howlers of Barro Colorado Island. In L. DeVore (Ed.), *Primate behavior*. New York: Holt, Rinehart & Winston, 1965.

COLLIAS, N. E. The analysis of socialization in sheep and goats. *Ecology*, 1956, *37*, 228–239.

DAVID, M., & APPELL, G. A study of nursing care and nurse-infant interaction. In B. M. Foss (Ed.), *Determinants of infant behavior*. I. New York: Wiley, 1961.

DE VORE, I. Mother-infant relations in free-ranging baboons. In H. L. Rheingold (Ed.), *Maternal behavior in mammals*. New York: Wiley, 1963.

EISENBERG, J. F. The behavior of heteromyid rodents. *University of California Publications in Zoology*, 1963, *69*, 1–78.

EPPLE, A. Comparative studies on vocalization in marmoset monkeys (*Hapalidae*). *Folia Primatologica,* 1968, *8,* 1–40.

ESPMARK, Y. Studies in dominance-subordination relationships in a group of semi-domestic reindeer (*Rangifer tarandus* L.) *Animal Behaviour,* 1964, *12,* 420–426.

FORMBY, D. Maternal recognition of infant's cry. *Developmental Medicine and Child Neurology,* 1967, *9,* 293–298.

FUCHS, A. R., & WAGNER, A. Quantative aspects of release of oxytocin by suckling in unanaesthetized rabbits. *Acta Endocrinologica,* 1963, *44,* 581–592.

GEIST, V. On the interrelation of external appearance, social behaviour and social structure of mountain sheep. *Zeitschrift für Tierpsychologie,* 1968, *25,* 199–215.

GERWITZ, H. B., & GEWIRTZ, J. L. Caretaking settings, background events, and behavior differences in four Israeli child-rearing environments: Some preliminary trends. In B. M. Foss (Ed.), *Determinants of infant behaviour.* IV. London: Methuen, 1969.

GOLDBERG, S., GODFREY, L., & LEWIS, M. Play behavior in the year-old infant: Early sex differences. Paper presented at biennial meeting of the Society for Research in Child Development. New York, March 1967.

GOSWELL, M. J., & GARTLAN, J. S. Pregnancy, birth, and early infant behaviour in the captive patas monkey, *Erythrocebus patas. Folia Primatologica,* 1965, *3,* 189–200.

GUNTHER, M. Infant behavior at the breast. In B. M. Foss (Ed.), *Determinants of infant behaviour.* I. New York: Wiley, 1961.

HALL, K. R. L., & MAYER, B. Social interactions in a group of captive patas monkeys (*Erythrocebus patas*). *Folia Primatologica,* 1967, *5,* 213–236.

HALVERSON, C. F., JR. Maternal behavior towards own and other children. Paper presented at the biennial meeting of the Society for Research in Child Development, Santa Monica, March 1969.

HAMPSON, J. L. Determinants of psychosexual orientation. In F. A. Beach (Ed.), *Sex and behavior.* New York: Wiley, 1965.

HAMPTON, J. K., JR., HAMPTON, S. H., & LANDWEHR, B. T. Observations on a successful breeding colony of the marmoset, *Oedipomidas oedipus. Folia Primatologica,* 1966, *4,* 265–287.

HANSEN, E. The development of maternal and infant behavior in the rhesus monkey. *Behaviour,* 1966, *27,* 107–149.

HARLOW, H. F., HARLOW, M. K., DODSWORTH, R. O., & ARLING, G. L. Maternal behavior of rhesus monkeys deprived of mothering and peer associations in infancy. *Proceedings of the American Philosophical Society,* 1966, *110,* 58–66.

HASKELL, H. S., & REYNOLDS, H. G. Growth, developmental food requirements and breeding in the California jackrabbit. *Journal of Mammalogy,* 1947, *28,* 129–136.

HERSHER, L., RICHMOND, J. B., & MOORE, A. U. Modifiability of the critical period for the development of maternal behavior in sheep and goats. *Behaviour,* 1963, *20,* 311–320.

HILTON, I. Differences in the behavior of mothers toward first- and later-born children. *Journal of Personality and Social Psychology,* 1967, *7,* 282–290.

HINDE, R. A., ROWELL, T. E., & SPENCER-BOOTH, Y. Behaviour of socially living rhesus monkeys in their first six months. *Proceedings of the Zoological Society of London,* 1964, *143,* 609–649.

JAY, P. Field studies. In A. M. Schrier, H. F. Harlow, & F. Stollnitz (Eds.), *Behavior of nonhuman primates.* Vol. 2. New York: Academic Press, 1965, 525–591.

JENSEN, G. D. Mother-infant relationship in the monkey *Macaca nemestrina:* Development of specificity of maternal responses to own infant. *Journal of Comparative and Physiological Psychology,* 1965, *59,* 305–308.

JOSLIN, P. W. B. Movements and home sites of timber wolves in Algonquin park. *American Zoologist*, 1967, *7*, 279–288.

KAUFMANN, J. H. Ecology and social behavior of the coati. *University of California Publications in Zoology*, 1962, *60*, 95–222.

KILEY-WORTHINGTON, M. The waterbuck (*Kobus defassa* Ruppel, 1835, and *K. ellipsiprimnus* Ogilby, 1833) in East Africa: Spatial distribution. A study of the sexual behavior. *Mammalia*, 1965, *29*, 177–204.

KING, J. A. Social behavior, social organization, and population dynamics in a black-tailed prairiedog town in the black hills of South Dakota. *Contributions of the Laboratory of Vertibrate Biology*, 1955, Whole No. 67.

KLOPFER, P. H., & GAMBLE, J. Maternal "imprinting" in goats: The role of chemical senses. *Zeitschrift für Tierpsychologie*, 1966, *23*, 588–592.

KLOPFER, P. H., & GILBERT, B. K. A note on retrieval and recognition of young in the elephant seal. *Mirounga angustirostris. Zeitschrift für Tierpsychologie*, 1966, *23*, 757–760.

KOFORD, C. B. The vicuna and the puna. *Ecological Monographs*, 1957, *27*, 153–219.

KOHLBERG, L. Development of moral character and moral ideology. In L. W. Hoffman, & M. L. Hoffman (Eds.), *Review of child development research.* Vol. *1*. New York: Russell Sage Foundation, 1964.

KUMMER, H. *Social organization of hamadryas baboons.* Chicago: University of Chicago Press, 1968.

LENT, P. C. Calving and related social behavior in the barren-ground caribou. *Zeitschrift für Tierpsychologie*, 1966, *23*, 701–756.

LOCKLEY, R. M. Social structure and stress in the rabbit warren. *Journal of Animal Ecology*, 1961, *30*, 385–423.

MANDLER, A. Parent and child in the development of the Oedipus complex. *Journal of Nervous and Mental Diseases*, 1963 *136*, 227–235.

MARLER, P., & HAMILTON, W. J., II. *Mechanisms of animal behavior.* New York: Wiley, 1966.

MCCARLEY, H. Annual cycle, population dynamics and adaptive behavior of *Citellus tridecemlineatus. Journal of Mammalogy*, 1966, *47*, 294–316.

MECH, L. D. *The wolves of Isle royale.* (Fauna of the National Parks of the United States, Fauna Series 7) Washington, D.C.: United States Government Printing Office, 1966.

MICHELSON, K., VUORENKOSKI, V., PARTANEN, T., VALANNE, E., & WASZ-HOCKERT, O. Identification of the baby's preverbal communication. (Trans. by Division of Research Services, National Institute of Mental Health) *Finsk Lakaresellsk Handl*, 1965, *109*, 43–47.

MOLTZ, H., LEVIN, R., & LEON, M. Differential effects of progesterone on the maternal behavior of primiparous and multiparous rats. *Journal of Comparative and Physiological Psychology*, 1969, *67*, 36–40.

MOLTZ, H., & WIENER, E. Effects of ovariectomy on maternal behavior of primiparous and multiparous rats. *Journal of Comparative and Physiological Psychology*, 1966, *62*, 382–387.

MOSS, H. A. Laboratory and field studies of mother-infant interaction. Bethesda, Md.: National Institute of Mental Health, 1964. (Mimeo)

———. Sex, age, and state as determinants of mother-infant interaction. *Merrill-Palmer Quarterly*, 1967, *13*, 19–36.

MOSS, H. A., & ROBSON, K. S. The role of protest behavior in the development of mother-infant attachment. Paper presented at the meeting of the American Psychological Association, San Francisco, 1968.

NEWTON, N. R., & NEWTON, M. Relation of the let-down reflex to the ability to breast feed. *Pediatrics,* 1950, *5,* 726–733.

NICOLL, C. S., & MEITES, J. Prolongation of lactation in the rat by litter replacement. *Proceedings of the Society for Experimental Biology and Medicine,* 1959, *101,* 81–82.

NOIROT, E. Changes in responsiveness to young in the adult mouse. I. The problematical effect of hormones. *Animal Behaviour,* 1964, *12,* 52–58. (a)

———. Changes in responsiveness to young in the adult mouse. IV. The effect of an initial contact with a strong stimulus. *Animal Behaviour,* 1964, *12,* 442–445. (b)

———. Changes in responsiveness to young in the adult mouse III. The effect of immediately preceding performances. *Animal Behaviour,* 1965, *24,* 318–325.

———. Ultrasounds in young rodents I. Changes with age in albino mice. *Animal Behaviour,* 1966, *14,* 459–462.

———. Ultrasounds in young rodents II. Changes with age in albino rats. *Animal Behaviour,* 1968, *16,* 129–134.

OSTWALD, P. F. *Soundmaking.* Springfield, Ill.: Charles C Thomas, 1963.

O'TOOLE, R., & DURBIN, R. Baby feeding and body sway: An experiment in George Herbert Mead's "Taking the role of the other." *Journal of Personality and Social Psychology,* 1968, *10,* 59–65.

PLOGG, D. W. Biological bases for instinct and behavior: Studies on the development of social behavior in squirrel monkeys. In J. Wortis (Ed.), *Recent advances in biological psychiatry.* Vol. 8. New York: Plenum Press, 1966.

PRECHTL, H. F. R. The mother-child interaction in babies with minimal brain damage. In B. M. Foss (Ed.), *Determinants of infants behavior.* II. New York: Wiley, 1963.

PROVENCE, S., & LIPTON, R. C. *Infants in institutions.* New York: International Universities Press, 1962.

RHEINGOLD, H. L. The effect of environmental stimulation upon social and exploratory behaviour in the human infant. In B. M. Foss (Ed.), *Determinants of infant behaviour.* I. New York: Wiley, 1961.

RICHARDS, M. P. M. Maternal behaviour in the golden hamster: Responsiveness to young in virgin, pregnant, and lactating females. *Animal Behaviour,* 1966, *14,* 310–313.

———. Maternal behaviour in rodents and lagomorphs. In A. McLaren (Ed.), *Advances in reproductive physiology.* Vol. 2. London: Logos Press, 1967.

RIDDLE, O., LAHR, E. L., & BATES, R. W. The role of hormones in the initiation of maternal behavior in rats. *American Journal of Physiology,* 1942, *137,* 299–317.

ROBSON, K. S., & MOSS, H. A. Subjective aspects of maternal attachment in man. Unpublished manuscript. National Institute of Mental Health, Bethesda, Maryland, 1969.

ROSENBLATT, J. S. Nonhormonal basis of maternal behavior in the rat. *Science,* 1967, *156,* 1512–1514.

ROSENBLATT, J. S., & LEHRMAN, D. S. Maternal behavior of the laboratory rat. In H. L. Rheingold (Ed.), *Maternal behavior in mammals.* New York: Wiley, 1963.

ROSENBLUM, L. A., & KAUFMAN, I. C. Laboratory observations of early mother-infant relations in pigtail and bonnet macaques. In S. A. Altmann (Ed.), *Social communication among primates.* Chicago: University of Chicago Press, 1967.

ROWELL, T. E. The family group in golden hamsters: Its formation and break-up. *Behaviour,* 1960, *17,* 81–94.

———. Forest living baboons in Uganda. *Journal of Zoology (London),* 1966, *149,* 344–364. (a)

———. Hierarchy in the organization of a captive baboon group. *Animal Behaviour,* 1966, *14,* 430–443. (b)

SACKETT, G., GRIFFIN, G. A., PRATT, C., JOSLYN, G. D., & RUPPENTHAL, G. Mother-infant and adult female choice behavior in rhesus monkeys after various rearing experiences. *Journal of Comparative and Physiological Psychology,* 1967, *63,* 376–381.

SAUER, E. G. F. Mother-infant relationship in galagos and the oral child-transport among primates. *Folia Primatologica,* 1967, *7,* 127–149.

SCHALLER, G. B. *The mountain gorilla.* Chicago: University of Chicago Press, 1963.

———. *The deer and the tiger.* Chicago: University of Chicago Press, 1967.

SCHNEIRLA, T. C., & ROSENBLATT, J. S. Behavioral organization and genesis of the social bond in insects and mammals. *American Journal of Orthopsychiatry,* 1961, *31,* 223–253.

———. "Critical periods" in the development of behavior. *Science,* 1963, *139,* 1110–1115.

SCHNEIRLA, T. C., ROSENBLATT, J. S., & TOBACH, E. Maternal behavior in the cat. In H. L. Rheingold (Ed.), *Maternal behavior in mammals.* New York: Wiley, 1963.

SCOTT, J. P., & FULLER, J. L. *Genetics and the social behavior of the dog.* Chicago: University of Chicago Press, 1965.

SEAY, B. Maternal behavior in primiparous and multiparous monkeys. *Folia Primatologica,* 1966, *4,* 146–168.

SEAY, B., ALEXANDER, B. K., & HARLOW, H. F. Maternal behavior of socially deprived rhesus monkeys. *Journal of Abnormal and Social Psychology,* 1964, *69,* 345–354.

SEITZ, P. F. D. The maternal instinct in animal subjects. I. *Psychosomatic Medicine,* 1958, *20,* 215–226.

SELYE, H., & MC KEOWN, T. Further studies on the influence of suckling. *Anatomical Record,* 1934, *60,* 323–332.

SHAINESS, N. The structure of the mothering encounter. *Journal of Nervous and Mental Diseases,* 1963, *136,* 146–161.

SMITH, F. V., VAN-TOLLER, C., & BOYES, T. The "critical period" in the attachment of lambs and ewes. *Animal Behaviour,* 1966, *14,* 120–125.

VALANNE, E. H., VUORENKOSKI, V., PARTANEN, T. J., LIND, J., & WASZ-HOCKERT, O. The ability of human mothers to identify the hunger cry signals of their own new-born infants during the lying-in period. *Experientia,* 1967, *23,* 768.

VAN HOOFF, J. A. R. A. M. The facial displays of catarrhine monkeys and apes. In D. Morris (Ed.), *Primate ethology.* Chicago: Aldine, 1967.

VAN LAWICK-GOODALL, J. Mother-offspring relationships in free-ranging chimpanzees. In D. Morris (Ed.), *Primate ethology.* Chicago: Aldine, 1967.

VYGOTSKY, L. S. *Thought and language.* Cambridge, Mass.: M.I.T. Press, 1962.

WASZ-HOCKERT, O., PARTANEN, T., VUORENKOSKI, V., VALANNE, E., & MICHELSON, K. Effect of training on ability to identify preverbal vocalizations. *Developmental Medicine and Child Neurology,* 1964, *6,* 393–396.

WIESNER, B. P., & SHEARD, N. M. *Maternal behaviour in the rat.* Edinburgh, Scotland: Oliver & Boyd, 1933.

CHAPTER 5: SUGGESTED FURTHER READING

ARIÈS, PHILLIPPE. *Centuries of Childhood.* New York: Random House, 1962.

BELL, N. W., and VOGEL, E. F. (Eds.) *The Family* (2nd ed.) Glencoe, Ill.: Free Press, 1968.

CLAUSEN, J. A. Family structure, socialization, and personality. In Hoffman, L. W., and Hoffman, M. L. (Eds.) *Review of Child Development Research.* Vol. 2. New York: Russell Sage Foundation, 1966. Pp. 1–54.

———. (Ed.) *Socialization and Society.* Boston: Little, Brown, 1968.

FESHBACH, S. Aggression. In Mussen, P. (Ed.) *Carmichael's Manual of Child Psychology,* Vol. 2. New York: Wiley, 1970. Pp. 159–259.

FREUD, A., and DANN, S. An experiment in group upbringing. *The Psychoanalytic Study of the Child.* New York: International University Press, 1951.

HESS, R., and HANDEL, G. *Family Worlds.* Chicago: University of Chicago Press, 1959.

HOFFMAN, M. Moral development. In Mussen, P. (Ed.) *Carmichael's Manual of Child Psychology,* Vol. 2. New York: Wiley, 1970. Pp. 261–359.

HOFFMAN, L. W., and LIPPITT, R. The measurement of family life variables. In Mussen, P. (Ed.) *Handbook of Research Methods in Child Development.* New York: Wiley, 1960. Pp. 945–1013.

MCCANDLESS, B. R. Childhood socialization. In Goslin, D. (Ed.) *Handbook of Socialization Theory and Research.* Chicago: Rand McNally, 1969. Pp. 791–819.

RHEINGOLD, H. L. The social and socializing infant. In Goslin, D. (Ed.) *Handbook of Socialization Theory and Research.* Chicago: Rand McNally, 1969. Pp. 779–790.

part two selected aspects of development

chapter six
socialization: beyond the family

Although, in the last chapter, we focused our attention on the family factors that influence socialization, do not think that the family is the only influence. The family may be the first and, perhaps, therefore one of the most important influences. However, each of us grows up, not in a vacuum known as home, but in a neighborhood with friends, schoolmates, teachers, and the ubiquitous television. Therefore, in this chapter, we have chosen articles that reflect the socialization inherent in some of these other features of the environment.

We are currently in a period of time where our "traditional" standards of sex role and behavior are being questioned by some people. Sex roles and standards are arbitrary entities determined by a certain culture. They are not absolutes, as can be witnessed by cross cultural data. There are or have been tribes and cultures where the women did (or do) the heavy labor such as lifting and plowing, while the men did lighter work. So, too, within a single society we see changes in sex-appropriate work and behaviors, such as the fact that secretaries were generally males a century ago.

Levitin and Chananie indicate that some school teachers like those children who exhibit appropriate sex-typed behavior, dependent girls, but also liked both achieving boys and girls. This may indicate that at least some teachers are liking and, probably in some way, reinforcing a behavior achievement that at one time was very much seen as "males only" behavior. The fact that they still liked "dependent" girls means that they are still rewarding some behaviors differentially by sex of child.

There is no fixed genetic pattern that says girls are and must be passive, dependent, and weak while boys are and must be dominant, aggressive, and strong. Both boys and girls are at birth equally capable of being all the above things. The article from *Ms.* that is included in this section is a hypothetical research project based on this idea. It raises many interesting questions: Why do we feel so frustrated not knowing a baby's sex? Why do we feel compelled to attribute sex-linked adjectives to a newborn? It is hoped the article will lead you off into many discussions on current and changing patterns of behavior.

The Walker article on body build and behavior suggests that both boys and girls with similar body builds have similar personality traits. It may be that part of one's socialization is dependent on one's body type. But this can lead to an issue as important as the sex-typing issue. Is it that one's body type in fact determines one's personality or is it that we tend to label children and others with certain body types as having certain characteristics? Maybe the same answer works here, that given a chance at nontyping, children of certain body builds can develop any type of personality, that all types of learning are equally available to all body builds, or perhaps that certain types of traits and behaviors are easier for people of certain builds than others. We have ended this section with an article on the Ik, a culture which has a perhaps slight resemblance to the ways ours is heading and it may be seen as a "chilling possible end for Man." It is included, not to imply that this must happen to all of us, but to indicate one of the ways in which a group of humans has dealt with the effects of overpopulation, density, and progress.

28. RESPONSES OF FEMALE PRIMARY SCHOOL TEACHERS TO SEX-TYPED BEHAVIORS IN MALE AND FEMALE CHILDREN

TERESA E. LEVITIN and J. D. CHANANIE

The responses of 40 female primary school teachers to descriptions of aggressive or dependent behaviors attributed to hypothetical male or female students was studied using a 2 × 2 factorial design. Ten teachers were randomly assigned to 1 of the 4 sex (male or female) and behavior (aggression or dependency) pairings. Half the teachers in each group were also randomly assigned a female-name/achievement-behavior pairing; half, a male-name/achievement-behavior pairing. Children showing sex-typed behavior (the aggressive boy and dependent girl) were judged typical. Particular behaviors were significantly more approved; particular sex/behavior pairings were significantly more liked. Results were interpreted in terms of teachers' professional and personal values.

The aims and activities of primary school teachers include transmitting cultural values and norms as well as providing instruction in academic skills such as reading and writing (Clausen, 1968). Among the most central of values and norms are those that define and regulate sex-typed behaviors. Sex-typed behaviors are those behaviors considered desirable and appropriate when emitted by one sex, undesirable and inappropriate when emitted by the other sex.

There may be disagreement about whether any particular behavior is more appropriate or even more common in males or in females. However, two classes of behaviors—dependency and aggression—are so regularly associated with females and males, respectively, that these behaviors have become the major referents for sex-typing; and "most research on sex differences has dwelt on aggression and dependency". (Mischel, 1970, p. 6). These sex-typed behaviors are apparent in children by the time they are 5–7 years old (Hartup & Zook, 1960; Kagan, Hosken, & Watson, 1961). Preschool boys are rather consistent in aggressive behaviors across situations but show almost no consistent patterns of dependent behaviors, and the reverse is true for preschool girls (Lansky, Crandall, Kagan, & Baker, 1961; Sears, Rau, & Alpert, 1965).

It may be clear that young boys tend to be aggressive and young girls tend to be acquiescent and dependent, that boys tend to be active and ignore the teacher and girls tend to be quiet and dependent on the teacher (Brown, 1957). However, how the teachers themselves respond to, teach, and encourage such sex-typed behaviors is less clear. There are two different views on the general expectations of primary school teachers about how boys and girls should behave. The first view is that teachers fundamentally do not evaluate young children in terms of sex-typed behavior. They may recognize that aggression is typical of young boys and that dependency is typical of young girls, but they neither teach such behavior nor respond more positively to children who behave in sex-typed ways than to children who do not. The second view is that teachers promulgate traditional sex-typed behaviors, expecting, encouraging, and rewarding assertiveness in little boys and dependency in little girls (Rossi, 1964). The present investigation was designed to see which of these two views better described the responses of female primary school teachers to the sex-typed behaviors of aggression and dependency in male and female students.

Predictions

To see how teachers responded to these two sex-typed behaviors, descriptions of hypothetical children were presented. This strategy was based on the notion that teachers will perceive hypothetical students in much the same way that they perceive actual students. Consequently, the teachers will agree that aggression is more typical of the hypothetical boy than of the hypothetical girl and that dependency is more typical of the hypothetical girl than of the hypothetical boy presented in this study, a response that does not indicate their evaluation of the appropriateness of such sex-typed behavior.

Predictions 1 and 2 present the two contrasting views of how teachers actually evaluate these sex-typed behaviors:

1. If teachers prefer that children exhibit sex-typed behaviors, they will respond more positively to the aggressive boy and the dependent girl than to the aggressive girl and the dependent boy. There will be a significant sex-and-behavior interaction effect.

2. If teachers do not prefer that children exhibit sex-typed behaviors, they will respond more positively to particular behaviors than to particular sex/behavior combinations. There will be a significant behavior main effect. Dependent behavior will be preferred over aggressive behavior because aggressive children are more difficult to teach. In addition, responses to a third behavior, achievement behavior, were also assessed. Since children who try to do well permit the teacher to exercise her teaching skills, it was assumed that achievement behavior would be the most preferred behavior for both the hypothetical boy and girl.

Method

Subjects

The subjects were 40 white, female, first- and second-grade teachers selected from nine suburban, middle-class schools that were part of the same large Midwestern public school system. The teachers had 1–25 years of teaching experience; the modal interval of teaching experience was 6–10 years.

Procedure and Design

Every first- and second-grade teacher in each of the schools selected was simultaneously administered a 10-minute questionnaire by the second author within a 2-week period. The first page of the questionnaire was identical for all teachers; each was asked to assume that children, to be described on the next pages, were children in her classroom and to answer a few questions about each child. Confidentiality was guaranteed, questions asked by the teachers were answered at the end of the session, and a summary of this study has been sent to all the participating teachers.

Each of the 40 teachers rated two hypothetical children. Each child was described as performing one of three different behaviors—dependency, aggression, or achievement.

The dependent and aggressive behaviors were used in a two-by-two factorial design and provided the major data for this study. In this analysis of variance, the first factor was sex of child as indicated by either a male or a female name. The second factor was behavior of child as indicated by a short phrase describing either dependent or aggressive activity. Ten teachers were randomly assigned to each of these four sex/behavior pairings.

In addition to evaluating either the aggressive or the dependent behavior paired with either a male or a female name, each teacher rated a second hypothetical child who was described as performing an achievement behavior. Half of the 10 teachers in each of the four groups defined by the two-by-two factorial design were randomly assigned a female-name/achievement-behavior pairing. The other half were randomly assigned a male-name/achievement-behavior pairing. Achievement behavior was used for information about a behavior that, particularly in a classroom, was not clearly sex-typed, and responses to achievement behaviors were not part of the two-by-two analysis of variance.

In sum, each teacher received one of the following four sets of descriptions of two hypothetical children from this universe of six sex/behavior pairings: (1) a male name paired with aggressive behavior and either a male or female name paired with achievement behavior; (2) a female name paired with aggressive behavior and either a male or female name paired with achievement behavior; (3) a male name paired with dependent behavior and either a male or female name paired with achievement behavior, (4) a female name paired with dependent behavior and either a male or female name paired with achievement behavior. The two sex/behavior pairings given each teacher were rotated to control for order effects. Using identical information paired with either a male or female name was suggested in a study by Goldberg (1968).

The following sentences were used to describe achievement, aggressive, and dependent behaviors:

Joan (Bob) is a good student. She (he) often tries harder than other children in her (his) class.

Tom (Alice) is an assertive child. He (she) is sometimes disobedient to the teacher and often aggressive with other children in his (her) class.

Carol (John) is a dependent child. She (he) is obedient to the teacher and often acquiescent with other children in her (his) class.

The dependent variables were the responses of the teachers to these various sex/behavior pairings. The teachers were asked what sex/behavior pairings they preferred (questions 1–2). They were also asked what sex/behavior pairings they typically encountered (question 3). The following three questions were constructed: (1) How much do you approve of (name of child)'s behavior? (2) How much do you think you would like (name of child)? (3) How typical is (name of child) of boys (or girls) his (or her) age you have taught? Each item was measured by a seven-point scale, ranging, for example, from "greatly approve" to "greatly disapprove." Responses were coded so that a high score represented approval, liking, or typicality. An additional open-ended question asking teachers about the purpose of the study indicated that none thought sex-typed behaviors were being examined.

Results

Table 6.1 presents mean scores on each of the three measures of response for each sex/behavior pairing. Achievement behavior was seen as somewhat typical of both the boy and the girl and met with equal approval in either sex. However, the achieving girl was significantly more liked than the achieving boy, $t(38) = 2.04$, $p < .05$

In a two-by-two analysis of variance on the ratings of typicality, the hypothetical children described as behaving in appropriate sex-typed ways (the aggressive boy and the dependent girl) were seen as significantly more typical of real children the teachers had taught than the hypothetical children described as behaving in inappropriate sex-typed ways (the aggressive girl and the dependent boy), $F(1,36) = 4.35$, $p < .05$.

Predictions 1 and 2 were tested by a two-by-two analysis of variance on the ratings of the teachers' approval and liking

Table 6.1. Teachers' mean ratings of hypothetical children characterized by sex and type of behavior

Sex/Behavior Pairing	Response to Child		
	Approval	Liking	Typicality
Male/achievement	6.7	6.3	4.8
Female/achievement	6.7	6.8	5.0
Male/aggression	2.8	4.7	5.8
Female/aggression	2.9	4.2	4.2
Male/dependency	3.6	4.6	4.1
Female/dependency	4.8	5.8	4.4

Note.—Each mean for the achievement scores is based on 20 evaluations; each mean for the aggression and for the dependency scores is based on 10 evaluations.

of the hypothetical children. The factors were two categories of sex and two kinds of behavior, dependency and aggression.

In the analysis of ratings of approvals, there was no significant interaction of sex and behavior, $F(1,36) = 3.03$, N.S. Therefore, prediction 1, that teachers would respond more favorably to appropriate sex-typed behavior (the aggressive boy and the dependent girl) than to inappropriate sex-typed behavior (the aggressive girl and the dependent boy), was not supported.

Prediction 2, that teachers would respond to particular behaviors rather than to particular sex/behavior combinations was supported by the significant behavior effect, $F(1,36) = 8.37$, $p < .05$. As predicted, dependent behavior rated significantly more approval than aggressive behavior. There was no significant main effect due to sex, $F(1,36) = 1.94$, N.S. Achievement behavior was the most preferred behavior for both the hypothetical boy and girl. Table 6.1 indicates the expected, unqualified approval of achievement behavior.

The pattern of results for liking the child were different from those for approving the child's behavior. The analysis of variance applied to the teachers' ratings on liking of child showed a significant interaction effect of sex and behavior, $F(1,36) = 4.67$, $p < .05$. Prior linear contrasts showed that the dependent girl was far more liked than the aggressive girl, $F(1,36) = 5.77$, $p < .05$, but this result provided only partial confirmation of prediction 1 because the aggressive boy was not significantly more liked than the dependent boy, $F(1,36) = 0.02$, N.S.

In the analysis of ratings of liking, there was no significant main effect due to behavior, $F(1,36) = 2.54$, N.S., and prediction 2 was not supported. There was also no significant main effect due to sex, $F(1,36) = 0.55$, N.S. Achievement behavior was, as expected, liked far more than dependent or aggressive behaviors. All correlations between scores for approval and for liking were low and nonsignificant.

Discussion

The requirements of the role of teacher and the putative values of the teachers themselves may answer two questions posed by the obtained results: (1) Why was the achieving girl significantly preferred over the other aggression or dependency and sex pairings? (2) Why were these sex/behavior preferences found only in the ratings of liking the child and not in the ratings of approving the child's behavior?

To answer the first question, it is important to note that schools are structured to encourage both achievement and dependency, the latter behavior facilitating the discipline and obedience required by most teachers (Postman & Weingartner,

1966; Sexton, 1969). A teacher in the role of teacher may best like achieving and dependent behaviors regardless of the sex of the child.

However, as Clausen has pointed out, most primary school teachers are also women drawn from the middle class; and "the implications of this sex linkage are worthy of more searching analysis than they have received. The classroom—its curriculum, activities, and trappings—tends to be markedly oriented to the interests and dispositions of the middle class and especially those of middle class girls" (1968, p. 156). Although as women teachers may identify with female students regardless of their behavior, as products of the middle class these same teachers may also adhere to middle-class values about what constitutes appropriate sex-typed behavior in children, tending to prefer children who behave in traditionally sex-typed ways.

The dependent girl might have been well liked for two reasons. First, she was exhibiting behavior congruent with the teachers' professional values about how students ought to behave. Second, she was exhibiting behavior congruent with the teachers' personal values about how girls ought to behave. In contrast, the aggressive girl, who was least liked, might have been violating both the professional and the personal values of the teacher. The hypothetical boys in the study might have violated either classroom norms (the aggressive boy) or personal values of the teachers (the dependent boy), but not both.

Both the achieving girl and the achieving boy were exhibiting the most preferred behavior, behavior congruent with the teachers' professional values about how students ought to behave. However, the achieving girl might have been better liked because the female teachers were apt to identify with members of their own sex.

The personal and professional orientations of these teachers may also answer the second question posed at the beginning of this section, that is, why preferences for particular sex/behavior pairings were reflected in the ratings of liking of the child but not in the ratings of approval of the child's behavior. Teachers are expected not to differentiate among children according to ascriptive criteria such as race or sex. Approval or disapproval of a particular behavior, regardless of the sex of the child performing that behavior, is a professionally appropriate response. However, how much a teacher likes a particular child is a more personal matter. So long as she does not respond to the same behaviors in liked and disliked children in different ways, so long as she displays neither favoritism nor discrimination, she is not violating her professional code. In order to understand the responses of teachers to their students, it may be critical to distinguish between a professional response of approval and a more personal or private response of liking.

Summary

Two predictions about the responses of teachers to various sex/behavior pairings were tested. In support of prediction 2, teachers clearly preferred dependent to aggressive behavior; they showed significantly more approval for dependent behavior, regardless of the sex of the hypothetical child. Achievement behavior was the most approved behavior, regardless of the sex of the child. However, in support of prediction 1, teachers clearly preferred the dependent girl to the other sex/behavior pairings; they showed significantly more liking for the dependent girl. Achieving girls were also significantly more liked than achieving boys. The response of approval was associated with particular behaviors, not particular sex/behavior pairings. The response of liking was associated with particular sex/behavior pairings, not particular behaviors. These results indicate that the type of response that is of interest must be clearly delineated, that different kinds of responses are associated with different patterns of relationships. The hypothetical dependent girl and aggressive boy were judged typical; these same sex/behavior pairings are typical of actual children.

A final word of caution is necessary: these results were based on data from white, middle-class, female teachers in suburban, middle-class schools. One cannot assume that these same results would be obtained from different populations of teachers in different kinds of school settings. Also, the responses of these teachers to questions, rather than their actual classroom behaviors, were the dependent variables. These limitations notwithstanding, this study has presented important data in support of predictions about the responses of female primary school teachers to sex-typed behaviors.

References

BROWN, D. Masculinity-feminity development in children. *Journal of Consulting Psychology,* 1957, *21,* 197–202.

CLAUSEN, J. A. Perspectives on childhood socialization. In J. A. Clausen (Ed.), *Socialization and society.* Boston: Little, Brown, 1968. Pp. 130–181.

GOLDBERG, P. Are women prejudiced against women? *Trans-Action,* 1968, *5,* 28–30.

HARTUP, W. W., & ZOOK, E. A. Sex role preferences in three- and four-year-old children. *Journal of Consulting Psychology,* 1960, *24,* 420–426.

KAGAN, J.; HOSKEN, B.; & WATSON, S. The child's symbolic conceptualization of the parents. *Child Development,* 1961, *32,* 625–636.

LANSKY, L. M.; CRANDALL, V. J.; KAGAN, J.; & BAKER, C. T. Sex differences in aggression and its correlates in middle-class adolescents. *Child Development,* 1961, *32,* 45–68.

MISCHEL, M. Sex-typing and socialization. In P. H. Mussen (Ed.), *Carmichael's manual of child psychology.* Vol. 2. New York: Wiley, 1970. Pp. 3–72.

POSTMAN, N., & WEINGARTNER, C. *Teaching as a subversive activity.* New York: Delacorte, 1966.

ROSSI, A. Equality between the sexes: an immodest proposal. *Daedalus,* 1964, *93,* 607–652.

SEARS, R. R.; RAU, L.; & ALPERT, R. *Identification and child rearing.* Stanford, Calif.: Stanford University Press, 1965.

SEXTON, P. *The feminized male.* New York: Vintage, 1969.

29. X: A FABULOUS CHILD'S STORY

LOIS GOULD

Once upon a time, a baby named X was born. This baby was named X so that nobody could tell whether it was a boy or a girl. Its parents could tell, of course, but they couldn't tell anybody else. They couldn't even tell Baby X, at first.

You see, it was all part of a very important Secret Scientific Xperiment, known officially as Project Baby X. The smartest scientists had set up this Xperiment at a cost of Xactly 23 billion dollars and 72 cents, which might seem like a lot for just one baby, even a very important Xperimental baby. But when you remember the prices of things like strained carrots and stuffed bunnies, and popcorn for the movies and booster shots for camp, let alone 28 shiny quarters from the tooth fairy, you begin to see how it adds up.

Also, long before Baby X was born, all those scientists had to be paid to work out the details of the Xperiment, and to write the *Official Instruction Manual* for Baby X's parents and, most important of all, to find the right set of parents to bring up Baby X. These parents had to be selected very carefully. Thousands of volunteers had to take thousands of tests and answer thousands of tricky questions. Almost everybody failed because, it turned out, almost everybody really wanted either a baby boy or a baby girl, and not Baby X at all. Also, almost everybody was afraid that a Baby X would be a lot more trouble than a boy or a girl. (They were probably right, the scientists admitted, but Baby X needed parents who wouldn't *mind* the Xtra trouble.)

There were families with grandparents named Milton and Agatha, who didn't see why the baby couldn't be named Milton or Agatha instead of X, even if it *was* an X. There were families with aunts who insisted on knitting tiny dresses and uncles who insisted on sending tiny baseball mitts. Worst of all, there were families that already had other children who couldn't be trusted to keep the secret. Certainly not if they knew the secret was worth 23 billion dollars and 72 cents—and all you had to do was take one little peek at Baby X in the bathtub to know if it was a boy or a girl.

But, finally, the scientists found the Joneses, who really wanted to raise an X more than any other kind of baby—no matter how much trouble it would be. Ms. and Mr. Jones had to promise they would take equal turns caring for X, and feeding it, and singing it lullabies. And they had to promise never to hire any baby-sitters. The government scientists knew perfectly well that a baby-sitter would probably peek at X in the bathtub, too.

The day the Joneses brought their baby home, lots of friends and relatives came over to see it. None of them knew about the secret Xperiment, though. So the first thing they asked was what kind of a baby X was. When the Joneses smiled and said, "It's an X!" nobody knew what to say. They couldn't say, "Look at her cute little dimples!" And they couldn't say, "Look at his husky little biceps!" And they couldn't even say just plain "kitchy-coo." In fact, they all thought the Joneses were playing some kind of rude joke.

But, of course, the Joneses were not joking. "It's an X" was absolutely all they would say. And that made the friends and relatives very angry. The relatives all felt embarrassed about having an X in the family. "People will think there's something wrong with it!" some of them whispered. "There *is* something wrong with it!" others whispered back.

"Nonsense!" the Joneses told them all cheerfully. "What could possibly be wrong with this perfectly adorable X?"

Nobody could answer that, except Baby X, who had just finished its bottle. Baby X's answer was a loud, satisfied burp.

Clearly, nothing at all was wrong. Nevertheless, none of the relatives felt comfortable about buying a present for a Baby X. The cousins who sent the baby a tiny football helmet would not come and visit any more. And the neighbors who sent a pink-flowered romper suit pulled their shades down when the Joneses passed their house.

The *Official Instruction Manual* had warned the new parents that this would happen, so they didn't fret about it. Besides, they were too busy with Baby X and the hundreds of different Xercises for treating it properly.

Ms. and Mr. Jones had to be Xtra careful about how they played with little X. They knew that if they kept bouncing it up in the air and saying how *strong* and *active* it was, they'd be treating it more like a boy than an X. But if all they did was cuddle it and kiss it and tell it how *sweet* and *dainty* it was, they'd be treating it more like a girl than an X.

On page 1,654 of the *Official Instruction Manual,* the scientists prescribed: "plenty of bouncing and plenty of cuddling, *both.* X ought to be strong and sweet and active. Forget about *dainty* altogether."

Meanwhile, the Joneses were worrying about other problems. Toys, for instance. And clothes. On his first shopping trip, Mr. Jones told the store clerk, "I need some clothes and toys for my new baby." The clerk smiled and said, "Well, now, is it a boy or a girl?" "It's an X," Mr. Jones said, smiling back. But the clerk got all red in the face and said huffily, "In *that* case, I'm afraid I can't help you, sir." So. Mr. Jones wandered helplessly up and down the aisles trying to find what X needed. But everything in the store was piled up in sections marked "Boys" or "Girls." There were "Boys' Pajamas" and "Girls' Underwear" and "Boys' Fire Engines" and "Girls' Housekeeping Sets." Mr. Jones went home without buying anything for X. That night he and Ms. Jones consulted page 2,326 of the *Official Instruction Manual.* "Buy plenty of everything!" it said firmly.

So they bought plenty of sturdy blue pajamas in the Boys' Department and cheerful flowered underwear in the Girls' Department. And they bought all kinds of toys. A boy doll that made pee-pee and cried, "Pa-pa." And a girl doll that talked in three languages and said, "I am the Pres-i-dent of Gen-er-al Mo-tors." They also bought a storybook about a brave princess who rescued a handsome prince from his ivory tower, and another one about a sister and brother who grew up to be a baseball star and a ballet star, and you had to guess which was which.

The head scientists of Project Baby X checked all their purchases and told them to keep up the good work. They also reminded the Joneses to see page 4,629 of the *Manual,* where it said, "Never make Baby X feel *embarrassed* or *ashamed* about what it wants to play with. And if X gets dirty climbing rocks, never say 'Nice little Xes don't get dirty climbing rocks.'"

Likewise, it said, "If X falls down and cries, never say 'Brave little Xes don't cry.' Because, of course, nice little Xes *do* get dirty, and brave little Xes *do* cry. No matter how dirty X gets, or how hard it cries, don't worry. It's all part of the Xperiment."

Whenever the Joneses pushed Baby X's stroller in the park, smiling strangers would come over and coo: "Is that a boy or a girl?" The Joneses would smile back and say, "It's an X." The strangers would stop smiling then, and often snarl something nasty—as if the Joneses had snarled at *them.*

By the time X grew big enough to play with other children, the Joneses' troubles had grown bigger, too. Once a little girl grabbed X's shovel in the sandbox, and zonked X on the head with it. "Now, now, Tracy," the little girl's mother began to scold, "little girls mustn't hit little—" and she turned to ask X, "Are you a little boy or a little girl, dear?"

Mr. Jones, who was sitting near the sandbox, held his breath and crossed his fingers.

X smiled politely at the lady, even though X's head had never been zonked so hard in its life. "I'm a little X," X replied.

"You're a *what?*" the lady exclaimed angrily. "You're a little b-r-a-t, you mean!"

"But little girls mustn't hit little Xes, either!" said X, retrieving the shovel with another polite smile. "What good does hitting do, anyway?"

X's father, who was still holding his breath, finally let it out, uncrossed his fingers, and grinned back at X.

And at their next secret Project Baby X meeting, the scientists grinned, too. Baby X was doing fine.

But then it was time for X to start school. The Joneses were really worried about this, because school was even more full of rules for boys and girls, and there were no rules for Xes. The teacher would tell boys to form one line, and girls to form another line. There would be boys' games and girls' games, and boys' secrets and girls' secrets. The school library would have a list of recommended books for girls, and a different list of recommended books for boys. There would even be a bathroom marked BOYS and another one marked GIRLS. Pretty soon boys and girls would hardly talk to each other. What would happen to poor little X?

The Joneses spent weeks consulting their *Instruction Manual* (there were 249½ pages of advice under "First Day of School"), and attending urgent special conferences with the smart scientists of Project Baby X.

The scientists had to make sure that X's mother had taught X how to throw and catch a ball properly, and that X's father had been sure to teach X what to serve at a doll's tea party. X had to know how to shoot marbles and how to jump rope and, most of all, what to say when the Other Children asked whether X was a Boy or a Girl.

Finally, X was ready. The Joneses helped X button on a nice new pair of red-and-white checked overalls, and sharpened six pencils for X's nice new pencilbox, and marked X's name clearly on all the books in its nice new bookbag. X brushed its teeth and combed its hair, which just about covered its ears, and remembered to put a napkin in its lunchbox.

The Joneses had asked X's teacher if the class could line up alphabetically, instead of forming separate lines for boys and girls. And they had asked if X could use the principal's bathroom, because it wasn't marked anything except BATHROOM. X's teacher promised to take care of all those problems. But nobody could help X with the biggest problem of all—Other Children.

Nobody in X's class had ever known an X before. What would they think? How would X make friends?

You couldn't tell what X was by studying its clothes—overalls don't even button right-to-left, like girls' clothes, or left-to-right, like boys' clothes. And you couldn't guess whether X had a girl's short haircut or a boy's long haircut. And it was very hard to tell by the games X liked to play. Either X played ball very well for a girl, or else X played house very well for a boy.

Some of the children tried to find out by asking X tricky questions, like "Who's your favorite sports star?" That was easy. X had two favorite sports stars, a girl jockey named Robyn Smith and a boy archery champion named Robin Hood. Then they asked, "What's your favorite TV program?" And that was even easier. X's favorite TV program was "Lassie," which stars a girl dog played by a boy dog.

When X said that its favorite toy was a doll, everyone decided that X must be a girl. But then X said that the doll was really a robot, and that X had computerized it, and that it was programmed to bake fudge brownies and then clean up the kitchen. After X told them that, the other children gave up guessing what X was. All that they knew was they'd sure like to see X's doll.

After school, X wanted to play with the other children. "How about shooting some baskets in the gym?" X asked the girls. But all they did was make faces and giggle behind X's back.

"How about weaving some baskets in the arts and crafts room?" X asked the boys. But they all made faces and giggled behind X's back, too,

That night, Ms. and Mr. Jones asked X how things had gone at school. X told them sadly that the lessons were okay, but otherwise school was a terrible place for an X. It seemed as if Other Children would never want an X for a friend.

Once more, the Joneses reached for their *Instruction Manual.* Under "Other Children," they found the following message: "What did you Xpect? *Other Children* have to obey all the silly boy-girl rules, because their parents taught them to. Lucky X—you don't have to stick to the rules at all! All you have to do is be yourself. P.S. We're not saying it'll be easy."

X liked being itself. But X cried a lot that night, partly because it felt afraid. So X's father held X tight, and cuddled it, and couldn't help crying a little, too. And X's mother cheered them both up by reading an Xciting story about an enchanted prince called Sleeping Handsome, who woke up when Princess Charming kissed him.

The next morning, they all felt much better, and little X went back to school with a brave smile and a clean pair of red-and-white checked overalls.

There was a seven-letter-word spelling bee in class that day. And a seven-lap boys' relay race in the gym. And a seven-layer-cake baking contest in the girls' kitchen corner. X won the spelling bee. X also won the relay race. And X almost won the baking contest, except it forgot to light the oven. Which only proves that nobody's perfect.

One of the Other Children noticed something else, too. He said: "Winning or losing doesn't seem to count to X. X seems to have fun being good at boys' skills *and* girls' skills."

"Come to think of it," said another one of the Other Children, "maybe X is having twice as much fun as we are!"

So after school that day, the girl who beat X at the baking contest gave X a big slice of her prizewinning cake. And the boy X beat in the relay race asked X to race him home.

From then on, some really funny things began to happen. Susie, who sat next to X in class, suddenly refused to wear pink dresses to school any more. She insisted on wearing red-and-white checked overalls —just like X's. Overalls, she told her parents, were much better for climbing monkey bars.

Then Jim, the class football nut, started wheeling his little sister's doll carriage around the football field. He'd put on his entire football uniform, except for the helmet. Then he'd put the helmet *in* the carriage, lovingly tucked under an old set of shoulder pads. Then he'd start jogging around the field, pushing the carriage and singing "Rockabye Baby" to his football helmet. He told his family that X did the same thing, so it must be okay. After all, X was now the team's star quarterback.

Susie's parents were horrified by her behavior, and Jim's parents were worried sick about his. But the worst came when the twins, Joe and Peggy, decided to share everything with each other. Peggy used Joe's hockey skates, and his microscope, and took half his newspaper route. Joe used Peggy's needlepoint kit, and her cookbooks, and took two of her three babysitting jobs. Peggy started running the lawn mower, and Joe started running the vacuum cleaner.

Their parents weren't one bit pleased with Peggy's wonderful biology experiments, or with Joe's terrific needlepoint pillows. They didn't care that Peggy mowed the lawn better, and that Joe vacuumed the carpet better. In fact, they were furious. It's all that little X's fault, they agreed. Just because X doesn't know what it is, or what it's supposed to be, it wants to get everybody *else* mixed up, too!

Peggy and Joe were forbidden to play with X any more. So was Susie, and then Jim, and then *all* the Other Children. But it was too late; the Other Children stayed mixed up and happy and free, and refused to go back to the way they'd been before X.

Finally, Joe and Peggy's parents decided to call an emergency meeting of the school's Parents' Association, to discuss "The X Problem." They sent a report to the principal stating that X was a "disruptive influence." They demanded immediate action. The Joneses, they said, should be *forced* to tell whether X was a boy or a girl. And then X should be *forced* to behave like whichever it was. If the Joneses refused to tell, the Parents' Association said, then X must take an Xamination. The school psychiatrist must Xamine it physically and mentally, and issue a full report. If X's test showed it was a boy, it would have to obey all the boys' rules. If it proved to be a girl, X would have to obey all the girls' rules.

And if X turned out to be some kind of mixed-up misfit, then X should be Xpelled from the school. Immediately!

The principal was very upset. Disruptive influence? Mixed-up misfit? But X was an Xcellent student. All the teachers said it was a delight to have X in their classes. X was president of the student council. X had won first prize in the talent show, and second prize in the art show, and honorable mention in the science fair, and six athletic events on field day, including the potato race.

Nevertheless, insisted the Parents' Association, X is a Problem Child. X is the Biggest Problem Child we have ever seen!

So the principal reluctantly notified X's parents that numerous complaints about X's behavior had come to the school's attention. And that after the psychiatrist's Xamination, the school would decide what to do about X.

The Joneses reported this at once to the scientists, who referred them to page 85,759 of the *Instruction Manual.* "Sooner or later," it said, "X will have to be Xamined by a psychiatrist. This may be the only way any of us will know for sure whether X is mixed up—or whether everyone else is."

The night before X was to be Xamined, the Joneses tried not to let X see how worried they were. "What if—?" Mr. Jones would say. And Ms. Jones would reply, "No use worrying." Then a few minutes later, Ms. Jones would say, "What if—?" and Mr. Jones would reply, "No use worrying."

X just smiled at them both, and hugged them hard and didn't say much of anything. X was thinking, What if—? And then X thought: No use worrying.

At Xactly 9 o'clock the next day, X reported to the school psychiatrist's office. The principal, along with a committee from the Parents' Association, X's teacher, X's classmates, and Ms. and Mr. Jones, waited in the hall outside. Nobody knew the details of the tests X was to be given, but everybody knew they'd be *very* hard, and that they'd reveal Xactly what everyone wanted to know about X, but were afraid to ask.

It was terribly quiet in the hall. Almost spooky. Once in a while, they would hear a strange noise inside the room. There were buzzes. And a beep or two. And several bells. An occasional light would flash under the door. The Joneses thought it was a white light, but the principal thought it was blue. Two or three children swore it was either yellow or green. And the Parents' Committee missed it completely.

Through it all, you could hear the psychiatrist's low voice, asking hundreds of questions, and X's higher voice, answering hundreds of answers.

The whole thing took so long that everyone knew it must be the most complete Xamination anyone had ever had to take. Poor X, the Joneses thought. Serves X right, the Parents' Committee thought. I wouldn't like to be in X's overalls right now, the children thought.

At last, the door opened. Everyone crowded around to hear the results. X didn't look any different; in fact, X was smiling. But the psychiatrist looked terrible. He looked as if he was crying! "What happened?" everyone began shouting. Had X done something disgraceful? "I wouldn't be a bit surprised!" muttered Peggy and Joe's parents. "Did X flunk the *whole* test?" cried Susie's parents. "Or just the most important part?" yelled Jim's parents.

"Oh, dear," sighed Mr. Jones.

"Oh, dear," sighed Ms. Jones.

"*Sssh,*" ssshed the principal. "The psychiatrist is trying to speak."

Wiping his eyes and clearing his throat, the psychiatrist began, in a hoarse whisper. "In my opinion," he whispered—you could tell he must be very upset—"in my opinion, young X here—"

"Yes? Yes?" shouted a parent impatiently.

"*Sssh!*" ssshed the principal.

"Young *Sssh* here, I mean young X," said the doctor, frowning, "is just about—"

"Just about *what?* Let's have it!" shouted another parent.

". . . just about the *least* mixed-up child I've ever Xamined!" said the psychiatrist.

"Yay for X!" yelled one of the children. And then the others began yelling, too. Clapping and cheering and jumping up and down.

"SSSH!" SSShed the principal, but nobody did.

The Parents' Committee was angry and bewildered. How *could* X have passed the whole Xamination? Didn't X have an *identity* problem? Wasn't X mixed up at *all*? Wasn't X *any* kind of a misfit? How could it *not* be, when it didn't even *know* what it was? And why was the psychiatrist crying?

Actually, he had stopped crying and was smiling politely through his tears. "Don't you see?" he said, "I'm crying because it's wonderful! X has absolutely no identity problem! X isn't one bit mixed up! As for being a misfit—ridiculous! X knows perfectly well what it is! Don't you, X?" The doctor winked. X winked back.

"But what *is* X?" shrieked Peggy and Joe's parents. "*We* still want to know what it is!"

"Ah, yes," said the doctor, winking again. "Well, don't worry. You'll all know one of these days. And you won't need me to tell you."

"What? What does he mean?" some of the parents grumbled suspiciously.

Susie and Peggy and Joe all answered at once. "He means that by the time X's sex matters, it won't be a secret any more!"

With that, the doctor began to push through the crowd toward X's parents. "How do you do," he said, somewhat stiffly. And then he reached out to hug them both. "If I ever have an X of my own," he whispered, "I sure hope you'll lend me your instruction manual."

Needless to say, the Joneses were very happy. The Project Baby X scientists were rather pleased, too. So were Susie, Jim, Peggy, Joe, and all the Other Children. The Parents' Association wasn't, but they had promised to accept the psychiatrist's report, and not make any more trouble. They even invited Ms. and Mr. Jones to become honorary members, which they did.

Later that day, all X's friends put on their red-and-white checked overalls and went over to see X. They found X in the back yard, playing with a very tiny baby that none of them had ever seen before. The baby was wearing very tiny red-and-white checked overalls.

"How do you like our new baby?" X asked the Other Children proudly.

"It's got cute dimples," said Jim.

"It's got husky biceps, too," said Susie.

"What kind of baby is it?" asked Joe and Peggy.

X frowned at them. "Can't you tell?" Then X broke into a big, mischievous grin. *"It's a Y!"*

30. PYGMALION BLACK AND WHITE

PAMELA C. RUBOVITS and MARTIN L. MAEHR

As a follow-up to work by Rosenthal and others, the present study observed teacher behavior following the manipulation of an expectancy regarding student potential. As in a previous study (Rubovits & Maehr), teachers gave preferential treatment to "gifted" students. Additionally, it was found that this pattern of treatment depended to some extent on the race of students. In general, black students were treated less positively than whites, with blacks labeled "gifted" apparently subjected to more discrimination than those labeled "nongifted." Moreover, the organismic variable of dogmatism *was found to play an important role in moderating the teacher's behavior in response to black students and white students. High-dogmatic teachers, while encouraging whites, tended to ignore blacks.*

It is not surprising that research on experimenter expectancies (Rosenthal, 1966; Rosenthal & Fode, 1963; Rosenthal & Lawson, 1964) has been quickly applied to the classroom, with some studies finding that students perform in line with their teachers' expectations for them (Meichenbaum, Bowers, & Ross, 1969; Rosenthal & Jacobson, 1968). These findings, controversial though they may be (Claiborne, 1969; Elashoff & Snow, 1970; Rosenthal, 1969; Snow, 1969; Thorndike, 1968, 1969), provide a perspective on a problem of major concern: the teaching of black students by white teachers. Black students have been found to believe that their white teachers have low estimates of their ability and worth (Brown, 1968; Davidson & Lang, 1960). It has also been well documented that white teachers expect less of lower-class children than they do of middle-class children (Becker, 1952; Deutsch, 1963; Warner, Havighurst, & Loeb, 1944; Wilson, 1963). In line with Rosenthal and Jacobson's proposal (1968) that teacher expectations affect teacher behavior in such a way that it is highly likely that student performance is in turn affected, it would seem probable that differential teacher expectation for black students and white students is related to differential school achievement. Few, if any, studies have, however, directly observed and compared teacher-expectancy effects on black students and white students. The present study was designed to do just that, and it yielded surprising results—results that can be interpreted as a paradigmatic instance of "white racism."

The present study is a replication and extension of a previous study (Rubovits & Maehr, 1971) that involved the systematic observation of teacher behavior following the experimental manipulation of expectations. The teachers, college undergraduates with limited classroom experience, each met with four students who had been randomly identified for the teacher as being "gifted" or "nongifted." The teachers did not differentiate in the amount of attention given to allegedly gifted and nongifted students; however, the pattern of attention did differ: Gifted students were called on and praised more than nongifted students. Thus, in this first study, teacher expectations were found to be related to teacher behavior in such a way that gifted students appeared to be encouraged and average students discouraged by their teachers.

The present study replicated the above

procedure with one new dimension. Whereas the previous study looked at interaction of white teachers with white students, this study considered the interaction of white teachers with white students and black students; one of the students labeled gifted and one of the students labeled nongifted were black. This provided an opportunity to investigate whether or not white teachers interact differently with white students and black students, both bright and average, in ways that would differentially affect their school performance. In addition, the study attempted to identify what kind of teacher would most likely be affected by race and label. Each teacher's level of dogmatism was, therefore, assessed under the assumption that high- and low-dogmatism teachers would react differently to the stereotyping effects of race and label.

Method

Subjects

Two different groups of subjects participated in the study. The group referred to as teachers was composed of 66 white female undergraduates enrolled in a teacher training course. All teachers had expressed interest in teaching, but not all were enrolled in an education curriculum, and none had yet had teaching experience. All teachers were volunteers; however, they were given course credit for participating in this project. The teachers knew nothing of the experimental manipulations; they simply thought they were taking advantage of a microteaching experience provided for them.

The group referred to as students was comprised of 264 seventh and eighth graders attending three junior high schools in a small midwestern city. These students were randomly selected within ability groups and given no instruction as to how they were to behave.

Measurement Procedures

In order to index the quality of teacher–student interaction, an instrument especially developed for this series of studies on teacher expectancy was employed. Although a more detailed description including reliability data may be found elsewhere (Rubovits, 1970; Rubovits & Maehr, 1971), the major features of this instrument should be noted. Briefly, the instrument is an observational schedule that requires a trained observer to record the incidence of six different teacher behaviors: (*a*) teacher *attention* to students' statements, subdivided into attention to requested statements and attention to spontaneous student statements; (*b*) teacher *encouragement* of students' statements; (*c*) teacher *elaboration* of students' statements; (*d*) teacher *ignoring* of students' statements; (*e*) teacher *praise* of students' statements; and (*f*) teacher *criticism* of students' statements.

The Rokeach Dogmatism Scale (Rokeach, 1960) was used to measure the teachers' authoritarianism. In addition, a questionnaire was given to each teacher in order to check the credibility of the experimental manipulations and to obtain some information on the teachers' perception of the students and the interpretations they gave to each student's behavior.

Experimental Procedure

One week before teaching, each teacher was given a lesson plan which outlined the topic to be taught and specified major points to be covered. As in the previous study, a lesson plan on the topic of television was employed. This topic and plan prompted considerable involvement on the part of both teacher and student. All students were found to be quite interested in discussing television and actively participated. The teachers had little or no difficulty in starting and sustaining a discussion on the topic and generally seemed at ease, improvising a great deal, adding and omitting points from the lesson plan, and using many original samples.

Attached to each teacher's lesson plan was a brief general description of the students she would be meeting. The teachers were told that an attempt would be made to have them teach as heterogeneous a group of students as possible. The teachers were also reminded that this was to be a learning experience for them, so they should be particularly alert to the differences between their students in terms of verbal ability, interest, quality of comments, etc.

The teachers were given no more information until just right before their teaching sessions, when each teacher was given a seating chart. This chart had on it each student's first name and also, under each name, an IQ score and a label indicating whether that student had been selected from the school's gifted program or from the regular track. The IQ score and a label had been *randomly* assigned to each student and did not necessarily bear any relation to the student's actual ability or track assignment.

For each teacher, a different group of four students was randomly selected from the same-ability-grouped class unit. Besides selecting from the same-ability units, one other restriction was placed on the selection of students; each session required two black students and two white students. One black student and one white student were randomly assigned a high IQ (between 130 and 135) and the label gifted. The other black student and the other white student were given lower IQs (between 98 and 102) and the label nongifted.

Each teacher was given the seating chart before the students arrived and was told to familiarize herself with the names and to examine closely the IQ scores and labels under each name. When the students arrived, the teacher was instructed to ask each student to sit in the seat designated on the chart. The teacher was further instructed before beginning the lesson to look at each student and read again, to herself, the IQ score and label of each child. The necessity for doing this was emphasized to the teacher and justified by explaining that being aware of each student's ability level could help a teacher to deal with that student during the session.

The teacher then introduced herself and explained that she had come from the University of Illinois to try out some new teaching materials. In the meantime, an observer seated herself two rows behind the students. The observer began categorizing the teacher's behavior as soon as the teacher had introduced herself and continued tallying behavior for 40 minutes. It must be emphasized that the observer did not know what label had been assigned to each student.

After the teaching session, the observer and the teacher discussed what had transpired, with the observer attempting to start the teacher thinking about each student's performance in relation to his reported intelligence. The teacher then filled out a questionnaire and two personality inventories. After all of the teachers had participated, the experimenters went to the two classes from which teachers had been recruited and explained the study in detail, discussing with them the results and implications of the study.

Results

Interaction Analysis

Frequency counts were collected on each teacher for each of eight categories. Each teacher met with four different kinds of students: gifted black, nongifted black, gifted white, and nongifted white. For each category, therefore, every teacher received four scores, with each score indicating her interaction with one kind of student. These scores were treated as repeated measures on the same individual.

A multivariate analysis of variance was used to analyze the data from seven of the categories (see Tatsuoka, 1971). Category 1, it will be remembered, measures the total number of times the teacher attended to the statements of the student. Attention to two specific kinds of statements were included in Category 1—attention to spontaneous responses to the teacher's questions (Category 1*a*) and attention to statements specifically requested by the teacher (Category 1*b*). Although the frequency of counts for Category 1 was not simply a combination of those for the subcategories 1*a* and 1*b*, Category 1 is clearly related to Categories 1*a* and 1*b*. For this reason, data on Category 1 were not included in the multivariate analysis of variance but were analyzed in a separate univariate analysis of variance.

In both of these analyses, there was one between-subjects variable—dogmatism (level of teacher dogmatism based on a high–low median split). This is referred to as the *teacher* variable. The two within-teachers variables are based on student differences and, for purposes of discussion, are referred to as *student* variables: race (black–white) and label (gifted–nongifted).

Table 6.2. Mean teacher interactions with gifted and nongifted black students and white students

Category	*Black*	*White*	*Combined*
1—Total attention			
Gifted	29.59	36.08	32.83
Nongifted	30.32	32.33	31.32
Combined	29.95	34.20	
1*a*—Attention to unsolicited statements			
Gifted	26.39	26.79	26.59
Nongifted	26.30	26.03	26.17
Combined	26.35	26.41	
1*b*—Attention to requested statements			
Gifted	3.88	10.64	7.70
Nongifted	4.77	5.67	5.22
Combined	4.32	8.15	
2—Encouragement			
Gifted	5.47	6.18	5.82
Nongifted	5.32	6.32	5.82
Combined	5.39	6.25	
3—Elaboration			
Gifted	2.09	2.08	2.08
Nongifted	2.44	2.15	2.30
Combined	2.26	2.11	
4—Ignoring			
Gifted	6.92	5.09	6.01
Nongifted	6.86	4.56	5.71
Combined	6.89	4.82	
5—Praise			
Gifted	.58	2.02	1.30
Nongifted	1.56	1.29	1.42
Combined	1.07	1.65	
6—Criticism			
Gifted	1.86	.77	1.32
Nongifted	.86	.68	.77
Combined	1.36	.73	

Student Variables: Race of Student

Each teacher met with two white students and two black students. Table 6.2 presents the mean number of teacher responses to black students and white students. Table 6.3 presents the *F* values from the analysis of variance and multivariate analysis of variance for the effects of race on the teacher–student interaction.

The analysis of variance for Category 1 (total attention) shows a significant difference in *quantity* of attention, with white students receiving far more attention from teachers than black students. This interpretation should be qualified in light of a Race × Label interaction and subsequent comparison of gifted and nongifted black and white means (see Tables 6.2 and 6.3 and Figure 6.1). Such a consideration would suggest that the significant main effect in this case is almost entirely attributable to the great amount of attention given the gifted whites. The multivariate analysis of variance analyzed *qualitative* differences in teacher attention, and it also shows a significant overall effect for race. From the discriminant coefficients (Table 6.4) it can be seen that treatment of black students and white students differed most on the dimensions of ignoring, praise, attention to requested statements, and criticism. Across all teachers and also

Table 6.3. F values associated with analysis of variance and multivariate analysis of variance

Source	*ANOVA (Category 1)*	*MANOVA*	*Univariate* Fs *for variables (categories) in MANOVA*						
			1a	*1b*	*2*	*3*	*4*	*5*	*6*
Dogmatism (A)	.56	5.25**	.00	2.48	.00	2.88	31.30**	.49	6.72*
Race (B)	9.51**	7.48**	.00	12.51**	3.85	.25	19.05**	11.68**	9.73**
Label (C)	2.12	3.28**	.15	9.21**	.00	.36	.71	.72	13.76**
A×B	1.17	3.74**	.16	.19	18.39**	.36	6.30*	.87	1.08
A×C	3.59	1.17	1.64	.24	.13	.47	4.59*	.02	.38
B×C	4.85*	5.60**	.08	4.02*	.10	.16	.49	26.95**	10.48**
A×B×C	.10	.32	.52	.12	.01	.10	.19	.19	.42

* $p<.05$.
** $p<.01$.

Table 6.4. Discriminant coefficients for significant effects in multivariate analysis of variance

Category	*Significant effects*				
	Dogmatism (A)	*Race (B)*	*Label (C)*	*A×B*	*B×C*
1a	.07	.02	.22	−.20	.34
1b	−.23	−.40	.67	−.28	−.50
2	.12	−.16	−.16	.94	−.34
3	−.23	.14	−.04	−.04	.02
4	−.83	.63	.09	−.39	−.30
5	−.11	−.56	−.17	−.12	−.91
6	.40	.36	.72	.20	.26

Note. A convenient explanation of discriminant coefficients can be found in Tatsuoka (1971, p. 162 ff.).

across labels, a pattern can be seen in the way teachers treated black students and white students. The directions of this pattern can be seen from the means in Table 6.2. Fewer statements were requested of blacks than of whites. More statements of blacks than of whites were ignored. Possibly most interesting of all, black students were praised less and criticized more.

Three dependent variables contributed little to the difference in treatment of black and white students. For one of these (Category 1*a*), it had been expected that little effect would be found. This category measures the amount of student initiated interaction. Little effect for this category would allow for the inference that there was no difference in the spontaneity of the students. Since this was the case, further confirmed by a nonsignificant univariate *F* for this category, it can be assumed that black students and white students were not treated differently by teachers because of differences in their verbosity.

Student Variables: Label of Student

Two students taught by each teacher, one black and one white, had been randomly given the label "gifted," and two, one black and one white, the label "nongifted." Table 6.2 presents the mean number of teacher responses in each category to gifted and nongifted students; Table 6.3 presents the *F* values for the analysis of variance and the multivariate analysis of variance.

The univariate analysis for Category 1 data shows no significant difference in total amount of attention to gifted and nongifted students. No differences had been expected for this category, as it was hypothesized that the *amount* of interaction between the teacher and the student would be fairly similar regardless of the student's label and that the crucial variable would be the *quality* of the interaction.

A significant multivariate effect was

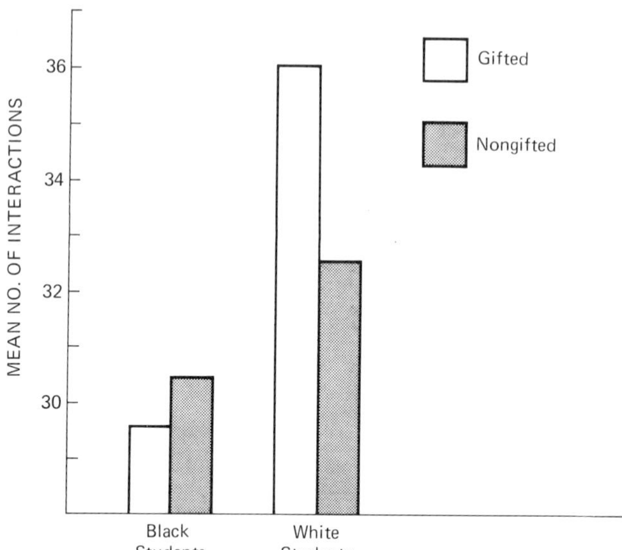

Figure 6.1. Teacher interaction with gifted and nongifted black and white students (Category 1: Total attention).

found for label, thus indicating qualitative differences in teacher interaction with gifted and nongifted students. From the discriminant coefficients in Table 6.4, it can be seen that two variables accounted for almost all of the difference in treatment of gifted and nongifted students. These two variables are Categories 1*b* (attention to requested statements) and 6 (criticism). From the means in Table 6.2, it can be seen that the significance occurs because more statements were requested of gifted than of nongifted students and also that gifted students were criticized more than nongifted students.

Once again, Category 1*a* contributed little to the total difference and also yielded a nonsignificant univariate *F*. This allows for the inference that gifted students were not called upon more often simply because they volunteered less.

Student Variables: Interaction of Race × Label

A prime consideration of this study was any difference in the effect of label depending on the race of the student. The univariate analysis for Category 1 revealed a significant interaction of Race × Label. Gifted white students received more attention than nongifted white students with a reverse tendency occurring in the case of black students.

A significant multivariate *F* was found for the interaction of Race × Label (see Table 6.3). The discriminant analysis showed this difference to be mostly attributable to Category 5 (praise) with Category 1*b* (attention to requested statements) also contributing toward the difference (see Table 6.4). In addition, Categories 1*a* (attention to unsolicited statements), 2 (encouragement), 4 (ignoring), and 6 (criticism) all contributed to the differences in treatment of differently labeled students of different races. Note from Tables 6.3 and 6.4 that Category 6 (criticism) contributed little to the overall interaction effect, although a highly significant univariate *F* was associated with it. This situation would suggest that the difference seemingly attributable to criticism in the univariate analysis is accounted for by the other variables with which it is correlated.

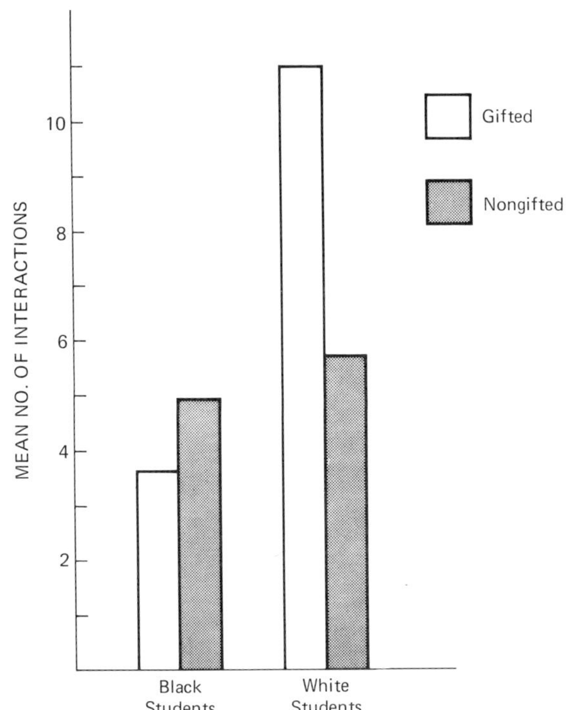

Figure 6.2. Teacher interaction with gifted and nongifted black and white students (Category 1*b*: Attention to requested statements).

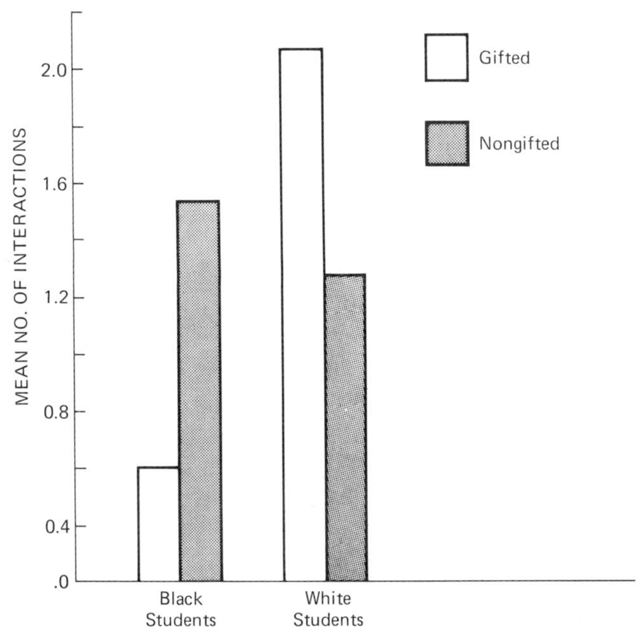

Figure 6.3. Teacher interaction with gifted and nongifted black and white students (Category 5: Praise).

The direction of these interactions can be ascertained from Table 6.2. In the case of Categories 1, 1*b*, and 5, the interactions are also portrayed in Figures 6.1, 6.2, and 6.3. Considering these interactions collectively, a pattern begins to emerge in which the expectation of giftedness is associated with a generally positive response of teachers—*if* the student is white. For black students, if anything, a reverse tendency is evident in which the expectation of giftedness is associated with *less* positive treatment.

Teacher Variables: Level of Dogmatism

It had been hypothesized that level of dogmatism might affect susceptibility to racial and labeling effects (see Table 6.5). Regardless of interaction with either student variable, level of dogmatism itself was found to affect overall teacher behavior. The analysis of variance on Category 1 (total attention) showed no quantitative differences in the attention given students by teachers high and low in dogmatism (see Table 6.3). The multivariate analysis of variance did, however, reveal a significant effect for dogmatism (see Table 6.3). This difference was due mostly to the effect of Category 4 (ignoring), with teachers higher in dogmatism ignoring many more statements than teachers lower in dogmatism. Some of the overall difference can also be attributed to Category 6 (criticism), with teachers higher in dogmatism criticizing more statements than teachers lower in dogmatism.

Interaction of Teacher and Student Variables: Dogmatism × Race

Of particular interest in this study was whether or not teachers with different levels of dogmatism would respond differ-

Table 6.5. Mean interaction with gifted and nongifted black and white students × teachers high and low in dogmatism

Category	*Black*	*White*	*Combined*	*Gifted*	*Nongifted*
1—Total attention					
High dogmatism	29.94	35.68	32.81	34.54	31.08
Low dogmatism	29.97	32.73	31.35	31.12	31.58
1*a*—Attention to unsolicited statements					
High dogmatism	26.06	26.67	26.36	27.27	25.45
Low dogmatism	26.64	26.15	26.39	25.91	26.88
1*b*—Attention to requested statements					
High dogmatism	5.47	8.82	7.14	8.85	5.44
Low dogmatism	3.18	7.48	5.33	6.56	4.11
2—Encouragement					
High dogmatism	4.44	7.17	5.80	5.88	5.73
Low dogmatism	6.35	5.33	5.84	5.77	5.91
3—Elaboration					
High dogmatism	2.50	2.53	2.52	2.53	2.50
Low dogmatism	2.03	1.70	1.86	1.64	2.09
4—Ignoring					
High dogmatism	9.39	6.14	7.76	8.29	7.24
Low dogmatism	4.39	3.52	3.95	3.73	4.18
5—Praise					
High dogmatism	1.06	1.48	1.27	1.20	1.35
Low dogmatism	1.08	1.82	1.45	1.39	1.50
6—Criticism					
High dogmatism	1.86	1.02	1.44	1.76	1.12
Low dogmatism	.86	.44	.65	.88	.42

ently to black students and white students. No significant interaction was found for Category 1 (total attention), but a significant multivariate F was found (see Table 6.3). Most of this interaction can be attributed to Category 2 (encouraging). Much less of the difference is contributed by the scores from Category 4 (ignoring). The univariate interactions for these two categories are shown in Figures 6.4 and 6.5. From Figure 6.4 it can be seen that dogmatism is associated with the encouraging of white rather than black students. Complementing the result is the finding that dogmatism was also associated with a tendency to ignore the statements of black students (see Figure 6.5).

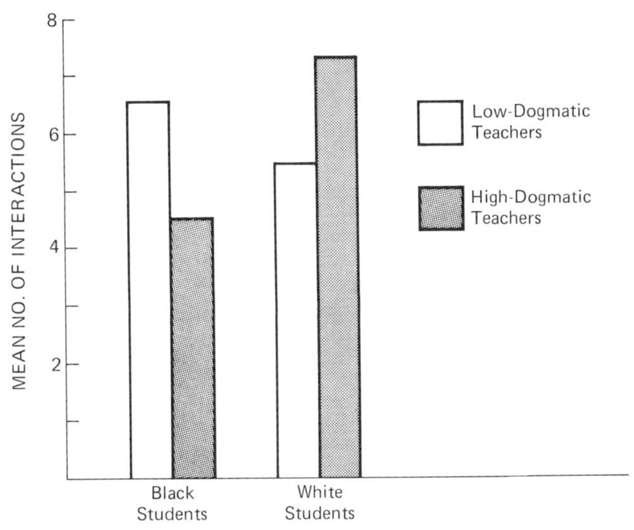

Figure 6.4. Interaction patterns of high- and low-dogmatic teachers (Category 2: Encourage).

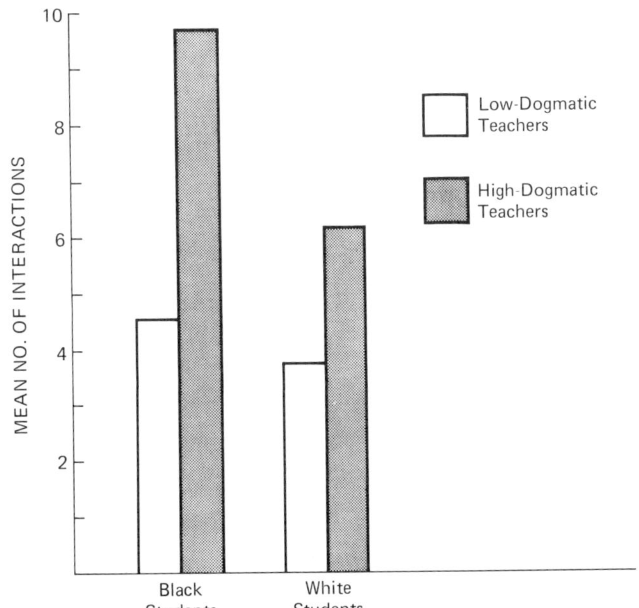

Figure 6.5. Interaction patterns of high- and low-dogmatic teachers (Category 4: Ignore).

Interaction of Teacher and Student Variables: Dogmatism × Label

A nonsignificant univariate F for Category 1 and also a nonsignificant multivariate F were found (see Table 6.3). One significant univariate F was found for the variables in the multivariate analysis of variance. However, since the multivariate F was not significant, this one significant univariate F may be attributed to chance.

Interaction of Teacher Variable and Student Variables: Dogmatism × Race × Label

No significant triple interactions were found for any category in any of the analyses, univariate or multivariate (see Table 6.3).

Credibility of Experimental Situation

A postexperiment questionnaire and an interview were given in order to check whether or not teachers accepted the experimental situation. No teacher expressed any suspicion of the experimental hypotheses. The teachers also showed great agreement with the assigned labels. One hundred and thirty-two students had been labeled gifted and 132 nongifted. Only in the case of 14 of the gifted students and 13 of the nongifted students did teachers express any reservations about accepting these labels as true indicants of the students' ability levels. These reports of the teachers, as well as clinical observations during the postexperimental interviews, suggest that the teachers not only accepted the situation as presented to them, but they also viewed each student in terms of the label assigned him.

Discussion

As in a previous study (Rubovits & Maehr, 1971), teachers were found to treat students labeled gifted different from students described as average. There was no difference in the *amount* of attention given to the supposedly different-ability groups, but there were differences in the *quality* of attention. Gifted students were called on more, thus replicating a previous finding (Rubovits & Maehr, 1971). Gifted students were also criticized more, but this difference may have been caused by the inclusion of black students in the gifted group as they were the recipients of almost all the criticism.

Considering the differences due to label for whites only, it can be seen that the gifted white student was given more attention than his nongifted counterpart, called on more, praised more, and also criticized a bit more. It is interesting, incidentally, that in the informal interviews with teachers the gifted white student was also chosen most frequently as the most liked student, the brightest student, and the certain leader of the class.

Of special interest, of course, are the comparisons of teacher interaction with black students and white students. In this regard, the present study provides what appears to be a disturbing instance of white racism. Black students were given less attention, ignored more, praised less and criticized more. More startling perhaps are the Race × Label interactions that suggest that it is the gifted black who is given the least attention, is the least praised, and the most criticized, even when comparing him to his nongifted black counterpart.

It is important to stress that these results not easily attributable to an experimental artifact of some kind. There is no reason to suppose that the expectancy communication varied for race. Moreover, it cannot be argued that teachers were responding to any actual intellectual differences between black students and white students or to any incongruity between label and actual potential. Recall that students were specifically selected so as to be of equivalent intellectual ability regardless of race.

An obvious question, of course, is

whether the expectancy resided in the observer or in the teacher. It is impossible to rule out observer expectancy effects completely. While the observer could not know which students were labeled gifted or average, it is obvious that she would know black from white. However, it is difficult to see how such knowledge might have determined the pattern of results that were obtained. First, the observational instrument is reasonably objective in nature, allowing for minimal judgment on the part of the observer (Rubovits, 1970). Second, the present authors in fact had no clear and obvious basis for postulating the results that did indeed occur. For example, it would have been equally logical to argue before the fact that young, idealistic teachers, most of whom expressed liberal beliefs, would make a special attempt to ingratiate themselves to blacks. Finally, the fact that high-dogmatic teachers were more inclined toward a prejudicial pattern than low-dogmatic teachers further suggests that the reported interactions were not just a figment of the observer's expectancy. If the observer were, in fact, the responsible agent, it would be difficult to see how, not knowing the dogmatism scores, she could have effected a generally predictable pattern for high and low dogmatists as well as the overall pattern. A bias leading toward differential observation of teacher–student interaction in the case of blacks and whites would presumably operate across all teachers regardless of dogmatism, thereby making it virtually impossible to obtain any meaningful Dogmatism × Race interaction. In brief, the most logical explanation of the results is that the teachers were indeed exhibiting the negative pattern toward blacks that the reported interactions indicate.

It is important to emphasize that this prejudicial pattern was not exhibited by all teachers. Teachers higher in dogmatism seemed to differentiate more in their treatment of blacks and whites. Moreover, one may wonder about the degree to which the patterns observed are unique to young, inexperienced teachers. After all, these teachers not only had little teaching experience but, as the questionnaire data would indicate, little experience of any kind with blacks. One might at least hope that the appropriate experience could be of benefit.

All in all, then, this study clearly suggests how teacher expectations may affect teacher behavior. Although the results must be interpreted within the limits of the study, with cautious generalization, the data do suggest answers to the question of why teachers are often able to do little to equalize the performance levels of blacks and whites.

References

BECKER, H. S. Social class variations in the teacher-pupil relationship. *Journal of Educational Sociology*, 1952, *25*, 451–465.

BROWN, B. The assessment of self-concept among four-year-old Negro and white children. (Cited by H. Proshansky & P. Newton: The nature and meaning of Negro self-identity) In M. Deutsch, I. Katz, & A. R. Jensen (Eds.), *Social class, race and psychological development*. New York: Holt, Rinehart & Winston, 1968.

CLAIBORNE, W. L. Expectancy effects in the classroom: A failure to replicate. *Journal of Educational Psychology*, 1969, *60*, 377–383.

DAVIDSON, H. H., & LANG, G. Children's perception of teachers' feelings toward them. *Journal of Experimental Education*, 1960, *29*, 107–118.

DEUTSCH, M. The disadvantaged child and the learning process. In A. H. Passow (Ed.), *Education in depressed areas*. New York: Bureau of Publications, Teachers College, Columbia University, 1963.

ELASHOFF, J. D., & SNOW, R. E. *A case study in statistical inference: Reconsideration of the Rosenthal-Jacobson data on teacher expectancy.* (Tech. Rep. No. 15) Stanford, Calif.: Stanford Center for Research and Development in Teaching, Stanford University, 1970.

MEICHENBAUM, D. H., BOWERS, K. S., & ROSS, R. R. A behavioral analysis of teacher expectancy effect. *Journal of Personality and Social Psychology,* 1969, *13,* 306–316.

ROKEACH, M. *The open and closed mind.* New York: Basic Books, 1960.

ROSENTHAL, R. *Experimenter effects in behavioral research.* New York: Appleton-Century-Crofts, 1966.

———. Empirical vs. decreed validation of clocks and tests. *American Educational Research Journal,* 1969, *6,* 689–691.

ROSENTHAL, R., & FODE, K. L. The effect of experimenter bias on the performance of albino rats. *Behavioral Science,* 1963, *8,* 183–189.

ROSENTHAL, R., & JACOBSON, L. *Pygmalion in the classroom: Teacher expectation and pupils' intellectual development.* New York: Holt, Rinehart & Winston, 1968.

ROSENTHAL, R., & LAWSON, R. A longitudinal study of the effects of experimenter bias on the operant learning of laboratory rats. *Journal of Psychiatric Research,* 1964, *2,* 61–72.

RUBOVITS, P. C. Teacher interaction with students labeled gifted and nongifted in a microteaching situation. Unpublished master's thesis, University of Illinois, 1970.

RUBOVITS, P. C., & MAEHR, M. L. Pygmalion analyzed: Toward an explanation of the Rosenthal-Jacobson findings. *Journal of Personality and Social Psychology,* 1971, *19,* 197–203.

SNOW, R. E. Unfinished pygmalion. *Contemporary Psychology,* 1969, *14,* 197–199.

TATSUOKA, M. *Multivariate analysis.* New York: Wiley, 1971.

THORNDIKE, R. L. Review of *Pygmalion in the classroom. American Educational Research Journal,* 1968, *5,* 708–711.

———. But do you have to know how to tell time? *American Educational Research Journal,* 1969, *6,* 692.

WARNER, W. L., HAVIGHURST, R. J., & LOEB, M. B. *Who shall be educated?* New York: Harper & Row, 1944.

WILSON, A. B. Social stratification and academic achievement. In A. H. Passow (Ed.), *Education in depressed areas.* New York: Teachers College, Columbia University, 1963.

31. BODY BUILD AND BEHAVIOR IN YOUNG CHILDREN: I. BODY BUILD AND NURSERY SCHOOL TEACHERS' RATINGS

RICHARD N. WALKER

Sample

The main subjects were 73 boys and 52 girls, all the children attending the Gesell Institute Nursery School during one or both of two consecutive years, with the exception of (a) children having physical handicaps, (b) children falling clearly outside the intelligence distribution of the rest of the group, (c) children of non-white racial background, (d) children whose stay in school was too short to permit teacher ratings, and (e) children who refused to be photographed. At the time of photographing, the children ranged in age from 2–6 to 2–11, 3–6 to 3–11, or 4–6 to 4–11. Socioeconomic status of the sample was biased upward and along academic lines: 95 per cent of the children's fathers held college degrees and over half held a degree at the doctoral level. As judged from the PARI scores of a subgroup, the children's mothers were relatively homogeneous in disagreeing with statements endorsing punitiveness and authoritarian control. The children formed a sample of well cared for, well nourished, healthy, bright subjects.

Procedure

Each child was photographed in the nude in standard pose in front, side, and back position. The physique evaluations were made from these photographs by three judges, two of whom never saw the subjects and one of whom was acquainted with the children. Each judge rated each child for manifest level of three physique dimensions; endomorphy (roughly speaking, fatness), mesomorphy (muscle and bone development), and ectomorphy (slenderness).

A set of 63 rating scales was assembled for appraising the children's nursery school behavior. Before any ratings were made, a set of predictions was drawn up concerning the probable direction of correlation of each behavior item with each physique variable. These predictions were based on Sheldon's report (1942) of physique-behavior relations in college men.

The children were then rated on the behavior scales. Each was rated independently by four or five teachers. Of the 15 teachers who contributed ratings, three knew that these were to be used for physique-behavior comparisons. At least three naïve judges' ratings were averaged with each rating by an informed judge. From the 63 individual items of the inventory, nine more general scales were developed, each composed of two to six intercorrelated items.

The Measuring Instruments

Physique Ratings

Along with the 125 photographs of children whose behavior was rated, the judges evaluated an additional 249 photographs of children in the same age range who had attended the nursery school in previous years. Standard scores were computed for endomorphy, mesomorphy, and ectomorphy for each judge's ratings at each age, and these were averaged for the three judges. These mean scores were transformed into somatotype-like scores with a mean of 3.5, a standard deviation of 1.0, and an interval of .5. Each physique component at each age then ranged by half steps from 1 or 1½ to 6½ or 7, with a mean of 3½. Coefficients of reliability for the average of the standard scores of the three judges fell near .90 for endomorphy and ectomorphy at each age. Interjudge agreement in rating mesomorphy was lower, represented by coefficients of around .85 for the boys and around .70 for the girls. For a subsample of children rated at more than one age (two judges did not know which were repeats), all retest correlations for a one-year-interval reached or exceeded .90, when corrected for attenuation. The small group of children rated at 2 and 4 years showed lower values, though all exceeded .70.

Behavior Ratings

A rating of the child's compliance-resistance in the photographing situation was made by the photographer and, during the second year of the study, by the teacher assisting. Correlations between the two were .93 for the 31 boys rated by both, .80 for the 32 girls.

For the individual items of the nursery school behavior scale, Horst's index of reliability of the average of scores of multiple judges was computed for the first year's ratings. Median reliability indices for the different age groups ranged from .71 to .81. Reliability coefficients for the cluster scores for the total sample were higher, ranging from .75 to .92 and with two thirds of the coefficients exceeding .85.

Results

Reaction to the Photographing Situation

While no age differences appeared in compliance ratings, marked differences appeared between the sexes, boys being the more resistant. Children of endomorphic physique tended to be resistant to the situation, while mesomorphs and ectomorphs tended to be compliant, in the case of both boys and girls. (Three of the six coefficients were significant.) Multiple correlations between the three physique variables and compliance reached .42 for boys, .67 for girls.

Outcome of the Predictions

Of the total of 292 predictions made for boys and girls for the three physique variables, 73 per cent were confirmed in direction and 21 per cent were confirmed beyond the .05 level while 3 per cent were disconfirmed beyond the .05 level. Sex differences in success of prediction were clear: over a third of predictions made for boys were significantly confirmed, less than 10 per cent for girls. The three physique components also showed differences in success ratios. Relations with mesomorphy were best predicted; for boys close to half the predictions made were confirmed at a significant level. Relations with ectomorphy were intermediate in success, though nearly as many predictions were confirmed significantly for boys. Relations with endomorphy were predicted with little better than chance success for the girls and slightly less than chance success for the boys.

Nursery School Behavior and Individual Physique Components

Endomorphy For boys, only one cluster score, aggressiveness, correlated significantly with endomorphy, and this evidently by virtue of the correlation of both with mesomorphy. Ten individual behavior items were associated with endomorphy, six of them in a direction opposite to that which had been predicted. Together with nine items significant only at the .10 level, these give a picture of assertive aggressiveness (self-assertive, revengeful, easily angered, inconsiderate, quarrelsome, etc.), high energy level (ambitious, daring, noisy, boyish), extraversion (does not daydream, social in play), and low sensitivity (insensitive to pain, feelings not easily hurt, few nervous habits). For girls also one cluster score, cooperativeness, correlated significantly with endomorphy. Only a single individual rating item was significantly associated with endomorphy, though together with the four items significant at the .10 level it contributed to a consistent picture of good personal-social adjustment (recovers quickly from upsets, not tense, does not daydream, direct in solving social problems, social in play).

Mesomorphy For boys, all but one of the nine cluster scores showed significant relation with mesomorphy, as did 24 of the individual rating items. The girls showed just three significant correlations between mesomorphy and the cluster scores, eight between mesomorphy and the individual rating items. Characteristic of both boys and girls high in mesomorphy is a dominating assertiveness (leader in play, competitive, self-assertive, easily angered, attacks others, etc.), high energy output, openness of expression, and fearlessness. The girls combine this assertiveness with socialness, cheerfulness, and warmth. The boys' items give more suggestion of hostility (quarrelsome, revengeful, inconsiderate) and of an impulsive, headlong quality to their activity (daring, noisy, quick, accident prone, self-confident, etc.).

Ectomorphy Boys and girls each showed two cluster scores which correlated with ectomorphy, but 27 individual items showed significant association with ectomorphy for the boys, just eight for the girls. In common for both sexes are items suggesting a certain aloofness (not social in play, does not attack others, daydreams, indirect in solving problems). Different items for boys and girls suggest an emotional restraint in both (boys: not easily angered, not expressive in movements, not talkative, etc.; girls: not dramatic, not open in expressing feelings, low verbal interests). For boys, the items in general define a cautious, quiet child, not self-assertive, hesitant to give offence, looking to adults rather than to children for approval, sensitive, slow to recover from upsets. He appears lacking in energy reserves (not energetic, dislikes gross motor play, enjoys hand activities, has few accidents). For girls, the composite picture is similar but tends more to indicate a somberness of outlook—unfriendly, tense, not gay or cheerful, irritable.

Total physique pattern Combination of the three physique components in multiple regression correlation with the cluster scores gave little increase over the highest single-component coefficients for the boys, somewhat greater increase for the girls. The multiple correlations ranged from .20 to .52.

A graphic technique of analysis suggests higher relations, particularly for the boys. In this method, the physique rating of each individual is plotted on a somatotype distribution chart, the plotted point indicating whether the subject is below or above average on the cluster score in question. A single, straight cutting line is then drawn which separates the total distribution of subjects into (approximately) equal halves and which gives a maximum of above-average subjects in one half. For this dichotomy a tetrachoric correlation can be computed. For a majority of the nine traits, the cutting lines chosen by inspection closely approximated a single, common cutting line. For boys, a dichotomy contrasting mesomorphs and mesomorphic endomorphs with ectomorphs and ectomorphic endomorphs produced differences in rates of aggressiveness, energy level, and sensitivity corresponding to tetrachoric correlations in the .60's. The traits of fearfulness, cheerfulness, and cooperativeness showed less striking separation by this common cutting line. Two other cutting lines showed some suggestion of association with behavior differences in boys, though the evidence was weaker. A line separating endomorphs and ectomorphs appears to separate boys more oriented to peer approval from boys more oriented to adult approval. And a line separating endomorphs from mesomorphs separates boys resistant in the photographing situation from boys compliant in that setting.

For girls, only a single cutting line was found which appeared associated with behavior differences. Girls plotted in the mesomorphic area of the chart differ from other girls in showing greater aggressiveness, cheerfulness, socialness, and energy, as well as fearfulness and less sensitivity.

Conclusions

It is concluded that in this group of preschool children important associations do exist between individuals' physiques and particular behavior characteristics. Further, these associations show considerable similarity to those described by Sheldon for college-aged men, though the strength of association is not as strong as he reports. It is suggested that the relations are multiply determined, arising from primary bodily conditions (e.g., strength, energy, sensory thresholds), from direct learnings concerning the efficacy of different modes of behavior and adjustment techniques, and from less direct learnings regarding expectations and evaluations accorded to different physiques by others. Other factors, possibly innate, as well as opportunity for and encouragement of particular behaviors, appear important in directing the physique-associated behavior. This is suggested by the mesomorphic girls' channeling of their energies more into social activities, the mesomorphic boys' more into physical, gross-motor activity. The young ages of the subjects would seem to give some weight to constitutional and direct-learning factors as contrasted with reputation variables, which others have pointed out as important at later ages. In particular, variations in physical energy, in bodily effectiveness for assertive or dominating behavior, and in bodily sensitivity appear as important mediating links between physique structure and general behavior.

32. SOME IMMEDIATE EFFECTS OF TELEVISED VIOLENCE ON CHILDREN'S BEHAVIOR

ROBERT M. LIEBERT and ROBERT A. BARON

The hypothesis that exposure to televised violence would increase the willingness of children to hurt another child was investigated. Boys and girls of two age groups (5–6 and 8–9 years) first viewed excerpts from actual television programs depicting either aggressive or nonaggressive scenes, and were then provided with an opportunity to aggress against a peer. All subjects were subsequently placed in a free play situation and the frequency of their aggressive responses observed. Results indicated that children exposed to the aggressive program engaged in longer attacks against an ostensible child victim than subjects exposed to the nonaggressive program. The aggressive program also elicited a higher level of aggressive play than the nonaggressive one, particularly among the younger boys.

In his review of the social and scientific issues surrounding the portrayal of violence in the mass media, Larsen (1968) noted that we may begin with two facts: "(1) Mass media content is heavily saturated with violence, and (2) people are spending more and more time in exposure to such content [p. 115]." This state of affairs has been used by both laymen and professionals as the basis for appeals to modify the entertainment fare to which viewers, particularly children and adolescents, are exposed (Merriam, 1964; Walters, 1966; Walters & Thomas, 1963; Wertham, 1966). Other writers, however, have argued that the kind of violence found on television or in movies does not necessarily influence observers' "real-life" social behavior (Halloran, 1964; Klapper, 1968). A few have even characterized the portrayal of violence as potentially preventing the overt expression of aggression, at least under some circumstances (Feshbach, 1961; Feshbach & Singer, 1971).

In view of the controversy, it is hardly surprising that recent years have seen a substantial increase in the number of experimental studies directed to this issue. An effort has been made to determine whether children will learn and/or be disinhibited in their performance of aggressive acts as a function of exposure to symbolic aggressive models (e.g., in cartoons, movies, stories, and simulated television programs). This research has indicated consistently that children may indeed *acquire*, from even a very brief period of observation, certain motoric and verbal behaviors which are associated with aggression in life situations. More specifically, it has been repeatedly shown that after viewing a film which depicts novel forms of hitting, kicking, and verbal abuse, children can, when asked to do so, demonstrate this learning by reproducing these previously unfamiliar behaviors with a remarkable degree of fidelity (Bandura, 1965; Hicks, 1965). Taken together with the large body of research on the observational learning of other behaviors (Flanders, 1968), the available evidence appears to leave little doubt that the learning of at least some aggressive responses can and does result from television or movie viewing.

Equally important, however, is the question of whether the observation of violence will influence children's performance of aggressive acts when they have *not* been specifically asked to show what they have seen or learned. Several experiments appear to provide evidence relating to this issue (Bandura, Ross, & Ross, 1961, 1963a, 1963b; Rosekrans & Hartup, 1967). In these studies, subjects have typically been exposed to live or filmed aggressive scenes, then placed in a free play situation with a variety of toys or other play materials. Results obtained with these procedures have shown repeatedly that the exposure of young children to aggression produces increments in such play activities as punching inflated plastic clowns, popping balloons, striking stuffed animals, and operating mechanized "hitting dolls."

It has been ragued by critics (Klapper, 1968) that findings such as those reviewed above are not directly relevant to the question of whether exposure to televised aggression will increase children's willingness to engage in behavior which might actually harm another person. Since this criticism was advanced, a human victim has replaced the inanimate target in at least four more recent investigations (Hanratty, 1969; Hanratty, Liebert, Morris, & Fernandez, 1969; Hanratty, O'Neal, & Sulzer, 1972; Savitsky, Rogers, Izard, & Liebert, 1971). These later studies have demonstrated clearly that exposure to the behavior of filmed aggressive models may lead young children to directly imitate aggression against a human, as well as a "toy," victim.

Despite the newer evidence, critics may still question whether exposure to the type of violence generally depicted on regularly broadcast television shows will produce similar effects. Likewise, it is important to consider the possible *disinhibitory* effects (cf. Lovaas, 1961; Siegel, 1956) rather than only the direct *imitative* effects of observing aggressive models. Although such effects have previously been observed with adult subjects and violent scenes taken from motion pictures (e.g., Berkowitz, 1965; Berkowitz & Rawlings, 1963; Walters & Thomas, 1963), in no previous investigation known to the authors has the influence of televised violence on interpersonal aggression been examined for young children. It was with these latter questions that the present research was primarily concerned. We sought to determine whether exposure to violent scenes taken directly from nationally telecast programs increases the willingness of young children to engage in aggressive acts directed toward another child.

Method

Participants

Population sample The sample was drawn both from Yellow Springs, Ohio, a small college town, and from a larger and more conservative neighboring community, Xenia. The participants were brought to Fels Research Institute in Yellow Springs by one of their parents, in response to a newspaper advertisement and/or a letter distributed in local public elementary schools asking for volunteers to participate in a study of the effects of television on children. To assure that no potential participants were turned away because of scheduling inconveniences, parents were invited to select their own appointment times (including evenings or weekends), and transportation was offered to those who could not provide it for themselves.

Subjects The subjects were 136 children, 68 boys and 68 girls. Sixty-five of the participants were 5 or 6 years of age at the time of the study; the remaining 71 subjects were 8 or 9 years of age. Within each age group and sex the children were assigned randomly to the treatment conditions. Approximately 20% of the children in this study were black; virtually all of the remainder were white. The economic backgrounds from which these participants came was widely varied. Although economic characteristics were not used as a basis for assignment to treatments, inspection suggested that the procedure of random assignment had adequately distributed them among the experimental groups.

Experimental personnel One of the investigators greeted the parent and child at the outset, served as the interviewer, and obtained informed parental consent for the child's participation. A 28-year-old white female served as experimenter for all the children, and two other adult females served as unseen observers throughout the experiment.

Design

A 2 × 2 × 2 factorial design was employed. The three factors were sex, age (5–6 or 8–9 years old), and treatment (observation of aggressive or nonaggressive television sequences).

Procedure

Introduction to the situation Upon the arrival of parent and child at the institute, the child was escorted to a waiting room containing nonaggressive magazines and other play materials while the parent was interviewed in a separate room. During the interview, the nature of the experiment was disclosed to the parent, questions were invited and answered, and a written consent to the child's participation was obtained.[1]

Experimental and control treatment After the interview, but without permitting the parent and the child to interact, the experimenter escorted each subject individually to a second waiting room containing children's furniture and a television video-tape monitor. The television was then turned on by the experimenter, who suggested that the child watch for a few minutes until she was ready for him. The experimenter left the child to watch television alone for approximately 6½ minutes; the subjects were in fact continuously observed through a concealed camera and video monitor. For all groups, the first 120 seconds of viewing consisted of two 1-minute commercials video-taped during early 1970. The first of these depicted the effectiveness of a certain paper towel, and the second advertised a humorous movie (rated G). The commercials were selected for their humor and attention-getting characteristics.

Thereafter, children in the experimental group observed the first 3½ minutes of a program from a popular television series, "The Untouchables." The sequence, which preserved a simple story line, contained a chase, two fist-fighting scenes, two shootings, and a knifing. In contrast, children in the control group viewed a highly active 3½-minute video-taped sports sequence in which athletes competed in hurdle races, high jumps, and the like. For all subjects, the final 60 seconds of the program contained a commercial for automobile tires. Before the end of this last commercial, the experimenter reentered the room and announced that she was ready to begin.

Assessment of willingness to hurt another child The subject was next escorted by the experimenter from the television room to a second room and seated at a response box apparatus modeled after the one employed by Mallick and McCandless (1966). The gray metal response box, which measured approximately 17 × 6 inches, displayed a red button on the left, a green button on the right, and a white light centered above these two manipulanda. The word "hurt" appeared beneath

---

[1] Since no specific information could be provided in public announcements or over the telephone, it appeared necessary to have parents accompany their children to the institute in order to assure that no child participated without the informed consent of his parents. In order to defray the costs of transportation, baby sitters for siblings who remained at home, and the like, and to eliminate economic biases which might otherwise have appeared in the sample, a $10 stipend was given the parent of each participant. No parent who appeared for the interview declined to allow his or her child to participate.

the red button, while the word "help" appeared beneath the green button. Several plastic wires led from the response box to a vent in the wall. The experimenter explained to the subject that these wires were connected to a game in an adjacent room and that "one of the other children is in the next room right now and will start to play the game in just a minute." She further explained that the game required the player in the other room to turn a handle and that the white light would come on each time the other child in the next room started to turn the handle, thus activating the red and green buttons.

The experimenter continued:

> When this white light comes on, you have to push one of these two buttons. If you push this green button, that will make the handle next door easier to turn and will help the child to win the game. If you push this red button, that will make the handle next door feel hot. That will hurt the child, and he will have to let go of the handle. Remember, this is the *help* button, and this is the *hurt* button [indicating]. See, it says *help* and *hurt*. . . . You have to push one of these two buttons each time the light goes on, but you can push whichever one you want to. You can always push the same button or you can change from one button to the other whenever you want to, but just remember, each time the light goes on, you can push only one. So if you push this green button then you help the other child and if you push this red button then you hurt the other child. Now if you push this green button for *just a second,* then you *help the other child just a little,* and if you push this red button down for *just a second,* then you *hurt the other child just a little.* But if you push this green button down a little longer, then you help the other child a little more, and if you push this red button down a little longer, then you hurt the other child a little more. *The longer you push the green button, the more you help the other child* and *the longer you push the red button, the more you hurt the other child.*

This explanation, with slightly varied wording, was repeated a second time if the child did not indicate comprehension of the instructions. After being assured that the subject understood the task, the experimenter left the room.[2]

Although all the subjects were led to believe that other children were participating, there was, in fact, no other child; the entire procedure was controlled in the next room so as to produce 20 trials, with an intertrial interval of approximately 15 seconds. Each child's response to each trial (appearance of the white light) and the duration of the response, recorded to the hundredth of a second, was automatically registered. When the subject had completed 20 trials, the experimenter reentered the room and announced that the game was over.

Assessment of aggressive play The influence of televised violence on the children's subsequent play activities was also explored, although this issue was of secondary interest in the present research (the study being primarily concerned with interpersonal aggression rather than aggression aimed at inanimate objects). After completing the button-pushing task, the child was escorted to a third room (designated the "play room") across the hallway. The room contained two large tables, on each of which appeared three attractive nonaggressive toys (e.g., a slinky, a cook-set, a space-station) and one aggressive toy (a gun or a knife). Two inflated plastic dolls, 36 inches and 42 inches in height,

[2] Nine children, all in the 5–6-year-old age group, were terminated prior to the collection of data because they refused to remain alone, cried, or left the experimental situation. Twenty-three other children participated in the entire experiment but were not included in the sample. Of these, 14 (5 in the younger age group and 9 in the older group) did not understand or follow instructions for the response box; 7 (3 younger and 4 older children) played or explored the room instead of watching television. The data for the remaining 2 children were not recorded properly due to the technical difficulties. All potential participants brought to the institute by their parents who were not eliminated for the reasons listed above were included in the experimental sample.

also stood in the room. The child was told that he would be left alone for a few minutes and that he could play freely with any of the toys.

All the children were observed through a one-way vision mirror, and their aggressive behavior was recorded using a time-sampling procedure. One point was scored for the occurrence of each of three predetermined categories of aggressive play (playing with the knife, playing with the gun, assaulting either of the dolls) during the first 10 seconds of each of ten ½-minute periods. In order to assess interobserver reliability for this measure, 10 subjects were observed independently by the two observers. Their agreement using the scoring procedures was virtually perfect ($r = .99$).

At the end of the play period, the experimenter reentered the room and asked the child to recall both the television program which he had seen and the nature of the game he had played. (All children included in the analyses were able to recall correctly the operation of the red and green buttons and the essential content of the television programs to which they had been exposed.) The child was then escorted to the lounge where the parent was waiting, thanked for his or her participation, rewarded with a small prize, and asked not to discuss the experiment with his or her friends.

Results

Willingness to Hurt Another Child

The single overall measure which appears to capture the greatest amount of information in this situation is the total duration in seconds of each subject's aggressive responses during the 20 trials. Since marked heterogeneity of variance was apparent among the groups on this measure, the overall 2 × 2 × 2 analysis of variance was performed on square-root transformed scores (i.e., $x' = \sqrt{x} + \sqrt{x + 1}$, Winer, 1962). The means for all groups on this measure are presented in Table 6.6. The analysis itself reveals only one significant effect: that for treatment conditions ($F = 4.16$, $p < .05$). Children who had observed the aggressive program later showed reliably more willingness to engage in interpersonal aggression than those who had observed the neutral program.

Several supplementary analyses, which may serve to clarify the nature of this overall effect, were also computed. For example, a subject's total duration score may be viewed as the product of the number of times he aggresses and the average duration of each of these aggressive responses. Moreover, these two measures are only moderately, although reliably, related in the overall sample ($r = +.30$, $p < .05$). Analysis of variance for the average duration of the hurt responses reveals only a significant program effect that directly parallels the effects for total duration ($F = 3.95$, $p < .05$). The means for all groups on this measure are presented in Table 6.7. In contrast, analysis of the frequency measure fails to show any significant effects, although the tendency for the younger children is in the same direction.

Helping Responses

One possible explanation of the higher total aggresssion scores shown by the aggressive program group is that these children were simply more aroused than their nonaggressive treatment counterparts. To check on this interpretation, an overall

Table 6.6. Mean total duration (transformed) of aggressive responses in all groups

	5–6-year-olds		*8–9-year-olds*	
Program shown	*Boys*	*Girls*	*Boys*	*Girls*
Aggressive	9.65	8.98	12.50	8.53
N	15	18	20	17
Nonaggressive	6.86	6.50	8.50	6.27
N	15	17	18	16

Table 6.7. Mean average durations (total duration/number of hurt responses) of aggressive responses in all groups

	5–6-year-olds		8–9-year-olds	
Program shown	*Boys*	*Girls*	*Boys*	*Girls*
Aggressive	3.42	2.64	5.18	3.07
Nonaggressive	2.55	2.09	2.07	1.57

Note.—The number of subjects for each cell in this analysis is the same as that shown in Table 6.6.

analysis of variance was performed on the total duration of the help responses, employing the same square-root transformation described above. Presumably, if general arousal accounted for the effects of the hurt measure, the aggressive program groups should also show larger help scores than the nonaggressive program groups. However, contrary to the general arousal hypothesis, the effect of the treatments on this measure was not significant; the overall F comparing the aggressive program subjects' prosocial responses with those of the nonaggressive program observers was only 1.17. The one effect of borderline significance which did appear in this analysis was a Program × Sex × Age interaction ($F = 3.91$, $p \cong .05$). As can be seen in Table 6.8, in which these data are presented, the interaction results from the very large helping responses shown by older girls who saw the aggressive program and the relatively large helping responses shown by younger girls who saw the nonaggressive one.

As a second check on the possibility that the longer durations in the aggressive program groups simply reflected a general arousal, a similar analysis was performed on the average duration scores of the help responses. In contrast to the comparable measure for aggressive responses, no significant differences for any of the main effects or interactions appeared on this measure (main effect for treatments, $F = 1.24$) although paralleling the total duration measure, the older girls who saw the aggressive program showed particularly long average durations. Finally, to show from a correlational approach that the overall help and hurt scores were not merely alternate measures of the same phenomenon, the product-moment correlation between the two sets of scores was computed. The resulting r of $-.24$ reflects a weak but significant ($p < .05$, two-tailed) negative relationship. Thus, overall, it appears clear that a specific disinhibition regarding *aggressive* behavior was produced by observing the televised aggression. This cannot be explained as a general arousal effect.

Aggression in the Play Situation

The mean aggressive play scores for all subjects are presented in Table 6.9. A 2 × 2 × 2 analysis of variance of these data revealed significant main effects for treatment ($F = 8.01$, $df = 1/128$, $p < .01$) and sex ($F = 37.87$, $df = 1/128$, $p < .001$). In addition, the Treatment × Sex ($F = 4.11$, $df = 1/128$, $p < .05$). Treatment × Age

Table 6.8. Mean total duration (transformed) of helping responses in all groups

	5–6-year-olds		8–9-year-olds	
Program shown	*Boys*	*Girls*	*Boys*	*Girls*
Aggressive	10.81	11.66	11.32	19.97
Nonaggressive	10.76	14.12	11.59	10.69

Note.—The number of subjects for each cell in this analysis is the same as that shown in Table 6.6.

Table 6.9. Mean number of time-sampled aggressive play responses in all groups

	5–6-year-olds		8–9-year-olds	
Program shown	*Boys*	*Girls*	*Boys*	*Girls*
Aggressive	7.13	2.94	5.65	3.00
Nonaggressive	3.33	2.65	5.39	2.63

Note.—The number of subjects for each cell in this analysis is the same as that shown in Table 6.6.

($F = 4.28$, $df = 1/128$, $p < .05$), and Treatment × Sex × Age ($F = 4.68$, $df = 1/128$, $p < .05$) interactions were all significant. As is apparent from inspection of Table 6.9, these interactions arose from the fact that, although children exposed to the aggressive program tended to show a higher level of aggressive play than children exposed to the nonaggressive one in all simple comparisons, the effect was much greater for the younger boys than for any of the remaining groups.

Discussion

The overall results of the present experiment provide relatively consistent evidence for the view that certain aspects of a child's willingness to aggress may be at least temporarily increased by merely witnessing aggressive television episodes. These findings confirm and extend many earlier reports regarding the effects of symbolically modeled aggression on the subsequent imitative aggressive behavior of young observers toward inanimate objects (e.g., Bandura, Ross, & Ross, 1963a; Hicks, 1965; Rosekrans & Hartup, 1967). Likewise, the present data are in accord with other studies which have shown disinhibition of both young children's aggressive play and older viewers' willingness to shock another person after observing filmed aggressive modeling. As in many earlier studies, subjects exposed to symbolic aggressive models regularly tended to behave more aggressively than control group subjects tested under identical circumstances. Further, the present results emerged despite the brevity of the aggressive sequences (less than 4 minutes), the absence of a strong prior instigation to aggression, the clear availability of an alternative helping response, and the use of nationally broadcast materials rather than specially prepared laboratory films.

The various measures employed, considered together, provide some clarification of the nature of the effects obtained in the overall analysis. The significant effect for the total duration measure appears to stem predominantly from the average duration of the subjects' aggressive responses. In fact, as seen in Table 6.7, the group means on this measure did not overlap; the *lowest* individual cell mean among those who observed the aggressive program was higher than the *highest* mean among those groups who observed the nonaggressive program.

It should also be recalled that the instructions given to all children emphasized that a brief depression of the hurt button would cause only minimal distress to the other child, while longer depressions would cause increasingly greater discomfort. This fact, coupled with the finding that the overall average duration of such responses was more than 75% longer in the aggressive program group than in the control group, suggests clearly that the primary effect of exposure to the aggressive program was that of reducing subjects' restraints against inflicting severe discomfort on the ostensible peer victim, that is, of increasing the *magnitude* of the hurting response. With the exception of the older girls, this effect was not paralleled by an increment in the corresponding measures of helping; thus it cannot be attributed to simple arousal effects.

It should be noted that the measure of aggressive play responses was obtained after all the subjects had been given an opportunity to help or hurt another child. Thus the observed effects might reflect an interaction between the programs and some aspect of the hurting/helping opportunity rather than the simple influence of the programs themselves. While the present data do not permit us to address the possibility of such interactions directly, it is clear that the obtained results are consistent with earlier studies in which other types of aggressive scenes were used and where there were no such intervening measures.

The present experiment was designed primarily to determine whether children's willingness to engage in interpersonal aggression would be affected by the viewing of violent televised material. Within the context of the experimental situation and dependent measures employed, it appeared that this was indeed the case. However, it is clear that the occurrence and magnitude of such effects will be influenced by a number of situational and personality variables. It is thus important to examine the antecedents and correlates of such reactions to violence in greater detail. In view of the fact that a child born today will, by the age of 18, have spent more of his life watching television than in any other single activity except sleep (Lesser, 1970), few problems seem more deserving of attention.

References

BANDURA, A. Influence of models' reinforcement contingencies on the acquisition of imitative responses. *Journal of Personality and Social Psychology*, 1965, *1*, 589–595.

BANDURA, A., ROSS, D., & ROSS, S. A. Transmission of aggression through imitation of aggressive models. *Journal of Abnormal and Social Psychology*, 1961, *63*, 575–582.

———. Imitation of film-mediated aggressive models. *Journal of Abnormal and Social Psychology*, 1963, *66*, 3–11. (a)

———. Vicarious reinforcement and imitative learning. *Journal of Abnormal and Social Psychology*, 1963, *67*, 601–607. (b)

BERKOWITZ, L. Some aspects of observed aggression. *Journal of Personality and Social Psychology*, 1965, *2*, 359–369.

BERKOWITZ, L., & RAWLINGS, E. Effects of film violence on inhibitions against subsequent aggression. *Journal of Abnormal and Social Psychology*, 1963, *66*, 405–412.

FESHBACH, S. The stimulating versus cathartic effects of a vicarious aggressive activity. *Journal of Abnormal and Social Psychology*, 1961, *63*, 381–385.

FESHBACH, S., & SINGER, R. D. *Television and aggression.* San Francisco: Jossey-Bass, 1971.

FLANDERS, J. P. A review of research on imitative behavior. *Psychological Bulletin*, 1968, *69*, 316–337.

HALLORAN, J. D. Television and violence. *The Twentieth Century*, 1964, *174*, 61–72.

HANRATTY, M. A. Imitation of film-mediated aggression against live and inanimate victims. Unpublished master's thesis, Vanderbilt University, 1969.

HANRATTY, M. A., LIEBERT, R. M., MORRIS, L. W., & FERNANDEZ, L. E. Imitation of film-mediated aggression against live and inanimate victims. *Proceedings of the 77th Annual Convention of the American Psychological Association*, 1969, *4*, 457–458. (Summary)

HANRATTY, M. A., O'NEAL, E., & SULZER, J. L. The effect of frustration upon imitation of aggression. *Journal of Personality and Social Psychology*, 1972, *21*, 30–34.

HICKS, D. J. Imitation and retention of film-mediated aggressive peer and adult models. *Journal of Personality and Social Psychology*, 1965, *2*, 97–100.

KLAPPER, J. T. The impact of viewing "aggression": Studies and problems of extrapolation. In O. N. Larsen (Ed.), *Violence and the mass media.* New York: Harper & Row, 1968.

LARSEN, O. N. *Violence and the mass media.* New York: Harper & Row, 1968.

LESSER, G. S. Designing a program for broadcast television. In F. F. Korten, S. W. Cook, & J. I. Lacey (Eds.), *Psychology and the problems of society.* Washington, D.C.: American Psychological Association, 1970.

LOVAAS, O. I. Effect of exposure to symbolic aggression on aggressive behavior. *Child Development*, 1961, *32*, 37–44.

MALLICK, S. K., & MCCANDLESS, B. R. A study of catharsis of aggression. *Journal of Personality and Social Psychology*, 1966, *4*, 591–596.

MERRIAM, E. We're teaching our children that violence is fun. *The Ladies' Home Journal,* 1964, *52,* 44, 49, 52.

ROSEKRANS, M. A., & HARTUP, W. W. Imitative influences of consistent and inconsistent response consequences to a model on aggressive behavior in children. *Journal of Personality and Social Psychology,* 1967, *7,* 429–434.

SAVITSKY, J. C., ROGERS, R. W., IZARD, C. E., & LIEBERT, R. M. The role of frustration and anger in the imitation of filmed aggression against a human victim. *Psychological Reports,* 1971, *29,* 807–810.

SIEGEL, A. E. Film-mediated fantasy aggression and strength of aggressive drive. *Child Development,* 1956, *27,* 365–378.

WALTERS, R. H. Implications of laboratory studies for the control and regulation of violence. *The Annals of the American Academy of Political and Social Science,* 1966, *364,* 60–72.

WALTERS, R. H., & THOMAS, E. L. Enhancement of punitiveness by visual and audiovisual displays. *Canadian Journal of Psychology,* 1963, *16,* 244–255.

WERTHAM, F. Is T.V. hardening us to the war in Vietnam? *New York Times,* December 4, 1966.

WINER, B. J. *Statistical principles in experimental design.* New York: McGraw-Hill, 1962.

33. EFFECTS OF FAMILIARIZATION ON CHILDREN'S RATINGS OF PICTURES OF WHITES AND BLACKS

GORDON N. CANTOR

Eighty 9- to 11-year-old white children (40 males, 40 females) were exposed to 10 10-second presentations of each of 3 pictures of white and each of 3 pictures of black boys. The Ss then rated these pictures and also those of 3 previously unseen whites and blacks on a 5-point rating scale, indicating the extent to which they "would like to bring the boy home to spend time with them and their families." The major results were: (a) the Ss as a group rated the blacks more highly than the whites; and (b) familiarization enhanced ratings made by both male and female Ss of the blacks, but not ratings of the whites (male Ss rated familiar whites below nonfamiliar whites, whereas female Ss gave these groups virtually identical ratings). These results were discussed with reference to earlier child studies on familiarization effects and the adult literature concerned with the effects of "mere exposure."

A provocative publication by Zajonc (1968) in which he maintained that "mere exposure" to a stimulus enhances one's attitude toward it has led to considerable work over the past few years on the attitudinal effects of stimulus familiarization. Some of the studies involved have been devoted to further documentation of the phenomenon in question (e.g., Zajonc & Rajecki, 1969), whereas others have been concerned with identifying the mechanism(s) mediating the phenomenon (e.g., Harrison, 1968; Matlin, 1970). The view offered by the latter two workers focuses on the suppositions that (*a*) nonfamiliar stimuli arouse competing response tendencies in the individual, (*b*) the presence of such tendencies is unpleasant, and (*c*) familiarization leads to a reduction in response competition associated with the familiarized stimuli and hence an increase in positive affective reactions to them. More recently, Zajonc, Swap, Harrison, and Roberts (1971) have reported evidence leading to the conclusion that the exposure effect (specifically, increasingly positive affective reactions as a function of increasing frequencies of exposure) occurs (by implication, without exception) when frequency of exposure is manipulated and ratings are obtained on a within-Ss basis, but "only if the stimuli differ in distribution or the scale values are unambiguous" when frequency of exposure is varied within-Ss and ratings are obtained on a between-Ss basis. Furthermore, these authors maintain that "the frequency variable cannot be considered to have been manipulated on a within-subject basis when some stimuli to be judged are shown to the individual a fixed number of times and others which he then also rates are never shown." Brickman and Redfield (1970) conclude, on the basis of their findings, that enhancement of attitude toward a stimulus due to familiarization occurs more markedly when S's initial attitude is neutral than when it is positive and that little or no enhancement (or even a decrement) occurs when initial predispositions are negative. Suedfeld, Epstein, Buchanan, and Landon (1971) also consider S's initial attitude to be of importance. These investigators introduced experimental manipulations designed to produce "favorable" or "unfavorable" attitudes toward stimuli that were subsequently exposed 0, 1, 2, 5, 10, or 25 times. The group given the favorable set behaved in accordance with Zajonc's original "mere exposure" findings, but the other group's function relating frequency of exposure and attitudinal ratings was curvilinear (the most negative ratings being associated with 0 and 25 exposures). Burgess and Sales (1971) argue that the "mere exposure" effect occurs because the experimental context within which stimulus exposure takes place is not affectively neutral; rather, they contend, the context is positively evaluated by S and this sort of affective reaction comes to be made to the familiarized stimuli in the course of their exposure via a classical conditioning process.

All of the research summarized above has dealt with adult Ss. Several studies in which children served as Ss provide data seemingly inconsistent with the Zajonc position. Some of these experiments (see Cantor, 1969, for a summary) show that nonfamilarized stimuli are projected for longer periods of time than are familiarized stimuli. More to the point, children give more positive attitudinal ratings to nonfamiliar than to familiar stimuli (Cantor, 1968; Cantor & Kubose, 1969). In attempting to reconcile these latter findings with those of Zajonc, Berlyne (1970) suggested that Zajonc's stimuli (English and foreign language words, Chinese characters, pictures of men's faces) were relatively "complex," whereas those used by Cantor (Welsh figures—i.e., relatively low-meaningful configurations and geometric patterns taken from the Welsh Figure Preference Test [Welsh, 1959]) were "simple." Berlyne (1970) reports an extensive series of studies on adults, the results of which he interprets as supporting the position that exposure enhances attitudes toward "complex" stimuli, but has the opposite effect on attitudes toward "simple" stimuli. Siebold (1971) attempted to test this assertion by familiarizing children with Welsh figures previously scaled by adults as "simple" or "complex." Siebold's results were not in accord with Berlyne's position, in that higher ratings were given to nonfamiliar than to familiar stimuli in the case of both classes of figures. As Siebold notes, his "complex" stimuli may not have been "complex enough," but in the absence of a means for scaling stimuli for complexity independent of the attitudinal data, one is dealing here with an unanswerable question.

Most relevant to the investigation reported here is a study by Perlman and Oskamp (1971) in which adults first rated the pictures of adult black and white males with reference to 12 different behavioral traits. The pictures used in this phase were designated "neutral," in the sense that they resembled yearbook-type, plain-background photographs of men dressed in clothing having no particular connotations with regard to status in life. In a subsequent treatment phase, the Ss were exposed to pictures of the same men for varying numbers of times (1, 5, or 10). For a third of the Ss, the same pictures used in the first phase (i.e., "neutral") were employed. For a second third, the same models appeared, but in clothing and settings designed to create a "positive" impression (e.g., clergyman, scientist, etc.). The remaining Ss also saw the same models, but in clothing and settings designed to create a "negative" impression (e.g., prisoner, unskilled workman, etc.). In a third phase of experiment, all Ss rated the "neutral" pictures once again. The results may be summarized as follows: (*a*) for black models, positive exposures enhanced evaluations (indexed by a composite measure that combined individual trait ratings), whereas negative exposures decreased them; (*b*) white models showed primarily the positive effect; (*c*) increasing frequency of exposure was associated with marked positive increments in evaluations in the case of the "positive" treatment; (*d*) with reference to the "neutral" treatment, almost no change occurred across frequencies (virtually identical and very small *decrements* for frequencies 0, 1, and 5, and a modest increment for 10 exposures); and (*e*) some slight evidence was obtained for larger decrements associated with higher frequencies in the case of the "negative" condition. The absence in these data of a substantial enhancement effect for the "neutral" condition is of fundamental concern, because this finding constitutes a failure to replicate the "mere exposure" effect itself.

It can be seen from the above review that the "mere exposure" effect may or may not be obtained with adult Ss and shows no signs of occurring when children serve as Ss. The purpose of the present study was to determine if either the "mere exposure" effect, the "reversed mere exposure" effect, or both would be obtained when children serve as Ss and the stimuli are photographs of black and white boys. On the basis of earlier child research involving Welsh figures as stimuli, it was expected that nonfamiliarized pictures would be rated more highly than familiarized ones. However, it was recognized that results not fitting this pattern might be obtained that could perhaps shed some light on one or more of the "theoretical" positions cited above.

Method

Subjects

Forty-three males and 44 females enrolled in two Iowa City public schools served as Ss. All but four males were enrolled in fifth grade, the four exceptions being fourth graders. All females were fifth graders. Three fifth-grade males and four females were eliminated from the study because of a failure to meet a criterion discussed below. The remaining Ss—40 males and 40 females—ranged in age from 9 [yrs.] 7 [mos.] to 11 [yrs.] 11 [mos.], with a mean of 10–8. The city (population approximately 50,000) in which the Ss reside and the schools they attend are both characterized by low minority-group representation.

Apparatus

The equipment included a Kodak RA 950 Carousel slide projector, Hunter timers used to control stimulus and interstimulus intervals, and a projection screen. Twelve 35-mm slides were used, each containing a different one of the photographs shown in Figure 6.6. The pictures included six white and six black boys, chosen for pleasantness of expression and general attractiveness. Additional materials included a supply of rating sheets. Each sheet measured 8½ × 11 inches and had arrayed across its center a series of five schematic faces. These consisted of circles, each with a radius of ⅞ inch, the adjacent pairs being separated by ⅜-inch gaps; small circles were drawn within each of the larger circles to represent the eyes and noses, the only difference among the faces being in the nature of the mouths. The mouth on the far left was drawn to suggest a "large frown," that on the far right a "large smile." The center face had a straight horizontal line representing the mouth. A face with a "small frown" and one with a "small smile" were located on appropriate sides of the center face. These are identical to rating scale drawings used by Siebold (1971).

Procedure

Each *S* participated individually in a session lasting approximately 15–20 minutes and conducted in a research trailer located on the school grounds. The *S* was seated before a table containing the projection screen, located about 2 ft from the table's edge. The slides were rear projected on the screen. The table top between S and the screen provided a surface on which rating forms were stacked and which *S* used in making his rating responses.

Rating instruction phase The *S* was told he would see pictures of some boys and would then be asked to indicate how he would feel about bringing each boy home to spend some time with him and his family. A sample rating sheet was then shown to *S* and it was explained that an X mark was to be drawn: (*a*) on the face with the "large frown" if *S* "really didn't want" to bring the boy home; (*b*) on the face with the "small frown" if *S* "kind of

Figure 6.6. The pictures used in the present experiment.

disliked" the idea of bringing the boy home; (c) on the face that "isn't frowning or smiling" if S "didn't care one way or the other"; (*d*) on the face with the "small smile" if S "kind of liked" the idea; and (*e*) on the face with the "large smile" if S "liked the idea a whole lot." The *E* marked each of the designated faces as the above instructions were presented. Following this, S was given five fresh rating sheets, one at a time, and told to place an X on the face that was to signify a particular judgment. The order of elicitation of the five responses for all Ss was 4, 1, 5, 3, and 2 (considering the faces as numbered from 1 to 5, starting on the extreme left).

Familiarization phase The familiarization phase was then administered. The S was told that some pictures of boys would be presented on the screen several times and that he was simply to look carefully at each picture the whole time it was projected. Each S was familiarized on three whites and three blacks. These were presented one at a time for 10-sec durations, each one on 10 different occasions, making a total of 60 familiarization exposures. For a given S, the six familiarization stimuli assigned to him (see below) occurred once within each block of 6 trials, the order of occurrence within each block being determined by separate random assignments. The interstimulus interval was only the time needed for the projector to change slides, the one exception being a 2-min rest interval given between familiarization trials 30 and 31.

Rating phase Following the final familiarization exposure, the rating phase was begun. The S was given a stack of 12 rating sheets and told to rate each picture he was about to see in this phase on a separate sheet. On a given rating trial, a picture was projected until S marked his rating sheet and turned it face down. At this point a blank slide was projected for approximately 5 sec and then the next picture to be rated was projected. Following completion of the twelfth and final rating, S was thanked and returned to his classroom.

Stimulus assignments and orders The numerals 1–6 were arbitrarily assigned to the six white (W) and six black (B) pictures (thus, W_1, W_2, . . . , W_6 and B_1, B_2, . . . , B_6). Each of the 20 possible W triads (W_1, W_2, W_3; W_1, W_2, W_4, . . . ; W_4, W_5, W_6) and the 20 possible B triads (B_1, B_2, B_3; etc.) were used equally often as familiar (F) and as nonfamiliar (NF) stimuli. In order to assign stimulus combinations, each of the 20 possible B triads (all designated for this purpose as F) was randomly paired with four different randomly selected W triads (designated NF). The resulting 80 combinations of three F-W, three NF-W, three F-B, and three NF-B were assigned S-numbers 1–80. The order of stimulus presentations during the familiarization phase was determined randomly for each S, with the restriction that all six familiarization stimuli (three W's, three B's) occur within each six-trial block. The order arrangements for the rating trials were determined as follows: (*a*) for rating trial 1, a fourth of the Ss rated an F-W, a fourth an NF-W, a fourth an F-B, and a fourth an NF-B stimulus; (*b*) in each block of two rating trials, every S rated one F-W and one NF-B or one NF-W and one F-B; (*c*) if F-W and NF-B occurred in a given block of two rating trials, then NF-W and F-B occurred in the next block, and vice versa; (*d*) except for the first pair of rating trials, the order of assignment of F and NF within blocks of two trials was determined randomly for each S; (*e*) the order of assignment of specific pictures to rating trial blocks (given the designation of the pictures as F or NF for each S) was random; and (*f*) the Ss were assigned S-numbers on a rotational basis that assured that a fourth of the males and a fourth of the females made their first rating on an F-W, an NF-W, an F-B, and an NF-B, and also that the sexes were spread evenly across S-numbers so as to avoid confounding sex with similarities across stimulus combinations.

Results

In order for S's data to be used, it was required that he respond correctly all five times when told to mark the various faces during the rating instruction phase. The data of seven Ss were discarded due to failures to meet this criterion. These Ss were replaced in order to obtain a final N of 80 (40 males, 40 females).

Each of S's ratings was scored by use of the values 1–5, 1 being assigned to ratings at the left end and 5 to ratings at the right end of the rating continuum. Thus, the higher the score, the more favorable the reaction. For each S, four means were computed: one based on his three F-W ratings, one on his three NF-W ratings, one on his three F-B ratings, and one on his three NF-B ratings. These means provided the basic scores entered into the analysis.

A mixed analysis of variance design was used, with sex of S as a between-Ss variable and familiar (F) versus nonfamiliar (NF) and white (W) versus black (B) as withins. Three significant effects were obtained: (*a*) the main effect of W versus B, $F(1,78) = 5.27$, $p < .05$; (*b*) the interaction between W versus B and F versus NF, $F(1,78) = 13.35$, $p < .01$, and (*c*) the interaction between W versus B and sex of S, $F(1,78) = 12.96$, $p < .01$.

The main effect of W versus B reflects the fact that a *lower* overall average rating was given to the whites ($\overline{X} = 3.20$) than to the blacks ($\overline{X} = 3.42$). The means involved in the two significant interactions are to be found in tables 6.10 and 6.11.

It may be seen in Table 6.10 that the Ss rated the NF-W pictures higher than the F-W pictures, but the F-B pictures higher than the NF-B. Both of these simple effects are significant, $F(1,78) = 4.00$, $p < .05$; $F(1,78) = 15.00$, $p < .01$. The difference between F-W and F-B, with F-B given the higher average ratings, is significant, $F(1,78) = 14.86$, $p < .01$; the difference in the opposite direction for NF-W and NF-B is not, $F(1,78) < 1.0$.

Table 6.10. Mean ratings involved in the interaction between white versus black and familiar versus nonfamiliar

Stimulus Type	Stimulus Color: White	Stimulus Color: Black	Overall
Familiar	3.10	3.61	3.35
Nonfamiliar	3.31	3.22	3.27
Overall	3.20	3.42	....

Table 6.11. Mean ratings involved in the interaction between white versus black and sex of S

Sex of S	Stimulus Color: White	Stimulus Color: Black	Overall
Male	3.15	3.70	3.43
Female	3.25	3.13	3.19
Overall	3.20	3.42	....

Table 6.11 shows that the female Ss rated the whites more highly than did the males, whereas the male Ss rated the blacks more highly than did the females. The first of these two simple effects is not significant, $F(1,78) < 1.0$; the second one is significant, $F(1,78) = 8.65$, $p < .01$. It may also be seen in Table 6.11 that the male Ss gave higher ratings to the blacks than to the whites, but that the female Ss gave slightly higher ratings to the whites than to the blacks. The former difference is significant, $F(1,78) = 17.14$, $p < .01$; but the latter is not, $F(1,78) < 1.0$.

It probably should be mentioned that the triple interaction (W vs. B × F vs. NF × sex of S), while not statistically significant, $F(1,78) = 3.51$, $p < .07$, reflects a differential pattern for the two sexes that is not revealed in Table 6.11. Specifically, the male Ss rated NF-W ($\overline{X} = 3.36$) above F-W ($\overline{X} = 2.95$) and F-B ($\overline{X} = 3.95$) above NF-B ($\overline{X} = 3.46$); in contrast, the females gave average ratings to F-W ($\overline{X}$ = 3.24), NF-W ($\overline{X}$ = 3.26); and F-B ($\overline{X}$ = 3.27) that were virtually identical and higher than the mean for NF-B ($\overline{X}$ = 2.99).

Discussion

The significantly higher ratings given by Ss of both sexes to the familiar as opposed to the nonfamiliar blacks constitute the first demonstration in the Institute laboratories of Zajonc's "mere exposure" effect (assuming one is willing to use that term with reference to an obtained difference that relates to a manipulation involving a constant number of exposures versus none). The finding just cited, considered in conjunction with the higher ratings given the nonfamiliar as opposed to the familiar whites (at least in the male data) plus the average ratings given the two types of nonfamiliarized stimuli by both sexes, provides a basis for discussing several of the "theoretical" positions mentioned in the introductory section of the present paper.

First, it would appear that the Burgess and Sales's (1971) viewpoint, attributing the "mere exposure" effect to a positive experimental context, would not be applicable in a situation such as the present one in which opposite effects (enhancement of *and* decrease in attitude) occurred for two different types of stimuli. Second, it is difficult to see how Berlyne's (1970) position regarding simple and complex stimuli would apply to the pictures used in the present study. The predisposition or initial set position (Brickman & Redfield, 1970; Suedfeld et al., 1971) is given some support by the female but not the male data, if we assume one can use the average ratings given the nonfamiliar stimuli to estimate initial attitudes (probably a questionable tack). The females did give the nonfamiliar blacks a neutral rating ($\overline{X}$ = 2.99) and the familiar blacks a fairly positive one ($\overline{X}$ = 3.27), whereas they gave the nonfamiliar whites a fairly favorable rating ($\overline{X}$ = 3.26) and the familiar whites virtually the same rating ($\overline{X}$ = 3.24). However, the males rated the nonfamiliar whites quite favorably ($\overline{X}$ = 3.36) and the familiar whites neutrally ($\overline{X}$ = 2.95) (a *reversed* "mere exposure" effect); furthermore, considering the substantial positive rating given the nonfamiliar blacks ($\overline{X}$ = 3.46) by the males, the enhancement effect due to familiarization on the blacks ($\overline{X}$ = 3.95) would seem to be quite unexpected from the set or predisposition viewpoint.

The competing response interpretation (Harrison, 1968; Matlin, 1970) assumes, of course, the occurrence of the "mere exposure" effect; it could not account for the clear reversed effect obtained for the white pictures in the male data.

The finding of higher affective ratings given nonfamiliar as compared with familiar stimuli has now been obtained a number of times in Institute studies involving children as Ss, including Cantor (1968), Cantor and Kubose (1969, Experiments I and II), Siebold (1971), and the present experiment (male data, white pictures). Zajonc et al. (1971) have made it clear they wish to think of the "mere exposure" effect (i.e., *enhancement* of attitude due to familiarization) as involving a within-Ss variation in frequency of exposure incorporating at least three frequency levels. The only Institute study of this nature that can be mentioned is an unpublished one in which 48 fifth-grade children were exposed to 1, 3, 5, and 7 presentations of different Welsh figures. These Ss gave the stimuli exposed for the above frequencies mean ratings of 7.67, 7.46, 7.46, and 6.81, respectively on a 12.7-cm graphic rating scale (higher score signifies more favorable rating). However, the frequency effect was not significant. Although the significant "reversed mere exposure" effects that *have* been obtained involved zero versus some constant number of exposures, it seems true that these results must be disquieting for those who believe "mere exposure" enhances but does not decrease the favorability of attitudes. It remains for those working with children to conduct experiments entailing manipulations that adhere to the Zajonc et al. boundary conditions, in order to determine if a significant "reversed mere exposure" effect can be demonstrated under such conditions.

It has no doubt occurred to the reader that different results might have been obtained in the present study had pictures of female as well as male whites and blacks been used. It is hoped that such a study will be conducted in the near future. A much more serious concern has to do with the possibility that effects obtained in a study such as the present one could be due at least in part to the *particular pictures* chosen to comprise the group of whites and the group of blacks. For example, one might wish to argue that the blacks who were used appear to be of an age more appropriate for association with fifth-graders than is the case for the whites. A difference of this sort could be appealed to in explaining the white versus black main effect and even, conceivably, the familiar versus nonfamiliar × white versus black interaction. The answer to this problem may lie in the use of pictures of whites and blacks drawn from a large pool, the members of which have been scaled on a number of dimensions (such as apparent age, attractiveness, etc.), with the white and black pictures to be used being equated on the basis of such scale values.

Whatever causal factors played a role in producing the results obtained in the present study, one cannot help but reflect on the substantially higher ratings given by both the males and females to the familiar as compared with the nonfamiliar blacks. Although one might wish to question whether any "real-life" implications reside in data produced in a laboratory session lasting 20 min per child, the author is enough of an optimist to hope that the "mere exposure" effect just mentioned (and also the effect stemming from the general tendency of the Ss to rate the blacks more highly than the whites) may have some social as well as statistical significance.

References

BERLYNE, D. E. Novelty, complexity, and hedonic value. *Perception & Psychophysics*, 1970, *8*, 279–286.

BRICKMAN, P., & REDFIELD, J. Drive and predisposition as factors in the attitudinal effects of mere exposure. Paper presented at the meeting of the American Psychological Association, Miami Beach, Florida, September 1970.

BURGESS, T. D. G., II, & SALES, S. M. Attitudinal effects of "mere exposure": a reevaluation. *Journal of Experimental Social Psychology*, 1971, *7*, 461–472.

CANTOR, G. N. Children's "like-dislike" ratings of familiarized and nonfamiliarized visual stimuli. *Journal of Experimental Child Psychology*, 1968, *6*, 651–657.

———. Effects of stimulus familiarization on child behavior. In J. P. Hill (Ed.), *Minnesota symposia on child psychology*. Vol. 3. Minneapolis: University of Minnesota Press, 1969.

CANTOR, G. N., & KUBOSE, S. H. Preschool children's ratings of familiarized and nonfamiliarized visual stimuli. *Journal of Experimental Child Psychology*, 1969, *8*, 74–81.

HARRISON, A. A. Response competition, frequency, exploratory behavior, and liking. *Journal of Personality and Social Psychology*, 1968, *9*, 363–368.

MATLIN, M. W. Response competition as a mediating factor in the frequency-affect relationship. *Journal of Personality and Social Psychology*, 1970, *16*, 536–552.

PERLMAN, D., & OSKAMP, S. The effects of picture content and exposure frequency on evaluations of Negroes and whites. *Journal of Experimental Social Psychology,* 1971, *7,* 503–514.

SIEBOLD, J. R. Children's rating responses as related to amount and recency of stimulus familiarization and stimulus complexity. Master's thesis, University of Iowa, 1971.

SUEDFELD, P.; EPSTEIN, Y. M.; BUCHANAN, E.; & LANDON, P. B. Effects of set on the "effects of mere exposure." *Journal of Personality and Social Psychology,* 1971, *17,* 121–123.

WELSH, G. S. *Welsh figure preference test.* (Research ed.) Palo Alto, Calif.: Consulting Psychologists Press, 1959.

ZAJONC, R. B. Attitudinal effects of mere exposure. *Journal of Personality and Social Psychology Monograph Supplement,* 1968, 9 (2, Pt. 2).

ZAJONC, R. B., & RAJECKI, D. W. Exposure and affect: field experiment. *Psychonomic Science,* 1969, *17,* 216–217.

ZAJONC, R. B.; SWAP, W. C.; HARRISON, A. A.; & ROBERTS, P. Limiting conditions of the exposure effect: satiation and relativity. *Journal of Personality and Social Psychology,* 1971, *18,* 384–391.

34. THE DEVELOPMENT OF POLITICAL ATTITUDES IN YOUNG CHILDREN

FREDA REBELSKY, CHERYL CONOVER, and PATRICIA CHAFETZ

Introduction

In recent years there has been a growing interest in the development of political attitudes. Studies of this topic come from a variety of disciplines though their main focus has been political attitudes of adolescents and young adults (7, 8, 9). Despite this emphasis on the development of political attitudes in adolescents, a series of studies by Hess and Easton (3, 4, 5) indicate that most political knowledge and attitudes have been acquired before adolescence. In a more recent study of 12,000 elementary school children, Hess and Torney (6, p. 23) found that "the acquisition of political attitudes proceeds rapidly, especially through fifth grade."

The present study was designed to investigate children's knowledge of and attitudes towards issues relevant to the 1968 Presidential election. Because of our interest in some of the cognitive components of children's development of political perceptions, our sample included preschoolers.

Method

Subjects

Subjects were 292 children from age two to age 13; half of each sex. Eighty percent of the children were white; the rest were of a variety of racial extractions.

Procedure

Children were interviewed with an open-ended questionnaire which permitted the child to explain his answers. Questions pertained to the President—his duties and possible successors—and issues of the 1968 Presidential election. Three of the items were scored for accuracy of information, three items were treated as attitude items, and responses to the remaining items were treated as qualitative data. The qualitative data were analyzed with the use of a frequency distribution of all responses given for each item, for each group of children.

Subjects were divided by age, sex, and race. Children up to age five comprised the young group; children from six to nine composed the middle group; the remaining children constituted the old group.

Results

Age Trends

As expected, the proportion of accurate answers on information items increased with age. For all three items, the largest difference was between the youngest and the middle group; scores for the middle group more closely resemble those for the older group. As can be seen in Table 6.12, more children knew that there was a war than knew the name of the President or Presidential candidates for all age groups. Moreover, more of the middle and older children knew the name of at least one Presidential candidate than knew the name of the President.

The tendency to give response of "I don't know" rather than to respond inaccurately also increased with age. *Es* interpreted this to mean that the older children were more aware that they did not know the answer to a question.

The three attitude-opinion items were: "Would you like to be a President someday?"; "Is war good or bad?"; and "Is peace good or bad?"

As Table 6.13 shows, the responses of the middle children more closely resemble the responses of the older children.

The data in response to the questions, "What does the President do?"; "Why do you or don't you want to be President?"; and "What's good/bad about war/peace?", reveal a large amount of overlap between the responses of the middle and the older children, but almost no overlap again between the responses of the younger and the middle groups. This similarity of the middle and the older groups is also true in terms of the distribution of response within each group. For example, the 247 middle and older children gave only nine different responses when asked "What does the President do?". In response to this same question, the 45 younger children gave 32 different responses.

Sex Differences

Since the age and race distributions were approximately equal for both sexes, it was possible to analyze sex differences without regard for age or racial biases. Approximately equal proportions of boys and girls knew at least one Presidential candidate and that there was a war somewhere. However, only 34 percent of the boys accurately knew the President's name, whereas 68 percent of the girls

Table 6.12. Percentage of children with accurate responses

Questions	*Young* *N*=45	*Middle* *N*=134	*Old* *N*=113
1. Who is President of the United States?	7%	55%	63%
2. Who wants to be the next President?	3%	62%	80%
3. Is there war any place now?	47%	80%	96%

Table 6.13. Percentage of children with indicated responses

Responses	Young N=45	Middle N=134	Old N=113
1. I would not like to be President someday.	38%	58%	76%
2. War is bad.	71%	88%	85%
3. Peace is good.	50%	95%	97%

knew his name. There was almost no difference between the attitudes of boys and girls: approximately equal proportions of each sex wanted to be President, felt that war was bad, and responded that peace was good. Boys and girls also tended to have a similar frequency of responses to those items that elicited qualitative data. However, girls were more likely than boys to respond that the President's job was to "take care of us." Despite this rather nurturant view of the Presidency, girls were also more likely to use their sex as an explanation for not wanting to be President.

Racial Differences

A racial comparison on the proportion of accurate responses to information items indicates a high rate of variation by items. A slightly higher percentage of nonwhites knew the name of the President; a slightly higher percentage of whites knew that there was a war; and 61 percent of the whites as compared to 31 percent of the nonwhites knew the name of at least one Presidential candidate. Whites responded "I don't know" more frequently than they responded inaccurately, while nonwhites responded inaccurately more frequently than they responded "I don't know."

A slightly higher proportion of nonwhites than whites responded that they would like to be President and that war was good. A somewhat higher proportion of nonwhites responded "I don't know" when asked if peace were bad or good. The qualitative responses of both groups were similar. Race was not mentioned as a reason for not wanting to be President.

Discussion

Our results suggest that there are consistent age-related learning patterns with regard to political information. Our data reveal a large difference between the responses of the younger group (two- through five-year-olds) and the older children in terms of both information and distribution of responses. There is much less difference between the middle and older children with respect to information, and almost no difference between these two groups with respect to the frequency distribution of responses. Thus, the data might be interpreted to suggest that there is a qualitative difference between the approach of the younger children and the other children which underlies and may explain the difference of information between them. This interpretation is supported by an examination of the content of the responses given by the younger as compared to the other children. For example, when the older children were asked what the President does, they most frequently responded that he makes laws, passes bills, and makes war. Responses of the younger children were more concrete and idiosyncratic: the President has birthdays, looks like Daddy, talks funny, rides horses, etc. This same concreteness is true for the items that are less related to information. For example, in response to the question "Why would you like to be President?" younger children answered things like to be tall, to have toys, to play drums, to "war my sister," and to run faster. These responses seem to indicate that the younger children were too egocentric and bound by the immediate to respond in an impersonal fashion. The nature of these responses would seem to support what Hess and Torney (6) have labeled the cognitive developmental model of political socialization. That is, children under six do not seem to have the cognitive maturity necessary to accumulate political information. On the other hand, the deceleration of political learning indicated by the similarity of responses of the middle and older children suggests that the accumulation model of political socialization (6) might apply to older children. This deceleration of political learning also supports Hess and Torney's conclusion that political knowledge increases rapidly in the early school years.

Our results are strikingly different from those found by Hess and Torney with respect to the President. The children in their sample knew more about the President than any other aspect of the political scene, whereas more of our children knew that there was a war and knew the name of at least one Presidential candidate than knew the name of the President. While 95 percent of their second graders knew the name of the President, only 55 percent of our middle group and 63 percent of our older group knew the name of the President. This difference of results is probably a reflection of the political developments between 1960 when Hess and Torney collected their data and 1968 when we collected our data. Their data were collected after the 1960 Presidential election which would tend to make the name of the new President more salient. Our data were collected just before the 1968 election in which the incumbent was not running. Thus, it is more likely that the children in our sample heard more comments regarding other candidates and the crucial issue of the war than they heard regarding the current President. While it is not surprising that young children are aware of the more controversial issues of the day, it does tend to disconfirm Hess and Torney's conclusion (6, p. 35) that "a young child's image of the national government is confined mainly to the President."

The children in our sample also reflect the political climate of their time on other issues. For example, of the middle and older children who wanted to be President, when asked why, over one third responded that they wanted to stop the war. Nearly one half of the middle children who did not want to be President said it was because they didn't want to get shot. Needless to say, both the war and the assassination of political figures were topics of discussion in autumn, 1968. Thus, our results seem to suggest that children's introduction to the political system is through the more salient topics of the day rather than through the person of the President.

These results are reminiscent of Converse's 1956 (2) re-evaluation of Centers' 1945 (1) study of American class structure and political attitudes. That is, it is difficult to generalize about political behavior from any one study, or even a group of studies, that are conducted in any one political era. With the change in political climate often comes a change in results of studies related to political behavior. This is especially important for the study of the development of political knowledge and attitudes, since it suggests great limitations to the interpretation of results of longitudinal studies in this area.

Summary

This study was an investigation of the acquisition of political knowledge and attitudes by children of ages two through 13. Two hundred and ninety-two children were interviewed on topics pertaining to politics. It was found that information increased with age, but that children under six responded in a very different way than did the older children. Results also showed that children knew more about the controversial issues of the day, such as the war, than knew the name of the President. This result seemingly contradicts Hess and Torney's (6) contention that the child initially relates to the political system through the person of the President. To reconcile this discrepancy of data, the authors suggest that children first learn whatever is politically important at the time. The person of the President was important at the time that Hess and Torney collected their data; the war was a larger issue at the time of our data collection. The authors conclude by pointing to the danger of generalization from political studies conducted during one political period.

References

1. CENTERS, R. The American class structure: A psychological analysis. In H. Proshansky & B. Seidenberg (Eds.), *Basic Studies in Social Psychology.* New York: Holt, Rinehart, & Winston, 1965.
2. CONVERSE, P. The shifting role of class in political attitudes and behavior. In H. Proshansky & B. Seidenberg (Eds.), *Basic Studies in Social Psychology.* New York: Holt, Rinehart, & Winston, 1965. Pp. 339–349.
3. HESS R. D., & EASTON, D. The child's changing image of the President. *Pub. Opin. Quart.*, 1960, *24*, 632–644.
4. ———. Youth and the political system. In S. W. Lipsitt & L. Lowenthal (Eds.), *Culture and Social Character: The Work of David Reisman Reviewed.* Glencoe, Illinois: Free Press, 1961.
5. ———. The role of elementary school in political socialization. *Schol. Rev.*, 1962, *70*, 253–265.
6. HESS, R. D., & TORNEY, J. V. *The Development of Political Attitudes in Children.* Chicago, Ill.: Aldine Publishing Co., 1967.
7. LEVIN, M. L. Social climate and political socialization. *Pub. Opin. Quart.*, 1961, *25* (4), 596–606.
8. O'NEIL, R. P. The development of political thinking during adolescence. *Diss. Abst.*, 1965, *25*(12), 7371–7372.
9. PUTNEY, S., & MIDDLETON, R. Some factors associated with student acceptance or rejection of the war. *Amer. Sociolog. Rev.* 1962, *27*(5), 655–677.

35. PLIGHT OF THE IK AND KAIADILT IS SEEN AS A CHILLING POSSIBLE END FOR MAN

JOHN B. CALHOUN

The Mountain—how pervasive in the history of man. A still small voice on Horeb, mount of God, guided Elijah. There, earlier, Moses standing before God received the Word. And Zion: "I am the Lord your God dwelling in Zion, my holy mountain."

Then there was Atum, mountain, God and first man, one and all together. The mountain rose out of a primordial sea of nothingness—Nun. Atum, the spirit of life, existed within Nun. In creating himself, Atum became the evolving ancestor of the human race. So goes the Egyptian mythology of creation, in which the Judaic Adam has his roots.

And there is a last Atum, united in his youth with another mountain of God, Mt. Morungole in northeasternmost Uganda. His people are the Ik, pronounced eek. They are the subject of an important new book, *The Mountain People,* by Colin M. Turnbull (Simon and Schuster, $6.95). They still speak Middle-Kingdom Egyptian, a language thought to be dead. But perhaps their persistence is not so strange. Egyptian mythology held that the waters of the life-giving Nile had their origin in Nun. Could this Nun have been the much more extensive Lake Victoria of 40 to 50 millennia ago when, near its borders, man groped upward to cloak his biological self with culture?

Well might the Ik have preserved the essence of this ancient tradition that affirms human beginnings. Isolated as they have been in their jagged mountain fastness, near the upper tributaries of the White Nile, the Ik have been protected from cultural evolution.

What a Shangri-la, this land of the Ik. In its center, the Kidepo valley, 35 miles across, home of abundant game; to the south, mist-topped Mt. Morungole; to the west the Niangea range; to the north, bordering the Sudan, the Didinga range; to the east on the Kenya border, a sheer drop of 2,000 feet into the Turkanaland of cattle herdsmen. Through ages of dawning history few people must have been interested in encroaching on this rugged land. Until 1964 anthropologists knew little of the Ik's existence. Their very name, much less their language, remained a mystery until, quite by chance, anthropologist Colin M. Turnbull found himself among them. What an opportunity to study pristine man! Here one should encounter the basic qualities of humanity unmarred by war, technology, pollution, over-population.

Turnbull rested in his bright red Land Rover at an 8,000-foot-high pass. A bit beyond this only "navigable" pass into the Kidepo Valley lay Pirre, a police outpost watching over a cluster of Ik villages. There to welcome him came Atum of the warm, open smile and gentle voice. Gray-haired at 40, appearing 65, he was the senior elder of the Ik, senior in authority if not quite so in age. Nattily attired in shorts and woolen sweater—in contrast to his mostly naked colleagues—Atum bounced forward with his ebony walking stick, greeted Turnbull in Swahili, and from that moment on took command as best he could of Turnbull's life. At Atum's village a plaintive woman's voice called out. Atum remarked that that was his wife—sick, too weak to work in the fields. Turnbull offered to bring her food and medicine. Atum suggested he handle

Turnbull's gifts. As the weeks wore on Atum picked up the parcels that Turnbull was supplying for Atum's wife.

One day Atum's brother-in-law, Lomongin, laughingly asked Turnbull if he didn't know that Atum's wife had been dead for weeks. She had received no food or medicine. Atum had sold it. So she just died. All of this was revealed with no embarrassment. Atum joined the laughter over the joke played on Turnbull.

Another time Atum and Lojieri were guiding Turnbull over the mountains, and at one point induced him to push ahead through high grass until he broke through into a clearing. The clearing was a sheer 1,500-foot drop. The two Iks rolled on the ground, nearly bursting with laughter because Turnbull just managed to catch himself. What a lovable cherub this Atum! His laughter never ended.

New Meaning of Laughter

Laughter, hallmark of mankind, not shared with any other animal, not even primates, was an outstanding trait of the Ik. A whole village rushed to the edge of a low cliff and joined in communal laughter at blind old Lo'ono who lay thrashing on her back, near death after stumbling over. One evening Iks around a fire watched a child as it crawled toward the flames, then writhed back screaming after it grasped a gleaming coal. Laughter erupted. Quiet came to the child as its mother cuddled it in a kind of respect for the merriment it had caused. Then there was the laughter of innocent childhood as boys and girls gathered around a grandfather, too weak to walk, and drummed upon his head with sticks or pelted him with stones until he cried. There was the laughter that binds families together: Kimat, shrieking for joy as she dashed off with the mug of tea she had snatched from her dying brother Lomeja's hand an instant after Turnbull had given it to him as a last token of their friendship.

Laughter there had always been. A few old people remembered times, 25 to 30 years ago, when laughter mirrored love and joy and fullness of life, times when beliefs and rituals and traditions kept a bond with the "millions of years" ago when time began for the Ik. That was when their god, Didigwari, let the Ik down from heaven on a vine, one at a time. He gave them the digging stick with the instruction that they could not kill one another. He let down other people. To the Dodos and Turkana he gave cattle and spears to kill with. But the Ik remained true to their instruction and did not kill one another or neighboring tribesmen.

For them the bow, the net and the pitfall were for capturing game. For them the greatest sin was to overhunt. Mobility and cooperation ever were part of them. Often the netting of game required the collaboration of a whole band of 100 or more, some to hold the net and some to drive game into it. Between the big hunts, bands broke up into smaller groups to spread over their domain, then to gather again. The several bands would each settle for the best part of the year along the edge of the Kidepo Valley in the foothills of Mt. Morungole. There they were once again fully one with the mountain. "The Ik, without their mountains, would no longer be the Ik and similarly, they say, the mountains without the Ik would no longer be the same mountains, if indeed they continued to exist at all."

In this unity of people and place, rituals, traditions, beliefs and values molded and preserved a continuity of life. All rites of passage were marked by ceremony. Of these, the rituals surrounding death gave greatest meaning to life. Folded in a fetal position, the body was buried with favorite possessions, facing the rising sun to mark celestial rebirth. All accompanying rituals of fasting and feasting, of libations of beer sprinkled over the grave, of seeds of favorite foods planted on the grave to draw life from the dust of the dead.

showed that death is merely another form of life, and reminded the living of the good things of life and of the good way to live. In so honoring the dead by creating goodness the Ik helped speed the soul, content, on its journey.

Such were the Ik until wildlife conservation intruded into their homeland. Uganda decided to make a national park out of the Kidepo Valley, the main hunting ground of the Ik. What then happened stands as an indictment of the myopia that science can generate. No one looked to the Ik to note that their hunter-gatherer way of life marked the epitome of conservation, that the continuance of their way of life would have added to the success of the park. Instead they were forbidden to hunt any longer in the Kidepo Valley. They were herded to the periphery of the park and encouraged to become farmers on dry mountain slopes so steep as to test the poise of a goat. As an example to the more remote villages, a number of villages were brought together in a tight little cluster below the southwest pass into the valley. Here the police post, which formed this settlement of Pirre, could watch over the Ik to see that they didn't revert to hunting.

These events contained two of the three strikes that knocked out the spirit of the Ik. *Strike No. 1:* The shift from a mobile hunter-gatherer way of life to a sedentary farming way of life made irrelevant the Ik's entire repertoire of beliefs, habits and traditions. Their guidelines for life were inappropriate to farming. They seemed to adapt, but at heart they remained hunters and gatherers. Their cultural templates fitted them for that one way of life.

Strike No. 2: They were suddenly crowded together at a density, intimacy and frequency of contact far greater than they had ever before been required to experience. Throughout their long past each band of 100 or so individuals only temporarily coalesced into a whole. The intervening breaking up into smaller groups permitted realignment of relationships that tempered conflicts from earlier associations. But at the resettlement, more than 450 individuals were forced to form a permanent cluster of villages within shouting distance of each other. Suppose the seven million or so inhabitants of Los Angeles County were forced to move and join the more than one million inhabitants of the more arid San Diego County. Then after they arrived all water, land and air communication to the rest of the world was cut off abruptly and completely. These eight million people would then have to seek survival completely on local resources without any communication with others. It would be a test of the ability of human beings to remain human.

Such a test is what Dr. Turnbull's book on the Mountain People is all about. The Ik failed to remain human. I have put mice to the same test and they failed to remain mice. Those of you who have been following SMITHSONIAN may recall from the April 1970 and the January 1971 issues something about the projected demise of a mouse population experiencing the same two strikes against it as did the Ik.

Fate of a Mouse Population

Last summer I spoke in London behind the lectern where Charles Darwin and Alfred Wallace had presented their papers on evolution—which during the next century caused a complete revision of our insight into what life is all about and what man is and may become. In summing up that session of 1858 the president remarked that nothing of importance had been presented before the Linnean Society at that year's meeting! I spoke behind this same lectern to a session of the Royal Society of Medicine during its symposium on "Man in His Place." At the end of my paper, "Death Squared: The Explosive Growth and Demise of a Mouse Population," the chairman admonished me to stick to my mice; the insights I had presented could have no implication for man. Wonderful if the chairman could be correct—but now I have read about the Mountain People, and I have a hollow feeling that perhaps we, too, are close to losing our "mountain."

Turnbull lived for 18 months as a member of the Ik tribe. His identity transfer became so strong that he acquired the Ik laughter. He laughed at seeing Atum suffer as they were completing an extremely arduous journey on foot back across the mountains and the Kidepo Valley from the Sudan. He felt pleasure at seeing Lokwam, local "Lord of the Flies," cry in agony from the beating given him by his two beautiful sisters.

Well, for five years I have identified with my mice, as they lived in their own "Kidepo Valley"—their contrived Utopia where resources are always abundant and all mortality factors except aging eliminated. I watched their population grow rapidly from the first few colonizers. I watched them fill their metal "universe" with organized social groups. I watched them bring up a host of young with loving maternal care and paternal territorial protection—all of these young well educated for mouse society. But then there were too many of these young mice, ready to become involved in all that mice can become, with nowhere to go, no physical escape from their closed environment, no opportunity to gain a niche where they could play a meaningful role. They tried, but being younger and less experienced they were nearly always rejected.

Rejecting so many of these probing youngsters overtaxed the territorial males. So defense then fell to lactating females. They became aggressive. They turned against their own young and ejected them before normal weaning and before adequate social bonds between mother and young had developed. During this time of social tension, rate of growth of the population was only one third of that during the earlier, more favorable phase.

Strike No. 1 against these mice: They lost the opportunity to express the capacities developed by older mice born during the rapid population growth. After a while they became so rejected that they were treated as so many sticks and stones by their still relatively well-adjusted elders. These rejected mice withdrew, physically and psychologically, to live packed tightly together in large pools. Amongst themselves they became vicious, lashing out and biting each other now and then with hardly any provocation.

Strike No. 2 against the mice: They reached great numbers despite reduced conceptions and increased deaths of newborn young resulting from the dissolution of maternal care. Many had early been rejected by their mothers and knew little about social bonds. Often their later attempts at interaction were interrupted by some other mouse intervening unintentionally as it passed between two potential actors.

I came to call such mice the "Beautiful Ones." They never learned such effective social interactions as courtship, mating and aggressive defense of territory. Never copulating, never fighting, they were unstressed and essentially unaware of their associates. They spent their time grooming themselves, eating and sleeping, totally individualistic, totally isolated socially except for a peculiar acquired need for simple proximity to others. This produced what I have called the "behavioral sink," the continual accentuation of aggregations to the point that much available space was unused despite a population increase to nearly 15 times the optimum.

All true "mousity" was lost. Though physically they still appeared to be mice, they had no essential capacities for survival and continuation of mouse society. Suddenly, population growth ceased. In what seemed an instant they passed over a threshold beyond which there was no likelihood of their ever recouping the capacity to become real mice again. No more young were born. From a peak population of 2,200 mice nearly three years ago, aging has gradually taken its toll until now there are only 46 sluggish near-cadavers comparable to people more than 100 years old.

It was just such a fading universe Colin Turnbull found in 1964. Just before he arrived, *Strike No. 3* had set in: starvation. Any such crisis could have added the coup de grace after the other two strikes. Normally the Ik could count on only making three crops every four years. At this time a two-year drought set in and destroyed almost all crops. Neighboring tribes survived with their cultures intact. Turkana herdsmen, facing starvation and death, kept their societies in contact with each other and continued to sing songs of praise to God for the goodness of life.

By the beginning of the long dought, "goodness" to the Ik simply meant to have food—to have food for one's self alone. Collaborative hunts were a thing of the past, long since stopped by the police and probably no longer possible as a social effort, anyway. Solitary hunting, now designated as poaching, became a necessity for sheer survival. But the solitary hunter took every precaution not to let others know of his success. He would gorge himself far off in the bush and bring the surplus back to sell to the police, who were not above profiting from this traffic. Withholding food from wife, children and aging parents became an accomplishment to brag and laugh about. It became a way of life, continuing after the government began providing famine relief. Those strong enough to go to the police station to get rations for themselves and their families would stop halfway home and gorge all the food, even though it caused them to vomit.

Village of Mutual Hatred

The village reflected this reversal of humanity. Instead of open courtyards around each group of huts within the large compound, there was a maze of walls and tunnels booby trapped with spears to ward off intrusion by neighbors.

In Atum's village a whole band of more than 100 individuals was crowded together in mutual hostility and aloneness. They would gather at their sitting place and sit for hours in a kind of suspended animation, not looking directly at each other, yet scanning slowly all others who might be engaged in some solitary task, watching for someone to make a mistake that would elicit the symbolic violence of laughter and derision. They resembled my pools of rejected withdrawn mice. Homemaking deteriorated, feces littered doorsteps and courtyard. Universal adultery and incest replaced the old taboo. The beaded virgins' aprons of eight-to-twelve-year-old girls became symbols that these were proficient whores accustomed to selling their wares to passing herdsmen.

One ray of humanity left in this cesspool was 12-year-old, retarded Adupa. Because she believed that food was for sharing and savoring, her playmates beat her. She still believed that parents were for loving and to be loved by. They cured her madness by locking her in her hut until she died and decayed.

The six other villages were smaller and their people could retain a few glimmers of the goodness and fullness of life. There was Kuaur, devoted to Turnbull, hiking four days to deliver mail, taunted for bringing food home to share with his wife and child. There was Losiké, the potter, regarded as a witch. She offered water to visitors and made pots for others. When the famine got so bad that there was no need for pots to cook in, her husband left her. She was no longer bringing in any income. And then there was old Nangoli, still capable of mourning when her husband died. She went with her family and village across Kidepo and into the Sudan where their village life turned for a while back to normality. But it was not normal enough to keep them. Back to Pirre, to death, they returned.

All goodness was gone from the Ik, leaving merely emptiness, valuelessness, nothingness, the chaos of Nun. They reentered the womb of beginning time from which there is no return. Urination beside the partial graves of the dead marked the death of God, the final fading of Mount Morungole.

My poor words give only a shadowy image of the cold coffin of Ik humanity that Turnbull describes. His two years with the Ik left him in a slough of despondency from which he only extricated himself with difficulty, never wanting to see them again. Time and distance brought him comfort. He did return for a brief visit some months later. Rain had come in abundance. Gardens had sprung up untended from hidden seeds in the earth. Each Ik gleaned only for his immediate needs. Granaries stood empty, not refilled for inevitable scarcities ahead. The future had ceased to exist. Individual and social decay continued on its downward spiral. Sadly Turnbull departed again from this land of lost hope and faith.

Last summer in London I knew nothing about the Ik when I was so publicly and thoroughly chastised for having the temerity to suspect that the behavioral and spiritual death my mice had exhibited might also befall man. But a psychiatrist in the audience arose in defense of my suspicion. Dr. Geoffrey N. Bianchi remarked that an isolated tribe of Australian Aborigines mirrored the changes and kinds of pathology I had among mice. I did not know that Dr. Bianchi was a member of the team that had studied these people, the Kaiadilt, and that a book about them was in preparation, *Cruel, Poor and Brutal Nations* by John Cawte (The University Press of Hawaii). In galley proof I have read about the Kaiadilt and find it so shattering to my faith in humanity that I now sometimes wish I had never heard of it. Yet there is some glimmer of hope that the Kaiadilt may recover—not what they were but possibly some new life.

A frail, tenacious people, the Kaiadilt never numbered more than 150 souls where they lived on Bentinck Island in the Gulf of Carpentaria. So isolated were they that not even their nearest Aboriginal neighbors, 20 miles away, had any knowledge of their existence until in this century; so isolated were the Kaiadilt from their nearest neighbors that they differ from them in such heredity markers as blood type and fingerprints. Not until the early years of this century did an occasional visitor from the Queensland Government even note their existence.

For all practical purposes the first real contact the Kaiadilt had with Western "culture" came in 1916 when a man by the name of McKenzie came to Bentinck with a group of male mainland Aborigines to try to establish a lime kiln. McKenzie's favorite sport was to ride about shooting Kaiadilt. His helpers' sport was to commandeer as many women as they could, and take them to their headquarters on a neighboring island. In 1948 a tidal wave poisoned most of the fresh-water sources. Small groups of Kaiadilt were rounded up and transported to larger Mornington Island where they were placed under the supervision of a Presbyterian mission. They were crowded into a dense cluster settlement just as the Ik had been at Pirre.

Here they still existed when the psychiatric field team came into their midst 15 years later. They were much like the Ik: dissolution of family life, total valuelessness, apathy. I could find no mention of laughter, normal or pathological. Perhaps the Kaiadilt didn't laugh. They had essentially ceased the singing that had been so much a part of their traditional way.

The spiritual decay of the Kaiadilt was marked by withdrawal, depression, suicide and tendency to engage in such self-mutilation as ripping one's testes or chopping off one's nose. In their passiveness some of the anxiety ridden children are accepting the new mold of life forced upon them by a benevolent culture they do not understand. Survival with a new mold totally obliterating all past seems their only hope.

So the lesson comes clear, and Colin Turnbull sums it up in the final paragraph of his book:

The Ik teach us that our much vaunted human values are not inherent in humanity at all, but are associated only with a particular form of survival called society, and that all, even society itself, are luxuries that can be dispensed with. That does not make them any the less wonderful or desirable, and if man has any greatness it is surely in his ability to maintain these values, clinging to them to an often very bitter end, even shortening an already pitifully short life rather than sacrifice his humanity. But that too involves choice, and the Ik teach us that man can lose the will to make it.

CHAPTER 6: SUGGESTED FURTHER READING

HARTUP, W. W. Peer interaction and social organization. In Mussen, P. (Ed.) *Carmichael's Manual of Child Psychology*, Vol. 2. New York: Wiley, 1970. Pp. 361–456.

KAGAN, J. Acquisition and significance of sex typing and sex role identity. In Hoffman, M. L., and Hoffman, L. W. (Eds.) *Review of Child Development Research*, Vol. 1. New York: Russell Sage Foundation, 1964. Pp. 137–167.

KOHLBERG, L. Development of moral character and moral ideology. In Hoffman, M. L., and Hoffman, L. W. (Eds.) *Review of Child Development Research*, Vol. 1. New York: Russell Sage Foundation, 1964. Pp. 383–431.

MACCOBY, E. E. (Ed.) *The Development of Sex Differences.* Stanford, Calif.: Stanford University Press, 1966.

MISCHEL, W. Sex-typing and socialization. In Mussen, P. (Ed.) *Carmichael's Manual of Child Psychology*, Vol. 2. New York: Wiley, 1970. Pp. 3–72.

MUSSEN, P. Early sex-role development. In Goslin, D. *Handbook of Socialization Theory and Research.* Chicago: Rand McNally, 1969. Pp. 707–731.

chapter seven
cognition and language

The birth cry signals the entrance of the human child into a complicated social world in which language is the primary tool of communication. At birth, the child has some of the physical rudiments that enable him to speak, but it is several years before the child is a fully active member of our language community. These are not fallow years, but ones in which the child is actively engaged in developing his cognitive capacities: thought, perception, and language. During the first two years, when the child is not a language-user in the true sense, he is busy comprehending his environment in a non-verbal way. Piaget calls this the sensori-motor period. The child learns about his environment through direct interaction with it, touching it, tasting it, manipulating it. As the child matures, he begins to speak, and with the abstraction that words provide, he is no longer solely dependent on physical contact with the matter to be learned. This is one of the great functions of language: it allows the user to communicate about objects and thoughts that do not exist in the immediate situation.

By the age of four, most children have mastered the fundamentals of their native language. We are not yet sure why this happens. We do know that important roles are played by the child's biological development, by his dependency on the environment, and by the fact that this is the earliest period of learning. The child himself is an active participant in the learning process. The young child will sit in his bed at night "rehearsing" the new things he has learned during the day. This is true for language and other cognitive skills. Often one can hear a three- or four-year-old counting, saying new words, and going through his thought processes out loud. It is from data like these that we know the child takes an active part, that the push from within is present in cognitive development, as it is in physical development when a child will try to walk despite repeated falls.

From earliest times, men have been concerned with how children learn their language. Early "experiments" to see what word a child will say when he has not had an opportunity to hear speech have been cited frequently in the literature.

Most descriptions of language development written before the second half of this century were done primarily from observations. They were often done by parents using their own children as subjects. Later observational studies have been done on more extensive samples and have relied on more complicated instrumentation. Experimental studies of language development have been done throughout this century.

In the 1940s and 1950s, linguists and psychologists who were concerned with the scientific study of language realized that one can only begin a scientific study of language by understanding both the nature of language (the syntactic and semantic rules) and the nature of the language user.

This communication between the two fields has led to the present exciting uncertainty about language development and to two major changes in approach. The two major changes concern questions about what constitutes language and the questions about the biological roots of language.

The first major change has been a shift in what is studied when one looks at language development. The earlier emphasis in both experimental and observational studies was on the development of vocabulary, sentence length and articulation—elements of a language that were considered of primary importance and easily measurable. These were the language habits that, once acquired, supposedly made a child a member of a language community.

Since the 1950s, more sophisticated notions of what constitutes language have been considered. Thus researchers are now concerned with the learning of syntax, intonation, and other such language elements. In addition, it is no longer clear what elements such as "words" are.

This is a far-reaching change. We have moved from studies of vocabulary to studies of smaller, yet just as meaningful language items, such as learning verb tenses (Brown and Bellugi, 1964) or the lingustic habits governing the use of negation (Miller, 1964). The study of language development has become more difficult. A modern investigator will no longer look only at vocabulary, but will have difficulty deciding what aspects of language should be studied, since it is presently unclear what children are learning when they are learning their language. In other words, the important linguistic units are not totally apparent at present.

The second major change has been a recognition that although speech may be a social acquisition, as had been assumed, it may also be, in some measure, a biological acquisition. The maturation-environment issue has again been raised, but on a different level due to more advanced understanding of the nature of language. For example, it is now possible to suggest that the presently unknown, solely human capacities for language learning may be transmitted genetically (Lenneberg, 1964).

There is almost universal consensus that language development is at present poorly understood. The need for more experimental research into the nature and functions of language is strongly felt. Sober researchers wax poetic in awe of the small child, "bathed" in language, who manages to comprehend words, grammatical structures, phonetic intricacies, and who in a few years moves from a nonverbal creature to a creatively active member of a linguistic community. This evolution is not understood. However, the acquisition of language is recognized as a major human development that changes an infant into a participant in a larger world.

As the child matures, his language changes and so do his cognitive skills. The changes are related: language influences what one sees and thinks, and what one sees and thinks influences one's language. According to Piaget, as soon as the child begins speaking, he is in a new stage of intellectual development, the preoperational stage. During this period, the child can speak and think aloud but has not yet developed the understanding that the world has a stability separate from the viewpoint of the observer. The child does not yet understand the fact that certain properties of matter, such as weight, volume, and mass, remain the same despite irrelevant changes, such as changes in shape. His thinking is very much tied to his perceptions and if he sees two things as being different in shape, he will say they are different in amount also. The typical example of the way in which Piaget measures conservation, or the ability to recognize the constancy of matter, is one in which two equal round balls of clay are shown to a child and he is asked if each contains the same amount of clay. When the child agrees, the tester flattens one of the balls as the child watches. He then asks if the two pieces are the same, and most children under five or six will now say that one has more clay, either the flatter one because it is now wider, or the round one because it is higher. The young child lacks conservation, but will have the concept by the time he is six or seven. Why conservation develops when it does, and how it develops, are questions that are at present unanswered. We no longer think of the young child as illogical, ignorant, and wrong when he gives non-adult-like answers to adults' questions. We understand that at any stage of his cognitive development, the thoughts that the child has and the answers that he gives to questions are logical for him, and quite predictable.

When the child has the concept of conservation and is capable of more logical thought, he is considered to be in the stage of formal operations. Thus, the child's thought processes and language change as he matures. The most dramatic cognitive change occurs between ages five and seven, when all processes seem to undergo a shift from child-like thought to more adult-like thought. This shift in cognition occurs in almost all children at about the same time despite wide cultural differences in their backgrounds. The underlying factors related to this change are the subjects of many research projects.

Research in the areas of cognitive and language development has changed much in the last twenty years, a change that reflects the interest in underlying processes as opposed to the previous interest in external behavior. The articles chosen for this section are examples of the current research in this area.

References

BROWN, R., and BELLUGI, U. Three processes in the child's acquisition of syntax. *Harvard Educational Review*, 1964, *34*, 133–151.

LENNENBERG, E. H. *Biological Foundations of Language*. New York: Wiley, 1967.

MILLER, G. A. Language and psychology. In Lenneberg, E. H. (Ed.) *New Directions in the Study of Language*. Cambridge, Mass.: M.I.T. Press, 1964. Pp. 89–108.

36. THE DEVELOPMENT OF LAUGHTER IN THE FIRST YEAR OF LIFE

L. ALAN SROUFE and JANE PICCARD WUNSCH

In a series of observational studies, based on more than 150 infants in the first year of life, clear evidence of age changes in both amount of laughter and the nature of stimuli eliciting laughter was found. Those stimuli that were primarily tactile or auditory elicited laughter in younger infants and then became less potent in the third or fourth trimester of life, while most visual items and some social items became increasingly successful across the age range studied. The results were discussed in terms of cognitive growth, the psychoanalytic notion of ambivalence, the role of stimulus context in eliciting laughter or fear, and a possible adaptive, stimulus-maintaining function of laughter.

Laughter is a highly stereotyped response pattern which is general within the human species and reliably makes its appearance at about the fourth month of life (Ambrose, 1963; Darwin, 1872; Washburn, 1929). From an evolutionary point of view, it is reasonable to assume that such a mechanism serves an important adaptive function for the organism. It is surprising, then, that this behavior pattern has received so little attention in the developmental literature. The data to be reported below, based on cross-sectional and longitudinal study of approximately 160 infants in a total of more than 300 observational sessions, will suggest both that laughter may provide a rich source of information concerning cognitive and emotional development in infancy and that a number of alternative conceptual notions currently compete in terms of integrative power.

While important theoretical papers are available (e.g., Ambrose, 1963), our work on laughter in infants is apparently antedated by only one major empirical study. Washburn (1929) observed 15 infants in a combination longitudinal–cross-sectional investigation. At least four babies were tested at each age level from 16 to 52 weeks, and the following conclusions were reached: (1) there were no developmental changes in amount of laughter or potency of different stimulus situations, and (2) there was no relationship between frequency of laughter and developmental status. While the study is important because of Washburn's careful description of the laughter response, it suffers due to the restricted range of the stimuli. For example, the two stimuli most frequently eliciting laughter, "threatening head" and "rhythmic hand clapping," both involved intense auditory and tactile stimulation. With only such intense stimuli, which may elicit laughter reflexively in even the youngest babies capable of the response, developmental changes may have been obscured. The studies described below utilized a wide variety of stimulus situations, only a few of which involved both tactile and auditory stimulation or were physically intense and a number of which were almost purely visual.

The items utilized in the following studies were developed from intensive experience with two infants over a period of 4 months. These items were supplemented by more formal observations of 30 babies and interviews with each infant's mother. This empirical base was further supplemented by certain rational considerations. First, it was assumed a priori that laughter would result from contact with the unexpected, the incongruous, the familiar yet unfamiliar (e.g., Bergson, 1911; Darwin, 1872; Koestler, 1964). Our thinking was not unlike Hebb's (1949) theorizing concerning the disruption of "phase sequences" in the production of fear. Second, we wanted to choose items that varied in terms of cognitive complexity, stimulus intensity, and sensory modality. Therefore, we selected a number of items that involved visual stimulation alone and only a few items that combined tactile and auditory stimulation or were physically intense, for example, "peek-a-boo" was played without any sound being made by the agent.

Study 1

As an optional component within an introductory child psychology course, 20 undergraduate students participated as experimenters. In addition to practice testing one or two infants (above), each student participated in four 2-hour training sessions devoted primarily to standardizing item administration. Only two of the sessions were devoted to rating procedures, and there were no checks on reliability of scoring during the study. However, it was later determined that agreement on laughter is rather easily achieved.

Method

Subjects Seventy healthy, white babies, 29 males and 41 females, ages 4 months through 12 months, were observed. The number of subjects observed at each age, respectively, was 6, 9, 9, 9, 4, 11, 9, 6, and 7.

Items The 24 test items employed in this study are presented in Table 7.1. Descriptions of the final form of these and other items, as used in studies 2 and 3, are found in the Appendix. Differences between item administration in study 1 and the descriptions in the Appendix are discussed in a later section. The grouping of these items is to some extent arbitrary; for example, "cover baby's face, pull off" is classified as visual, though it could have easily been grouped with the social or even tactile items. All items are in a sense social, since they involve the agent (the infant's mother) doing something in the baby's presence. Our use of the social category, however, is restricted to those items that have a gamelike quality. Such items often involve multiple sensory modalities. Likewise, all items are presented when the infant is oriented toward the agent, but we categorized items as visual only when they had no primary auditory or tactile component.

It was hypothesized that the visual items and the social items would make greater cognitive demands on the baby and would tend to elicit laughter later in development than the tactile and auditory items. The distinction made is not unlike that of William James (1890) concerning "passive immediate sensorial attention" and "associational attention" or that of some investigators concerning near versus far receptors (e.g., Schopler, 1965; White, 1964). We were not fully committed to either of these theoretical positions, and our classification was partly a matter of convenience.

Procedure Because of a priori notions concerning the role of context in infant laughter, all babies were tested in the home with the mother as stimulus agent. Prior to testing, all items were described to the mother, or demonstrated when exposure of the item to the infant could be avoided. Each baby received the items in a different random order, usually across two sessions lasting about 45 minutes. While babies were tested after napping and feeding, interruption of testing for feeding and other baby care was routine, especially with younger infants. An item was presented up to six times, but was discontinued if it produced laughter on two consecutive trials or in the rare instance where it elicited crying. Mothers were blind to any experimental hypothesis, and raters were blind except for the expectation of some developmental change. Each student observed three or four babies, often distributed across the age range studied. Mothers were routinely checked for corroboration on items judged to produce laughter.

Results

While ratings were made on a six-point scale (crying, distress, neutral, smile, active smile, and laughter), this paper will focus on the extensive and coherent results from the laughter data. Additional data analysis is in progress to determine the continuity or discontinuity of the laughter and smiling responses. The percentage of babies who laughed at each item is presented in Table 7.1. To increase clarity, the data have been collapsed into 3-month groupings.

Despite the fact that this study involved 20 different raters, minimally trained, teaching 70 different mothers to administer a complicated set of items, quite clear results emerged. With this wide range of items, there is a notable increase in the amount of laughter with age, with a cross-category average of 10%, 37%, and 43% for the 4–6-, 7–9-, and 10–12-month groups, respectively. There are also interesting developmental trends in the type of items eliciting laughter. This is most clear in comparing the 7–9-month-olds with the 10–12-month-olds;the oldest infants laughed more in response to 12 or 13 visual and social items ($p = .004$, two-tailed sign test), while the 7–9-month-olds showed more laughter than the 10–12-month-olds to 9 of 11 auditory and tactile items ($p = .066$). An overall test on this distribution of frequencies was also significant ($\chi^2 = 10.59$, $p < .01$). Even the two clear reversals from this pattern are suggestive: "jiggling high overhead," classed as tactile, has an obvious social component, while "cover baby's face—pull off," classed as visual, would seem to have a tactile aspect as well. Finally, of the 11 items that produced laughter in more than 10% of the 4–6-month-olds, all but two involved auditory or tactile stimulation. The best social item with these youngest babies ("gonna get you") includes both auditory and tactile stimulation.

Table 7.1. Percentage of laughter by item for study 1

	Age in Months		
Item	*4–6*	*7–9*	*10–12*
Auditory:			
Lip popping	12	25	14
Aaah	17	46	32
Boom, boom, boom	12	21	23
Synthesizer	8	21	9
Whispering	12	25	18
Squeaky voice	4	38	32
Tactile:			
Blowing hair	8	17	9
Kissing stomach	29	83	54
Coochy-coo	8	46	41
Bouncing on knee	12	46	9
Jiggling over head	25	75	86
Social:			
Playing tug	4	42	45
Cloth in mouth	4	25	59
Gonna get you	21	54	82
Covering baby's face	12	42	36
Peek-a-boo	12	62	82
Chasing, crawling after	4	38	68
Visual:			
Covered face	4	25	54
Disappearing object	4	25	32
Sucking baby bottle	4	17	36
Crawling on floor	4	21	36
Walking like Laurel	4	33	54
Shaking hair	21	54	86
Holding in air	8	42	68
Total	10	37	43

Studies 2 and 3

To determine the replicability of the finding in study 1, a second cross-sectional and a longitudinal study were conducted. The procedures in these two studies were similar to those of the initial study, but there were a number of methodological improvements. Items were sharpened, raters were extensively trained, there were checks for rater reliability, and a single rater made all of the observations in the longitudinal study.

Method

Items A modified item list was developed with carefully detailed rules for administration, as outlined in the Appendix. Unwanted confounding of items was removed; for example, "whispering in ear" was to be done at a distance to avoid producing tactile stimulation, and the final trial of "gonna get you" (no. 18) and "walking fingers" (no. 15) was done without touching, and only this trial was scored as "social." Six items were added (7, 13, 14, 15, 20, and 28), and one item was reclassified ("covering baby's face" was judged to be primarily social rather than visual), to yield a total of seven items in each category. Three other items were administered, but tallied separately: "chasing baby" (29) was pulled out because of its obvious bias against noncrawling infants, "holding in air" (30) was felt to be too confounded between visual and tactile stimulation, and having the baby "look in mirror" (31) was of great interest but was judged to be atypical in that the crucial feature of the stimulus situation is not an act of the agent.

Training of raters The five raters in these studies had each been involved in study 1, and they each tested additional pilot subjects. They also participated in group training sessions, three of which included group ratings of videotapes. Finally, each participated in live sessions independently rated by the first author, until the criterion of perfect agreement on laughter to an item was reached. This was easily achieved, never requiring more than two 45-minute sessions.

Subjects Subjects in study 2 were 13 7–8-month-old infants (10 males and three females) and 13 11–12-month-old infants (five males and eight females). Ten male babies participated in the longitudinal study. Each of these infants was observed at least seven times at about midmonth between the ages of 4 and 12 months. The number of infants seen at each age is indicated in Table 7.2. All infants were white and in good general health.

Procedure In contrast to study 1, a number of steps were taken to insure similar presentation of items from mother to mother. Efforts were made to have pauses uniform within trials of repetitive stimuli and between trials of all items, and to have intensity and duration of items constant. Generally, there was a mechanization of items that reduced spontaneity of the agent as well as variability. For example, "lip popping" (no. 1) became four pops, evently spaced, and of uniform low intensity; and "playing tug" (no. 16) became three even jerks, pause, three even jerks, etc. While item presentation was unavoidably less animated, mothers were still encouraged to be generally warm throughout the session. Items were again presented in a random order, with pauses between items to reduce contagion effects. In the longitudinal study, where standardization was promoted by having a single rater train each mother and make all observations, mothers were carefully instructed not to rehearse items with the baby between sessions. All of the longitudinal observations were made in the homes, while about half of the babies in study 2 were tested in an airy, carpeted room at the university.

Interrater reliability In addition to reliability checks prior to the start of studies 2 and 3, eight infants were independently rated by two observers during the longitudinal study. A total of 232 items were rated across 12 sessions. The primary rater scored laughter on 59 of these items, while the second judge recorded laughter on these 59 plus two other items rated by the primary rater as active smile. Agreement on these 61 laughter items, then, is 97%, and agreement on the total set of items is greater than 99%.

Table 7.2. Percentage of laughter by item for longitudinal study

Item	*Age in Months*								
	4 (6)	*5 (10)*	*6 (9)*	*7 (9)*	*8 (8)*	*9 (7)*	*10 (10)*	*11 (9)*	*12 (10)*
Auditory:									
1. Lip popping	0	10	0	0	0	0	10	0	10
2. Aaah	0	20	33	33	13	0	40	55	40
3. Boom, boom, boom	0	40	11	22	25	0	20	0	20
4. Synthesizer	0	20	0	0	0	0	0	0	10
5. Whispering	0	0	11	0	0	0	0	0	10
6. Squeaky voice	0	0	0	0	25	0	0	11	40
7. Horse sound	0	0	0	44	0	0	20	22	10
Tactile:									
8. Blowing in hair	0	0	0	11	0	0	10	11	20
9. Kissing stomach	33	30	44	77	50	43	20	33	50
10. Coochy-coo	0	20	22	44	25	14	30	0	0
11. Bouncing on knee	0	20	11	22	25	29	20	22	30
12. Jiggling baby	0	30	33	44	13	29	30	0	40
13. Tickling under chin	0	10	33	11	25	29	10	22	0
14. Mouthing back of neck	0	0	11	11	25	14	20	0	20
Social:									
15. Walking fingers (last trial)	17	20	11	33	25	29	20	22	30
16. Playing tug	0	20	22	33	25	43	20	11	20
17. Cloth in mouth	0	10	11	33	50	14	30	44	50
18. Gonna get you (last trial)	50	30	44	77	63	43	30	33	70
19. Covering baby's face	0	0	22	22	38	29	20	22	40
20. Stick out tongue	0	0	11	22	13	0	40	33	60
21. Peek-a-boo	0	10	11	55	38	0	10	11	30
Visual:									
22. Covered face	0	10	33	55	38	14	30	11	50
23. Disappearing object	0	10	11	11	25	0	30	0	30
24. Sucking baby bottle	0	0	0	11	13	0	40	11	40
25. Crawling on floor	0	10	11	11	50	29	30	22	60
26. Walking like Laurel	0	0	22	22	25	14	10	0	40
27. Shaking hair	0	0	11	44	38	57	40	66	50
28. Human mask	17	0	11	33	13	29	80	33	40
Extra items:									
29. Chasing	0	0	22	22	13	14	50	55	80
30. Holding in air	0	10	22	33	13	43	50	22	40
31. Mirror	0	10	22	33	0	0	0	0	0
32. Gonna get you (all trials)	50	40	55	77	75	57	50	33	90
33. Walking fingers (all trials)	0	20	11	44	38	43	60	22	80

Note.—Item numbers correspond to descriptions in the Appendix. Numbers in parentheses indicate number of babies tested.

Results, Study 2

The total amount of laughter observed in study 2 was sharply diminished compared with study 1. The 7–8-month-olds laughed at an average of 20% of the items across all categories, while the 11–12-month-olds laughed at 26% of all items (vs. 37% and 43% for comparable groups in study 1). This reduced affective responsiveness cannot be attributed to the testing away from home, because a laboratory–home difference was not found. Despite the overall reduction in laughter, the pattern of results was quite similar to that obtained in the original study. Tabulating the auditory and tactile items as "hits" if the younger babies laughed more, and the social and visual items as "hits" if the older babies laughed more, 15 hits, six misses, and seven ties resulted, $p < .10$, two-tailed sign test; t (27) = 2.69, $p < .02$. Thus, the overall pattern found in study 1 was replicated by these data.

Results, Study 3

Table 7.2 shows the percentage of laughter to each item, month by month. In Figure 7.1, these data are collapsed within categories, and Figure 7.2 presents the same data when collapsed further into 3-month age blocks, as in study 1.

Closely paralleling the results in study 2, total amount of laughter was diminished in this study in comparison with study 1 (12.5%, 24%, and 25%, vs. 10%, 37%, and 43% for 4–6-, 7–9-, and 10–12-month-olds). The low level of laughter in response to the auditory items is especially notable, 10.5% here across all ages compared with 21% in study 1. Because of the discontinuity in amount of laughter between the auditory and other categories (Figure 7.2),

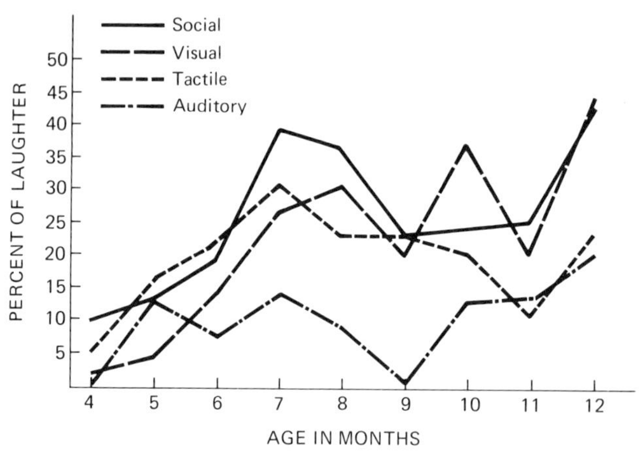

Figure 7.1. Month-by-month percentage of laughter in the longitudinal study, collapsed within categories.

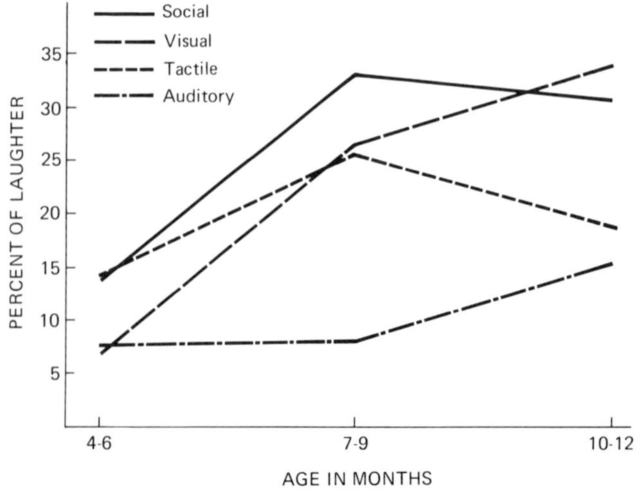

Figure 7.2. Percentage of laughter in the longitudinal study, collapsed into 3-month age blocks.

and the large number of zeros in the auditory data, nonparametic and parametric analyses presented below focus on the tactile, visual, and social categories. There were no significant age changes within the auditory category; for example, only six of 10 subjects showed increased responsiveness (Figure 7.2) between 7–9 and 10–12 months, t (9) = 1.44, $p > .10$.

A nonparametric analysis of the tactile, social, and visual categories generally confirms the impressions from Figure 7.2. Each of these categories elicited more laughter in 7–9-month-olds than was the case with 4–6-month-olds: eight of nine individual infants (one tie) showed the change for tactile ($p = .040$, two-tailed sign test), nine of 10 for social ($p = 0.22$), and eight of eight with two ties, for visual ($p = .008$). Then, between 7–9 months and 10–12 months, seven of 10 individual babies continued to show an increase to the visual items, while seven of 10 infants showed a decreased responsiveness for the tactile items.

To subject these data to parametric statistical analysis, some estimation is required to complete the partially filled blocks. Of the 90 possible observations (10 infants across 9 months), 78 observations were made. The missing observations were distributed across infants (no baby was missed more than twice), they were not systematic, and they never occurred in consecutive testing of the same infant. Because of the high number of zeros in the month-by-month data, iterative estimation procedures based on the performance of all subjects seemed inappropriate. Instead, each missing observation was simply estimated by interpolating from the infant's score at surrounding months (or month 5 in the case of the 4-month observations). It was felt that such procedures would not bias the F ratios presented below; nonetheless, a conservative test was made in the case of the important interaction to be reported.

An analysis of variance on the tactile, social, and visual categories collapsed into three age groups again confirmed the suggestions from Figure 7.2. There was a significant effect for age, F (2,18) = 15.702 $p < .005$, and for age × category, F (4,36) = 5.714, $p < .005$, but a nonsignificant main effect for category F (2,18) = 2.579, $p > .10$. Subsequent analysis revealed that the increases from ages 4–6 to 7–9 were, of course, all significant ($p < .01$), as was the increase for visual ($p < .05$) between 7–9 and 10–12 months, but the decrease for tactile failed to reach significance ($.10 > p < .05$). To be conservative, a separate analysis of variance was employed to test the important interaction between visual and tactile across the last two age blocks. A significant interaction was obtained from this analysis, F (1,9) = 9.910, $p < .025$, confirming the divergence of response to these two categories.

The results may also be summarized in terms of modal age of laughter for items in the four categories (Table 7.2). The following number of items showed clear modal tendencies (a 2-point percentage difference) for each category: auditory, 5; tactile, 6; social, 6; visual, 5. Based on these items, the median modal ages for the four categories were 7.0, 6.5, 8.0, and 10.5 months. While the ordering of the categories is in keeping with our initial developmental hypothesis, our classification of the items is to some extent arbitrary, and not explicitly in terms of cognitive demands. Therefore, four developmental psychologists at the University of Minnesota were asked specifically to select from the 28-item pool the nine items requiring the greatest "cognitive sophistication." There was little agreement in the rankings of the items, but all four raters included six in their selection (20, 22, 23, 24, 25, and 26). The median modal age for these items is 11.5 months. For other items nominated by more than one rater (6, 16, 17, 19, and 28), the median modal age was 10.0 months. Three of the four judges placed items 24–26, which all have a peak at 12 months, in the top three ranks.

In summary, there is both replication

and failure to replicate in these results. For tactile and visual items, results from the longitudinal study are quite consistent with studies 1 and 2; responsiveness to visual items increases between 4–6 and 7–9 months and continues to rise, while laughter to tactile items increases, then decreases. This was the pattern for individual babies as well as the group: seven of 10 babies showed a clear linear trend for the visual category, while a clear quadratic trend was exhibited by seven of 10 infants for the tactile category. Responsiveness to social items (Figure 7.2) rose to a high level by 7–9 months, as was the case in study 1, but then remained at that level, rather than continuing to rise. In all three studies, visual and social items were most successful in eliciting laughter from the oldest babies, with the social items peaking earlier in development than the visual items.

Qualitative results Item-by-item and month-by-month study of Table 7.2 reveals both consistency with the results outlined above and interesting anomalies. Some items show dramatic modal tendencies (e.g., "boom, boom, boom"; "horse sound"; and "human mask"); others are clearly bimodal, with modes generally at 7 months and 12 months. Only one item has a clear mode at 8 months and only one at 9 months, where the overall drop in laughter is significant, $t\ (6) = 2.88,\ p < .05$.

Consideration of the results from 9 months to 12 months reveals that at each month the strongest items were visual or social, whereas tactile and auditory items were most potent during the fifth and sixth months. At 7 months there was a dramatic increase in social responsivity, with peaks for both the social and tactile categories. Four-month-olds laughed most at "gonna get you," the only social item with an auditory component, and "kissing stomach." Based on the total set of observations we have thus far accumulated on 4-month-olds ($N = 14$), 16 or the 21 observed laughter responses were to "gonna get you" or other auditory or tactile stimuli.

Some reversals from predicted results for the oldest babies are especially interesting. For example, two of the auditory items were quite potent, "aaah swelling" and "squeaky voice," and both of these seem to have a heavy social component. The 12-month peak for "kissing stomach" and the relative peak for "coochy-coo" at 10 months are examples of important qualitative changes in response with age. Notes taken at each session suggest that older infants laughed earlier in the trial than younger infants. Rather than waiting for and responding to the completed stimulus, older babies often sought to engage the stimulus by reaching or leaning forward, and they generally laughed in anticipation. These observations raise questions concerning the changing meaning of the same "stimulus" with age.

Finally, the five nontabulated items can be summarized briefiy. All four social-visual items (29, 30, 32, 33) produced increasing laughter with age. "Gonna get you" (all trials, 32), which parallels Washburn's (1929) stimuli by combining auditory, tactile, and visual stimulation, was successful in eliciting laughter across all ages and was the peak item for the 4-month-olds, as was the case in study 1. The mirror item showed a precipitous drop after 7 months, never again eliciting laughter. Our observations suggested that this drop in laughter was followed by progressively increasing attentiveness to the mirror image in older infants.

Laughter and motor development These studies were exploratory and therefore no formal attempts were made to collect developmental status data. However, the age of onset of crawling is available, since crawling was a prerequisite for administration of the "chasing" item (29). An interesting relationship was obtained between age of crawling and age of first laughter to "mother crawling on floor" (25): in seven of the 10 babies, laughter to item 25 began at the same month or 1 month later than onset of crawling. One baby laughed 1 month before crawling, one 2 months after, and one 3 months after crawling. Onset of crawling varied between 6 and 10 months of age, and the correlation between the two variables was positive and significant, $r\ (9) = .69, p < .05$.

Discussion

The observations outlined on preceding pages can be summarized briefly. Subsequent to the onset of laughter, at about the fourth month of life, there is a clear increase with age in the number of situations eliciting laughter. With the items employed in our studies, this increase is most apparent between the second and third trimesters of life. In addition, there is a change in the nature of stimuli eliciting laughter with increasing age. Some stimuli, which were once potent, become less effective, while others become increasingly successful, often reaching their maximum at 12 months, the oldest age explored. Both a priori considerations and the independent ratings of judges suggested that stimuli which become potent with increasing age are those which make the greatest cognitive demands on the infant.

There were a number of inconsistencies in our data which provide a challenge for future research. The fact that laughter was diminished when items were presented in an automated fashion raises questions about the importance of such factors as spontaneity of the agent, uneven cadence, and uncertain termination point. For example, in our later studies the swelling "aaah" which was terminated abruptly, but at an unpredictable time, produced more laughter in the oldest infants than our mechanical version of "peek-a-boo." Individual visual items which produced laughter in younger babies and tactile and auditory items which elicited laughter in older infants raise further questions about relevant stimulus parameters and the changing meaning of a stimulus with age. At this point we can merely speculate that for an item such as "shaking hair in face" a factor-like rate of change of stimulation may be relevant for the youngest babies, whereas, for example, an "interpretation" of mock attack by mother may be crucial for older babies. Likewise, when "aaah" peaked for the second time at age 11 months, an interpretation concerning an auditory analog of maternal approach may have been involved, and an understanding of the communication in the "squeaky voice" may have contributed to the potency of this item with older babies. It was at least clear that for older babies laughter often anticipated stimulus termination, whereas laughter was generally elicited by the completed stimulus in the younger infants.

We plan to pursue the question of developmental changes in responsivity to different stimulus dimensions in two ways: (1) interitem correlational analysis at different ages, based on a larger sample; and (2) the interaction with age of dimensions such as stimulus intensity, experimentally manipulated within items.

Both our findings and conclusions are in sharp contrast to those of Washburn (1929). It seems likely that the intense, sudden nature of Washburn's stimuli failed to allow the cognitive capacities of older infants to become manifest. Our one multimodel, vigorous stimulus situation ("I'm gonna get you") produced results parallel to those of Washburn, while our numerous more subtle stimuli perhaps enabled the separation of what Darwin (1872) has called reflexive and nonreflexive laughter.[1]

Finding such developmental changes in laughter, we are persuaded that this affective response denotes an especially meaningful interaction between the infant and

---

[1] Darwin's distinction between "reflexive" and "nonreflexive" laughter would seem to refer to the necessity of attention to and processing of the stimulus situation (James's "association attention") in the latter case. Response to the stimulus without discernible time lag, as in tickling, characterized reflexive laughter.

his environment, not a random or incidental event. We will now turn our attention to four conceptual notions which ultimately may have potential for specifying that meaning.

Ambivalence

Ambrose (1963) argues cogently that laughter in infants is an expression of ambivalence in the psychoanalytic sense. Such ambivalence is produced by "stimulus situations which elicit simultaneously both stimulus-maintaining and stimulus-terminating tendencies with the former predominating" (p. 180). There is something frightening or angering in the situation and yet something, perhaps the mother's face, which is positive. Ambrose's argument is based both on an analysis of the laughter response, which he finds to have components of crying and the pleasure smile (see also Wolff, 1969), and a discussion of the type of stimuli previously reported to produce laughter.

This is a persuasive conceptualization. In rare instances we did observe wavering between smiling and crying or a change from laughing to crying within a single trial. Also, many of our items, such as "boom, boom, boom," which was moderately loud, the mock attack of "gonna get you," and the mask are readily handled by an ambivalence interpretation.

However, many of our observations were not consistent with an ambivalence position. We found little evidence of *behavioral* ambivalence. In our laboratory we have now videotaped 40 babies responding to the mask item. In the clear majority of cases the infant leaned forward toward the mother and strived to reach the mask, smiling or laughing during his attempt. There was sometimes hesitation but seldom vacillation, even in this laboratory setting, and there were only two instances of negative affect. Also, Ambrose argues that stimulus termination reduces the negative component of the situation, thus allowing the expression of laughter, but we found that laughter generally occurred at the height of stimulation. Moreover, most of the items in our studies were not sudden or intense, or even surprising after a number of presentations, and are more aptly described as incongruous. Finally, it is difficult to conceive of a stimulus-terminating motive with regard to many of our stimuli, such as "cloth in mouth." In fact, older babies often sought to reproduce the laughter situations, for example, by leaning toward the mother (in "coochy-coo"), taking her hand (in "walking fingers"), and putting the cloth back in her mouth. Still, Ambrose's theorizing is compelling, and we will return to a position quite similar to his below.

Cognitive Factors

Zigler, Levine, and Gould (1967) have suggested a cognitive challenge hypothesis, in addition to psychodynamic factors, to explain their findings on humor in third, fifth, and seventh graders. The maximal percentage of laughter for all age groups was for jokes independently rated as moderately difficult; neither too obvious nor beyond the child's comprehension. Zigler et al. related their findings to White's (1959) effectance concept and conclude that "children enjoy most that which lies at the growing edge of their capacities" (p. 335) (see also Shultz & Zigler [1970] and Zelazo & Komer [1971] for similar formulations). Such a formulation can be fitted readily to the general patterning of our findings, including the relationship between age of laughter and independently rated, "cognitive sophistication" of items.

Both Kagan (1971) and Lewis (1971) have argued that an infant's attention is directed in the service of developing and newly formed schemata. A number of our findings, including the relationship between age of crawling and laughter at mother crawling, suggest a parallel case for laughter. While such reasoning is highly speculative, it may be that laughter can provide an index to the infant's registry of developing concepts. Certainly, it has been commonly accepted that laughter occurs at the violation of expectation (Bergson, 1911; Koestler, 1964; Spencer, 1892), and expectations must relate to available schemata.

Fear versus laughter: the role of context Fear and laughter must be related in some way. As noted, the rationale underlying our item development was similar to that of investigators of fear (Bronson, 1968; Hebb, 1949). Also, it is common knowledge that stimuli quite potent in producing fear, such as loud sounds and loss of balance (Watson, 1920), can produce laughter. We too observed laughter at caretakers tossing their infants in the air, and documented laughter to "jiggling baby," "boom, boom, boom," and "aaah."

Cognitive factors seem to play an important role in the evocation of fear or laughter. This can be illustrated by a consideration of the results with the mask. Others (e.g., Scarr & Salapatek, 1970) have found such a stimulus to be quite adequate for fear production, showing peaks at ages 9–11 and 11–13 months, yet we noted crying or avoidance in only two cases out of more than 150 observations with this item. Differences in procedure seem clearly implicated. In the Scarr and Salapatek study, the masks were nonhuman and were put on by the unfamiliar experimenter out of the baby's view. In our work the agent was the infant's mother, and she placed our human-looking mask over her face while the infant was watching. The same mask, used in the absence of the infant's caretaker, elicited crying and behavioral avoidance in each of three infants when the agent was the experimenter. Even with the mother as agent, laughter to the mask was sharply reduced in our laboratory (18% of 11 9–11-month-olds compared with 50% across these three ages in the longitudinal study), though an avoidance response occurred only once, and smiling was the rule. We are only beginning to explore such factors as partial versus total transformation of the face, human quality of the mask, and the suddenness of the mother's approach; nonetheless, context seems clearly implicated. In fact, context and stimulus may be inseparable. Like Gibson (1960), we are persuaded that the effective stimulus in our studies is complex, including setting, agent, prior stimulation, dynamic aspects of presentation and, for example, features of the mask, which may be of minimal importance.

The Function of Laughter

Less than 100 years ago Herbert Spencer (1892) suggested a functional role for laughter in the response to incongruity:

> a large amount of nervous energy, instead of being allowed to expend itself in producing an equivalent amount of new thoughts and emotion which were nascent, is suddenly checked in its flow. . . . The excess must discharge itself in some other direction, and there results an efflux through the motor nerves to various classes of muscles, producing the half-convulsive acts we term laughter (p. 114).

Like the social smile, laughter may have a positive effect on caretaker-infant interaction, but Spencer's tension-discharge notion suggests an important role for laughter in cognitive development as well. Such a notion makes possible an integration of much of our previous discussion. When an unexpected or incongruous event occurs, appropriate to the infant's cognitive level and important because it does not mesh with developing schemata, dramatic attention and processing of the stimulus situation occurs. Tension is produced. If the infant's "interpretation" of this event is negative, because of context and possibly prepotent aspects of the stimulus situation, he will *cry and engage in avoidance behavior*. If his interpretation is positive, he will smile or, depending on context and the amount of tension produced, *laugh and engage in approach behavior*.

Our observations are fully consistent with such an analysis. We have observed repeatedly that when an infant cries he pulls back in the highchair and turns from the stimulus, whereas when laughter occurs the baby maintains an orientation toward the agent, reaches for the object, and seeks to reproduce the situation. Also, when an infant becomes distressed in our laboratory, stimuli previously eliciting laughter produce crying, suggesting that the infant's interpretation of the situation has changed. (Wolff [1969] has reported that in each of five infants, when the baby was fussing, tickling in the most sensitive places repeatedly produced crying.) Moreover, we find routinely that laughter builds from smiling responses on initial trials and fades again to smiling on later trails. Based on the present analysis, we would speculate that the infant laughs on those trials when the incongruity is fully processed and the tension is maximal, then smiles again as the incongruity is brought into harmony with existing schemata. An explanation based on an ambivalence notion must rest on the assumption that the infant processes positive aspects of the situation first, and then somehow must overlook or forget the slowly developing negative aspects on trials following laughter. Interestingly, we do not observe trial-by-trial patterns of, for example, smile, smile, laugh, cry or smile, cry, laugh, which would be expected to occur occasionally based on an ambivalence position. Likewise, we observed crying only about once in every four testings (one of every 125 items), much less than would be expected from an ambivalence position. We have observed wavering between smiling and distress within a trial, which we would suggest derives from an uncertain interpretation on the part of the infant.

We are now beginning to gather data on the relationship between emotional expression and attention to further test the strength of a cognitive interpretation formulation. We have already observed that if an infant smiles immediately in the mask situation, a common occurrence in younger babies, laughter on subsequent trials is rare. If, on the other hand, activity completely ceases and the infant fixates on the mask then smiles, laughter on subsequent trials is much more likely. In our laboratory we have also observed consistent, dramatic cardiac rate decelerations preceding laughter, with the slowest heartbeat just prior to the response. We are now recording concurrent muscle activity, skin conductance, and respiration to further explore such relationships.

Conclusion

Our data suggest that laughter signifies the occurrence of an important transaction between the infant and his environment. At the present time we can only speculate that laughter plays a functional role in the maintenance of such commerce; that the consequent discharge of tension enables continued orientation to and approach toward the incongruous stimulus situation. Our reasoning, if correct, suggests an important tie between cognitive development and emotional growth and expression, including the relationship between security and exploration. Such assumptions concerning laughter are based on the belief that highly stereotyped, general-within-the-species behavior patterns are functional for the organism's adaptation. In the human organism, approach toward the incongruous may be part of that adaptation (Berlyne, 1960; Charlesworth, 1964; Piaget, 1953; White, 1959).

APPENDIX

These are the instructions for the individual items used in the studies. The numbers correspond to the items listed in Table 7.2. Unless otherwise stipulated, there was a 4-second pause between trials.

Auditory:

1. Four pops in a row, then pause. Starts with lips pursed, checks full.
2. Starts low, then crescendo in a loud voice, abrupt cutoff; 6-second pause.
3. Using a loud, deep voice pronounce "boom, boom, boom" at 1-second intervals.

4. Mechanical type of sound, varying voice pitch from low to high and back down again.
5. With mouth 1 foot from baby's ear, whisper, "Hi baby, how are you?" Avoid blowing in ear.
6. Falsetto voice (like Mickey Mouse), say, "Hi baby, how are you?"
7. With lips relaxed, blow through them as a horse does when he is tired.

Tactile:

8. Blow gently at hair for 3 seconds. Blow from the side, across the top of his head.
9. Four quick pecks, on bare stomach.
10. Gently stroke cheek three times with soft object.
11. Place baby on knees facing away. Five vigorous bounces.
12. Hold baby waist high, horizontal, face toward floor, and jiggle vigorously 3 seconds.
13. Using finger, gently tickle under baby's chin for 3 seconds.
14. Open mouth wide, press lips on back of neck and create a suction for 2 seconds.

Social:

15. Focus baby's attention on your fingers. Walk fingers toward baby, then give baby a poke in the ribs. If laughter is achieved, do another trial *not* followed by poking.
16. Allow baby to grasp yarn, then tug three times trying not to pull it away from him. Pause and repeat.
17. Put cloth in mouth and lean close enough for baby to grasp. Allow baby to pull cloth out and replace it if this is his tendency. Place the end of the cloth in his hand if this is necessary.
18. Say lyrically, "I'm gonna get you" ("I'm" quite protracted), while leaning toward baby with hands poised to grab. Then grab baby around stomach. If laughter is achieved, do another trial *not* followed by grabbing.
19. Stand at baby's side. If he does not uncover his face immediately, uncover for him. Do not drag cloth across baby's face. Emphasis is on baby getting out from underneath.
20. Stick out tongue until baby touches it (make his hand touch it if necessary). Quickly pull tongue back in as soon as he touches it.
21. Using blank cardboard, get baby's attention with face uncovered, cover face for 2 seconds, uncover quickly and pause 3 seconds. Do *not* say "Peek-a-boo."

Visual:

22. Using a white cloth, proceed as in no. 28 below.
23. Use one of baby's favorite toys. Focus his attention on it (out of reach). Cover it 2 seconds, uncover quickly.
24. First make sure that the baby is not hungry, then take bottle, bring toward lips, take three pretend sucks, lower bottle.
25. Place baby in highchair or infant seat. Crawl *across* his field of vision, *not* toward him. *Stand*, return to starting point.
26. Stand with arms extended to sides, walk in an exaggerated waddle, across baby's field of vision. Return to starting point walking normally.
27. Shake head vigorously at a distance of 1 foot from baby's face three times. Do not allow hair to touch baby.
28. Obtain baby's attention. Hold mask up so he can see it. Place mask in front of your face, lean slowly to within 1 foot of baby's face, pause 2 seconds. Lean back slowly, remove mask slowly.

Extra items:

29. Crawl behind baby, ostentatiously chasing him, slapping hands on floor.

30. Lift baby slowly to position overhead, looking down back. Minimize tactile and kinesthetic aspects.
31. To reduce peek-a-boo effects move baby slowly in front of full-length mirror. Hold 3 seconds, remove slowly, then pause 4 seconds.
32. As in no. 18.
33. As in no. 15.

References

AMBROSE, A. The age of onset of ambivalence in early infancy: indications from the study of laughing. *Journal of Child Psychology and Psychiatry*, 1963, *4*, 167–181.

BERGSON, H. L. *Laughter: an essay on the meaning of the comic* (trans. Cloudesley Brereton). New York: Macmillan, 1911.

BERLYNE, D. E. *Conflict, arousal and curiosity*. New York: McGraw-Hill, 1960.

BRONSON, G. W. The fear of novelty. *Psychological Bulletin*, 1968, *69*, 350–358.

CHARLESWORTH, W. R. Instigation and maintenance of curiosity behavior as a function of surprise versus novel and familiar stimuli. *Child Development*, 1964, *35*, 1169–1186.

DARWIN, C. *The expression of emotions in man and animals*. New York: Philosophy Library, 1872.

FREUD, S. *Female sexuality*. (Standard ed., vol. *21*.) London: Hogarth, 1931.

GIBSON, J. J. The concept of the stimulus in psychology. *American Psychologist*, 1960, *15*, 694–703.

HEBB, D. O. *The organization of behavior*. New York: Wiley, 1949.

JAMES, W. *The principles of psychology*. New York: Holt, 1890.

KAGAN, J. *Change and continuity in infancy*. New York: Wiley, 1971.

KOESTLER, A. *The act of creation*. New York: Macmillan, 1964.

LEWIS, M. Individual differences in the measurement of early cognitive growth. In J. Hellmuth (Ed.), *Exceptional infant*, vol. 2. New York: Brunner/Mazel, 1971.

PIAGET, J. *The origin of intelligence in the child*. London: Routledge & Kegan Paul, 1953.

SCARR, S., & SALAPATEK, P. Patterns of fear development during infancy. *Merrill-Palmer Quarterly*, 1970, *16*, 53–87.

SCHOPLER, E. Early infantile autism and receptor processes. *Archives of General Psychiatry*, 1965, *13*, 327–335.

SCHULTZ, T. R., & ZIGLER, E. Emotional concomitants of visual mastery in infants: the effects of stimulus movement on smiling and vocalizing. *Journal of Experimental Child Psychology*, 1970, *10*, 390–402.

SPENCER, H. The physiology of laughter. In *Essays*, vol. 2 (1863). New York: Appleton, 1892.

WASHBURN, R. W. A study of the smiling and laughing of infants in the first year of life. *Genetic Psychology Monographs*, 1929, *6*, 397–537.

WATSON, J. B., & RAYNER, R. Conditioned emotional reactions. *Journal of Experimental Psychology*, 1920, *3*, 1–14.

WHITE, R. W. Motivation reconsidered: the concept of competence. *Psychological Review*, 1959, *66*, 297–333.

WHITE, S. H. Age differences in reaction to stimulus variation. Paper presented at ONR Conference on Adaptation to Complex and Changing Environment at Boulder, Colorado, March 1964.

WOLFF, P. H. The natural history of crying and other vocalizations in early infancy. In B. M. Foss (Ed.), *Determinants of infant behavior*, vol. *4*. London: Methuen, 1969.

ZELAZO, P. R., & KOMER, J. Infant smiling to nonsocial stimuli and the recognition bypothesis. *Child Development*, 1971, *42*, 1327–1339.

ZIGLER, E.; LEVINE, J.; & GOULD, L. Cognitive challenge as a factor in children's humor appreciation. *Journal of Personality and Social Psychology*, 1967, *6*, 332–336.

37. EXCERPTS FROM *FROM TWO TO FIVE*

KORNEI CHUKOVSKY

About the Beginning and the End of Being

We must make use of this peculiarity of the child's mind when he poses questions which we cannot answer with complete directness. Questions of this type include those concerning birth.

The more inquisitive children, in most instances, have already begun in their fourth year to wonder about how they appeared in the world. At that time they also begin to wonder how all that lives appeared on the earth; and there probably is not a child who does not formulate his own hypothesis on this.

Of course, all such hypotheses are, without exception, wrong; but each one of them testifies loudly to the tireless effort of the child's mind. The contemplation of the beginning of everything that exists is the law governing the mental development of the child. And when the child asks: "Who gave birth to the first mother?" —he expresses thereby one of the earliest efforts of his mind to reach out in search of the primary causes of the material world.

Experienced teachers apply a special method by means of which it is possible, without turning away too much from the truth, to satisfy the child in the early stages of his inquisitiveness, when he tries to penetrate the mystery of how human beings are born. "And why is father never pregnant?" a youngster asked his kindergarten teacher. She answered him with that "caution" recommended to teachers by Gorki: "Children are borne only by mothers but fathers also love their children and are concerned about them. You saw how the pigeons fed their baby birds —both the mother and the father gave the babies their food. Only the mother laid the eggs in the nest, but when the mother pigeon flew away for a while, the father pigeon sat in the nest and kept the eggs warm. . . ." This is the good, intelligible way to answer such questions put by children.

Whether this is the only way, I do not know. There are differences in children, and we have no universal "prescriptions." We sometimes need an individual approach; furthermore, a lot depends on the teacher's sensitivity, on his skill and tact. A general norm, equally suitable to every child under all circumstances, does not and cannot exist. For this reason we are obliged to limit ourselves in the following pages to a simple reproduction of characteristic examples illustrating how many-faceted and how ardent is the interest in these young minds in this, for them, insoluble problem.

Here, for example, is a curious note

about my great-granddaughter, Mashen'ka:

"Up to the age of four she was persuaded that children were bought in stores. But, recently, after her fourth birthday, a shower of questions: 'In what kind of store? Where? How?,' and so on. We were forced to explain that children are not bought but born: the tummy is cut open and the child lifted from it. For example, Mother gave birth to Mashen'ka, and Grandmother Marina gave birth to Mother, and so forth. 'And Grandfather Kolia—whom did he give birth to? Do women give birth to girls and men to boys?' And she was perturbed when she found out that men do not give birth and that only women's tummies are cut open. Another shower of questions: 'Why did Aunt Galia give birth to Seriozha and not you? He didn't want to be in *your* tummy? Why? And why was Liudochka born after me and now she is smaller than I? Why didn't she want to be born together with me?' "

"My six-year-old Tus'ka," writes her father, "saw a pregnant woman and said, laughing:

" 'Oh, what a belly!'

"I said to her: 'Don't laugh at the woman—there's a baby in her tummy.'

"Tus'ka, with horror:

" 'She ate up a baby?!' "

. . .

"Mothers give birth to boys too? Then what are fathers for?"

. . .

"How I was born I know. But how were you and father born?"

. . .

"Mother, who gave birth to me? You? I knew it! If daddy had given birth to me I'd have a mustache."

. . .

And, again—on the same subject:

"What kind of librarian is she? With a mustache?"

"Yes."

"And why does she have a mustache?"

"I don't know."

"Her father must have given birth to her."

. . .

"The rooster, could he completely, completely, completely forget that he is a rooster, and lay an egg?"

. . .

"What do you mean—where did I come from? You yourself gave birth to me, with your own hands."

. . .

"Out of what does one make people? Out of bones?"

. . .

"Uncle, uncle, so many tiny rabbits came pouring out of the big rabbit! Come, quicker, or they'll all crawl back and you'll never see them!"

. . .

"Oh, Mommie, Mommie, why did you give birth to this awful Guk? It would have been better if he had remained in your stomach forever and be lonely there all his life."

. . .

In Vera Panova's novel, *Seriozha*, its five-year-old hero has a discussion with himself:

"Where do children come from—that's well known: they are bought at the hospital. The hospital trades in children. One woman bought two at the same time. Why did she buy two that were alike?—they say she tells them apart by a birthmark—one has a birthmark on his neck, the other has none. It's strange; why does she need identical children? It would have been better to buy two that were different."

Generally, the legend that parents buy their children is one of the most widespread among the younger preschoolers.

A persistent, teasing old man said to five-year-old Natasha, about her younger sister:

"Give me this little girl as a gift!"

"That's impossible!" Natasha objected stolidly. "We paid money for her."

. . .

The father of six-year-old Svetlana had just sold his television set.

"That's good!" pronounced Svetlana. "Now you have money with which to buy me a little brother."

. . .

Three-year-old Irina was convinced that her mother was not "buying" a baby because babies were too expensive. With this in mind, every penny [*kopeika*] that she happened to find on the street, in the yard, or around the house she brought to her mother with the same directive:

"Only for buying the baby! Don't spend it on anything else!"

. . .

Ira Gmuzhina asked her mother to buy her a little Tania.

"Tanias are very expensive," the mother answered. "Would you like a doll?"

Ira refused the doll. Within a few days a decrease in prices was announced over the radio.

"Now," Ira exclaimed, "you can buy me a Tania!"

. . .

This happened during the war—the little girl's nanny [*niania*] had stood in line for a long time but did not receive the rations for which she came. Trying to console the disappointed nanny, the little girl said:

"Nanny, dear, don't be so upset! Mommie went to the hospital, she stood and stood in line, but instead of a boy they gave her a girl!"

. . .

I remember, twenty years ago, when there were still horse-drawn carriages in Leningrad, six-year-old Anton, when he found out that baby horses are born "from the belly," asked:

"But do coachmen have such a large belly?"

. . .

"Say, Mother, when I was born, how did you find out that I was—Yurochka?"

. . .

"Had I known that you'd be so mean, I'd not have gotten born to you."

. . .

Five-year-old Eric, boasting in the communal kitchen:

"My father promised Mother a wrist watch if she gave birth to a girl. If he'd give *me* a watch I'd bear him ten of them."

. . .

Not seldom do we meet children who consider various methods of procreation equally possible:

"Mommie, did you buy me or give birth to me?"

"I gave birth to you."

"Oh! But Lion'ka you bought?"

. . .

A threat:

"I'll run away to Rostov, will give birth there to a baby, and I will never write you its name."

. . .

"Why did you give birth to such a mean daddy?"

. . .

"Mommie, darling, give birth to a little one."

"Don't nag. I have no time to bear a baby."

"But you have a day off sometimes!"

. . .

"What did I see when I was in mommie's tummy?"

"You didn't see anything!"

"That's not true—when mommie opened her mouth I'd look out and see things."

. . .

"All right, if you don't want me to be your son then ungive birth to me." (Then he cried all day, oppressed by his scoffing insolence.)

. . .

"Mommie, please give birth to a baby or a puppy. I beg you! You know how much I'll love them."

I have been convinced many times over of how well the child is armored against thoughts and information that he does not yet need and that are prematurely offered to him by too-hasty adults. If the mother or the father, not taking into account the needs of the child's age, does attempt to reveal to him the full and candid truth about conception, pregnancy, birth, and so forth, he, in accordance with the laws of his childish nature, will inevitably transform this truth into material for boundless fantasy.

. . .

The child himself turns away from the information supplied by grownups, for which he is not yet ready. He thoroughly eliminates such information from his consciousness, as if to convince the grownups that this mental food offered by them is, in this instance, not yet needed.

The mother of Tolia Bozhinskii told me:

"I explained to Tolia what pregnancy was. When Tinochka was born I talked to him at length about how she emerged from my tummy. But some time later I told him a fairy tale about a stork. After that, when anyone asked how Tinochka was born, he would say with utter conviction:

" 'The stork brought her.'

"I never told him that Tinochka was brought by a stork."

. . .

There were guests in the house and one of them asked about three-year-old Volia:

> "Whose eyes does Volia have?"
> "His father's."
> "And poor daddy remained without eyes," thought Volia, and he at once formulated the following hypothesis:
> "When I was not yet born, daddy had many eyes, big ones and little ones; and when mommie bought me, daddy gave me the big eyes and he left for himself the small ones."

With what delightful ease does the child solve such problems! All this is pure improvisation, akin to the inspired "impromptus" that he utters while he plays. These inspirations are as spontaneous with him as they are unexpected by his interlocutor. Not even a moment earlier does he usually know what he is going to say, but when he says it, he does so with conviction and firmness, not doubting at all the reality of his inventions.

These inventions are transitory; they are not workable hypotheses. Within a minute the child is ready to express opposite thoughts, since at times he plays games with thoughts. Even when, by accident, he happens to witness the birth of an animal, he is ready even then to explain what is going on in a most fantastic way.

V. I. Kachalov told me that when his son and his little friend, Mitya, found out that the cat was about to give birth to kittens, they could not guess from where the kittens would make their appearance.

Mitya looked into the cat's ear and announced:

"It will be soon now! I see a little paw already."

. . .

> "My mother went to a house in Moscow to buy me a brother or a sister."
> "They don't sell children in the Soviet Union, only in America."
> "They don't sell them in America either; they are born there from monkeys."
>
> . . .
>
> "Was my mother a monkey . . . and Nadezhda Nikitichna?" (Nadezhda Nikitichna is the kindergarten teacher.)
>
> . . .

Here is another scientific discussion about the creation of man, according to Darwin:

> Nina asked her grandmother:
> "Granny, were you once a monkey?"
> "No, never."
> "And your mother?"
> "Not either."
> "Then who was a monkey? Grandpa?"
> "God be with you, child! No, grandpa not either."
> "Oh, well, that means that my Moscow granny was the monkey."

38. THE ROLE OF BODY PARTS AND READINESS IN ACQUISITION OF NUMBER CONSERVATION

FRANK CURCIO, OWEN ROBBINS, and SUSAN SLOVIN ELA

167 preschoolers were tested on 2 number-conservation tasks, 1 for fingers, and 1 for external objects. Results showed that the first task was mastered before the second. Children then trained to generalize their number conservation ability with fingers to external objects were more successful than children lacking this ability who received counting or addition/subtraction training. However, since type of training and readiness were confounded, additional groups were selected for training, and comparisons showed that a combination of readiness and body-part training was the most effective combination in producing number conservation with external objects.

Many studies have tried to delineate specific experiences affecting acquisition of number conservation. This study examined an additional factor which has received little attention: one's own body or body parts. Although not conclusive, some anecdotal evidence suggests that one's own body may be involved in number conservation. For instance, children's counting games which center upon their fingers and toes may contribute to the mastery of number conservation. Also, Piaget, Inhelder, and Szeminska (1960) have noted that, before using an independent measuring instrument, children often use parts of their bodies to measure objects (as if the child acquires conservation of length with his own body before generalizing this principle to external objects).

From this suggestive, although highly speculative, material, it seemed possible that number conservation involving body parts precedes number conservation with external objects. In the present study, number conservation was tested by presenting two rows of objects equal in length and number, then rearranging one row into a different length or shape. An analogous procedure could be performed with the five fingers of each hand. Equality of fingers could be established, fingers of one hand could be rearranged, etc. These two procedures constituted the initial part of this study to determine if number conservation with fingers precedes number conservation with external objects.

The Ss were 167 nursery school children (age range = 42–64 mo; X = 54 mo). Materials used in all procedures were red and yellow pipe cleaners (PCs). Subject was asked to choose the color of PCs he would like to have; *E* then placed S's chosen PCs on S's side of the table and left the remaining PCs on *E*'s side. Depending on the task, various numbers of PCs from each pile were brought to the center of the table.

Initially, all Ss were tested on five tasks: addition/subtraction, counting, one-to-one correspondence of objects, number conservation with objects, and number conservation with fingers. The first three tasks were given to ensure that Ss used for possible training had certain abilities with which to participate meaningfully in such training. The tasks were given in the following order: (1) *Counting*—Subject was asked to give *E* five PCs and then four PCs. (2) *One-to-one correspondence*—Experimenter lined up five PCs and asked S to "make a row just like mine." This was repeated with three PCs. (3) *Number conservation with objects.*—From S's and E's piles, E placed two rows of five PCs in one-to-one correspondence and asked, "Who has more pipe cleaners, you or I, or do we both have the same number of pipe cleaners?" This was the standard question (Q) used to test number conservation. Then E spread his row out to twice the length of S's and repeated Q. With minor variations, this procedure was repeated in two additional trials. (4) *Addition/subtraction.*—Five yellow and five red PCs were placed in two piles, and E indicated to S that each pile had the same number. Then E removed two PCs from S's pile and asked Q. This was repeated twice more with minor variations. (5) *Number conservation with fingers.*—Subject was asked to hold up his hands, palms outward, fingers slightly spread. Experimenter asked, "Do you have more fingers on this hand [pointing to left hand] or on this hand [pointing to right hand] or do you have the same number of fingers on both hands?" This was the standard question for finger conservation. Then S was asked to spread apart his left hand and leave the fingers of his right hand together. Again Q for fingers was asked. With some minor variations, this procedure was repeated twice. The verbal instructions were usually accompanied by some gestural demonstration.

To pass a task, S had to perform correctly on both trials in each of the counting and correspondence tasks and on at least two of three trials in the remaining three tasks. Under these criteria, the number of Ss passing each of the five tasks was 150 for addition/subtraction, 122 for correspondence, 119 for counting, 52 for conservation with fingers, and 13 for conservation with objects. Further examination of the data showed that number conservation with fingers generally precedes conservation with external objects. The number of Ss passing both tasks was 11, whereas 113 failed both tasks. More important, 41 Ss passed number conservation with fingers but failed conservation with objects; only two Ss showed the reverse pattern.

Thus, the results indicate that, in general, number conservation of fingers precedes number conservation of external objects; however, this does not mean that they are functionally related (e.g., walking and reading). Therefore, to explore this issue, a second study was undertaken to examine the effectiveness of training number conservation with objects by utilizing number conservation with fingers in training. For comparison, two additional groups were trained with counting and addition/subtraction procedures.

From Ss pretested, three groups of Ss, 16 per group, were selected for training and posttesting. One to 3 days after pretesting, 32 Ss who had passed the counting, addition/subtraction, and correspondence tasks but had failed both conservation tasks were randomly assigned either to rote-counting (RC) or addition/subtraction (A/S) training groups. In RC training, Ss were given a number-conservation task with five PCs per row. When the PCs were in one-to-one correspondence, Q was asked; after S's reply, E asked, "How do you know? Count them." This procedure, with different transformations (rows were condensed, expanded, etc.), was repeated in seven more trials. In A/S training, Ss were also given a number-conservation task with five PCs per row. When the PCs were in one-to-one correspondence, Q was asked, and, after S's reply, one row was lengthened and Q asked again. When S said one row contained more, a single PC was added to the other row which, by inference, contained less; Q was then repeated. If S still maintained that the first row contained more, another PC was added to the second row and Q repeated. If S's response implied that it contained less, the previously added PC was removed and Q repeated. This oscillation between adding and subtracting PCs was performed three times or until S asserted the equality of the rows. After the first trial, this procedure, with different transformations, was repeated for four additional trials.

The 16 Ss used for body-part (BP) training had also passed the counting, addition/subtraction, and correspondence tasks, but, unlike the A/S and RC groups, they had passed at least two of three trials in the pretest on conservation with fingers, a necessary prerequisite to meaningfully participating in BP training. In this training procedure, the primary intent was to foster generalization from number conservation with fingers to number conservation with external objects. Five yellow and five red PCs were bent into rings and placed on the 10 slightly spread fingers of S's raised hands. Experimenter asked, "Do you have more rings on this hand [pointing to right hand] or on this hand [pointing to left hand] or do they both have the same?" Subject was then asked to spread the fingers on his right hand and close those on his left hand. The question was repeated. The rings were then removed from S's fingers and placed on the table so that those on the closed hand were placed close together and those on the spread hand were placed further apart. Then the standard conservation Q for objects was asked. The rings were then moved into rows of one-to-one correspondence, and Q was repeated. This procedure constituted one trial. The rings were then replaced on S's fingers, and the procedure was repeated twice more with some minor variations.

All training groups received two identical posttests of number conservation with objects: immediately after training and 1 week later. Unlike the number used in pretest and training sessions, six or seven PCs per row were used in the posttests. In the first trial, two rows of seven PCs were placed in one-to-one correspondence, Q was asked, *E*'s row was lengthened, and Q was asked again. This was repeated in a second trial with six PCs and S's row lengthened, and in a third trial with six PCs and S's row transformed into a star-like configuration.

Correctly responding on at least two of three trials in the posttest counted as a pass. The numbers of subjects (out of 16 per group) passing the immediate posttest for the A/S, RC, and BP training groups were 2, 3, and 11 respectively. In the delayed posttest, two Ss in A/S, two in RC, and 12 in the BP training group passed. Chi-square analyses of the numbers of Ss failing and passing the posttests for the three training groups yielded χ^2s of 13.7 for the immediate posttest and 18.8 for the delayed posttest ($p < .01$).

The results clearly indicate that the BP training group is superior to the other two groups; however, this superiority may be due, not to training, but simply to the fact that this group was "closer" to acquisition of number conservation with objects. Specifically, the BP training group possessed all the abilities of the A/S and RC groups *plus* number conservation of fingers before training. In fact, type of training may be irrelevant, and with the greater closeness or "readiness" of the group any type of training may have induced number conservation with external objects.

To clarify this issue, two additional training groups (eight Ss per group) were selected which showed number conservation with fingers, but not with objects, in the pretest. In addition, they had passed the remaining three pretest tasks. One group received RC and one group received A/S training as described above. Thus, these groups were only one step removed from conservation of external objects (since they possessed finger conservation), but they received training irrelevant to conservation of fingers. As before, training was given 1–3 days after pretesting, and posttests were given immediately and 1 week after training.

Since preliminary analyses revealed no major differences between the A/S and

RC groups, the results for these groups were combined. As a first comparison, the posttest performances of this combined group were compared with those of the group which possessed number conservation with fingers and which received training specific to this ability (BP training). In the immediate posttest, of those receiving A/S or RC training, 7 out of 16 Ss passed, whereas of those receiving BP training 11 out of 16 Ss passed. Although the latter group, which received BP training, was slightly superior to the group receiving A/S or RC training, a χ^2 analysis of the numbers of Ss failing and passing the immediate posttest for the two training groups was not significant ($\chi^2 = 2.03$; $p > .05$). However, in the delayed posttest, three Ss from the A/S, RC group who had previously passed the immediate posttest were absent from this category; two failed, and one S was ill. Thus, in the delayed posttest, 4 out of 15 receiving A/S or RC training passed, whereas 12 out of 16 Ss receiving BP training passed. Chi-square analysis of these results yielded a χ^2 of 8.58 ($p < .01$). Had the absent S from the A/S, RC group passed the delayed posttest, the χ^2 would have been 6.14 ($p < .05$).

Summarizing thus far, the specific training received by the BP training group was of some special importance in acquiring and maintaining number conservation with external objects. The closeness or readiness of a group, when coupled with *some* form of training involving addition/subtraction or counting, may temporarily induce number conservation, but it is not sufficient to maintain it.

Also, another comparison is made possible by contrasting the posttest performances of the A/S and RC training groups which already possessed number conservation with fingers ($N = 16$) with the performance of the A/S and RC training groups originally trained which did not show finger conservation in the pretest ($N = 32$). Thus, readiness or closeness of the groups varies, and training procedures are equated. In a comparison of Ss with finger conservation and those without this ability, 7 of 16 *Ss* (42%) with finger conservation passed the immediate posttest, whereas only 5 out of 32 *Ss* (16%) who had not shown finger conservation in the pretest passed this posttest. In the delayed posttest 4 out of 15 Ss (27%) with finger conservation passed, while 4 out of 32 (13%) without finger conservation passed. While some trend showing a superiority of the group possessing finger conservation exists, χ^2 analyses of the immediate and delayed posttests revealed no significant group differences ($\chi^2 = 4.5$ and 1.5; $p > .05$).

In summary, the strongest training effect emerges when the following groups are compared: Ss who possess number conservation with fingers trained to generalize this ability and Ss who do not possess finger conservation trained on A/S or RC procedures. When closeness or readiness is equated and training is different, the BP training group tends to maintain acquisition of number conservation 1 week later, while the other groups do not, which suggests the special contribution made by this type of training. Thus, when readiness of a child is coupled with a form of training appropriate to the child's current level of development, acquisition of number conservation is strongest—a finding, incidentally, which provides support for Hunt's (1961) match-mismatch hypothesis. Also, when training experiences of the groups are the same (but not tied to experiences involving fingers) and closeness or readiness is different, there is a nonsignificant trend for more Ss in the closer group to acquire number conservation with objects.

These findings offer a conceptual distinction between two factors affecting cognitive development: the kinds of experiences a child receives and readiness or closeness of the child to the criterion concept. With few exceptions (e.g., Kingsley & Hall, 1967), most attention has been directed toward the kinds of experiences affecting cognitive development. Perhaps some of the disparity between studies which succeed and those which fail to train conservation may lie as much in the closeness of a sample of children to the criterion concept as in the type of training provided. To assess meaningfully the effects of different training experiences it would be essential to diagnose and equate children on their closeness to the criterion concept.

Concerning the *horizontal decalage* between number conservation with fingers and that with external objects, perhaps the "provoked correspondence" (Piaget 1952) in pairing thumbs, index fingers, etc., contributes to the recognition of number conservation with fingers before that with external objects. Also, some evidence suggests that training in reversibility may be involved in acquisition of number conservation (Wallach & Sprott 1964). The large variety of transformations and reversible operations that a pair of human hands can easily perform indicates that such activity may contribute to a mastery of number conservation with fingers before mastery of number conservation with external objects. Of some theoretical import here is the fact that reversibility of this type is sensory-motor, which suggests (as Piaget has claimed) that sensory-motor reversibility precedes reversibility of a more mental type.

References

HUNT, J. MC V. *Intelligence and experience.* New York: Ronald, 1961.

KINGSLEY, R. C., & HALL, V. C. Training conservation through the use of learning sets. *Child Development,* 1967, *38,* 1111–1126.

PIAGET, J. *The child's conception of number.* London: Routledge & Kegan Paul, 1952.

PIAGET, J.; INHELDER, B.; & SZEMINSKA, A. *The child's conception of geometry.* New York: Harper & Row, 1960.

WALLACH, L., & SPROTT, R. L. Inducing number conservation in children. *Child Development,* 1964, *35,* 1057–1071.

39. SAMPLE ITEMS FROM *STANFORD-BINET SCALE*

LEWIS M. TERMAN and MAUDE E. MERRILL

The Stanford-Binet is one of the most widely used tests of intelligence. It consists of six items at each age level from age 2 to 14. Also included are tests for ages 2½, 3½, and 4½, and four adult tests. When an item appears at a certain age, it means that 50 percent of the tested population of that age will pass the item. Obviously 50 percent of the population will fail the item also.

Some sample items from different age levels are presented below:

Year II: The child can identify several parts of the body.
Year II–6: Copies a tower of blocks.
Repeats 2 numbers.
Obeys the command "Put the button in the box."
Year III: Copies a circle.
Year IV: Identifies objects, such as "which do we cook on."
Year V: Can define 2 simple objects.
Year VI: Can define "orange, envelope, straw."
Can tell the difference between a bird and a dog.
Can trace a simple maze.
Year VIII: Names the days of the week, specifying which comes after Tuesday, Thursday, Friday.
Can tell similarities and differences between objects.
Year IX: Repeats 4 digits reversed (such as 5–8–2–6).
Can draw designs from memory.
Year X: Names at least 28 words in one minute.
Defines abstract words.

The vocabulary that begins at year VI is given at VIII and at every year after that, including such words as *muzzle, tolerate, stave,* and *harpy*. The number of correct definitions required changes with the age level. At age 6, six correct are usual, while at age 10, eleven words must be defined.

40. UNKNOWNS IN THE IQ EQUATION: A REVIEW OF THREE MONOGRAPHS

SANDRA SCARR-SALAPATEK

IQ scores have been repeatedly estimated to have a large heritable component in United States and Northern European white populations (*1*). Individual differences in IQ, many authors have concluded, arise far more from genetic than from environmental differences among people in these populations, at the present time, and under present environmental conditions. It has also been known for many years that white lower-class and black groups have lower IQs, on the average, than white middle-class groups. Most behavioral scientists comfortably "explained" these group differences by appealing to obvious environmental differences between the groups in standards of living, educational opportunities, and the like. But recently an explosive controversy has developed over the heritability of between-group differences in IQ, the question at issue being: If individual differences within the white population as a whole can be attributed largely to heredity, is it not plausible that the average differences between social-class groups and between racial groups also reflect significant genetic differences? Can the former data be used to explain the latter?

To propose genetically based racial and social-class differences is anathema to most behavioral scientists, who fear any scientific confirmation of the pernicious racial and ethnic prejudices that abound in our society. But now that the issue has been openly raised, and has been projected into the public context of social and educational policies, a hard scientific look must be taken at what is known and at what inferences can be drawn from that knowledge.

The public controversy began when A. R. Jensen, in a long paper in the *Harvard Educational Review*, persuasively juxtaposed data on the heritability of IQ and the observed differences between groups. Jensen suggested that current large-scale educational attempts to raise the IQ's of lower-class children, white and black, were failing because of the high heritability of IQ. In a series of papers and rebuttals to criticism, in the same journal and elsewhere (*2*), Jensen put forth the hypothesis that social-class and racial differences in mean IQ were due largely to differences in the gene distributions of these populations. At least, he said, the genetic-differences hypothesis was no less likely, and probably more likely, than a simple environmental hypothesis to explain the mean difference of 15 IQ points between blacks and whites (*3*) and the even larger average IQ differences between professionals and manual laborers within the white population.

Jensen's articles have been directed primarily at an academic audience. Herrnstein's article in the *Atlantic* and Eysenck's book (first published in England) have brought the argument to the attention of the wider lay audience. Both Herrnstein and Eysenck agree with Jensen's genetic-differences hypothesis as it pertains to individual differences and to social-class groups, but Eysenck centers his attention on the genetic explanation of racial-group differences, which Herrnstein only touches on. Needless to say, many other scientists will take issue with them.

Eysenck's Racial Thesis

Eysenck has written a popular account of the race, social-class, and IQ controversy in a generally inflammatory book. The provocative title and the disturbing cover picture of a forlorn black boy are clearly designed to tempt the lay reader into a pseudo-battle between Truth and Ignorance In this case Truth is genetic-environmental interactionism (*4*) and Ignorance is naive environmentalism. For the careful reader, the battle fades out inconclusively as Eysenck admits that scientific evidence to date does not permit a clear choice of the genetic-differences interpretation of black inferiority on intelligence tests. A quick reading of the book, however, is sure to leave the reader believing that scientific evidence today strongly supports the conclusion that U.S. blacks are genetically inferior to whites in IQ.

The basic theses of the book are as follows:

1. IQ is a highly heritable characteristic in the U.S. white population and probably equally heritable in the U.S. black population.

2. On the average, blacks score considerably lower than whites on IQ tests.
3. U.S. blacks are probably a non-random, lower-IQ, sample of native African populations.
4. The average IQ difference between blacks and whites probably represents important genetic differences between the races.
5. Drastic environmental changes will have to be made to improve the poor phenotypes that U.S. blacks now achieve.

The evidence and nonevidence that Eysenck cites to support his genetic hypothesis of racial differences make a curious assortment. Audrey Shuey's review (5) of hundreds of studies showing mean phenotypic differences between black and white IQ's leads Eysenck to conclude:

> All the evidence to date suggests the strong and indeed overwhelming importance of genetic factors in producing the great variety of intellectual differences which we observe in our culture, and much of the difference observed between certain racial groups. This evidence cannot be argued away by niggling and very minor criticisms of details which do not really throw doubts on the major points made in this book [p. 126].

To "explain" the genetic origins of these IQ mean IQ differences he offers these suppositions:

> White slavers wanted dull beasts of burden, ready to work themselves to death in the plantations, and under those conditions intelligence would have been counter-selective. Thus there is every reason to expect that the particular sub-sample of the Negro race which is constituted of American Negroes is not an unselected sample of Negroes, but has been selected throughout history according to criteria which would put the highly intelligent at a disadvantage. The inevitable outcome of such selection would of course be a gene pool lacking some of the genes making for higher intelligence [p. 42].

Other ethnic minorities in the U.S. are also, in his view, genetically inferior, again because of the selective migration of lower IQ genotypes:

> It is known [*sic*] that many other groups came to the U.S.A. due to pressures which made them very poor samples of the original populations. Italians, Spaniards, and Portuguese, as well as Greeks, are examples where the less able, less intelligent were forced through circumstances to emigrate, and where their American progeny showed significantly lower IQ's than would have been shown by a random sample of the original population [p. 43].

Although Eysenck is careful to say that these are not established facts (because no IQ tests were given to the immigrants or nonimmigrants in question?), the tone of his writing leaves no doubt about his judgment. There is something in this book to insult almost everyone except WASP's and Jews.

Despite his conviction that U.S. blacks are genetically inferior in IQ to whites, Eysenck is optimistic about the potential effects of radical environmental changes on the present array of Negro IQ phenotypes. He points to the very large IQ gains produced by intensive one-to-one tutoring of black urban children with low-IQ mothers, contrasting large environmental changes and large IQ gains in intensive programs of this sort with significant environmental improvements and small IQ changes obtained by Head Start and related programs. He correctly observes that, whatever the heritability of IQ (or, it should be added, of any characteristic), large phenotypic changes may be produced by creating appropriate, radically different environments never before encountered by those genotypes. On this basis, Eysenck calls for further research to determine the requisites of such environments.

Since Eysenck comes to this relatively benign position regarding potential improvement in IQ's, why, one may ask, is he at such pains to "prove" the genetic inferiority of blacks? Surprisingly, he expects that new environments, such as that provided by intensive educational tutoring, will not affect the black-white IQ differential, because black children and white will probably profit equally from such treatment. Since many middle-class white children already have learning environments similar to that provided by tutors for the urban black children, we must suppose that Eysenck expects great IQ gains from relatively small changes in white, middle-class environments.

This book is an uncritical popularization of Jensen's ideas without the nuances and qualifiers that make much of Jensen's writing credible or at least responsible. Both authors rely on Shuey's review (5), but Eysenck's way of doing it is to devote some 25 pages to quotes and paraphrases of her chapter summaries. For readers to whom the original Jensen article is accessible, Eysenck's book is a poor substitute; although he defends Jensen and Shuey, he does neither a service.

It is a maddeningly inconsistent book filled with contradictory caution and incaution; with hypotheses stated both as hypotheses and as conclusions; with both accurate and inaccurate statements on matters of fact. For example, Eysenck thinks evoked potentials offer a better measure of "innate" intelligence than IQ tests. But on what basis? Recently F. B. Davis (6) has failed to find any relationship whatsoever between evoked potentials and either IQ scores or scholastic achievement, to which intelligence is supposed to be related. Another example is Eysenck's curious use of data to support a peculiar line of reasoning about the evolutionary inferiority of blacks: First, he reports that African and U.S. Negro babies have been shown to have precocious sensorimotor development by white norms (the difference, by several accounts, appears only in gross motor skills and even there is slight). Second, he notes that by three years of age U.S. white exceed U.S. black children in mean IQ scores. Finally he cites a (very slight) negative correlation, found in an early study, between sensorimotor intelligence in the first year of life and later IQ. From exaggerated statements of these various data, he concludes:

> These findings are important because of a very general view in biology according to which the more prolonged the infancy the greater in general are the cognitive or intellectual abilities of the species. This law appears to work even within a given species [p. 79].

Eysenck would apparently have us believe that Africans and their relatives in the U.S. are less highly evolved than Caucasians, whose longer infancy is related to later higher intelligence. I am aware of no evidence whatsoever to support a within-species relationship between longer infancy and higher adult capacities.

Herrnstein's Social Thesis

Thanks to Jensen's provocative article, many academic psychologists who thought IQ tests belonged in the closet with the Rorschach inkblots have now explored the psychometric literature and found it to be a trove of scientific treasure. One of these is Richard Herrnstein, who from a Skinnerian background has become an admirer of intelligence tests—a considerable leap from shaping the behavior of pigeons and rats. In contrast to Eysenck's book, Herrnstein's popular account in the *Atlantic* of IQ testing and its values is generally responsible, if overly enthusiastic in parts.

Herrnstein unabashedly espouses IQ testing as "psychology's most telling accomplishment to date," despite the current controversy over the fairness of testing poor and minority-group children with IQ items devised by middle-class whites. His historical review of IQ test development, including tests of general intelligence and multiple abilities, is interesting and accurate. His account of the validity and usefulness of the tests centers on the fairly accurate prediction that can be made from IQ scores to academic and occupational achievement and income level. He clarifies the pattern of relationship between IQ and these criterion variables: High IQ is a necessary but not sufficient condition for high achievement, while low IQ virtually assures failure at high academic and occupational levels. About the usefulness of the tests, he concludes:

> An IQ test can be given in an hour or two to a child, and from this infinitesimally small sample of his output, deeply important predictions follow—about schoolwork, occupation, income, satisfaction with life, and even life expectancy. The predictions are not perfect, for other factors always enter in, but no other single factor matters as much in as many spheres of life [p. 53].

One must assume that Herrnstein's enthusiasm for intelligence tests rests on population statistics, not on predictions for a particular child, because many children studied longitudinally have been shown to change IQ scores by 20 points or more from childhood to adulthood. It is likely that extremes of giftedness and retardation can be sorted out relatively early by IQ tests, but what about the 95 percent of the population in between? Their IQ scores may vary from dull to bright normal for many years. Important variations in IQ can occur up to late adolescence (8). On a population basis Herrnstein is correct; the best early predictors of later achievement are ability measures taken from age five on. Predictions are based on correlations, however, which are not sensitive to absolute changes in value, only to rank orders. This is an important point to be discussed later.

After reviewing the evidence for average IQ differences by social class and race, Herrnstein poses the nature-nurture problem of "which is primary" in determining phenotypic difference in IQ. For racial groups, he explains, the origins of mean IQ differences are indeterminate at the present time because we have no information from heritability studies in the black population or from other, unspecified, lines of research which could favor primarily genetic or primarily environmental hypotheses. He is thoroughly convinced, however, that individual differences and social-class differences in IQ are highly heritable at the present time, and are destined, by environmental improvements, to become even more so:

> If we make the relevant environment much more uniform (by making it as good as we can for everyone), then an even larger proportion of the variation in IQ will be attributable to the genes. The average person would be smarter, but intelligence would run in families even more obviously and with less regression toward the mean than we see today [p. 58].

For Herrnstein, society is, and will be even more strongly, a meritocracy based largely on inherited differences in IQ. He presents a "syllogism" [p. 58] to make his message clear.

1. If differences in mental abilities are inherited, and
2. If success requires those abilities, and
3. If earnings and prestige depend on success,
4. Then social standing (which reflects earnings and prestige) will be based to some extent on inherited differences among people.

Five "corollaries" for the future predict that the heritability of IQ will rise; that social mobility will become more strongly related to inherited IQ differences; that most bright people will be gathered in the top of the social structure, with the IQ dregs at the bottom; that many at the bottom will not have the intelligence needed for new jobs; and that the meritocracy will be built not just on inherited intelligence but on all inherited traits affecting success, which will presumably become correlated characters. Thus from the successful realization of our most precious egalitarian, political and social goals there will arise a much more rigidly stratified society, a "virtual caste system" based on inborn ability.

To ameliorate this effect, society may

have to move toward the socialist dictum, "From each according to his abilities, to each according to his needs," but Herrnstein sees complete equality of earnings and prestige as impossible because high-grade intelligence is scarce and must be recruited into those critical jobs that require it, by the promise of high earnings and high prestige. Although garbage collecting is critical to the health of the society, almost anyone can do it; to waste high-IQ persons on such jobs is to misallocate scarce resources at society's peril.

Herrnstein points to an ironic contrast between the effects of caste and class systems. Castes, which established artificial hereditary limits on social mobility, guarantee the inequality of opportunity that preserves IQ heterogeneity at all levels of the system. Many bright people are arbitrarily kept down and many unintelligent people are artifically maintained at the top. When arbitrary bounds on mobility are removed, as in our class system, most of the bright rise to the top and most of the dull fall to the bottom of the social system, and IQ differences between top and bottom become increasingly hereditary. The greater the environmental equality, the greater the hereditary differences between levels in the social structure. The thesis of egalitarianism surely leads to its antithesis in a way that Karl Marx never anticipated.

Herrnstein proposes that our best strategy, in the face of increasing biological stratification, is publicy to recognize genetic human differences but to reallocate wealth to a considerable extent. The IQ have-nots need not be poor. Herrnstein does not delve into the psychological consequences of being publicly marked as genetically inferior.

Does the evidence support Herrnstein's view of hereditary social classes, now or in some future Utopia? Given his assumptions about the high heritability of IQ, the importance of IQ to social mobility, and the increasing environmental equality of rearing and opportunity, hereditary social classes are to some extent inevitable. But one can question the limits of genetic homogeneity in social-class groups and the evidence for his syllogism at present.

Is IQ as highly heritable throughout the social structure as Herrnstein assumes? Probably not. In a recent study of IQ heritability in various racial and social-class groups (*9*), I found much lower proportions of genetic variance that would account for aptitude differences among lower-class than among middle-class children, in both black and white groups. Social disadvantage in prenatal and postnatal development can substantially lower phenotypic IQ and reduce the genotype-phenotype correlation. Thus, average phenotypic IQ differences between the social classes may be considerably larger than the genotypic differences.

Are social classes largely based on hereditary IQ differences now? Probably not as much as Herrnstein believes. Since opportunities for social mobility act at the phenotypic level, there still may be considerable genetic diversity for IQ at the bottom of the social structure. In earlier days arbitrary social barriers maintained genetic variability throughout the social structure. At present, individuals with high phenotypic IQ's are often upwardly mobile; but inherited wealth acts to maintain genetic diversity at the top, and nongenetic biological and social barriers to phenotypic development act to maintain a considerable genetic diversity of intelligence in the lower classes.

As P. E. Vernon has pointed out (*10*), we are inclined to forget that the majority of gifted children in recent generations have come from working-class, not middle-class, families. A larger percentage of middle-class children are gifted, but the working and lower classes produce gifted children in larger numbers. How many more disadvantaged children would have been bright if they had had middle-class gestation and rearing conditions?

I am inclined to think that intergenerational class mobility will always be with us, for three reasons. First, since normal IQ is a polygenic characteristic, various recombinations of parental genotypes will always produce more variable genotypes in the offspring than in the parents of all social-class groups, especially the extremes. Even if both parents, instead of primarily the male, achieved social-class status based on their IQ's, recombinations of their genes would always produce a range of offspring, who would be upwardly or downwardly mobile relative to their families of origin.

Second, since, as Herrnstein acknowledges, factors other than IQ—motivational, personality, and undetermined—also contribute to success or the lack of it, high IQ's will always be found among lower-class adults, in combination with schizophrenia, alcoholism, drug addiction, psychopathy, and other limiting factors. When recombined in offspring, high IQ can readily segregate with facilitating motivational and personality characteristics, thereby leading to upward mobility for many offspring. Similarly, middle-class parents will always produce some offspring with debilitating personal characterisics which lead to downward mobility.

Third, for all children to develop phenotypes that represent their best genotypic outcome (in current environments) would require enormous changes in the present social system. To improve and equalize all rearing environments would involve such massive intervention as to make Herrnstein's view of the future more problematic than he seems to believe.

Race as Caste

Races are castes between which there is very little mobility. Unlike the social-class system, where mobility based on IQ is sanctioned, the racial caste system, like the hereditary aristocracy of medieval Europe and the caste system of India, preserves within each group its full range of genetic diversity of intelligence. The Indian caste system was, according to Dobzhansky (*11*), a colossal genetic failure—or success, according to egalitarian values. After the abolition of castes at independence, Brahmins and untouchables were found to be equally educable despite—or because of—their many generations of segregated reproduction.

While we may tentatively conclude that there are some genetic IQ differences between social-class groups, we can make only wild speculations about racial groups. Average phenotypic IQ differences between races are not evidence for genetic differences (any more than they are evidence for environmental differences). Even if the heritabilities of IQ are extremely high in all races, there is still no warrant for equating within-group and between-group heritabilities (*12*). There are examples in agricultural experiments of within-group differences that are highly heritable but between-group differences that are entirely environmental. Draw two random samples of seeds from the same genetically heterogeneous population. Plant one sample in uniformly good conditions, the other in uniformly poor conditions. The average height difference between the populations of plants will be entirely environmental, although the individual differences in height within each sample will be entirely genetic. With known environments, genetic and environmental variances between groups can be studied. But racial groups are not random samples from the same population, nor are members reared in uniform conditions within each race. Racial groups are of unknown genetic equivalence for polygenic characteristics like IQ, and the differences in environments within and between the races may have as yet unquantified effects.

There is little to be gained from approaching the nature-nuture problem of race differences in IQ directly (*13*). Direct comparisons of estimated within-group heritabilities and the calculation of between-group heritabilities require assumptions that few investigators are willing to make, such as that all environmental differences are quantifiable, that differences in the environments of blacks and whites can be assumed to affect IQ in the same way in the two groups, and that differences in environments between groups can be "statistically controlled." A direct assault on race differences in IQ is vulnerable to many criticisms.

Indirect approaches may be less vulnerable. These include predictions of parent-child regression effects and admixture studies. Regression effects can be predicted to differ for blacks and whites if the two races indeed have genetically different population means. If the population mean for blacks is 15 IQ points lower than that of whites, then the offspring of high-IQ black parents should show greater regression (toward a lower population mean) than the offspring of whites of equally high IQ. Similarly, the offspring of low-IQ black parents should show less regression than those of white parents of equally low IQ. This hypothesis assumes that assortative mating for IQ is equal in the two races, which could be empirically determined but has not been studied as yet. Interpretable results from a parent-child regression study would also depend upon careful attention to intergenerational environmental changes, which could be greater in one race than the other.

Studies based on correlations between degree of white admixture and IQ scores *within* the black group would avoid many of the pitfalls of between-group comparisons. If serological genotypes can be used to identify persons with more and less white admixture, and if estimates of admixture based on blood groups are relatively independent of visible characteristics like skin color, then any positive correlation between degree of admixture and IQ would suggest genetic racial differences in IQ. Since blood groups have not been used directly as the basis of racial discrimination, positive findings would be relatively immune from environmentalist criticisms. The trick is to estimate individual admixture reliably. Several loci which have fairly different distributions of alleles in contemporary African and white populations have been proposed (*14*). No one has yet attempted a study of this sort.

h^2 and Phenotype

Suppose that the heritabilities of IQ differences within all racial and social-class groups were .80, as Jensen estimates, and suppose that the children in all groups were reared under an equal range of conditions. Now, suppose that racial and social-class differences in mean IQ still remained. We would probably infer some degree of genetic difference between the groups. So what? The question now turns from a strictly scientific one to one of science and social policy.

As Eysenck, Jensen, and others (*14*) have noted, eugenic and euthenic strategies are both possible interventions to reduce the number of low-IQ individuals in all populations. Eugenic policies could be advanced to encourage or require reproductive abstinence by people who fall below a certain level of intelligence. The Reeds (*15*) have determined that one-fifth of the mental retardation among whites of the next generation could be prevented if no mentally retarded persons of this generation reproduced. There is no question that a eugenic program applied at the phenotypic level of parents' IQ would substantially reduce the number of low-IQ children in the future white population. I am aware of no studies in the black population to support a similar program, but some proportion of future retardation could surely be eliminated. It would be extremely important, however, to sort out genetic and environmental sources of low IQ both in racial and in social-class groups before advancing a eugenic program. The request or demand that some persons refrain from any reproduction should be a last resort, based on sure knowledge that their retardation is caused primarily by genetic factors and is not easily remedied by environmental intervention. Studies of the IQ levels of adopted children with mentally retarded natural parents would be most instructive, since some of the retardation observed among children of retarded parents may stem from the rearing environments provided by the parents.

In a pioneering study of adopted children and their adoptive and natural parents, Skodak *(16)* reported greater *correlations* of children's IQ's with their natural than with their adoptive parents' IQ's. This statement has been often misunderstood to mean that the children's *levels* of intelligence more closely resembled their natural parents' which is completely false. Although the rank order of the children's IQ's resembled that of their mothers' IQ's, the children's IQ's were higher, being distributed, like those of the adoptive parents, around a mean above 100, whereas their natural mothers' IQ's averaged only 85. The children, in fact, averaged 21 IQ points higher than their natural mothers. If the (unstudied) natural fathers' IQ's averaged around the population mean of 100, the mean of the children's would be expected to be 94, or 12 points lower than the mean obtained. The unexpected boost in IQ was presumably due to the better social environments provided by the adoptive families. Does this mean that phenotypic IQ can be substantially changed?

Even under existing conditions of child rearing, phenotypes of children reared by low IQ parents could be markedly changed by giving them the same rearing environment as the top IQ group provide for their children. According to DeFries *(17)*, if children whose parents average 20 IQ points below the population mean were reared in environments such as usually are provided only by parents in the top .01 percent of the population, these same children would average 5 points *above* the population mean instead of 15 points below, as they do when reared by their own families.

Euthenic policies depend upon the demonstration that different rearing conditions can change phenotypic IQ sufficiently to enable most people in a social class or racial group to function in future society. I think there is great promise in this line of research and practice, although its efficacy will depend ultimately on the cost and feasibility of implementing radical intervention programs. Regardless of the present heritability of IQ in any population, phenotypes can be changed by the introduction of new and different environments. (One merit of Eysenck's book is the attention he gives to this point.) Furthermore, it is impossible to predict phenotypic outcomes under very different conditions. For example, in the Milwaukee Project *(18)*, in which the subjects are ghetto children whose mothers' IQ's are less than 70, intervention began soon after the children were born. Over a four-year period Heber has intensively tutored the children for several hours every day and has produced an enormous IQ difference between the experimental group (mean IQ 127) and a control group (mean IQ 90). If the tutored children continue to advance in environments which are radically different from their homes with retarded mothers, we shall have some measure of the present phenotypic range of reaction *(19)* of children whose average IQ's might have been in the 80 to 90 range. These data support Crow's comment on h^2 in his contribution to the *Harvard Educational Review* discussion (p. 158):

> It does not directly tell us how much improvement in IQ to expect from a given change in the environment. In particular, it offers no guidance as to the consequences of a new kind of environmental influence. For example, conventional heritability measures for height show a value of nearly 1. Yet, because of unidentified environmental influences, the mean height in the United States and in Japan has risen by a spectacular amount. Another kind of illustration is provided by the discovery of a cure for a hereditary disease. In such cases, any information on prior heritability may become irrelevant. Furthermore, heritability predictions are less dependable at the tails of the distribution.

To illustrate the phenotypic changes that can be produced by radically different environments for children with clear genetic anomalies, Rynders (*20*) has provided daily intensive tutoring for Down's syndrome infants. At the age of two, these children have average IQ's of 85 while control-group children, who are enrolled in a variety of other programs, average 68. Untreated children have even lower average IQ scores.

The efficacy of intervention programs for children whose expected IQ's are too low to permit full participation in society depends on their long-term effects on intelligence. Early childhood programs may be necessary but insufficient to produce functioning adults. There are critical research questions yet to be answered about euthenic programs, including what kinds, how much, how long, how soon, and toward what goals?

Does h^2 Matter?

There is growing disillusionment with the concept of heritability, as it is understood and misunderstood. Some who understand it very well would like to eliminate h^2 from human studies for at least two reasons. First, the usefulness of h^2 estimates in animal and plant genetics pertains to decisions about the efficacy of selective breeding to produce more desirable phenotypes. Selective breeding does not apply to the human case, at least so far. Second, if important phenotypic changes can be produced by radically different environments, then, it is asked, who cares about the heritability of IQ? Morton (*21*) has expressed these sentiments well:

> Considerable popular interest attaches to such questions as "is one class or ethnic group innately superior to another on a particular test?" The reasons are entirely emotional, since such a difference, if established, would serve as no better guide to provision of educational or other facilities than an unpretentious assessment of phenotypic differences.

I disagree. The simple assessment of phenotypic performance does not suggest any particular intervention strategy. Heritability estimates can have merit as indicators of the effects to be expected from various types of intervention programs. If, for example, IQ tests, which predict well to achievements in the larger society, show low heritabilities in a population, then it is probable that simply providing better environments than those which now exist will improve average performance in that population. If h^2 is high but environments sampled in that population are largely unfavorable, then (again) simple environmental improvement will probably change the mean phenotypic level. If h^2 is high and the environments sampled are largely favorable, then novel environmental manipulations are probably required to change phenotypes, and eugenic programs may be advocated.

The most common misunderstanding of the concept "heritability" relates to the myth of fixed intelligence: if h^2 is high, this reasoning goes, then intelligence is genetically fixed and unchangeable at the phenotypic level. This misconception ignores the fact that h^2 is a population statistic, bound to a given set of environmental conditions at a given point in time. Neither intelligence nor h^2 estimates are fixed.

It is absurd to deny that the frequencies of genes for behavior may vary between populations. For individual differences within populations, and for social-class differences, a genetic hypothesis is almost a necessity to explain some of the variance in IQ, especially among adults in contemporary white populations living in average or better environments. But what Jensen, Shuey, and Eysenck (and others) propose is that genetic racial differences are necessary to account for the current phenotypic differences in mean IQ between populations. That may be so, but it would be extremely difficult, given current methodological limitations, to gather evidence that would dislodge an environmental hypothesis to account for the same data. And to assert, despite the absence of evidence, and in the present social climate, that a particular race is genetically disfavored in intelligence is to scream "FIRE! . . . I think" in a crowded theater. Given that so little is known, further scientific study seems far more justifiable than public speculations.

References

1. For a review of studies, see L. Erlenmeyer-Kimling and L. F. Jarvik, *Science 142*, 1477 (1963). Heritability is the ratio of genetic variance to total phenotype variance. Heritability is used in its broad sense of total genetic variance/total phenotypic variance.
2. The *Harvard Educational Review* compilation includes Jensen's paper, "How much can we boost IQ and scholastic achievement?," comments on it by J. S. Kagan, J. McV. Hunt, J. F. Crow, C. Bereiter, D. Elkind, L. J. Cronbach and W. F. Brazziel, and a rejoiner by Jensen. See also A. R. Jensen, in J. Hellmuth, *Disadvantaged Child*, vol. 3 (Special Child Publ., Seattle, Wash., 1970).
3. P. L. NICHOLS, thesis, University of Minnesota (1970). Nichols reports that in two large samples of black and white children, seven-year WISC IQ scores showed the same means and distributions for the two racial groups, once social-class variables were equated. These results are unlike those of several other studies, which found that matching socio-economic status did not create equal means in the two racial groups [A. Shuey (5); A. B. Wilson, *Racial Isolation in the Public Schools*, vol. 2 (Government Printing Office, Washington, D.C., 1967)]. In Nichols's samples, prenatal and postnatal medical care was equally available to blacks and whites which may have contributed to the relatively high IQ scores of the blacks in these samples.
4. By interaction, Eysenck means simply $P=G+E$, or "heredity and environment acting together to produce the observed phenotype" (p. 111). He does not mean what most geneticists and behavior geneticists mean by interaction; that is, the *differential* phenotypic effects produced by various combinations of genotypes and environments, as in the interaction term of analysis-of-variance statistics. Few thinking people are not interactionists in Eysenck's sense of the term, because that's the only way to get the organism and the environment into the same equation to account for variance in any phenotypic trait. How much of the phenotypic variance is accounted for by each of the terms in the equation is the real issue.
5. A. SHUEY, *The Testing of Negro Intelligence* (Social Science Press, New York, 1966), pp. 499–519.
6. F. B. DAVIS, *The Measurement of Mental Capacity Through Evoked-Potential Recordings* (Educational Records Bureau, Greenwich, Conn., 1972). "As it turned out, no evidence was found that the latency periods obtained . . . displayed serviceable utility for predicting school performance or level of mental ability among pupils in preschool through grade 8" (p. v).
7. *New York Times*, 8 Oct. 1971, p. 41.
8. J. KAGAN, and H. A. MOSS, *Birth to Maturity* (Wiley, New York, 1962).
9. S. SCARR-SALAPATEK, *Science*, in press.
10. P. E. VERNON, *Intelligence and Cultural Environment* (Methuen, London, 1969).
11. T. DOBZHANSKY, *Mankind Evolving* (Yale Univ. Press, New Haven, 1962), pp. 234–238.
12. J. THODAY, *J. Biosocial Science 1*, suppl. 3, 4 (1969).
13. L. L. CAVALLI-SFORZA, and W. F. BODMER, *The Genetics of Human Populations* (Free-

man, San Francisco, 1971), pp. 753–804. They propose that the study of racial differences is useless and not scientifically supportable at the present time.

14. T. E. REED, *Science 165*, 762 (1969); *Am. J. Hum. Genet. 21*, 1 (1969); C. MacLean and P. L. Workman, paper at a meeting of the American Society of Human Genetics (1970, Indianapolis).

15. E. W. REED, and S. C. REED, *Mental Retardation: A Family Study* (Saunders, Philadelphia, 1965); *Social Biol. 18*, suppl., 42 (1971).

16. M. SKODAK, and H. WM. SKEELS, *J. Genet. Psychol. 75*, 85 (1949).

17. J. C. DE FRIES, paper for the C.O.B.R.E. Research Workshop on Genetic Endowment and Environment in the Determination of Behavior (3–8 Oct. 1971, Rye, N.Y.).

18. R. HEBER, *Rehabilitation of Families at Risk for Mental Retardation* (Regional Rehabilitation Center, Univ. of Wisconsin, 1969); S. P. Strickland, *Am. Ed. 7*, 3 (1971).

19. I. I. GOTTESMAN, in *Social Class, Race, and Psychological Development*, M. Deutsch, I. Katz, and A. R. Jensen, Eds. (Holt, Rinehart, and Winston, New York, 1968), pp. 11–51.

20. J. RYNDERS, personal communication, November 1971.

21. N. E. MORTON, paper for the C.O.B.R.E. Research Workshop on Genetic Endowment and Environment in the Determination of Behavior (3–8 Oct. 1971, Rye, N.Y.).

41. FIVE MYTHS ABOUT YOUR IQ

MARY JO BANE and CHRISTOPHER JENCKS

Standard IQ Tests purport to measure "intelligence," which is widely viewed as the key to adult success. As a result, children with low IQ scores* are the subjects of anxious solicitude from their parents, while groups that test badly, notably blacks, are constantly on the defensive. This is doubly true when, as usually happens, those who do poorly on IQ tests also do poorly on school achievement tests that measure things like reading comprehension and arithmetic skills.

Parents' and teachers' anxieties have been further intensified as a result of claims that IQ scores are largely determined by heredity. If an individual's genes determine his IQ, and if IQ then determines his chances of adult success, it is a short step to the conclusion that there is nothing he can do to improve his prospects. Moreover, if life chances are determined at birth, many recent efforts at social reform have obviously been doomed from the start.

The controversy over IQ and achievement tests has become so bitter that it is almost impossible to discuss the subject rationally. Neither social scientists nor lay-

* An intelligence quotient is computed by ascertaining a person's mental age on the basis of a standardized intelligence test, and multiplying the result by 100. That result is then divided by the person's chronological age, to yield the IQ. Thus, the average IQ of the population is (and arithmetically must be) 100. About one person in six has an IQ under 85, and about one in six has an IQ over 115. About one in forty is under 70, and about one in forty is over 130.

men seem to have much interest in the actual facts, which are extremely complex. The best currently available evidence suggests that:

1. IQ tests measure only one rather limited variety of intelligence, namely the kind that schools (and psychologists) value. Scores on the tests show remarkably little relationship to performance in most adult roles. People with high scores do a little better in most jobs than people with low scores, and they earn somewhat more money, but the differences are surprisingly small.
2. The poor are seldom poor because they have low IQ scores, low reading scores, low arithmetic scores, or bad genes. They are poor because they either cannot work, cannot find adequately paying jobs, or cannot keep such jobs. This has very little to do with their test scores.
3. Claims that "IQ scores are 80 percent hereditary" appear to be greatly exaggerated. Test results depend almost as much on variations in children's environments as on variations in their genes.
4. While differences in the environments that children grow up in explain much of the variation in their test scores, differences in their school experiences appear to play a relatively minor role. But even socioeconomic background has a quite modest impact on test scores. Many factors that influence the scores seem to be unrelated to either school quality or parental status. At present, nobody has a clear idea what these factors are, how they work, or what we can do about them.
5. If school quality has a modest effect on adult test scores, and if test scores then have a modest effect on economic success, school reforms aimed at teaching basic cognitive skills are likely to have minuscule effects on students' future earning power.

Each of these conclusions contradicts a commonly accepted myth about IQ.

Myth 1: IQ Tests Are the Best Measure of Human Intelligence

When asked whether IQ tests really measure "intelligence," psychologists are fond of saying that this is a meaningless question. They simply define intelligence as "whatever IQ tests measure." This is rather like Humpty-Dumpty, for whom words meant whatever he wanted them to mean, and it was just a question of who was to be master. The trouble is that psychologists are *not* the masters of language, and they cannot assign arbitrary meanings to words without causing all kinds of confusion. In the real world, people cannot use a term like intelligence without assuming that it means many different things at once—all very important. Those who claim that "intelligence is what intelligence tests measure" ought logically to assume, for example, that "intelligence is of no more consequence in human affairs than whatever intelligence tests measure." But people do not think this way. Having said that "intelligence is what IQ tests measure," psychologists always end up assuming that what IQ tests measure *must* be important, because "intelligence" is important. This road leads through the looking glass.

What, then, does the term "intelligence" really mean? For most people, it includes all the mental abilities required to solve whatever theoretical or practical problems they happen to think important. At one moment intelligence is the ability to unravel French syntax. At another it is the intuition required to understand what ails a neurotic friend. At still another it is the capacity to anticipate future demand for hog bristles. We know from experience that these skills are only loosely related to one another. People who are "intelligent" in one context often are remarkably "stupid" in another. Thus, in weighing the value of IQ tests, one must ask exactly what *kinds* of intelligence they really measure and what kinds they do not measure.

The evidence we have reviewed suggests that IQ tests are quite good at measuring the kinds of intelligence needed to do school work. Students who do well on IQ tests are quite likely to get good grades in school. They are also likely to stay in school longer than average. But the evidence also suggests that IQ tests are *not* very good at measuring the skills required to succeed in most kinds of adult work.

Myth 2: The Poor Are Poor Because They Have Low IQs. Those With High IQs End Up in Well-Paid Jobs

The fact is that people who do well on IQ and achievement tests do not perform much better than average in most jobs. Nor do they earn much more than the average. There have been more than a hundred studies of the relationship between IQ and people's performance on different jobs, using a wide variety of techniques for rating performance. In general, differences in IQ account for less than 10 percent of the variation in actual job performance. In many situations, there is no relationship at all between a man's IQ and how competent he is at his job. IQ also plays a modest role in determining income, explaining only about 12 percent of the variation. Thus, 88 precent of the variation in income is unrelated to IQ.

Nor do IQ differences account for much of the economic gap between blacks and whites. Phillips Cutright of the University of Indiana has conducted an extensive investigation of blacks who were examined by the Selective Service System in 1952. These men all took the Armed Forces Qualification Test, which measures much the same thing as an IQ test. In 1962, the average black in this sample earned 43 percent less than the average white. Blacks with AFQT scores as high as the average white's earned 32 percent less than the average white. Equalizing black and white test scores therefore reduced the income gap by about a quarter. Three quarters of the gap had nothing to do with test scores. This same pattern holds for whites born into working-class and middle-class families. Whites with middle-class parents earn more than whites with working-class parents, but only 25–35 percent of the gap is traceable to test-score differences between the two groups.

None of this means that a child with a high IQ has no economic advantage over a child with a low IQ, nor that a child with high reading and math scores has no economic advantage over a child with low scores. It just means that the economic effect is likely to be much smaller than anxious parents or educational reformers expect. Among white males, those who score in the top fifth on standardized tests appear to earn about a third more than the national average. Those who score in the bottom fifth earn about two-thirds of the national average. These differences are by no means trivial. But they do not look very impressive when we recall that the best paid fifth of all workers earns six or seven times as much as the worst paid fifth. Most of that gap has nothing to do with test scores, and cannot be eliminated by equalizing test scores.

How can this be? We know that test scores play a significant role in determining school grades, in determining how long students stay in school, and in determining what kinds of credentials they eventually earn. We also know that credentials play a significant role in determining what occupations men enter. Occupations, in turn, have a significant effect on earnings. But at each stage in this process there are many exceptions, and the cumulative result is that exceptions are almost commonplace. A significant number of students with relatively low test scores earn college degrees, for example. In addition, a significant number of individuals without college degrees enter well-paid occupations, especially in business. Finally, people in relatively low-status occupations (such as plumbers and electricians) often earn more than professionals (think of teachers and clergymen). Overall, then, there are a lot of people with rather low test scores who nonetheless make above-average incomes, and a lot of people with high IQs but below-average incomes.

The limited importance of test scores is also clear if we look at the really poor—those who have to get by on less than half the national average. Nearly half of all poor families have no earner at all, either because they are too old, because they are headed by a woman with young children, or because the father is sick, alcoholic, mentally ill, or otherwise incapacitated. These problems are a bit more common among people with low IQs, but that is not the primary explanation for any of them.

This does not mean that financial success depends primarily on socioeconomic background, as many liberals and radicals seem to believe. Socioeconomic background has about the same influence as IQ on how much schooling a person gets, on the kind of occupation he enters, and on how much money he makes. Thus we can say that *neither* socioeconomic background *nor* IQ explains much of the variation in adult occupational status or income. Most of the economic inequality among adults is due to other factors.

Unfortunately, we do not know enough to identify with much precision the other factors leading to economic success. All we can do is suggest their complexity. First, there is a wide variety of skills that have little or no connection with IQ but have a strong relationship to success in some specialized field. The ability to hit a ball thrown at high speed is extremely valuable, if you happen to be a professional baseball player. The ability to walk along a narrow steel beam 600 feet above the ground without losing your nerve is also very valuable, if you happen to be a construction worker. In addition, many personality traits have substantial cash value in certain contexts. A man who is good at figuring out what his boss wants, or good at getting his subordinates to understand and do what he wants, is at a great premium in almost any large hierarchical organization. While these talents are doubtless related to IQ, the connection is obviously very loose. Similarly, a person who inspires confidence is likely to do well regardless of whether he is a doctor, a clergyman, a small businessman, or a Mafioso, and inspiring confidence depends as much on manner as on mental abilities.

Finally, there is the matter of luck. America is full of gamblers, some of whom strike it rich while others lose hard-earned assets. One man's farm has oil on it, while another man's cattle get hoof-and-mouth disease. One man backs a "mad inventor" and ends up owning a big piece of Polaroid, while another backs a mad inventor and ends up owning a piece of worthless paper. We cannot say much about the relative importance of these factors, but when it comes to making a dollar, IQ is clearly a small part of a big, complicated picture.

Myth 3: Your IQ Is Overwhelmingly Determined by Your Genetic Endowment

Over the past decade, an enormous number of school reform programs have attempted to raise the scores of those who do poorly on standardized tests. These programs have involved preschool education, curriculum development, teacher training, compensatory education, administrative reorganization, and many other innovations. None appears to have produced the promised results on a permanent basis. This has led many people to the conclusion that variations in IQ scores must reflect innate genetic differences between individuals and groups. This is a logical non sequitur. But more important, the theory that IQ scores are determined at the moment of conception is not supported by the evidence. Genes clearly have a significant influence on IQ and school achievement scores, but so does environment. The reason reform programs have failed to improve test scores is not that the environment is irrelevant but that the reforms have not altered the most important features of the environment.

Much of the continuing furor over IQ scores derives from Arthur Jensen's controversial claim that genes "explain" something like 80 percent of the variation in children's performance on IQ tests. We have reviewed the same evidence as Jensen, and while it certainly shows that genes have *some* effect on IQ, we believe that his 80 percent estimate is much too high. The details of the argument are extremely complicated, but the basic reasons that Jensen overestimated the role of heredity and underestimated the role of environment are fairly easy to understand.

First, Jensen estimated the influence of genes on IQ scores largely by using data from studies of twins. Some of these studies dealt with identical twins who had been separated early in life and brought up by different parents. Identical twins have exactly the same genes. When they are brought up in different environments, all differences between them can be attributed to the effects of their environments.

Other studies compared identical twins who had been reared together with fraternal twins who had been reared together. Fraternal twins have only about half their genes in common; identical twins have all their genes in common. Thus if identical twins were no more alike on IQ tests than fraternal twins, we would have to conclude that genetic resemblance did not affect the children's test scores. But identical twins are in fact considerably more alike than fraternal twins, so it seems reasonable to suppose that genes have a significant effect on test scores. (Identical twins may also be treated somewhat more alike than fraternal twins, but the effect of this appears to be small.)

It is perfectly legitimate to use twin studies to estimate the relative influence of heredity and environment on test scores. But we can also estimate the effects of environment by measuring the degree of resemblance between adopted children reared in the same home. When we do this, environment appears to have somewhat more effect than it does in twin studies, while genes appear to have somewhat less effect. No one has ever offered a good explanation for this discrepancy, but that does not justify ignoring it. The most reasonable assumption is that the true effect of heredity is somewhat less than that suggested by twin studies but somewhat more than that suggested by studies of unrelated children in the same home.

A second difficulty with Jensen's estimate is that it is based on twin studies in England as well as in the United States. When we separate the American and English studies, we find that genetic factors appear to be more important in England than in America. This suggests that children's environments are more varied in the United States than they are in England. Other evidence, as well as commonsense observation of the two cultures, supports this interpretation. Consequently, when Jensen pools English and American data to arrive at his estimate of the effects of genes on IQ scores, he overestimates the relative importance of genes in America and underestimates their importance in England.

A third problem: Jensen assumes that the effects of genes and those of environment are completely independent of one another. In fact, since parents with favorable genes tend to have above-average cognitive skills, they tend to provide their children with usually rich home environments. Our calculations suggest that this double advantage accounts for about a fifth of the variation in IQ scores.

After correcting all these biases, our

best estimate is that genes explain 45 rather than 80 percent of the variation in IQ scores in contemporary America. This 45 percent estimate could easily be off by 10 percent either way, and it might conceivably be off by as much as 20 percent either way. The estimate would change if the range of environments were to increase or decrease for any reason. Genes are relatively more important in small homogeneous communities, where children's environments are relatively similar, than in America as a whole. By the same token, genes are relatively less important among groups whose environments are unusually diverse. If, for example, there were a sharp increase in the number of children suffering from acute malnutrition, or if large numbers of children were excluded from schools, environmental inequality would increase, and the relative importance of genes in determining IQ scores would decrease.

While genes probably account for something like 45 percent of the variation in IQ scores, it does not follow that genetic differences in actual learning capacity account for anything like this much variation. Genes influence test scores in two quite different ways. First, they influence what an individual learns from a given environment. Placed in front of the same TV program, one child may remember more of what he sees than another. Confronted with subtraction, one child may "catch on" faster than another. These differences derive partly from genetically based differences in learning capacity. In addition, however, genes can influence the environments to which people are exposed. Imagine a nation that refuses to send children with red hair to school. Under these circumstances having genes that cause red hair will lower your reading scores. This does not tell us that children with red hair cannot learn to read. It tells us only that in this particular situation there is a socially imposed relationship between genes and opportunities to learn. In America, the genes that affect skin color have an indirect influence on an individual's opportunities and incentives to learn many skills. So too hereditary appearance and athletic ability influence a youngster's chance of getting into many colleges, and thus affect his or her later test scores.

Beyond all that, a person's genes may influence his actual learning capacity, which may then affect his opportunities and incentives to learn. If an individual has low test scores for genetic reasons, he may be assigned to a "slow" class where he learns less. Or he may be excluded from college. Such practices tend to widen the initial test score gap between the genetically advantaged and the genetically disadvantaged. The resulting inequality is thus due *both* to genes *and* to environment. Yet conventional methods of estimating heritability impute the entire difference to genes.

When we say that genes "explain" 45 percent of the variation in test scores, we are talking about their overall effect, including their effect both on the capacity to learn and on opportunities and incentives to learn. No one has yet devised a method for separating these two effects. But if opportunities and incentives to learn were absolutely equal, genetically determined differences in learning capacity would account for considerably less than 45 percent of the variation in IQ scores.

Myth 4: The Main Reason Black Children and Poor White Children Have Low IQ Scores Is That They Have "Bad" Genes

Children from poor families tend to get lower scores on both IQ and school achievement tests than children from middle-class families. This difference is apparent when children enter school, and it does not seem to change much as children get older. Many liberals argue that the reason poor children do badly on these tests is that the tests are biased. Most of the tests contain items that are culturally loaded, in the sense that they presume familiarity with certain objects or assume the correctness of certain attitudes. The bias in these items always appears to favor children from middle-class backgrounds. Yet when psychologists have examined children's answers to these "loaded" items, they have not found that poor children did particularly badly on them. Nor have they found that eliminating such items from tests reduced the disparity in overall performance between poor and middle-class children. Middle-class children outscore poor children by as much on "culture free" tests as on "culturally loaded" tests. This suggests that what poor children lack is not specific information but more basic skills that are relevant to many different kinds of tests.

These findings seem to support the theory that test-score differences between rich and poor derive from genetic differences between rich and poor children. Like the "cultural bias" explanation, this "genetic" explanation has considerable logical appeal. Everyone who has studied the matter agrees that genes have *some* influence on test scores, that test scores have *some* influence on education attainment, and that education has *some* influence on adult success. It follows that there must be *some* genetic difference, however small, between economically successful and unsuccessful adults. If this is true, there must also be some genetic difference between children with successful and unsuccessful parents.

The evidence suggests, however, that genetic differences between successful and unsuccessful families play a very minor role in determining children's IQs. Studies of adopted children indicate that genes may account for as much as half the observed correlation between parental status and children's test scores. Indirect evidence, derived from the relationship between test scores and parental success, suggests that the relationship is even weaker. Overall, our best guess is that genetic differences between social classes explain no more than 6 percent of the variation in IQ scores, while cultural differences between social classes explain another 6–9 percent.

This conclusion means that the average middle-class child may have a small genetic advantage over the average working-class child. But it also means that there are more working-class children than middle-class children with high genetic potential. This is because there are more working-class children to begin with. While their average score is a little lower than that of middle-class children, the difference is very small, and nearly half of all working-class children are above the middle-class average.

Furthermore, while differences between rich and poor whites are probably partly genetic, this tells us nothing about the origins of differences between whites and blacks. Blacks have lower IQ and achievement scores than whites, even when their parents have similar economic positions. But blacks also grow up in very different social and cultural environments from whites, even when their parents have the same occupations and incomes. We have no way of measuring the effects of these cultural differences. Our personal feeling is that black-white cultural differences could easily explain the observed IQ difference, which is only about 15 points. Differences of this magnitude are often found between white subcultures. Both black and white scores on military tests rose about 10 points between World I and World War II, for example. Whites in eastern Tennessee improved by almost this much between 1930 and 1940, apparently as a result of the introduction of schools, roads, radios, etc.

The key point is that *it doesn't much matter whether IQ differences between blacks and whites are hereditary or envimental.* IQ accounts for only a quarter of the income gap between blacks and whites. Therefore, even if genes accounted for *all* the IQ gap between blacks and whites, which is hardly likely, they would account for only a quarter of the economic gap. In all probability their role is far smaller. The widespread obsession with possible genetic differences between races is thus a diversion from the real problem. We ought to worry about eliminating the discrimination that still accounts for most of the observed economic difference between blacks and whites. If this could be done, the average black would be earning almost as much as the average white, and the pointless debate about possible genetic differences would no longer seem important to most sensible people.

Myth 5: Improving the Quality of the Schools Will Go a Long Way Toward Wiping Out Differences in IQ and School Achievement and Therefore in Children's Life Chances

Whether we like it or not, the quality of a child's school has even less effect than his social class on his test scores. The best evidence on this still comes from the 1965 Equality of Educational Opportunity Survey, whose first and most famous product was the Coleman Report. This survey did not give individual IQ tests to children, but it did give "verbal ability" tests that are very similar. It also gave reading and math tests. The results of this survey have aroused all sorts of controversy, but they have been confirmed by several other large surveys, notably the national study of high schools conducted by Project Talent throughout the 1960s. These surveys show that the differences among students in the same school are far greater than the difference between the average student in one school and the average student in another.

The surveys also show that test score difference between the alumni of different schools are largely due to differences among the entering students. Those from high-status families who enter school with high test scores tend to end up with high scores no matter what school they attend. Conversely, students from low-status families with low initial scores tend to end up with low scores even in what most people define as "good" schools. It follows that even if all schools had exactly the same effects on students' scores, the variation in students' IQ and achievement scores would decline very little. Qualitative differences among elementary schools seem to account for less than 6 percent of the variation in IQ test scores. Qualitative differences among high schools account for less than 2 percent.

In theory, of course, we could give students with low initial scores *better* schooling than students with high initial scores. This would allow us to reduce initial differences by more than 6 percent. The difficulty is that nobody knows how to do this. There is no consistent relationship between the amount of money we spend on a school and the rate at which children's test scores improve after they enter. Indeed, while school expenditures nearly doubled during the 1960s, a recent Project Talent survey shows that eleventh graders' school achievement scores hardly changed at all during that decade. Nor is there a consistent relationship between any specific school resource and the rate at which students' test scores rise. Neither small classes, well-paid teachers, experienced teachers, teachers with advanced degrees, new textbooks, nor adequate facilities have a consistent effect on students' scores.

Compensatory educational programs aimed at boosting the test scores of disadvantaged students have also produced discouraging results. Some studies report big gains, but others show that students who were not in the program gained more than those who were. Taken as a group, these studies suggest that students' scores do not improve any faster in compensatory programs than elsewhere. Thus, while there are good theoretical reasons for assuming that we can improve the test scores of those who enter school at a disadvantage, there is also strong evidence that educators simply do not know how to do this at the present time. (Neither, we should add, do educational critics, including ourselves.)

Racial and economic segregation may have slightly more effect than school expenditures on IQ test scores. The evidence, however, is by no means conclusive. Blacks who attend what we might call "naturally" desegregated schools, that is, schools in racially mixed neighborhoods, generally have higher test scores than blacks who attend segregated schools. These differences are apparent when students enter first grade, but they increase over time. This suggests that attending a racially mixed school boosts test scores somewhat faster than attending an all-black school. But the cumulative difference over six years of elemetnary school is small enough so that the effect in any one year is likely to be almost undetectable.

When we turn from "naturally" desegregated schools to schools that have been desegregated by busing, the evidence is more ambiguous. Some busing studies report that blacks showed appreciable gains. Very few report losses. Most show no statistically reliable difference. Since most of the studies involve small samples and short periods of time, this is not surprising. Taken together, the studies suggest that *on the average* busing probably increases black students' test scores, but that there are plenty of exceptions. Our best guess, based on evidence from both studies of busing and studies of naturally desegregated schools, is that desegregated schools would eventually reduce the test score gap between blacks and whites by about 20 percent. This is, however, only an educated guess. The evidence on this question remains inconclusive, despite some recent extravagant claims to the contrary.

Nor is there any obvious reason to suppose that either decentralization or community control will improve students' test scores. Among whites, relatively small districts score at about the same level as large ones, once other factors are taken into account. Neither decentralization nor community control has been tried on a large enough scale in black communities to prove very much. But predominantly black suburban school districts, like Ravenswood and Compton in California, do not appear to have produced particularly impressive results. Neither have they done particularly badly.

None of this means that we should spend less on schools, stop trying to desegregate them, or reject decentralization or community control. Quite the contrary. If additional expenditures make schools better places for children, then they are justified regardless of their effects on reading comprehension, or IQ scores. If school desegregation reduces racial antagonism over the long run, then we should desegregate even though the students' test scores remain unaffected. And if community control gives parents the feeling that the schools belong to "us" rather than "them," this too is worthwhile for its own sake. Given the slim connection between test scores and adult successes, it would be myopic to judge any sort of school reform primarily in terms of its effect on either IQ or school achievement.

Because a student's mastery of the skills taught in school provides a very poor measure of how well he will do once he graduates, reforms aimed at teaching these skills more effectively are not likely to take us very far toward economic prosperity or equality among adults. We have noted that only 12 percent of the variation in men's earnings is explained by their test scores. We have also seen that reducing inequality in test scores is very difficult. Under these circumstances it makes little sense for economic egalitarians to concentrate on equalizing IQ and achievement scores. Instead, they should concentrate on eliminating the other sources of income inequality, which cause 88 percent of the problem.

To be sure, this is more easily said than done. Those who do well in the present economic system inevitably resist reforms that would reduce their privileges. Those who do poorly in the present system are for the most part too demoralized to protest in any effective way. So long as this persists, there will be little chance of reducing economic inequality.

The complacency of the rich and the demoralization of the poor are reinforced by theories that attribute economic success to genetic superiority and economic failure to genetic deficiency. These theories are nonsense. In 1968, the income difference between the best and worst paid fifth of all workers was about $14,000. Of this, perhaps $500 or $1000 was attributable to genetically determined differences in IQ scores. The idea that genetic inequality explains economic inequality is thus a myth. Like the divine right of kings, such myths help legitimize the status quo. But they should not be taken seriously by those who really want to understand the modern world, much less those who want to change it.

42. THE MAINTENANCE OF VERBAL EXCHANGES BETWEEN YOUNG CHILDREN

EDWARD MUELLER

Although spontaneous verbal interaction among preschool children is reputed to be limited as the result of their egocentrism, a direct examination revealed that 4-year-olds almost always displayed social interest and usually received replies to the things they said in free play. The maintenance of verbal interaction was found to be multidetermined; however, when many causative factors operated in 1 direction, the outcome was perfectly predictable. The two most powerful predictors of whether a given message would receive a reply were its technical quality and the visual attention of the listener at its beginning.

There are two conceptual problems underlying this research: one is the degree of egocentrism in children's verbal interaction; the other involves a delineation of the situational factors which facilitate or impede reciprocal communication.

The concept of egocentrism implies that young children do not really talk with one another in spontaneous play settings (Piaget 1926). Part of the time, this is because they are talking to no one other than themselves. For example, they audibly give directions as to how to assemble a toy—directions that they will later perform mentally. At other times, the child may intend to communicate with another child, but the message is so poorly adapted to the listener's perspective that it cannot be understood. For example, a child might say "I bet Charlie could beat you up," but he fails to take into account that the listener does not know Charlie.

This view of the young children's speech suggests that verbal interaction will be frequently disjointed or unsuccessful. Yet, previous tests of these ideas have followed Piaget in focusing on the children's speech itself (e.g., Kohlberg, Yaeger, & Hjertholm 1968) rather than on the interpersonal consequences of that speech. In addition, most of the evidence supporting the idea that children's utterances are hard to understand comes from experiments where the communication task is very narrowly defined and often quite difficult (Flavell 1968; Krauss & Glucksberg 1969).

While considerable progress has recently been made in explaining the acquisition of language in the child, little is known about the acquisition of skills for successful communication (Cazden 1970). There has been no previous work on the factors that facilitate or impede children's communication. Therefore, it seemed advisable to examine additional antecedents, not deriving from the egocentric-speech literature, as possible sources of verbal interaction success and failure. Thus, in addition to studying intent in speaking and utterance adaptation to the listener, we will examine factors such as the listener's visual attention at the start of the utterance, the physical distance between the children, and the use of attention-getting techniques.

Methods

Subjects

Twenty-four pairs of children participated. They were from upper-middle-class families and their ages ranged from 3½ to 5½. They were divided into three 8-month age groups and paired in such a way that both members came from a single group. There were four pairs of boys and four pairs of girls for each age group. On the average, pairs had birthdays 1.9 months apart.

Procedures

Same-sexed pairs of children were introduced to each other just outside a playroom where they had been brought by their mothers. The room was equipped with a variety of toys and games appropriate for preschool children. They were told that they could do whatever they liked and if they wanted anything just to knock on the door "and we would come." Most of the pairs remained in the playroom for a full hour; no pairs in the playroom less than 20 minutes.

All sessions were recorded on video tape; split-screen recording and the use of two cameras concealed behind one-way mirrors permitted both children's faces to be visible at all times. All analyses derived from the video-tape record.

Method of Data Analysis

In order to determine rates of interaction success and failure, one coder categorized all utterances occurring during four 5-minute periods distributed evenly across the entire play period. This coder was blind with respect to the purposes of the study.

Operationally, success and failure were the extreme values of the code describing the "social effect" of individual utterances on the listener's behavior. A given utterance was coded as a success only when the listener clearly responded to it. This response could consist of nonverbal behavior such as shaking one's head "yes" or "no" or carrying out some action requested by the speaker (e.g., "Bring me the doll"). The response could also consist of a verbal reply such as "What did you say?" This example was chosen to illustrate that success in verbal interaction as defined here did not imply a highly efficient exchange of information. Nevertheless, success did imply that the listener's behavior was uniquely contingent on the speaker utterance; instances where the listener merely spoke immediately after the speaker but said something totally unrelated were not rated successes.

Verbal interaction was said to "fail" when the listener did not reply and did not display any other behavior which may have been in response to the utterance. Instances where the listener visually attended to the speaker as a result of the utterance but did not otherwise reply constituted the intermediate category of possible social effects. The reliability of categorizing the three-value social effect code, utilizing Scott and Wertheimer's (1962) index of intercoder agreement, was .87.

Other coders, unaware of the results of the previous classification, coded 10 potential causes of interaction success or failure. These antecedents, the independent variables of the study, were selected to index both properties of utterances and of the speaker's and listener's engagement at the time of an utterance. The mean intercoder agreement for these categories was .82. Some categories were predicted to make success more likely (S) while others were thought to make failure more likely (F). It is in terms of these predictions that the categories are described:

1. *Clarity*
   (S) Words are clear.
   (F) All or some of the words are unclear.
2. *Fragments*
   (S) Grammatical form of the utterance is clear and complete.
   (F) Grammatical form is unclear or incomplete (e.g., "He's got all the . . .").
3. *Social adaptation*
   (S) Utterance is adapted to the perspective of the listener.
   (F) Utterance is not adapted (e.g., "There are just those things like there ought to be," where listener can't tell from context what "things" refers to).
4. *Attention-getting devices (AGDs)*
   (S) AGDs are present (e.g., "Hey," touching, use of proper name).
   (F) AGDs are absent.
5. *Content*
   (S) Content is about listener's activity or things directly relevant to listener.
   (F) Content is about speaker's activity, wishes, etc.
6. *Form*
   (S) Utterance is a command or question.
   (F) Utterance is of declarative form.
7. *Context*
   (S) Utterance is a direct reply.
   (F) Utterance is not a reply.
8. *Speaker attention*
   (S) Speaker glances at or sustains attention to the listener.
   (F) Speaker never visually attends to listener.
9. *Listener attention*
   (S) Listener is watching speaker as utterance begins.
   (F) Listener is not watching speaker.
10. *Distance*
    (S) Children are within 4 feet.
    (F) Children are more than 4 feet apart.

In analyzing the importance of each of these antecedents, it was desirable to represent each pair of children equally. Therefore, in advance, 20 successes and 20 failures were selected from each pair of children. The procedure involved finding a success that had occurred about 30 seconds prior to a selected failure. It insured that both members of each utterance pair came from the same time period but were still enough apart so as to not be uniquely related to one another.

An example will help explain how this utterance sample was used: It was predicted (distance) that, when the children were within 4 feet of each other, the probability of success was enhanced. Several outcomes were possible. If being close together had no effect whatever on listener responsiveness, then, in this sample of equal numbers of both outcomes, the probability of success would not differ substantially from .50. If the probability of success was substantially below .50, then it was concluded that the prediction was incorrect and being close together was more likely to result in failure than in success. Finally, as the observed probability approached 1.00 it was clear that being close to one another was a powerful predictor of verbal interaction success.

Results

For the group as a whole, utterances occurred at the average rate of one utterance every 9 seconds. Thus, there was abundant verbal behavior available for analysis despite the fact that the children were not acquainted initially. An analysis of variance of amount of talking showed that late-3-year-old children talked significantly less than either of the older groups ($p < .05$). In addition, boys talked significantly more than girls ($p < .05$). However, there was no significant main effect for amount of talking across a session; that is, pairs of children spoke at about the same rate at the beginning, middle, and end of the play session. Finally, none of the interactions in this analysis were statistically significant.

An additional analysis of variance indicated no age or sex differences in the proportion of successes or failures. (The use of proportions in this analysis controlled for differences in total talking just reported.) Therefore, the results can be summarized for the entire group of children as follows: 62% of all utterances were successes in that they produced a definite response from the listener, while 15% were failures. The remaining 23% of all utterances fell into the intermediate category of possible social effects, namely, the listener visually attended to the speaker but did not otherwise reply.

It is important to keep in mind two aspects of the 10 antecedents listed above. One is their frequency of occurrence, while the other is their power as predictors of success or failure. Since these two aspects may be independent, they will be considered separately. Analyses of variance tested for age- and sex-group differences in the frequencies of occurrence of the antecedent events. The overall result was similar to that obtained for success and failure rates: the occurrence of the antecedents did not vary significantly across age and sex. Because of this invariance, the frequency data can be presented for all the children as a group.

Considering some of the more theoretically interesting frequencies that will be discussed later, it was found that a surprisingly small number of utterances (12%) were unclear or fragmentary. Furthermore, only 0.4% of all utterances were found to be poorly adapted to the listener's perspective. (Social adaptation was excluded from further analysis since lack of adaptation was so rare.)

Additionally, if the speaker's visual attention is considered as the sole measure of his intent to communicate with the listener, it would appear that he was not too socially oriented, since the speaker only looked at the listener during 45% of the things he said. However, in addition to this measure, if talking about things of interest to the listener or using attention-getting techniques are considered sufficient to indicate "social intent," fully 94% of all utterances showed such intent; that is, 94% of all utterances evidenced one or more of these three indicators.

The power of nine antecedents as predictors of success and failure is shown in figure 7.3. The summation measure was devised by assigning a value of +1 to the success-predicting value of each code and −1 to the failure-predicting value. A score of +9 indicated utterances where success was simultaneously predicted by all nine codes, while −9 indicate utterances where failure was predicted by all nine codes. It is clear that, when many codes predicted success or failure at once, the likelihood of its being observed approached and reached 1.00. However, the interpretation of this result is contingent on the extent of interdependence of these codes. Using informational analysis (Garner 1962), it was found that, with the exception of a relation between form and content, the antecedent factors were fully independent of one another. Therefore, the individual antecedents were seen to have an additive influence on the social effectiveness of an utterance.

Turning to the individual measures, it was found that all nine codes predicted in

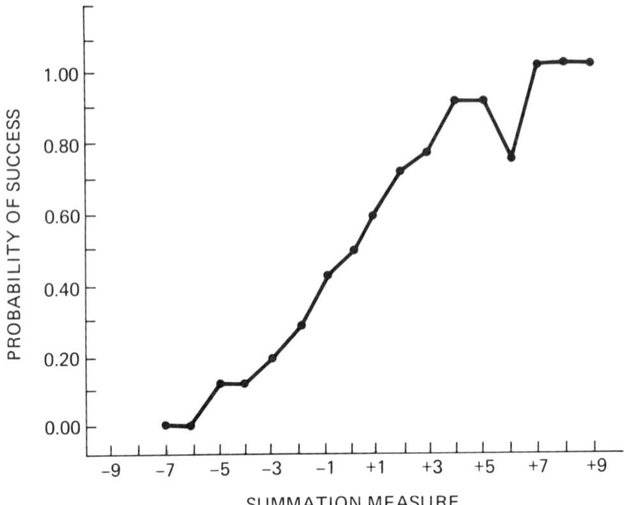

Figure 7.3. The probability of success after summating the predictions of nine codes.

the expected directions; however, their power varied considerably (see Table 7.3). The two most powerful predictors of success were listener attention (.89) and context (.78). Both these measures had reference to the *listener's* behavior rather than to anything the *speaker* did or said. Specifically, when the listener watched the speaker as the utterances began or when the utterance was itself a reply to something that the listener had just said, success was highly probable. Conditional probability analysis showed the following: having the listener's attention at the start of the utterance was so powerful that, even if the speaker talked about his own activity, an antecedent category predictive of failure, he received replies to three out of every four attempts. By contrast, the overall rate of getting replies when talking about one's own activity was but once in three attempts.

The two most powerful predictors of failure both indexed difficulties in producing utterances of good technical quality. The probability of failure was .83, given unclear utterances, and .79, given fragmentary or grammatically unclear utterances.

Beyond measures of technical quality, the next most powerful predictor of failure was the measure of social intent described above. Under this measure, when the speaker did not look at the listener, used no attentional techniques, and spoke about his own activity, the probability of failure was .72.

In the previous analyses, the power of the predictive categories was assessed independently of their frequency of occurrence. For example, it was reported that unclear utterances predicted failure with considerable accuracy; yet 95% of all utterances were clear (see Table 7.3). When they *were* clear, predicting success or failure was little better than random guesswork. Thus, one may ask which single code or pair of codes had the greatest utility, given both its predictive power and its frequency of occurrence.

Informational analysis was used to answer this question, and the results are given in detail elsewhere (Mueller 1971). Here, it suffices to say that form and listener attention had the greatest overall utility. Context and speaker attention were also relatively high. By contrast, clarity and fragments were of less relative value due to the infrequency of occurrence of their powerful category. This analysis also showed that prediction of social effect was not attributable to one or two antecedents

Table 7.3. Observed probability of occurrence of each category and observed probability of success or failure when predicted by each category

Category Name[a]	Observed probability of occurrence of specified category[b]	Observed probability of predicted outcome, given occurrence of specified category
Categories predicting success:		
Listener attention: watching speaker	.19	.89
Context: direct reply	.17	.78
Form: command or question	.43	.68
Speaker attention: looks at listener	.42	.66
Content: about listener's activity	.46	.65
Attention-getting techniques: present	.27	.61
Distance: within 4 feet	.72	.53
Clarity: words are clear	.95	.53
Fragments: grammar is clear and complete	.94	.52
Categories predicting failure:		
Clarity: words unclear	.05	.83
Fragments: grammar unclear or incomplete	.07	.79
Content: about speaker's activity	.21	.64
Speaker attention: never looks at listener	.55	.61
Form: declarative	.49	.60
Listener attention: not watching speaker	.71	.57
Distance: more than 4 feet apart	.28	.57
Context: not a reply	.83	.56
Attention-getting techniques: absent	.73	.53

[a] The social adaptation code is excluded since lack of adaptation was so rare (.004).
[b] In other words, frequency of occurrence of utterances with the event described by a given category divided by all utterances in the sample. Success- and failure-predicting categories need not total 1.00, since there was sometimes a third category for utterances on which the judgment in question could not be made or for which no prediction could be made (see Mueller 1971).

alone. Instead, social effect was responsive to the additive and largely independent influence of all the antecedents. When they acted in harmony, the outcome was highly predictable (Figure 7.3).

Discussion

The results did not support previous work suggesting large amounts of communication failure in the spontaneous talk of 4-year-old children. Most of the children's language was clear, grammatically well formed and well adapted to the listener's perspective. In addition, much of what was said related to the activity of the potential listener. In almost all instances, speakers revealed that they were interested in the listener's reaction to what they said. In addition, 85% of all utterances received replies or at least attracted the listener's attention. However, the discrepancy between these results and past research findings should not be overstated. This study examined natural interaction in an unstructured setting, while previous work focused on structured setting with precisely specified communication tasks (Krauss & Glucksberg 1969). Also, this study examined different aspects of communication than had been focused upon previously. Whereas previous work stressed the accurate transmission of information, this research stressed the maintenance of verbal interchanges and the role of attentional variables and social intent in this process.

When this study was designed, it was expected that the age period $3\frac{1}{2}$–$5\frac{1}{2}$ would involve dramatic improvements in communication success. This expectation was not confirmed: even the youngest children were successful in receiving replies to their messages. Thus, it appears that the processes found to be important in the maintenance of verbal exchanges emerged at still younger ages. These processes were the production of technically good utterances, the display of social intent when speaking, and the maintenance of mutual engagement between children. Utilizing some of the techniques for assessing dyadic interaction developed for this research, future investigations might examine the emergence of these processes in a younger age sample.

References

CAZDEN, C. B. The neglected situation in child language research and education. In F. Williams (Ed.), *Language and poverty.* Chicago: Markham, 1970.

FLAVELL, J. H. (in collaboration with Botkin, P. T.; Fry, C. L.; Wright, H. W. & Jarvis, P. E.). *The development of role-taking and communication skills in children.* New York: Wiley, 1968.

GARNER, W. R. *Uncertainty and structure as psychological concepts.* New York: Wiley, 1962.

KOHLBERG, L.; YAEGER, J.; & HJERTHOLM, E. Private speech: four studies and a review of theories. *Child Development,* 1968, *39,* 691–736.

KRAUSS, R. M., & GLUCKSBERG, S. The development of communication: competence as a function of age. *Child Development,* 1969, *40,* 255–266.

MUELLER, E. C. An analysis of children's communication in free play. Unpublished doctoral dissertation, Cornell University, 1971.

PIAGET, J. *The language and thought of the child.* London: Routledge & Kegan Paul, 1926.

SCOTT, W. A., & WERTHEIMER, M. *Introduction to psychological research.* New York: Wiley, 1962.

43. THE EFFECT OF NAMING AND OBJECT PERMANENCE ON TOY PREFERENCES

GAIL C. ROBERTS and
KATHRYN NORCROSS BLACK

Forty children, 18–22 months, were presented with 16 toys, one at a time, with half of the toys named for the child and half not named. Timed preference choices between named and unnamed pairs were then obtained. Stage of object permanence was also assessed. It was found that if children have achieved the stage of object permanence where they can follow an object through a sequence of invisible displacements they manipulate named toys more than unnamed toys. These results are interpreted as being consistent with formulations by both Luria and Piaget.

The purpose of the present study was to determine whether a name for a toy affects an infant's attentional preference for a toy and whether this process is related to the infant's concept of object permanence.

Theoretical statements by Luria (1961), Luria and Yudovich (1959), Piaget (1947, 1951), and Piaget and Inhelder (1969) concerning the relationship between the name of an object and the perception of the object to which the name refers are relevant.

Luria (1961) states that having a name for an object affects the object's perceptual properties. According to Luria, speech associations influence the perceptual processes to the extent that there is a readjustment of the relevant strength of stimuli. Luria writes: "By naming various surrounding objects and giving the child orders and instructions, his mother shapes his behavior. Having carefully observed the objects named by his mother, after he acquires the faculty of speech, the child begins to name objects actively and thus to organize his acts of perception and his deliberate attention" (Luria, 1961, p. 17).

Luria and Yudovich (1959) also say that stating the function role of an object, in addition to the name of the object, isolates the essential properties of an object and inhibits the less essential properties of an object, making perception of the object permanent and generalized. Thus, to Luria, the relationship between an object and its name is fundamental. By helping to define the salient cues, speech substantially modifies the child's perceptions and permits the working out of a system of stable differentiated associations.

Piaget (1951) and Piaget and Inhelder (1969), in contrast, conceive of language development as dependent upon the development of images and thought processes. The development of the symbolic function makes representational thought possible and allows the child to evoke persons, objects, or events not perceived at that particular moment. The child begins to acquire the symbolic function at the end of the sensorimotor period, around 18–24 months. This symbolic function includes: symbolic play, dreams, deferred imitation, drawing, mental images, and language (Piaget, 1951). The symbolic function arises from sensorimotor development, including the development of the permanence of objects in general. The child has the concept of object when he can conceive of things as substantial, independent of himself, and existing in a context of spatial and causal relations even when they are not present to his perception. Thus, according to Piaget, by the end of the sensorimotor period the child has the ability mentally to represent reality, to operate with symbols, and to begin to learn language. Images of objects are established, and the child acquires verbal signs for those which correspond to language.

Although there have been theoretical statements on the topic, there have been no systematic observations on the relationship between object permanence and the effect of object names on an infant's attention to particular objects.

Method

Subjects

Forty-one children between the ages of 18 and 22 months were seen for this study. Testing was discontinued with one potential subject, age 18 months, because of his unwillingness to cooperate with the experimenter. Usable data were collected from 20 boys and 20 girls. All of the children, with the exception of two children who were seen at the Child Development Laboratory, were tested in their own homes. All of the subjects were children of staff or students at Purdue University. The sample was evenly divided with half of each sex group older than 20 months and half younger than 20 months. The mean age of the subjects was 20.1 months. Birth order was recorded for the subjects with 23 of the subjects found to be first borns and 17 being later borns.

Design

Each of the children was seen twice. In the first session information about the child's language was obtained from the mother. Sixteen toys were then presented to the child one at a time for play. One of each of a pair of toys was named for the child, and the other was not. Immediately following this naming manipulation, a series of timed preference choices between named and unnamed toy pairs were obtained. During the second session, which followed no more than 7 days later, the object permanence and the vocal imitation subscales of the Infant Psychological Development Scale (Uzgiris & Hunt, 1966) were administered. This order of administration was planned so that the experimenter would not know the child's stage of object permanence during the naming manipulation and the test of preferences.

Procedure

Session 1 Prior to presentation of the toys, a report was obtained from the mother by asking her to check off on a list, which, if any, of the names of 16 toys the child was saying. In addition, the mother was asked the approximate number of total vocabulary words the child used and whether or not the child was producing two-word phrases.

The toys used were chosen to appeal to children of this age, and the two toys of a pair had a similar use. The paired toys (with their names italicized) were as follows: stuffed *dog* and stuffed *donkey*; plastic *boat* and plastic *hourglass*, both filled with water and colored beads; pop-it *beads* and pop-it *blocks*; plastic *banana* and plastic *pear*; plastic *orange* and plastic *apple*; rubber squeaky *kitty* and rubber squeaky *fish*; Tonka *car* and Tonka *truck*; Fisher Price pull *train* and pull *pig*.

The child was presented with one toy at a time to play with for 1 minute. During this time, one of each of the eight pairs of toys was named for the child and the match of the pair was not named. If the child was already saying one of the names of a pair, that toy was assigned to the naming condition. Otherwise, the assigning of a name to one of a pair of toys was essentially random. In the "named" condition, the name of the toy was taught for comprehension by using the name of the toy in a variety of sentences during play. The following are examples of some of the types of sentences used: "Here is a *train*." "You can pull the *train*. "Take the *train* for a walk." "What does the *train* say?" "What is this?" "That's right, *train*." The name of the toy was used approximately 10 times during the 1 minute. In the "not named" condition, a similar conversation was carried on with the child, but the toy was not named. Instead, the toy was referred to as "it" or "the toy." The order of presentation of the toys was randomized. It was also recorded which of the toys, if any, were identical to ones the child already owned.

After all of the toys had been shown, the child was presented with a series of preference tests using the named versus the unnamed toy pairs. The experimenter seated the child at a table in a high chair and presented the toy pairs to the child in a 7 × 15-inch choice box, partitioned in the middle. The time spent looking at and the time spent manipulating the toy on the left and the toy on the right were recorded in seconds by the experimenter using a four-channel print-out event recorder which was activated by four push buttons. Each toy pair was presented to the child, and the responses recorded for 1 minute. The particular order of presentation of pairs and left-right position of each pair were randomized for each subject. The time record for the eight pairs was transcribed onto a data sheet for each subject immediately after the session.

Session 2 During the second session the child was administered the object permanence and the vocal imitation subscales of the Infant Psychological Development Scale (Uzgiris & Hunt, 1966). The children were first given the following parts of the permanence-of-objects scale to familiarize them with the procedure: finding an object hidden under one of three screens and following an object through one hidden displacement with three screens. All of the children were then tested on their ability to follow an object through a series of invisible displacements in sequence (Section VI, No. 15, of IPDS). Three screens were used: a plain green cloth, a plain blue cloth, and a green pillow. The hidden object was one of a variety of small toys but usually a small car or doll.

The procedure is to get the child's attention and interest, then hide the object in the closed hand, and then hide the hand under each of the three screens in succession, leaving the object under the last of the three screens. At least three trials were given. If the child searched directly under the last screen in the series of invisible displacements, then the child's ability to develop a representation of the series was tested in a final trial by hiding the object under the first screen in the sequence, while continuing to move the now empty hand under the next two screens. The following scoring system was used: 1 = no search or searches only in *E*'s hand; 2 = searches only under first screen in series; 3 = searches in order of path of hand or under the first screen and then the last screen; 4 = searches in order of path of hand or under the first then last screen on first trial but searches directly under last screen by third trial; 5 = searches directly under the last screen; 6 = searches systematically from the last screen to the first in test of representation of the sequence. The vocal imitation subscale was used to assess the development of imitation of words including both the imitation of familiar words and of new words.

Results

Language Behavior

Language production was scored on a three-point scale: 1 = less than 50 words, no two-word phrases; 2 = more than 50 words, no two-word phrases; 3 = more than 50 words, two-word phrases. The mean score obtained for the 40 children on the scale was 2.15. There were no significant differences between mean scores on reported language for different sexes or ordinal positions.

On the vocal imitation subscale of the IPDS, 30 of the 40 children imitated new words for the examiner. All of the children who were reported to produce at least 50 words ($N = 26$) imitated new words extensively.

Object Permanence

The mean score obtained by the children on the object permanence scale was 3.9. There were no significant differences between mean scores on object permanence for different sexes or ordinal positions. The mean scores suggest that an average performance for a child of this age would be for the child to be able to find the toy after a sequence of invisible hidings but not necessarily by looking directly under the last screen on the first trial.

Table 7.4 presents the intercorrelations between the variables of object permanence, age, and language. For the total sample, the correlation between object permanence and age in months is statistically significant, $r = .48$, $p < .01$, as is the correlation between object permanence and language, $r = .32$, $p < .05$. When computed separately for the sexes, these correlations are significant for girls but not for boys.

Age norms, as such, do not exist for the IPDS so it is not possible to compare this sample to the general population on stage of object permanence.

Table 7.4. Intercorrelations of age, object permanence, and language

	Boys	*Girls*	*Total*
Age by object permanence	.35	.62**	.48**
Language by object permanence	.25	.43*	.32*
Language by age	.06	.29	.14
df	(18)	(18)	(38)

* $p<.05$.
** $p<.01$.

Preference for Toys

The primary variable of interest in this study was the child's preference for named and unnamed toy pairs. During the test of toy preferences, the child was presented with pairs of toys for 1 minute per pair and the time spent manipulating and looking at each object was recorded. Since the child could play with both toys simultaneously, the maximum amount of time the child could spend with the eight pairs of toys was 960 seconds.

The mean time spent in tactual manipulation was 295.2 sec, SD = 94.70, and for visual attention 152.1 sec, SD = 47.83. The longer manipulation than looking time may result from the fact that the child could look at the mother or the experimenter while still holding one or both of the toys. The experimenter found it more difficult to record visual attention than manipulation and when in doubt that the child was actually focusing on a toy, the experimenter did not record the behavior as visual attention. There were no significant differences between the boys and girls on total tactual or visual time spent with the toys.

Responses were recorded for all toy pairs including those toy pairs where one of the toys was already familiar to the child because it was identical to one he owned. However, for the analysis of differences between named and unnamed toys such pairs are omitted because of the predominant preference of children of this age for novelty. For all subjects together, 25 object pairs were omitted for this reason.

The mean time spent in tactual manipulation for named objects was 153.7 sec, SD = 58.37, and for unnamed objects was 118.8 sec, SD = 59.06. For visual attention the mean time for named objects was 88.9 sec, SD = 36.08, and for unnamed objects was 55.2 sec, SD = 34.05. Significantly more time was spent playing with the named toys than with the unnamed toys for both tactual manipulation, $t(39)$

= 3.51, $p < .001$, and visual attention, $t(39) = 4.42$, $p < .001$.

The differences in total amount of time spent on the eight named and unnamed toy pairs were computed for all the subjects. The average difference scores, for the total sample, between time spent with the named toy and time spent with the unnamed toy was +34.9 sec for tactual manipulation and +33.7 sec for visual attention with SD's of 62.83 and 48.17, respectively.

The amount of time that the children spent on the named and unnamed toy pairs is presented separately for boys and girls in Table 7.5. The average difference score between time spent with the named toy and time spent with the unnamed toy was greater for the boys on the visual variable than the tactual variable, +40.9 versus +23.9, whereas for the girls the average difference score was greater on the tactual variable than on the visual variable, +45.9 versus +31.5. A two-way analysis of variance for repeated measures was done with tactual and visual times as two measures and the sex variable. A significant interaction between the tactual and visual measures and sex was obtained, $F(1,38) = 7.37$, $p < .01$. Although both boys and girls spent more time manipulating than looking at the toys, boys showed more differentiation between the named and unnamed toys in the visual mode, while the girls showed more differentiation in the tactual mode.

The tactual manipulation difference scores and the visual attention difference scores are highly correlated, $r = .84$, $p < .01$, for the total sample although the tactual and visual variable are more highly correlated, $z = 2.5$, $p < .02$, for boys, $r = .93$, $p. < .01$, than for girls, $r = .67$, $p < .01$. These correlations reflect the fact that generally when the children were looking at a toy it was the same one they were manipulating.

To assure ourselves that named-unnamed differences were not due to some special familiarity or preference on the part of those children who already had names for some objects, a subanalysis was done comparing the difference scores for those pairs decided by the S's vocabulary and those pairs where the name condition was essentially random. The difference scores were numerically larger for those pairs with random name assignment. This difference, however, did not reach statistical significance, $t(39) = 1.91$, $p < .10$.

The Pearson product-moment correlations for the tactual and visual (named-unnamed) difference scores with age, language, and object permanence appear in Table 7.6. The correlations between the difference scores and age were not significant, except for the visual difference score by age for boys, $r = .47$, $p < .05$. The correlations between the difference scores and language did not reach significance but were higher for girls than for boys.

The correlations between the tactual (named-unnamed) difference scores and stage of object permanence were signifi-

Table 7.5. Time spent on named and unnamed pairs by sex

	Boys		*Girls*	
	Tactual	*Visual*	*Tactual*	*Visual*
Mean time on named	144.55 sec	89.0 sec	162.9 sec	88.9 sec
SD	68.25	43.42	46.45	30.34
Mean time on unnamed	120.65 sec	48.1 sec	117.0 sec	57.4 sec
SD	63.90	40.66	55.40	28.27
Mean (named-unnamed) difference score	+23.9 sec	+40.9 sec	+45.9 sec	+31.5 sec
SD	78.15	55.30	41.67	33.85
N	(20)	(20)	(20)	(20)

Table 7.6. Intercorrelations of (named-unnamed) difference scores for object permanence, language, and age

	Boys		*Girls*		*Total*	
	Tactual	*Visual*	*Tactual*	*Visual*	*Tactual*	*Visual*
Age by difference scores	.31	.47*	.23	−.27	.27	.21
Language by difference scores	−.02	−.07	.37	.41	.14	.11
Object performance by difference scores	.51**	.47*	.50**	.08	.45**	.32*
df	(18)	(18)	(18)	(18)	(38)	38

* $p<.05$.
** $p<.01$.

cant for the total sample, $r = .45$, $p < .01$, and for boys and girls separately. The correlations between the visual difference scores and object permanence were significant for the total sample, $r = .32$, $p < .05$, and for boys but not for girls. Thus, there exists a stronger and more general positive relationship between stage of object permanence and preference for named over unnamed toys as measured by time spent on tactual manipulation than as measured by time spent looking at the toys.

In particular, the mean difference scores of the tactual and visual variables for the six levels of object permanence show increasing magnitude of differences from low object permanence to high object permanence (see Table 7.7). This progression is greater for the tactual variable than for the visual variable.

One-way analyses of variance were computed for the six levels of object permanence using the tactual and visual difference scores. Significant results were obtained for the tactual (named-unnamed) difference scores, $F(5,34) = 3.58$, $p < .02$, but not for the visual (named-unnamed) difference scores, $F(5,34) = 2.04$, $p < .10$.

An examination of the means, together with the analysis of variance, leads us to conclude that children do spend more time on tactual manipulation of named objects than unnamed objects if they have achieved the stage of object permanence where they can follow an object through a sequence of invisible displacements (stage 3) and that this difference is greatest when they have acquired a complete concept of object permanence (stage 6).

A series of two-way analyses of variance was done using the tactual (named-unnamed) difference scores and object permanence, sex, age, birth order, and language. Because of the limited size of the appropriate samples, only two levels of object permanence were used for the two-way analyses. It should be noted that a one-way analysis of variance of the tactual difference scores with two levels of object permanence (stages 1–3 and stages 4–6) was significant, $F(1,38) = 4.78$, $p < .05$. None of the variables, other than that of

Table 7.7. Means for (named-unnamed) difference scores for six levels of object permanence

	Stage of Object Permanence					
	1	*2*	*3*	*4*	*5*	*6*
Mean for tactual	−76.5	−4.7	+39.8	+58.2	+22.7	+74.9
Mean for visual	−29.5	+6.7	+37.1	+62.5	+38.7	+43.6
N	(2)	(6)	(10)	(6)	(7)	(9)

object permanence, produced any significant main effects or interactions although the effect of sex and the interaction effect with birth order approached significance with p values of about .067.

Discussion

In this study it was found that children from 18 to 22 months will spend more time manipulating and looking at toys for which a name has been given than toys without a name if they have achieved the stage of object permanence where they can follow an object through a sequence of invisible displacements (stage 3). Further, children who have acquired a complete concept of object permanence (stage 6) will be more likely to perform in this way than children who do not yet have a complete concept of object. These results are interpreted as being consistent with formulations by both Luria and Piaget. Naming does affect perception in young children, as Luria suggested, but this effect is associated with certain cognitive structures of the child, particularly the development of object permanence, as Piaget has held. Although the data obtained in this study are correlational in nature, it seems more likely that the naming effect of language, at least at this age, is dependent upon the development of object permanence, rather than the development of object permanence being dependent upon the naming effect of language.

It should be emphasized that the naming manipulation consisted of using the names embedded in sentences descriptive of the toy and the child's ongoing activity. A simple labeling procedure might not have produced the same effect.

The naming effect does not seem to be directly related to language, as measured by number of vocabulary words and two-word phrases. This may be due to possible inaccuracy of the mother's report or the fact that one is a comprehension measure and the other is a production measure of language. However, both the naming effect of language and language in general are related to the stage of object permanence. This finding is consistent with recent formulations of Piagetian psycholinguistics by Sinclair-de-Zwart (1967, 1969), who writes: "The coordination of sensorimotor schemas which are actively built up during the first 18 months of life . . . is a necessary condition for language acquisition to become possible" (Sinclair-de-Zwart, 1969, p. 333).

As pointed out by McNeill (1970), in the past little attention has been paid to the relationship between cognition and language in the young child. Usually linguistic structures have been studied in isolation from the cognitive structures of the child. An exception to this pattern has been the recent statements by Brown (1970) that the meanings expressed during the earliest stage of language development are extensions of sensorimotor intelligence. Brown (1970) goes on to say that "If the meanings of the first utterances are an extension of sensorimotor intelligence, then they are probably universal in mankind" (Brown, 1970, p. 223).

If language development occurs within the framework of general cognitive development then it seems inappropriate to specify innate language acquisition devices as explanatory mechanisms without taking into consideration the associated cognitive capacities of the child.

The relationship between the naming effect and object permanence seems to have considerable generality across sexes and birth orders. A sex difference was found in the sensory mode the children used to differentiate between the named and unnamed toys. Although both boys and girls spent more time manipulating than looking at the toys, boys showed more differentiation between the named and unnamed toys in the visual mode, while girls showed more differentiation in the tactual mode.

The present research raises the possibility that when teaching infants one should first emphasize activities that would enhance sensorimotor intelligence. When it is clear that the child has attained the concept of the permanence of objects and is able to maintain a mental image of objects, then is the time that one may most profitably help the child to organize his environment by emphasizing the names of the objects around him.

References

BROWN, R. The first sentences of child and chimpanzee. In *Psycholinguistics: selected papers.* New York: Free Press, 1970.

LURIA, A. R. *The role of speech in the regulation of normal and abnormal behavior.* New York: Liveright, 1961.

LURIA, A. R., & YUDOVICH, F. *Speech and development of mental processes in the child.* London: Staples, 1959.

MC NEILL, D. *The acquisition of language.* New York: Harper & Row, 1970.

PIAGET, J. *The psychology of intelligence.* London: Routledge & Kegan Paul, 1947.

———. *Play, dreams, and imitation in children.* New York: Norton, 1951.

PIAGET, J., & INHELDER, B. *The psychology of the child.* New York: Basic, 1969.

SINCLAIR-DE-ZWART, H. *Acquisition du langage et développement de la pensée.* Paris: Dunod, 1967.

———. Developmental psycholinguistics. In D. Elkind & H. Flavell (Eds.), *Studies in cognitive development.* London: Oxford University Press, 1969.

UZGIRIS, I., & HUNT, J. MC V. An instrument for assessing infant psychological development. Mimeographed paper, University of Illinois, 1966.

44. BLACK CHILDREN, BLACK SPEECH

DOROTHY Z. SEYMOUR

"Cmon, man, les git goin'!" called the boy to his companion. "Dat bell ringin'. It say, 'Git in rat now!' " He dashed into the school yard.

"Aw, f'get you," replied the other. "Whe' Richuh? Whe' da' muvvuh? He be goin' to schoo'."

"He in de' now, man!" was the answer as they went through the door.

In the classroom they made for their desks and opened their books. The name of the story they tried to read was "Come." It went:

Come, Bill, come.
Come with me.
Come and see this.
See what is here.

The first boy poked the second. "Wha' da' wor'?"

"Da' wor' *is*, you dope."

"*Is*? Ain't no wor' *is*. You jivin' me? Wha da' wor' mean?"

"Ah dunno. Jus' *is*."

To a speaker of Standard English, this exchange is only vaguely comprehensible.

But it's normal speech for thousands of American children. In addition it demonstrates one of our biggest educational problems: children whose speech style is so different from the writing style of their books that they have difficulty learning to read. These children speak Black English, a dialect characteristic of many inner-city Negroes. Their books are, of course, written in Standard English. To complicate matters, the speech they use is also socially stigmatized. Middle-class whites and Negroes alike scorn it as low-class poor people's talk.

Teachers sometimes make the situation worse with their attitudes toward Black English. Typically, they view the children's speech as "bad English" characterized by "lazy pronunciation," "poor grammar," and "short, jagged words." One result of this attitude is poor mental health on the part of the pupils. A child is quick to grasp the feeling that while school speech is "good," his own speech is "bad," and that by extension he himself is somehow inadequate and without value. Some children react to this feeling by withdrawing; they stop talking entirely. Others develop the attitude of "F'get you, honky." In either case, the psychological results are devastating and lead straight to the dropout route.

It is hard for most teachers and middle-class Negro parents to accept the idea that Black English is not just "sloppy talk" but a dialect with a form and structure of its own. Even some eminent black educators think of it as "bad English grammar" with "slurred consonants" (Professor Nick Aaron Ford of Morgan State College in Baltimore) and "ghettoese" (Dr. Kenneth B. Clark, the prominent educational psychologist).

Parents of Negro school children generally agree. Two researchers at Columbia University report that the adults they worked with in Harlem almost unanimously preferred that their children be taught Standard English in school.

But there is another point of view, one held in common by black militants and some white liberals. They urge that middle-class Negroes stop thinking of the inner-city dialect as something to be ashamed of and repudiated. Black author Claude Brown, for example, pushes this view.

Some modern linguists take a similar stance. They begin with the premise that no dialect is intrinsically "bad" or "good," and that a non-standard speech style is not defective speech but different speech. More important, they have been able to show that Black English is far from being a careless way of speaking the Standard; instead, it is a rather rigidly constructed set of speech patterns, with the same sort of specialization in sounds, structure, and vocabulary as any other dialect.

The Sounds of Black English

Middle-class listeners who hear black inner-city speakers say "dis" and "tin" for "this" and "thin" assume that the black speakers are just being careless. Not at all; these differences are characteristic aspects of the dialect. The original cause of such substitutions is generally a carryover from one's original language or that of his immigrant parents. The interference from that carryover probably caused the substitution of /d/ for the voiced *th* sound in *this*, and /t/ for the unvoiced *th* sound in *thin*. (Linguists represent language sounds by putting letters within slashes or brackets.) Most speakers of English don't realize that the two *th* sounds of English are lacking in many other languages and are difficult for most foreigners trying to learn English. Germans who study English, for example, are surprised and confused about these sounds because the only Germans who use them are the ones who lisp. These two sounds are almost nonexistent in the West African languages which most black immigrants brought with them to America.

Similar substitutions used in Black English are /f/, a sound similar to the unvoiced *th,* in medial word-position, as in *birfday* for *birthday,* and in final word-position, as in *roof* for *Ruth* as well as /v/ for the voiced *th* in medial position, as in *bruvver* for *brother.* These sound substitutions are also typical of Gullah, the language of black speakers in the Carolina Sea Islands. Some of them are also heard in Caribbean Creole.

Another characteristic of the sounds of Black English is the lack of /l/ at the end of words, sometimes replaced by the sound /w/. This makes a word like *tool* sound like *too.* If /l/ occurs in the middle of a Standard English word, in Black English it may be omitted entirely: 'I can hep you." This difference is probably caused by the instability and sometimes interchangeability of /l/ and /r/ in West African languages.

One difference that is startling to middle-class speakers is the fact that Black English words appear to leave off some consonant sounds at the end of words. Like Italian, Japanese and West African words, they are more likely to end in vowel sounds. Standard English *boot* is pronounced *boo* in Black English. *What* is *wha. Sure* is *sho. Your* is *yo.* This kind of difference can make for confusion in the classroom. Dr. Kenneth Goodman, a psycholinguist, tells of a black child whose white teacher asked him to use *so* in a sentence—not "sew a dress" but "the other *so.*" The sentence the child used was "I got a *so* on my leg."

A related feature of Black English is the tendency in many cases not to use sequences of more than one final consonant sound. For example, *just* is pronounced *jus', past* is *pass, mend* sounds like *men* and *hold* like *hole. Six* and *box* are pronounced *sick* and *bock.* Why should this be? Perhaps because West African languages, like Japanese, have almost no clusters of consonants in their speech. The Japanese, when importing a foreign word, handle a similar problem by inserting vowel sounds between every consonant, making *baseball* sound like *besuboru.* West Africans probably made a simpler change, merely cutting a series of two consonant sounds down to one. Speakers of Gullah, one linguist found, have made the same kind of adaptation of Standard English.

Teachers of black children seldom understand the reason for these differences in final sounds. They are apt to think that careless speech is the cause. Actually, black speakers aren't "leaving off" any sounds; how can you leave off something you never had in the first place?

Differences in vowel sounds are also characteristic of the non-standard language. Dr. Goodman reports that a black child asked his teacher how to spell rat. "R-a-t," she replied. But the boy responded "No ma'am, I don't mean rat mouse, I mean rat now." In Black English, *right* sounds like *rat.* A likely reason is that in West African languages, there are very few vowel sounds of the type heard in the word *right.* This type is common in English. It is called a glided or dipthongized vowel sound. A glided vowel sound is actually a close combination of two vowels; in the word *right* the two parts of the sound "eye" are actually "ah-ee." West African languages have no such long, two-part, changing vowel sounds; their vowels are generally shorter and more stable. This may be why in Black English, *time* sounds like *Tom, oil* like *all,* and *my* like *ma.*

Language Structure

Black English differs from Standard English not only in its sounds but also in its structure. The way the words are put together does not always fit the description in English grammar books. The method of expressing time, or tense, for example, differs in significant ways.

The verb *to be* is an important one in Standard English. It's used as an auxiliary verb to indicate different tenses. But Black English speakers use it quite differently. Sometimes an inner-city Negro says "He coming"; other times he says "He be coming." These two sentences mean different things. To understand why, let's look at the tenses of West African languages; they correspond with those of Black English.

Many West African languages have a tense which is called the habitual. This tense is used to express action which is always occurring and it is formed with a verb that is translated as *be*. "He be coming" means something like "He's always coming," "He usually comes," or "He's been coming."

In Standard English there is no regular grammatical construction for such a tense. Black English speakers, in order to form the habitual tense in English, use the word *be* as an auxiliary: *He be doing it. My Momma be working. He be running.* The habitual tense is not the same as the present tense, which is constructed in Black English without any form of the verb *to be*: *He do it. My Momma working. He running.* (This means the action is occurring right now.)

There are other tense differences between Black English and Standard English. For example, the non-standard speech does not use changes in grammar to indicate the past tense. A white person will ask, "What did your brother say?" and the black person will answer, "He say he coming." (The verb *say* is not changed to *said.*) "How did you get here?" "I walk." This style of talking about the past is paralleled in the Yoruba, Fante, Hausa, and Ewe languages of West Africa.

Expression of plurality is another difference. The way a black child will talk of "them boy" or "two dog" makes some white listeners think Negroes don't know how to turn a singular word into a plural word. As a matter of fact, it isn't necessary to use an *s* to express plurality. In Chinese and Japanese, singular and plural are not generally distinguished by such inflections; plurality is conveyed in other ways. For example, in Chinese it's correct to say "There are three book on the table." This sentence already has two signals of the plural, *three* and *are*; why require a third? This same logic is the basis of plurals in most West African languages, where nouns are often identical in the plural and the singular. For example, in Ibo, one correctly says *those man,* and in both Ewe and Yoruba, one says *they house.* American speakers of Gullah retain this style; it is correct in Gullah to say *five dog.*

Gender is another aspect of language structure where differences can be found. Speakers of Standard English are often confused to find that the non-standard vernacular often uses just one gender of pronoun, the masculine, and refers to women as well as men as *he* or *him.* "He a nice girl," even "Him a nice girl" are common. This usage probably stems from West African origins, too, as does the use of multiple negatives, such as "Nobody don't know it."

Vocabulary is the third aspect of a person's native speech that could affect his learning of a new language. The strikingly different vocabulary often used in Negro Non-standard English is probably the most obvious aspect of it to a casual white observer. But its vocabulary differences don't obscure its meaning the way different sounds and different structure often do.

Recently there has been much interest in the African origins of words like *goober* (peanut), *cooter* (turtle), and *tote* (carry), as well as others that are less certainly African, such as *to dig* (possibly from the Wolof *degan,* "to understand"). Such expressions seem colorful rather than low-class to many whites; they become assimilated faster than their black originators do. English professors now use *dig* in their scholarly articles, and current advertising has enthusiastically adopted *rap.*

Is it really possible for old differences in sound, structure, and vocabulary to persist from the West African languages of slave days into present-day inner-city Black English? Easily. Nothing else really explains such regularity of language habits, most of which persist among black people in various parts of the Western Hemisphere. For a long time scholars believed that certain speech forms used by Negroes were merely leftovers from archaic English preserved in the speech of early English settlers in America and copied by their slaves. But this theory has been greatly weakened, largely as the result of the work of a black linguist, Dr. Lorenzo Dow Turner of the University of Chicago. Dr. Turner studied the speech of Gullah Negroes in the Sea Islands off the Carolina coast and found so many traces of West African languages that he thoroughly discredited the archiac-English theory.

When anyone learns a new language, it's usual to try speaking the new language with the sounds and structure of the old. If a person's first language does not happen to have a particular sound needed in the language he is learning, he will tend to substitute a similar or related sound from his native language and use it to speak the new one. When Frenchman Charles Boyer said "Zees ees my heart," and when Latin American Carmen Miranda sang "Souse American way," they were simply using sounds of their native languages in trying to pronounce sounds of English. West Africans must have done the same thing when they first attempted English words. The tendency to retain the structure of the native language is a strong one, too. That's why a German learning English is likely to put his verb at the end: "May I a glass beer have?" The vocabulary of one's original language may also furnish some holdovers. Jewish immigrants did not stop using the word *bagel* when they came to America; nor did Germans stop saying *sauerkraut*.

Social and geographical isolation reinforces the tendencies to retain old language habits. When one group is considered inferior, the other group avoids it. For many years it was illegal to give any sort of instruction to Negroes, and for slaves to try to speak like their masters would have been unthinkable. Conflict of value systems doubtless retards changes, too. As Frantz Fanon observed in *Black Skin, White Masks,* those who take on white speech habits are suspect in the ghetto, because others believe they are trying to "act white." Dr. Kenneth Johnson, a black linguist, put it this way: "As long as disadvantaged black children live in segregated communities and most of their relationships are confined to those within their own subculture, they will not replace their functional nonstandard dialect with the nonfunctional standard dialect."

Linguists have made it clear that language systems that are different are not necessarily deficient. A judgment of deficiency can be made only in comparison with another language system. Let's turn the tables on Standard English for a moment and look at it from the West African point of view. From this angle, Standard English: (1) is lacking in certain language sounds, (2) has a couple of unnecessary language sounds for which others may serve as good substitutes, (3) doubles and drawls some of its vowel sounds in sequences that are unusual and difficult to imitate, (4) lacks a method of forming an important tense, (5) requires an unnecessary number of ways to indicate tense, plurality and gender, and (6) doesn't mark negatives sufficiently for the result to be a good strong negative statement.

Now whose language is deficient?

How would the adoption of this point of view help us? Say we accepted the evidence that Black English is not just a sloppy Standard but an organized language style which probably has developed many of its features on the basis of its West African heritage. What would we gain?

The psychological climate of the classroom might improve it teachers understood why many black students speak as they do. But we still have not reached a solution of the main problem. Does the discovery that Black English has pattern and structure mean that it should not be tampered with? Should children who speak Black English be excused from learning the Standard in school? Should they perhaps be given books in Black English to learn from?

Any such accommodation would surely result in a hardening of the new separatism being urged by some black militants. It would probably be applauded by such people as Roy Innis, Director of C.O.R.E., who is currently recommending dual autonomous education systems for white and black. And it might facilitate learning to read, since some experiments have indicated that materials written in Black English syntax aid problem readers from the inner city.

But determined resistance to the introduction of such printed materials into schools can be expected. To those who view inner-city speech as bad English, the appearance in print of sentences like "My mama, he work" can be as shocking and repellent as a four-letter word. Middle-class Negro parents would probably mobilize against the move. Any stratagem that does not take into account such practicalities of the matter is probably doomed to failure. And besides, where would such a permissive policy on language get these children in the larger society, and in the long run? If they want to enter an integrated America they must be able to deal with it on its own terms. Even Professor Toni Cade of Rutgers, who doesn't want "ghetto accents" tampered with, advocates mastery of Standard English because, as she puts it, "if you want to get ahead in this country, you must master the language of the ruling class." This has always been true, wherever there has been a minority group.

The problem then appears to be one of giving these children the ability to speak (and read) Standard English without denigrating the vernacular and those who use it, or even affecting the ability to use it. The only way to do this is to officially espouse bi-dialectism. The result would be the ability to use either dialect equally well—as Dr. Martin Luther King did—depending on the time, place, and circumstances. Pupils would have to learn enough about Standard English to use it when necessary, and teachers would have to learn enough about the inner-city dialect to understand and accept it for what it is —not just a "careless" version of Standard English but a different form of English that's appropriate in certain times and places.

Can we accomplish this? If we can't, the result will be continued alienation of a large section of the population, continued dropout trouble with consequent loss of earning power and economic contribution to the nation, but most of all, loss of faith in America as a place where a minority people can at times continue to use those habits that remind them of their link with each other and with their past.

45. LANGUAGE ACQUISITION FROM AGE FIVE ONWARD

DAVID S. PALERMO and DENNIS L. MOLFESE

It has become a commonplace in recent years to point to the impressive accomplishments evidenced in the developing language of the child between the ages of 18 months, when two-word utterances begin to be heard, and 4 or 5 years of age, when the child has succeeded "in mastering the exceedingly complex structure of his native language [Slobin, 1971a, p. 1]." While the accumulated observations of the language development of the preschool child do leave one with a sense of awe, especially when viewed within the theoretical framework of recent linguistic and psycholinguistic theory (e.g., McNeill, 1970), it seems to the present authors that the emphasis upon what goes on between the ages of 18 months and 4½ years has led to the relative neglect of development in language from age 5 onward.

Thus, without minimizing the important character of the language accomplishments up to age 5, this article attempts to show that considerable additional development occurs from age 5 to adolescence. A review of the literature indicates that the 5-year old is far from having the equivalent of an adult native speaker's facility with the language. Scattered through the literature is evidence that at the phonological, syntactic, and the semantic levels a good deal more facility needs to be acquired before the adult level is reached.

Phonological Development

Perhaps the most neglected aspect of language acquisition is that of phonological development. The relative lack of research is surprising in light of the advanced state of phonological theory in general (e.g., Chomsky & Halle, 1968; Halle & Keyser, 1971) and the recently translated developmental theory of phonology advanced by Jacobson (1968).

Our review of the literature provides us with little more than anecdotal evidence about the receptive or comprehension aspects of the phonological capacities of the child. Most of the research discussed will allow us to make statements only about the productive capacities of the child. This is an unfortunate state of affairs considering the valuable insights provided by studies of comprehension at the level of syntax. While the problems associated with the study of comprehension at the phonological level may be different than those at the syntactic level, it seems useful to examine phonological development through experiments that use methodology along the lines of the Fraser, Bellugi, and Brown (1963) study, for example, to add to what we know about the productive capacities.

Beginning with the comprehensive study of Templin (1957), we have strong evidence that the articulatory skills of the child at his fifth birthday are far from complete. Although there are other studies that preceded Templin's (e.g., Poole, 1934; Wellman, Case, Mengert, & Bradbury, 1931), hers is based upon a carefully selected sample, a set of 176 sounds tested in initial, medial, and final positions, and the broad age range from 3 to 8 years. The sounds were elicited by pictures, written words, or repetition of the experimenter's oral example.[1] In general, the results show a marked increase in performance from age 3 to 4, a plateau from age 4 to 5, and then significant increases in performance from age 5 to 7. At age 8 the child's articulation is essentially the same as that of the adult. Phonemes in the initial position are articulated correctly prior to those in the medial position, and the latter tend to precede correct articulation in the final position. Most of the errors at age 5 and beyond occurred on double and triple consonant blends. Only 14 sounds or sound combinations tested in initial position were failed by 25% or more of the children at this age, but some 50 other sounds or sound combinations in medial and final positions were failed by 25% or more of the sample.

It seems from Templin's data that while most individual phonemes in English are

[1] It is of interest to note that no significant differences were obtained in the child's responses when the experimenter correctly articulated the sound in a word and the child repeated it as compared to spontaneous articulation of the same sounds. This fact is, of course, reminiscent of Ervin's (1964) report on syntactic imitation and suggests that additional study of this phenomenon, perhaps along the lines of Slobin's analysis of imitation (Slobin, 1968; Slobin & Welch, in press), may be fruitful.

correctly articulated in most positions in words by age 5, there is considerably more difficulty in combining a series of consonants in clusters. Such consonant clusters are undoubtedly less frequent in the language, thus affording the child less opportunity to acquire the rules involved in their production. In addition, the phonological rules for production of such strings of consonants in English are surely more complex than those involving consonant-vowel clusters. It also appears from these data that the consonant features +continuant and +strident tend to be late in coming into the phonological repertoires of these children.

Recently, Menyuk (1968) reported an analysis of the role of distinctive features in children's acquisition of phonology. Her data are based upon the consonant substitutions produced by children while spontaneously generating sentences. She reported on the percentage of usage of six features for children from ages 2 years, 6 months, to 5 years. The features nasality, gravity, and voicing appear to be correctly used nearly 100% of the time by 4½ years; the diffuseness feature comes in a bit later; and the features of continuancy in combination with stridency are not completely mastered until after the sixth birthday. Additional data collected from Japanese children in a narrower age range suggest the same rank ordering of the correct usage of these features.

A study by Snow (1964) analyzed the sound substitutions that 438 Grade 1 children, aged 6 to 8 years, made on an articulation test. While the mean number of errors for each child was small, the large sample and number of sound tests produced a substantial set of errors upon which to base generalizations. The major findings indicate that unvoiced plosives are replaced by other unvoiced plosives, and unvoiced fricatives are replaced by unvoiced fricatives. Similarly, voiced plosives and fricatives are replaced by other voiced plosives and fricatives. Semivowels are replaced by other semivowels. If a change in voicing occurs, it is nearly always an unvoiced phoneme substituted for a voiced phoneme and seldom the reverse. The most frequent errors, /*f*/ for /*θ*/ and /*v*/, /*θ*/ for /*s*/, /*k*/ for /*t*/, and /*n*/ for /*m*/, are the errors most frequently made in adult perceptual confusions and in substitutions made at all ages. The fact that these substitutions reflect sounds differing on but one distinctive feature is of interest, but of greater interest would be some indication of why particular single features are confused and not other single features and why single-feature confusions occur with some phonemes and not with others.

The production difficulties that children evidence from age 5 to 8 seem to center on (*a*) sounds that occur in the medial or final position of a word; (*b*) consonant sounds that involve the features of continuancy and stridency; and (*c*) sounds that involve a sequence or cluster of consonants as in the case of *-lfth* (twe*lfth*), which Templin found was difficult even for 8-year-olds. As Menyuk (1971) has indicated, these production difficulties may result from the fact that the sounds involved lack clear acoustic differences that the child can distinguish. If the child fails to discriminate the acoustic cues, he will fail, in turn, to articulate them. On the other hand, if he can make the acoustic discriminations, the production errors may be attributable to difficulties with the articulatory gestures involved.

While it would be helpful to have some perceptual data to resolve this question, it would seem from what little evidence we have that the difficulty resides in the articulatory gestures and not the acoustic cues. First, it would seem from casual evidence that speech sound perception is more advanced than production and certainly begins long before production (e.g., Eimas, Siqueland, Jusczyk, & Vigorito, 1971). Second, the fact that sounds in the initial position cause little difficulty, while the same sounds in medial or final position may lead to errors, suggests that articulatory factors associated with preceding articulatory contexts may be problematical. The child may have no difficulty in producing a sound from a resting position, but when that same sound must be produced from the position of the articulators after making another sound in the sequence composing a word, the child finds the task more difficult. Even in correct articulation by adults there is a good deal more variability in articulatory movements in medial and final positions than initial position (MacNeilage, 1970). Third, the child has difficulty with consonant blends that seem to involve a rapid series of complicated articulatory gestures unrelieved by interruption of an easier vowel sound. Fourth, the errors that do occur seem to be near misses in articulation. Plosives are replaced by other plosives, fricatives by other fricatives, and so on. Children make errors that seem to result from imprecise articulation rather than incorrect articulation. Finally, the errors that are made after age 5 seem to be made on sounds such as fricatives and liquids in which partial closure in the middle of the vocal tract is required. The bilabial sounds formed with the front of the vocal tract come in early, the sounds made at the back of the vocal tract come in somewhat later, but when rather precise control of the tongue shape and position in the region from the dental ridge to the front third of the hard palate is required, production errors persist to relatively older ages. Thus, the child can identify easily, with respect to his own motor movements, the end points of the vocal tract, and he can make more easily the grosser muscular movements associated with articulating sounds at each end of the vocal tract. However, when partial closure of the vocal tract is required with constriction in various parts of the central region, more errors are made. Thus, the target that the articulators must hit seems to be smaller for fricatives and liquids, varies with context in the case of a broader range of sounds, and requires greater muscular control in the case of consonant blends.

A somewhat different approach to the understanding of phonological development was begun by Berko (1958)[2] and expanded by Anisfeld and his colleagues. Berko was interested primarily in the acquisition of the morphological rules associated with the formation of plurals, possessives, and third-person singular of the verb, and with the inflections for the past tense of regular verbs. Since all of the sounds used in producing these inflections were within the articulatory abilities of the children, the question of concern was whether the children had acquired the phonological rules that determine the particular inflectional ending for each phonological context, that is, the three allomorphs for past tense and the three allomorphs for pluralization.

Berko's procedure involved presenting the child with pictures that were referred to with nonsense or real English names and then eliciting from the child the appropriate names with an inflection. A comparison of the 4- and 5-year-old group with the 6- and 7-year-old group of children indicates that of 28 items used in her test, there were 12 items on which significantly more adultlike performance was evidenced in the productions of the older children. Pluralization of the nonsense words was generally 70% correct or better for all ages when the */s/* and */z/* allomorphs were required but less than 40% correct when the */əz/* allomorph was correct, despite the fact that 99% of the older children correctly inflected *glass* for the plural form. Similarly, when the */əz/* inflection was required in forming the third-person singular of a verb or the possessive form of a noun, performance was poor. In the case of past-tense inflection, per-

[2] The methodological weaknesses of this pioneering research have been pointed out by Natalicio and Natalicio (1969) and should be consulted by those interested in extensions of this work.

formance ranged approximately from 50% to 85% correct when the /t/ or /d/ inflection was called for, but was less than 35% correct at all ages when the /əd/ inflection was correct for the nonsense words, although the verb *melt* was correctly inflected by better than 70% of all children.

It would appear that in both the case of the pluralization rules and the past-tense inflection rules, the child at this age has collapsed the three rules involved into two rules, at least insofar as the productive extension of the rules is concerned. The child is able to extend the /s/ and /z/ plural allomorphs and the /t/ and /d/ past-tense allomorphs to new forms, but he fails to use the /əz/ and /əd/ allomorphs. Another interpretation is that the child has three rules in each case, but, for nouns ending in a sibilant or verbs ending in /t/ or /d/, pluralization and past tense, respectively, are formed by a zero allomorph. Alternatively, Berko favored the argument that there is only one rule in each case, a rule that /z/ added to a noun makes that word plural and a rule that /d/ added to a verb makes it past tense, and under certain conditions the /z/ becomes /s/ and the /d/ becomes a /t/ automatically by a more general phonological rule. Anisfeld's research reported below provides some additional data relative to these alternatives.

One other point with respect to Berko's study pertains to the fact that the plural of some nouns, for example, *heaf*, and the past tense of some verbs, for example, *gling*, were treated as irregular forms by a significant number of adults who offered the plural form *heaves* (42%) and the past form *glung* or *glang* (75%), which the children seldom produced. This finding suggests that children learn some irregular forms by rote and later acquire an alternative rule that is based upon a few irregular words in the language and may be extended to new words that have a similar overall phonological form to the irregular words already known. The fact that the /əz/ plural for *glass* was used correctly by 99% of the older children but not generalized to new words suggests that rote learning may be a general initial strategy in language acquisition, at least for this aspect of language, and only when the memory load or some other factor makes rote learning unmanageable does the use of more general rules come into play. Even when the rules are acquired, Berko's data on the relatively better performance with the /əz/ allomorph, both for possessive forms and for the third-person singular verbs relative to the plural form, may imply that the rules are sensitive to other factors, such as syntactic context, before they are applied only on phonological bases.

In discussing some aspects of her data, Berko suggested that children may generalize responses on the basis of phonological similarity rather than on the basis of phonetic similarity, that is, on the basis of feature similarity and not sound similarity. This point has been cleverly investigated by Anisfeld in a series of three studies that have examined some aspects of the development of phonological rules in young children.

In the first of this series, Anisfeld and Tucker (1967) revealed a number of interesting aspects of the development of the pluralization rules. An initial experiment with 6-year-old children not only established that children of this age have difficulty with the pluralization rule in which /ɨz/[3] is used but that they are aware both of the concept of plurality and the phonological problems involved with words ending in sounds that require the /ɨz/ plural form. These aspects of the child's conceptual as well as linguistic processes are revealed by the fact that the children tended to use numbers in their responses when they were not sure of the correct pluralization rule, usually when /ɨz/ was

---

[3] Anisfeld and his collaborators use the /ɨz/ and /ɨd/ phonetic symbols where Berko uses the /əz/ and /əd/. Presumably this difference reflects dialect differences of the subjects used in the experiments.

required. Thus, the children responded as if they knew that their pluralization might not convey the semantic concept, and therefore they preceded the word by the appropriate number to achieve the same effect.

A second study indicated that children seem to have a concept that the plural form of a name is the singular form with something appended. It would seem that children of this age have the concepts of one and more than one, the ability to recognize when they do not know how to correctly pluralize a word, and the concept that pluralization demands some sort of phonological addition to the word to make it plural—although they may not know what that addition should be.

Finally, the authors attempted to determine both the recognitory and productive capacities of the child at 6 years of age for the specific English pluralization rules. The results confirmed the difficulty that children at this age have with the productive use of the /ɨz/ inflection and the relative lack of difficulty with the /s/ and /z/ inflections. The mean error rate for the /ɨz/ forms was somewhat more than 50%, while it was less than 25% for the other two forms. In the recognition task, however, the error rate was high for the /s/ as well as the /ɨz/ form, although the overall error rate was less for recognition than production.

A study by Anisfeld, Barlow, and Frail (1968) delves specifically into the child's generalization of phonological rules in relation to the distinctive features of the sounds. Four groups of subjects, 6, 7, 8, and 19 years of age, were used. Consonant-vowel-consonant trigrams ending in /*l*/, /*r*/, or /*n*/ were presented to them as a singular name, and they were asked to choose which of a pair of plural alternatives they preferred. The plural alternatives were formed by adding to the singular form one of the following sounds: /*p*/, /*b*/, /*m*/, /*f*/, /*v*/, /*k*/, /*g*/, /*t*/, /*d*/, /*n*/, and /*ch*/.

All of the singular forms called for the /*z*/ ending so that the results were tabulated in terms of the distinctive features with the same sign that the chosen consonants had in common with the correct /*z*/ plural form. Obviously a random distribution of choices would be expected if the generalization of phonological rules played no part in affecting the choice of responses. It was found that +continuant (/*f*/ and /*v*/) and +strident (/*f*/, /*v*/, and /*ch*/) sounds were preferred significantly by the first- and second-grade subjects and the adults, although not by the 6-year-old kindergarten children. Further, it was found that the older groups tended to select the artificial plural marker with the fewest feature differences compared to the regular one. The authors argued that the features of +continuant and +strident are more important than the features +diffuse, −grave, +voice, and −nasal, which also characterize /*z*/ because it is the two features +continuant and +strident that distinguish the plural marker /*z*/ from more other consonants than any of the other features. The additional fact that voicing was not an important distinguishing feature was interpreted to indicate that pluralization rules are not formulated in terms of the voiced /*z*/ and voiceless /*s*/. Rather, a more general rule, which states that an inflectional suffix has the same sign on voicing as the preceding sound, pertains to all suffixes and therefore is not an important feature distinction in a particular instance such as pluralization. The fact that the kindergarteners did not show the same systematicity as the older subjects may be attributed to the lack of development of the phonological rules involved or, as the authors suggested, to the influence of a rule irrelevant to phonology that led them to select the second of the two alternatives presented.

A study by Anisfeld and Gordon (1968) more thoroughly examined the problem of inflectional rules. In this case, a larger number of consonantal endings were used. The subjects were first- and fourth-grade children and adults. In addition, the inflection of synthetic verbs for past tense was investigated with fifth-grade children. Otherwise, essentially the same procedures were used as in the earlier study. The use of the past-tense test was added for two reasons: First, to demonstrate that the findings of this and the previous study were not due merely to particular sound preferences regardless of the task; and, second, to show that the voicing feature is a part of a more general voicing-assimilation rule applicable to inflections in general rather than pluralization in particular.

The results showed that adults restricted their choices when possible to sounds that were +strident (*/ch/* and */j/*), +continuant (*/th/*) or both (*/f/*, */v/*, and */sh/*). The first- and fourth-grade children showed preferences only for */sh/*, */ch/*, and */j/*, which make up the subclass of sounds that along with */s/* and */z/* are the functionally significant sounds in English pluralization is that they all take the */ɨz/* form for pluralization when they occur at the end of a noun. The children's rules thus seem more restrictive than those of the adults. Although they showed some tendency to prefer the */f/*, */v/*, and the */th/*, found acceptable by the adults, their preferences for all sounds were less strong than those of the adults. Further evidence that the children's phonological rules are not as well developed nor as complete as those of the adults was reflected by the fact that the adults favored */m/* and */n/* endings often used in irregular forms of pluralization in English, while the children showed no such preferences, a finding that seems to corroborate Berko's results with *heaf* and *gling*.

In the case of the past-tense choices, the fifth-grade children showed significant preferences for */ch/* and */j/*. The authors attributed this result to the fact that there are no other sounds relevant to past tense as there are in the case of pluralization. They argued that the */ch/* and */j/* sounds contain within them the regular past-tense markers */t/* and */d/*; that is, in the articulation of */ch/* and */j/*, the */t/* and */d/* sounds are part of the more complex */ch/* and */j/*, respectively. In addition, the children showed a significant rejection of the */s/* and */z/* sounds that are relevant to the pluralization inflection and thus in grammatical opposition to the past-tense inflection.

In contrast to the efforts of Anisfeld to determine the phonological rules for appending a sound, in the form of an inflection, to an already complete word, Bruce (1964) attempted to examine the child's ability to analyze the component sounds comprising a word unit. His approach was to present a series of words to 5–7½-year-old children (from 5 to 9 years mental age) and to ask them to delete one sound from the word and pronounce the word with the sound deleted. All of the deletions resulted in other real English words. Both the sound and position of the elision were included in the instructions for each word. The strategies employed in the task by the children at various ages are perhaps most revealing of the phonological development indicated by this task. Up to about mental age 6, the children were not able to separate sound from word. They could produce isolated sounds and words, but they were unable to take from a word one of its component sounds, regardless of whether that sound was at the beginning, middle, or end of the word. At mental age 6, the child began to be able to take a part of the word and form a new word, but the relation of the word they formed and the satisfactory solution of the task was often remote. While the 6-year-old child has begun to get the idea of sounds within words, it appears that word units merely were being substituted for word units. The last stage prior to correct performance was characterized by elision, but errors of overdeletion or incorrect deletion were prominent, and deletion from the middle of a word was particularly likely to lead to error.

These data, along with those from a study by Bryant and Anisfeld (1969) which show that children have difficulty parsing the singular form from a plural form, suggest that children take a holistic approach to words as sound units. It may be that at earlier ages the child treats whole sentences as undivided units, and as he acquires more language he parses the larger units into parts. At least in the age range from 5 to 8 years, it would appear that the word, or syllable, is the sound unit with which the child deals. He lacks the analytic abilities required to isolate and manipulate phonemic units within words. Savin and Bever (1970) presented some data that suggest that adults analyze the syllable unit prior to the phonemic unit. They argued that phonemes are abstract entities that are perceived only by an analysis of previously perceived syllables. It may be the case that young children learning inflection rules are learning new words that express semantic concepts rather than new phonemes that convert singular words to their plural form. Only at a later age, sometime after the child generalizes the /ɨd/ and /ɨz/ inflectional forms, will the children make the latter analysis. The child may have developed a complex system of phonological rules by the time he is 6 or 7 years old, but he still has not abstracted the phoneme from that system of rules and mastered the complex relationships which it has to acoustic stimuli and to articulatory movements.

Another bit of data that may relate to the same point is provided by Warren and Warren (1966). Their results indicate that compared to college-age subjects, 5- and 6-year-old children do not hear as many verbal transitions nor as many different verbal forms in a verbal transformation task. When children do report transformations, they tend to involve several sound changes at once, and sometimes additional sounds, rather than gradual single sound changes more characteristic of the older subjects. Children from 8 to 10 years of age tend to respond in a manner more similar to the adults.

Warren and Warren (1966) interpreted their results to indicate that the younger children organize the repeating stimulus in terms of individual phonemes because they report sound sequences not permitted in English. Just the opposite interpretation might be indicated since the adults tend to change only single phonemes when they report transformations while the children report fewer but larger transformations. Children cannot break up the word unit. When they do report transformations, the form of the word changes by several phonemes. These results do not seem contradictory to the hypothesis that words or syllables are the perceptual units for young children—as Savin and Bever have argued that they are for adults—and that, in contrast to the adult, the child prior to about 8 years of age has not yet developed the conceptual ability to abstract the phonemes from the word unit.

In summary, it seems that there are ample data here to allow us to agree fully with Chomsky's comment that "It is by no means obvious that a child of six has mastered his phonological system in full—he may not yet have been presented with all of the evidence that determines the general structure of the English sound pattern [Chomsky, 1964, p. 7]." It seems equally clear that the area of phonological development deserves a good deal more attention both before and after age 5 than it has received from researchers to date. In particular, the examination of the perceptual as well as the productive aspects of the system requires further research effort. Perhaps an expansion and elaboration of the sound-discrimination task, reported only briefly by Templin (1957), would be a valuable place to start. In addition, the relationship between acoustic characteristics of sounds and the production difficulties of the child might be revealing in light of Liberman's (1966, p. 193) comments indicating that /*s*/, /*sh*/, /*l*/, and /*r*/ are some of the most stable acoustic phonemes, but they tend to cause articulatory problems for the child. Finally, little or no research has been done on the prosodic aspects of the phonology of children this age.

Syntactic Development

Turning now to syntax, we find considerably more research available and a large number of studies conceived within the general transformational-generative framework. The results of these studies have frequently been interpreted to support the contention that "All the basic structures used by adults to generate their sentences can be found in the grammar of nursery school children [Menyuk, 1963, p. 419]." The interpretation turns, of course, upon what is meant by the phrase "basic structures." Without trying to quibble about what is or is not a basic structure, some data suggest that important syntactic advances occur long after the child has passed his fifth birthday.

The first set of studies that is examined here attempted to evaluate syntactic development by the procedure of collecting a corpus of language from children of various ages, followed by an analysis of that corpus in terms of a set of grammatical rules that could be used to describe it. The rules that describe the corpus are, in turn, compared to the rules presumed to account for adult language, and evaluations of development are made. The methodological and interpretative difficulties with such an approach are, of course, serious, although they are not discussed here.

The studies of Menyuk (1963, 1964, 1968), Loban (1963, 1966), and O'Donnell, Griffin, and Norris (1967) are particularly extensive examples of this type of approach. Menyuk examined the language of children from 2 to 7 years of age. Approximately 80 to 120 sentences were collected from each child, although no indication was given of how the sentences were selected from the running speech of the child. On the basis of grammars written to describe the sentences of the children, Menyuk concluded that nursery-school children have completed the phrase structure and morphological levels of grammar. Her analyses focused upon transformation rules in which some developmental trends were observed. Menyuk suggested that nearly all transformations used in adult language are present in some of the nursery-school-aged children, but even the first graders, as well as the kindergarten children, in the age range of 5 to 7 years failed to exhibit full development of the auxiliary *have,* participial complement, iteration, nominalization, pronominalization, and conjunctions with *if* and *so.* In addition, there were some 17 types of restricted transformations used only by children and not apparent in the language of adults. For example, noun phrase redundancy, as in "She took it away the hat," actually increased significantly in frequency from nursery school to Grade 1. Finally, there were some structures used by adults that never appeared in the children's language at any age level although these were not specified. Little can be said about whether the latter failed to appear because of lack of opportunity or lack of the competence to produce such structures.

Loban (1963, 1966) conducted a longitudinal study of language development over a 10-year period for a group of 220 children carefully selected in terms of socioeconomic level and a number of other variables. The study began when the children were in kindergarten and continued through ninth grade. Each subject was individually interviewed annually, and his spoken responses recorded. The results indicate that as children get older their speech performance improves, as indicated by decreases in incomplete syntactic structures, increases in the variety of structural patterns used, and greater variation in the structures within sentences in terms of vocabulary, positions of phrases (such as adverbial modifiers), nominalizations, and so on.

In a similar study, O'Donnell et al.

(1967) collected samples of oral and written language from 5- to 14-year-old children. The analyses of the data were similar to those of Loban but based upon terminal syntactic units (T units) used by Hunt (1965) in an earlier study of children's written language. Simple or complex sentences were defined as T units, but a compound sentence was analyzed in the smaller T units of which it was composed.

The length of the T units increased from about 7 words for kindergarteners to about 10 for the seventh graders. Of more interest, however, is the evidence for two periods in which sudden changes in performance appear to occur. Between kindergarten and first grade and between fifth grade and seventh grade are developmental periods when large increases in new grammatical constructions, or sudden increases in the use of constructions previously evidenced at low frequencies, and high error rates on some kinds of constructions seem to occur. Mean number of sentence-embedding transformations within T units increased significantly at both of these transition periods. Marked increases in nominal, abverbial, and coordinate constructions also occurred at both of these developmental points. Nominals containing adjectives and prepositional phrases particularly increased from Grade 5 to 7. Finally, frequency of coordinate nominals and coordinate predicates increased significantly from Grade 5 to 7.

In addition, O'Donnell et al. reported that only 2.6% of the seventh graders' utterances (excluding garbles) could not be accounted for by 1 of 11 common structural descriptions (e.g., subject-verb-object, etc.), while 12.5% of the kindergarten children's utterances fell outside of these categories. Most of the excluded utterances, however, did not involve gross grammatical errors. The subject-verb and subject-verb-object structural forms accounted for approximately 77% of the grammatical utterances of kindergarten children and nearly 90% of the seventh-grade children's utterances. Passive constructions accounted for less than 1% of the sentences of any of the grades, although there was a slight rise in these forms with age. These results are consistent with those of Loban and fit well with the data reported by Goldman-Eisler and Cohen (1970), who found that only 4% of adult utterances were passive, while 87% were of the simple, active, affirmative, declarative form.

In summary, the Menyuk (1963, 1964), Loban (1963, 1966), and O'Donnell et al. (1967) research provides a general overview of further language development in the child after 5 years of age. The overall results suggest that there is a general but gradual consolidation of language structures from kindergarden to seventh grade but also abrupt shifts in performance, which occur between kindergarten and first grade and between the fifth and seventh grades. More research focused upon these two periods may be of particular interest in revealing what is happening at these ages. It may be that the child is acquiring rules for different syntactic structures at these ages and that these rules affect and disrupt other structures that the child previously has dealt with in a competent manner. Language is an integrated system in which a change in one structure cannot help but affect other structures within the system. Examples of this latter phenomenon are seen in the data reported by Chomsky (1969) and Kessel (1970) using more controlled experimental procedures in which specific linguistic constructions were investigated.

[C.] Chomsky (1969) studied aspects of comprehension as a function of a number of factors including sentence complexity, selectional restrictions, and subcategorization restrictions. She was concerned with the developmental control over deep structure—surface structure relations when particular lexical items do not conform to rules that frequently relate surface structure to deep structure. She focused her attention upon the lexical entries *ask, tell,* and *promise;* pronominalization; and the syntactic comprehension of sentences in which the surface structure subject is not the deep structure subject. Her subjects ranged in age from 5 to 10 years. A Piagetian interviewing method with structured tasks and specified initial questions was used with more open questioning to evaluate the child's comprehension of the language-task relations.

In the case of *promise*, the so-called minimal distance principle applicable to most verbs is violated. In sentences that conform to the minimal distance principle, the noun phrase that immediately precedes an infinitive complement verb is the subject of that verb. Thus, in "John wanted Bill to leave" it is Bill who does the leaving, but in "John promised Bill to leave" it is John who does the leaving.

Chomsky's results indicate that while even the youngest children in this age range seem to know the meaning of *promise,* although there is some doubt as to the adequacy of Chomsky's check on this, they show systematic developmental trends suggesting that they do not correctly comprehend sentences involving both *promise* and the minimal distance principle until they are about 8 years old. The children appeared to pass through a stage in which they first applied the minimal distance principle to all cases across the board. Next, as children began to recognize exceptions to the rule, they made errors with sentences that followed the minimal distance principle as well as those that did not. In the third stage, the children finally straightened out the cases to which the minimal distance principle applied but continued to mix their responses to the exceptions so that sometimes they treated *promise* appropriately and sometimes overgeneralized the principle. Only at the fourth stage was errorless performance achieved in all cases. While there was a good deal of variability with respect to the ages of the children who achieved each stage, the sequence of achieving the stages was orderly and nontransitive. Similar results were found when *ask* and *tell* were used in another experimental task in which *ask* was used both as a command and a question. *Tell* consistently follows the minimal distance principle, while *ask* is inconsistent and does not when used in the command or request form. Development of the correct interpretation of *ask* in the command form was correlated with the development of *promise,* and similar stages of confusion with *tell* were apparent. Comprehension of *promise,* which consistently violates the minimal distance principle, always preceded the comprehension of *ask,* which is inconsistent with respect to this rule.

Kessel (1970) also investigated the *ask–tell* relationships with a group of children ranging from kindergarten to fifth grade. His results were highly correlated with Chomsky's (1969). The major difference was that Kessel's subjects tended to achieve the various stages described by Chomsky at somewhat earlier ages. Like Chomsky, Kessel found that children passed through an invariant and nontransitive sequence in their acquisition of *ask* and *tell.*

Chomsky's (1969) examination of the comprehension of sentences in which the surface structure subject is not the deep structure subject made use of the child's response to the sentence "Is this doll easy to see or hard to see?" in the context of a blindfolded doll. Her results indicated that 5-year-old children tend to interpret the sentence to mean that the doll is hard to see, that is, that *doll* is the deep structure subject of the sentence rather than the object of the infinitive. By 9 years of age no child incorrectly interpreted the question.

Both Kessel (1970) and Cromer (1970) have challenged Chomsky's (1969) methodology in this task. Kessel argued that the blindfold is an unnecessarily distracting cue in the task and that poor performance may be attributed to the fact that the younger children did not recognize that the blindfold was irrelevant to the question. Further, Kessel noted that Chomsky did not test comprehension of superficially similar sentences in which the deep and surface structures are the same.

Kessel used a simulated hide-and-seek game in which the child responded to eight declarative sentences. Half of the sentences were of the form "Lucy was sure to see," and half were of the form "Lucy was impossible to see." The results indicated that 6-year-old children have little difficulty with sentences in which the deep and surface structure subjects are the same, but they do have difficulty in the comprehension of sentences in which the deep and surface structure subjects are not congruent. The children's errors indicated that the difficulty in sentences of the latter form is manifest in the assignment of the incorrect subject to the infinitive verb. In line with Chomsky's results, Kessel found that by 9 years of age children have little difficulty with such sentences. Again, a nontransitive sequence of stages was found in the acquisition of sentences of this type.

Cromer (1970) examined the comprehension of sentences in which the nouns and verbs were held constant, but adjectives, such as *eager* and *easy*, determined the relation of the deep and surface structure subjects. His subjects used hand puppets to act out the sentences uttered by the experimenter. Cromer used four adjectives that unambiguously require the noun to be interpreted as the subject of the sentence, four adjectives that unambiguously require the noun to be interpreted as the object of the infinitive verb, and four adjectives that render the sentences ambiguous. The results indicate that children of mental age up to 5 years, 7 months, tend to interpret all sentences as if the noun were the subject of the sentence; between 5 years, 9 months, and 6 years, 6 months, the children are in a transition stage in which the first type of sentence is correctly interpreted, but there are both correct and incorrect interpretations of the second type of sentence; and children over mental age 6 years, 8 months, interpret both the first and second sentence types correctly and interpret some of the ambiguous sentences one way and some the other. Cromer divided his groups by mental age rather than chronological age because the apparent developmental trends seem to emerge more clearly. This may be an important finding that others should note more carefully in future studies plotting the course of langauge acquisition.

Cromer also found that all but two of the youngest children had no difficulty with comprehension of passives, indicating that these children knew that what appears to be the surface subject in sentences need not necessarily be the deep structure subject. Finally, he presented the children two nonsense words in sentence frames, which required them to be differentiated with respect to what was to be taken as the deep structure subject and then tested for comprehension of the two nonsense words. Children in the first stage failed to make the differentiation; some of the children in the transition stage correctly interpreted the two new words, but most of the children did not; and, finally, those children who were in the third stage correctly interpreted the two new nonsense words on the basis of hearing them used in only one repeated sentence. Thus, it would appear that Chomsky's results have some generality when tested under different conditions.

In the case of pronominalization, Chomsky found that children learned the nonidentity restriction for pronominalization between 5 and 6 years of age, while seven-year-olds were able to handle, in addition, the identity case. Thus, kindergarten children were able to comprehend sentences such as, "He knew that John was going to win the race," in which *he* and *John* refer to two different persons. Not until the children were older, however, did the identity situation, as in "John knew that he was going to win the race"—where *John* and *he* refer to the same person—no longer present any difficulties. Chomsky (1969) argued that since the second form requires a more complex set of rules, because of the ambiguity involved, it would be acquired later. Since the ability to deal with pronominals in these situations is basically dependent upon two rules, she theorized that this would account for such structures being acquired relatively early, while other constructions such as the *ask–tell* distinction would require more time to be mastered because a more specific and complex set of rules is necessary to account for them.

Other investigators, however, have found that difficulties with pronominal forms persist into the junior-high-school level.[4] Loban (1963), for example, found a marked increase in errors of pronominalization at the seventh grade which did not decrease to the performance level of the sixth graders until after grade 9. Chai (1967), in a controlled experimental procedure, also reported that difficulty in comprehending pronominal referents in compound sentences extends into the junior-high-school range. It seems that the development of structures involving pronominalization are far from complete by 5 years of age, as evidenced in both production and comprehension capacities of children well beyond that age.

There are a number of studies that have focused on comprehension and production of question, negative, and, particularly, passive sentences by children in the age range we have been considering. Slobin (1966) reported a rather extensive developmental study of the comprehension of various sentence structures including passives. His data for 6-, 8-, 10-, and 12-year-old children and for adults indicate a developmental trend toward increasing performance in comprehending passive, negative, and passive-negative sentences. Unfortunately he reported only latency data, and the more revealing error data collected are not reported in the published paper. It is of interest to note, however, that performance on passive sentences is superior if the subject and object of the passive sentence are not reversible, a result that was especially clear for the 6- and 8-year-old children. In fact, the nonreversible passive sentences were nearly as easy as the simple, active, affirmative, declarative sentences. Slobin argued that the difficulty in keeping track of which noun is the actor is eliminated on a semantic basis in the nonreversible passive sentence.

Turner and Rommetveit (1967a) provided support for Slobin's hypothesis. In a developmental study of active and passive sentence imitation, comprehension, and production, they found that 94.5% of the errors made in the various tasks involved inversion of the two noun elements. Most of the errors occurred on the reversible sentences, but a surprisingly large percentage (32.6%) occurred on the nonreversible sentences, which suggests that even with semantic support, children in the age range from 4 to 9 years continue to have difficulty with comprehension and production of passive sentences. Not until second grade (mean age 8.11 years) was performance with reversible passive sentences better than 60% correct on either comprehension or performance tests, although the kindergarten children (mean age 5.87 years) performed at approximately the same level on nonreversible sentences.

A second study by Turner and Rommetveit (1967b), using the same subjects as in the previous study, tried to provide contexts in which children would be likely to use the passive structure. The children were presented pictures and encouraged by the experimenter to describe the pictures with passive sentences by focusing attention upon the acted-upon noun rather than the actor noun.

[4] L. S. Golub, W. C. Frederick, & S. L. Johnson. Development and refinement of measures of linguistic abilities. (Working Paper No. 33) Madison, Wisconsin: Wisconsin Research and Development Center for Cognitive Learning, 1970. Golub et al. used a multiple-choice format to test comprehension of sentences containing a pronoun and found that a large percentage of fourth and sixth graders had difficulty identifying the referents of pronouns in sentences, particularly when relative pronouns were involved.

The results indicated that spontaneous use of passive forms was minimal. Not until first grade (mean age 7.00 years) was it possible to induce the children to give more than 50% passive sentences even after an example had been given and the acted-upon object was shown first in the picture. When questions were asked about the object, kindergarteners gave approximately 50% passive responses. Those who did use the passive forms tended to show advanced linguistic abilities on the independent measure of imitation, comprehension, and production reported in the previous study. Thus, there appear to be individual difference variables involved, and most children do not seem to have command of passive forms until after age 5. There was a tendency to give passive constructions more frequently when nonreversible actor-object relations were involved.

Hayhurst (1967) also found that children between the ages of 5 and 9 have a great deal of difficulty producing passive constructions even when the experimenter provides passive examples in the context of describing a picture. If the passive sentences are negated, the child's difficulty is compounded, but if the passive is truncated, that is, without an expressed actor, the child's difficulty is reduced. Under no condition, however, was performance as high as 50% correct for the 5- and 6-year-old children in Hayhurst's study.

Another study confirms the difficulty that children have with passive constructions (Gaer, 1969). Not until 6 years of age did Gaer's subjects show comprehension of passives that was well above chance, and Gaer's production test yielded little evidence of ability to produce passives at that age. Gaer also found that 5-year-old children have considerable difficulty in comprehending and producing sentences with embeddings, particularly when there are two embeddings or a single center embedding.

In summary, it would appear from these data that the 5-year-old child is just beginning to fully comprehend the passive construction and very seldom uses the passive in his own spontaneous speech. The various experimental attempts to elicit passive constructions yield results that make it difficult as yet to judge when production capacity is well developed. Clearly, there are marked individual differences that are, perhaps, more evident with this construction than most others that have received research attention. It may be fruitful to examine variables that are considered to affect language acquisition in general with the acquisition of passive forms. The technique, used with adults by Wright (1969), of giving sentences in passive (or active) form and then asking questions about the sentence in active (or passive) form might be used effectively in revealing some of the difficulties that children have with passive sentences.

Finally, in this section we consider some data pertaining to connectives, which could, perhaps, be discussed in the next section on semantics since there seems to be a strong semantic component involved in the results, although the specific words of interest are usually considered function rather than content words. A study by Katz and Brent (1968) provided some information about the comprehension and production of the connectives *because*, *then*, *therefore*, *but*, *although*, and *and*. Their data are based upon a corpus of spontaneous speech, responses to pairs of sentences in which various connectives were contrasted, and explanations for choices made in the latter situation. The subjects were first- and sixth-grade children and a college student group. Some of the data clearly suggest that the meaning of *because*, *then*, and *therefore* changes between first and sixth grade. While the first grader may use these words in his spontaneous speech, it would appear that the temporal relations of *because*, for example, are better understood than the causal ones, and the younger children probably do not have more than a sequential, as opposed to a causal, meaning for *because.* In other words, all three of these words are used as if they were marked semantically as *then,* with no causal relations implied. In addition, it appeared that when the adversative connectives *but* and *although* were used, children in the first grade showed little evidence of comprehending such constructions, and the sixth graders, while better in the identification of sentences correctly using the words, showed little ability to account for their choice. Finally, there was a developmental trend revealing an increase from Grade 1 to Grade 6 in the preference for the linguistic order of clauses to mirror the temporal order of cause and effect events. Thus, sixth graders seemed more aware than first graders of the cause and effect relations in such sentences as, "The benches were wet, we did not sit down" and showed a marked preference for stating the sentence in that order rather than in the order, "We did not sit down, the benches were wet." The college students showed no preference for order. These results may reflect a general cognitive developmental awareness of cause and effect by the older children and, at a somewhat more abstract level, may reflect the same kind of perceptual linguistic interrelationship showed by Huttenlocher in her studies (Huttenlocher, Eisenberg, & Strauss, 1968; Huttenlocher & Strauss, 1968) and Bever in some of his work (Bever, 1970).

In a series of studies concerned with logical thinking within a Piagetian framework, Neimark reported some surprising results related to the connectives *and* and *or.* In the first study (Neimark & Slotnick, 1970), children in Grades 3 through 9 and college students were presented with a sequence of 16 problems dealing with class inclusion and exclusion, class intersect, and class union. The results indicate that none of the subjects had any difficulty with class inclusion and exclusion, only the third-grade children had any difficulty with class intersection, but only the college students achieved success on the majority of the union problems. Children in Grade 9 responded correctly only 30% of the time when given instructions to select A or B, and performance was still poorer when the presumably clearer instruction to select A or B or both was given. According to the authors, these results are not culture bound since they replicate findings with Japanese children. An analysis of the errors revealed that most of the children interpreted *or* as *and,* a result also apparent in a study by Shine and Walsh (1971).

A second study (Neimark, 1970), conducted with children in Grades 9 through 12, indicated that correct performance on union problems increases steadily from Grade 9 to 12. A particularly interesting finding comes from the children's descriptions of the union sets in one form of the test used. It would appear from the children's own efforts to describe the sets that they do not use the word *or* spontaneously, at least under these circumstances. Only 6 of 39 subjects used *or* in describing union sets. Instead of using *or* they used *and* in describing the sets. They did not even use *except* or *all but* with any frequency. This failure of children as old as high school age to be able to comprehend a word as superficially simple and frequently used as *or* suggests that syntactic and/or semantic development extends over an unexpectedly long period and that it must be carefully examined throughout childhood.

Along similar lines, Olds (1968) has developed a game for children which cleverly allows exploration of the comprehension of various syntactic forms. He has shown, among other things, that children as old as 9 years do not comprehend the conditional *unless.* Children of age 9 and younger interpret *unless* as if the word *if* had been used.

Finally, a study by Goodglass, Gleason, and Hyde (1970) may be mentioned here. As a part of their study, they tested normal children between the ages of 3 and 10 years for comprehension of prepositions. In one test the subject was shown sets of three pictures and asked to identify, for example, the picture with the girl standing *behind* (as opposed to *in front of* or *next to*) the car. In the other test, the subjects were asked to indicate which of two sentences involving a contrast in prepositions was a better description of a picture.

Performance was relatively good on the first test and showed a steady increase from about 73% correct for the 3- and 4-year-old children to about 97% for the 10-year-old children. The biggest increase occurred between 5 and 6 years. On the second test, however, performance was near chance level until the age of 6 when performance jumped to a level indicating full comprehension of the correct prepositional forms. Further inevstigation of the comprehension of prepositions will be required before firm conclusions may be dawn.

The results of these studies of syntactic development point to a close interrelationship between general cognitive development and the comprehension and production of syntactic forms. Slobin (1971b) recently has suggested that this is the case, and he has outlined a model beginning with semantic intentions, which are based upon the general cognitive developmental level of the child, and relating those semantic intentions to the means for expressing them in a linguistic form. Particular lingustic forms are not comprehended nor produced until the underlying cognitive aspects are developed. Once such cognitive development has occurred, the child will look to the language for the means to express the new cognitive structures. Thus, examination of the language development of children, which reveals errors of various kinds at different ages, indicates either that cognitive development has not reached the point where the linguistic forms in question have any meaning for the child or the child has not as yet discovered the appropriate linguistic means for expressing the meaning he does know, a point that McNeill (1970) discussed in terms of weak and strong linguistic universals. In some cases it may be quite easy to distinguish which problem the child is having, while in others a theory of cognitive development may be a more important prerequisite to the understanding of language acquisition. For example, in the previous section the research of Anisfeld and Tucker (1967) clearly indicated that 5-year-old children had the cognitive concept of plurality but did not always know how to express it in a linguistically correct form. Slobin's examples with bilingual children make this point in a particularly convincing fashion. On the other hand, the review of the studies of pronominalization present an unusually complex picture in which the child seems to grasp pronominal constructions at one age only to lose them and reacquire them again, with final errorless performance coming relatively late in language acquisition. Surely the child acquires the concept of the pronoun as a noun substitute rather early. The erroneous linguistic structures that occur at later stages result either from attempts to express more complex cognitive relations in which the pronoun and its noun substitute become confused in the form of linguistic expression, or from the development of new cognitive structures to which pronominalization is differently related.

While the research reviewed in this section reflects a steady development of linguistic form from age 5 to adolescence, there is an indication across a number of the studies that the periods between 5 and 8 years and between 10 and 13 years are marked by instability in linguistic development, and these periods are followed by growth to new levels and subsequent stable linguistic performance. It may not be coincidental that these are precisely the periods in cognitive development marked by Piaget (1970) as transition points from preoperational thought to concrete operations in the first case and from concrete operations to formal operations in the second case.[5] It is during these two periods that large increases in new grammatical constructions and high error rates on some kinds of constructions are reported. The minimal distance principle is worked out during the first of these periods, as is the passive construction. Pronominalization performance advances during both of these periods. The work of Katz and Brent (1968) provided some specific hints about the relation between cognitive development and linguistic expression. The indication of a shift in the use of *because* from a mere expression of time sequencing to cause and effect relations, and the ordering of phrases in sentences, are two examples that seem to indicate that even when the same surface structure forms are used, the underlying syntactic and semantic relations may change as the child develops cognitively. Finally, the research of Neimark and her associates on union problems appears to fit very nicely with Piaget's notions of formal operations and gives additional support to the cognitive basis of language development.

Semantic Development

Since the research that might be considered relevant to semantic development has not been integrated by any particular theoretical point of view, it is difficult to interrelate it or to determine which kinds of data are of importance in the evaluation of the child's semantic system. To begin with, it is obvious that additions to the vocabulary are made throughout the life span. The fact that we add a new word to our lexicon, however, may have relatively little effect upon our semantic system. It is probably insignificant to a consideration of the semantic system if a new word merely acts as a label or shortcut for expressing something that it is possible to express using other words. For example, an unmarried male expresses adequately what is meant by bachelor, and the addition of the latter word to the vocabulary says little about language development. Thus, developmental studies of vocabulary growth, while gross indexes of semantic development, may not be very revealing of the system itself.

The problem, of course, is to identify the significant aspects of semantic change as the child develops. This problem is not limited to the nature of the semantic features in the narrow sense but must also include the interword semantic restrictions. We must examine not only the acquisition of the semantic features that mark the words *wish* and *want*, for example, as nearly synonymous but also the semantic restrictions and syntactic restrictions that allow us to say, "The man wishes that she would go home," but not, "The chair wishes that she would go home" or "The man wants that she would go home."

Thus, the expansion of the semantic system involves not merely the meaning of isolated words, however described, but the interrelations of those words with others. Research in this area, threfore, needs to be devoted to a consideration, in studies of both comprehension and production, of the development of semantic markers and selection restrictions, both syntactic and semantic.

Turning now to the data, we devote our attention to some evidence for the evolving meaning of lexical items in the dictionary, avoiding research reviewed in other discussions of the topic (e.g., McNeill, 1970). A number of studies scattered through the literature indicate that the elementary-school-aged child may have a substantial set of words in his vocabulary that have different meanings than those same words have for adults. Asch and Nerlove (1960), for example, investigated the development of what they call "double function" words. Such words as *bright,*

---

[5] Sinclair-de-Zwart (1969) has argued along similar lines and has noted the fact that the beginning of structured language occurs as the child's cognitive development shifts from the sensorimotor to the preoperational stage at about 18 months to 2 years of age.

hard, and *sweet*, for example, have both a physical and a psychological meaning in the sense that they may refer to both physical characteristics of objects and to psychological characteristics of persons. The authors studied the development of these two functions of such words in children between the ages of 3 and 12 years. In a Piagetian type of interview situation, the children were presented a series of objects and asked if any of the objects could be called *sweet*, or *cold*, or *crooked*, etc. If the child could identify correctly the object associated with the words, he then was asked if a person could be "sweet." If the child used the word in the psychological sense, he was asked about the relation of that meaning to the physical meaning.

The results indicated that the 3- and 4-year-old children could correctly use the words with respect to the physical objects, but, with the possible exception of *sweet*, they had no idea that the words could be applied to people, and, in fact, they denied specifically that these words could be so used. The 5- and 6-year-old children showed little evidence of change from the performance of the youngest children. In the 7 -and 8-year-old group, however, about half of the words were correctly applied to people, but the children could not relate the physical meaning of the word to the psychological meaning with any great success. By 9 to 10 years of age, half of the children could correctly use all of the words in both contexts, and the ability to indicate the relation between the two uses began to be evident. While all of the 11- and 12-year-old groups did not perform perfectly, they did show marked advances in the comprehension of the dual function of the words.

The authors concluded that children first master the object reference of double function words, then the psychological sense of these terms as independent meanings, and, finally, the dual or relational aspects of the words are acquired. It appears that the two related meanings of these words are acquired independently by the children first, and only later are the common features of the meanings integrated. If the semantic markers associated with the two meanings of each of these words are functionally independent and, therefore, entered separately into the dictionary at first and only later unified, then these results seem most consonant with what McNeill (1970) has called vertical development of the dictionary. The latter hypothesis is that lexical items enter the dictionary list with a nearly complete set of semantic markers, and semantic development consists primarily of establishing the relations among entries through the vertical organization of common markers.

The results also may be interpreted as an indication of the relation between semantic development and general conceptual development of children who give other indications of moving from the ability to conceptualize primarily in terms of concrete operations to more abstract levels at about 11 or 12 years of age (Piaget, 1970). Additional evidence for the development of more abstract conceptualization of words, which may be conceived as the vertical organization of semantic markers, may be found in some developmental studies of word definitions (e.g., Al-Issa, 1969; Wolman & Baker, 1965), which indicate that concrete and functional definitions of words give way to abstract definitions at about 10 to 12 years of age. Similarly, in some recently reported research, Anglin (1970) emphasized the concrete to abstract developmental trend in semantic development.

At about the same time that Asch and Nerlove were studying the developmental convergence of the meanings of words, Ervin and Foster (1960) were examining the developmental differentiation within sets of words that are frequently correlated in usage but that are not synonymous. Children in Grades 1 and 6 were presented with objects that could be described in terms of weight, strength, and size and pictures of faces that could be described as *happy, pretty, clean,* and *good.* The materials within each set were presented in pairs such that one of the dimensions was contrasted in the pairs and the other dimension held constant. The children were asked about all of the dimensions. The results revealed that both first and sixth graders indicated that the dimensions held constant also varied in addition to the one actually contrasted in the objects presented. The effects were so strong with the words *good, pretty,* and *happy* that the authors concluded that these three words are interchangeable synonyms for first-grade children. The tendency to treat the *big, strong, heavy* set as synonyms was less strong, and in both cases the effects decreased with age. In contrast with the results of the Asch and Nerlove study, these results point to the interpretation of what McNeill calls the horizontal development of semantic markers rather than vertical development. These sets of common words appear to have entered the dictionary without all of the semantic markers required to differentiate among them. As semantic development progresses, additional markers are associated with each entry so that eventually words that were once treated as synonyms are differentiated.

A more recent study by Lumsden and Poteat (1968) points to the same interpretation. They were concerned only with the concept of "bigger" in children 5 and 6 years of age and a high school control group. They presented children with pairs of geometric figures in which the area was equal but the vertical dimension was varied, and the child was asked which of the two was bigger. For example, one pair consisted of an 8 × 8 inch square and a 13 × 4.8 inch rectangle with a vertical axis of 13 inches. Two additional pairs were used in which the area as well as the vertical dimension varied.

The results indicated that the 5- and 6-year-old children selected the object with the greatest vertical dimension in approximately 72%–97% of the pairs. Even when the area of the alternate object was four times as great as the object with the greater vertical dimension, 85% of the children selected the smaller object with the greater vertical dimension. Since rectangles were used and therefore the vertical lines did not bisect the horizontal lines, there is little likelihood that these results are attributable to the vertical-horizontal illusion. This illusion actually increases from 6 years of age to adulthood when bisection is not involved (Fraisse & Vautrey, 1956).[6] If we assume that these results are attributable to a lack of the appropriate semantic markers on the lexical entry *bigger*, rather than to some factor associated with the perceptual salience of the vertical dimension in the experimental task, then these data may be interpreted as supporting the hypothesis of horizontal semantic development.

Finally, another study that attacks the same problem with still another technique is reported by Bradshaw and Anderson (1968). Their interest was in adverbial modifiers. They investigated the problem by asking their subjects to compare each of nine adverbial modifiers with all of the other modifiers using a paired-comparison procedure. The modifiers were *slightly, somewhat, rather, pretty, quite, decidedly, unusually, very,* and *extremely,* and all were modifying the word *large.* The subjects were drawn from Grades 1 through 6, 8, 10, 12, and college. The procedure proved to the highly reliable at all grades, and developmental differences in meaning were evidenced at the younger grade levels. Specifically, the modifiers *slightly* and *somewhat* were neutral modifiers for the children in the first two grades. *Slightly* shifted to the most extreme position by Grade 4, and *somewhat* moved into its adult position next to *slightly* more gradually and was not located where adults place it until Grade 8. *Very,* at the other

[6] We are grateful to Charles N. Cofer (personal communication, May 1971) who pointed out that this illusion might be relevant here.

end of the continuum, was considered the equivalent of *extremely* by first graders and gradually shifted toward the neutral position in ranking and was located at the adult position by fifth-grade children. The fact that *slightly large*, for example, is considered by the first-grade children as meaning larger than *rather large, large,* or *quite large* implies that the markers associated with the adverbial modifier *slightly* are either different or incomplete, relative to those that the adult has. While these data seem to support the horizontal semantic development hypothesis of McNeill, they also suggest the possibility that a third hypothesis may be tenable. It is conceivable that the young child may enter incorrect markers for some lexical entries in the dictionary, and semantic development may consist of acquiring enough knowledge about entries to not only add markers as in horizontal development but in some cases subtract markers associated with particular entries.

In summary our examination of the literature in this area has been far from complete, but the data reviewed seem to leave us in the same position that McNeill found himself in evaluating the characteristics of a set of developmental data dealing primarily with word associations, word recognition, and recall of word strings. Both the horizontal and vertical semantic developmental hypothesis seem to be supported by parts of the data. Perhaps both processes take place, but some additional research, focused on attempting to directly test the hypothesis, is needed since it is always difficult to evaluate research within one framework when it was collected within another.

Conclusions

In conclusion, while this review has not been exhaustive, there are a number of general impressions that emerge. First, there are rather clear indications that language development is far from complete when the child reaches his fifth birthday. Regardless of whether we examine phonology, syntax, or semantics, we find data already in the literature that indicate that further development is required before adult language competence may be reached. Furthermore, there are numerous hints in the literature reviewed that additional research will reveal other areas, not yet fully explored, in which development is incomplete. For example, at the phonological level there are indications that adults have a set of rules that subsume subsets of the so-called irregular inflectional forms. Young children, on the other hand, evidence no such rules and seem to acquire the irregular forms by rote memory. Presumably after enough experience with enough examples within each subset of irregular forms, the child infers rules that govern subsequent inflections for new words. It also may be possible that a hierarchy of rules is acquired such that in this case, for example, the regular or more frequently used rule is applied first, but other rules are available if the regular rule is inappropriate.

Second, this review suggests that in the analysis of children's performance it is becoming more difficult to clearly distinguish phonological, syntactic, and semantic aspects of language as separate levels that can be studied independently; for example, children seem to be aware of the semantic aspects of inflections, and when they do not know the phonological rules required to convey a semantic concept, they use some other method of conveying the concept. At the syntactic level the so-called function words, which in and of themselves are semantically empty, do involve meaning, and the analysis of the comprehension and use of these words cannot treat them from a syntactic point of view alone.

Third, the interrelationship of phonology, syntax, and semantics with overall cognitive development was continually apparent throughout our consideration of the research reviewed. It is clear that a theory of language development must be embedded within the larger context of a theory of cognitive development. While cognitive development may precede its expression in language, it is obvious that the reverse is unlikely. Thus, for example, the use of plural inflections must be preceded by a concept of number, and the full comprehension of the logical connective *or* must be preceded by the concept of set union. In addition, the suggestions in the data that the age ranges of from 5 to 7 and from 12 to 14 may be important transition points in language development are also the age ranges in which other more general cognitive changes are assumed to occur, at least within a Piagetian framework. White (1965) has documented many other changes that occur in various cognitive skills at the 5–7 year age range. Further exploration of the 12–14-year age range may prove fruitful both from a cognitive and a language point of view. The general point that cognitive development and language development are related intimately has also been emphasized strongly by Slobin (1971b) and Olson (1970) as well as Piaget (Sinclair-de Zwart, 1969). In this connection, mental age has been shown to be related closely to performance measures of language development in two studies reported here (Bruce, 1964; Cromer, 1970). It may be appropriate in future studies to look more closely at this relationship.

References

AL-ISSA, I. The development of word definitions in children. *The Journal of Genetic Psychology,* 1969, *114,* 25–28.

ANGLIN, J. M. *The growth of word meaning.* Cambridge: M. I. T. Press, 1970.

ANISFELD, M., BARLOW, J., & FRAIL, C. M. Distinctive features in the pluralization rules of English speakers. *Language and Speech,* 1968, *11,* 31–37.

ANISFELD M., & GORDON, M. On the psychophonological structure of English inflectional rules. *Journal of Verbal Learning and Verbal Behavior,* 1968, *7,* 973–979.

ANISFELD, M., & TUCKER, G. R. English pluralization rules of six-year-old children. *Child Development,* 1967, *38,* 1201–1217.

ASCH, S. E., & NERLOVE, H. The development of double function terms in children: An exploratory investigation. In B. Kaplan & S. Wapner (Eds.), *Perspectives in psychological theory: Essays in honor of Heinz Werner.* New York: International Universities Press, 1960.

BERKO, J. The child's learning of English morphology. *Word,* 1958, *14,* 150–177.

BEVER, T. G. The cognitive basis for linguistic structures. In J. R. Hayes (Ed.), *Cognition and the development of language.* New York: Wiley, 1970.

BRADSHAW, W. L., & ANDERSON, H. E., JR. Developmental study of the meaning of adverbial modifiers. *Journal of Educational Psychology,* 1968, *59,* 111–118.

BRUCE, D. J. The analysis of word sounds by young children. *British Journal of Educational Psychology,* 1964, *34,* 158–159.

BRYANT, B., & ANISFELD, M. Feedback versus no-feedback in testing children's knowledge of English pluralization rules. *Journal of Experimental Child Psychology,* 1969, *8,* 250–255.

CHAI, D. T. *Communication of pronominal referents in ambiguous English sentences for children and adults.* Unpublished doctoral dissertation, University of Michigan, 1967.

CHOMSKY, C. *The acquisition of syntax in children from 5 to 10.* Cambridge: M. I. T. Press, 1969.

CHOMSKY, N. Comments for project literacy meeting. (Project Literacy Rep., No. 2) Ithaca, N. Y.: Cornell University, 1964. (Mimeo) (Also available from ERIC Document No. ED 010 308.)

CHOMSKY, N., & HALLE, M. *The sound pattern of English.* New York: Harper & Row, 1968.

CROMER, R. F. "Children are nice to understand": Surface structure clues for the recovery of deep structure. *British Journal of Psychology,* 1970, *61,* 397–408.

EIMAS, P. D., SIQUELAND, E. R., JUSCZYK, P., & VIGORITO, J. Speech perception in infants. *Science,* 1971, *171,* 303–306.

ERVIN S. M. Imitation and structural change in children's language. In E. H. Lenneberg (Ed.), *New directions in the study of language.* Cambridge: M. I. T. Press, 1964.

ERVIN, S. M., & FOSTER, G. The development of meaning in children's descriptive terms. *Journal of Abnormal and Social Psychology,* 1960, *61,* 271–275.

FRAISSE, P., & VAUTREY, P. The influence of age, sex, and specialized training on the vertical-horizontal illusion. *The Quarterly Journal of Experimental Psychology,* 1956, *8,* 114–120.

FRASER, C., BELLUGI, U., & BROWN, R. Control of grammar in imitation, comprehension, and production. *Journal of Verbal Learning and Verbal Behavior,* 1963, *2,* 121–135.

GAER, E. P. Children's understanding and production of sentences. *Journal of Verbal Learning and Verbal Behavior,* 1969, *8,* 289–294.

GOLDMAN-EISLER, F., & COHEN, M. Is N, P, and NP difficulty a valid criterion of transformational operations? *Journal of Verbal Learning and Verbal Behavior,* 1970, *9,* 161–166.

GOODGLASS, H., GLEASON, J. G., HYDE, M. R. Some dimensions of auditory language comprehension in aphasia. *Journal of Speech and Hearing Research,* 1970, *13,* 595–606.

HALLE, M., & KEYSER, S. *English stress: Its form, its growth, and its role in verse.* New York: Harper & Row, 1971.

HAYHURST, H. Some errors of young children in producing passive sentences. *Journal of Verbal Learning and Verbal Behavior,* 1967, *6,* 634–639.

HUNT, K. W. *Grammatical structures written at three grade levels.* (Research Rep. No. 3) Champaign, Ill.: National Council of Teachers of English, 1965.

HUTTENLOCHER, J., EISENBERG, K., & STRAUSS, S. Comprehension: Relation between perceived actor and logical subject. *Journal of Verbal Learning and Verbal Behavior,* 1968, *7,* 527–530.

HUTTENLOCHER, J., & STRAUSS, S. Comprehension and a statement's relation to the situation it describes. *Journal of Verbal Learning and Verbal Behavior,* 1968, *7,* 300–304.

JACOBSON, R. *Child language, aphasia and phonological universals.* The Hague: Mouton, 1968.

KATZ, E. W., & BRENT, S. B. Understanding connectives. *Journal of Verbal Learning and Verbal Behavior,* 1968, *7,* 501–509.

KESSEL, F. S. The role of syntax in children's comprehension from ages six to twelve. *Monographs of the Society for Research in Child Development,* 1970, *35* (6, Whole No. 139).

LIBERMAN, A. M. General discussion. In F. Smith & G. A. Miller (Eds.), *The genesis of language.* Cambridge: M. I. T. Press, 1966.

LOBAN, W. D. *The language of elementary school children.* (Research Rep. No. 1) Champaign, Ill.: National Council of Teachers of English, 1963.

———. *Problems in oral English.* (Research Rep. No. 5), Champaign, Ill.: National Council of Teachers of English, 1966.

LUMSDEN, E. A., JR., & POTEAT, B. W. S. The salience of the vertical dimension in the concept of "bigger" in five and six year olds. *Journal of Verbal Learning and Verbal Behavior,* 1968, *7,* 404–408.

MAC NEILAGE, P. F. Motor control of serial ordering of speech. *Psychological Review,* 1970, *77,* 182–196.

MC NEILL, D. *The acquisition of language: The study of developmental psycholinguistics,* New York: Harper & Row, 1970.

MENYUK, P. Syntactic structures in the language of children. *Child Development,* 1963, *34,* 407–422.

———. Syntactic rules used by children from preschool through first grade. *Child Development,* 1964, *35,* 533–546.

———. The role of distinctive features in children's acquisition of phonology. *Journal of Speech and Hearing Research,* 1968, *11,* 138–146.

———. *The acquisition and development of language.* Englewood Cliffs, N. J.: Prentice-Hall, 1971.

NATALICIO, D. S., & NATALICIO, L. F. S. "The child's learning of English morphology" revisited. *Language Learning,* 1969, *19,* 205–215.

NEIMARK, E. D. Development of comprehension of logical connectives: Understanding of "or." *Psychonomic Science,* 1970, *21,* 217–219.

NEIMARK, E. D., & SLOTNICK, N. S. Development of the understanding of logical connectives. *Journal of Educational Psychology,* 1970, *61,* 451–460.

O'DONNELL, R. C., GRIFFIN, W. J., & NORRIS, R. C. *Syntax of kindergarten and elementary school children: A transformational analysis.* (Research Rep. No. 8) Champaign, Ill.: National Council of Teachers of English, 1967.

OLDS, H. F., JR. *An experimental study of syntactic factors influencing children's comprehension of certain complex relationships.* (Center for Research and Development of Educational Difficulties Rep. No. 4) Cambridge, Mass.: Harvard University Press, 1968.

OLSON, D. R. Language and thought: Aspects of a cognitive theory of semantics. *Psychological Review,* 1970, *77,* 257–273.

PIAGET, J. Piaget's theory. In P. H. Mussen (Ed.), *Carmichael's manual of child psychology.* New York: Wiley, 1970.

POOLE, I. Genetic development of articulation of consonant sounds in speech. *Elementary English Review,* 1934, *11,* 158–161.

SAVIN, H. B., & BEVER, T. G. The nonperceptual reality of the phoneme. *Journal of Verbal Learning and Verbal Behavior,* 1970, *9,* 295–302.

SHINE, D., & WALSH, J. F. Developmental trends in the use of logical connectives. *Psychonomic Science,* 1971, *23,* 171–172.

SINCLAIR-DE-ZWART, H. Developmental psycholinguistics. In D. Elkind & J. H. Flavell (Eds.), *Studies in cognitive development: Essays in honor of Jean Piaget.* Oxford: Oxford University Press, 1969.

SLOBIN, D. I. Grammatical transformations and sentence comprehension in childhood and adulthood. *Journal of Verbal Learning and Verbal Behavior,* 1966, *5,* 219–227.

———. Imitation and grammatical development in children. In N. S. Endler, L. R. Boulter, & H. Osser (Eds.), *Contemporary issues in developmental psychology.* New York: Holt, Rinehart & Winston, 1968.

———. *The ontogenesis of grammar: Facts & theories.* New York: Academic Press, 1971. (a)

———. Developmental psycholinguistics. In W. O. Dingwell (Ed.), *A survey of linguistic science.* College Park, Md.: Linguistics Program, University of Maryland, 1971. (b)

SLOBIN, D. I., & WELCH, C. A. Elicited imitation as a research tool in developmental psycholinguistics. In C. A. Ferguson & D. I. Slobin (Eds.), *Readings on child language acquisition.* New York: Holt, Rinehart & Winston, in press.

SNOW, K. A comparative study of sound substitutions used by "normal" first grade children. *Speech Monographs,* 1964, *31,* 135–142.

TEMPLIN, M. C. *Certain language skills in children: Their development and interrelations.* (Monographs Series No. 26) Minneapolis: University of Minnesota, Institute of Child Welfare, 1957.

TURNER, E. A. & ROMMETVEIT, R. The acquisition of sentence voice and reversibility. *Child Development,* 1967, *38,* 649–660. (a)

———. Experimental manipulation of the production of active and passive voice in children. *Language and Speech,* 1967, *10,* 169–180. (b)

WARREN, R. M., & WARREN, R. P. A comparison of speech perception in childhood, maturity, and old age by means of the verbal transformation effect. *Journal of Verbal Learning and Verbal Behavior,* 1966, *5,* 142–146.

WELLMAN, B. L., CASE, I. M., MENGERT, I. G., & BRADBURY, D. Speech sounds of young children. *University of Iowa Studies in Child Welfare,* 1931, *5,* No. 2.

WHITE, S. H. Evidence for a hierarchical arrangement of learning processes. In L. P. Lipsitt & C. C. Spiker (Eds.), *Advances in child development and behavior. Vol. 2.* New York: Academic Press, 1965.

WOLMAN, R. N., & BAKER, E. N. A developmental study of word definitions. *Journal of Genetic Psychology,* 1965, *107,* 159–166.

WRIGHT, P. Transformations and the understanding of sentences. *Language and Speech,* 1969, *12,* 156–166.

46. THE DEVELOPMENT OF COMPETENCE IN AN EXCEPTIONAL LANGUAGE STRUCTURE IN OLDER CHILDREN AND YOUNG ADULTS

PAMELA E. KRAMER, ELISSA KOFF, and ZELLA LURIA

Ss between 8 and 20 years of age were tested for competence on an exception to a grammatical rule, the Minimal Distance Principle. No age group tested was found with all Ss competent. Older groups had 2 competent Ss for every S who lacked the competence. Stages found by C. Chomsky (1969) for Ss below 8 were duplicated above age 8. Two years after the original experiment, Ss who had not been found competent originally were retested. All age groups improved; no evidence for greater improvement of competency for the younger "language-plastic"-aged Ss was found.

There appears to be an interesting class of exceptional linguistic structures which, because of their relative linguistic complexity and infrequency, are acquired rather late in life and may never be acquired by all adult speakers. Such linguistic structures allow the process of language acquisition to be studied not only in young children, but also in young adults.

Our work is based directly upon the

work of Carol Chomsky (1969). In her research, subjects ranging in age from 5 to 10 years were tested on their ability to decode sentences involving an exceptional structure in English, the exception to the Minimal Distance Principle. "I tell him where to go" follows the Minimal Distance Principle; the subject of the complement verb phrase "where to go" is the noun phrase most closely preceding that verb phrase, or the object of the main clause. "I ask him where to go" violates the Minimal Distance Principle. Here, the subject of the complement "where to go" is the main clause subject, the noun phrase more distant from the complement.

"Ask" is an unusual verb in that it can follow the Minimal Distance Principle as in the sentence "John asked Bill to leave," or violate the Minimal Distance Principle as in the sentence "John asked Bill what to do." Presumably, children who have not learned when to apply the exception to the Minimal Distance Principle will apply the Minimal Distance Principle, the regular rule. Therefore, Carol Chomsky predicted, such children would interpret the sentence "(you) ask John what to paint" as "ask John what he should paint." Consequently, these children should respond to this sentence with "John, what do you want to paint?" when "what should I paint?" is the correct response.

In addition to the above response, however, Carol Chomsky found that over half of the subjects, especially the younger children—5- and 6-years-olds—were responding to "ask" in such sentences as "Ask John what to paint" as if "ask" were synonymous with "tell." Subjects were responding, moreover, to "ask" in less complicated sentences such as "ask John what color this is" in a similar manner. (Subjects would respond "it's red.") While this is an understandable mistake in that "ask" in the sense of a request often does mean the same thing as "tell," it nonetheless seemed startling that the structural meaning of such common and everyday words should fail to be distinguished by such large numbers of children.

On the basis of these findings, Carol Chomsky decided to investigate structures involving "ask" and "tell" in a more general manner, with the exception to the Minimal Distance Principle as the most difficult structure tested. She tested for children's understandings of three kinds of sentences: case 1, "Ask Laura what time it is"; case 2, "Ask Laura her last name"; case 3, "Ask Laura what to feed the doll." She found five stages in the acquisition of competence in these constructions. In the first, Ss would *tell* rather than *ask* in response to simple sentences such as "Ask Mary what color this is" (case 1). In the second, Ss would respond correctly to the preceding sentence (where all elements of the response are present in the complement) but would *tell* in response to sentences such as "Ask Mary her last name" (case 2). In the third stage, Ss would respond correctly to the simple "ask" constructions of cases 1 and 2, but would *tell* in response to sentences calling for the violation of the Minimal Distance Principle in case 3. In the fourth stage, Ss would "ask" in response to sentences calling for the exception, but would choose the wrong subject for the Wh-clause. Finally, in the fifth stage, Ss would respond correctly to all of the test sentences. Because these stages follow an orderly progression, and because the stage of the subject correlates with age (younger Ss tend to be in lower stages than are older Ss), the five stages which have been described appear to represent developmental stages in the acquisition of competence in "ask" constructions.

The purpose of the current study was to investigate the acquisition of the exception to the Minimal Distance Principle in sentences with the main verb "to ask" in older children and adults. We hypothesized that:

1. Although competence in the exception to the Minimal Distance Principle in-

creases with age, differences in competence will be found even in adults. No age group should demonstrate 100% competence.

2. Based upon the Lenneberg hypothesis of a critical period for language learning, (*a*) after the age of 12 the proportion of Ss within any given age group who demonstrate competence will not vary significantly; (*b*) Ss under 12 (the "language-plastic" period) who do not have the competence in question will more readily acquire the rule for the exception after modeling by a peer than will those over 12; (*c*) Ss who upon first testing do not have the exceptional structure, and who are within the language-plastic age range, will be more likely to induce the rule than will Ss aged 12 and over when retested some 2 years later.
3. The later developmental stages in the acquisition of the exception to the Minimal Distance Principle found by Carol Chomsky will be found in our sample.
4. IQ and competence in the exceptional structure will be related.

Study 1

Method

Subjects The Ss were 122 white, middle-class children and young adults–61 boys and 61 girls–who were divided into six age groups (mean ages: 8-10; 10-7; 12-10; 14-6; 15-8; and 19-0). Each group consisted of 10 boys and 10 girls with the exception of the college sample, which consisted of 11 men and 11 women. All of the Ss ranged in IQ from 106 to 148.

Procedure The Ss were required to respond to a four-part interview. During the entire interview, a second child or helper was present in addition to S. The "helper" was always a child who had demonstrated competence in the exception to the Minimal Distance Principle (MDP) on a pretest.

After instructions, Ss responded to sentences involving "to ask" in its regular, nonexceptional use (part 1). Inasmuch as it was not anticipated that any of the Ss would have difficulty with this portion of the interview, and none did, these sentences were intended primarily as a warm-up. If there were no questions, part 2 followed.

Test Sentences

Part 1: Cases 1 and 2
- (S) ask *H* (helper) what time it is (case 1, stage A)
- (*H*) tell (S) how many pencils there are
- (S) ask (*H*) his last name (case 2, stage B)
- (*H*) tell (S) where you live

Part 2: Test trials (case 3, exception to MDP, stages C,D,E)
- (S) ask (*H*) which book to read
- (*H*) tell (S) which pencil to use
- (S) ask (*H*) which comb to use
- (*H*) tell (S) which hammer to pound with

Optional (for Ss who missed one of the above)
- (S) ask (*H*) which cup to use
- (*H*) tell (S) which spoon to use

If optional omitted (cue sentence, case 1)
- (S) ask (*H*) which cup *you* should use
- (*H*) tell (S) which spoon to use

If optional included (cue sentence, case 1)
- (S) ask (*H*) which book *you* should read
- (*H*) tell (S) which pencil to use

Part 2 was the critical section of the experimental interview. Here, test instruction sentences were used which tested the S's ability to decode the exception to the MDP. The helper, in turn, responded to nonexceptional sentences including the verb "to tell" rather than "to ask" (i.e., "John, tell Bill which pencil to use" [John, the helper, responds]. "Bill, ask John which book to read" [Bill, the S, responds]).

In part 3, an attempt was made to test the S's knowledge of the exceptional structure without requiring a verbal response. The Ss made a series of choices between pairs of pictures as possible depictions of sentences spoken by the *E*, calling for the violation of the MDP. Following each choice, the *S* was required to explain why the picture chosen corresponded with the sentence which had been given. Some sample sentences are: "Mother told Sally what to wear," "John asked Mary what to paint."

In part 4 of the experimental interview, S responded to sentences similar to those in part 2 after the correct response to sentences violating the MDP had been modeled by the "helper."

The Ss were scored as having demonstrated competence on any given portion of the interview if they responded correctly to at least two out of three of the test sentences, duplicating Chomsky's requirements. The entire interview was tape-recorded. Objects referred to in the test sentences and the pictures that were correct within each pair were alternated such that half of the subjects received sentences referring to one set of objects or pictures (part A), and the other half of the Ss received sentences referring to the opposite set (part B). For each S the number and order of sibs, and IQ were recorded.

Results

Our first hypothesis consisted of two parts: (1) that differences in competence would be found in our six age groups, and (2) that no age group would have 100% competence. Both parts of this hypothesis were confirmed, as can be seen in Table 7.8. In our sample of 122 subjects, 69 performed to criterion on part 2 of the experimental interview and 53 did not. The breakdown of the Ss according to age can be found in Table 7.8. Part 3 of the experimental interview was not used as an index of competence because it was revealed to be an inadequate test of whether or not the Ss had the exceptional structure. The Ss elaborated reasons for choosing either of the two pictures shown which seemed plausible to us.

Our second hypothesis, based on the idea of a critical period in the development of langauge, stated that after the critical period the proportion of Ss who demonstrate competence in exceptional structures will remain roughly the same. Again referring to Table 7.8, it can be seen that the proportion of Ss who perform to criterion on part 2 within each age group does not vary substantially from seventh grade on. Calculation of exact probabilities for difference in two independent proportions supports this assertion in that significant differences are found when subjects over 12 are compared with all younger children. Thus, competence in the exception to the MDP may be seen as increasing in our sample until somewhere between the ages of 10 and 12, after which age most, but never all, of our subjects may be expected to demonstrate competence. It appears that for every two competent adults, there is one noncompetent adult, even in this college group.

We had predicted (hypothesis 2*b*) that

Table 7.8. *N* successes and failures for each age group for exceptional use of "ask"

Age Group	*Successes* (N)		*Failures* (N)	*Total*
College	15	(68)	7	22
Sophomore high school	12	(60)	8	20
Ninth grade	11	(55)	9	20
Seventh grade	14	(70)	6	20
Fifth grade	10	(50)	10	20
Third grade	7	(35)	13	20
Total	69		53	122

Note.—Percentage of successes in parentheses.

children under 12 should more readily acquire the exception after the correct response had been modeled by a peer. While our data do *not* support this hypothesis, we also found that our method allowed Ss to parrot the model. Since Ss were often not able to supply the correct response when it was no longer available in the environment (and since we did not discover this until half the Ss had been run), we feel that this portion of the interview was not an adequate test of the hypothesis.

The follow-up testing of hypothesis 2*c*, that Ss who on first trial did not have the exceptional structure would be more likely on retest some two years later to have the structure *if* the original test had been given before age 12, rather than after that age, will be reported below as study 2.

A third hypothesis predicted that the responses of Ss to the test sentences in part 2 would correspond to the last three developmental stages described by Carol Chomsky. In fact, all of the incorrect responses on part 2 fell into one of two categories. First, Ss would *tell* rather than *ask* in response to these sentences (e.g., "John, ask Bill which comb to use." John: "Use that one"). Second, Ss would formulate a question but would choose the wrong subject (e.g., "Arthur, ask Nancy which book to read." Arthur: "Which book do you want to read, Nancy?"). An χ^2 ($df = 2$) for the age of the S and the type of error made by S was significant at $p < .01$. Younger subjects tend to "tell" whereas older subjects tend to choose the incorrect subject. Thus, our data confirm Carol Chomsky's findings. We have duplicated her last three stages for a sample older than the one which she used.

A fourth hypothesis predicted that there would be a significant and positive correlation between successful performance on part 2 and IQ. With a correction for the restricted range of the IQ scores, we obtained an estimate of r of .49 for our sample (significant at $p < .01$).

Study 2

Method

Subjects The Ss were 34 children and young adults who participated in the original study 2 years earlier and who failed to demonstrate competence in the exception to the MDP in sentences with the main verb *to ask*. These were 10 10–11-year-olds (4 girls, 6 boys), six 12–13-year-olds (3 girls, 3 boys), four 15-year-olds (1 girl, 3 boys), nine 16–18-year-olds (4 girls, 5 boys), and five 20–21-year-olds (1 girl, 4 boys). The IQ range in the original study was between 106 and 148; the IQ range of this group was 108 to 134.

Although an attempt was made to reach all 53 Ss in study 1 who had failed to meet the criterion, only 34 Ss were still available for interviewing in this follow-up study.

Procedure Each S was required to repeat parts 1 and 2 of the original experimental interview. Part 1 was identical with part 1 of the original interview, and functioned as a warmup. No one experienced difficulty with this part of the interview. The only change in part 2 was the inclusion of the optional sentences cited in study 1. This was done purely to make the interview, which was extremely brief, seem slightly longer. The criterion for demonstrating competence remained the same: correct responses to at least two out of three of the test sentences.

The interview was tape-recorded. Approximately one half the Ss received part A and one half part B. There was no difference between these two parts in the original study; this assignment was done only in order to replicate the conditions of the first study.

Results

In this sample of 34 Ss, 19 performed to criterion in response to the test sentences in part 2, and 15 failed to do so. These results, by age group, appear in Table 7.9. They give no basis for support of the hypothesis that Ss tested originally at ages 12–13 and under would be more likely to pick up the exceptional structure than would older Ss. It must be noted, however, that the group is quite small at each age. We have, however, not found any startling difference.

As found in the original study, the incorrect responses fall into one of two categories. The Ss would *tell* instead of *ask* (e.g., "use this cup") or they would phrase a question but use the wrong subject for the Wh-clause (e.g., "which pencil will you use?"), or echo the second part of the instruction sentence (e.g., "which to use?"), omitting the noun. The latter mode was used by only one S, a fifth grader.

Tell responses decreased with age, and the older Ss (eleventh grade to college) chose incorrect subjects for the Wh-clause exclusively. Of the 15 failures, seven were *tell* errors and eight were "wrong subject" errors. The distribution of types of errors duplicates the results in our original sample and in Chomsky's sample in that only the last three stages appear. Younger Ss make more third-stage errors (failing case 3) and older Ss make more fourth-stage errors (wrong subject for case 3).

In study 1, Ss tended to be highly consistent in their responses to the test instruction sentences. Out of the 15 Ss in study 2 who failed to reach criterion, 12 gave consistent responses throughout the series, and three gave inconsistent responses. If *Ss* switched responses, they tended to switch from the *you* (wrong subject error to the *tell* error (to regress from the fourth to the third stage), rather than from incorrect to correct responses. There were two *Ss* who switched spontaneously from incorrect to correct responses after the first test sentence, and one who did so on the third sentence. Of the first two *Ss*, one was a fifth grader who switched from "which book to read?" to the correct response, and the other a college student who went from "which book would you like to read?" to the correct response. Consistency of responses is generally high as in the first study. The IQs of those succeeding in study 2 are not different from those failing on the exceptional structure.

It appears that Ss over the age of 12 who failed to demonstrate competence succeeded in doing so 2 years later in about

Table 7.9. *N* successes and failures for each group on study 2

Age Group	*Successes* (N)		*Failures* (N)	*Total Tested/ Total Possible*[a]
College (20–21 yr)	3	(60)	2	5/7
Twelfth grade (17–18 yr)	4	(100)	0	4/8
Eleventh grade (16–17 yr)	3	(60)	2	5/8
Ninth grade (15 yr)	1	(25)	3	4/6
Seventh grade (12–13 yr)	5	(83)	1	6/10
Fifth grade (10–11 yr)	3	(30)	7	10/14
Total	19		15	34/53

Note.—Percentages of successes in parentheses.

[a] Total possible represents the number of failures from the original study; not all were able to be found this time.

the same proportion as those who were 12 or under at the original testing. It is not possible to perform any meaningful statistical analysis on the data due to the restrictions of the small N and the nonrandomness of the sample.

Discussion

The exceptional structure studied here is not the only complex structure with which young children have difficulty. It is clear from Carol Chomsky's work on some other exceptional structures that there are a series of such structures which have a cognitive complexity such that children over 6 are still acquiring competence.

We have found no solid evidence to confirm the hypothesis that acquisition of a structure is *more* likely for children of language-plastic ages. We have, however, some inkling from our Ss' statements during the second study that some older Ss who have mastered the exceptional structure after failure in the first study are not comfortably sure of themselves. One college student told us that she knew she had been wrong in the first study, had actively tried to figure it out, but that even now "I have to think about it; I'm never sure I've got it right." No child under 12 behaved as though the task was difficult, regardless of whether the child was competent or not. It seems possible that syntactic structures in one's native language that are learned late in life (after age 12) may be associated with longer latencies and may never be quite as automatic as structures learned earlier. We have only hints of this, but no firm evidence.

Kessel (1970) has recently reported that by 8 years of age all of his Ss were responding to "ask" and "tell" sentences (similar to those studied here) correctly. Kessel appears to believe his results are discrepant from both Chomsky's and ours because of differing linguistic task requirements in the two Boston as compared with his Minnesota studies. Unfortunately he has not been sufficiently aware of extraneous cues which could amply account for his results.

In both Chomsky's (1969) and our study an interview situation was used. The S had to decode a stimulus utterance in the absence of extralinguistic cues. Kessel objects to this method on the grounds that the stimulus utterance is an imperative, which may encourage a set to "tell." Therefore, Kessel used a picture-choice situation in which the child must decode a simple declarative utterance by choosing and explaining which of two pictures represents the utterance. Part 3 of our interview was very much like Kessel's. We finally discarded the results because of the ambiguities of interpretation. Every child offered us reasons for his choice of picture which were thoroughly reasonable on contextual, nonlinguistic grounds. We, therefore, concluded we were not testing any psycholinguistic hypothesis after all. Unfortunately, the introduction of pictures into a linguistic comprehension task raises two additional and interrelated problems.

First, on what basis does the child choose? When Kessel used the utterance "the girl asked the boy which pencil to sharpen," the child does not need to determine that the girl, and not the boy, will be doing the action (Chomsky's stage D vs. stage E). The S need only determine *who* is asking, and *who* is telling (stage B or C vs. stage D or E). If the child looks at the pictures, the girl is clearly asking in Kessel's picture where she is holding out the two pencils, and telling in the picture where she is pointing and the boy is holding the two pencils. Therefore, a child who fails to violate the MDP and chooses the wrong subject for the complement clause can still choose the correct picture if the child does not confuse "ask" and "tell." Supposedly, Kessel's two follow-up questions: (1) Why did you choose that one? (2) What is she (he) saying? should detect when a child is depending upon extralinguistic cues in the manner described above. However, in response to the first question, all the child need do is parrot the original stimulus utterance ("because the girl is asking the boy"), a feat which in no way demonstrates that S has the competence in question (as we found to our chagrin in part 4 of our experimental interview). Furthermore, in response to the second question, if the child has chosen correctly, the answer may be read from the picture. The girl has the pencils; therefore, she must be planning to sharpen one of them for herself. In short, the follow-up questions do not appear to yield unambiguous information concerning the linguistic or nonlinguistic basis of the child's initial choice.

Second, implicit in the preceding is that the reasons for correct or incorrect choice of pictures are not clearly separated out by Kessel. Stage C is characterized by the achievement of the semantic distinction between "ask" and "tell" for all but complex statements ("ask John what to do"). The simple statement ("ask John his name") does not require any violation of the MDP; moreover there is no need for the S to recover a deleted subject for his answer. It is somewhat surprising that Kessel's Ss so often failed this item.

Stage D is the point where the ask-tell distinction (semantic) extends to the complex sentence with the deleted subject: "ask John what to do." Stage-D Ss ask correctly, but they fail to violate the MDP ("John, what are you going to do?"). Thus, only at stage E do Ss have both the semantic distinction and the grammatical exception: "John, what should I do?"

Our impression is that Kessel has judged Ss giving stages B, C, and D answers as incompetent and only stage E as competent. This makes it altogether more curious that he gets so many competent 8-year-olds.

We believe that his Ss are making, for the most part, semantic distinctions about ask-tell, which stage-C children can do. Kessel's failure to distinguish clearly between the semantic and grammatical has blinded him to the role of nongrammatical cues in the child's picture choices. Thus, his high-scoring 8-year-olds may well be our stage-C children, with the ask-tell distinction available for the simple but not complex distinction. In that case, Chomsky's results and ours are not so discrepant from Kessel's. Future researchers should especially take note of the difficulties of making two picture-alternatives represent, on purely linguistic grounds, large numbers of reasonably grammatical constructions.

We have wondered how an adult fares without competence in these exceptional structures and have attended to real-life situations with adults who lacked some syntactic structure. It seems to us that adult speakers have enough redundancy in their everyday speech to cover up lack of competence. They may respond incorrectly but they often continue talking, thus providing the answer to the question posed. Adults rarely correct other adults' linguistic errors. Thus, once the information requested is given, the form of the response is rarely remarked upon. Language is for communication; the redundant answer "corrects" the linguistic error.

References

CHOMSKY, C. *The acquisition of syntax in children from five to ten.* Cambridge, Mass.: M.I.T. Press, 1969.

KESSEL, F. S. The role of syntax in children's comprehension from ages six to twelve. *Monographs of the Society for Research in Child Development,* 1970, *35* (6, Serial No. 139).

CHAPTER 7: SUGGESTED FURTHER READING

BAYLEY, N. Development of mental abilities. In Mussen, P. (Ed.) *Carmichael's Manual of Child Psychology*. Vol. 1. New York: Wiley, 1970. Pp. 1163–1209.

BERKO, J., and BROWN, R. Psycholinguistic research methods. In Mussen, P. *Handbook of Research Methods in Child Development*. New York: Wiley, 1960. Pp. 517–557.

BERLYNE, D. E. Children's reasoning and thinking. In Mussen, P. (Ed.) *Carmichael's Manual of Child Psychology*. Vol. 1. New York: Wiley, 1970. Pp. 939–981.

CHURCH, J. *Language and the Discovery of Reality*. New York: Random House, 1961.

ELKIND, D., and FLAVELL, J. *Studies in Cognitive Development*. New York: Oxford University Press, 1969.

ERVIN-TRIPP, S. Language development. In Hoffman, L. W. and Hoffman, M. L. (Eds.) *Review of Child Development Research*. Vol. 2. New York: Russell Sage Foundation, 1966. Pp. 55–105.

FLAVELL, J. H. Concept development. In Mussen, P. (Ed.) *Carmichael's Manual of Child Psychology*. Vol. 1. New York: Wiley, 1970. Pp. 983–1059.

HESS, R. D., and BEAR, R. D. (Eds.) *Early Education*. Chicago: Aldine, 1968.

HUNT, J. MCV. *Intelligence and Experience*. New York: Ronald Press, 1961.

KAGAN, J., and KOGAN, N. Individuality and cognitive performance. In Mussen, P. (Ed.) *Carmichael's Manual of Child Psychology*. Vol. 1. New York: Wiley, 1970. Pp. 1273–1365.

LENNEBERG, E. *New Directions in the Study of Language*. Cambridge, Mass.: M.I.T. Press, 1964.

MCNEILL, D. The development of language. In Mussen, P. (Ed.) *Carmichael's Manual of Child Psychology*. Vol. 1. New York: Wiley, 1970. Pp. 1061–1161.

———. *The Acquisition of Language*. New York: Harper & Row, 1970.

OPIE, I., and OPIE, P. *The Love and Language of Schoolchildren*. London: Oxford University Press, 1959.

REBELSKY, F., STARR, R., and LURIA, Z. Language development: The first four years. In Brackbill, Y. (Ed.) *Infancy and Early Childhood*. New York: Free Press, 1967. Pp. 289–357.

SIGEL, I. E., and HOOPER, F. H. (Eds.) *Logical Thinking in Children*. New York: Holt, Rinehart, and Winston, 1968.

STEVENSON, H. W. Learning in children. In Mussen, P. (Ed.) *Carmichael's Manual of Child Psychology*. Vol. 1. New York: Wiley, 1970. Pp. 849–938.

WEIR, R. *Language in the crib*,. The Hague: Mouton, 1966.

chapter eight possible application of knowledge

The basic data of every field have possible application in other areas. Psychology is one field where application seems almost probable and uncontrollable; but that is not the whole picture. Some of the areas to which our developmental knowledge can rightfully be applied are fields that more or less refuse to hear what we have to say. And in addition, in the easy application of partially understood material, the basic premise behind the research is often hidden. If we found that children learned math better while being beaten, we should not start beating children. Just because children can do certain things does not mean that they should be taught these things earlier and earlier. Our magazines and newspapers abound with examples of research cited and used poorly.

One of the areas to which psychology is readily applicable is education. Education is also an area with great resistance to change. For example, we know that labeling children as "smart," "average," and "dumb" (even though such labels may be bluebirds, sparrows, and robins) makes them behave in accordance with the label. We also know that heterogeneous groupings help all children in the class. Yet many schools still have a traditional tracking system, with children of the "same intellectual level" in the same class. Some schools have learned that all children are not equally proficient at all subjects, so they track differently for different subjects, but the kids are still tracked. How can a child learn about differences in people and learn to help others and be helped if all during the day he or she is with others like him or her? What happens to the teacher who knows that the class is "bright" or "dumb"? Does she become intellectually equivalent to the class? Does she like her job as much? One's attitude toward a job determines the way one behaves and this may be the most important feature in teaching–one has to like and respect the children in the class. In addition, it is not clear to us that we carry a certain amount of intelligence around in a bundle. Most of us recognize that we are smarter in certain situations, with certain people, at certain times of the day.

We know that children can't sit all day, and shouldn't have to, yet we ask them to do that in most schools. How many adults can sit for a minimum of two hours? Most college students dread the thought of a two- or three-hour class yet we expect first and second graders to sit from morning until afternoon with brief respites from the desk.

Education isn't the only area where ideas about children's development might lead to new practices. Few of the laws about children are based on a modern understanding of development. Children have few legal rights in our society. A parent can have a child "put away" for misbehaving–the "stubborn child" law still exists in some states. Persons under the age of eighteen or twenty-one have few legal resources open to them; often they are not allowed an attorney to represent them in juvenile court. A young offender may spend more time locked up for a crime than an older person accused of the same crime. Granted, the younger offender may not be locked up in an adult prison, but the institution in which incarceration takes place is almost equivalent. Children, as well as adults, have certain rights, and we are now beginning to be made aware of this. In addition, we are now more aware of the nature of children's understandings of right and wrong, and this information could be beneficially used by courts. Children may be our greatest resource, but they are presently often not receiving the care they need. Children can't be ignored or treated as third-class citizens during their youth and suddenly become responsible, caring adults. They must be responded to and cared for during youth. We know from much research that adult presence and support helps a child to ultimately become an independent person, yet many still believe that ignoring a child is what leads to independence. A whole new field of advocacy has recently been created to help adults stand up for children in situations where they cannot represent their needs adequately.

Our society in general has a long way to go in its concerns for children. The authors in this section reflect on some current problems and suggest ways that we might make healthy environments for children, and eventually for all people.

47. NOT SO GOLDEN RULE DAYS

JOHN HOLT

Our compulsory school attendance laws are an impediment to good education. They should be relaxed, amended, repealed, or overturned in the courts.

I once felt this was necessary in the interests of children. I now have come to feel equally strongly that it is also in the best interests of the schools. It is time for our schools to get themselves, or us to get them, out of the jail business. No one can doubt that this is where they are. The public has, in effect, said to our schools, "Lock up our children for six or more hours a day for a hundred and eighty or so days a year, so that they will be out of our hair and out of trouble—and, by the way, while you have them locked up, try to educate them." The two demands are contradictory and self-canceling. The schools can be in the jail business or in the education business, but not in both. To the extent that they are in the one they cannot be in the other.

There are many reasons why it would benefit our schools to get out of the jail business. One of these has to do with money. I have heard the assistant superintendent of schools in Baltimore, Maryland, describe the millions of dollars his system has to spend every year to repair broken windows and other kinds of vandalism. Who broke those windows? Who did the damage? Kids who hated being in school and therefore hated the school they were in. Vandalism by students is an act of revenge. Do away with the cause for hatred and the need for revenge, and the vandalism will stop. Teen-age youths do not walk the streets, except under the most exceptional circumstances, throwing stones through the windows of banks, hotels, drug stores. It is the schools they hate; it is the schools they try to destroy. Not long ago I heard a very intelligent and articulate young man in one of our major cities suggest, quite seriously, and altogether apart from any other kind of rioting, that all the schools in his community should be burned down simultaneously.

There is no way of estimating how much time, effort, and money the schools spend trying to find ways to take care of the many youngsters who do not want to be there. Countless special schools, special classes, special personnel, special disciplinary regulations, special therapeutic guidance, etc.—all exist almost solely to handle the problem of the child who hates being in school. It is also impossible to assess how much of the time and energy of teachers is taken up with the problem of controlling unruly prisoners.

The jail business is expensive in still another way. Since the schools have been given the job of keeping all our children in prison for a certain number of hours each day, it follows that they are responsible for seeing that the prisoners are in fact there, and if they are not there, why not, and where they are instead. This is a major source of the inordinate amount of paper work that plagues administrators and teachers alike. All the complicated attendance records that schools keep have one and only one purpose—to prove that all the prisoners were there or that they had a lawful excuse to be absent. If we overturn the compulsory attendance laws, all this will instantly disappear.

I see a great many students in the Boston Public Library. They behave as reasonably, sensibly, and considerately as anyone else. Nobody has ever even hinted that their behavior might be a problem. Why not? For one thing, when you are in a place because you want to be there, you tend to behave in an appropriate way. In the second place, the students know that if they raise hell in the library they will not be allowed to return. Nothing else need be said. The kind of monitors, spies, corridor-watchers, and so on who infest our schools—to say nothing of armed, uniformed police—are not found in libraries, even in the toughest parts of our cities. There is no need for them. If the school becomes a resource to be used by the people who want it, there will be no need for such policing there either.

But it is in the classroom itself that the jail business does the most harm. It wholly corrupts the relationship between the teacher and the student. It makes the teacher into a mixture of taskmaster and cop. It means that, however many smiles there may be, however much the teacher may enjoy his material and want to get it across to the children, his primary function must be, by methods however subtle, to threaten and coerce. In short it makes the schoolroom into a battleground. Nothing in the way of technological or other educational devices or gimmicks can do much to change this. The results are plain. People who go into teaching full of hope and good intentions gradually become used to thinking of themselves as policemen and of the children as their natural enemies. They become cynical about their teaching and helping functions and in many cases grow, in time, to hate and despise the children they are working with. This is not their fault, and very little can be done in the way of special training or selection to change it. It is no more possible to have open, friendly, and mutually helpful relationships between most teachers and students than it is between prison guards and prison convicts —and for exactly the same reasons. If, on the other hand, compulsory attendance were abolished, the relationship would be entirely different, for the teacher would not be a jailer, therefore not an enemy.

I have offered a number of reasons why I think compulsory school attendance is against the best interests of the schools; but I oppose it largely because I believe it is harmful and unfair to children. In speaking to many parent groups around the country, most of them in suburban areas where one might reasonably suppose the school systems to be among the best, I have heard more stories than I can remember about children being hurt and injured, and perhaps in important ways crippled, by their schools or their teachers. As a result, I have come to think that these laws are a most serious and fundamental violation of the civil liberties of the children and their parents. I believe they should be challenged—and perhaps can be overturned—on constitutional grounds.

I am aware that from time to time, in various parts of the country, parents have attempted to challenge the compulsory school attendance laws, usually with no success. These challenges have been made on rather different grounds from mine—not so much that what the school was doing was bad or harmful to the child but that the parents could do as well or better at home. To this essentially elitist argument the schools have countered, reasonably enough, that the school provides certain kinds of educational resources, among them the opportunity to come in contact with large numbers of other children, that cannot be provided in the home. Their case has been strong enough so that the courts have usually been willing to uphold it. The challenge I propose is different. I say that the schools have no right to demand a child's attendance unless they are in fact helping him, that the burden of proof is on them to show, at any time, that they are in fact helping, and that where they cannot show this or where, for whatever reasons, their effects on the child are negative rather than positive, they have no right to demand that he be there. In short, though it often talks and acts as though it was, school is not the Army. The historical and legal justification for schools has been that they are good for children, every child. We have not yet decided to have universal conscription for six-year-olds.

It is worth noting that when the compulsory attendance laws were enacted, they were rightly considered a pro- rather than anti-civil liberties measure. They were enacted to defend the right of children to an education against those adults who, in order to exploit their economic labor, would have denied it to them. The farmers and small shopkeepers and artisans of America, many of whom had not themselves had formal schooling, naturally preferred to have their children at work in the shop or mine or mill, or on the farm. The law was passed to prevent such exploitation. But times and customs have changed and the condition that the laws were passed to remedy no longer exists. There is no large market for the labor of young children; very few, if any, parents would want to keep their children home from school for economic reasons. The fact is that the only exploiters and destroyers of children today are the schools themselves.

What should the law say? It should say that if in the opinion of a child and his parents the school is doing him no good, or is indeed doing him harm, he should not be required to attend any more frequently than he wishes. There should be no burden of proof on the parents to show that they can provide facilities, companionship with other children, and all the other things the schools happen to provide. If Billy Smith hates school, and his parents feel that he is right in hating it, they are constitutionally entitled to relief. They are not obliged to demonstrate that they can give him a perfect education as against the bad one the school is giving him. It is a fundamental legal principle that if we can show that a wrong is being done, we are not compelled to say what ought to be done in its place before we are permitted to insist that it be stopped.

I know many children who find school hateful and intolerable who might discover that it was not only bearable but interesting if they were not obliged to be there every day. Even those who hate school most do not want to be away from it all the time. After all it is where their friends are and where the action is. Many who cannot stand five days a week might actually enjoy two or three and get more education and more satisfaction than they now get out of the five.

Anyone who knows anything about schools—including almost all students—recognizes that children who use any substantial part of their intelligence and energy can do in two days or less what schools ask them to do in five. If the law said that children could go to school only as much as they wanted, they would be able in non-school time to undertake a great many serious projects for which they now have no time. It is worth noting that the eleven-year-old Rumanian girl who was the favorite of the crowd at the Olympic figure-skating championships at Grenoble last winter does all her studying at home. I find it both interesting and sad that a Communist dictatorship should allow at least one of its children a freedom to learn that the supposedly free United States will not.

My proposal raises some thorny questions for which I do not have all the answers. What about situations in which the child and his parents do not agree about the worth or harmfulness of the school? I would say that if a child wants to go to school, and his parents do not want him to, his wish should prevail over theirs. If, on the other hand, the situation is reversed, the question is more difficult, but I would tend to put the child's wishes first. This runs counter to the generally accepted and generally reasonable notion that the parents are the proper directors of a young child's life. However, I agree with Edgar Friedenberg that it is both a serious mistake and a grave injustice for our young people to have no inalienable rights of their own, with the possible exception of the right to life. (I say "possible" because I have read that there are some states in which a school may kill a child while administering "corporal punishment" without incurring any legal penalty.)

I doubt that any state legislature at the moment can be persuaded to modify the school attendance laws. I suspect that most parents value the babysitting or jailing function of the school, and that any attempt to change the laws would meet with a good deal of opposition. I think, therefore, that they must be challenged in the courts, and on the constitutional libertarian grounds that I have suggested.

I do not want to imply, however, that unless and until the courts overturn these laws, nothing can be done. One example may be cited: A nine-year-old child who attends the leading elementary school in a fairly civilized community came home in tears one day. From her first day in school this girl has been a model student. On this particular day she had had a substitute teacher in her class. She had finished a piece of assigned "seatwork" and, having nothing else to do, drew a picture of a rabbit on a small piece of paper. The teacher stole up behind her, saw the drawing, and, without warning, snatched the paper and pencil away, crumpled up the paper, threw both pencil and paper against the wall, and at the top of her voice said, "If I catch you drawing another picture in class, I am going to make you write 'I shall not draw pictures in class' until your hand hurts!" The child's mother, when she heard this story after school, was furious. She called up the principal, described what had happened, and then said that although she understood why it might not be possible for him to fire the substitute teacher, she would not return her child to the class as long as this teacher was there. The decision of the principal was to ignore the absence of the child—and in my view this was the wise decision. In other words, a policy of resistance to the school attendance laws can acheive some results, even before the courts formally repeal or overturn them.

48. CHAPTER TWO FROM *DEATH AT AN EARLY AGE*

JONATHAN KOZOL

Many people in Boston are surprised, even to this day, to be told that children are beaten with thin bamboo whips within the cellars of our public schools and that they are whipped at times for no greater offense than for failing to show respect to the very same teachers who have been describing them as niggers. Some rules exist about these whippings and a number of public statements have been made by the school administration in their defense. Some of the rules and some of the public statements are in themselves revelatory of the attitudes which still prevail within the system. One of the present School Committee members, Mr. Thomas Eisenstadt, has made the following remarks in regard to the use of the rattan:

> The conditions . . . under which it may be employed are very explicit; for example, a written report must be made and kept on file in the principal's office stating the reason for

using the rattan. Also a witness must be present when the rattan is administered, and the name of the said witness must be recorded in the principal's report. Since I have been a member of the School Committee, and that has been over three and one-half years, not one instance of abuse of this prerogative by a teacher or by anyone else has been brought to my attention. The rattan is used conservatively and not indiscriminately.[1]

Another statement on the subject is that given to a Boston newspaper by Miss Marguerite Sullivan, until recently the Deputy Superintendent for elementary schools in Boston. "She noted that the extent of the rattanning is usually limited to three blows on the hand: 'And the child is never held by the teacher. If he won't put out his hand, the matter is taken up with the parents.'"[2]

The Boston Teachers' Handbook also contains these rules: "Corporal punishment shall not be inflicted when it might aggravate an existing physical impairment or produce or threaten to produce permanent or lasting injury. . . . Violent shaking or other gross indignities are expressly forbidden. Cases of corporal punishment shall be reported by each teacher on the dates of their occurrence in writing. . . . These reports shall state the name of the pupil, the name of the witness, the amount of punishment, and the reason therefore . . ."[3]

These stipulations are daydreams to anyone who knows certain of the Boston schools. Whippings were frequently given at my school without a witness present. Cards were commonly not filed, if for no other reason than that this task alone would have taken some of the teachers several hours. Students were repeatedly grabbed, shaken and insulted. Parents were rarely notified. And at least one child in my school was whipped in such a way as to leave on his hand a physical impairment in the form of a large raised scar which may be with him all his life. I know this boy well, for he was a student in my room. His name is Frederick. When I first noticed the curious protrusion that rose up near the end of his finger, I asked him about it immediately and he explained it in these words:

"It happened in September before you were my teacher. I was talking and I was sent down to the cellar and when I got the stick I was scared and I must have pulled back my hand a little so I got it on the knuckle instead of on the finger part. I already had a bad infection. They said it was my fault for not keeping my hand still."

It is never simple to accept the idea that these things happen. It came to me that the only conceivable way in which this sort of thing might go unnoticed in a civilized city in the middle of the 1960's would be if the boy had been too terrified to report what had happened to any grown-up outside school, or if that grown-up in turn were too scared to pass it on to anybody else. This was not the case. As Frederick reported it to me, he had indeed told someone. He told his mother. His mother, with whom I have confirmed the remaining details, did not do anything until evening but then became greatly alarmed when she saw the infected knuckle swelling up into the size of a small ball. She took her child to a doctor. Nothing had been exaggerated. The finger was in a highly inflamed state. The boy was not merely treated at City Hospital but it was felt necessary by the doctor that he be put into the hospital for a period that lasted several days. Frederick's medical records afford confirmation of this injury although of course the records do not make any mention of the whipping.

When I spoke to Frederick's mother, I

---

[1] Statement of Thomas Eisenstadt presented to Boston parents and press, July 28, 1965.

[2] Marguerite Sullivan quoted in Boston *Globe*, Oct. 4, 1964.

[3] Boston "Teachers' Handbook," School Document Number One, 1961. See pages 18 and 19 [of the Handbook].

asked her whether she had gone up to school to demand an explanation. She told me that she had but that she had not gotten further than the Art Teacher. Frederick had been in art class at the time the trouble started; she believed, therefore, that the Art Teacher would be the one to know about it. This turned out to be so. The Art Teacher did know about it. She knew what had happened, and she knew that the boy had been hurt badly and she even knew that he had been subsequently hospitalized, and she did not deny any of it. What she did do, however, was to tell the mother that there was no reason to be angry or to pursue the matter further, for she had, she said, already checked with the male teacher who had given the rattanning and had found out that he had "done the whipping right." I wondered whether she felt this could in any way justify the injury or whether she believed that it could in any way provide exoneration either for herself, as the teacher in charge of the child, or for the man who did the whipping. Because it was done right, according to a rule, did that mean it was permissible? It reminded me of the way that many people in wartime Germany had exonerated themselves for their participation in the deaths of Jewish people on the grounds that what they had done had been done correctly. The truth, of course, in this instance, is that the whipping *hadn't* been done correctly. The rules had not been followed, or else a child with an infected finger would not have been beaten. And possibly the Art Teacher knew this and may have had some doubts about it. For she followed through with an act which suggests that she may have had some later worries. The mother of the child has shown me a handsome card that her son received while he was recuperating from his whipping in the hospital. The card is a get-well card and it is signed with a flourishing hand: *"To Frederick. Get well soon and come back to school again! With Love, from your Art Teacher."* Underneath that, she has signed her name. The envelope bears the address of City Hospital.

It seems to me too simple to call the Art Teacher a blatant hypocrite for sending this message, although the thought occurred to me when I read it. I think that she was no more a hypocrite to send him that card than I was a hypocrite to chat with her in a friendly way day after day after I knew all of these things, or to go out and have a friendly beer and shake hands warmly with the pleasant casual man who did the whipping. All white people, I think, are implicated in these things so long as we participate in America in a normal way and attempt to go on leading normal lives while any one race is being cheated and tormented. But now I believe that we probably will go on leading our normal lives, and will go on participating in our nation in a normal way, unless there comes a time when Negroes can compel us by methods of extraordinary pressure to interrupt our pleasure.

To whip a normal child and scar his fingers seems bad enough, but to whip an emotionally disturbed child and to devastate his heart and mind is to go a step further. This happened also in my school building. There were two children to whom it happened in my immediate knowledge. One was Stephen. I don't know how many times he underwent those whippings and I am certain that whatever records exist at school would not be accurate. Unquestionably it happened for a while as often as once every month and probably more often, probably closer to once or twice a week. It happened, I noticed, very often when the class was having math instruction, and this, I came to believe, was closely connected to the nature of the feelings that the Math Teacher at our school tended to show toward kids like Stephen. I ought to explain briefly, although it will become more apparent in the sections that come later, that our school was loaded with a certain number of experts in different subject areas, for art, for math, for reading; and the reason for this was that we were participating in the Boston version of a compensatory education program for Negro children. The compensation involved was of a questionable nature, in fact, and when our city lost the prospect of obtaining two million dollars in federal aid for compensatory education, the reason given was that the federal government just did not consider Boston's program to be providing any kind of legitimate compensation. But even if the program had itself been a wise and splendid one, the experts who arrived on the scene, or who were drafted to serve in it, would have compromised it anyway.

Among the various experts with whom I found that I must deal, and under whose general authority I worked, were such people as the Art and the Math and the Reading Teachers. Each of the latter two came into my classroom for a particular part of every morning, the Art Teacher twice weekly. During these periods I was either to observe or else to go out and do remedial work with other classes. In this way, it was imagined that a novice teacher would learn from the old-timers. In the case of the Mathematics Teacher, in the same way as with the Art Teacher—although—I cannot say that I learned anything at all except how to suppress and pulverize any sparks of humanity or independence or originality in children. What I learned from them specifically of the techniques of teaching I have had to do my best to unlearn since. The Math Teacher, like the Art Teacher, did not seem very fond of Stephen. She told me so freely on more than one occasion. Yet she was also very much aware of his mental instability and it was she, rather than I, who was the first to come out in the open and speak of him as a child who was not well.

I remember the day that she told me this, snapping it out with sureness: "The child's not in his right mind." I asked her, when she said this, if she had thought of helping him into any kind of treatment. This was a mistake, however, for it developed that the Math Teacher was not at all keen about psychiatry. When I asked about treatment for Stephen, she answered only that she had not thought of it but that, now that I mentioned it, she was going to have to admit that she could not go along. When I asked her why, her answer to me was that "he would just lie and tell the psychiatrists that we weren't kind to him. He'd tell them that we were all prejudiced up here." Within days, Stephen was sent to the cellar for another rattanning and the comment of the Math Teacher, with no sense of incongruity or injustice, was, again, that he was "not in his right mind." Others in the school made similar statements about Stephen. The Assistant Principal, a man who was generally kind and—within the context of this school—relatively enlightened, told me almost exactly the same thing. The man was aware of the situation, as were many people. Nothing was done about it, however, and Stephen continued to get whippings. Nor did I do anything myself. I am afraid that many people may not wish to believe that these were real whippings, or that they honestly scared a child, or that they actually involved substantial pain. If this is the case, then I would like to describe what Stephen was like and how he seemed and behaved when he went downstairs to take his beating.

I have said how little he was. Sixty pounds isn't very heavy. He was skinny, with tiny arms, and he couldn't have been more than four feet tall. He had light-brown skin and a Red Sox baseball jersey. He had terrified tiny little hopeless eyes. He had on corduroy pants, which were baggy. He had on basketball sneakers which looked a few sizes too large. His hair had oil on it and had been shaved down almost to the scalp. He was standing near the men's smoke-room. Up above were the pipes of the cellar ceiling. Nearby was the door to the basement boys' toilet. Out of that doorway urine stank. He looked at the floor. He wouldn't look up. He wouldn't let his eyes depart from one chosen spot. His elbows froze at his sides. The teacher who administered the whipping gave the order to hold out his hands. He wouldn't answer. He was the image of someone in torture. Again the teacher, standing above him, passed down the order. He wouldn't do it. The teacher, now losing his patience, ordered it a third time. And still he wouldn't answer or comply. A fourth time. Yet still this frozen terror. So the decision is made: He will get it twice as many times. The stink still from the toilet. Comment from a passing teacher: "The little bastards don't mind acting up but when it's time for them to take their punishment they suddenly lose all their nerve." He can't hold out forever. And finally he gives in. He breaks down and stops resisting. Hands out. He gets the beating.

The teacher who gives the beating may, in all other instances, seem a decent man. Moreover, even in giving this beating, he may do it absolutely as he is supposed to and in every little detail by the rules. Yet —well done or not, and whatever the man's intent—the tears still come and the welts still are formed upon the light-brown hand. The stick is flexible, light and quick and it must hurt badly or else those winces of screwed-up agony and those tears are an incredibly good act. As for the teacher, in most cases, he behaves with a sense of sobriety. Most teachers do not treat the matter lightly. On the other hand, there are always a couple of teachers (there were some in my school and there are many elsewhere) who will speak about a rattanning in a manner of cynicism and humor and open cruelty and who will not hesitate to intersperse their talk with some pretty straightforward remarks. There are also male teachers who, in the very act of giving a whipping, cannot prevent themselves from manifesting a really unmistakable kind of satisfaction. In my own school and elsewhere I have heard any number of proud and boastful statements about the kind of pain that you can get across.

"When you do it, you want to snap it abruptly or else you are not going to get the kind of effect you want."

"Leave it over-night in vinegar or water if you want it to really sting the hands."

I asked, soon after I had started teaching and observing the acts of other teachers, whether it was within the rules to strike a child or whether that was against the law.

"Don't worry about the law. You just make damn sure that no one's watching."

Other counsel: "Don't let them get too close to you. No matter how you feel. The ones you help the most are the first ones who will axe you in the back."

From a teacher at my school: "The ones I can't stand are the goddamn *little* buggers. The First Graders. And the Second Graders. There's nothing you can do to them—you can't even lift up your goddamn hand."

In special regard to a child like Stephen, one question remains and still poses itself repeatedly: Why would *any* teacher, whatever his bent or inclination, just go ahead and whip a boy whom he knows it will not in any way help or correct for something which that teacher has already acknowledged, both to himself and to others, to be beyond the child's ability to prevent? The beginning of one answer may be found in the fact that segregated schools seem often to require this kind of brutal discipline because of the uneasy feelings which are so often present. The children, enough of them anyway, are quietly smoldering with a generally unimagined awareness of their own degradation. The atmosphere that grows out of this may be one of real danger to the equanimity of a teacher or administrator. I am sure this is one reason at least why discipline comes so fast and so strong and, at times, so unjustly. Possibly, in the case of some of the best teachers, this was the entire story. Thinking of some of the other teachers, however, I am convinced that there was also at times something else happening and once you had seen it in action, and watched it, you would know exactly what it was and would never deny that it was there. You would have to have watched certain people doing it, and to have seen their eyes, to have any idea of what was going on.

"This hurts me," says the old expression, "more than it hurts you." Yet this is said easily and it is just not always so. Sadism has its signs and they are unmistakable. There are moments when the visible glint of gratification becomes undeniable in the white teacher's eyes. Would any teacher be able to say with absolute certainty that he has not sometimes taken pleasure in that slash of the rattan and that he has not felt at times an almost masculine fortification out of the solemnity and quietude and even authoritive control and "decency" with which he struck the child? I have watched a teacher giving the rattan with a look on his face which was certainly the very opposite of abhorrence, and I have heard a teacher speak of it as if it were somehow a physical accomplishment or even some kind of military feat. I am sure that teachers as a class are no more sadistic than any other people, and possibly in this the teachers in Boston are no worse than the teachers anywhere else. But many human beings do take pleasure in inflicting pain on others, and those who have the least to be proud of or to be happy about are often the ones who take that pleasure most.

Sometimes the argument is put forward by white Bostonians that corporal punishment did not begin with Negro children and that it is, in fact, a very old tradition within our public schools. I have never found this a convincing argument. The fact that a crime might have been committed with impunity in the past may make it seem more familiar and less gruesome to certain people but surely it does not give it any greater legality. And the fact that some boys may have been whipped unjustly fifty years ago does not make that injustice more palatable today. Whatever it was once, it just seems wrong in its present context. It does not matter whether it was done once by Yankees to Irish children. And it does not matter, either, if it was done once by Irish to Jews. What does matter is that today it is being used by whites on Negroes and that it is being used in too many cases to act out, on a number of persuasive pretexts, a deeply seated racial hate. If you hear of just any tough teen-ager being beaten on the fingers by his teacher you can assume that a school offcial someplace is going to be able to pass it off as discipline. But when you hear of a sixty-pound mentally ill Fourth Grader being guarded by two men and whipped by a third for acts that are manifestly crazy, and when the teacher who prepares the punishment is not only gleaming with excitement but has, not ten days before, been speaking calmly of the niggers Down South or the little bastards causing trouble up there in room four, then it seems to me that anyone, including the administrator of such a system, is going to have to admit that something has gone wrong. A School Committee member, as I have shown, has put it into the public record that he has never yet heard of a case of the abuse of corporal punishment in the Boston Public Schools. I think that he and all others who share responsibility for these matters ought to recognize quite clearly that they are hearing of one now.

49. WHO CARES FOR AMERICA'S CHILDREN?

URIE BRONFENBRENNER

I shall be short, but not very sweet. America's families and their children are in trouble. Trouble so deep and pervasive as to threaten the future of our nation. The source of the trouble is nothing less than a national neglect of children, and of those primarily engaged in their care; and neglect of America's parents.

We like to think of America as a child-centered society, but our actions belie our words. A hard look at our institutions and ways of life reveals that our national priorities lie elsewhere. The pursuit of affluence, the worship of material things, the hard sell and the soft; the willingness to accept technology as a substitute for human relationships; the imposition of responsibility upon families without support, and the readiness to blame the victims of evil for the evil itself, have brought us to the point where a broken television set or a broken computer provokes more indignation and more action than a broken family or a broken child.

Our national rhetoric not withstanding, the actual patterns of life in America are such that children and families come last. Our society expects its citizens first of all to meet the demands of their jobs, and then to fulfill civic and social obligations. Responsibilities to children are to be met, of course, but this is something one is expected to do in his spare time.

But when, where and how? In today's world, parents find themselves at the mercy of a society which imposes pressures and priorities that allow neither time nor place for meaningful activities and relations between children and adults, which downgrade the role of parent and the functions of parenthood, and which prevent the parent from doing the things he wants to do as a guide, friend and companion to his children.

The frustrations are greatest for the family of poverty, where the capacity for human response is crippled by hunger, cold, filth, sickness and despair. No parent who spends his days in search of menial work and his nights in keeping rats away from the crib can be expected to find the time, let alone the heart, to engage in constructive activities with his children or serve as a stable source of love and discipline. The fact that some families in poverty do manage to do this is a tribute to them, but not to the society or community in which they live.

For families who can get along, the rats are gone but the rat race remains. The demands of a job, or often two jobs, which claim mealtimes, evenings and weekends as well as days; the trips and moves one must make to get ahead or simply hold one's own; the ever increasing time spent in commuting; the parties, the evenings out, the social and community obligations; all of the things one has to do if he is to meet his primary responsibilities produce a situation in which a child often spends more time with a passive babysitter than with a participating parent or adult.

Even when the parent is at home, a compelling force cuts off communication and response among family members. Although television could, if used creatively, enrich the activities of children and families, it now only undermines them. Like the sorcerer of old, the television set casts its magic spell, freezing speech and action, turning the living into silent statues so long as the enchantment lasts. The primary danger of the television screen lies not so much in the behavior it produces—although there is danger there—as in the behavior it prevents; the talks, the games, the family festivities and arguments through which much of the child's learning takes place and through which his character is formed. Turning on the television set can turn off the process that transforms children into people.

In our modern way of life it is not only parents of whom children are deprived, it is people in general. A host of factors conspire to isolate children from the rest of society: the fragmentation of the extended family, the separation of residential and business areas, the disappearance of neighborhoods, the elimination of small stores in favor of supermarkets, zoning ordinances, occupational mobility, child labor laws, the abolishment of the apprentice system, consolidated schools, television, telephones, the substitution of the automobile for public transportation or just plain walking, separate patterns of social life for different age groups, the working mother, the delegation of child care to specialists; all these manifestations of progress operate to decrease opportunity and incentive for meaningful contact between children and persons older or younger than themselves.

And here we confront a fundamental and disturbing fact: *Children need people in order to become human.* The fact is fundamental because it is firmly grounded both in scientific research and in human experience. It is disturbing because the isolation of children from adults simultaneously threatens the growth of the individual and the survival of the society. The young cannot pull themselves up by their own bootstraps. It is primarily through observing, playing and working with others older and younger than himself that a child discovers both what he can do, and who he can become, that he develops both his ability and his identity. It is primarily through exposure and interaction with adults and children of different ages that a child acquires new interests and skills, and learns the meaning of tolerance, cooperation and compassion.

Hence, to relegate children to a world of their own is to deprive them of their humanity and to deprive ourselves of humanity as well. Yet, this is what is happening in America today. We are experiencing a breakdown in the process of making human beings human. By isolating our children from the rest of society, we abandon them to a world devoid of adults and ruled by the destructive impulses and compelling pressures, both of the age segregated peer group and the aggressive and exploitive television screen. By setting our priorities elsewhere and by putting children and families last, by claiming one set of values while pursuing another, we leave our children bereft of standards and support, and our own lives impoverished and corrupted.

This reversal of priorities, which amounts to a betrayal of our children, underlies the growing disillusionment and alienation among young people in all segments of American society. Those who grew up in settings where children, families, neighborhoods and communities still counted are able to act out their frustration in positive ways through constructive protest, through participation and through public service. Those who come from circumstances in which the family, the neighborhood and the community could not function—be it in slum or suburb—can only strike out against an environment they have experienced as indifferent, callous, cruel and unresponsive. One cannot condone the destruction and violence manifested by young people in widely disparate and desperate parts of our society. But one can point to the roots of a process which if not reversed will continue to spread.

The failure to reorder our priorities, the insistence on business as usual, and the continued reliance on rhetoric as a substitute for radical reforms can have only one result: the far more rapid and pervasive growth of alienation, apathy, drugs, delinquency and violence among the young and among the not so young in all segments of our national life. We face the prospect of a society which resents its own children and fears its youth.

What is needed is a change in our patterns of living which will once again bring people back into the lives of children, and children back into the lives of people. But how? The verse in Isaiah says, "a little child shall lead them." I propose we act upon that text. But perhaps to do so one must speak not in the language of Isaiah, but in the language of our contemporary times.

What I am proposing is the seduction of America by its children. What do I mean? Let me give you some examples, concrete actions we could take at all levels in our society: business, industry, mass media, communities, local, state and Federal governments, right down to the local neighborhood; concrete actions that would have the effect of bringing people back into the lives of children, and back into the lives of people.

One of these suggested actions comes from the U.S.S.R., which is not the only country that does this; it's also done in Scandinavia. This is the custom for which there's no English word, so I've used the word "adoption," in which a business or an industry adopts a group of children or a children's program with the aim of becoming friends, of acquainting children with the people who work in the world of work.

My colleague in the Forum Planning Committee, Dr. David Goslin of the Russell Sage Foundation, decided to Americanize this idea, because he felt, as I do, that the values are human rather than parochial. He persuaded the *Detroit Free Press* to try an experiment. Recently that newspaper saw in its composing room, press room, dispatch room, city room and other offices, young children 12 years of age from two schools in the city of Detroit. It was a fascinating thing to watch.

When we first talked to the people at the *Free Press* they said, "Gee! kids? You know we're a newspaper here. What will we do with them, sit there all day and watch them? Besides, you know this is a busy place." As one lady in the advertising section said to me, "Professor, you mean you're going to have kids around here—you really mean that?"

On the last day, that same lady said to me, "Professor, it's going to be so lonely here next week—those kids are easier to talk to than people." They were from two schools, one in a slum area, the other in a middle-class area, both black and white. The children were just themselves. They said things like, "This is a place to meet, a way to understand people." "If every kid in Detroit and all around the United States got to do this, I don't think there would be so many problems in the world." It was a two-way street that came alive there. People rediscovered children, and children rediscovered people.

Other Actions Can Be Taken

Another idea is the notion of encouraging business and industry to place day care centers in or near the place of business—not as the only location for day care and preschool centers, but as one of the options available to parents, so that during the coffee breaks and during the lunch hours, people could visit the kids. Perhaps then children would once again become a subject of conversation in places where children don't get talked about as much as they used to.

We are about to propose that every moderately sized place of business or branch of a business in the country establish a Commission on Children to ask how the policies and practices of that business affect the lives of their employees and their children as family members. On such a commission, obviously the employees as well as the management and the union should participate.

We recommend that business explore and maximize half-time and part-time jobs for comparable rates of pay and status so that those parents who choose to work part-time may do so, instead of having to make the choice between full-time work or full-time no work, or part-time work at a reduced rate of pay, reduced status and reduced job security. We're talking about flexible work schedules so that parents can be at home when the kids arrive at home.

We emphasize especially family-oriented industrial planning and development: so that when plants are established, locations are determined and housing is planned, consideration is given to the fact that employees have families and have to be concerned with how and where they can spend time as families. It should be kept in mind in planning the buildings, the apartments and residences that there will be children and parents living in these places. In short, we are asking for a family-oriented business and industrial policy in America. We speak also of actions to be taken in the realm of the mass media and the advertising industry.

We ask that urgent attention be paid to the creation of an entirely new kind of television programming, one which no longer casts the viewer in the role of a passive and isolated bystander, but which instead involves family members and neighbors in activities with each other. That is, involving children, adults, older kids, younger kids and grandparents in games, conversations and joint creative activity. And we assert that there is nothing inherent in television technology which precludes this kind of possibility.

The community, of course, is the family of families. And it is there, perhaps, more than anywhere else that the family needs support. Because the thesis I am presenting to you is that just as children cannot function unless they have healthy and human parents and caretakers to deal with them, so these caretakers, parents and all those who carry the responsibility for children in our society need the support of the community and of the society in order for them to be able to function effectively in their roles. It is not the family that's breaking down, it is not the staff of people engaged in work with children that is breaking down, it is the support in the society for the family and for those who are faced with the responsibility and the delight of raising a new generation of human beings that is being withdrawn.

There are many other measures we are considering. I will mention one or two, in relation to the schools. We point out the sterility of courses in parent education for junior and senior high school, where there are no children in evidence. We suggest that preschool programs and Head Start centers be located in or near school programs, that school curricula utilize these as learning opportunities and opportunities for responsibility. Then the older children get some notion of what a child is like, what a child's needs are and how much fun a child is, so we do not have a generation of young people who don't discover what a child is until they have one.

These are new kinds of suggestions. They bring difficulties, but they also bring promise. They bring a very important element into the lives of older school-aged children. If one looks at the problems of human development cross-culturally, as I've been privileged to do during this past decade, one is struck by the fact that American society is characterized by the inutility of children. We in our own country do not give children anything really important to do. We give them duties, not responsibilities. And yet, there are things they could do if we but looked around.

One of the most important responsibilities that the older child can have, both as an individual and as a group, is responsibility for the young. Evidence indicates that older children are very effective as models, as re-enforcers, as praise-givers to the young, but in our age-segregated society such opportunities are seldom given.

Oldsters Offer Vital Assistance

Similarly, there is another group for whom children can be a delight and a genuine help, and who in turn can serve a very important purpose in providing a humanizing experience for children. I refer to older people. The pleasure which a child gets from recognizing how much he's appreciated by an older person is a special kind of pleasure on both sides.

It's perhaps paradoxical that in our discussions and preparation for the White House Conference on a forum which is to deal with children and families, we make very few recommendations to families. Our position is essentially this: that given sun, soil, air and water, a plant does not need to be told how to grow. If America's parents, and those bearing the responsibility for the upbringing of the young, are given the place and the power and the prestige, to enable them to function as guides, companions and sources of love and discipline for children; and to have a decisive role in determining the environments and programs in which our children live and grow, the great majority of these parents and these professional workers will be able to take full advantage of that opportunity to enhance the quality of life both for children and for the nation.

There is but one caution to be borne in mind. The crucial factor, of course, is not how much time is spent with a child, but how the time is spent. A child learns, he becomes human, primarily through participation in challenging activity with those whom he loves and admires. It is the example, challenge and re-enforcement provided by people who care that enable a child to develop both his ability and his identity. An everyday example of the operation of this principle is the mother who daily talks with her young child and, usually without thinking much about it, responds more warmly when he uses new words or expressions or new motions. And as he does so, she gradually introduces new and more complex activities in her activity with the child.

So it is this way, in work and in play with children: in games, in projects, in shared responsibilities with parents, adults and older children, that the child develops the skills, motives and qualities of character that enable him to live a life that is gratifying both to himself and to those around him. But this can happen only in a society that lets it happen, and makes it happen, a society in which the needs of families and children become a primary concern, not merely of special organizations and interest groups, but of all the major institutions—government, industry, business, mass media, communities, neighborhoods and individual citizens.

It is the priorities that they set that will determine our children's present and America's future.

50. THE RIGHTS OF CHILDREN

LOIS G. FORER

I am delighted to have the opportunity to discuss the problems of the child and the law with those responsible for the education of young children. We have assumed that adults spoke for children, protected them, provided for them and disciplined them. If the system failed in any way, then the adults would take action. A child, in the words of the court, had "no right to liberty, only to custody." Even the word "custody" has a nonhuman connotation. The law defines custody as "the care or keeping of anything."

We know that simply the keeping of a child in a home or a classroom is not enough. We have been warehousing children in institutions (including schools) long enough. It is time to look at children as persons—individuals with rights, dignities, needs and separate individualities.

In considering this important area of the rights of children, educators, physicians and interested citizens often look to the lawyer in vain.

"What are the rights of children? What is the law?" These questions are being asked by nonlawyers with increasing frequency.

What Law?

The lawyer who is asked this question may well reply, "What law?" It is an anomalous and incredible fact that there is very little case and statutory law setting forth the rights of children. Although the United States Supreme Court passes on some 2,500 cases a year and decides on the merits of approximately 400 cases a year, it was not until 177 years after the founding of this nation that the court ruled on a case raising the constitutional rights of a child. The much discussed *Gault* case (337 U.S. 1), which was decided the following year, 1967, was limited to four procedural points in delinquency hearings in juvenile court. Even these rulings are hedged with limitations. The decision did, however, signal a radical change in jurisprudential theory. Contrary to the prior state cases and the views of the many authorities on the juvenile court, the *Gault* decision indicates that children do have some constitutional rights. The extent and limits of those rights have not been clarified.

Thoughtful persons who deal with the minds and bodies of children are deeply disturbed by many difficult and sensitive decisions affecting the lives of children that they are required to make, and they seek legal guidance. There are few clear legal answers to their questions. To date the legal profession appears to be oblivious of the vast unchartered area of legal problems involving the lives of children.

It is interesting to speculate on the reasons for this legal vacuum. Almost half of all Americans are under the age of 21. In our highly structured, complex society, many agencies of government take actions affecting children's lives, often with drastic results. Yet there are few cases challenging such actions or alleging that the constitutional rights of the child have been infringed. Other issues of limited importance and involving comparatively few people have been before the courts again and again and have been the subjects of exhaustive scholarship.

Probably there are many psychological and sociological reasons for the law's neglect of the rights of children. In America's youth-oriented society, adults may have ambivalent feelings toward children. Today a child is an economic liability. He is no longer a source of cheap or unpaid labor on the farm or in the family business. Few parents can look forward to being supported by their children in old age. Campus unrest and the growing juvenile delinquency rate provoke cries of "Get tough!" Such conditions do not give rise to a concern for the rights of young people.

A simpler explanation for the scarcity of law involving the rights of children is the fact that very few children have been represented by counsel. Most of the children in institutions, whether for the delinquent, the neglected or the mentally ill, are indigent. Prior to the *Gault* decision, it was considered inappropriate, if not unauthorized, for counsel to appear in juvenile delinquency proceedings. Conferences are held on the subject, "What is the role of a lawyer in Juvenile Court?" There is still the subconscious assumption that a lawyer should not function like a lawyer in Juvenile Court. In innumerable other situations in which children's welfare and liberty are involved, there is no requirement that the matter be judicially determined or that children have counsel. In many proceedings affecting the lives of children, they are not now represented by counsel—for example, neglect and dependency cases which may result in the child being institutionalized. The battered baby has no one to speak for him while the parents or foster parents who have abused him are represented by counsel, often at public expense. No provision is made to furnish lawyers for these children. Without counsel, there are seldom appeals or written opinions that would form the basic materials for legal scholarship. Consequently, there is little research or analysis of these problems.

The principal legislation governing children is the Juvenile Court Act. Every state has by statute established a special court to handle cases of neglect, dependent and delinquent children. The primary purpose of such legislation and the principal activity of these courts is the processing of children whose behavior is disruptive to the community, the schools or their families. With minor variations these acts create courts with broad powers and loose procedures. Nowhere in the standard juvenile court law or the new Model Juvenile Court Act are there any specifications of the rights of a child or the procedures that he may invoke for his protection or to obtain redress for wrongs done to him. These wrongs may be mistreatment by parents or custodians, the school system, the police, the welfare department, or others. The laws governing the treatment of animals are more specific than those with respect to children.

A Blank Slate Is at Least a Clean Slate

Since there is so little precedent, we are in the unusual position of being able to consider what the law ought to be. Social reformers often engage in Utopian speculations about restructuring society, the family or government. Lawyers frequently err in the other extreme by presenting a legislative package that deals with specific abuses but fails to consider basic injustices structured in the larger system. This paper tries to avoid both pitfalls. Although urging those concerned with the problem of children to give their attention to the wide range of legal issues involving the rights of minors, it seeks primarily to ask questions, explore concepts and suggest avenues of inquiry.

Legal rights do not exist separate and apart from daily life. Constitutional and statutory guarantees are meaningful only if they protect the individual from real hazards. If lawyers, courts and legislatures are to devise substantive and procedural laws to guarantee and implement the rights of children today, they will need factual information with respect to life as it is actually lived in the inner cities, in the affluent suburbs, in small towns and rural areas. They must put aside preconceived notions of childhood innocence, Biblical ideals of filial devotion, the ethic of hard work and frugality. They must examine reality, unpleasant and shocking though it may be. They must learn how such institutions as schools, reformatories, juvenile courts and hospital clinics actually function, not simply read the reports of statistics and goals. They must study the lives of America's children as they are lived day by day in the family, in school and on the streets. This is not a task for lawyers alone. It requires the *expertise* of many disciplines—especially the teachers who know the child and his needs, who see him meeting challenges, succeeding, failing, dropping out.

Don't Ask a Lawyer "Who Is a Child?"

Perhaps the first inquiry should be to determine who is a child. At present there is no clear answer. One might say that under the law anyone who is not an adult is a child. But this reply is deceptively simple. A quick glance at the pertinent statutes reveals a patchwork of inconsistent, anomalous and conflicting age levels.

If the child, at whatever age, is denied full legal rights, then what duties of protection does society owe to him? Concepts of right develop imperceptibly, without scientific proof, technical argument or documentation. When the time is ripe, a declaration is made that certain rights, not heretofore formulated in law, are inalienable, inherent or self-evident. And society grudgingly concedes that such is the fact. Freedom from want, for example, is a peculiarly twentieth century notion. It is hard to think of another time in history when society would have recognized a right to sustenance on the part of the individual and a correlative obligation on the part of government to support the citizenry. Perhaps we are now ready to recognize that there are certain human rights which all children have and certain corresponding obligations on the part of society to implement those rights.

Four Rights Are Inherent in All Children

I suggest that in formulating a juvenile jurisprudence there are four basic rights which the law should recognize as inherent in all children; i.e. (1) the right to life, (2) the right to a home, (3) the right to an education and (4) the right to liberty.

Liberty is the only one of these postulated rights that the courts have considered even indirectly. The decisions are fragmentary and based upon inexact analogies to the criminal law. They turn on due process questions of the procedures by which a child is institutionalized, but skirt the fundamental issue of the right of the state to deprive a child of his liberty under circumstances in which an adult could not be removed from society. Children are deprived of liberty in our complex contemporary world for many reasons. Alleged delinquency is only one. A child may be removed from his home, immured and isolated from society and deprived of an education because he is mentally retarded, emotionally disturbed, nonconforming, difficult, refuses to attend school or perhaps is just unloved or unlovable. These are the majority of children whom the state places in institutions.

The emerging doctrine of right to treatment is an indirect and perhaps clumsy judicial attempt to mitigate the harshness of depriving the noncriminal person of his liberty. Significantly, the seminal cases involve adults, not children, although vastly larger numbers of children are placed in institutions.

The perplexing problem of what to do with these difficult children, who are often sloughed off on the state by their parents, should be considered in the context of the child's right to freedom. Legality of the commitment would then be the issue—not the procedures by which he was committed or the quantum of care that he receives or the existence of institutional peonage. These are inexact and difficult facts to prove and really peripheral to the question of whether the child (or adult) must be incarcerated to protect society or to save his own life.

The Right to Life Is Not Self-Evident

The right to life seems self-evident. I am not discussing abortion. But once an infant is born, it should be clear that no one has a legal right to take its life. In 1972, we would be shocked at the thought that a parent would be permitted to kill his child. We would also reject the notion that a parent has the right to maim or deform his child.

The parent who fails or refuses to provide medical care for his child may be little different from these other parents whose conduct shocks the contemporary American conscience. Natural parents, foster parents and institutions in which children are housed frequently fail to provide necessary medical care and treatment. Often the young infant is literally starved to death. It is not only infants who are denied care. Older children are equally at the mercy of adults with respect to obtaining medical care. Few children are able to consult a physician on their own. Parental consent is required for hospital treatment and perhaps for psychiatric care even when a teenager has money of his own and voluntarily seeks help.

There is little statutory law governing health care for children. Medical treatment is not yet a recognized consitutional right. Although the government does provide some free clinics and the law prescribes certain entitlements under aid to dependent children programs, there are few procedures by which a child may claim these benefits for himself. If medical treatment or surgery is necessary to save the life of a child, most courts will order that such treatment be provided irrespective of the wishes of the parent. These cases usually arise when a child is already in a hospital and the parent refuses to give consent to a blood transfusion or surgery. The cases of battered or abused children require much thought. Society simply ignores this problem though, of course, many teachers are certain that their pupils are mistreated —and the numbers are incredible. It is estimated that there are from 500,000 to 2,500,000 of these children each year in the United States. Often these children are denied necessary medical care because society will not pay for it. Children are put out of hospitals too soon because the hospital cannot afford to maintain such nonpaying patients. They are placed in foster homes because these are cheaper than hospitals, although the foster parents cannot provide the care which these very sick babies require. Medical care in public institutions for children is often deplorable.

There are many other situations, not life or death emergencies, but very serious illnesses, in which a child is denied medical care because of the ignorance, poverty or neglect of parents or guardian. Although few statistics are available with respect to the incidence of childhood illness as related to the economic status of the family, it is undoubtedly true that there is more preventable and curable illness among children of poor families than of middle-class and well-to-do families. The law fails to provide a structure by which these children can obtain necessary treatment and care. Unless a child is actually committed to a mental hospital or a correctional institution, the juvenile courts do not order medical treatment. Thus a child who is delinquent (criminal) may receive some treatment, whereas a child who is discharged (acquitted) will not receive any medical care unless it is voluntarily provided by his family.

Twenty years ago Medicare for the aged sounded improbable and visionary. Today it is a fact. Some system of financing medical care for the poor children in America is a necessity. The poor child may be physically crippled by accident or disease or mentally stunted by malnutrition. The right to life should include a structure by which medical care to cure and prevent such conditions is available and a legal mechanism to protect children from abuse.

The right of a child to have a home would appear to be self-evident to most Americans. In the United States, children are not permitted to sleep in the streets, on vacant lots or park benches. If there is no other place for a child without family or friends, he will be put in a detention center until some place can be found for him.

Homes for the Friendless

No one believes that a child, if he is incapable of caring for himself or if he does not have a safe dwelling, should be permitted to roam the streets and forage for himself. Society must provide a home for him. In the nineteenth century, orphan asylums were a popular form of charity. They were indeed an improvement over the workhouse and the indenturing or apprenticing of orphans who had to work for their keep. The *de facto* orphan, the child who has a parent but no home, is a commonplace. Often a parent refuses to provide for his child. "You take him, Judge. I can't do nothin' with him," says the mother or father. Very few judges will compel an unwilling parent to care for his child. If the parent does not want him, the child will be sent to an institution even though he has not committed any crime.

The institutions in which such adolescents are placed have all the characteristics of a jail. A detention center is not a hotel or boarding school. The children may not leave. They are locked behind bars or walls. They cannot attend public school. They have none of the pleasures of life. In the United States today a child who is deprived of a home is also deprived of his liberty. Little thought is given to the critical need for nonpenal shelters for such children. It would cost less to provide boarding schools than jails. Both the right to a home and the right to liberty are violated when unfortunate noncriminal children and youths are held in detention. There have been few legal challenges to this common and deplorable practice.

The Inverse of an Old Law

The right to an education is basic. It is really the inverse of an old law. For more than half a century, America has had compulsory school attendance statutes. If a child refuses to go to school, his parents can be fined and he can be sent to jail. In twentieth century America there is no place for functional illiterates. Thus, although the law requires the child to attend school, it seldom requires the school to educate him nor does it explicitly give the child a right to attend school. We are all familiar with the school dropout. But the pushout—the child put out of school—is an equally serious problem.

Compulsory school attendance laws operate like a penal sentence. They prescribe the number of hours, days and years a child must spend in school. When he has served his time, he is released regardless of his skills or lack of them. Often the most ignorant are permitted to leave school early and are encouraged to drop out at or before legal school-leaving age. Possibly a different type of attendance law should be drafted, one that makes legal school leaving dependent upon skills rather than time served. If a child is functionally literate, reasonably well informed and employable at 16, why must he remain in school another year if he prefers to get a job? Conversely, just because he is 17, should he be permitted to leave if he cannot read or function in the adult world?

Children are often excluded from the public schools because they are disruptive. Many of these children are not "bad" or delinquent. At age eight how bad can a child be? Whether one agrees with Skinner or Rousseau, we reject the notion of the bad seed. Children can be helped. Often they are made antisocial and hostile by their treatment in school. Undoubtedly, many of these boys and girls are difficult to manage in classes of 25 to 35 pupils. Consequently, brain-damaged, emotionally disturbed and nonconforming children are pushed out of the school system. Whether these children have a legal or possibly a constitutional right to attend school is unclear. Since most of the children who have been excluded from public school are too poor to afford to retain counsel, this question has not been litigated.

The law has largely ignored the rights of the child vis-à-vis the school system, except for cases on haircuts and discipline, and these generally involve the well-to-do suburban child. Again the few reported cases turn on procedural points adopted by analogy from administrative law—the right to a hearing and the right to counsel. While such aspects of due process are important, they are of relative insignificance if the child has no substantive right to attend school. The unresolved and largely unformulated question I would pose as follows: "Does every child have a right to elementary and secondary education suitable to his physical, intellectual and emotional needs at public expense?" And I urge you to make your community give an affirmative answer to this question.

It is obvious that some children, because of physical handicaps, severe mental retardation or emotional disturbance cannot function in a regular school program. There are also many normal children who are simply putting in time at school but not learning. They are being deprived of an education as surely as the child who is excluded from the classroom. Neither the educational bureaucracy nor the lawyers have faced the question of the rights and remedies of these pupils. In some communities special public schools have been established for the retarded, the emotionally disturbed, pregnant girls and those who want to drop out of the standard classroom program. Many of these are very successful. We need more of them.

I should like to mention briefly the question of freedom of choice in education. Certainly it should be the right of parents to provide forms of education for their children other than the public schools if they wish to do so, meet state standards and pay for it. These schools often provide experimentation that is useful and may become a model for the public schools. But the base of elementary and secondary education in America has been the public schools.

Today there are many proposals which, if effectuated, would not merely erode but destroy the public schools. One such program is the voucher plan which would give the parents a sum equivalent to the cost of maintaining a child in the public school and let him use it to purchase private education. In theory some believe that under this plan the poor child will have equal opportunity with the rich to have freedom of choice in attending a nonpublic school. However, there are not enough private schools to accept all these children. Few private schools will accept difficult, culturally deprived or academically untalented children. Private school fees are often higher than public expenditures per child. Few poor parents have the time or skills to establish and operate their own schools. The result will be again a public subsidy of the middle class and an impoverishment of the poor with a resultant loss in the quality and character of public education.

The public schools could, however, offer a freedom of choice to the student by operating different kinds of schools. They could have traditional schools, Montessori-type schools, English-type open classrooms and a wide variety of programs so that the parents could with the help of guidance counsellors and teachers choose the school best suited to the needs of the child. There are many possibilities and great opportunities with the help of federal and state monies to try newer and better ways of educating our children in these difficult and restless times.

We know that we must do better in all areas of life in America. We know that the rising demand among suppressed people all over the world—colonials, blacks, women—will impel change either peacefully or, if we resist necessary improvements, by force. Children are also a suppressed group. Children are demanding a place and a voice in the larger society. A group of high school students in Philadelphia, for example, intends to sue for student representation on the school board.

We cannot wait for these problems to be resolved piecemeal in 51 different jurisdictions by the aleatory processes of litigation. More direct and speedy remedies are required. Lawyers and teachers, in cooperation with doctors and sociologists, must devise statutes, rules, regulations and government institutions to formulate and enforce the rights of American children.

Young people today are restless and impatient. They have little faith that the customary legal processes will solve their problems. Neither appeals to belief in law and order and the democratic way nor threats of repressive measures will quiet them. Society will either recognize now the rights of the young and the obligations of government to provide a decent environment, meaningful education and an opportunity to live a healthy, free life to every child, or it will have to provide jails and mental institutions later. The price of delay may be far greater than the cost of action.

CHAPTER 8: SUGGESTED FURTHER READING

Action for Children's Television. New York: Avon, 1971.

BREMNER, R. H. (Ed.) *Children and Youth in America.* 3 vols. Cambridge, Mass.: Harvard University Press, 1970.

Government Research on the Problems of Children and Youth. Washington, D.C.: U.S. Government Printing Office, 1971. (#5270–1198)

KATZ, S. N. *When Parents Fail.* Boston: Beacon Press, 1971.

PIVEN, F. F., and CLOWARD, R. A. *Regulating the Poor.* New York: Random House, 1971.

REIN, M. *Social Policy.* New York: Random House, 1970.

Report of the White House Conference on Youth. Washington, D.C.: U.S. Government Printing Office, 1971. (#4000–0267)

name index

*Boldface page numbers refer to pages on which an article in this text begins.

concept index

about the authors

Freda Rebelsky is currently a Professor of Psychology at Boston University, where she also directs the doctoral program in Developmental Psychology. She received her B.A. and M.A. degrees at the University of Chicago and her Ph.D. from Radcliffe. Professor Rebelsky has previously held research and teaching positions at the University of Chicago, Harvard University, and Massachusetts Institute of Technology. During 1965-1967, Professor Rebelsky was a visiting lecturer at Utrecht University in Holland and also lectured at universities in Germany and England. She has contributed articles to *Child Development, Journal of Genetic Psychology, Contemporary Psychology,* and many other journals. In 1970 Professor Rebelsky received the Distinguished Teacher of Psychology Award from the American Psychological Foundation. She also received the 1971 E. Harris Harbison Award for Gifted Teaching from the Danforth Foundation.

Lynn Dorman is presently teaching at Boston University. She received her B.A. degree at Queens College and her M.A. and Ph.D. degrees at Boston University. Before receiving her Ph.D., Dr. Dorman was a kindergarten teacher. She has also taught at Framingham State College and Wheaton College. During 1969-1970 Dr. Dorman was a postdoctoral fellow at the Institute of Human Development at the University of California, Berkeley. She has also contributed articles to *Child Development* and the *Journal of Genetic Psychology.*

a note on the type

The text of this book is set in CALEDONIA, *a Linotype face designed by W. A. Dwiggins. It belongs to the family of printing types called "modern face" by printers—a term used to mark the change in style of type-letters that occurred about 1800. Caledonia borders on the general design of Scotch Modern, but is more freely drawn than that letter.*

The book was composed by Cherry Hill Composition, Pennsauken, N.J. It was printed and bound by the Kingsport Press, Kingsport, Tenn.